MONSTER MANUAL D&D DESIGN TEAM

Monte Cook, Jonathan Tweet, Skip Williams

MONSTER MANUAL DESIGN
Skip Williams

ADDITIONAL DESIGN & DIRECTION
Peter Adkison

ADDITIONAL DESIGN
Jason Carl, William W. Connors,
Sean K Reynolds

EDITORS
Jennifer Clarke Wilkes, Jon Pickens

EDITORIAL ASSISTANCE
Julia Martin, Jeff Quick, Rob Heinsoo,
David Noonan, Penny Williams

MANAGING EDITOR
Kim Mohan

CORE D&D CREATIVE DIRECTOR
Ed Stark

DIRECTOR OF RPG R&D
Bill Slavicsek

BRAND MANAGER
Ryan Dancey

CATEGORY MANAGER
Keith Strohm

PROJECT MANAGERS
Larry Weiner, Josh Fischer

VISUAL CREATIVE DIRECTOR
Jon Schindehette

ART DIRECTOR
Dawn Murin

D&D CONCEPTUAL ARTISTS
Todd Lockwood, Sam Wood

D&D LOGO DESIGN
Matt Adelsperger, Sherry Floyd

COVER ART
Henry Higgenbotham

GRAPHIC DESIGNERS
Sean Glenn, Sherry Floyd

TYPOGRAPHERS
Erin Dorries, Angelika Lokotz,
Nancy Walker

DIGI-TECH SPECIALIST
Joe Fernandez

PHOTOGRAPHER
Craig Cudnohufsky

PRODUCTION MANAGER
Chas DeLong

INTERIOR ARTISTS

Glen Angus, Carlo Arellano, Daren Bader, Tom Baxa, Carl Critchlow, Brian Despain,
Tony Diterlizzi, Larry Elmore, Scott Fischer, Rebecca Guay, Paul Jaquays,
Michael Kaluta, Dana Knutson, Todd Lockwood, David Martin, Matthew Mitchell,
Monte Moore, rk Post, Adam Rex, Wayne Reynolds, Richard Sardinha, Brian Snoddy,
Mark Tedin, Anthony Waters

SPECIAL THANKS:
Jim Lin, Richard Garfield, Andrew Finch, Skaff Elias

OTHER WIZARDS OF THE COAST RPG R&D CONTRIBUTORS
Eric Cagle, Michele Carter, Bruce R. Cordell, Dale Donovan, David Eckelberry,
Jeff Grubb, Miranda Horner, Gwendolyn FM Kestrel, Steve Miller, Roger Moore,
John D. Rateliff, Rich Redman, Thomas M. Reid, Mike Selinker, Stan!, JD Wiker,
James Wyatt
Based on the original Dungeons & Dragons® rules created by E. Gary Gygax and Dave Arneson

U.S., CANADA,
ASIA, PACIFIC, & LATIN AMERICA
Wizards of the Coast, Inc.
P.O. Box 707
Renton WA 98057-0707

EUROPEAN HEADQUARTERS
Wizards of the Coast, Belgium
P.B. 2031
2600 Berchem
Belgium
+32-70-23-32-77

Questions? 1-800-324-6496   620-T11552
First Printing   October 2000

Visit our website at www.wizards.com/dnd

Alphabetical Listing of Monsters

MONSTERS BY TYPE (AND SUBTYPE)

Aberration: aboleth, athach, beholder, carrion crawler, choker, chuul, cloaker, delver, destrachan, drider, ethereal filcher, ettercap, gibbering mouther, grick, mimic, mind flayer, nagas, otyugh, rust monster, skum, umber hulk, will-o'-wisp.

(Air): cloud giant, green dragon, silver dragon, will-o'-wisp.

Animal: animals (Appendix 1), dire animals.

(Aquatic): aboleth, aquatic elves, crocodile, dire shark, dragon turtle, elasmosaurus, giant crocodile, giant octopus, kraken, kuo-toa, lizardfolk, locathah, merfolk, merrow, octopus, porpoise, sahuagin, sea hag, sharks, skum, squids, water naga, whales.

Beast: ankheg, bulette, dinosaurs, girallon, gray render, griffon, hippogriff, hydras, owlbear, purple worm, roc, sea lion, stirge.

(Cold): cryohydra, frost giant, frost worm, ice mephit, white dragon, winter wolf.

Construct: animated objects, golems, homunculus, retriever, shield guardian.

Dragon: dragons, dragon turtle, half-dragon (red)/half-ogre, pseudodragon, wyvern.

(Earth): blue dragon, copper dragon, gargoyle, stone giant.

(Electricity): behir, storm giant.

Elemental (Air): belker, air elementals, invisible stalker.

Elemental (Earth): earth elementals, thoqqua.

Elemental (Fire): fire elementals, magmin, thoqqua.

Elemental (Water): water elementals.

Fey: dryad, grig, nixie, nymph, pixie, satyr.

(Fire): brass dragon, fire giant, gold dragon, pyrohydra, red dragon.

Giant: ettin, giants, ogre, ogre mage, troll.

Humanoid: bugbear, dwarf, elf, gnoll, gnome, goblin, halfling, hobgoblin, kobold, lizardfolk, locathah, merfolk, orc, sahuagin, troglodyte.

Magical Beast: abyssal dire rat, basilisk, blink dog, celestial lion, chimera, cockatrice, darkmantle, digester, displacer beast, dragonne, ethereal marauder, frost worm, giant eagle, giant owl, gorgon, kraken, krenshar, lamia, lammasu, manticore, pegasus, phase spider, remorhaz, roper, shocker lizard, sphinxes, spider eater, tarrasque, unicorn, winter wolf, worg, yrthak.

Monstrous Humanoid: centaur, grimlock, hags, harpy, kuo-toa, medusa, minotaur, yuan-ti.

Ooze: black pudding, gelatinous cube, gray ooze, ochre jelly.

Outsider: aasimar, janni, ravid, tiefling.

Outsider (Air): arrowhawks, djinni, air mephit, dust mephit, ice mephit.

Outsider (Chaotic): chaos beast, demons, ghaele, half-celestial/half-unicorn, djinni, howler, lillend, slaadi, titan.

Outsider (Evil): achaierai, barghest, demons, devils, efreeti, half-fiend/half-medusa, hell hound, howler, night hag, nightmare, rakshasa, shadow mastiff, vargouille, xill, yeth hound.

Outsider (Earth): earth mephit, salt mephit, xorns.

Outsider (Fire): azer, efreeti, hell hound, fire mephit, magma mephit, steam mephit, rast, salamanders.

Outsider (Good): celestials, couatl, djinni, half-celestial/half-unicorn, lillend, titan.

Outsider (Lawful): achaierai, archons, azer, barghest, couatl, devils, formians, efreeti, half-fiend/half-medusa, hell hound, rakshasa, xill.

Outsider (Water): ooze mephit, water mephit, tojanidas, triton.

Plant: assassin vine, fungus, phantom fungus, shambling mound, tendriculos, treant.

(Reptilian): basilisk, kobold, lizardfolk, troglodyte.

Shapechanger: aranea, doppelganger, lycanthropes, phasm.

Undead: allip, bodak, devourer, ghast, ghost, ghoul, lich, mohrg, mummy, nightshades, shadow, skeletons, spectre, vampire spawn, wight, wraith, zombie.

Vermin: vermin (Appendix 2).

(Water): black dragon, bronze dragon.

Introduction

This book contains entries for more than 500 creatures, both hostile and benign, for use in DUNGEONS & DRAGONS® adventures.

This introduction explains how to read a creature's write-up, including summaries of the most common attacks and abilities.

Entries for creatures are listed alphabetically by name. Some creatures, such as giants, are ordered from weakest to strongest in the entry.

Appendix 1 describes mundane animals, in alphabetical order within the listing. Appendix 2 describes vermin (a type of creature; see below), again in alphabetical order. Variable-sized creatures are ordered from weakest to strongest. Appendix 3 explains and describes a group of creatures that are created by adding a "template" to an existing creature type. An example of this is a vampire, which adds the "vampire" template to a range of eligible creatures.

At the end of the book, a list of monsters organized by Challenge Rating makes it easy for the Dungeon Master to tailor encounters to the party level of the player characters.

READING THE ENTRIES

Each monster entry is organized in the same general format, as described below. The information is in a condensed form. For complete information about the characteristics of monsters, consult the *Player's Handbook* or the *DUNGEON MASTER's Guide*.

MAIN STATISTICS BLOCK

This text contains basic game information on the creature.

Name

This is the name by which the creature is generally known. The descriptive text (following the main statistics block and secondary statistics block) may give other names.

Size and Type

This line begins with the creature's size (Huge, for example). The eight size categories are briefly described in the table below. A size modifier can apply to the creature's Armor Class (AC) and attack bonus, as well as to certain skills. A creature's size also determines how far it can reach to make a melee attack and how much space it occupies in a fight (see Face/Reach, below, and also Big and Little Creatures in Combat, page 131 in the *Player's Handbook*).

CREATURE SIZES

Size	AC/Attack Modifier	Dimension*	Weight**
Fine	+8	6 in. or less	1/8 lb. or less
Diminutive	+4	6 in.–1 ft.	1/8 lb.–1 lb.
Tiny	+2	1 ft.–2 ft.	1 lb.–8 lb.
Small	+1	2 ft.–4 ft.	8 lb.–60 lb.
Medium	0	4 ft.–8 ft.	60 lb.–500 lb.
Large	–1	8 ft.–16 ft.	500 lb.–4,000 lb.
Huge	–2	16 ft.–32 ft.	4,000 lb.–32,000 lb.
Gargantuan	–4	32 ft.–64 ft.	32,000 lb.–250,000 lb.
Colossal	–8	64 ft. or more	250,000 lb. or more

*Biped's height, quadruped's body length (nose to base of tail).
**Assumes that the creature is roughly as dense as a regular animal. A creature made of stone will weigh considerably more. A gaseous creature will weigh much less.

The size and type line continues with the creature's type (giant, for example). Type determines how magic affects a creature; for example, the *hold animal* spell affects only creatures of the animal type. Type also determines many of the creature's characteristics and abilities, as described below.

Aberration: An aberration has a bizarre anatomy, strange abilities, an alien mindset, or any combination of the three. Unless noted otherwise, aberrations have darkvision with a range of 60 feet (see page 74 in the *DUNGEON MASTER's Guide*). Example: beholder.

Animal: An animal is a nonhumanoid creature, usually a vertebrate. All the animals included in this book lived on the planet Earth in historical times, or are larger versions of such creatures. All animals have Intelligence scores of 1 or 2. Unless noted otherwise, animals have low-light vision (see page 79 in the *DUNGEON MASTER's Guide*). Example: bear.

Beast: A beast is a nonhistorical, vertebrate creature with a reasonably normal anatomy and no magical or unusual abilities. Unless noted otherwise, beasts have low-light vision and darkvision with a range of 60 feet. Example: owlbear.

Construct: A construct is an animated object or artificially constructed creature. Constructs usually have no Intelligence scores and never have Constitution scores. A construct is immune to mind-influencing effects (charms, compulsions, phantasms, patterns, and morale effects) and to poison, sleep, paralysis, stunning, disease, death effects, and necromantic effects.

Constructs cannot heal damage on their own, though they can be healed. Constructs can be repaired in the same way an object can (see the creature's description for details). A construct with the regeneration and fast healing special qualities still benefits from those qualities.

A construct is not subject to critical hits, subdual damage, ability damage, ability drain, or energy drain. It is immune to any effect that requires a Fortitude save (unless the effect also works on objects). A construct is not at risk of death from massive damage (see page 129 in the *Player's Handbook*), but when reduced to 0 hit points or less, it is immediately destroyed. Since it was never alive, a construct cannot be raised or resurrected.

Unless noted otherwise, constructs have darkvision with a range of 60 feet. Example: golem.

Dragon: A dragon is a reptilian creature, usually winged, with magical or unusual abilities. Dragons are immune to sleep and paralysis effects. Unless noted otherwise, dragons have darkvision with a range of 60 feet and low-light vision. Example: red dragon.

Elemental: An elemental is composed of one of the four classical elements: air, earth, fire, or water. It is immune to poison, sleep, paralysis, and stunning. Elementals have no clear front or back and are therefore not subject to critical hits or flanking. Unless noted otherwise, they have darkvision with a range of 60 feet.

A slain elemental cannot be raised or resurrected, although a *wish* or *miracle* spell can restore it to life. Example: invisible stalker.

Fey: A fey is a creature with supernatural abilities and connections to nature or to some other force or place. Fey are usually human-shaped. Unless noted otherwise, fey have low-light vision. Example: dryad.

Giant: A giant is a humanoid creature of great strength, usually of at least Large size. Giants are proficient with all simple weapons and with any weapons listed in their entries. Unless noted otherwise, giants have darkvision with a range of 60 feet. Example: ogre.

Humanoid: A humanoid usually has two arms, two legs, and one head, or a humanlike torso, arms, and head. Humanoids have few or no supernatural or extraordinary abilities, and usually are Small or Medium-size. Every humanoid creature also has a type modifier (see below). Humanoids are proficient with all simple weapons and with any weapons mentioned in their entries. Example: goblin.

Magical Beast: Magical beasts are similar to beasts but have supernatural or extraordinary abilities. Unless noted otherwise, magical beasts have darkvision with a range of 60 feet and low-light vision. Example: displacer beast.

Monstrous Humanoid: These are humanoid creatures with monstrous or animalistic features, often having supernatural abilities. Unless noted otherwise, monstrous humanoids have darkvision with a range of 60 feet. Monstrous humanoids are proficient with all simple weapons and with any weapons mentioned in their entries. Example: medusa.

Ooze: An ooze is an amorphous or mutable creature. Oozes are immune to poison, sleep, paralysis, stunning, and polymorphing. They have no clear front or back and are therefore not subject to critical hits or flanking. Oozes are blind but have the blindsight special quality. They have no Intelligence scores and are therefore immune to all mind-influencing effects (charms, compulsions, phantasms, patterns, and morale effects).

Oozes have no natural armor ratings, but they are nevertheless difficult to kill because their bodies are mostly simple protoplasm. This is reflected by bonus hit points (in addition to those from Hit Dice and Constitution scores) according to size, as shown in the table below. Example: gelatinous cube.

Ooze Size	Bonus Hit Points
Fine	—
Diminutive	—
Tiny	—
Small	5
Medium-size	10
Large	15
Huge	20
Gigantic	30
Colossal	40

Outsider: An outsider is a nonelemental creature that comes from another dimension, reality, or plane. Unless noted otherwise, outsiders have darkvision with a range of 60 feet.

A slain outsider cannot be raised or resurrected, although a *wish* or *miracle* spell can restore it to life. Example: devil.

Plant: This type comprises vegetable creatures. Plants are immune to poison, sleep, paralysis, stunning, and polymorphing. They are not subject to critical hits or mind-influencing effects (charms, compulsions, phantasms, patterns, and morale effects). Unless otherwise noted, plants have low-light vision. Example: shambling mound.

Shapechanger: This type of creature has a stable body but can assume other forms. Unless noted otherwise, shapechangers have darkvision with a range of 60 feet. Example: doppelganger.

Undead: Undead are once-living creatures animated by spiritual or supernatural forces. Undead are immune to poison, sleep, paralysis, stunning, disease, death effects, and necromantic effects, and they ignore mind-influencing effects (charms, compulsions, phantasms, patterns, and morale effects). Undead are not subject to critical hits, subdual damage, ability damage, ability drain, or energy drain. They have no Constitution scores and are therefore immune to any effect requiring a Fortitude save (unless it affects objects). An undead spellcaster uses its Charisma modifier when making Concentration checks.

Undead with no Intelligence scores cannot heal damage on their own, though they can be healed. Negative energy (such as an *inflict wounds* spell) can heal undead creatures. The regeneration and fast healing special qualities work regardless of the creature's Intelligence score.

An undead creature is not at risk of death from massive damage, but when reduced to 0 hit points or less, it is immediately destroyed. Most undead have darkvision with a range of 60 feet.

Undead cannot be raised. *Resurrection* can affect them, but since undead creatures usually are unwilling to return to life, these attempts generally fail (see Bringing Back the Dead, page 153 in the *Player's Handbook*). Example: zombie.

Vermin: This type includes insects, arachnids, arthropods, worms, and similar invertebrates. Vermin have no Intelligence scores and are immune to all mind-influencing effects (charms, compulsions, phantasms, patterns and morale effects). Unless noted otherwise, vermin have darkvision with a range of 60 feet. Poisonous vermin get a bonus to the DC for their poison based on their size, as shown on the following table. Example: monstrous spider.

Vermin Size	Poison DC Bonus
Medium-size	+2
Large	+4
Huge	+6
Gargantuan	+8
Colossal	+10

Type Modifiers

A parenthetical note following the creature type indicates a type modifier (fire, for example), indicating that the creature is associated with an element, a form of energy, a state of being, or the like. A type modifier creates a subtype within a larger type, such as undead (incorporeal); links creatures that share characteristics, such as humanoid (goblinoid); or connects members of different types. For example, white dragons and frost giants belong to the dragon and giant types, respectively, but they are also of the cold subtype.

Some common type modifiers that affect a creature's abilities are described below.

Cold: A cold creature is immune to cold damage. It takes double damage from fire unless a saving throw for half damage is allowed, in which case it takes half damage on a success and double damage on a failure.

Fire: A fire creature is immune to fire damage. It takes double damage from cold unless a saving throw for half damage is allowed, in which case it takes half damage on a success and double damage on a failure.

Incorporeal: An incorporeal creature has no physical body. It can be harmed only by other incorporeal creatures, +1 or better magic weapons, and spells, spell-like abilities, or supernatural abilities. It is immune to all nonmagical attack forms. Even when hit by spells or magic weapons, it has a 50% chance to ignore any damage from a corporeal source (except for force effects, such as *magic missile*, or attacks made with *ghost touch* weapons). An incorporeal creature has no natural armor but has a deflection bonus equal to its Charisma modifier (always at least +1, even if the creature's Charisma score does not normally provide a bonus).

An incorporeal creature can pass through solid objects at will, but not force effects. Its attack passes through (ignores) natural armor, armor, and shields, although deflection bonuses and force effects (such as *mage armor*) work normally against it. An incorporeal creature moves silently and cannot be heard with Listen checks if it doesn't wish to be. It has no Strength score, so its Dexterity modifier applies to both its melee and its ranged attacks.

Hit Dice

This line gives the number and type of Hit Dice the creature has and any bonus hit points. A parenthetical note gives the creature's average hit points.

A creature's Hit Dice total is also its level for determining how spells affect the creature, its rate of natural healing, and its maximum ranks in a skill.

Initiative

This line shows the creature's modifier to initiative rolls. A parenthetical note tells where the modifier comes from (most commonly the creature's Dexterity modifier and the Improved Initiative feat, if the creature has it).

Speed

This line gives the creature's tactical speed on land (the amount of distance it can cover in one move). If the creature wears armor that reduces its speed, this fact is given along with a parenthetical note indicating the armor type; the creature's base unarmored speed follows.

If the creature has other modes of movement, these are listed after the main entry. Unless noted otherwise, modes of movement are natural (not magical).

Burrow: The creature can tunnel through dirt, but not through rock unless the descriptive text says otherwise. Creatures cannot use the run action while burrowing.

Climb: A creature with a climb speed has the Climb skill at no cost and gains a +8 racial bonus to all Climb checks. The creature must make a Climb check to climb any wall or slope with a DC of more than 0, but it always can choose to take 10 (see Checks without Rolls, page 61 in the *Player's Handbook*), even if rushed or threatened while climbing. The creature climbs at the listed speed while climbing. If it chooses an accelerated climb (see Climb, page 64 in the *Player's Handbook*), it moves at double the listed climb speed (or its normal land speed, whichever is less) and makes a single Climb check at a −5 penalty. Creatures cannot use the run action while climbing.

Fly: The creature can fly at the listed speed if carrying no more than a medium load (see Carrying Capacity, page 141 in the *Player's Handbook*, and Strength, below). All fly speeds include a parenthetical note indicating maneuverability, as follows.

Perfect: The creature can perform almost any aerial maneuver it wishes. It moves through the air as well as a human does over smooth ground.

Good: The creature is very agile in the air (like a housefly or hummingbird), but cannot change direction as readily as those with perfect maneuverability.

Average: The creature can fly as adroitly as a small bird.

Poor: The creature flies as well as a very large bird.

Clumsy: The creature can barely fly at all.

Creatures that fly can make dive attacks. A dive attack works just like a charge, but the diving creature must move a minimum of 30 feet. It can make only claw attacks, but these deal double damage. Creatures can use the run action while flying, provided they fly in a straight line.

For more information, see Tactical Aerial Movement, page 69 in the DUNGEON MASTER's Guide.

Swim: A creature with a swim speed can move through water at the listed speed without making Swim checks. It gains a +8 racial bonus to any Swim check to perform some special action or avoid a hazard. The creature always can choose to take 10, even if rushed or threatened when swimming. Creatures can use the run action while swimming, provided they swim in a straight line.

Armor Class

The Armor Class line gives the creature's AC for normal combat and includes a parenthetical mention of the modifiers contributing to it (usually size, Dexterity, and natural armor).

Attacks

This line gives all the creature's physical attacks, whether with natural or manufactured weapons.

Natural Weapons: These include teeth, claws, sting, and the like. The entry gives the number of attacks along with the weapon (2 claws, for example), attack bonus, and form of attack (melee or ranged). The first listing is for the creature's primary weapon, with an attack bonus including modifications for size and Strength (for melee attacks) or Dexterity (for ranged attacks). A creature with the Weapon Finesse feat can use its Dexterity modifier on melee attacks.

The remaining weapons are secondary and have −5 to the attack bonus, no matter how many there are. Creatures with the Multiattack feat (see "Feats" below) suffer only a −2 penalty to secondary attacks.

All of the foregoing assumes that the creature makes a full attack (see Attack Actions, page 122 in the *Player's Handbook*) and employs all its natural weapons. If a creature instead chooses the attack option (and thus makes only a single attack), it uses its primary attack bonus.

Unless noted otherwise, natural weapons threaten critical hits on a natural attack roll of 20.

Manufactured Weapons: Creatures that use swords, bows, spears, and the like follow the same rules as characters, including those for multiple attacks and two-weapon fighting penalties. All the steps in a multiple attack sequence are given and include all modifications.

Damage

This line shows the damage each of the creature's attacks deals. Damage from an attack is always at least 1 point, even if a subtraction from a die roll brings the result to 0 or lower.

Natural Weapons: A creature's primary attack damage includes its full Strength modifier (one and a half times its Strength bonus if it is the creature's sole attack). Secondary attacks add only one-half the creature's Strength bonus.

If any attacks also cause some special effect other than damage (poison, disease, etc.), that information is given here.

Unless noted otherwise, creatures deal double damage on critical hits.

Natural weapons have types just as other weapons do. The most common are summarized below.

Bite: The creature attacks with its mouth, dealing piercing, slashing, and bludgeoning damage.

Claw or Rake: The creature rips with a sharp appendage, dealing piercing and slashing damage.

Gore: The creature spears the opponent with an antler, horn or similar appendage, dealing piercing damage.

Slap or Slam: The creature batters opponents with an appendage, dealing bludgeoning damage.

Sting: The creature stabs with a stinger, dealing piercing damage. Stings are usually envenomed.

Manufactured Weapons: Creatures that use swords, bows, spears, and the like follow the same rules as characters do. The bonus for attacks with two-handed weapons is one and a half times the creature's Strength modifier (if it is a bonus), while secondary weapons add only one-half the Strength bonus.

Face/Reach

This line describes how much space the creature needs to fight effectively and how close it has to be to an opponent to threaten that square. This is written in the format [feet] by [feet]/[feet]: The numbers before the slash show the creature's fighting space (width first, length second). The number after the slash is the creature's natural reach. If the creature has exceptional reach due to a weapon, tentacle, or the like, the extended reach and its source are noted in parentheses.

Special Abilities

Many creatures have unusual abilities, which can include special attack forms, resistance or vulnerability to certain types of damage, and enhanced senses, among others. A monster entry breaks these abilities into Special Attacks and Special Qualities. The latter category includes defenses, vulnerabilities, and other special abilities that are not modes of attack.

A special ability is either extraordinary (Ex), spell-like (Sp), or supernatural (Su).

Extraordinary: Extraordinary abilities are nonmagical, don't go away in an *antimagic field*, and are not subject to anything that disrupts magic. Using an extraordinary ability is a free action unless noted otherwise.

Spell-Like: Spell-like abilities are magical and work just like spells (though they are not spells and so have no verbal, somatic, material, focus, or XP components). They go away in an *antimagic field* and are subject to spell resistance.

Spell-like abilities usually have a limit on the number of times they can be used. A spell-like ability that can be used "at will" has no use limit. Using a spell-like ability is a standard action unless noted otherwise, and doing so while threatened provokes an attack of opportunity. A spell-like ability can be disrupted just as a spell can be. Spell-like abilities cannot be used to counterspell, nor can they be counterspelled.

For creatures with spell-like abilities, a designated caster level serves to define how difficult it is to dispel their spell-like effects and to define any level-dependent variable (such as range and duration) the abilities might have. The creature's caster level never affects which spell-like abilities the creature has; sometimes the given caster level is lower than the level a spellcasting character would need to cast the spell of the same name. If no caster level is specified, the caster level is equal to the creature's Hit Dice.

The saving throw (if any) for a spell-like ability is 10 + the level of the spell the ability resembles or duplicates + the creature's Charisma modifier.

Supernatural: Supernatural abilities are magical and go away in an *antimagic field* but are not subject to spell resistance. Using a supernatural ability is a standard action unless noted otherwise. Supernatural abilities may have a use limit or be usable at will, just like spell-like abilities. However, supernatural abilities do not provoke attacks of opportunity and never require Concentration checks. Unless otherwise noted, a supernatural ability has an effective caster level equal to the creature's Hit Dice.

Special Attacks

This line lists all the creature's special attacks in the order they are most likely to be used. If the creature has no special attacks, this line does not appear. Details of the most common special attacks are given here, with additional information in the creatures' descriptive text. In general, "creature" means the creature using the special attack, while "opponent" is the target of the attack.

Ability Score Loss (Su): Some attacks reduce the opponent's score in one or more abilities. This loss can be permanent or temporary (see Ability Score Loss, page 72 in the DUNGEON MASTER's *Guide*).

Permanent Ability Drain: This effect permanently reduces a living opponent's ability score when the creature hits with a melee attack. The creature's descriptive text lists the ability and the amount drained. If an attack that causes permanent ability drain scores a critical hit, it drains twice the listed amount (if the damage is expressed as a die range, roll two dice). A draining creature heals 5 points of damage (10 on a critical hit) whenever it drains an ability score no matter how many points it drains. If the amount of healing is more than the damage the creature has suffered, it gains any excess as temporary hit points.

Some ability drain attacks allow a Fortitude save with a DC of 10 + 1/2 draining creature's HD + draining creature's Charisma modifier (the exact DC is given in the creature's descriptive text). If no saving throw is mentioned, none is allowed.

Temporary Ability Damage: This attack damages an opponent's ability score. The creature's descriptive text gives the ability and the amount of damage. If an attack that causes ability damage scores a critical hit, it deals twice the listed amount (if the damage is expressed as a die range, roll two dice). Temporary ability damage returns at the rate of 1 point per day.

Breath Weapon (Su): A breath weapon attack usually causes damage and is often based on some type of energy (such as fire breath). It allows a Reflex save for half damage with a DC of 10 + 1/2 breathing creature's HD + breathing creature's Constitution modifier (the exact DC is given in the creature's descriptive text). A creature is immune to its own breath weapon unless otherwise noted. Breath weapons are described in an abbreviated form in the monster entry.

Constrict (Ex): The creature crushes the opponent, dealing bludgeoning damage, after making a successful grapple check (see Grapple, page 137 in the *Player's Handbook*). The amount of damage is given in the creature's entry. If the creature also has the improved grab ability (see below), it deals constriction damage in addition to damage dealt by the weapon used to grab.

Energy Drain (Su): This attack saps a living opponent's vital energy and happens automatically when a melee or ranged attack hits. Each successful energy drain inflicts one or more negative levels (the descriptive text specifies how many). See Energy Drain, page 75 in the DUNGEON MASTER's *Guide*, for details. If an attack that includes an energy drain scores a critical hit, it drains twice the given amount. For each negative level inflicted on an opponent, the draining creature heals 5 points of damage (10 on a critical hit). If the amount of healing is more than the damage the creature has suffered, it gains any excess as temporary hit points.

The affected opponent suffers a –1 penalty to all skill and ability checks, attacks, and saving throws, and loses 1 effective level or Hit Die (whenever level is used in a die roll or calculation) for each negative level. A spellcaster loses one spell slot of the highest level she can cast and (if applicable) one prepared spell of that level; this loss persists until the negative level is removed.

Negative levels remain until 24 hours have passed or until removed with a spell, such as *restoration*. At that time, the afflicted opponent must attempt a Fortitude save with a DC of 10 + 1/2 draining creature's HD + draining creature's Charisma modifier (the exact DC is given in the creature's descriptive text). On a success, the negative level goes away with no harm to the creature. On a failure, the negative level goes away, but the creature's level is also reduced by one. A separate saving throw is required for each negative level.

Fear (Su or Sp): Fear attacks can have various effects.

Fear Aura (Su): This ability either operates continuously or can be used at will. In either case, it's a free action. This can freeze an opponent (such as a mummy's despair) or function like the *fear* spell (for example, the aura of a lich). Other effects are possible.

Fear Cones (Sp) and Rays (Su): These usually work like the *fear* spell.

If a fear effect allows a saving throw, it is a Will save with a DC of 10 + 1/2 fearsome creature's HD + fearsome creature's Charisma modifier (the exact DC is given in the creature's descriptive text).

Frightful Presence (Ex): This ability makes the creature's very presence unsettling to foes. It takes effect automatically when the creature performs some sort of dramatic action (such as charging, attacking, or snarling). Opponents within range who witness the action may become frightened or shaken (see pages 84 and 85 in the DUNGEON MASTER's *Guide*).

Actions required to trigger the ability are given in the creature's descriptive text. The range is usually 30 feet, but the entry will give any exceptions. The duration is usually 5d6 rounds.

This ability affects only opponents with fewer Hit Dice or levels than the creature has. An affected opponent can resist the effects with a successful Will save with a DC of 10 + 1/2 frightful creature's HD + frightful creature's Charisma modifier (the exact DC is given in the creature's descriptive text). An opponent who succeeds at the saving throw is immune to that creature's frightful presence for one day.

Gaze (Su): A gaze attack takes effect when opponents look at the creature's eyes (see Gaze Attacks, page 77 in the DUNGEON MASTER's *Guide*). The attack can have almost any sort of effect: petrification, death, charm, and so on. The typical range is 30 feet, but check the creature's entry for details.

The type of saving throw for a gaze attack varies, but it is usually a Will or Fortitude save. The DC is 10 + 1/2 gazing creature's HD + gazing creature's Charisma modifier (the exact DC is given in the creature's descriptive text). A successful saving throw negates the effect. Gaze attacks are described in an abbreviated form in the monster entry.

Each opponent within range of a gaze attack must attempt a saving throw each round at the beginning of his or her turn in initiative order. Only looking directly at a creature with a gaze attack leaves an opponent vulnerable. Opponents can avoid the saving throw by not looking at the creature, in one of two ways.

Averting Eyes: The opponent avoids looking at the creature's face, instead looking at its body, watching its shadow, tracking it in a reflective surface, and so on. Each round, the opponent has a 50% chance to not need to make a saving throw against the gaze attack.

Wearing a Blindfold: The opponent cannot see the creature at all (also possible by turning one's back on the creature or shutting one's eyes.) The creature with the gaze attack gains total concealment against the opponent.

A creature with a gaze attack can actively gaze as an attack action by choosing a target within range. That opponent must attempt a saving throw but can try to avoid this as described above. Thus, it is possible to save against a creature's gaze twice during the same round, once before the opponent's action and once during the creature's turn.

Gaze attacks can affect ethereal opponents. A creature is immune to its own gaze attack unless otherwise noted.

Improved Grab (Ex): If the creature hits with a melee weapon (usually a claw or bite attack), it deals normal damage and attempts to start a grapple as a free action without provoking an attack of opportunity (see Grapple, page 137 in the *Player's Handbook*). No initial touch attack is required, and Tiny and Small creatures do not suffer a special size penalty. Unless otherwise stated, improved grab works only against opponents at least one size category smaller than the creature. The creature has the option to conduct the grapple normally, or simply use the part of its body it used in the improved grab to hold the opponent. If it chooses to do the latter, it suffers a –20 penalty to grapple checks, but is not considered grappled itself; the creature does not lose its Dexterity bonus to AC, still threatens an area, and can use its remaining attacks against other opponents.

A successful hold does not deal any additional damage unless the creature also has the constrict ability. If the creature does not constrict, each successful grapple check it makes during successive rounds automatically deals the damage listed for the attack that established the hold. Otherwise, it deals constriction damage as well (the amount is listed in the creature's descriptive text).

When a creature gets a hold after an improved grab attack, it pulls the opponent into its space. This act does not provoke attacks of opportunity. The creature is not considered grappled while it holds the opponent, so it still threatens adjacent squares and retains its Dexterity bonus. It can even move (possibly carrying away the opponent), provided it can drag the opponent's weight.

Poison (Ex): Poison attacks deal initial damage, such as temporary ability damage (see above) or some other effect, to the opponent on a failed Fortitude save. Unless otherwise noted, another saving throw is required 1 minute later (regardless of the first save's result) to avoid secondary damage. The creature's descriptive text lists the details.

The Fortitude save against poison has a DC of 10 + 1/2 poisoning creature's HD + poisoning creature's Constitution modifier (the exact DC is given in the creature's descriptive text). A successful save averts the damage.

Psionics (Sp): These are abilities that the creature generates with the power of its mind. Psionic abilities are always at will (no use limit).

Ray (Su or Sp): A ray behaves like a ranged attack (see Aiming a Spell, page 148 in the *Player's Handbook*). It requires a ranged touch attack roll, ignoring armor and shield and using the creature's ranged attack bonus. Ray attacks are always made at short range (no range increment). The creature's descriptive text specifies the maximum range, effects, and any applicable saving throw.

Sonic Attacks (Su): Unless noted otherwise, sonic attacks follow the rules for spreads (see Aiming a Spell, page 148 in the *Player's Handbook*); the range of the spread is measured from the creature using the sonic attack. Once a sonic attack has taken effect, deafening the subject or stopping its ears does not break the effect. Stopping one's ears ahead of time allows opponents to avoid having to make saving throws against mind-affecting sonic attacks, but not other kinds of sonic attacks (such as those that inflict damage). Stopping one's ears is a full-round action and requires wax or other soundproof material to stuff into the ears.

Spells (Sp): Some creatures can cast arcane or divine spells just as members of a spellcasting class can (and can activate magic items accordingly). These creatures are subject to the same spellcasting rules as characters are.

Spellcasting creatures are not actually members of a class unless their entries say so, and they do not gain any class abilities. For example, a creature that casts arcane spells as a sorcerer cannot acquire a familiar. A creature with access to cleric spells must prepare them in the normal manner and receives no bonus spells.

Swallow Whole (Ex): The creature can swallow opponents it holds (see Improved Grab, above). If it makes a second successful grapple check after a grab, it swallows its prey. Unless otherwise noted, the opponent can be up to one size category smaller than the swallowing creature. Damage is usually bludgeoning, often accompanied by acid damage from the creature's digestive juices. The consequences of being swallowed vary with the creature and are explained in its descriptive text.

Trample (Ex): As a standard action during its turn each round, the creature can literally run over an opponent at least one size category smaller than itself. The creature merely has to move over the opponent. The trample deals bludgeoning damage, and the creature's descriptive text lists the amount.

Trampled opponents can attempt attacks of opportunity, but these incur a –4 penalty. If they do not make attacks of opportunity, trampled opponents can attempt Reflex saves for half damage. The save DC is 10 + 1/2 trampling creature's HD + trampling creature's Strength modifier (the exact DC is given in the creature's descriptive text).

Special Qualities

This line gives all the creature's special qualities, in the order they are most likely to be used. If the creature has no special qualities, this line does not appear. Details of the most common special qualities are provided here.

Blindsight (Ex): Using nonvisual senses, such as sensitivity to vibrations, scent, acute hearing, or echolocation, the creature maneuvers and fights as well as a sighted creature. Invisibility and darkness are irrelevant, though the creature still can't discern ethereal beings. The ability's range is specified in the creature's descriptive text. The creature usually does not need to make Spot or Listen checks to notice creatures within range of its blindsight ability.

Damage Reduction (Su): The creature ignores damage from most weapons and natural attacks. Wounds heal immediately, or the weapon bounces off harmlessly (in either case, the opponent knows the attack was ineffective). The creature takes normal damage from energy attacks (even nonmagical ones), spells, spell-like abilities, and supernatural abilities. A magic weapon or a creature with its own damage reduction can sometimes damage the creature normally, as noted below.

The entry indicates the amount of damage ignored (usually 5 to 25 points) and the type of weapon that negates the ability. For example, the werewolf's entry reads "damage reduction 15/silver": Each time a foe hits a werewolf with a weapon, the damage dealt by that attack is reduced by 15 points (to a minimum of 0). However, a silver weapon deals full damage.

Any weapon more powerful than the type listed in the note also negates the ability. (For details, see Table 3–13: Damage Reduction Rankings, page 74 in the *Dungeon Master's Guide*.)

For example, the werewolf (damage reduction 15/silver) takes normal damage from weapons with +1 or better magical bonuses, but not from nonmagical weapons made from material other than silver, and not from keen weapons or weapons with other special magical properties.

For purposes of harming other creatures with damage reduction, a creature's natural weapons count as the type that ignore its own innate damage reduction. However, damage reduction from spells, such as *stoneskin*, does not confer this ability. The amount of damage reduction is irrelevant. For example, a Large air elemental (damage reduction 10/+1) deals full damage to a werewolf, as if the elemental's attack were with a +1 weapon.

Fast Healing (Ex): The creature regains hit points at an exceptionally fast rate, usually 1 or more hit points per round, as given in the entry (for example, a vampire has fast healing 5). Except where noted here, fast healing is just like natural healing (see page 129 in the *Player's Handbook*). Fast healing does not restore hit points lost from starvation, thirst, or suffocation, and it does not allow a creature to regrow or reattach lost body parts.

Regeneration (Ex): Creatures with this ability are difficult to kill. Damage dealt to the creature is treated as subdual damage. The creature automatically heals subdual damage at a fixed rate per round, as given in the entry (for example, a troll has regeneration 5). Certain attack forms, typically fire and acid, deal normal damage to the creature, which doesn't go away. The creature's descriptive text describes the details.

A regenerating creature that has been rendered unconscious through subdual damage can be killed with a coup de grace (see Helpless Defenders, page 133 in the *Player's Handbook*). The attack cannot be of a type that automatically converts to subdual damage.

Attack forms that don't deal hit point damage (for example, most poisons and disintegration) ignore regeneration. Regeneration also does not restore hit points lost from starvation, thirst, or suffocation.

Regenerating creatures can regrow lost portions of their bodies and can reattach severed limbs or body parts; details are in the creature's entry. Severed parts that are not reattached wither and die normally.

Resistance to Energy (Ex): The creature ignores some damage of the listed type each round (commonly acid, cold, fire, or electricity). The listing indicates the amount and type of damage ignored. For example, a janni has fire resistance 30, so it ignores the first 30 points of fire damage dealt to it each round.

Scent (Ex): This ability allows the creature to detect approaching enemies, sniff out hidden foes, and track by sense of smell. Creatures with the scent ability can identify familiar odors just as humans do familiar sights.

The creature can detect opponents within 30 feet by sense of smell. If the opponent is upwind, the range increases to 60 feet; if downwind, it drops to 15 feet. Strong scents, such as smoke or rotting garbage, can be detected at twice the ranges noted above. Overpowering scents, such as skunk musk or troglodyte stench, can be detected at triple normal range.

When a creature detects a scent, the exact location is not revealed—only its presence somewhere within range. The creature can take a partial action to note the direction of the scent. If it moves within 5 feet of the source, the creature can pinpoint that source.

A creature with the scent ability can follow tracks by smell, making a Wisdom check to find or follow a track. The typical DC for a fresh trail is 10 (no matter what kind of surface holds the scent). This DC increases or decreases depending on how strong the quarry's odor is, the number of creatures, and the age of the trail. For each hour that the trail is cold, the DC increases by 2. The ability otherwise follows the rules for the Track feat. Creatures tracking by scent ignore the effects of surface conditions and poor visibility.

Spell Resistance (Ex): The creature can avoid the effects of spells and spell-like abilities that directly affect it. The listing includes a numerical rating. To determine if a spell or spell-like ability works, the spellcaster must make a level check (1d20 + caster level). If the result equals or exceeds the creature's spell resistance (SR) rating, the spell works normally, although the creature is still allowed a saving throw. See Spell Resistance, page 81 in the DUNGEON MASTER's Guide, for details.

Turn Resistance (Ex): The creature (usually undead) is less easily affected by clerics or paladins (see Turn and Rebuke Undead, page 139 in the *Player's Handbook*). When resolving a turn, rebuke, command, or bolster attempt, add the listed bonus to the creature's Hit Dice total. For example, a shadow has +2 turn resistance and 3 HD. Attempts to turn, rebuke, command, or bolster treat the shadow as though it had 5 HD, though it is a 3 HD creature for any other purpose.

Saves

This line gives the creature's Fortitude, Reflex, and Will save modifiers, which take into account its type, ability score modifiers, and any special qualities.

Abilities

This line lists all six of the creature's ability scores, in order: Str, Dex, Con, Int, Wis, Cha. Most abilities work exactly as described in Chapter 1: Abilities in the *Player's Handbook*, with the following exceptions.

Strength: Quadrupeds can carry heavier loads than characters can. To determine a quadruped's carrying capacity limits, use Table 9-1: Carrying Capacity, page 142 in the *Player's Handbook*, multiplying by the appropriate modifier for the creature's size: Fine 1/4, Diminutive 1/2, Tiny 3/4, Small 1, Medium 1 1/2, Large 3, Huge 6, Gargantuan 12, and Colossal 24.

Intelligence: A creature can speak all the languages mentioned in its descriptive text, plus one additional language per point of Intelligence bonus. Any creature with an Intelligence score of 3 or higher understands at least one language (Common unless noted otherwise).

Nonabilities: Some creatures lack certain ability scores. These creatures do not have an ability score of 0—they lack the ability altogether. The modifier for a nonability is +0. Other effects of nonabilities are as follows.

Strength: Any creature that can physically manipulate other objects has at least 1 point of Strength.

A creature with no Strength score can't exert force, usually because it has no physical body (a ghost, for example) or because it doesn't move (a shrieker). The creature automatically fails Strength checks. If the creature can attack, it applies its Dexterity modifier to its base attack instead of a Strength modifier.

Dexterity: Any creature that can move has at least 1 point of Dexterity.

A creature with no Dexterity score can't move (a shrieker, for example). If it can act (such as by casting spells), it applies its Intelligence modifier to initiative checks instead of a Dexterity modifier. The creature fails all Reflex saves and Dexterity checks.

Constitution: Any living creature has at least 1 point of Constitution.

A creature with no Constitution has no body (a spectre, for example) or no metabolism (a golem). It is immune to any effect that requires a Fortitude save unless the effect works on objects. For example, a zombie is unaffected by any type of poison but is susceptible to a *disintegrate* spell. The creature is also immune to ability damage, ability drain, and energy drain, and always fails Constitution checks.

Intelligence: Any creature that can think, learn, or remember has at least 1 point of Intelligence.

A creature with no Intelligence score is an automaton, operating on simple instincts or programmed instructions. It is immune to all mind-influencing effects (charms, compulsions, phantasms, patterns and morale effects) and automatically fails Intelligence checks.

Wisdom: Any creature that can perceive its environment in any fashion has at least 1 point of Wisdom.

Anything with no Wisdom score is an object, not a creature. Anything without a Wisdom score also has no Charisma score, and vice versa.

Charisma: Any creature capable of telling the difference between itself and things that are not itself has at least 1 point of Charisma.

Anything with no Charisma score is an object, not a creature. Anything without a Charisma score also has no Wisdom score, and vice versa.

Skills

This line lists all the creature's skills by name along with each skill's score, which includes adjustments for ability scores and any bonuses from feats or racial abilities unless otherwise noted in the descriptive text. All listed skills were purchased as class skills unless the creature has a character class (noted in the entry). If you wish to customize the creature with new skills, use the table below to determine its total skill points. Treat any skill not mentioned in the creature's entry as a cross-class skill unless the creature has a character class, in which case it can purchase the skill as any other member of that class can.

A creature's type and Intelligence score determine the number of skill points it has. Some creatures receive bonus skill points for having Hit Dice in excess of what is normal for creatures of their size, as listed in the accompanying table.

The "Skills" section of the creature's descriptive text recaps racial and other bonuses for the sake of clarity; these bonuses should not be added to the listed skill scores unless otherwise noted. An asterisk (*) beside the relevant score and in the "Skills" section indicates a conditional adjustment.

Feats

The line lists all the creature's feats by name. The creature's descriptive text may contain additional information if a feat works differently than described in this section or Chapter 5: Feats in the *Player's Handbook*.

Most creatures use the same feats that are available to characters, but some have access to one or more unique feats. See the sidebar on this page for descriptions of these feats.

Type	Base Skill Points	Bonus Skill Points
Aberration	2 × Int score	+2/EHD*
Animal	10–15	—
Beast	2 × Int score	+1/EHD
Construct	—	—
Dragon	(6 + Int mod) × HD	—
Elemental	2 × Int score	+2/EHD
Fey	3 × Int score	+2/EHD
Giant	6 + Int mod	+1/EHD
Humanoid	6 + Int mod	+1/EHD
Magical beast	2 × Int score	+1/EHD
Monstrous humanoid	2 × Int score	+2/EHD
Ooze	—	—
Outsider	(8 + Int mod) × HD	—
Plant	—	—
Shapechanger	2 × Int score	+1/EHD
Undead	3 × Int score	+2/EHD
Vermin	10–15	—

*EHD: Extra Hit Die. To calculate EHD, subtract 1 from the creature's total Hit Dice if it is Medium-size or smaller; 2 if Large; 4 if Huge; 16 if Gargantuan; and 32 if Colossal. Treat results less than 0 as 0.

SECONDARY STATISTICS BLOCK

This section includes information that the DM needs for campaign purposes but not (usually) during an encounter. In many cases when the main statistics block includes information about a number of related creatures (elementals, for instance), and the secondary statistics block for all those creatures is identical, the secondary statistics block appears only once, at the end of the main statistics blocks for all the creatures.

Climate/Terrain

This entry describes the locales where the creature is most often found.

Cold: Arctic and subarctic climes. Any area that has winter conditions for the greater portion of the year is cold.

Temperate: Any area that has alternating warm and cold seasons.

Warm: Tropical and subtropical climes. Any area that has summer conditions for the greater portion of the year is warm.

FLYBY ATTACK [General]

The creature can attack on the wing.

Prerequisite: Fly speed.

Benefit: When flying, the creature can take a move action (including a dive) and another partial action at any point during the move. The creature cannot take a second move action during a round when it makes a flyby attack.

Normal: Without this feat, the creature takes a partial action either before or after its move.

MULTIATTACK [General]

The creature is adept at using all its natural weapons at once.

Prerequisite: Three or more natural weapons.

Benefit: The creature's secondary attacks with natural weapons suffer only a –2 penalty.

Normal: Without this feat, the creature's secondary natural attacks suffer a –5 penalty.

MULTIDEXTERITY [General]

The creature is adept at using all its hands in combat.

Prerequisite: Dex 15+, three or more arms.

Benefit: The creature ignores all penalties for using an off hand.

Normal: Without this feat, a creature who uses an off hand suffers a –4 penalty to attack rolls, ability checks, and skill checks. A creature has one primary hand, and all the others are off hands; for example, a four-armed creature has one primary hand and three off hands.

Special: This feat replaces the Ambidexterity feat for creatures with more than two arms.

MULTIWEAPON FIGHTING [General]

A creature with three or more hands can fight with a weapon in each hand. The creature can make one extra attack each round with each extra weapon.

Prerequisite: Three or more hands.

Benefit: Penalties for fighting with multiple weapons are reduced by 2.

Normal: A creature without this feat suffers a –6 penalty to attacks made with its primary hand and a –10 penalty to attacks made with its off hands. (It has one primary hand, and all the others are off hands.) See Attacking with Two Weapons, page 124 in the *Player's Handbook*.

Special: This feat replaces the Two-Weapon Fighting feat for creatures with more than two arms. The Multidexterity feat further reduces penalties for off-hand attacks.

Aquatic: Fresh or salt water.

Desert: Any dry area with sparse vegetation.

Forest: Any area covered with trees.

Hill: Any area with rugged but not mountainous terrain.

Marsh: Low, flat, waterlogged areas; includes swamps.

Mountains: Rugged terrain, higher than hills.

Plains: Any fairly flat area that is not a desert, marsh, or forest.

Underground: Subterranean areas.

Organization

This line describes the kinds of groups the creature might form. A range of numbers in parentheses indicates how many combat-ready adults are in each type of group. Many groups also have a number of noncombatants, expressed as a percentage of the fighting population. Noncombatants can include young, the infirm, slaves, or other individuals who are not inclined to fight. A creature's Society entry may include more details on non-combatants.

Challenge Rating

This is the average level of a party of adventurers for which one creature would make an encounter of moderate difficulty. Assume a party of four fresh characters (full hit points, full spells, and equipment appropriate to their levels). Given reasonable luck, the party should be able to win the encounter with some damage but no casualties. For more information about Challenge Ratings, see pages 101 and 167 in the DUNGEON MASTER'S Guide.

Treasure

This entry reflects how much wealth the creature owns and refers to the treasure table on page 170 in the DUNGEON MASTER'S Guide. In most cases, a creature keeps valuables in its home or lair and has no treasure with it when it travels. Intelligent creatures that own useful, portable treasure (such as magic items) tend to carry and use these, leaving bulky items at home.

Note: The random dungeon generation tables in Chapter 4: Adventures in the DUNGEON MASTER'S Guide provide their own treasure information. Use that information instead of the monster's Treasure line whenever you refer to those tables.

Treasures include coins, goods, and items. Creatures can have varying amounts of each, as follows.

Standard: Roll once under each type of treasure's column on the appropriate row for the creature's Challenge Rating (for groups of creatures, use the Encounter Level for the encounter instead).

Some creatures have double, triple, or even quadruple standard treasure; in these cases roll under each treasure column two, three, or four times.

None: The creature collects no treasure of its own.

Nonstandard: Some creatures have quirks or habits that affect the types of treasure they collect. These creatures use the same treasure tables, but with special adjustments.

Fractional Coins: Roll on the Coins column for the creature's Challenge Rating, but divide the result as indicated.

% Goods or Items: The creature has goods or items only some of the time. Before checking for goods or items, roll d% against the listed percentage. On a success, make a normal roll on the Goods or Items column (which may still result in no goods or items).

Double Goods or Items: Roll twice on the Goods or Items column.

Parenthetical Notes: Some entries for goods or items include notes that limit the types of treasure a creature collects.

When a note includes the word "no," it means the creature does not collect or cannot keep that thing. If a random roll generates such a result, treat the result as "nothing" instead. For example, if a creature's "items" entry reads "no flammables," and a random roll generates a scroll, the creature instead has no item at all (the scroll burned up, or the creature left it behind).

When a note includes the word "only," the creature goes out of its way to collect treasure of the indicated type. If an entry for Goods indicates "gems only," roll on the Goods column and treat any "art" result as "gems" instead.

It sometimes will be necessary to reroll until the right sort of item appears. For example, if a creature's "items" entry reads "non-flammables only," roll normally on the Items column. If you get a flammable item, reroll on the same table until you get a nonflammable one. If the table you rolled on contains only flammable items, back up a step and reroll until you get to a table that can give you an appropriate item.

Alignment

This entry gives the alignment that the creature is most likely to have. Every entry includes a qualifier that indicates how broadly that alignment applies to the species as a whole.

Always: The creature is born with the listed alignment. The creature may have a hereditary predisposition to the alignment or come from a plane that predetermines it. It is possible for individuals to change alignment, but such individuals are either unique or one-in-a-million exceptions.

Usually: The majority (more than 50%) of these creatures have the given alignment. This may be due to strong cultural influences, or it may be a legacy of the creatures' origin. For example, most elves inherited their chaotic good alignment from their creator, the deity Corellon Larethian.

Often: The creature tends toward the listed alignment, either by nature or nurture, but not strongly. A plurality (40–50%) of individuals have the given alignment, but exceptions are common.

Advancement

This book lists only the weakest and most common version of each creature. The Advancement line shows how tough the creature can get, in terms of extra Hit Dice. (This is not an absolute limit, but exceptions are extremely rare.)

Improvement

As its Hit Dice increase, the creature's attack bonuses and saving throw modifiers might improve, and it could gain more feats and skills, depending on its type. The Creature Advancement by Type sidebar shows how creature types advance.

Saving throw bonuses are listed on Table 3-1: Base Save and Base Attack Bonuses, page 22 in the *Player's Handbook*. A "good" saving throw uses the higher of the listed values.

Note that if the creature acquires a character class, it improves according to its class, not its type.

Size Increases

Creatures may become larger as they gain Hit Dice (the new size is noted parenthetically).

A size increase affects a creature's ability scores, AC, attack bonuses, and damage ratings as indicated on the following tables.

Old Size*	New Size	Str	Dex	Con	Natural Armor	AC/Attack
Fine	Diminutive	Same	−2	Same	Same	−4
Diminutive	Tiny	+2	−2	Same	Same	−2
Tiny	Small	+4	−2	Same	Same	−1
Small	Medium-size	+4	−2	+2	Same	−1
Medium-size	Large	+8	−2	+4	+2	−1
Large	Huge	+8	−2	+4	+3	−1
Huge	Gargantuan	+8	Same	+4	+4	−2
Gargantuan	Colossal	+8	Same	+4	+5	−4

*Repeat the adjustment if the creature moves up more than one size. For example, if a creature advances from Medium-size to Huge size, it gains +16 Strength, −2 Dexterity, and −2 to attack bonus and Armor Class.

CREATURE ADVANCEMENT BY TYPE

Aberration
Hit Die: d8
Attack Bonus: Total HD × 3/4 (as cleric)
Good Saving Throws: Will
Skill Points: +2 per extra HD
Feats: +1 per 4 extra HD

Animal
Hit Die: d8
Attack Bonus: Total HD × 3/4 (as cleric)
Good Saving Throws: Usually Fortitude and Reflex
Skill Points: 10–15
Feats: —

Beast
Hit Die: d10
Attack Bonus: Total HD × 3/4 (as cleric)
Good Saving Throws: Fortitude and Reflex
Skill Points: +1 per extra HD
Feats: —

Construct
Hit Die: d10
Attack Bonus: Total HD × 3/4 (as cleric)
Good Saving Throws: —
Skill Points: —
Feats: —

Dragon
Hit Die: d12
Attack Bonus: Total HD (as fighter)
Good Saving Throws: Fortitude, Reflex, Will
Skill Points: +6 (+ Intelligence modifier) per extra HD
Feats: +1 per 4 extra HD

Elemental
Hit Die: d8
Attack Bonus: Total HD × 3/4 (as cleric)
Good Saving Throws: Variable by type—Reflex (Air, Fire);
   Fortitude (Earth, Water)
Skill Points: +2 per extra HD
Feats: +1 per 4 extra HD

Fey
Hit Die: d6
Attack Bonus: Total HD × 1/2 (as wizard)
Good Saving Throws: Reflex and Will
Skill Points: +2 per extra HD
Feats: +1 per 4 extra HD

Giant
Hit Die: d8
Attack Bonus: Total HD × 3/4 (as cleric)
Good Saving Throws: Fortitude
Skill Points: +1 per extra HD
Feats: +1 per 4 extra HD

Humanoid
Hit Die: d8
Attack Bonus: Total HD × 3/4 (as cleric)
Good Saving Throws: Variable (Fortitude or Reflex or Will)
Skill Points: +1 per extra HD
Feats: +1 per 4 extra HD

Magical Beast
Hit Die: d10
Attack Bonus: Total HD (as fighter)
Good Saving Throws: Fortitude and Reflex
Skill Points: +1 per extra HD
Feats: +1 per 4 extra HD

Monstrous Humanoid
Hit Die: d8
Attack Bonus: Total HD (as fighter)
Good Saving Throws: Reflex and Will
Skill Points: +2 per extra HD
Feats: +1 per 4 extra HD

Ooze
Hit Die: d10
Attack Bonus: Total HD × 3/4 (as cleric)
Good Saving Throws: —
Skill Points: —
Feats: Blindsight

Outsider
Hit Die: d8
Attack Bonus: Total HD (as fighter)
Good Saving Throws: Fortitude, Reflex, Will
Skill Points: +8 (+ Intelligence modifier) per extra HD
Feats: +1 per 4 total HD

Plant
Hit Die: d8
Attack Bonus: Total HD × 3/4 (as cleric)
Good Saving Throws: Fortitude
Skill Points: —
Feats: —

Shapechanger
Hit Die: d8
Attack Bonus: Total HD × 3/4 (as cleric)
Good Saving Throws: Fortitude, Reflex, Will
Skill Points: +1 per extra HD
Feats: +1 per 4 extra HD

Undead
Hit Die: d12
Attack Bonus: Total HD × 1/2 (as wizard)
Good Saving Throws: Will
Skill Points: +2 per extra HD
Feats: +1 per 4 extra HD

Vermin
Hit Die: d8
Attack Bonus: Total HD × 3/4 (as cleric)
Good Saving Throws: Fortitude
Skill Points: 10–12
Feats: —

Old Damage (Each)*	New Damage
1d2	1d3
1d3	1d4
1d4	1d6
1d6	1d8
1d8 or 1d10	2d6
1d12	2d8

*Repeat the adjustment if the creature moves up more than one size category. For example, if a Medium-size creature with two claw attacks dealing 1d4 points of damage each advances from Medium-size to Huge, the damage dealt by each of its claw attacks increases to 1d8.

Creatures With Character Classes

If a creature acquires a character class, it follows the rules for multiclassing described on pages 55–56 in the *Player's Handbook*. The creature's character level equals the number of class levels it has, plus the total Hit Dice for such beings. For example, an ogre normally has 4 HD. If it picks up one barbarian level, it becomes a 5th-level character: 1st-level barbarian/4th-level ogre (its "monster class") and adds 1d12 to its hit point total. Creatures with 1 or fewer HD use only their character levels (see Monsters as Races, page 22 in the *Dungeon Master's Guide*, for details).

A creature's monster class is always its favored class, and the creature never suffers XP penalties for having it.

Additional Hit Dice from a character class never affect a creature's size.

DESCRIPTIVE TEXT

The descriptive text opens with a short description of the monster: what it does, what it looks like, and what is most noteworthy about it. Special sections describe how the creature fights and give details on special attacks, special qualities, skills, and feats.

EXAMPLE OF MONSTER ADVANCEMENT

An otyugh is a Large aberration with an advancement of 7–8 HD (Large) and 9–15 HD (Huge). Creating a more powerful otyugh with 15 HD requires the following adjustments.

	Old Statistics	New Statistics	Notes
Size/Type:	Large Aberration	Huge Aberration	New size due to 15 HD.
Hit Dice:	6d8+6 (33 hp)	15d8+45 (112 hp)	Constitution increases from 13 to 17 for becoming Huge.
Initiative:	+0	+3 (–1 Dex, Improved Initiative)	Dexterity decreases from 10 to 8 for becoming Huge; Improved Initiative added as a new feat (one of two from +9 HD).
Speed:	20 ft.	20 ft.	No change.
AC:	17 (–1 size, +8 natural)	19 (–2 size, –1 Dex, +12 natural)	Natural armor increases by +4 for becoming Huge, but size modifier reduces AC –2.
Attacks:	2 tentacles +3 melee, bite –2 melee	2 tentacles +13 melee, bite +11 melee	Base attack bonus for a 15 HD aberration is +11 + 4 (Strength 19) – 2 (Huge size) for a primary attack bonus of +13; added Multiattack feat (two of two from +9 HD), so secondary attacks are at –2.
Damage:	Tentacle 1d6, bite 1d4	Tentacle 1d8+4, bite 1d6+2	Each d6 damage becomes d8, each d4 damage becomes d6; Strength 19 gives +4 attack bonus for primary attacks and +2 for secondary attacks.
Face/Reach:	5 ft. by 5 ft./5 ft. (15 ft. with tentacle)	10 ft. by 10 ft./15 ft. (25 ft. with tentacle)	Increased face and reach for Huge size.
Special Attacks:	Improved grab, constrict, disease	Improved grab, constrict, disease	No changes.
Special Qualities:	Scent	Scent	No changes.
Saves:	Fort +3, Ref +2, Will +6	Fort +8, Ref +4, Will +10	At 15 HD, normal saves have a +5 bonus and good saves have a +9 bonus, all adjusted for ability scores and feats.
Abilities:	Str 11, Dex 10, Con 13, Int 5, Wis 12, Cha 6	Str 19, Dex 8, Con 17, Int 5, Wis 12, Cha 6	Strength increases by +8, Dexterity decreases by –2, Constitution increases by +4.
Skills:	Hide +5, Listen +6, Spot +9	Hide +9, Listen +11, Spot +13	Adding 9 HD raises maximum skill rank to 18 and adds 18 skill points. (+9 to Hide, +5 to Listen, +4 to Spot). Hide skill suffers a –8 penalty because of Huge size. All skill scores adjusted for ability scores.
Feats:	Alertness	Alertness, Improved Initiative, Multiattack	Adding 9 HD adds two feats: Improved Initiative and Multiattack.

Challenge Rating: The otyugh's Challenge Rating remains unchanged, but the experience award increases by the same ratio as the increase in Hit Dice. This creature grew from 6 to 15 HD, a multiplication of 2 1/2. Parties who defeat this monster receive 2 1/2 times the normal experience award.

ABOLETH

Huge Aberration (Aquatic)
Hit Dice: 8d8+40 (76 hp)
Initiative: +1 (Dex)
Speed: 10 ft., swim 60 ft.
AC: 16 (–2 size, +1 Dex, +7 natural)
Attacks: 4 tentacles +12 melee
Damage: Tentacle 1d6+9 and transformation
Face/Reach: 10 ft. by 20 ft./10 ft.
Special Attacks: Transformation, psionics, enslave
Special Qualities: Mucus cloud
Saves: Fort +7, Ref +3, Will +11
Abilities: Str 26, Dex 12, Con 20, Int 15, Wis 17, Cha 17
Skills: Concentration +16, Knowledge (any one) +7, Listen +16, Spot +16
Feats: Alertness, Combat Casting, Iron Will

Climate/Terrain: Any underground
Organization: Solitary, brood (2–4), or slaver brood (1d3+1 plus 7–12 skum)
Challenge Rating: 7
Treasure: Double standard
Alignment: Usually lawful evil
Advancement: 9–16 HD (Huge); 17–24 HD (Gargantuan)

The aboleth is a revolting fish-like amphibian found primarily in subterranean lakes and rivers. It despises all nonaquatic creatures and attempts to destroy them on sight.

Aboleths are both cruel and highly intelligent, making them very dangerous predators. They know many ancient and terrible secrets, for they inherit their parents' knowledge at birth and assimilate the memories of all they consume.

An aboleth resembles an enormous, prehistoric fish, measuring some 20 feet in length from snout to tail, with four 10-foot-long tentacles sprouting from behind its massive head. Its rubbery skin is blue-green with regular gray splotches running along its sides. The pink belly of the creature is interrupted by a lampreylike mouth and four pulsating organs that secrete a foul-smelling gray slime.

Aboleths are smart enough to refrain from immediately attacking land dwellers who draw near. Instead they hang back, hoping their prey will enter the water, which they often make appear cool, clear, and refreshing with their powers of illusion. Aboleths also use their psionic abilities to enslave individuals for use against their own companions.

Aboleths have both male and female reproductive organs. They breed in solitude, laying 1d3 eggs every five years. These eggs grow for another five years before hatching into full-grown aboleths. Although the young are physically mature, they remain with their parent for some ten years, obeying the older creature utterly.

Aboleth speak their own language, as well as Undercommon and Aquan.

COMBAT

An aboleth attacks by flailing with its long, slimy tentacles, though it prefers to fight from a distance using its illusion powers.

Transformation (Ex): A blow from an aboleth's tentacle can cause a terrible transformation. Affected creatures must succeed at a Fortitude save (DC 19) or begin to transform over the next 1d4+1 minutes, the skin gradually becoming a clear, slimy membrane. A transformed creature must remain moistened with cool, fresh water or suffer 1d12 points of damage every 10 minutes.

A *remove disease* spell cast before the transformation is complete will restore an afflicted creature to normal. Afterward, however, only a *heal* or *mass heal* spell can reverse the change.

Psionics (Sp): At will—*hypnotic pattern, illusory wall, mirage arcana, persistent image, programmed image, project image,* and *veil.* These effects are as the spells cast by a 16th-level sorcerer (save DCs, where applicable, are 13 + spell level).

Enslave (Su): Three times a day, an aboleth can attempt to enslave any one living creature within 30 feet. The target must succeed at a Will save (DC 17) or be affected as though by a *dominate person* spell cast by a 16th-level sorcerer. An enslaved creature obeys the aboleth's telepathic commands (but will not fight on its behalf) until freed by *remove curse* or *dispel magic,* and can attempt a new Will save every 24 hours to break free. The control is also broken if the aboleth dies or travels more than one mile from its slave.

Mucus Cloud (Ex): An aboleth underwater surrounds itself with a viscous cloud of mucus roughly 1 foot thick. Any creature coming into contact with and inhaling this substance must succeed at a Fortitude save (DC 19) or lose the ability to breathe air for the next 3 hours. The affected creature suffocates in 2d6 minutes if removed from the water. Renewed contact with the mucus cloud and failing another Fortitude save continues the effect for another 3 hours.

ACHAIERAI

Large Outsider (Evil, Lawful)
Hit Dice: 6d8+12 (39 hp)
Initiative: +1 (Dex)
Speed: 50 ft.
AC: 20 (–1 size, +1 Dex, +10 natural)
Attacks: 2 claws +9 melee, bite +4 melee
Damage: Claw 2d6+4, bite 4d6+2
Face/Reach: 5 ft. by 5 ft./10 ft.
Special Attacks: Black cloud
Special Qualities: SR 19
Saves: Fort +7, Ref +6, Will +7
Abilities: Str 19, Dex 13, Con 14, Int 13, Wis 14, Cha 16
Skills: Climb +13, Jump +13, Listen +11, Move Silently +10, Sense Motive +11, Spot +11
Feats: Dodge, Mobility

Climate/Terrain: Any land and underground
Organization: Solitary or flock (5–8)
Challenge Rating: 5
Treasure: Double standard
Alignment: Always lawful evil
Advancement: 7–12 HD (Large); 13–18 HD (Huge)

Achaierai are massive, flightless birds that inhabit the infernal plane of Acheron and are only occasionally encountered elsewhere. They are evil, clever, and predatory, with a distinct taste for torture.

Standing some 15 feet tall, achaierai have plump bodies resembling quails' and four stork legs. Their soft feathers range in color through a variety of browns and earth tones. The claws and beak of an achaierai have a metallic glint.

Achaierai speak Infernal.

COMBAT

In close combat, achaierai lash out with two of their four legs and snap with their powerful beaks. These attack modes alone would make them deadly warriors.

Black Cloud (Ex): Up to three times per day an achaierai can release a choking, toxic black cloud. Those other than achaierai within 10 feet instantly take 2d6 points of damage. They must also succeed at a Fortitude save (DC 15) or be affected for 3 hours as though by an *insanity* spell cast by a 16th-level sorcerer.

ALLIP

Medium-Size Undead (Incorporeal)
Hit Dice: 4d12 (26 hp)
Initiative: +5 (+1 Dex, +4 Improved Initiative)
Speed: Fly 30 ft. (perfect)
AC: 15 (+1 Dex, +4 deflection)
Attacks: Incorporeal touch +3 melee
Damage: Incorporeal touch 1d4 permanent Wisdom drain
Face/Reach: 5 ft. by 5 ft./5 ft.
Special Attacks: Babble, Wisdom drain, madness
Special Qualities: Undead, incorporeal, +2 turn resistance
Saves: Fort +1, Ref +2, Will +4
Abilities: Str —, Dex 12, Con —, Int 11, Wis 11, Cha 18
Skills: Hide +8, Intimidate +11, Intuit Direction +4, Listen +7, Search +7, Spot +7
Feats: Improved Initiative

Climate/Terrain: Any land and underground
Organization: Solitary
Challenge Rating: 3
Treasure: None
Alignment: Always neutral evil
Advancement: 5–12 HD (Medium-size)

An allip is the spectral remains of someone driven to madness and suicide. Allips crave only revenge and unrelentingly pursue those who pushed them over the brink.

An allip looks more or less as it did in life, but its features are distorted with madness. The mouth is often twisted in an anguished moan, and the eyes are bright with terror. From the waist down, it trails away into vaporous nothingness, leaving a faint trace of fog behind it as it moves.

COMBAT

Allips are unable to cause physical harm, although they don't appear to know that. They keep flailing away at their enemies, yet they inflict no wounds.

Babble (Su): An allip constantly mutters and whines to itself, creating a hypnotic effect. All sane creatures within 60 feet of the allip must succeed at a Will save (DC 16) or be affected as though by a *hypnotism* spell for 2d4 rounds. This is a sonic, mind-affecting compulsion. Opponents who successfully save cannot be affected by the same allip's babble for one day.

Wisdom Drain (Su): Those whose Wisdom is reduced to 0 by the allip become helpless until at least 1 point of Wisdom is restored.

Madness (Su): Anyone targeting the allip with a mind-control or telepathic ability makes direct contact with its tortured mind and takes 1d4 points of temporary Wisdom damage.

Undead: Immune to mind-influencing effects, poison, sleep, paralysis, stunning, and disease. Not subject to critical hits, subdual damage, ability damage, energy drain, or death from massive damage.

Incorporeal: Can be harmed only by other incorporeal creatures, +1 or better magic weapons, or magic, with a 50% chance to ignore any damage from a corporeal source. Can pass through solid objects at will, and own attacks pass through armor. Always moves silently.

	Tiny Animated Object Tiny Construct	Small Animated Object Small Construct	Medium-Size Animated Object Medium-Size Construct
Hit Dice:	1/2 d10 (2 hp)	1d10 (5 hp)	2d10 (11 hp)
Initiative:	+2 (Dex)	+1 (Dex)	+0
Speed:	40 ft. (50 ft. legs, 60 ft. multiple legs, 80 ft. wheels)	30 ft. (40 ft. legs, 50 ft. multiple legs, 70 ft. wheels)	30 ft. (40 ft. legs, 50 ft. multiple legs, 70 ft. wheels)
AC:	14 (+2 size, +2 Dex)	14 (+1 size, +1 Dex, +2 natural)	14 (+4 natural)
Attacks:	Slam +1 melee	Slam +1 melee	Slam +2 melee
Damage:	Slam 1d3–1	Slam 1d4	Slam 1d6+1
Face/Reach:	2 1/2 ft. by 2 1/2 ft./0 ft.	5 ft. by 5 ft./5 ft.	5 ft. by 5 ft./5 ft.
Special Attacks:	See text	See text	See text
Special Qualities:	See text	See text	See text
Saves:	Fort +0, Ref +2, Will –5	Fort +0, Ref +1, Will –5	Fort +0, Ref +0, Will –5
Abilities:	Str 8, Dex 14, Con —, Int —, Wis 1, Cha 1	Str 10, Dex 12, Con —, Int —, Wis 1, Cha 1	Str 12, Dex 10, Con —, Int —, Wis 1, Cha 1

	Large Animated Object Large Construct	Huge Animated Object Huge Construct	Gargantuan Animated Object Gargantuan Construct
Hit Dice:	4d10 (22 hp)	8d10 (44 hp)	16d10 (88 hp)
Initiative:	+0	–1 (Dex)	–2 (Dex)
Speed:	20 ft. (30 ft. legs, 40 ft. multiple legs, 60 ft. wheels)	20 ft. (30 ft. legs, 40 ft. multiple legs, 60 ft. wheels)	10 ft. (20 ft. legs, 30 ft. multiple legs, 50 ft. wheels)
AC:	14 (–1 size, +5 natural)	13 (–2 size, –1 Dex, +6 natural)	12 (–4 size, –2 Dex, +8 natural)
Attacks:	Slam +5 melee	Slam +9 melee	Slam +15 melee
Damage:	Slam 1d8+4	Slam 2d6+7	Slam 2d8+10
Face/Reach:	5 ft. by 10 ft./5 ft. (long) 5 ft. by 5 ft./10 ft. (tall)	10 ft. by 20 ft./10 ft. (long) 10 ft. by 10 ft./15 ft. (tall)	20 ft. by 40 ft./10 ft. (long) 20 ft. by 20 ft./20 ft. (tall)
Special Attacks:	See text	See text	See text
Special Qualities:	See text	See text	See text
Saves:	Fort +1, Ref +1, Will –4	Fort +2, Ref +1, Will –3	Fort +5, Ref +3, Will +0
Abilities:	Str 16, Dex 10, Con —, Int —, Wis 1, Cha 1	Str 20, Dex 8, Con —, Int —, Wis 1, Cha 1	Str 24, Dex 6, Con —, Int —, Wis 1, Cha 1

	Colossal Animated Object Colossal Construct
Hit Dice:	32d10 (176 hp)
Initiative:	–3 (Dex)
Speed:	10 ft. (20 ft. legs, 30 ft. multiple legs, 50 ft. wheels)
AC:	11 (–8 size, –3 Dex, +12 natural)
Attacks:	Slam +25 melee
Damage:	Slam 4d6+13
Face/Reach:	40 ft. by 80 ft./15 ft. (long) 40 ft. by 40 ft./25 ft. (tall)
Special Attacks:	See text
Special Qualities:	See text
Saves:	Fort +10, Ref +7, Will +5
Abilities:	Str 28, Dex 4, Con —, Int —, Wis 1, Cha 1

Climate/Terrain:	Any land and underground
Organization:	Tiny: Group (4); Small: Pair; Medium-size, Large, Huge, Gargantuan, and Colossal: Solitary
Challenge Rating:	Tiny 1/2; Small 1; Medium-size 2; Large 3; Huge 5; Gargantuan 7; Colossal 10
Treasure:	None
Alignment:	Always neutral
Advancement:	—

Animated objects come in all sizes, shapes, and colors. They owe their existence as creatures to spells or supernatural abilities such as *animate objects*.

COMBAT

Animated objects fight only as directed by the animator. They follow orders without question and to the best of their abilities. Since they do not need to breathe and never tire, they can be extremely capable minions.

Construct: Immune to mind-influencing effects, poison, disease, and similar effects. Not subject to critical hits, subdual damage, ability damage, energy drain, or death from massive damage.

An animated object can have one or more of the following special abilities, depending on its form.

Blind (Ex): A sheetlike animated object such as a carpet or tapestry can grapple an opponent up to three sizes larger. The object makes a normal grapple check. If it gets a hold, it wraps itself around the opponent's head, blinding that creature until removed. The blinded creature cannot make Spot, Search, or Track checks and suffers a –6 circumstance penalty to other checks related to perception, such as Listen.

Constrict (Ex): A flexible animated object such as a rope, vine, or rug deals automatic slam damage with a successful grapple check against creatures up to one size larger than itself.

An object of at least Large size can make constrict attacks against multiple creatures at once, if they all are at least two sizes smaller than the object and fit under it.

Trample (Ex): An animated object of at least Large size and with a hardness of at least 10 can trample creatures two or more sizes smaller for the object's slam damage. Opponents who do not make attacks of opportunity against the object can attempt Reflex saves (DC 10 + 1/2 object's HD) to halve the damage.

Hardness (Ex): An animated object has the same hardness it had before it was animated (see Attack an Object, page 135 in the *Player's Handbook*).

Improved Speed (Ex): The base speeds given in the statistics block assume that animated objects lurch, rock, or slither along. Objects with two legs (statues, ladders) or a similar shape that allows faster movement have a speed bonus of 10 feet. Objects with multiple legs (tables, chairs) have a speed bonus of 20 feet. Wheeled objects gain a speed bonus of 40 feet.

Objects might have additional modes of movement. A wooden object can float and has a swim speed equal to half its land speed. A rope or similar sinuous object has a climb speed equal to half its land speed. A sheetlike object can fly (clumsy maneuverability) at half its normal speed.

The ankheg is a burrowing monster with a taste for fresh meat. One bite of its powerful mandibles can snap a small tree.

An ankheg looks like a huge segmented worm or caterpillar with six slender legs, each ending in a sharp claw. A tough chitinous shell, usually brown or yellow, covers its entire body. It has glistening black eyes and two sensitive antennae. An ankheg is about 10 feet long and weighs about 800 pounds.

An ankheg uses its legs and mandibles to dig a winding tunnel up to 40 feet below the surface in the rich soil of forests or farmlands. The tunnel is about 5 feet tall and wide, and from 60 to 150 feet long. The hollowed ends of the tunnel serve as temporary lairs for sleeping, eating, or hibernating.

Ankhegs can eat decayed organic matter but prefer fresh meat. Though a hungry ankheg might kill a farmer, the creature is quite beneficial to farmland. Its tunnel system laces the soil with passages for air and water, while its wastes add rich nutrients.

COMBAT

An ankheg usually lies 5 to 10 feet below the surface until its antennae detect the approach of prey. It then burrows up to attack. (Treat this as a charge.)

Clusters of ankhegs share the same territory but do not cooperate. If several attack, each tries to grab a different foe. If there aren't enough targets, two might grab the same creature in a tug of war.

Improved Grab (Ex): To use this ability, the ankheg must hit with its bite attack. If it gets a hold, it deals automatic bite damage each round the hold is maintained. If the ankheg is damaged after grabbing its prey, it retreats backward down its tunnel at burrowing speed, dragging the victim with it.

Acid (Ex): Acidic enzymes drip from an ankheg's mouth each round it maintains a hold. It automatically deals 1d4 points of acid damage each round in addition to bite damage.

Spit Acid (Ex): Stream of acid 5 feet high, 5 feet wide, and 30 feet long, once every 6 hours; damage 4d4, Reflex half DC 14. One such attack depletes the ankheg's acid supply for 6 hours. It cannot spit acid or deal acid damage during this time.

Ankhegs do not use this ability unless they are desperate or frustrated. They most often spit acid when reduced to fewer than half their hit points or when they have not successfully grabbed an opponent.

Tremorsense (Ex): Ankhegs can automatically sense the location of anything within 60 feet that is in contact with the ground.

ANKHEG

Large Beast
Hit Dice: 3d10+9 (25 hp)
Initiative: +0
Speed: 30 ft., burrow 20 ft.
AC: 18 (–1 size, +9 natural)
Attacks: Bite +6 melee
Damage: Bite 2d6+7
Face/Reach: 5 ft. by 10 ft./5 ft.
Special Attacks: Improved grab, acid, spit acid
Special Qualities: Tremorsense
Saves: Fort +6, Ref +3, Will +2
Abilities: Str 21, Dex 10, Con 17, Int 1, Wis 13, Cha 6
Skills: Listen +4

Climate/Terrain: Temperate and warm plains, forest, and underground
Organization: Solitary or cluster (2–4)
Challenge Rating: 3
Treasure: None
Alignment: Always neutral
Advancement: 4 HD (Large); 5–9 HD (Huge)

ARANEA

Medium-Size Shapechanger
Hit Dice: 3d8+6 (19 hp)
Initiative: +6 (+2 Dex, +4 Improved Initiative)
Speed: 50 ft., climb 25 ft.
AC: 13 (+2 Dex, +1 natural)
Attacks: Bite +4 melee; or web +4 ranged
Damage: Bite 1d6 and poison
Face/Reach: 5 ft. by 5 ft./5 ft.
Special Attacks: Spells, web, poison
Special Qualities: Alternate form
Saves: Fort +5, Ref +5, Will +4
Abilities: Str 11, Dex 15, Con 14, Int 14, Wis 13, Cha 14
Skills: Climb +14, Concentration +8, Craft (weaving) +8, Escape Artist +8, Jump +6, Listen +3, Spot +3
Feats: Alertness, Improved Initiative, Weapon Finesse (bite)

Climate/Terrain: Temperate and warm forest and underground
Organization: Solitary or colony (3–6)
Challenge Rating: 4
Treasure: Standard coins; double goods; standard items
Alignment: Usually neutral
Advancement: By character class

The aranea is an intelligent, shapechanging spider with sorcerous powers.

In its natural form, an aranea resembles a large spider. Its body is 3 feet across, its legs span 7 feet, and it weighs about 150 pounds. An odd-shaped lump on its back houses its brain. A pair of mandibles sprout from the front of its body. Two small arms, each about 2 feet long, lie below the mandibles. Each arm has a hand with four many-jointed fingers and a double-jointed thumb.

Araneas speak Common and Sylvan.

COMBAT

Araneas avoid physical combat and use their webs and spells when they can. In a battle, they try to immobilize or distract the most aggressive opponents first. Araneas often subdue opponents for ransom.

Spells: Araneas cast spells as 3rd-level sorcerers (save DC 12 + spell level). They prefer illusions and charms but avoid fire spells.

Web (Ex): In spider or hybrid form (see Alternate Form, below), an aranea can cast a web up to six times per day. This is similar to an attack with a net but has a maximum range of 50 feet, with a range increment of 10 feet, and is effective against targets of up to Large size (see page 102 in the *Player's Handbook* for details on net attacks). The web anchors the target in place, allowing no movement.

An entangled creature can escape with a successful Escape Artist check (DC 20) or burst the web with a successful Strength check (DC 26). The web has 6 hit points and takes double damage from fire.

Poison (Ex): Bite, Fortitude save (DC 13); initial damage 1d6 temporary Strength, secondary damage 2d6 temporary Strength.

Alternate Form (Su): An aranea's natural form is that of a Large monstrous spider. It can assume two other forms. The first is a Small or Medium-size humanoid (the exact form is fixed at birth). The second form is a Medium-size, spider-humanoid hybrid. Changing form is a standard action.

In humanoid form, the aranea gains all the abilities of the form (for example, an aranea in dwarf form has dwarven racial traits). The aranea keeps its ability scores and can cast spells, but it cannot use webs or poison in humanoid form.

In hybrid form, an aranea looks like a humanoid at first glance, but a successful Spot check (DC 18) reveals the creature's fangs and spinnerets. The aranea can use weapons and webs in this form.

An aranea remains in one form until it chooses to assume a new one. A change in form cannot be dispelled, nor does the aranea revert to its natural form when killed. A *true seeing* spell, however, reveals its natural form if it is in humanoid or hybrid form.

ARROWHAWK

	Juvenile	Adult	Elder
	Small Outsider (Air)	**Medium-Size Outsider (Air)**	**Large Outsider (Air)**
Hit Dice:	3d8+3 (16 hp)	7d8+7 (38 hp)	15d8+45 (112 hp)
Initiative:	+5 (Dex)	+5 (Dex)	+5 (Dex)
Speed:	Fly 60 ft. (perfect)	Fly 60 ft. (perfect)	Fly 60 ft. (perfect)
AC:	20 (+1 size, +5 Dex, +4 natural)	21 (+5 Dex, +6 natural)	22 (–1 size, +5 Dex, +8 natural)
Attacks:	Electricity ray +9 ranged touch; or bite +9 melee	Electricity ray +12 ranged touch; or bite +12 melee	Electricity ray +19 ranged touch; or bite +20 melee
Damage:	Electricity ray 2d6; or bite 1d6+1	Electricity ray 2d8; or bite 1d8+2	Electricity ray 2d8; or bite 2d6+9
Face/Reach:	5 ft. by 5 ft./5 ft.	5 ft. by 5 ft./5 ft.	5 ft. by 10 ft./5 ft.
Special Attacks:	Electricity ray	Electricity ray	Electricity ray
Special Qualities:	Immunities, fire and cold resistance 20	Immunities, fire and cold resistance 20	Immunities, fire and cold resistance 20
Saves:	Fort +4, Ref +8, Will +4	Fort +6, Ref +10, Will +6	Fort +12, Ref +14, Will +10
Abilities:	Str 12, Dex 21, Con 12, Int 10, Wis 13, Cha 13	Str 14, Dex 21, Con 12, Int 10, Wis 13, Cha 13	Str 22, Dex 21, Con 16, Int 10, Wis 13, Cha 13
Skills:	Intuit Direction +2, Listen +7, Search +7, Sense Motive +7, Spot +7	Escape Artist +15, Intuit Direction +7, Listen +11, Search +10, Sense Motive +11, Spot +11	Escape Artist +23, Intuit Direction +16, Knowledge (Plane of Air) +15, Listen +19, Search +18, Sense Motive +19, Spot +19

Feats:	Weapon Finesse (bite)	Dodge, Weapon Finesse (bite)	Blind-Fight, Combat Reflexes, Dodge, Weapon Finesse (bite)
Climate/Terrain:	Any land and underground	Any land and underground	Any land and underground
Organization:	Solitary or clutch (2–4)	Solitary or clutch (2–4)	Solitary or clutch (2–4)
Challenge Rating:	3	5	8
Treasure:	None	None	None
Alignment:	Always neutral	Always neutral	Always neutral
Advancement:	4–6 HD (Small)	8–14 HD (Medium-size)	16–24 HD (Large); 25–32 HD (Gargantuan)

Arrowhawks are predators and scavengers from the Elemental Plane of Air. They are consummate fliers that spend their entire lives on the wing.

An arrowhawk has a sinuous, snakelike body with a long neck and tail. Its central body is bulbous and has two pairs of yellow, feathered wings, one on the top and another on the bottom. Most of the body is covered with iridescent blue scales, with tufts of yellow feathers at the base of the neck and the tail. The head has a black, toothed beak and four eyes, one pair above the beak and the other below. The tail has alternating bands of feathers and rows of blue spines, with a mass of feathers and spines at the tip.

Arrowhawks are always in motion while they live. They can fly from the moment they hatch, and they eat, sleep, and mate on the wing. By twisting its body and varying the cadence of its wingbeats, an arrowhawk can fly at top speed in any direction.

Arrowhawk eggs have an innate levitation ability. Females lay clutches of 2d4 eggs in midair and leave them to float until they hatch. The female guards the eggs and collects them if the wind scatters them, but otherwise leaves them alone.

A juvenile arrowhawk (one to ten years old) is about 5 feet long from beak to tail, with the body accounting for about a third of the length. Its wingspan is about 7 feet, and it weighs about 20 pounds. An adult (aged eleven to forty years) is about 10 feet long from beak to tail, with a wingspan of about 15 feet and a weight of about 100 pounds. An elder arrowhawk (aged forty-one to seventy-five years) is about 20 feet long with a wingspan of 30 feet and a weight of about 800 pounds.

Arrowhawks speak Auran, but they are not talkative creatures.

COMBAT

Arrowhawks are extremely territorial and always hungry. They attack almost any other creature they meet, seeking a meal or trying to drive away a rival. The primary mode of attack is an electricity ray, fired from the tail. The creature also bites, but it prefers to stay out of reach.

Electricity Ray (Su): An arrowhawk can fire this ray once a round, with a range of 45 feet.

Immunities (Ex): Arrowhawks have acid, electricity, and poison immunity.

Illus. by T. Lockwood

ASSASSIN VINE

Large Plant
Hit Dice: 4d8+12 (30 hp)
Initiative: +0
Speed: 0 ft.
AC: 15 (–1 size, +6 natural)
Attacks: Slam +7 melee
Damage: Slam 1d6+7
Face/Reach: 5 ft. by 5 ft./10 ft. (20 ft. with vine)
Special Attack: Entangle, improved grab, constrict 1d6+7
Special Qualities: Camouflage, electricity immunity, cold and fire resistance 20, blindsight
Saves: Fort +7, Ref +1, Will +2
Abilities: Str 20, Dex 10, Con 16, Int —, Wis 13, Cha 9

Climate/Terrain: Temperate and warm forest and underground
Organization: Solitary or patch (2–4)
Challenge Rating: 3
Treasure: 1/10th coins; 50% goods; 50% items
Alignment: Always neutral
Advancement: 5–16 HD (Huge); 17–32 HD (Gargantuan); 33+ HD (Colossal)

The assassin vine is a semimobile plant that collects its own grisly fertilizer by grabbing and crushing animals and depositing the carcasses near its roots.

The mature plant consists of a main vine as thick as a human's forearm and about 20 feet long. Smaller vines up to 5 feet long branch off from the main vine about every 6 inches. These small vines bear clusters of leaves shaped curiously like human hands, and in late summer they produce bunches of small fruits that resemble wild grapes. The woody parts of the vine are coiled and gnarled, covered with brown, stringy bark, making the whole plant resemble a robust grapevine. The fruit is tough and has a hearty flavor, but is widely believed to be poisonous. Assassin vine berries make a heady wine.

A subterranean version of the assassin vine grows near hot springs, volcanic vents, and other sources of thermal energy. These plants have thin, wiry stems and gray leaves shot through with silver, brown, and white veins so that they resemble mineral deposits. An assassin vine growing underground usually generates enough offal to support a thriving colony of mushrooms and other fungi, which spring up around the plant and help conceal it.

COMBAT

Assassin vines use simple tactics: They lie still until prey comes within reach, then attack. They use their entangle ability both to catch prey and to deter counterattacks.

Entangle (Su): An assassin vine can animate plants within 30 feet of itself as a free action. The effect lasts until the vine dies or decides to end it (also a free action). The ability is otherwise similar to *entangle* as cast by a 4th-level druid (save DC 13).

Improved Grab (Ex): To use this ability, the assassin vine must hit with its slam attack.

Constrict (Ex): An assassin vine deals 1d6+7 points of damage with a successful grapple check against Medium-size or smaller creatures.

Blindsight (Ex): Assassin vines have no visual organs but can ascertain all foes within 30 feet using sound, scent, and vibration.

Camouflage (Ex): Since an assassin vine looks like a normal plant when at rest, it takes a successful Spot check (DC 20) to notice it before it attacks. Anyone with Wilderness Lore or Knowledge (plants or herbs) can use those skills instead of Spot to notice the plant. Dwarves can use stonecunning to notice the subterranean version.

ATHACH

Huge Aberration
Hit Dice: 14d8+70 (133 hp)
Initiative: +1 (Dex)
Speed: 50 ft.
AC: 20 (–2 size, +1 Dex, +3 hide, +8 natural)
Attacks: Huge club +12/+7 melee, 2 Huge clubs +12 melee, bite +14 melee; or rock +5/+0 ranged, 2 rocks +5 ranged
Damage: Huge club 2d6+8, 2 Huge clubs 2d6+4, bite 2d8+4 and poison; or rock 2d6+8, 2 rocks 2d6
Face/Reach: 10 ft. by 10 ft./15 ft.
Special Attacks: Poison
Saves: Fort +9, Ref +5, Will +10
Abilities: Str 27, Dex 12, Con 21, Int 7, Wis 12, Cha 6
Skills: Climb +16, Jump +16, Listen +7, Spot +7
Feats: Multiattack, Multidexterity, Multiweapon Fighting

Climate/Terrain: Temperate and warm hill, mountains, and underground
Organization: Solitary, gang (2–4), or tribe (7–12)
Challenge Rating: 7
Treasure: 1/2 coins; double goods; standard items
Alignment: Often chaotic evil
Advancement: 15–28 HD (Huge)

The athach is a hulking, misshapen biped. Its flabby, pear-shaped body has a third arm growing from its chest. Immensely strong, an athach can hammer most opponents to gory paste.

An athach has a wide, slobbering mouth. Curving tusks like a boar's jut from its lower jaw. Its other teeth are small and peglike. It has tiny eyes, a small nose, and lopsided ears: one huge, one tiny. An athach dresses in shabby rags and furs. It rarely bathes, and smells particularly foul. An adult stands some 18 feet tall and weighs about 4,500 pounds.

Athachs are fond of gems and crystals of all types. They often jam bracelets on their chubby fingers, necklaces around their fat wrists, and other jewelry where they can. They have been known to sit for hours, polishing and admiring their jewels. The only other things athachs tend to be passionate about are food and violence. They despise hill giants and, unless outnumbered, attack them on sight. They fear other giants and most other Huge creatures.

Athachs speak a crude dialect of Giant.

COMBAT

Athachs charge into melee combat unless their opponents are out of reach, in which case they throw rocks. They sometimes try to overrun armored opponents to reach unarmored opponents in back ranks. With their first few melee attacks, athachs tend to flail about indiscriminately. After a few rounds, they concentrate on foes that have been hitting them most often and use their bites on whoever has dealt them the most damage.

Poison (Ex): Bite, Fortitude save (DC 22); initial damage 1d6 temporary Strength, secondary damage 2d6 temporary Strength.

AZER

Medium-Size Outsider (Fire, Lawful)
Hit Dice: 2d8+2 (11 hp)
Initiative: +1 (Dex)
Speed: 30 ft.
AC: 19 (+1 Dex, +6 natural, +2 large shield)
Attacks: Warhammer +3 melee; or halfspear +3 ranged
Damage: Warhammer 1d8+1 and 1 fire; or halfspear 1d6+1 and 1 fire
Face/Reach: 5 ft. by 5 ft./5 ft.
Special Attacks: Heat
Special Qualities: SR 13, fire subtype
Saves: Fort +4, Ref +4, Will +4
Abilities: Str 13, Dex 13, Con 13, Int 12, Wis 12, Cha 9
Skills: Climb +2, Craft (any one) +6, Hide −1, Listen +4, Search +4, Spot +5
Feats: Power Attack

Climate/Terrain: Any land and underground
Organization: Solitary, pair, team (2–4), squad (11–20 plus 2 3rd-level sergeants and 1 leader of 3rd–6th level), or clan (30–100 plus 50% non-combatants plus 1 3rd-level sergeant per 20 adults, 5 5th-level lieutenants, and 3 7th-level captains)
Challenge Rating: 2
Treasure: Standard coins; double goods (nonflammables only); standard items (nonflammables only)
Alignment: Always lawful neutral
Advancement: By character class

Azers are dwarves native to the Elemental Plane of Fire. They have metallic, brass-colored skin, and flames lick their heads where a normal dwarf would have hair and a beard. They wear kilts of brass, bronze, or copper.

Azers speak Ignan and Common.

COMBAT

Azers use broad-headed spears or well-crafted hammers in combat. When unarmed, they attempt to grapple foes. They wear no armor, for their tough skin provides ample protection.

Although unfriendly and taciturn, azers rarely provoke a fight except to relieve a foe of gems, which they love. If threatened, they fight to the death, but they see the value of taking prisoners themselves.

Heat (Ex): Azers' bodies are intensely hot, so their unarmed attacks deal additional fire damage. Their metallic weapons also conduct this heat.

Fire Subtype (Ex): Fire immunity, double damage from cold except on a successful save.

AZER SOCIETY

Azers maintain a tightly regimented society in which every member has a specific place. The state always takes precedence over the individual. Azer nobles are prodigiously strong and wield absolute power. Azers dwell within bronze fortresses on their home plane, only rarely visiting other planes to gather gems. They hate efreet, with whom they wage an eternal war for territory and slaves.

BARGHEST

	Barghest Medium-Size Outsider (Evil, Lawful)	Greater Barghest Large Outsider (Evil, Lawful)
Hit Dice:	6d8+6 (33 hp)	9d8+18 (58 hp)
Initiative:	+6 (+2 Dex, +4 Improved Initiative)	+6 (+2 Dex, +4 Improved Initiative)
Speed:	30 ft. or 60 ft.	30 ft. or 60 ft.
AC:	18 (+2 Dex, +6 natural)	20 (−1 size, +2 Dex, +9 natural)
Attacks:	Bite +9 melee, 2 claws +4 melee	Bite +12 melee, 2 claws +7 melee
Damage:	Bite 1d6+3, claw 1d4+1	Bite 1d8+4, claw 1d6+2
Face/Reach:	5 ft. by 5 ft./5 ft.	5 ft. by 5 ft./10 ft. (goblin form) 5 ft. by 10 ft./5 ft. (wolf form)
Special Attacks:	Spell-like abilities, feed	Spell-like abilities, feed
Special Qualities:	Damage reduction 15/+1, scent, alternate form	Damage reduction 15/+1, scent, alternate form
Saves:	Fort +6, Ref +7, Will +7	Fort +8, Ref +8, Will +10
Abilities:	Str 17, Dex 15, Con 13, Int 14, Wis 14, Cha 14	Str 19, Dex 15, Con 15, Int 18, Wis 18, Cha 18
Skills:	Bluff +11, Hide +11*, Intimidate +11, Jump +12, Listen +11, Move Silently +10, Spot +11	Bluff +16, Concentration +14, Hide +10*, Intimidate +18, Jump +16, Listen +16, Move Silently +14, Sense Motive +16, Spot +16
Feats:	Combat Reflexes, Improved Initiative	Combat Casting, Combat Reflexes, Improved Initiative
Climate/Terrain:	Any land and underground	Any land and underground
Organization:	Solitary or pack (3–6)	Solitary or pack (3–6)
Challenge Rating:	4	5
Treasure:	Double standard	Double standard
Alignment:	Always lawful evil	Always lawful evil
Advancement:	7–8 HD (Medium-size)	10–14 HD (Large); 15–18 HD (Huge)

Though they resemble big goblins, barghests are fiends that can change into lupine form. They come into the world to feed on blood and souls and thus grow stronger.

As whelps, barghests are nearly indistinguishable from goblins, except for their size. As they grow larger and stronger, their skin darkens to bluish-red and eventually becomes blue altogether. A full-grown barghest stands about 6 feet tall and weighs 180 pounds. A barghest's eyes glow orange when the creature becomes excited.

Barghests speak Goblin, Worg, and Infernal.

COMBAT

Barghests can claw and bite, no matter what their form, and usually disdain weapons. Though they love killing, they have little stomach for direct combat and attack from ambush whenever possible. Once battle is joined, barghests hide and use *project image* to conceal their true numbers and locations, with *emotion* and *charm person* to keep opponents off balance. They try to pit as many of themselves against as few of the enemy as possible, and use their high speed to stay way from the enemy's main strength.

Spell-Like Abilities: At will—*levitate, misdirection,* and *project image;* 1/day—*charm monster, charm person, dimension door,* and *emotion.* These abilities are as the spells cast by a sorcerer whose level equals the barghest's HD (save DC 12 + spell level).

Feed (Su): When a barghest slays a humanoid opponent, it can feed on the corpse, devouring both flesh and life force, as a full-round action. For every 8 HD or levels a barghest consumes, it gains 1 Hit Die. Feeding destroys the victim's body and prevents any form of raising or resurrection that requires part of the corpse. A *wish, miracle,* or *true resurrection* spell can restore a devoured victim to life, but there is a 50% chance that even such powerful magic will fail.

Alternate Form (Su): A barghest can assume the form of a goblin or a large wolf as a standard action. This ability is similar to the *polymorph self* spell, except that it allows only goblin and wolf forms.

*While in wolf form, a barghest gains the higher of the two listed speeds and a +4 circumstance bonus to Hide checks.

Pass Without Trace (Ex): A barghest in wolf form can pass without trace (as the spell) as a free action.

Greater Barghest

These creatures are about 8 feet tall and weigh about 300 pounds in goblin form.

Combat

Occasionally, a greater barghest uses a magic two-handed weapon in combat, giving it multiple attacks (attack bonus +13/+8). It can also make one bite attack (attack bonus +8) each round. The save DC against a greater barghest's spell-like abilities is 14 + spell level.

Medium-Size Magical Beast (Reptilian)
Hit Dice: 6d10+12 (45 hp)
Initiative: –1 (Dex)
Speed: 20 ft.
AC: 16 (–1 Dex, +7 natural)
Attacks: Bite +8 melee
Damage: Bite 1d8+3
Face/Reach: 5 ft. by 5 ft./5 ft.
Special Attacks: Petrifying gaze
Saves: Fort +9, Ref +4, Will +3
Abilities: Str 15, Dex 8, Con 15, Int 2, Wis 12, Cha 10
Skills: Hide +0*, Listen +7, Spot +7
Feats: Alertness, Great Fortitude

Climate/Terrain: Any land and underground
Organization: Solitary or colony (3–6)
Challenge Rating: 5
Treasure: None
Alignment: Always neutral
Advancement: 7–10 HD (Medium-size); 11–18 HD (Large)

The basilisk is a reptilian monster that petrifies living creatures with a mere gaze. Fighting a basilisk requires either careful preparation or considerable good fortune.

Basilisks are found in nearly every climate, and often in subterranean areas as well. They tend to lair in shallow burrows, caves, or other sheltered areas. The entrance to a basilisk lair is sometimes distinguished by lifelike stone statues or carvings, actually creatures that ran afoul of the creature's gaze. Basilisks are omnivorous and able to consume their petrified victims. They make effective guardians, if one has the magical or monetary resources to capture and contain them.

A basilisk usually has a dull brown body with a yellowish underbelly. A single row of bony spines lines its back, and some specimens sport a short, curved horn atop the nose. The creature's most distinctive feature is its eyes, which glow with an eerie, pale green incandescence. An adult basilisk's body grows to about 6 feet long, not including its tail, which can reach an additional length of 5 to 7 feet. The creature weighs about 300 pounds.

COMBAT

Basilisks rely on their gaze attack, biting only when opponents come within reach. Though they have eight legs, their slow metabolism renders them relatively sluggish, so they do not expend energy unnecessarily. Intruders who flee the basilisk rather than fight can expect, at best, a halfhearted pursuit.

These creatures tend to spend most of their time lying in wait for prey, which includes small mammals, birds, reptiles, and similar creatures. When not hunting, basilisks are usually sleeping off the meal in their lairs. Basilisks sometimes gather in small colonies for mating or for mutual defense in unusually hostile terrain, and a colony will attack intruders in concert.

Barghest illus. by S. Wood

23

Petrifying Gaze (Su): Turn to stone permanently, range 30 feet; Fortitude negates DC 13.

Skills: *The basilisk's dull coloration and its ability to remain motionless for long periods of time grant it a +4 racial bonus to Hide checks in natural settings.

BEHIR

Huge Magical Beast (Electricity)
Hit Dice: 9d10+45 (94 hp)
Initiative: +1 (Dex)
Speed: 40 ft., climb 15 ft.
AC: 16 (–2 size, +1 Dex, +7 natural)
Attacks: Bite +15 melee, 6 claws +10 melee
Damage: Bite 2d4+8, claw 1d4+4
Face/Reach: 10 ft. by 30 ft./10 ft.
Special Attacks: Breath weapon, improved grab, swallow whole, constrict 2d8+8
Special Qualities: Electricity immunity, scent, can't be tripped
Saves: Fort +11, Ref +7, Will +5
Abilities: Str 26, Dex 13, Con 21, Int 7, Wis 14, Cha 12
Skills: Climb +18, Hide +5, Spot +7
Feats: Cleave, Power Attack

Climate/Terrain: Any land and underground
Organization: Solitary or pair
Challenge Rating: 8
Treasure: Standard
Alignment: Often neutral
Advancement: 10–13 HD (Huge); 14–27 HD (Gargantuan)

The behir is a snakelike monster whose dozen legs allow it to move with considerable speed.

A behir is about 40 feet long and weighs about 4,000 pounds. It can fold its limbs close to its long, narrow body and slither in snake fashion if it desires. The head looks more crocodilian than snakelike, but the mouth can open wide enough to swallow prey whole, as a snake's does.

Behirs have bandlike scales of great hardness. Their color ranges from ultramarine to deep blue with bands of gray-brown. The belly is pale blue. The two large horns curving back over the head look dangerous but are actually used for preening the creature's scales, not for fighting.

Behirs are never friendly with dragonkind and won't coexist with any type of dragon. If one enters a behir's territory, the behir does everything it can to drive the dragon out. If the behir fails, it moves off to find a new home. A behir never knowingly enters the territory of a dragon.

Behirs speak Common.

COMBAT

A behir usually bites and grabs its prey first, then either swallows or constricts the opponent. If beset by a large number of foes, it uses its breath weapon.

Breath Weapon (Su): Line of lightning 5 feet wide, 5 feet high, and 20 feet long, once a minute; damage 7d6, Reflex half DC 19.

Improved Grab (Ex): To use this ability, the behir must hit with its bite attack. If it gets a hold, it can attempt to swallow or constrict the opponent.

Swallow Whole (Ex): A behir can try to swallow a grabbed Medium-size or smaller opponent by making a successful grapple check. A behir that swallows an opponent can use its Cleave feat to bite and grab another opponent.

The swallowed creature takes 2d8+8 points of crushing damage and 8 points of acid damage per round from the behir's gizzard. A swallowed creature can also cut its way out by using claws or a Small or Tiny slashing weapon to deal 25 points of damage to the gizzard (AC 20). Once the creature exits, muscular action closes the hole; another swallowed opponent must again cut its own way out.

The behir's gizzard can hold two Medium-size, four Small, eight Tiny, sixteen Diminutive, or thirty-two Fine or smaller opponents.

Constrict (Ex): A behir deals 2d8+8 damage with a successful grapple check against Gargantuan or smaller creatures. It can use its claws against the grappled foe as well.

BEHOLDER

Large Aberration
Hit Dice: 11d8+11 (60 hp)
Initiative: +4 (Improved Initiative)
Speed: 5 ft., fly 20 ft. (good)
AC: 20 (–1 size, +11 natural)
Attacks: Eye rays +7 ranged touch, bite +2 melee
Damage: Bite 2d4
Face/Reach: 5 ft. by 5 ft./5 ft.
Special Attacks: Eye rays
Special Qualities: All-around vision, antimagic cone, fly
Saves: Fort +4, Ref +3, Will +11
Abilities: Str 10, Dex 10, Con 12, Int 17, Wis 15, Cha 15
Skills: Hide +7, Knowledge (arcana) +10, Listen +15, Search +18, Spot +20
Feats: Alertness, Flyby Attack, Improved Initiative, Iron Will, Shot on the Run

Climate/Terrain: Any land and underground
Organization: Solitary, pair, or cluster (3–6)
Challenge Rating: 13
Treasure: Double standard
Alignment: Usually lawful evil
Advancement: 12–16 HD (Large); 17–33 HD (Huge)

The beholder is the stuff of nightmares. This creature, also called the "sphere of many eyes" or "eye tyrant," is known among adventurers as a deadly adversary.

A beholder is a 6-foot-wide orb dominated by a central eye and a large, toothy maw. Ten smaller eyes on stalks sprout from the top of the orb.

Beholders speak their own language and the Common tongue.

COMBAT

Beholders often attack without provocation. Though not powerful physically, they often plow right into groups of opponents to use as many of their eyes as they can. When closing with an enemy, a beholder tries to cause as much disruption and confusion as possible.

Eye Rays (Su): Each of the ten small eyes can produce a magical ray once a round, even when the beholder is attacking physically or moving at full speed. The creature can easily

Illus. by M. Tedin after T. Lockwood

BEHIR

aim all its eyes upward, but its own body tends to get in the way when it tries to aim the rays in other directions. During a round, the creature can aim only three eye rays at targets in any one arc other than up (forward, backward, left, right, or down). The remaining eyes must aim at targets in other arcs or not at all. A beholder can tilt and pan its body each round to change which rays it can bring to bear in an arc.

Each eye's effect resembles a spell cast by a 13th-level sorcerer but follows the rules for a ray (see Aiming a Spell, page 148 in the *Player's Handbook*). All rays have a range of 150 feet and a save DC of 18.

Charm Person: The target must succeed at a Will save or be affected as though by the spell. Beholders use this ray to confuse the opposition, usually employing it early in a fight. The beholder generally instructs a *charmed* target to either restrain a comrade or stand aside.

Charm Monster: The target must succeed at a Will save or be affected as though by the spell. Beholders use this ray in the same manner as the *charm person* ray.

Sleep: This works like the spell, except that it affects one creature with any number of Hit Dice. The target must succeed at a Will save to resist. Beholders like to use this ray against warriors and other physically powerful creatures. They know their foes can quickly awaken the sleepers, but they also know that doing so takes time and can delay an effective counterattack.

Flesh to Stone: The target must succeed at a Fortitude save or be affected as though by the spell. Beholders like to aim this ray at enemy spellcasters. They also use it on any creature whose appearance they find interesting. (After the fight, the beholder takes the statue to its lair as a decoration.)

Disintegrate: The target must succeed at a Fortitude save or be affected as though by the spell. The beholder likes to use this ray on any foe it considers a real threat.

Fear: This works like the spell, except that it targets one creature. The target must succeed at a Will save or be affected as though by the spell. Beholders like to use this ray against warriors and other powerful creatures early in a fight, to break up the opposition.

Slow: This works like the spell, except that it affects one creature. The target must make a Will save to resist. Beholders often use this ray against the same creature targeted by their *disintegrate*, *flesh to stone*, or *finger of death* rays. If one of the former rays fails to eliminate the foe, this ray might at least hamper it.

Inflict Moderate Wounds: This works just like the spell, causing 2d8+10 points of damage (Will half).

Finger of Death: The target must succeed at a Fortitude save or be slain as though by the spell. The target suffers 3d6+13 damage if his saving throw succeeds. Beholders use this ray to eliminate dangerous foes quickly.

Telekinesis: The beholder can move objects or creatures that weigh up to 325 pounds, as though with a *telekinesis* spell. Creatures can resist the effect with a successful Will save.

All-Around Vision (Ex): Beholders are exceptionally alert and circumspect. Their many eyes give them a +4 racial bonus to Spot and Search checks, and they can't be flanked.

Antimagic Cone (Su): A beholder's central eye continually produces a 150-foot antimagic cone extending straight ahead from the creature's front. This functions just like *antimagic field* cast by a 13th-level sorcerer. All magical and supernatural powers and effects within the cone are suppressed— even the beholder's own eye rays. Once each round, during its turn, the beholder decides which way it will face, and whether the *antimagic cone* is active or not (the beholder deactivates the cone by shutting its central eye). Note that a beholder can bite only creatures to its front.

Flight (Ex): A beholder's body is naturally buoyant. This buoyancy allows it to fly as the spell, as a free action, at a speed of 20 feet. This buoyancy also grants it a permanent *feather fall* effect with personal range.

BEHOLDER SOCIETY

Beholders are hateful, aggressive, and avaricious, attacking or dominating others whenever they can get away with it. They exhibit a xenophobic intolerance, hating all creatures not like themselves. The basic body type comprises a great variety of beholder subspecies. Some are covered with overlapping chitinous plates; some have smooth hides or snakelike eye tentacles; some have crustacean joints. But even a difference as small as hide color or size of the central eye can make two groups of beholders sworn enemies. Every beholder declares its own unique form to be the "true ideal of beholderhood," the others being nothing but ugly copies fit only to be eliminated.

Beholders usually carve out underground lairs for themselves using their *disintegrate* rays. Beholder architecture emphasizes the vertical, and a lair usually has a number of parallel tubes, with chambers stacked on top of each other. Beholders prefer inaccessible locations that earthbound foes can reach only with difficulty.

BELKER

Large Elemental (Air)
Hit Dice: 7d8+7 (38 hp)
Initiative: +5 (Dex)
Speed: 30 ft., fly 50 ft. (perfect)
AC: 22 (–1 size, +5 Dex, +8 natural)
Attacks: 2 wings +9 melee, bite +4 melee, 2 claws +4 melee
Damage: Wing 1d6+2, bite 1d4+1, claw 1d3+1
Face/Reach: 5 ft. by 5 ft./10 ft.
Special Attacks: Smoke claws
Special Qualities: Smoke form
Saves: Fort +3, Ref +10, Will +2
Abilities: Str 14, Dex 21, Con 13, Int 6, Wis 11, Cha 11
Skills: Listen +9, Move Silently +9, Spot +9
Feats: Multiattack, Weapon Finesse (wing)

Climate/Terrain: Any land and underground
Organization: Solitary or clutch (2–4)
Challenge Rating: 6
Treasure: None
Alignment: Usually neutral evil
Advancement:
8–10 HD (Large);
11–21 HD
(Huge)

Belkers are composed primarily of smoke. Although undeniably evil, they are very reclusive and usually have no interest in the affairs of others.

The black, winged shapes of these creatures makes them look distinctly demonic. Because of their semigaseous nature, however, they shift and change shape with every puff of wind.

COMBAT

In most cases, a belker fights with its nasty claws and painful bite.

Smoke Claws (Ex): A belker in smoke form (see below) can engulf opponents by moving on top of them. It fills the air around one Medium-size or smaller opponent without provoking an attack of opportunity. The target must succeed at a Fortitude save (DC 14) or inhale part of the creature. Smoke inside the victim solidifies into a claw or talon and begins to rip at the surrounding organs, dealing 3d4 points of damage per round. The affected creature can attempt another Fortitude save each subsequent round to cough out the semivaporous menace.

Smoke Form (Su): Most of the time a belker is more or less solid, but at will it can assume a smoke form. It can switch forms once a round as a free action and can spend up to 20 rounds per day in smoke form. A belker in smoke form can fly at a speed of 50 feet (perfect maneuverability). The ability is otherwise similar to a *gaseous form* spell cast by a 7th-level sorcerer.

BLINK DOG

Medium-Size Magical Beast
Hit Dice: 4d10 (22 hp)
Initiative: +3 (Dex)
Speed: 30 ft.
AC: 16 (+3 Dex, +3 natural)
Attacks: Bite +4 melee
Damage: Bite 1d6
Face/Reach: 5 ft. by 5 ft./5 ft.
Special Qualities: Blink, dimension door, scent
Saves: Fort +4, Ref +7, Will +4
Abilities: Str 10, Dex 17, Con 10, Int 10, Wis 13, Cha 11
Skills: Hide +8, Listen +8, Sense Motive +5, Spot +8
Feats: Iron Will

Climate/Terrain: Temperate plains
Organization: Solitary, pair, or pack (7–16)
Challenge Rating: 2
Treasure: None
Alignment: Always lawful good
Advancement: 5–7 HD (Medium-size); 8–12 HD (Large)

The blink dog is an intelligent canine that has a limited teleportation ability.

Blink dogs have yellow-brown fur and are larger and stockier than other kinds of wild dogs. They are social animals, traveling in packs, and eat equal amounts of meat and plant matter. They avoid human lands but drive off evil humanoids that enter their territory.

They speak their own language, a complex mixture of barks, yaps, whines, and growls that can transmit complex information. When not hunting, they are playful with each other but very protective of their pups, which outsiders sometimes steal to train as guard animals. Blink dogs and displacer beasts are natural enemies.

COMBAT

Blink dogs hunt in packs, teleporting in a seemingly random fashion until they surround their prey, allowing some of them to make flank attacks.

Blink (Su): A blink dog can blink as the spell cast by an 8th-level sorcerer, and can evoke or end the effect as a free action.

Dimension Door (Su): A blink dog can teleport as *dimension door* cast by an 8th-level sorcerer, once per round as a free action. The ability affects only the blink dog, which never appears within a solid object and can act immediately after teleporting.

BODAK

Medium-Size Undead
Hit Dice: 9d12 (58 hp)
Initiative: +6 (+2 Dex, +4 Improved Initiative)
Speed: 20 ft.
AC: 15 (+2 Dex, +3 natural)
Attacks: Slam +6 melee
Damage: Slam 1d8+1
Face/Reach: 5 ft. by 5 ft./5 ft.
Special Attacks: Death gaze
Special Qualities: Damage reduction 15/silver, fire and acid resistance 20, electricity immunity, sunlight vulnerability, flashbacks
Saves: Fort +3, Ref +5, Will +7
Abilities: Str 13, Dex 15, Con —, Int 6, Wis 12, Cha 12
Skills: Listen +11, Move Silently +14, Spot +13
Feats: Dodge, Improved Initiative, Weapon Focus (slam)

Climate/Terrain: Any land and underground
Organization: Solitary or gang (2–4)
Challenge Rating: 8
Treasure: None
Alignment: Always chaotic evil
Advancement: 10–13 HD (Medium-size); 14–27 HD (Large)

Bodaks are the undead remnants of those who have been destroyed by the touch of absolute evil.

A bodak looks more or less as it did in life, although its face is twisted into an expression of mingled madness and horror. Bodaks have gray, hairless flesh and empty, white eyes. The statistics above are for a formerly human bodak.

COMBAT

Bodaks love to approach their opponents at a leisurely pace, letting their gaze do its work before closing.

Death Gaze (Su): Death, range 30 feet, Fortitude negates DC 15. Humanoids who die from this attack are transformed into bodaks in one day.

Sunlight Vulnerability (Ex): Bodaks loathe sunlight, for its merest touch burns their impure flesh. Each round of exposure to the direct rays of the sun deals 1 point of damage to the creature.

Flashbacks (Ex): From time to time, a bodak sees something that reminds it of its almost-forgotten life. At the start of every encounter, there is a 5% chance that it notices something about an opponent (randomly determined, if more than one opponent is present) that causes it to recall its life. If this happens, the bodak takes no action for 1 round and thereafter suffers a –2 morale penalty to all attacks directed at that opponent.

BUGBEAR

Medium-Size Humanoid (Goblinoid)
Hit Dice: 3d8+3 (16 hp)
Initiative: +1 (Dex)
Speed: 30 ft.
AC: 17 (+1 Dex, +3 natural, +2 leather, +1 small shield)
Attacks: Morningstar +4 melee; or javelin +3 ranged
Damage: Morningstar 1d8+2; or javelin 1d6+2
Face/Reach: 5 ft. by 5 ft./5 ft.
Special Qualities: Darkvision 60 ft.
Saves: Fort +2, Ref +4, Will +1
Abilities: Str 15, Dex 12, Con 13, Int 10, Wis 10, Cha 9
Skills: Climb +2, Hide +3, Listen +3, Move Silently +6, Spot +3
Feats: Alertness

Climate/Terrain: Any underground
Organization: Solitary, gang (2–4), or band (11–20 plus 150% noncombatants plus 2 2nd-level sergeants and 1 leader of 2nd–5th level)
Challenge Rating: 2
Treasure: Standard
Alignment: Usually chaotic evil
Advancement: By character class

The biggest and strongest of the goblinoids, bugbears are even more aggressive than their relatives. They live by hunting any creature weaker than themselves.

Bugbears are large and very muscular, standing 7 feet tall. Their hides vary in color from light yellow to yellow-brown, with thick, coarse hair of brown to brick red. Their eyes resemble those of a savage animal, being greenish-white with

red pupils, and they have wedge-shaped ears. A bugbear's mouth is full of long, sharp fangs, and its nose is much like that of a bear, with the same fine sense of smell. This feature earned them their name, though they are not related to bears. Their tough hides and sharp claws also resemble those of bears, but they are far more dexterous.

Bugbears speak Goblin and Common.

COMBAT

Bugbears prefer to ambush opponents whenever possible. When hunting, they normally send scouts ahead of the main group who, if they spy prey, return to report and bring up reinforcements. Bugbear attacks are coordinated, and their tactics are sound if not brilliant.

Skills: Bugbears receive a +4 racial bonus to Move Silently checks.

BUGBEAR SOCIETY

Bugbears prefer subterranean locations such as caverns and dungeons, dwelling in small tribal units. A single bugbear, usually the biggest and meanest, leads each tribe. A tribe has as many young as it has adults. Children do not join the adults in the hunt, but they will fight to protect themselves or their lairs.

Bugbears have only two genuine goals in life: food and treasure. Prey and intruders are considered a valuable source of both. The extremely greedy creatures prize anything shiny, including arms and armor. They never miss an opportunity to increase their hoards through theft, plunder, and ambush. On rare occasions they parley with other beings if they believe something can be gained, but they are not skilled negotiators, losing their patience quickly if such encounters run overlong. They are sometimes found commanding goblins and hobgoblins, whom they bully mercilessly.

These creatures survive primarily by hunting, and they eat whatever they can bring down. Any creature is a legitimate source of food, including monsters and even their own smaller kin. When game is scarce, bugbears turn to raiding and ambush to fill their stewpots.

Most bugbears revere a deity called Hruggek, who delights in ambushes followed by furious combat.

BUGBEAR CHARACTERS

A bugbear's favored class is rogue. Most bugbear leaders are fighters or fighter/rogues. Bugbear clerics worship Hruggek (favored weapon: morningstar) and can choose any two of the following domains: Chaos, Evil, Trickery, and War.

Climate/Terrain: Temperate land and underground
Organization: Solitary or pair
Challenge Rating: 7
Treasure: None
Alignment: Always neutral
Advancement: 10–16 HD (Huge); 17–27 HD (Gargantuan)

Aptly called a "landshark," the bulette is a terrifying predator that lives only to eat. It is universally shunned, even by other monsters.

It is said by some that the bulette is a cross between an armadillo and a snapping turtle, but this is only conjecture. The bulette's head and hind portions are blue-brown, covered with plates and scales ranging from gray-blue to blue-green. Its nails and teeth are dull ivory. The area around its eyes is brown-black, and its eyes are yellowish with blue-green pupils.

Fortunately for the rest of the world, the bulette is a solitary animal, although mated pairs (very rare) might share the same territory. Since its appetite is so voracious, each landshark has a large territory that can range up to thirty square miles. Other predators rarely share territory with one, for fear of being eaten. The bulette has no lair, preferring to wander above and below ground and burrowing beneath the soil to rest.

Bulettes consume their victims clothing, weapons, and all. Their powerful stomach acids quickly destroy armor, weapons, and even magic items. They are not above nibbling on chests or sacks of coins either, the bulette motto being "Eat first and think later." When it has eaten everything in the territory, a bulette moves on. The sole criterion for a suitable territory is the availability of food, so bulettes occasionally move in near human and halfling settlements and terrorize the residents.

COMBAT

A bulette attacks anything it regards as edible, choosing the easiest or closest prey first. The only creatures it refuses to eat are elves, and it dislikes dwarves. When burrowing underground, the landshark relies on vibrations to detect prey. When it senses something edible (that is, senses movement), it breaks to the surface, crest first, and begins its attack.

The landshark has a foul temperament—stupid, mean, and fearless. The size, strength, and number of its opponents mean nothing.

Leap (Ex): A bulette can jump into the air during combat. This allows it to make four claw attacks instead of two, but it cannot bite. The attack bonus is +12.

Tremorsense (Ex): Bulettes can automatically sense the location of anything within 60 feet that is in contact with the ground.

BULETTE

Huge Beast
Hit Dice: 9d10+45 (94 hp)
Initiative: +2 (Dex)
Speed: 40 ft., burrow 10 ft.
AC: 22 (–2 size, +2 Dex, +12 natural)
Attacks: Bite +12 melee, 2 claws +7 melee
Damage: Bite 2d8+8, claw 2d6+4
Face/Reach: 10 ft. by 20 ft./10 ft.
Special Attacks: Leap
Special Qualities: Scent, tremorsense
Saves: Fort +11, Ref +8, Will +4
Abilities: Str 27, Dex 15, Con 20, Int 2, Wis 13, Cha 6
Skills: Jump +12, Listen +6

Illus. by T. Lockwood

CARRION CRAWLER

Large Aberration

Hit Dice: 3d8+6 (19 hp)
Initiative: +2 (Dex)
Speed: 30 ft., climb 15 ft.
AC: 17 (–1 size, +2 Dex, +6 natural)
Attacks: 8 tentacles +3 melee, bite –2 melee
Damage: Tentacle paralysis, bite 1d4+1
Face/Reach: 5 ft. by 10 ft./5 ft.
Special Attacks: Paralysis
Special Qualities: Scent
Saves: Fort +3, Ref +3, Will +5
Abilities: Str 14, Dex 15, Con 14, Int 1, Wis 15, Cha 6
Skills: Climb +10, Listen +6, Spot +6
Feats: Alertness

Climate/Terrain: Any underground
Organization: Solitary or cluster (2–5)
Challenge Rating: 4
Treasure: None
Alignment: Always neutral
Advancement: 3–4 HD (Large); 5–9 HD (Huge)

Carrion crawlers are aggressive subterranean scavengers, greatly feared for their paralyzing attacks. They scour their underground territory for dead and decaying flesh but also attack and kill living creatures. The crawler's multilegged and segmented body grows to about 9 feet long and looks like a cross between a giant green cutworm and a cephalopod. Eight slender tentacles protrude from its head, directly above its mandibles. Each tentacle is about 2 feet long and secretes a sticky, paralyzing substance. A rank odor often accompanies the creature and warns adventurers of its approach. Like so many other hybrid monsters, the carrion crawler may well be the result of genetic experimentation.

COMBAT

Carrion crawlers use their keen senses of sight and smell to detect carcasses and potential prey. When attacking, a crawler lashes out with all eight tentacles and tries to paralyze its victim. The tentacles deal no other damage. The creature then kills the paralyzed victim with its bite and devours the flesh. Multiple crawlers do not fight in concert, but each paralyzes as many opponents as possible. The unintelligent creature continues to attack as long as it faces any moving opponents.

Paralysis (Ex): Those hit by a carrion crawler's tentacle attack must succeed at a Fortitude save (DC 13) or be paralyzed for 2d6 minutes.

CELESTIAL

	Lantern Archon Small Outsider (Good, Lawful)	Hound Archon Medium-Size Outsider (Good, Lawful)	Avoral (Guardinal) Medium-Size Outsider (Good)
Hit Dice:	1d8 (4 hp)	6d8+6 (33 hp)	7d8+7 (38 hp)
Initiative:	+4 (Improved Initiative)	+4 (Improved Initiative)	+7 (+3 Dex, +4 Improved Initiative)
Speed:	Fly 60 ft. (perfect)	40 ft. or 60 ft.*	40 ft., fly 90 ft. (good)
AC:	15 (+1 size, +4 natural)	19 (+9 natural)	21 (+3 Dex, +8 natural)
Attacks:	2 light rays +2 ranged touch	Bite +8 melee, 2 slams +3 melee; or greatsword +8/+3 melee, bite +3 melee	2 claws +9 melee; or 2 wings +9 melee
Damage:	Light ray 1d6	Bite 1d8+2, slam 1d4+1; greatsword 2d6+2, bite 1d8+1	Claw 2d6+2; wing 2d8+2
Face/Reach:	5 ft. by 5 ft./5 ft.	5 ft. by 5 ft./5 ft.	5 ft. by 5 ft./5 ft.
Special Attacks:	Spell-like abilities	Spell-like abilities	Spell-like abilities, fear aura
Special Qualities:	Damage reduction 20/+1, celestial qualities	Damage reduction 10/+1, SR 16, celestial qualities, scent, alternate form	Damage reduction 10/+1, SR 25, celestial qualities, lay on hands, animal telepathy, true seeing
Saves:	Fort +2, Ref +2, Will +2	Fort +6, Ref +5, Will +6	Fort +6, Ref +8, Will +8
Abilities:	Str 1, Dex 11, Con 10, Int 6, Wis 11, Cha 10	Str 15, Dex 10, Con 13, Int 10, Wis 13, Cha 12	Str 15, Dex 17, Con 12, Int 15, Wis 16, Cha 16
Skills:	—	Concentration +8, Hide +7*, Jump +9, Listen +8, Move Silently +7, Sense Motive +8, Spot +7, Wilderness, Lore +1*	Animal Empathy +10, Concentration +8, Hide +10, Knowledge (any two) or Craft (any two) +9, Listen +10, Move Silently +10, Sense Motive +10, Spellcraft +9, Spot +18
Feats:	Improved Initiative	Improved Initiative, Track	Improved Initiative, Flyby Attack
Climate/Terrain:	Any land and underground	Any land and underground	Any land and underground
Organization:	Solitary, pair, or squad (3–5)	Solitary, pair, or squad (3–5)	Solitary, pair, or squad (3–5)
Challenge Rating:	2	4	9
Treasure:	None	No coins; double goods; standard items	No coins; double goods; standard items
Alignment:	Always lawful good	Always lawful good	Always neutral good
Advancement:	2–4 HD (Small)	7–9 HD (Medium-size); 10–18 HD (Large)	8–14 HD (Medium-size); 15–21 HD (Large)

	Ghaele (Eladrin) Medium-Size Outsider (Chaotic, Good)	Trumpet Archon Medium-Size Outsider (Good, Lawful)	Astral Deva Medium-Size Outsider (Good)
Hit Dice:	10d8+20 (65 hp)	12d8+12 (66 hp)	12d8+48 (102 hp)
Initiative:	+5 (+1 Dex, +4 Improved Initiative)	+7 (+3 Dex, +4 Improved Initiative)	+8 (+4 Dex, +4 Improved Initiative)
Speed:	50 ft., fly 150 ft. (perfect)	40 ft., Fly 90 ft. (good)	50 ft., fly 100 ft. (good)
AC:	25 (+1 Dex, +14 natural)	27 (+3 Dex, +14 natural)	29 (+4 Dex, +15 natural)
Attacks:	+4 greatsword +21/+16 melee; or 2 light rays +11 ranged touch	+4 greatsword +21/+16/+11 melee	+3 heavy mace of disruption +21/+16/+11 melee
Damage:	+4 greatsword 2d6+14 and positive energy; light ray 2d12	+4 greatsword 2d6+11	+3 heavy mace of disruption 1d8+12 and stun
Face/Reach:	5 ft. by 5 ft./5 ft.	5 ft. by 5 ft./5 ft.	5 ft. by 5 ft./5 ft.
Special Attacks:	Spell-like abilities, spells, gaze, positive energy	Spell-like abilities, spells, trumpet	Stun, spell-like abilities
Special Qualities:	Damage reduction 25/+3, SR 28, celestial qualities, alternate form	Damage reduction 10/+1, SR 29, celestial qualities	Damage reduction 10/+1, SR 30, celestial qualities, uncanny dodge
Saves:	Fort +9, Ref +8, Will +10	Fort +9, Ref +11, Will +11	Fort +12, Ref +12, Will +12
Abilities:	Str 25, Dex 12, Con 15, Int 17, Wis 16, Cha 16	Str 20, Dex 17, Con 13, Int 16, Wis 16, Cha 16	Str 22, Dex 18, Con 18, Int 18, Wis 18, Cha 20
Skills:	Animal Empathy +13, Concentration +12, Escape Artist +11, Hide +11, Knowledge (any three) or Craft (any three) +13, Listen +15, Move Silently +11, Sense Motive +13, Spot +15	Animal Empathy +15, Concentration +13, Escape Artist +15, Hide +15, Knowledge (any three) +15, Listen +15, Move Silently +15, Sense Motive +15, Spot +15	Concentration +19, Escape Artist +19, Hide +19, Knowledge (any three) or Craft (any three) +17, Listen +25, Move Silently +19, Sense Motive +19, Spot +25
Feats:	Alertness, Blind-Fight, Improved Initiative	Blind-Fight, Cleave, Improved Initiative, Power Attack	Alertness, Cleave, Improved Initiative, Power Attack
Climate/Terrain:	Any land and underground	Any land and underground	Any land and underground
Organization:	Solitary, pair, or squad (3–5)	Solitary, pair, or squad (3–5)	Solitary, pair, or squad (3–5)
Challenge Rating:	13	14	14
Treasure:	No coins; double goods; standard items	No coins; double goods; standard items	No coins; double goods; standard items
Alignment:	Always chaotic good	Always lawful good	Always good (any)
Advancement:	11–15 HD (Medium-size); 16–30 HD (Large)	13–18 HD (Medium-size); 19–36 HD (Large)	13–18 HD (Medium-size); 19–36 HD (Large)

	Planetar Large Outsider (Good)	Solar Large Outsider (Good)
Hit Dice:	14d8+70 (133 hp)	22d8+110 (209 hp)
Initiative:	+8 (+4 Dex, +4 Improved Initiative)	+9 (+5 Dex, +4 Improved Initiative)
Speed:	30 ft., fly 90 ft. (good)	50 ft., fly 150 ft. (good)
AC:	32 (–1 size, +4 Dex, +19 natural)	35 (–1 size, +5 Dex, +21 natural)
Attacks:	+3 greatsword +23/+18/+13 melee	+5 dancing, vorpal greatsword +35/+30/+25/+20/15 melee; or +2 mighty composite longbow (+5) +28/+23/+18/+13/+8 ranged
Damage:	+3 greatsword 2d6+13	+5 dancing, vorpal greatsword 2d6+18; +2 mighty composite longbow (+5) 1d8+7 and slaying
Face/Reach:	5 ft. by 5 ft./10 ft.	5 ft. by 5 ft./10 ft.
Special Attacks:	Spell-like abilities, spells	Spell-like abilities, spells
Special Qualities:	Damage reduction 30/+3, SR 30, celestial qualities, regeneration 10	Damage reduction 35/+4, SR 32 celestial qualities, regeneration 15
Saves:	Fort +14, Ref +13, Will +15	Fort +18, Ref +18, Will +20
Abilities:	Str 25, Dex 19, Con 20, Int 22, Wis 23, Cha 22	Str 28, Dex 20, Con 20, Int 23, Wis 25, Cha 25
Skills:	Concentration +16, Escape Artist +20, Hide +17, Knowledge (any five) or Craft (any five) +21, Listen +23, Move Silently +17, Sense Motive +23, Search +19, Spot +23	Concentration +16, Escape Artist +30, Hide +26, Knowledge (any five) or Craft (any five) +28, Listen +32, Move Silently +30, Search +30, Sense Motive +32, Spellcraft +19, Spot +32
Feats:	Blind-Fight, Cleave, Improved Initiative, Power Attack	Cleave, Dodge, Great Cleave, Improved Initiative, Mobility, Power Attack
Climate/Terrain:	Any land and underground	Any land and underground
Organization:	Solitary or pair	Solitary or pair
Challenge Rating:	16	19
Treasure:	No coins; double goods; standard items	No coins; double goods; standard items
Alignment:	Always good (any)	Always good (any)
Advancement:	15–21 HD (Large); 22–42 HD (Huge)	23–33 HD (Large); 34–66 HD (Huge)

The term "celestial" refers to many beings who live on the planes of Good. Celestials positively drip with goodness—every fiber of their bodies and souls is suffused with it.

They are the natural enemies of the fiends (creatures of the infernal realms). Examples of three types of celestials are presented here: archons (lawful good), guardinals (neutral good), and eladrins (chaotic good). Also included are devas, planetars, and solars, who can be of any good alignment.

All celestials are blessed with comely looks, though their actual appearances vary widely.

Celestials speak Celestial, Infernal, and Draconic.

COMBAT

Celestials never attack without provocation (though their overwhelming goodness often makes them easily provoked). They avoid harming other good creatures if they can, using nonlethal spells or subdual attacks if possible. An angry celestial can be vengeance itself, however, no matter what the foe's alignment is.

Celestials with few magical abilities generally prefer to meet a foe head-on if it is prudent to do so, but if outmatched, they do what they can to even the odds. Because most celestials are very mobile, they favor hit-and-run tactics. Magically powerful celestials usually stand off and engage a foe with spells before moving into melee.

Celestial Qualities

Aura of Menace (Su): A righteous aura surrounds archons that fight or get angry. Any hostile creature within a 20-foot radius of an archon must succeed at a Will save to resist its effects. The save DC varies with the type of archon. Those who fail suffer a −2 morale penalty to attacks, AC, and saves for one day or until they successfully hit the archon that generated the aura. A creature that has resisted or broken the effect cannot be affected again by that archon's aura for one day.

Magic Circle against Evil (Su): A *magic circle against evil* effect always surrounds archons, identical with the spell cast by a sorcerer whose level equals the archon's Hit Dice. The effect can be dispelled, but the archon can create it again during its next turn as a free action. (The defensive benefits from the circle are not included in the statistics block.)

Protective Aura (Su): As a free action, ghaeles, devas, planetars, and solars can surround themselves with a nimbus of light having a radius of 20 feet. This acts as a double-strength *magic circle against evil* and as a *minor globe of invulnerability*, both as cast by a sorcerer whose level equal to the celestial's Hit Dice. The aura can be dispelled, but the celestial can create it again as a free action on its next turn.

Teleport (Su): Archons can teleport without error at will, as the spell cast by a 14th-level sorcerer, except that the creature can transport only itself and up to 50 pounds of objects.

Tongues (Su): All celestials can speak with any creature that has a language, as though using a *tongues* spell cast by a 14th-level sorcerer. This ability is always active.

Immunities (Ex): All celestials are immune to electricity and petrification attacks. Devas, planetars, and solars are also immune to cold and acid.

Resistances (Ex): Guardinals and eladrins have cold and acid resistance 20. Devas, planetars, and solars have fire resistance 20.

All celestials receive a +4 racial bonus to Fortitude saves against poison.

Keen Vision (Ex): All celestials have low-light vision and 60-foot darkvision.

LANTERN ARCHON

Lantern archons appear as floating balls of light that glow about as brightly as a torch. Only their destruction can extinguish the glow, though they can try to hide it.

Lantern archons are very friendly and usually eager to give what assistance they can. However, their bodies are just gaseous globes, and they are much too weak to render any material aid. Lantern archons speak in soft, musical voices.

Combat

A lantern archon has little reason to get within melee range. It usually hovers just close enough to bring the enemy within its aura of menace, then blasts away with its light rays. Lantern archons prefer to concentrate on a single opponent, seeking to reduce enemy numbers quickly. This tactic can be devastating when a large group gather for a fight.

Light Ray (Ex): A lantern archon's light rays have a range of 30 feet.

Spell-Like Abilities: At will—*aid*, *detect evil*, and *continual flame*. These abilities are as the spells cast by a 3rd-level sorcerer.

Celestial Qualities: Aura of menace (save DC 11), magic circle against evil, electricity and petrification immunity, teleport, tongues, +4 save against poison.

HOUND ARCHON

Hound archons look like well-muscled humans with canine heads. They seek to defend the innocent and the helpless against evil.

Their broad shoulders and meaty fists mark hound archons as able combatants. Likewise, their strong legs indicate that fleeing enemies won't get very far.

Combat

Hound archons always fight with a will. They prefer to attack with their natural weapons but occasionally use greatswords.

Spell-Like Abilities: At will—*aid, continual flame, detect evil,* and *message.* These abilities are as the spells cast by a 6th-level sorcerer.

Celestial Qualities: Aura of menace (save DC 16), magic circle against evil, electricity and petrification immunity, teleport, tongues, +4 save against poison.

Alternate Form (Su): Hound archons can assume any canine form (except that of a werewolf or other lycanthrope) as a standard action. This ability is similar to the *polymorph self* spell but allows only canines.

*While in canine form, a hound archon gains the higher of the two listed speeds and a +4 circumstance bonus to Hide and Wilderness Lore checks.

AVORAL

Avorals have the bodies of tall, muscular humans, but their arms are long, powerful wings.

An avoral's wings feature small hands at the midpoints. When its wings are folded, these appendages are about where human hands would be and can do nearly anything hands can.

Avorals' lower legs feature strong talons and feathery vanes to act as a tail in flight. Their faces are more human than avian, but the hair resembles a feathery cowl, and the eyes are bright gold. Their chests are exceptionally deep and powerful, anchoring their wing muscles. Their bones are strong but hollow, so even the largest avorals weigh no more than 120 pounds.

Their visual acuity is unbelievable: They can see detail on objects up to 10 miles away and are said to be able to discern the color of a creature's eyes at 200 paces.

Combat

On the ground, an avoral can lash out with its wings to deliver punishing blows. However, it prefers to meet its foes in the air, where it can employ its rock-hard talons and make full use of its aerial speed and agility. It can't make wing attacks while flying, however.

Spell-Like Abilities: At will—*aid, blur* (self only), *command, detect magic, dimension door, dispel magic, gust of wind, hold person, light, magic circle against evil* (self only), *magic missile,* and *see invisibility;* 1/day—*lightning bolt.* These abilities are as the spells cast by an 8th-level sorcerer (save DC 13 + spell level).

Fear Aura (Su): Once per day an avoral can create an aura of fear in a 20-foot radius. It is otherwise identical with *fear* as cast by an 8th-level sorcerer (save DC 17).

Celestial Qualities: Electricity and petrification immunity, cold and acid resistance 20, tongues, +4 save against poison.

Lay on Hands (Su): This works just like the paladin's ability, but the avoral can heal as much damage per day as its own undamaged hit point total.

Animal Telepathy (Su): An avoral can mentally communicate with animals as a free action. This works exactly like *speak with animals* as cast by an 8th-level druid but does not require sound.

True Seeing (Su): This is identical with *true seeing* as cast by a 14th-level cleric, except that it has personal range and the avoral must concentrate for 1 full round before it takes effect. Thereafter it remains in effect as long as the avoral concentrates on it.

Skills: An avoral's sharp eyes give it a +8 racial bonus to Spot checks.

GHAELE

Ghaeles are the knights-errant of the celestials. Wherever evil and tyranny raise their ugly heads, the ghaeles respond.

Working behind the scenes more than other eladrins, ghaeles quietly muster resistance and offer guidance to any of good heart with the courage to stand against their oppressors.

Ghaeles might easily be mistaken for noble elves if not for their pearly, opalescent eyes and radiant aura. They can also take the form of an incorporeal globe of eldritch colors, 5 feet in diameter.

Combat

Ghaeles who enter combat prefer direct confrontation and damaging attacks to more subtle or insidious methods. They usually fight in their humanoid forms, wielding incandescent +4 greatswords. If a ghaele desires mobility, it assumes its globe form and blasts the enemy with light rays.

Spell-Like Abilities: At will—*aid, alter self, charm monster, color spray, comprehend languages, continual flame, cure light wounds, dancing lights, detect evil, detect thoughts, dispel magic, hold monster, improved invisibility* (self only), *major image, see invisibility,* and *teleport without error* (self plus 50 pounds of objects only); 1/day—*chain lightning, prismatic spray,* and *wall of force.* These abilities are as the spells cast by a 12th-level sorcerer (save DC 13 + spell level).

Spells: Ghaeles in humanoid form can cast divine spells from the cleric list and the Air, Animal, Chaos, Good, and Plant domains as 14th-level clerics (save DC 13 + spell level).

Gaze (Su): In humanoid form—slay evil creatures of 5 or fewer HD, range 60 feet, Will negates DC 18. Even if the save succeeds, the creature is affected as though by a *fear* spell for 2d10 rounds. Nonevil creatures, and evil creatures with more than 5 HD, must succeed at a Will save (DC 18) or suffer the *fear* effect.

Positive Energy (Ex): The ghaele's incandescent sword deals an additional 2d6 points of positive energy damage to evil creatures.

Light Ray (Ex): A ghaele in globe form can project light rays with a range of 300 feet.

Celestial Qualities: Protective aura, electricity and petrification immunity, cold and acid resistance 20, tongues, +4 save against poison.

Alternate Form (Su): A ghaele can shift between its humanoid and globe forms as a standard action. In humanoid form, it cannot fly or use its light rays, but it can use its gaze attack and spell-like abilities, make physical attacks, and cast spells. In globe form, it can fly, use its light rays, and use spell-like abilities, but it cannot cast spells or use its gaze attack.

A ghaele remains in one form until it chooses to assume a new one. A change in form cannot be dispelled, nor does the ghaele revert to any particular form when killed. A *true seeing* spell, however, reveals both forms simultaneously.

TRUMPET ARCHON

Trumpet archons look like beautiful, winged elves. They serve as celestial messengers and heralds, though their martial skills are considerable. Each carries a gleaming silver trumpet about 6 feet long.

Combat

Trumpet archons usually disdain physical combat, preferring to obliterate the foe with spells quickly and return to their duties. If forced into an extended battle, though, they sound their trumpets and attack with a vengeance.

Spell-Like Abilities: At will—*detect evil, continual flame,* and *message.* These abilities are as the spells cast by a 12th-level sorcerer.

Celestial Qualities: Aura of menace (save DC 19), magic circle against evil, electricity and petrification immunity, teleport, tongues, +4 save against poison.

Spells: Trumpet archons can cast divine spells from the cleric list and from the Air, Destruction, Good, Law, and War domains as 14th-level clerics (save DC 13 + spell level).

Trumpet (Su): The archon's trumpet produces music of utter clarity, piercing beauty, and, if the trumpet archon wills it, paralyzing awe. All creatures except archons within 100 feet of the blast must succeed at a Fortitude save (DC 19) or be paralyzed for 1d4 rounds. The archon can also command its trumpet to become a +4 *greatsword* as a free action.

If the trumpet is ever stolen, it becomes a chunk of useless lead until the archon can recover it. Woe betide any thief caught with it.

ASTRAL DEVA

Astral devas watch over lesser beings of good alignment and help when they can. In particular, they are patrons of planar travelers and powerful creatures undertaking good causes.

Supple and lithe, devas look like beautiful humans with long, feathery wings. They can be of any good alignment.

Combat

Astral devas are not afraid to enter melee combat. They take a fierce joy in bashing evil foes with their powerful +3 *heavy maces of disruption.*

Stun (Su): If an astral deva strikes an opponent twice in one round with its mace, that creature must succeed at a Fortitude save (DC 15) or be stunned for 1d6 rounds.

Spell-Like Abilities: At will—*aid, continual flame, detect evil, discern lies, dispel evil, dispel magic, holy aura, holy smite, holy word, invisibility sphere* (self only), *polymorph self, remove curse, remove disease,* and *remove fear;* 7/day—*see invisibility* and *cure light wounds;* 1/day—*heal* and *blade barrier.* These abilities are as the spells cast by a 12th-level sorcerer (save DC 15 + spell level).

Celestial Qualities: Protective aura; fire resistance 20, tongues; electricity, cold, acid, and petrification immunity, +4 save against poison.

Uncanny Dodge (Ex): Astral devas are never caught flat-footed and cannot be flanked.

Skills: Extremely alert, astral devas receive a +4 racial bonus to Spot and Listen checks.

PLANETAR

Planetars serve as mighty generals of celestial armies. They also help powerful mortals on missions of good, particularly those that involve battles with fiends.

Planetars resemble massively muscular humans with smooth emerald skin, white-feathered wings, and hairless heads.

Combat

Despite their vast array of magical powers, planetars are likely to wade into melee with their +3 *greatswords.* They particularly enjoy fighting fiends.

Spell-Like Abilities: At will—*continual flame, dispel magic, holy smite, improved invisibility* (self only), *lesser restoration, remove curse, remove disease, remove fear,* and *speak with dead;* 3/day—*blade barrier, flame strike,* and *raise dead;* 1/day—*earthquake, greater restoration, shapechange,* and *symbol* (any). These abilities are as the spells cast by a 17th-level sorcerer (save DC 16 + spell level).

The following abilities are always active on the planetar's person, as the spells cast by a 17th-level sorcerer: *detect evil, detect snares and pits, discern lies, see invisibility,* and *true seeing.* They can be dispelled, but the planetar can reactivate them as a free action.

Spells: Planetars can cast divine spells from the cleric list and from the Air, Destruction, Good, Law, and War domains as 17th-level clerics (save DC 16 + spell level).

Celestial Qualities: Protective aura, fire resistance 20, tongues, electricity, cold, acid, and petrification immunity, +4 save against poison.

SOLAR

Solars are the greatest of the celestials, usually close attendants to a deity or champions of some cosmically beneficent task (such as eliminating a particular type of wrongdoing).

A 9-foot-tall humanoid with brilliant topaz eyes, silvery or golden skin, and gleaming white wings, a solar has a deep and commanding voice.

Combat

Solars are virtually unmatched in power. Other than demon princes, archdevils, and deities, nothing else in the multiverse approaches them. Even more fearsome than their +5 *vorpal, dancing greatswords* are their +2 *mighty composite longbows* that create any sort of *slaying arrow* when drawn.

Spell-Like Abilities: At will—*aid, animate objects, commune, continual flame, dimensional anchor, greater dispelling, holy smite, imprisonment, improved invisibility* (self only), *lesser restoration, remove curse, remove disease, remove fear, resist elements, summon monster VII,* and *speak with dead;* 3/day—*blade barrier, earthquake, heal, permanency, resurrection,* and *shapechange;* 1/day—*greater restoration, mass charm, power word blind, power word kill, power word stun, prismatic spray, symbol* (any), and *wish.* These abilities are as the spells cast by a 20th-level sorcerer (save DC 17 + spell level).

The following abilities are always active on the solar's person, as the spells cast by a 20th-level sorcerer: *detect evil, detect snares and pits, discern lies, see invisibility,* and *true seeing.* They can be dispelled, but the solar can reactivate them as a free action.

Spells: Solars can cast divine spells from the cleric list and from the Air, Destruction, Good, Law, and War domains as 20th-level clerics (save DC 17 + spell level).

Celestial Qualities: Protective aura, fire resistance 20, tongues, electricity, cold, acid, and petrification immunity, +4 save against poison.

CENTAUR

Large Monstrous Humanoid
Hit Dice: 4d8+8 (26 hp)
Initiative: +2 (Dex)
Speed: 50 ft.
AC: 15 (–1 size, +2 Dex, +2 natural, +2 large shield)
Attacks: Greatclub +7 melee (or heavy lance +7 melee), 2 hooves +3 melee; or mighty composite longbow (+4) +5 ranged
Damage: Greatclub 1d10+4 (or heavy lance 1d8+4), hoof 1d6+2; or mighty composite longbow 1d8+4
Face/Reach: 5 ft. by 10 ft./5 ft.
Saves: Fort +3, Ref +6, Will +5
Abilities: Str 18, Dex 14, Con 15, Int 8, Wis 13, Cha 11
Skills: Hide +2 Listen +4, Move Silently +4, Spot +4, Wilderness Lore +5
Feats: Weapon Focus (hoof)

Climate/Terrain: Temperate forest
Organization: Solitary, company (5–8), troop (8–18 plus 1 leader of 2nd–5th level), or tribe (20–200 plus 10 3rd-level sergeants, 5 5th-level lieutenants, and 1 leader of 5th–9th level)
Challenge Rating: 3
Treasure: Standard
Alignment: Usually neutral good
Advancement: By character class

Centaurs are woodland beings who shun the company of outsiders. They are deadly archers and even more fearsome in melee.

A centaur's appearance is unmistakable: The upper torso, arms, and head are humanoid, while the lower body is that of a large horse. Both human and equine physiques are well muscled.

Centaurs speak Sylvan and Elven.

COMBAT

Although generally mild-tempered, centaurs are always armed. Their favorite melee weapons are massive oaken clubs. When scouting or hunting, they carry shields and mighty composite bows. If armed for war, they also carry heavy lances.

Centaurs usually don't provoke a fight. Their normal response to aggression is swift retreat, perhaps launching a few arrows to discourage pursuit. Against creatures dangerous to their communities, they use much the same tactics, except that about half their number will circle around to lie in ambush or attack the foe from the rear.

CENTAUR SOCIETY

Among their own kind, centaurs are sociable creatures, but they have been known to become rowdy, boorish, and aggressive when under the influence of alcohol.

Lone centaurs are usually males out hunting or scouting. Companies and troops are usually males hunting or scouting in force. Centaur tribes remain near their lairs. At any given time, most of the centaurs in the tribal lair are female; while the males are out hunting and scouting, the females lead and administer the tribe. A third of a tribe's population is young.

The typical centaur lair is located deep within a forest. It consists of a large hidden glade and pastures, with a good supply of running water. Depending upon the climate, the lair may contain huts or lean-tos to shelter individual families. Hearths for cooking and warmth are in an open area, away from the trees.

Centaurs are skilled in horticulture and may cultivate useful plants near their lair. In dangerous, monster-infested areas they plant thick barriers of thorn bushes around the lair, dig pits, and set snares.

Centaurs survive through a mixture of hunting, foraging, fishing, agriculture, and trade. Though they shun dealings with humans, centaurs do trade with elves, especially for food and wine. The elves are paid from the group treasury: the booty of slain monsters.

A centaur tribe's territory varies with its size and the nature of the area it inhabits. Centaurs do not object to sharing territory with elves. The attitude of a centaur toward a stranger in its territory varies with the visitor. Humans and dwarves are politely asked to leave, halflings or gnomes are tolerated, and elves are welcomed. Centaurs deal with monsters according to the threat to the welfare and survival of the tribe: If a giant or dragon were to enter the territory, the centaurs would relocate, but they would kill trolls, orcs, and the like.

The patron deity of the centaurs is Skerrit, a god of nature and community.

CENTAUR CHARACTERS

Centaurs sometimes become bards, rangers, or druids. Their favored class is ranger. Centaur rangers often choose a magical beast or some variety of humanoid as their favored enemy. A centaur druid is usually a tribe's designated leader and speaker. Centaur clerics (who are rare) worship Skerrit and can choose any two of the following domains: Animal, Good, and Plant.

CHAOS BEAST

Medium-Size Outsider (Chaotic)
Hit Dice: 8d8+8 (44 hp)
Initiative: +5 (+1 Dex, +4 Improved Initiative)
Speed: 20 ft.
AC: 16 (+1 Dex, +5 natural)
Attacks: 2 claws +10 melee
Damage: Claw 1d3+2 and corporeal instability
Face/Reach: 5 ft. by 5 ft. to 10 ft. by 10 ft./5 ft.
Special Attacks: Corporeal instability
Special Qualities: SR 15, immune to transformation, immune to critical hits
Saves: Fort +7, Ref +7, Will +6
Abilities: Str 14, Dex 13, Con 13, Int 10, Wis 10, Cha 10
Skills: Climb +12, Escape Artist +11, Hide +10, Jump +10, Listen +9, Spot +9, Tumble +10
Feats: Dodge, Improved Initiative, Mobility

Climate/Terrain: Any land and underground
Organization: Solitary
Challenge Rating: 7
Treasure: None
Alignment: Always chaotic neutral
Advancement: 9–12 HD (Medium-size); 13–24 HD (Large)

These horrific creatures have mutable, everchanging forms. Their deadly touch can make opponents melt into formless goo.

There's no telling what a chaos beast will look like. One moment it might be a towering horror of hooks and fangs, all pulpy flesh and exposed veins, and the next, a slithering mass of ropy, vermilion-tipped tentacles. A moment later it may be a bulbous thing with ten eyes swimming in a viscous sac at the top of the body, in turn surrounded by a ring of smacking mouths, then become a mighty creature, all muscle and fury. A chaos beast's dimensions vary, but it weighs about 200 pounds.

Chaos beasts do not speak.

COMBAT

How many different attacks can a creature capable of any form have? In this case, only two.

For all its fearsome appearances, whether it has claws, fangs, pincers, tentacles, or spines, a chaos beast does little physical harm. Regardless of form, the creature seems unable to manage more than two attacks per round. Its continual transmutations prevent the coordination needed to do more.

Corporeal Instability (Su): A blow from a chaos beast can cause a terrible transformation. A living creature must succeed at a Fortitude save (DC 15) or become a spongy, amorphous mass. Unless controlled through an act of will, the victim's shape melts, flows, writhes, and boils.

The affected creature is unable to hold or use any item. Clothing, armor, rings, helmets, and backpacks become useless. Large items—armor, backpacks, even shirts—hamper more than help, reducing the creature's Dexterity score by 4. Soft or misshapen feet and legs reduce speed to 10 feet or one-quarter normal, whichever is less. Searing pain courses along the nerves, so strong that the creature cannot act coherently. It cannot cast spells or use magic items, and it attacks blindly, unable to distinguish friend from foe (–4 penalty to hit and a 50% miss chance, regardless of the attack roll).

Each round the creature spends in an amorphous state deals 1 point of permanent Wisdom drain from mental shock. If the creature's Wisdom score falls to 0, it becomes a chaos beast itself.

A creature with a strong sense of self can regain its own shape by taking a standard action to attempt a Charisma check (DC 15). A success reestablishes the creature's normal form for 1 minute. On a failure, the creature can still repeat the check each round until successful.

Corporeal instability is not a disease or a curse and so is hard to remove. A *shapechange* or *stoneskin* spell does not cure the afflicted creature but fixes its form for the duration of the spell. A *restoration, heal,* or *greater restoration* spell removes the affliction (a separate *restoration* is necessary to restore any lost Wisdom).

Immune to Transformation (Ex): No mortal magic can affect or fix a chaos beast's form. Effects such as *polymorph* or petrification force the creature into a new shape for a moment, but it immediately returns to its mutable form as a free action.

CHIMERA

Large Magical Beast
Hit Dice: 9d10+27 (76 hp)
Initiative: +1 (Dex)
Speed: 30 ft., fly 50 ft. (poor)
AC: 16 (–1 size, +1 Dex, +6 natural)
Attacks: Bite +12 melee, bite +10 melee, butt +10 melee, 2 claws +10 melee
Damage: Bite 2d6+4, bite 1d8+2, butt 1d8+2, claw 1d6+2
Face/Reach: 5 ft. by 10 ft./5 ft.
Special Attacks: Breath weapon
Special Qualities: Scent
Saves: Fort +9, Ref +7, Will +4
Abilities: Str 19, Dex 13, Con 17, Int 4, Wis 13, Cha 10
Skills: Hide +4, Listen +9, Spot +9
Feats: Alertness, Multiattack

Climate/Terrain: Any land and underground
Organization: Solitary, pride (3–5), or flight (6–13)
Challenge Rating: 7
Treasure: Standard
Alignment: Usually chaotic evil
Advancement: 10–13 HD (Large); 14–27 HD (Huge)

The chimera is a bizarre, three-headed predator that hunts on the ground and on the wing. It can defeat even the hardiest opponent with a flurry of claws and fangs.

A chimera has the hindquarters of a large black goat and the forequarters of a great lion. It has brownish-black dragon wings and the heads of a goat, a lion, and a fierce dragon. The pitch-black goat head has glowing amber eyes and long ochre horns. The maneless lion head has green eyes. The scaly dragon head has black eyes, and the scales might be black, blue, green, red, or white. The creature is about 5 feet tall at the shoulder, nearly 10 feet long, and weighs about 4,000 pounds.

Chimeras can speak Draconic but seldom bother to do so, except when toadying to more powerful creatures.

COMBAT

A deadly foe, the chimera prefers to surprise prey. It often swoops down from the sky or lies concealed until it charges. The dragon head can loose a breath weapon instead of biting. Several chimeras attack in concert.

Breath Weapon (Su): Every 1d4 rounds, damage 3d8, Reflex half DC 17. Use all rules for dragon breath of the appropriate variety (see the Dragon entry) except as specified in the table below.

To determine the head color and breath weapon randomly, roll 1d10 and consult the table.

1d10	Head Color	Breath Weapon
1–2	Black	Line of acid*
3–4	Blue	Line of lightning
5–6	Green	Cone of gas**
7–8	Red	Cone of fire
9–10	White	Cone of cold

*A line is always 5 feet high, 5 feet wide, and 40 feet long.
**A cone is always 20 feet long.

Skills: The chimera's three heads give it a +2 racial bonus to Spot and Listen checks.

Chimera illus. by C. Critchlow

LOCKWOOD

really tentacles with multiple knobby joints of cartilage. Thus, it appears bowlegged, and its movements seem peculiar and fluid.

Chokers speak Undercommon.

COMBAT

A choker likes to perch near the ceiling, often at intersections, archways, wells, or staircases, and reach down to attack its prey.

A choker attacks creatures of almost any size, but prefers lone prey of at least Small size. If very hungry, it may attack a group, but it waits to grab the last creature in line.

Chokers are sly and greedy. Quick-thinking parties that spot one before it attacks might be able to bribe a choker with food and question it about the area around its lair.

Haste (Su): Although not particularly dexterous, a choker is supernaturally quick. It can take an extra partial action each round, as if affected by a *haste* spell.

Improved Grab (Ex): To use this ability, the choker must hit an opponent of up to Large size with a tentacle attack. If it gets a hold, it can constrict.

Constrict (Ex): A choker deals 1d3+3 points of damage with a successful grapple check against Large or smaller creatures. Because it seizes victims by the neck, a creature in the choker's grasp cannot speak or cast spells with verbal components.

CHUUL

Large Aberration
Hit Dice: 11d8+44 (93 hp)
Initiative: +7 (+3 Dex, +4 Improved Initiative)
Speed: 30 ft., swim 20 ft.
AC: 22 (−1 size, +3 Dex, +10 natural)
Attacks: 2 claws +12 melee
Damage: Claw 2d6+5
Face/Reach: 5 ft. by 5 ft./10 ft.
Special Attacks: Improved grab, squeeze, paralysis
Special Qualities: Paralysis and poison immunity
Saves: Fort +7, Ref +6, Will +9
Abilities: Str 20, Dex 16, Con 18, Int 10, Wis 14, Cha 5
Skills: Hide +13, Jump +11, Listen +13, Spot +13
Feats: Alertness, Improved Initiative

Climate/Terrain: Temperate and warm forest, marsh, and underground
Organization: Solitary or pack (2–5)
Challenge Rating: 7
Treasure: 1/10th coins; 50% goods; standard items
Alignment: Usually chaotic evil
Advancement: 12–16 HD (Large); 17–33 HD (Huge)

A horrible mix of crustacean, insect, and serpent, the chuul is an abomination that lurks submerged or partially submerged, awaiting intelligent prey to devour.

A chuul has huge pincerlike claws, four webbed legs, a wide tail, and a mandibled mouth surrounded by squirming tentacles. Its entire body is encased in an orange and black carapace.

Although amphibious, chuuls are clumsy swimmers and actually prefer to be on land or in very shallow water. They love to prey on lizardfolk.

Chuuls are known to collect trophies from their kills. Although unable to use weapons, armor, or most other belongings, chuuls keep these items in their lairs. If a victim has no interesting possessions, the chuul takes its skull.

Although most live in swamps and jungles, some chuuls have adapted to subterranean life, hunting in and near underground streams and lakes. These underground varieties have 60-foot darkvision and prey on troglodytes and unwary drow. They are sometimes in the thrall of beholders or mind flayers.

CHOKER

Small Aberration
Hit Dice: 3d8+3 (16 hp)
Initiative: +4 (Improved Initiative)
Speed: 20 ft., climb 10 ft.
AC: 16 (+1 size, +5 natural)
Attacks: 2 tentacle slaps +6 melee
Damage: Tentacle slap 1d3+3
Face/Reach: 5 ft. by 5 ft./10 ft.
Special Attacks: Haste, improved grab, constrict 1d3+3
Saves: Fort +2, Ref +1, Will +4
Abilities: Str 16, Dex 10, Con 13, Int 4, Wis 13, Cha 7
Skills: Climb +16, Hide +7, Move Silently +4
Feats: Improved Initiative

Climate/Terrain: Any underground
Organization: Solitary
Challenge Rating: 2
Treasure: 1/10 coins; 50% goods; 50% items
Alignment: Usually chaotic evil
Advancement: 4–6 HD (Small); 7–12 HD (Medium-size)

These vicious little predators lurk underground, grabbing whatever prey happens by.

A choker has mottled gray or stony brown flesh. It looks humanoid at first glance: The head and torso are as small and compact as a halfling's, but the arms and legs (and fingers and toes) are incredibly spindly and long. The hands and feet have spiny pads that help the choker grip almost any surface. The creature weighs about 35 pounds.

The choker's skull, spine, and rib cage are bony, but its limbs are

COMBAT

A chuul prefers to wait by the shore, submerged in murky water, until it hears nearby prey (in or out of the water) that it can attack with surprise.

A chuul facing multiple opponents grabs with its claws and crushes its foes, then passes one opponent to its tentacles. It tries to always have one claw free, so if it faces a great number of opponents, it drops paralyzed or dead victims without eating them and continues grabbing, crushing, and paralyzing the rest.

Improved Grab (Ex): To use this ability, the chuul must hit with a claw attack.

Squeeze (Ex): A chuul that gets a hold automatically deals claw damage, with an additional 1d6 points of bludgeoning damage from the crushing force, each round the hold is maintained.

Paralysis (Ex): The chuul can transfer grabbed victims from a claw to its tentacles as a partial action. The tentacles grapple with the same strength as the claw but deal no damage. However, they exude a paralytic secretion. Those held in the tentacles must succeed at a Fortitude save (DC 19) or be paralyzed for 6 rounds. While held in the tentacles, paralyzed or not, the victim automatically takes 1d8+2 points of damage each round from the creature's mandibles.

CLOAKER

Large Aberration
Hit Dice: 6d8+18 (45 hp)
Initiative: +7 (+3 Dex, +4 Improved Initiative)
Speed: 10 ft., fly 40 ft. (average)
AC: 19 (–1 size, +3 Dex, +7 natural)
Attacks: Tail slap +8 melee, bite +3 melee
Damage: Tail slap 1d6+5, bite 1d4+2
Face/Reach: 5 ft. by 5 ft./10 ft. (5 ft. with bite)
Special Attacks: Moan, engulf
Special Qualities: Shadow shift
Saves: Fort +5, Ref +5, Will +7
Abilities: Str 21, Dex 16, Con 17, Int 14, Wis 15, Cha 15
Skills: Hide +12, Listen +11, Move Silently +12, Spot +11
Feats: Alertness, Improved Initiative

Climate/Terrain: Underground
Organization: Solitary, mob (3–6), or flock (7–12)
Challenge Rating: 5
Treasure: Standard
Alignment: Usually chaotic neutral
Advancement: 7–9 HD (Large); 10–18 HD (Huge)

Cloakers are bizarre creatures that lurk in dark places far beneath the surface. They kill intruders without remorse or pause, except to plan cruel amusement.

When resting or lying in wait, these creatures are almost impossible to distinguish from common black cloaks. Black eyespots in a row on the back resemble buttons, and the cloaker's ivory claws look very much like bone clasps. Only when it unfurls, revealing its wide, toothy mouth and piercing red eyes, does the horrific nature of the creature become apparent.

Cloakers pursue their own mysterious goals. While they are certainly intelligent, their minds work in a way so alien that few if any human beings have ever been able to make meaningful contact with them.

COMBAT

Cloakers usually lie still, watching and listening for prey. If facing a single opponent, a cloaker uses its engulf attack. Against multiple foes, it lashes with its tail in concert with its moan and shadow shift abilities to reduce the opposition's numbers, then engulfs a survivor. Multiple cloakers usually split up, leaving one or two behind to use special abilities while the rest attack.

Moan (Ex): A cloaker can emit a dangerous subsonic moan instead of biting. By changing the frequency, the cloaker may cause one of four effects. Cloakers are immune to these sonic, mind-affecting attacks. Unless noted otherwise, creatures who successfully save against these effects cannot be affected by the same moan effect from the same cloaker for one day.

Unnerve: All within an 80-foot spread automatically suffer a –2 morale penalty to attack and damage rolls. Those forced to hear the moan for more than 6 consecutive rounds must succeed at a Will save (DC 15) or enter a trance, unable to attack or defend themselves until the moaning stops. Even on a success, they must repeat the save in each round the moaning continues.

Fear: All those within a 30-foot spread must succeed at a Will save (DC 15) or flee in terror for 2 rounds.

Nausea: Everyone in a 30-foot cone must succeed at a Fortitude save (DC 15) or be overcome by nausea and weakness. Affected characters fall to the ground and are unable to take any actions, including defending themselves, for 1d4+1 rounds.

Stupor: A single creature within 30 feet of the cloaker must succeed at a Fortitude save (DC 15) or be affected as though by a *hold person* spell for 5 rounds. Even after a successful save, the creature must repeat the save if the cloaker uses this effect again.

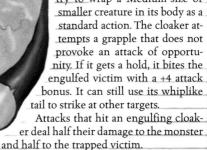

Engulf (Ex): A cloaker can try to wrap a Medium-size or smaller creature in its body as a standard action. The cloaker attempts a grapple that does not provoke an attack of opportunity. If it gets a hold, it bites the engulfed victim with a +4 attack bonus. It can still use its whiplike tail to strike at other targets.

Attacks that hit an engulfing cloaker deal half their damage to the monster and half to the trapped victim.

Shadow Shift (Su): Cloakers can manipulate shadows. This ability is effective only in shadowy areas and has several possible effects.

Obscure Vision: The cloaker gains one-quarter concealment (10% miss chance) for 1d4 rounds.

Illus. by D. Knutson & T. Lockwood

Dancing Images: This duplicates a *mirror image* spell cast by a 6th-level sorcerer.

Silent Image: This duplicates a *silent image* spell cast by a 6th-level sorcerer.

COCKATRICE

Small Magical Beast
Hit Dice: 5d10 (27 hp)
Initiative: +3 (Dex)
Speed: 20 ft., fly 60 ft. (poor)
AC: 14 (+1 size, +3 Dex)
Attacks: Bite +4 melee
Damage: Bite 1d4–2
Face/Reach: 5 ft. by 5 ft./5 ft.
Special Attacks: Petrification
Special Qualities: Petrification immunity
Saves: Fort +4, Ref +7, Will +2
Abilities: Str 6, Dex 17, Con 11, Int 2, Wis 13, Cha 9
Skills: Listen +7, Spot +7
Feats: Alertness, Dodge

Climate/Terrain: Any temperate and warm land and underground
Organization: Solitary, flight (2–4), or flock (6–13)
Challenge Rating: 3
Treasure: None
Alignment: Always neutral
Advancement: 6–8 HD (Small); 9–15 HD (Medium-size)

The cockatrice is an eerie, repulsive hybrid of lizard, cockerel, and bat. It is infamous for its ability to turn flesh to stone.

A cockatrice is about the size of a large goose or turkey. It has the head and body of a cockerel, bat wings, and the long tail of a lizard, tipped with a few feathers. The cockatrice's wattles, comb, and eyes are bright red. Its beak is yellow, its wings gray, its tail green, and its feathers golden brown.

Females, much rarer than males, differ only in that they have no wattles or comb.

The feathers of the cockatrice are prized as quills for scribing scrolls.

COMBAT

The cockatrice fiercely attacks anything that it deems a threat to itself or its lair. Flocks of cockatrices do their utmost to overwhelm and confuse their foes, and sometimes fly directly into their opponents' faces.

Petrification (Su): A cockatrice can turn beings to stone with a touch. Creatures hit by a cockatrice must succeed at a Fortitude save (DC 15) or instantly turn to stone.

Petrification Immunity (Ex): Cockatrices are immune to the petrifying ability of other cockatrices, but other petrifying attacks affect them normally (a medusa's gaze, gorgon's breath, a *flesh to stone* spell, etc.).

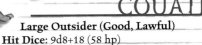

COUATL

Large Outsider (Good, Lawful)
Hit Dice: 9d8+18 (58 hp)
Initiative: +7 (+3 Dex, +4 Improved Initiative)
Speed: 20 ft., fly 60 ft. (good)
AC: 15 (–1 size, +3 Dex, +3 natural)
Attacks: Bite +12 melee
Damage: Bite 1d3+6 and poison
Face/Reach: 5 ft. by 5 ft. (coiled)/5 ft.
Special Attacks: Spells, psionics, poison, constrict 2d8+6
Special Qualities: Telepathy, ethereal jaunt
Saves: Fort +8, Ref +9, Will +10
Abilities: Str 18, Dex 16, Con 14, Int 17, Wis 19, Cha 17
Skills: Concentration +14, Knowledge (any three) +8, Listen +16, Search +15, Sense Motive +16, Spellcraft +15, Spot +16, Tumble +15
Feats: Dodge, Improved Initiative, Still Spell

Climate/Terrain: Warm forest
Organization: Solitary, pair, or flight (3–6)
Challenge Rating: 10
Treasure: Standard
Alignment: Always lawful good
Advancement: 10–13 HD (Large); 14–27 HD (Huge)

The couatl is legendary for its sheer beauty, vast magical powers, and unwavering virtue. Its intelligence and goodness have made it an object of reverence in the regions it inhabits.

The couatl is one of the most beautiful creatures in existence: It has the body of a serpent and feathered wings the color of the rainbow. The creature is about 12 feet long, with a wingspan of about 15 feet. It weighs about 1,800 pounds.

Couatls speak Common, Draconic, and Celestial and also have the power of telepathy.

COMBAT

A couatl seldom attacks without provocation, though it always attacks evildoers caught red-handed. Since it is highly intelligent, a couatl usually casts spells from a distance before closing. If more than one couatl is involved, they discuss their strategy before a battle.

Spells: A couatl casts spells as a 9th-level sorcerer, except that it does not need material components. It can also cast spells from the cleric list and from the Air, Good, and Law domains as arcane spells.

Psionics (Su): At will—*detect chaos, detect evil, detect good, detect law, detect thoughts, invisibility, plane shift,* and *polymorph self.* These abilities are as the spells cast by a 9th-level sorcerer (save DC 13 + spell level).

Poison (Ex): Bite, Fortitude save (DC 16); initial damage 2d4 temporary Strength, secondary damage 4d4 temporary Strength.

Constrict (Ex): A couatl deals 2d8+6 points of damage with a successful grapple check against Huge or smaller creatures. Often, a couatl uses a stilled and quickened spell against other opponents while constricting a foe.

Telepathy (Su): A couatl can communicate telepathically with any creature within 90 feet that has an Intelligence score of at least 1. The creature can respond to the couatl if it wishes—no common language is needed.

Ethereal Jaunt (Su): This works like the spell as cast by a 16th-level sorcerer.

Skills: Arcana, history, and nature are favored Knowledge skills among couatls.

DARKMANTLE

Small Magical Beast
Hit Dice: 1d10+1 (6 hp)
Initiative: +4 (Improved Initiative)
Speed: 20 ft., fly 30 ft. (poor)
AC: 17 (+1 size, +6 natural)
Attacks: Slam +5 melee
Damage: Slam 1d4+4
Face/Reach: 5 ft by 5 ft./5 ft.
Special Attacks: Darkness, improved grab, constrict 1d4+4
Special Qualities: Blindsight
Saves: Fort +3, Ref +2, Will +0
Abilities: Str 16, Dex 10, Con 13, Int 2, Wis 10, Cha 10
Skills: Hide +11, Listen +5*
Feats: Improved Initiative

Climate/Terrain: Any underground
Organization: Solitary, pair, clutch (3–9), or swarm (6–15)
Challenge Rating: 1
Treasure: None
Alignment: Always neutral
Advancement: 2–3 HD (Small)

The darkmantle lurks near cavern roofs, waiting for prey to pass beneath. Its ability to create magical darkness makes it difficult to defeat.

A darkmantle is a species of gastropod resembling a squid or octopus, with a stonelike shell covering its body and a tough membrane stretched between its tentacles. The darkmantle hangs from a ceiling by a muscular "foot" at the top of its body. It can look like a stalactite, by holding its tentacles stiffly under itself, or like a lump of rock, spreading its tentacles so the membrane between them covers its body. Its shell and skin usually resemble limestone, but the darkmantle can slowly change its color to match almost any type of stony background.

Scholars believe the darkmantle has recently evolved from a similar but far less capable subterranean predator.

COMBAT

A darkmantle attacks by dropping onto its prey and wrapping its tentacles around the opponent's head. Once attached, it squeezes and tries to suffocate the foe. A darkmantle that misses its initial attack often flies up and tries to drop on the opponent again.

Darkness (Su): Once per day a darkmantle can cause darkness as the spell cast by a 5th-level sorcerer. It most often uses this ability just before attacking.

Improved Grab (Ex): To use this ability, the darkmantle must hit with its slam attack. If it gets a hold, it can constrict.

Constrict (Ex): A darkmantle deals 1d4+4 damage with a successful grapple check.

Blindsight: A darkmantle can "see" by emitting high-frequency sounds, inaudible to most other creatures, that allows it to ascertain objects and creatures within 90 feet. A *silence* spell negates this and effectively blinds the darkmantle.

Skills: A darkmantle receives a +4 racial bonus to Listen checks. *This bonus is lost if its blindsight is negated. The creature's variable coloration gives it a +4 racial bonus to Hide checks.

DELVER

Huge Aberration
Hit Dice: 15d8+75 (142 hp)
Initiative: +5 (+1 Dex, +4 Improved Initiative)
Speed: 30 ft., burrow 10 ft.
AC: 14 (–2 size, +1 Dex, +5 natural)
Attacks: 2 slams +17 melee
Damage: Slam 1d6+8 and 2d6 acid
Face/Reach: 10 ft. by 20 ft./10 ft.
Special Attacks: Acid
Special Qualities: Acid immunity, corrosive slime, tremorsense, stone shape
Saves: Fort +10, Ref +6, Will +11
Abilities: Str 27, Dex 13, Con 21, Int 14, Wis 14, Cha 12
Skills: Intuit Direction +9, Knowledge (geology) +9, Listen +13, Move Silently +19, Spot +13
Feats: Alertness, Blind-Fight, Improved Initiative, Power Attack

Climate/Terrain: Any underground
Organization: Solitary
Challenge Rating: 9
Treasure: None
Alignment: Usually neutral
Advancement: 16–30 HD (Huge); 31–45 HD (Gargantuan)

Illus. by B. Despain

SARDINHA

These bizarre creatures live in the depths of the earth, burrowing through solid stone with a corrosive slime they secrete from their skins.

Delvers are shy and mostly inoffensive creatures, but rogue specimens with murderous streaks are not unknown. They feed on stone and may even devour creatures such as xorns and earth elementals.

A delver resembles a cross between a giant slug and a sea turtle. It has a teardrop-shaped body that glistens with slime, mottled gray, brown, and ochre all over. Two great flippers tipped with blunt claws sprout from the forebody. The creature feeds by dissolving rock with its slime and shoving the resulting goo under its body, the underside of which is almost all mouth.

Delvers eat rock but enjoy various nonmetallic minerals as seasonings in the same way that humans enjoy spices. Adventurers might secure information and assistance from delvers by offering them tasty minerals (usually gems) or pick-me-ups (such as coins). Metal is an intoxicant to delvers. Some, however, become addicted and are a menace to miners and anyone who carries metal equipment.

Delvers speak Terran and Undercommon.

COMBAT

Delvers prefer to fight from their tunnels, which they use to protect their flanks while lashing out with their flippers.

A delver expecting trouble may honeycomb an area with tunnels, leaving most closed with layers of stone 1 or 2 inches thick.

The delver can quickly dissolve the stone cover and pop up to attack unexpectedly.

Corrosive Slime (Ex): Delvers produce a mucuslike slime that contains a highly corrosive substance. The slime is particularly effective against stone.

A delver's mere touch deals 2d6 points of damage to organic creatures or objects. Against metallic creatures or objects, a delver's slime deals 4d8 points of damage, and against stony creatures (including earth elementals) or objects it deals 8d10 points of damage. A slam attack by a delver leaves a patch of slime that deals 2d6 points of damage on contact and another 2d6 points of damage in each of the next 2 rounds. A large quantity (at least a quart) of water or weak acid, such as vinegar, washes off the slime.

An opponent's armor and clothing dissolve and become useless immediately unless the wearer succeeds at a Reflex save (DC 22). Weapons that strike a delver also dissolve immediately unless the wielder succeeds at a Reflex save (DC 22).

Creatures attacking the delver with natural weapons take damage from the slime each time their attacks hit unless they succeed at Reflex saves (DC 22).

Tremorsense (Ex): A delver can automatically sense the location of anything within 60 feet that is in contact with the ground.

Stone Shape (Ex): A delver can alter its slime to temporarily soften stone instead of dissolving it. Once every 10 minutes, a delver can soften and shape up to 25 cubic feet of stone, as *stone shape* cast by a 15th-level druid.

	Dretch (Tanar'ri)	Quasit	Succubus (Tanar'ri)
	Small Outsider (Chaotic, Evil)	**Tiny Outsider (Chaotic, Evil)**	**Medium-Size Outsider (Chaotic, Evil)**
Hit Dice:	2d8 (9 hp)	3d8 (13 hp)	6d8+6 (33 hp)
Initiative:	+0	+3 (Dex)	+1 (Dex)
Speed:	20 ft.	20 ft., fly 50 ft. (perfect)	30 ft., fly 50 ft. (average)
AC:	16 (+1 size, +5 natural)	18 (+2 size, +3 Dex, +3 natural)	20 (+1 Dex, +9 natural)
Attacks:	2 claws +3 melee, bite +1 melee	2 claws +8 melee, bite +3 melee	2 claws +7 melee
Damage:	Claw 1d4, bite 1d4	Claw 1d3–1 and poison, bite 1d4–1	Claw 1d3+1
Face/Reach:	5 ft. by 5 ft./5 ft.	2 1/2 ft. by 2 1/2 ft./0 ft.	5 ft. by 5 ft./5 ft.
Special Attacks:	Spell-like abilities, summon tanar'ri	Spell-like abilities, poison	Spell-like abilities, energy drain, summon tanar'ri
Special Qualities:	Damage reduction 5/silver, SR 5, tanar'ri qualities	Damage reduction 5/silver, SR 5, poison immunity, fire resistance 20, alternate form, regeneration 2	Damage reduction 20/+2, SR 12, tanar'ri qualities, alternate form, tongues
Saves:	Fort +3, Ref +3, Will +3	Fort +3, Ref +6, Will +4	Fort +6, Ref +6, Will +7
Abilities:	Str 10, Dex 10, Con 10, Int 5, Wis 11, Cha 11	Str 8, Dex 17, Con 10, Int 10, Wis 12, Cha 10	Str 13, Dex 13, Con 13, Int 16, Wis 14, Cha 20
Skills:	—	Hide +14, Listen +6, Move Silently +6, Search +4, Spellcraft +4, Spot +6	Bluff +11, Concentration +7, Disguise +11*, Escape Artist +7, Hide +7, Knowledge (any one) +9, Listen +16, Move Silently +7, Ride +7, Search +9, Spot +16
Feats:	Multiattack	Weapon Finesse (bite, claw)	Dodge, Mobility
Climate/Terrain:	Any land and underground	Any land and underground	Any land and underground
Organization:	Solitary, gang (2–4), swarm (6–15), or mob (10–40)	Solitary	Solitary
Challenge Rating:	2	3	9
Treasure:	None	None	Standard
Alignment:	Always chaotic evil	Always chaotic evil	Always chaotic evil
Advancement:	3–6 HD (Small)	4–6 HD (Tiny)	7–12 HD (Medium-size)

	Bebilith	Retriever	Vrock (Tanar'ri)
	Huge Outsider (Chaotic, Evil)	**Huge Construct**	**Large Outsider (Chaotic, Evil)**
Hit Dice:	12d8+48 (102 hp)	10d10 (55 hp)	8d8+24 (60 hp)
Initiative:	+5 (+1 Dex, +4 Improved Initiative)	+1 (Dex)	+2 (Dex)
Speed:	40 ft., climb 20 ft.	50 ft.	30 ft., fly 50 ft. (average)
AC:	25 (–2 size, +1 Dex, +16 natural)	22 (–2 size, +1 Dex, +13 natural)	25 (–1 size, +2 Dex, +14 natural)
Attacks:	Bite +19 melee, 2 claws +14 melee	4 claws +12 melee	2 claws +11 melee, bite +9 melee, 2 rakes +9 melee
Damage:	Bite 2d6+9 and poison, claw 2d4+4 and armor damage	Claw 2d6+7	Claw 1d8+4, bite 1d6+2, rake 1d4+2
Face/Reach:	15 ft. by 15 ft./10 ft.	10 ft. by 10 ft./10 ft.	5 ft. by 5 ft./10 ft.
Special Attacks:	Web, poison, armor damage	Eye rays +6 ranged touch, improved grab, find target	Spell-like abilities, spores, screech, dance of ruin, summon tanar'ri
Special Qualities:	Damage reduction 30/+3, protective aura, plane shift, scent, telepathy	Construct, regeneration 5	Damage reduction 20/+2, SR 22, tanar'ri qualities
Saves:	Fort +12, Ref +9, Will +9	Fort +3, Ref +4, Will +3	Fort +9, Ref +8, Will +8
Abilities:	Str 28, Dex 12, Con 18, Int 11, Wis 13, Cha 13	Str 25, Dex 13, Con —, Int —, Wis 11, Cha 1	Str 19, Dex 15, Con 17, Int 14, Wis 14, Cha 12
Skills:	Climb +21, Hide +11, Jump +21, Listen +17, Move Silently +15, Search +14, Sense Motive +15, Spot +17	—	Concentration +14, Hide +9, Knowledge (any one) +12, Listen +13, Move Silently +13, Search +13, Sense Motive +13, Spellcraft +12, Spot +12
Feats:	Alertness, Cleave, Improved Initiative, Power Attack	—	Cleave, Multiattack, Power Attack
Climate/Terrain:	Any land and underground	Any land and underground	Any land and underground
Organization:	Solitary	Solitary	Solitary, gang (2–4), or squad (6–10)
Challenge Rating:	9	10	13
Treasure:	None	None	Standard
Alignment:	Always chaotic evil	Always chaotic evil	Always chaotic evil
Advancement:	13–18 HD (Huge); 19–36 HD (Gargantuan)	11–15 HD (Huge); 16–30 HD (Gargantuan)	9–12 HD (Large); 13–24 HD (Huge)

	Hezrou (Tanar'ri)	Glabrezu (Tanar'ri)	Nalfeshnee (Tanar'ri)
	Large Outsider (Chaotic, Evil)	Huge Outsider (Chaotic, Evil)	Huge Outsider (Chaotic, Evil)
Hit Dice:	9d8+27 (67 hp)	10d8+40 (85 hp)	11d8+44 (93 hp)
Initiative:	+0	+0	+1 (Dex)
Speed:	30 ft.	40 ft.	30 ft., fly 40 ft. (poor)
AC:	26 (−1 size, +17 natural)	27 (−2 size, +19 natural)	28 (−2 size, +1 Dex, +19 natural)
Attacks:	Bite +13 melee, 2 claws +8 melee	2 pincers +15 melee, 2 claws +13 melee, bite +13 melee	Bite +15 melee, 2 claws +13 melee
Damage:	Bite 4d4+5, claw 1d6+2	Pincer 2d6+7, claw 1d3+3, bite 1d4+3	Bite 2d4+6, claw 1d4+3
Face/Reach:	5 ft. by 5 ft./10 ft.	5 ft. by 10 ft./15 ft.	10 ft. by 10 ft./15 ft.
Special Attacks:	Spell-like abilities, stench, improved grab, summon tanar'ri	Spell-like abilities, improved grab, summon tanar'ri	Spell-like abilities, smite, summon tanar'ri
Special Qualities:	Damage reduction 20/+2, SR 23, tanar'ri qualities, half damage	Damage reduction 20/+2, SR 21, tanar'ri qualities, detect magic, true seeing	Damage reduction 20/+2, SR 24, tanar'ri qualities, know alignment, see invisibility
Saves:	Fort +9, Ref +6, Will +8	Fort +11, Ref +7, Will +10	Fort +11, Ref +8, Will +13
Abilities:	Str 21, Dex 10, Con 17, Int 14, Wis 14, Cha 14	Str 25, Dex 10, Con 19, Int 16, Wis 16, Cha 16	Str 23, Dex 13, Con 19, Int 22, Wis 22, Cha 16
Skills:	Concentration +15, Hide +14, Listen +22, Move Silently +12, Search +14, Spellcraft +14, Spot +22	Bluff +13, Concentration +14, Hide +2, Knowledge (any one)+13, Listen +21, Move Silently +10, Scry +13, Search +13, Sense Motive +13, Spellcraft +13, Spot +21	Bluff +17, Concentration +18, Diplomacy +17, Hide +7, Knowledge (arcana) +16, Listen +26, Move Silently +15, Scry +19, Search +20, Sense Motive +19, Spellcraft +20, Spot +26
Feats:	Blind-Fight, Cleave, Power Attack	Cleave, Multiattack, Power Attack	Cleave, Multiattack, Power Attack
Climate/Terrain:	Any land and underground	Any land and underground	Any land and underground
Organization:	Solitary or gang (2–4)	Solitary or troupe (1 glabrezu, 1 succubus, and 2–5 vrocks)	Solitary or troupe (1 nalfeshnee, 1 hezrou, and 2–5 vrocks)
Challenge Rating:	14	15	16
Treasure:	Standard	Standard coins; double goods; standard items	Standard coins; double goods; standard items
Alignment:	Always chaotic evil	Always chaotic evil	Always chaotic evil
Advancement:	10–13 HD (Large); 14–27 HD (Huge)	11–15 HD (Huge); 16–30 HD (Gargantuan)	12–17 HD (Huge); 18–33 HD (Gargantuan)

	Marilith (Tanar'ri)	Balor (Tanar'ri)
	Large Outsider (Chaotic, Evil)	Large Outsider (Chaotic, Evil)
Hit Dice:	9d8+45 (85 hp)	13d8+52 (110 hp)
Initiative:	+2 (Dex)	+5 (+1 Dex, +4 Improved Initiative)
Speed:	40 ft.	40 ft., fly 90 ft. (good)
AC:	29 (−1 size, +2 Dex, +18 natural)	30 (−1 size, +1 Dex, +20 natural)
Attacks:	Weapon +13/+8 melee, 5 weapons +13 melee, tail slam +11 melee	+1 vorpal greatsword +18/+13/+8 melee, whip +17 melee; or 2 slams +19 melee
Damage:	Weapon 1d8+5, weapons 1d8+2, tail slam 4d6+2	+1 vorpal greatsword 2d6+8, whip 1d4+3 and entangle; or slam 1d6+7 and fear
Face/Reach:	5 ft. by 5 ft./10 ft.	5 ft. by 5 ft./10 ft. (15 ft. with whip)
Special Attacks:	Spell-like abilities, improved grab, constrict 4d6+7, summon tanar'ri	Spell-like abilities, fear, entangle, body flames, summon tanar'ri
Special Qualities:	Damage reduction 20/+2, SR 25, tanar'ri qualities	Damage reduction 30/+3, SR 28, tanar'ri qualities, death throes
Saves:	Fort +11, Ref +8, Will +10	Fort +12, Ref +9, Will +13
Abilities:	Str 21, Dex 15, Con 21, Int 18, Wis 18, Cha 16	Str 25, Dex 13, Con 19, Int 20, Wis 20, Cha 16
Skills:	Bluff +14, Concentration +15, Hide +10, Listen +24, Move Silently +12, Scry +14, Search +14, Sense Motive +15, Spellcraft +14, Spot +24	Bluff +18, Concentration +19, Diplomacy +17, Hide +13, Knowledge (any one) +13, Listen +28, Move Silently +13, Scry +21, Search +20, Sense Motive +20, Spellcraft +21, Spot +29
Feats:	Cleave, Multiattack, Multidexterity, Multiweapon Fighting, Power Attack	Ambidexterity, Cleave, Improved Initiative, Two-Weapon Fighting
Climate/Terrain:	Any land and underground	Any land and underground
Organization:	Solitary or pair	Solitary or troupe (1 balor, 1 marilith, and 2–5 hezrous)
Challenge Rating:	17	18
Treasure:	Standard coins; double goods; standard items, plus 1d4 magic weapons	Standard coins; double goods, plus whip; standard items, plus +1 vorpal greatsword
Alignment:	Always chaotic evil	Always chaotic evil
Advancement:	10–13 HD (Large); 14–27 HD (Huge)	14–19 HD (Large); 20–39 HD (Huge)

Demons are native to the Abyss, a realm of unmitigated chaos and evil. They are the most violent, greedy, fickle, and perverse of the fiends (creatures from the infernal planes).

Many demons, not satisfied with their own iniquity, take pleasure in tempting mortals to become as depraved as they are.

The largest and most diverse group of demons is the tanar'ri, unchallenged masters of the Abyss. But demons come in an overwhelming variety of forms, and no one has ever cataloged them all. Those most familiar to mortals are described here.

Except where noted below, demons speak Abyssal, Celestial, and Draconic.

COMBAT

Demons are ferocity personified and will attack any creature just for the sheer fun of it—even other demons. They enjoy terrifying their victims before slaying them and often devour the slain. Many demons can create darkness, and a group of demons frequently blanket the enemy with darkness before joining battle.

Summon Tanar'ri (Sp): Tanar'ri can summon other tanar'ri much as though casting a *summon monster* spell, but they have only a limited chance of success. Roll d%: On a failure, no tanar'ri answer the summons. Summoned creatures automatically return whence they came after 1 hour. A tanar'ri that has just been summoned cannot use its own summon ability for 1 hour.

Most tanar'ri do not use their summon ability lightly, since it leaves them beholden to the summoned creature. In general, they use it only when necessary to save their own lives.

TANAR'RI QUALITIES

Immunities (Ex): Tanar'ri are immune to poison and electricity.

Resistances (Ex): Tanar'ri have cold, fire, and acid resistance 20.

Telepathy (Su): Tanar'ri can communicate telepathically with any creature within 100 feet that has a language (although dretches are more limited).

DRETCH

Dretches are pathetic but wicked creatures that spend most of their time milling about in massive hordes or serving as rank-and-file troops in tanar'ri armies.

Dretches look like squat humanoids with blubbery, almost hairless bodies. Their skin is pale white to beige, giving way to sickly blue in some areas. They have slack and slobbery mouths with many small fangs, and their hair is sparse and bristly. Dretches are about 4 feet tall.

Dretches cannot speak but can communicate telepathically.

Combat

Dretches are slow, stupid, and not very effective combatants. They depend on sheer numbers to overcome foes and immediately summon other dretches to improve the odds in battle. They flee at the first sign of adversity unless more powerful demons are present to intimidate them into fighting. Dretches' fear of their greater kin is stronger then even their fear of death.

When fighting on their own, dretches often forget to use their spell-like abilities.

Spell-Like Abilities: At will—*darkness, scare,* and *telekinesis;* 1/day—*stinking cloud.* These abilities are as the spells cast by a 2nd-level sorcerer (save DC 10 + spell level).

Summon Tanar'ri (Sp): Once per day a dretch can attempt to summon another dretch with a 35% chance of success.

Telepathy (Su): Dretches can communicate telepathically with creatures within 100 feet that speak Abyssal.

QUASIT

Quasits are insidious demons often found serving chaotic evil spellcasters as councilors and spies.

In their natural forms, quasits stand some 2 feet tall and weigh about 8 pounds. They look like tiny humanoids with spiky horns and bat wings. The hands and feet are long and slender, with very long, claw-tipped digits. Their skin is pustulent and green.

Combat

Although quasits thirst for victory in combat as other demons do, they are cowards at heart. They typically attack from ambush, using *polymorph* and *invisibility* to get within reach, then try to scuttle away. When retreating, they use their fear ability to deter pursuit.

Spell-Like Abilities: At will—*detect good, detect magic,* and *invisibility* (self only); 1/day—*cause fear* (as the spell, except that its area is a 30-foot radius from the quasit). These abilities are as the spells cast by a 6th-level sorcerer (save DC 10 + spell level).

Once per week a quasit can use *commune* to ask six questions (this is otherwise as the spell cast by a 12th-level cleric).

Poison (Ex): Claw, Fortitude save (DC 13); initial damage 1d4 temporary Dexterity, secondary damage 2d4 temporary Dexterity.

Alternate Form (Su): A quasit can assume other forms at will as a standard action. This ability functions as *polymorph self* cast by a 12th-level sorcerer, except that any individual quasit can assume only one or two forms no larger than Medium-size. Common forms include bat, monstrous centipede, toad, and wolf.

Regeneration (Ex): Quasits take normal damage from acid, and from holy and blessed weapons.

SUCCUBUS

Succubi are the most comely of the tanar'ri (perhaps of all demons), and they live to tempt mortals.

A succubus usually appears as a stunningly beautiful humanoid, with perfect build and flawless skin. Succubi usually take a female form but occasionally appear as males (called incubi). Their natural appearance is decidedly demonic: statuesque humanoid bodies, large bat wings, and sinister, glowing eyes. Succubi are about 6 feet tall.

Combat

Succubi are not warriors and flee combat whenever they can. If forced to fight, they can attack with their claws, but they prefer to turn foes against one another.

Spell-Like Abilities: At will—*charm monster, clairaudience/clairvoyance, darkness, desecrate, detect good, detect thoughts, doom, ethereal jaunt* (self plus 50 pounds of objects only), *suggestion,* and *teleport without error* (self plus 50 pounds of objects only); 1/day—*unholy blight.* These abilities are as the spells cast by a 12th-level sorcerer (save DC 15 + spell level).

Energy Drain (Su): A succubus drains energy from a mortal it lures into some act of passion, or by simply planting a kiss on the victim. If the target is not willing to be kissed, the succubus must start a grapple, which provokes an attack of opportunity. The succubus's kiss or embrace inflicts one negative level; the victim must succeed at a Wisdom check (DC 15) to even notice. The Fortitude save to remove the negative level has a DC of 18.

Summon Tanar'ri (Sp): Once per day a succubus can attempt to summon one balor with a 10% chance of success.

Alternate Form (Su): Succubi can assume any humanoid form of Small to Large size as a standard action. This ability is similar to the *polymorph self* spell but allows only humanoid forms.

*While using this ability, a succubus gains a +10 circumstance bonus to Disguise checks.

Tongues (Su): A succubus has a permanent *tongues* ability as the spell cast by a 12th-level sorcerer. Succubi usually use verbal communication with mortals and save telepathic communication for conversing with other fiends.

Skills: Succubi receive a +8 racial bonus to Listen and Spot checks.

*When using alternate form, a succubus receives an additional +10 circumstance bonus to Disguise checks.

BEBILITH

Bebiliths are huge, predatory, arachnid demons that hunt other demons. While their favorite prey is tanar'ri, they aren't picky—they will stalk and attack any type of creature.

Bebiliths look like misshapen spiders with dark, mottled, chitinous bodies. Their forelegs end in wicked barbs, and their fanged mouths drip poisonous goo.

Bebiliths do not speak but understand Abyssal. Their telepathy allows them to communicate silently with one another.

COMBAT

Bebiliths attack any creature they see. They usually pick one target and concentrate their attacks on that opponent, using their webs to isolate the chosen target from its comrades.

Web (Ex): Four times per day a bebilith can shoot webs from its abdomen. This attack is like a *web* spell, with a few exceptions. The range is 30 feet, and the webs are permanent, nonmagical, and cannot be dispelled. The DC for evading or breaking free from the webs is 20, and there is a 75% chance that the webbing won't burn if any sort of fire is applied to it (check each round).

Poison (Ex): Bite, Fortitude save (DC 20); initial damage 1d6 temporary Constitution, secondary damage 2d6 temporary Constitution. Bebilith venom is highly perishable, losing its potency

and becoming inert, foul-smelling goo almost as soon as it comes into contact with air.

Armor Damage (Ex): A bebilith's claws can catch and tear an opponent's armor. If the opponent has both armor and a shield, roll 1d6: A roll of 1–4 affects the armor and a roll of 5–6 affects the shield.

Make a grapple check whenever the bebilith hits with a claw attack, adding to the opponent's roll any magical bonus for the armor or shield. If the bebilith wins, the affected armor or shield is torn away and ruined.

Protective Aura (Su): A *magic circle against chaos, evil, good,* or *law* effect always surrounds a bebilith, identical with the spell cast by a 12th-level sorcerer. The bebilith usually chooses *magic circle against chaos* but can change the aura each round as a free action. The aura can be dispelled, but the bebilith can create it again during its next turn as a free action. (The defensive benefits from the aura are not included in the creature's statistics.)

Plane Shift (Su): This ability affects only the bebilith. It is otherwise similar to the spell of the same name.

Skills: The bebilith's mottled coloration gives it a +8 racial bonus to Hide checks.

RETRIEVER

Retrievers were created through foul sorcery to be assassins, warriors, and servants to powerful demon nobles.

A retriever resembles a huge spider with the four frontmost legs ending in cleaverlike claws. As its name suggests, it specializes in recovering lost or desired objects, runaway slaves, and enemies and bringing them back to its master.

Combat

Retrievers attack with four claws, but their eye rays are far more deadly.

Eye Rays (Su): A retriever's eyes can produce four different magical rays with a range of 100 feet. Each round, it can fire two rays, but an individual ray is usable only once every 6 rounds. It cannot fire rays in the same round as it makes physical attacks.

Each effect follows the rules for a ray (see Aiming a Spell, page 148 in the *Player's Handbook*). Save DC is 16.

The four eye effects are:

Fire: Deals 12d6 fire damage to the target and to all those within 5 feet (those nearby are allowed Reflex saves to halve the damage).

Cold: Deals 12d6 cold damage to the target.

Electricity: Deals 12d6 electricity damage to the target.

Petrification: The target must succeed at a Fortitude save or turn to stone permanently.

Improved Grab (Ex): To use this ability, the retriever must hit with its bite attack. If it gets a hold, it holds the opponent fast in its mouth. This is how it usually "retrieves" things.

Illus. by D. Knutson

Find Target (Sp): When ordered to find an item or being, a retriever does so unerringly, as though guided by *discern location*.

Construct: Immune to mind-influencing effects, poison, disease, and similar effects. Not subject to critical hits, subdual damage, ability damage, energy drain, or death from massive damage.

Regeneration (Ex): Blessed and holy weapons deal normal damage to retrievers.

A retriever that loses a limb or body part can reattach it by holding the severed member to the stump. Reattachment takes 1 minute. A retriever regrows lost body parts in one day (lost parts become inert).

VROCK

Vrocks look like crosses between large humans and vultures. They serve as guards to more powerful demons and as elite troops.

A vrock is about 8 feet tall, with strong, sinewy limbs covered in fine gray feathers and a long neck topped with a vulture's head. Vrocks have wickedly sharp claws and beaks.

Combat

Vrocks are vicious fighters who like to wade into the enemy and cause as much damage as possible. They prance about in battle, taking briefly to the air and bringing their clawed feet into play. They make sparing use of *darkness*, since this nullifies *mirror image*.

Spell-Like Abilities: At will—*darkness, desecrate, detect good, detect magic, mass charm, mirror image, telekinesis,* and *teleport without error* (self plus 50 pounds of objects only). These abilities are as the spells cast by a 12th-level sorcerer (save DC 11 + spell level).

Spores (Ex): A vrock can release masses of spores from its body once every 3 rounds. The spores automatically deal 1d8 points of damage to all creatures within 5 feet of the vrock. They then penetrate the skin and grow, dealing an additional 1d2 points of damage each round for 10 rounds. At the end of this time, the victim is covered with a tangle of viny growths. A *delay poison* spell

stops the spores' growth for its duration. *Bless, neutralize poison,* or *remove disease* kills the spores, as does sprinkling the victim with a vial of holy water.

Stunning Screech (Su): Once per hour a vrock can emit a piercing screech. Every creature within a 30-foot radius must succeed at a Fortitude save (DC 17) or be stunned for 1 round.

Dance of Ruin (Su): To use this ability, a group of five or more vrocks join hands in a circle, dancing wildly and chanting. If they dance for 3 rounds, a wave of crackling energy flashes outward in a 100-foot radius. All nondemon creatures within the radius take 2d20 points of damage (Reflex half DC 15). Forcing the vrocks to break the circle stops the dance.

Summon Tanar'ri (Sp): Once per day a vrock can attempt to summon 2d10 dretches or another vrock with a 35% chance of success.

Skills: Vrocks receive a +8 racial bonus to Listen and Spot checks.

HEZROU

Hezrous are demonic sergeants, overseeing the formation of armies and commanding units in battle.

Hezrous look like massive, roughly humanoid toads with arms in place of forelegs. They walk both upright and on all fours but always fight standing up. Their wide mouths have rows of blunt, powerful teeth, and long spines run the length of their backs. Hezrous are about 7 feet tall.

Combat

Hezrous enjoy melee combat even more than vrocks do. They eagerly press the attack, so their stench can take effect as quickly as possible.

Spell-Like Abilities: At will—*animate object, blasphemy, blink, chaos hammer, deeper darkness, desecrate, detect good, detect magic, dispel good, magic circle against good, produce flame, summon swarm, teleport without error* (self plus 50 pounds of objects only), and *unholy blight;* 3/day—*gaseous form.* These abilities are as the spells cast by a 13th-level sorcerer (save DC 12 + spell level).

Stench (Ex): A hezrou's skin produces a foul-smelling, toxic liquid whenever it fights. All creatures (except other tanar'ri) within 10 feet must succeed at a Fortitude save (DC 17) or be overwhelmed by nausea. They are rendered helpless from gagging and vomiting for as long as they remain in the affected area and for 1d4 rounds afterward. Creatures who successfully save suffer a –2 morale penalty to attack rolls but cannot be affected again by the same hezrou's stench for one day. A *delay poison* or *neutralize poison* spell removes the effect from one creature.

Improved Grab (Ex): To use this ability, the hezrou must hit a Medium-size or smaller opponent with both claw attacks.

Summon Tanar'ri (Sp): Once per day a hezrou can attempt to summon 4d10 dretches or another hezrou with a 35% chance of success.

Half Damage (Ex): Any nonmagical attack against a hezrou, including hits from enchanted weapons, deals only half damage. This effect does not stack with the hezrou's damage reduction; apply either the damage reduction or the half damage, whichever results in the least amount of damage suffered.

Skills: Hezrous receive a +8 racial bonus to Listen and Spot checks.

GLABREZU

Like succubi, glabrezu occupy themselves with tempting mortals into ruin, but prefer to lure them with power rather than passion. They also make formidable opponents in battle.

Glabrezu are towering (15 feet tall), broad, and well muscled, with four arms, two ending in clawed hands and two in powerful pincers. They have doglike heads with sharp fangs and penetrating violet eyes, and their skin color ranges from deep russet to pitch black.

Combat

Glabrezu prefer subterfuge to combat. However, if their attempts do not fool the opposition, they attack with a vengeance.

Spell-Like Abilities: At will—*burning hands, chaos hammer, charm person, confusion, death knell, deeper darkness, desecrate, detect good, dispel magic, enlarge, mirror image, reverse gravity, shatter,* and *unholy blight.* These abilities are as the spells cast by a 10th-level sorcerer (save DC 13 + spell level).

A glabrezu also can *teleport without error* (self plus 50 pounds of objects only) at will as the spell cast by a 12th-level sorcerer. Seven times per day it can cast *power word, stun* as a 15th-level sorcerer.

Improved Grab (Ex): To use this ability, the glabrezu must hit a Medium-size or smaller opponent with a pincer attack. If it gets a hold, it deals automatic pincer damage each round the hold is maintained.

Summon Tanar'ri (Sp): Once per day a glabrezu can attempt to summon 4d10 dretches or 1d2 vrocks with a 50% chance of success, or another glabrezu with a 20% chance of success.

Detect Magic (Su): Glabrezu continuously detect magic as the spell cast by a 12th-level sorcerer.

True Seeing (Su): Glabrezu continuously use true seeing as the spell cast by a 12th-level cleric.

Skills: Glabrezu receive a +8 racial bonus to Listen and Spot checks.

NALFESHNEE

A nalfeshnee stands 20 feet tall and looks like a huge, gross cross between an ape and a boar. These demons often enjoy judging doomed souls.

A nalfeshnee needs all its vast strength to support its massive body. The small, feathered wings that sprout from its back are seemingly unable to lift its bulk. Nevertheless, nalfeshnees can fly. Their red eyes glow like embers and seem to pierce the mind and draw energy from just a glance.

Combat

Nalfeshnees disdain combat as something beneath them, but they often succumb to blood lust and do battle anyway. They prefer to disable opponents with their smite ability and slaughter them while they can't fight back.

Spell-Like Abilities: At will—*alter self, call lightning, chaos hammer, chill touch, death knell, deeper darkness, desecrate, detect magic, feeblemind, forget, greater dispelling, invisibility* (self only), *magic circle against good* (self only), *mirror image, raise dead, slow, teleport without error* (self plus 50 pounds of objects only), *unholy aura, unholy blight,* and *web.* These abilities are as the spells cast by a 12th-level sorcerer (save DC 13 + spell level).

Smite (Su): Three times per day a nalfeshnee can create a nimbus of unholy light. When the demon triggers the ability, rainbow-colored beams play around its body. One round later they burst in a 60-foot radius. Affected creatures take 15 points of damage (Reflex half DC 18). They also must succeed at a Will save (DC 18) or be in a stupor for 1d10 rounds as visions of their worst fears hound them. They receive full Dexterity and shield bonuses to AC if attacked but can take no actions. Other tanar'ri are immune to this effect.

Summon Tanar'ri (Sp): Twice per day a nalfeshnee can attempt to summon 1d4 vrocks, 1d4 hezrous, or one glabrezu with a 50% chance of success, or another nalfeshnee with a 20% chance of success.

Know Alignment (Su): Nalfeshnees always know the alignment of any creature that they look upon.

See Invisibility (Su): Nalfeshnees continuously see invisibility as the spell cast by a 12th-level sorcerer.

Skills: Nalfeshnees receive a +8 racial bonus to Listen and Spot checks.

MARILITH

Mariliths are generals and tacticians, often rivaling balors in sheer brilliance and cunning. Some also serve as chief lieutenants for major demon royalty.

Mariliths appear as giant snakes from the waist down, with green, scaly coils, and attractive female humanoids above the waist. Besides their half-snake bodies, mariliths are distinguished by their six arms, each one usually holding some exotic weapon and sporting many bangles and jewels. Mariliths stand about 7 feet tall and measure about 20 feet from head to tip of tail.

Combat

Though mariliths thrive on grand strategy and army-level tactics, they love physical combat and never shirk an opportunity to fight. Each of a marilith's six arms can wield a weapon, and the creature gets an additional weapon attack with its primary arm. Mariliths seldom rush headlong into battle, however, preferring to hang back and size up the situation first. They always seek to gain the best possible advantage from the local terrain, obstacles, and any vulnerability or weakness in their opponents.

Spell-Like Abilities: At will—*animate dead, bestow curse, chaos hammer, cloudkill, comprehend languages, darkness, desecrate, detect good, detect law, detect magic, inflict serious wounds, magic circle against good* (self only), *magic weapon, project image, polymorph self, pyrotechnics, see invisibility, shatter, telekinesis, teleport without error* (self plus 50 pounds of objects only), *unholy aura,* and *unholy blight.* These abilities are as the spells cast by a 13th-level sorcerer (save DC 13 + spell level).

Improved Grab (Ex): To use this ability, the marilith must hit a Medium-size or smaller opponent with its tail slam attack. If it succeeds, it can constrict.

Constrict (Ex): A marilith deals 4d6+7 points of damage with a successful grapple check against Medium-size or smaller creatures. The constricted creature must succeed at a Fortitude save (DC 19) or lose consciousness for at long as it remains in the coils and for 2d4 rounds thereafter.

Summon Tanar'ri (Sp): Once per day a marilith can attempt to summon 4d10 dretches, 1d4 hezrou, or one nalfeshnee with a 50% chance of success, or one glabrezu or another marilith with a 20% chance of success.

Skills: Mariliths receive a +8 racial bonus to Listen and Spot checks.

Feats: A marilith receives the Multidexteriry and Multiweapon Fighting feats as bonus feats. In combination with its natural abilities, these feats allow the marilith to attack with all its arms at no penalty.

BALOR

Balors are among the greatest and most terrible of the demons. They motivate their kindred to spread fear and misery.

A balor is a repulsive, towering humanoid (about 12 feet tall) with dark red skin and massive, clawed hands. Its huge wings can propel it through the air with unnatural speed, and its body is often wrapped in lurid flames.

Combat

Balors love to join battle armed with their swords and whips. If they face stiff resistance, they may teleport away to loose a few *symbols* and fear effects at the foe.

Spell-Like Abilities: At will—*blasphemy, deeper darkness, desecrate, detect good, detect law, fear, greater dispelling, pyrotechnics, read magic, suggestion, symbol* (any), *telekinesis, teleport without error* (self plus 50 pounds of objects only), *tongues* (self only), *unhallow, unholy aura, unholy blight,* and *wall of fire;* 1/day—*fire storm* and *implosion.* These abilities are as the spells cast by a 20th-level sorcerer (save DC 13 + spell level).

Fear (Su): A creature hit by a balor's slam attack must succeed at a Will save (DC 19) or flee in terror for 1d6 rounds.

Entangle (Ex): A balor's whip entangles foes much like an attack with a net. The whip has a maximum range of 40 feet, with a range increment of 10 feet, and 20 hit points (see page 102 in the *Player's Handbook* for details on net attacks). The whip needs no folding. If it hits, the target and the balor immediately make opposed Strength checks; if the balor wins, it drags the target against its flaming body (see below). The target remains anchored against the balor's body until it escapes the whip.

Body Flames (Su): Balors can wreathe their bodies in roaring flames as a free action. The balor suffers no harm, but anyone grappling with it takes 4d6 points of fire damage each round.

Vorpal Sword (Su): Every balor carries a *+1 vorpal greatsword* that looks like a flame or a bolt of lightning. The sword also has the spell-like ability to *detect good* as cast by a 12th-level sorcerer, except that its range is 30 feet.

Detect Magic (Su): Balors continuously detect magic as the spell cast by a 20th-level sorcerer.

See Invisibility (Su): Balors continuously see invisibility as the spell cast by a 20th-level sorcerer.

Summon Tanar'ri (Sp): Once per day a balor can automatically summon 4d10 dretches, 1d4 hezrous, or one nalfeshnee, glabrezu, marilith, or balor.

Death Throes (Ex): When killed, a balor explodes in a blinding flash of light that deals 50 points of damage to everything within 100 feet (Reflex half DC 20).

Skills: Balors receive a +8 racial bonus to Listen and Spot checks.

DESTRACHAN

Large Aberration
Hit Dice: 8d8+24 (60 hp)
Initiative: +5 (+1 Dex, +4 Improved Initiative)
Speed: 30 ft.
AC: 16 (−1 size, +1 Dex, +6 natural)
Attacks: 2 claws +9 melee
Damage: Claw 1d6+4
Face/Reach: 5 ft. by 10 ft./5 ft.
Special Attacks: Destructive harmonics, reverberating harmonics
Special Qualities: Blindsight, protection from sonics
Saves: Fort +5, Ref +3, Will +10
Abilities: Str 18, Dex 12, Con 16, Int 12, Wis 18, Cha 12
Skills: Hide +7, Intuit Direction +10, Listen +25, Move Silently +10
Feats: Dodge, Improved Initiative

Climate/Terrain: Any underground
Organization: Solitary or pack (3–5)
Challenge Rating: 8
Treasure: None
Alignment: Usually neutral evil
Advancement: 9–16 HD (Large); 17–24 HD (Huge)

The dungeon-dwelling destrachan looks like some bizarre, unintelligent beast, but it's an incredibly evil and crafty sadist.

This vaguely reptilelike monster has a stooped frame, large claws for hands, and an almost tubelike head that is featureless except for its large ear structures and toothless maw. The destrachan has two complex, three-part ears that it can adjust to be more or less sensitive to various sounds. It is blind, yet hunts with a sense of sound more precise than most creatures' sight.

From its tubular mouth a destrachan emits carefully focused harmonics, producing sonic energy so powerful it can shatter a stone wall. So skilled is the destrachan at controlling the sounds it emits that it can choose what type of material to affect with its attack.

Destrachans feed on death and misery. They haunt inhabited underground complexes, spreading woe for evil's own sake. They can blast their way through stone well enough to travel beneath the surface as they wish. Sometimes a destrachan subdues its victims and brings them back to its horrible lair for torture and imprisonment.

No living thing would ever willingly ally itself with this monster, although sometimes undead or evil outsiders accompany a destrachan as it attacks and slays other creatures.

A destrachan speaks no language but understands Common. If one must communicate, it does so through action.

COMBAT

A destrachan uses its claws only as a last resort or to finish off foes weakened by its sonic attacks. Being extremely intelligent, it often enters battle with surprise if possible. It first focuses on destroying metal armor and weapons and then changes to harmonics that disrupt flesh.

Destructive Harmonics (Su): A destrachan can blast sonic energy in a cone up to 80 feet long. It can tune the harmonics of this destructive power to affect different types of targets.

Flesh: Disrupting tissue and rending bone, this horrible attack deals 4d6 points of damage to all within the cone (Reflex half DC 15).

Nerves: The destrachan can focus its harmonics to subdue rather than slay. This attack plays havoc with nerves and sensory systems, dealing 6d6 points of subdual damage to all within the cone (Reflex half DC 15).

Material: The destrachan chooses wood, stone, metal, or glass. All objects made of that material within the cone must succeed at a Fortitude save (DC 15) or shatter. Objects (or portions of objects) that have up to 30 hit points are potentially affected by this attack.

Reverberating Harmonics (Su): The destrachan can use a wall, a ceiling, or even a floor to reflect any of the sonic attacks listed above (except those that would damage the reflecting surface). This attack affects all within 30 feet of the destrachan, which is immune to the effects of its own ability.

Blindsight (Ex): A destrachan can use hearing to ascertain all foes within 100 feet as a sighted creature would.

Protection from Sonics (Ex): While they can be affected by loud noises and sonic spells (such as *ghost sound* or *silence*), destrachans are less vulnerable to sound-based attacks (+4 circumstance bonus on all saves) because they can protect their ears. A destrachan whose sense of hearing is impaired is effectively blind, treating all targets as totally concealed (see Concealment, page 133 in the *Player's Handbook*).

Skills: With perhaps the most sophisticated auditory organs in existence, the destrachan gains a +10 racial bonus to Listen checks.

	Lemure (Baatezu) Medium-Size Outsider (Evil, Lawful)	Imp Tiny Outsider (Evil, Lawful)	Osyluth (Baatezu) Large Outsider (Evil, Lawful)
Hit Dice:	2d8 (9 hp)	3d8 (13 hp)	5d8+10 (32 hp)
Initiative:	+0	+3 (Dex)	+4 (Improved Initiative)
Speed:	20 ft.	20 ft., fly 50 ft. (perfect)	40 ft.
AC:	13 (+3 natural)	18 (+2 size, +3 Dex, +3 natural)	17 (−1 size, +8 natural)
Attacks:	2 claws +2 melee	Sting +8 melee	Bite +9 melee, 2 claws +4 melee, sting +4 melee
Damage:	Claw 1d3	Sting 1d4 and poison	Bite 1d8+5, claw 1d4+2, sting 3d4+2 and poison
Face/Reach:	5 ft. by 5 ft./5 ft.	2 1/2 ft. by 2 1/2 ft./0 ft.	5 ft. by 5 ft./10 ft.
Special Attacks:	—	Spell-like abilities, poison	Spell-like abilities, fear aura, poison, summon baatezu
Special Qualities:	Damage reduction 5/silver, SR 5, baatezu qualities, mindless	Damage reduction 5/silver, SR 5, poison immunity, fire resistance 20, see in darkness, polymorph, regeneration 2	Damage reduction 10/+1, SR 22, baatezu qualities, know alignment
Saves:	Fort +3, Ref +3, Will +3	Fort +3, Ref +6, Will +4	Fort +6, Ref +4, Will +6
Abilities:	Str 10, Dex 10, Con 10, Int —, Wis 11, Cha 5	Str 10, Dex 17, Con 10, Int 10, Wis 12, Cha 10	Str 21, Dex 10, Con 15, Int 14, Wis 14, Cha 14
Skills:	—	Hide +15, Listen +5, Move Silently +5, Search +5, Spellcraft +5, Spot +5	Concentration +8, Hide +3, Listen +11, Move Silently +8, Search +8, Sense Motive +10, Spot +12
Feats:	—	Dodge, Weapon Finesse (sting)	Alertness, Improved Initiative
Climate/Terrain:	Any land and underground	Any land and underground	Any land and underground
Organization:	Solitary, gang (2–4), swarm (6–15), or mob (10–40)	Solitary	Solitary, team (2–4), or squad (6–10)
Challenge Rating:	1	2	6
Treasure:	None	None	Standard
Alignment:	Always lawful evil	Always lawful evil	Always lawful evil
Advancement:	3–6 HD (Small)	4–6 HD (Tiny)	6–8 HD (Large); 9–15 HD (Huge)

	Kyton Medium-Size Outsider (Evil, Lawful)	Hellcat Large Outsider (Evil, Lawful)	Barbazu (Baatezu) Medium-Size Outsider (Evil, Lawful)
Hit Dice:	8d8+8 (44 hp)	7d8+21 (52 hp)	6d8+6 (33 hp)
Initiative:	+4 (Improved Initiative)	+6 (+2 Dex, +4 Improved Initiative)	+4 (Improved Initiative)
Speed:	30 ft.	40 ft.	40 ft.
AC:	18 (+8 natural)	14 (−1 size, +2 Dex, +3 natural)	17 (+7 natural)
Attacks:	2 chain rakes +9 melee	2 claws +12 melee, bite +7 melee	Glaive +8/+3 melee; or claws +8 melee, beard (see text)
Damage:	Chain rake 1d8+1	Claw 1d4+6, bite 2d6+3	Glaive 1d10+3 and wounding; claw 1d4+2; beard 1d8+2 and disease
Face/Reach:	5 ft. by 5 ft./10 ft.	5 ft. by 10 ft./5 ft.	5 ft. by 5 ft./5 ft.
Special Attacks:	Dancing chains, unnerving gaze	Pounce, improved grab, rake 1d4+3	Wounding, beard, battle frenzy, summon baatezu
Special Qualities:	Damage reduction 20/+2, SR 17, cold immunity, regeneration 2	Scent, invisible in light, SR 16, damage reduction 20/+2, fire resistance 20	Damage reduction 10/+1, SR 23, baatezu qualities
Saves:	Fort +7, Ref +6, Will +6	Fort +8, Ref +7, Will +7	Fort +6, Ref +5, Will +5
Abilities:	Str 13, Dex 11, Con 13, Int 6, Wis 10, Cha 12	Str 23, Dex 15, Con 17, Int 10, Wis 14, Cha 10	Str 15, Dex 11, Con 13, Int 6, Wis 10, Cha 10
Skills:	Climb +12, Craft (blacksmithing) +10, Escape Artist +11, Listen +13, Spot +13	Climb +16, Jump +16, Listen +16, Move Silently +16, Spot +12, Swim +12	Concentration +7, Hide +6, Listen +6, Move Silently +6, Sense Motive +6, Spot +6
Feats:	Alertness, Improved Critical (chain), Improved Initiative	Dodge, Improved Initiative	Cleave, Improved Initiative
Climate/Terrain:	Any land and underground	Any land and underground	Any land and underground
Organization:	Solitary, gang (2–4), band (6–10), or mob (11–20)	Solitary, pair, or pride (6–10)	Solitary, team (2–4), or squad (6–10)
Challenge Rating:	6	7	7
Treasure:	Standard	None	Standard
Alignment:	Always lawful evil	Always lawful evil	Always lawful evil
Advancement:	9–16 HD (Medium-size)	8–10 HD (Large); 11–21 HD (Huge)	7–9 HD (Medium-size); 10–18 HD (Large)

	Erinyes (Baatezu) Medium-Size Outsider (Evil, Lawful)	Hamatula (Baatezu) Medium-Size Outsider (Evil, Lawful)	Cornugon (Baatezu) Large Outsider (Evil, Lawful)
Hit Dice:	6d8+6 (33 hp)	9d8+9 (49 hp)	11d8+33 (82 hp)
Initiative:	+1 (Dex)	+0	+1 (Dex)
Speed:	30 ft., fly 50 ft. (average)	30 ft.	20 ft., fly 50 ft. (average)
AC:	20 (+1 Dex, +9 natural)	22 (+12 natural)	25 (−1 size, +1 Dex, +15 natural)
Attacks:	Longsword +8/+3 melee; or longbow +7/+2 ranged; or rope +7 ranged	2 claws +12 melee	Whip +15/+10/+5 melee (or 2 claws +15 melee), bite +9 melee, tail +9 melee
Damage:	Longsword 1d8+3; or longbow 1d8; or rope entangle	Claw 2d4+3 and fear	Whip 1d6+5 and stun, claw 1d4 +5; bite 1d4+2, tail 1d3+2 and wound
Face/Reach:	5 ft. by 5 ft./5 ft.	5 ft. by 5 ft./5 ft.	10 ft. by 10 ft./15 ft.
Special Attacks:	Rope entangle, charm person, summon baatezu	Fear, improved grab, impale 3d4+4, summon baatezu	Spell-like abilities, fear aura, stun, wound, summon baatezu
Special Qualities:	Damage reduction 10/+1, SR 12, baatezu qualities, tongues	Damage reduction 10/+1, SR 23, baatezu qualities	Damage reduction 20/+2, SR 24, baatezu qualities, regeneration 5
Saves:	Fort +6, Ref +6, Will +7	Fort +7, Ref +6, Will +8	Fort +10, Ref +8, Will +9
Abilities:	Str 14, Dex 13, Con 13, Int 14, Wis 14, Cha 20	Str 17, Dex 11, Con 13, Int 12, Wis 14, Cha 10	Str 21, Dex 12, Con 17, Int 14, Wis 14, Cha 14
Skills:	Concentration +9, Disguise +11, Escape Artist +8, Hide +9, Listen +10, Move Silently +9, Search +9, Spot +10	Concentration +13, Hide +12, Listen +15, Move Silently +12, Search +13, Sense Motive +13, Spot +15	Bluff +14, Climb +16, Concentration +15, Hide +7, Listen +14, Move Silently +14, Search +14, Sense Motive +14, Spot +14
Feats:	Dodge, Mobility	Alertness, Cleave, Power Attack	Cleave, Power Attack, Sunder
Climate/Terrain:	Any land and underground	Any land and underground	Any land and underground
Organization:	Solitary	Solitary, team (2–4), or squad (6–10)	Solitary, team (2–4), or squad (6–10)
Challenge Rating:	7	8	10
Treasure:	Standard, plus rope	Standard	Standard coins; double goods; standard items
Alignment:	Always lawful evil	Always lawful evil	Always lawful evil
Advancement:	7–12 HD (Medium-size)	10 HD (Medium-size); 11–21 HD (Large)	12–15 HD (Large); 16–30 HD (Huge)

	Gelugon (Baatezu) Large Outsider (Evil, Lawful)	Pit Fiend (Baatezu) Large Outsider (Evil, Lawful)
Hit Dice:	12d8+60 (114 hp)	13d8+65 (123 hp)
Initiative:	+1 (Dex)	+5 (+1 Dex, +4 Improved Initiative)
Speed:	40 ft.	40 ft., fly 60 ft. (average)
AC:	28 (−1 size, +1 Dex, +18 natural)	30 (−1 size, +1 Dex, +20 natural)
Attacks:	Longspear +17/+12/+7 melee (or 2 claws +17 melee), bite +12 melee, tail +12 melee	2 claws +19 melee, 2 wings +14 melee, bite +14 melee, tail slap +14 melee
Damage:	Longspear 1d8+9 and cold, claw 1d8+6, bite 2d4+3, tail 3d4+3 and cold	Claw 1d6+7, wing 1d4+3, bite 2d6+3 and poison plus disease, tail slap 2d4+3
Face/Reach:	10 ft. by 10 ft./15 ft.	5 ft. by 5 ft./10 ft.
Special Attacks:	Spell-like abilities, fear aura, cold, summon baatezu	Spell-like abilities, fear aura, improved grab, constrict 2d4+10, summon baatezu
Special Qualities:	Damage reduction 20/+2, SR 25, baatezu qualities, regeneration 5	Damage reduction 25/+2, SR 28, baatezu qualities, regeneration 5
Saves:	Fort +13, Ref +9, Will +14	Fort +13, Ref +9, Will +13
Abilities:	Str 23, Dex 13, Con 21, Int 22, Wis 22, Cha 16	Str 25, Dex 13, Con 21, Int 20, Wis 20, Cha 16
Skills:	Bluff +16, Climb +20, Concentration +20, Disguise +17, Jump +19, Knowledge (arcana) +20, Listen +22, Move Silently +16, Search +20, Sense Motive +20, Spellcraft +20, Spot +22	Bluff +17, Climb +20, Concentration +19, Disguise +17, Hide +4, Jump +19, Knowledge (arcana) +20, Listen +21, Move Silently +17, Search +21, Spellcraft +21, Spot +21
Feats:	Alertness, Cleave, Dodge, Power Attack	Cleave, Great Cleave, Improved Initiative, Power Attack
Climate/Terrain:	Any land and underground	Any land and underground
Organization:	Solitary, team (2–4), squad (6–10), or troupe (1–2 gelugons, 7–12 barbazu, and 1–4 osyluths)	Solitary, team (2–4), or troupe (1–2 pit fiends, 2–5 cornugons, and 2–5 hamatulas)
Challenge Rating:	13	16
Treasure:	Standard coins; double goods; standard items	Standard coins; double goods; standard items
Alignment:	Always lawful evil	Always lawful evil
Advancement:	13–18 HD (Large); 19–33 HD (Huge)	14–20 HD (Large); 21–39 HD (Huge)

Devils are fiends from the plane of Baator, a lawful evil realm. The most numerous are the baatezu, who are infamous for their strength, evil temperament, and ruthlessly efficient organization.

Baatezu have a rigid caste system, in which authority derives not only from power but also from station. They occupy themselves mainly with extending their influence throughout the planes by corrupting mortals. Baatezu who further this goal are usually rewarded with improved stations.

Most baatezu have a Gothic gargoyle look, grotesque and unsightly by human standards.

Except where noted below, all devils speak Infernal, Celestial, and Draconic.

COMBAT

Devils enjoy bullying those weaker than themselves and often attack good creatures just to gain a trophy or three. Most devils are surrounded by an aura of fear, which they use to break up powerful groups and defeat opponents piecemeal. The baatezu also use their illusion abilities to delude and confuse foes as much as possible. A favorite trick is to create illusory reinforcements; enemies can never be entirely sure if a threat is only a figment or real summoned devils joining the fray.

Summon Baatezu (Sp): Most baatezu can summon other baatezu much as though casting a *summon monster* spell, but they have only a limited chance of success. Roll d%: On a failure, no baatezu answer the summons. Summoned creatures automatically return whence they came after 1 hour. A baatezu that has just been summoned cannot use its own summon ability for 1 hour.

Baatezu do not use their summon ability lightly, since it leaves them beholden to the summoned creature. In general, they use it only when necessary to gain victory or save their own lives.

BAATEZU QUALITIES

Immunities (Ex): Baatezu are immune to fire and poison.

Resistances (Ex): Baatezu have cold and acid resistance 20.

See in Darkness (Su): All devils can see perfectly in darkness of any kind, even that created by *deeper darkness* spells.

Telepathy (Su): Baatezu (except lemures) can communicate telepathically with any creature within 100 feet that has a language.

LEMURE

Lemures are revolting blobs of molten flesh, about 5 feet tall, with vaguely humanoid torsos and heads. Their features are twisted into permanent expressions of anguish.

Lemures are mindless and thus cannot communicate, but they are sensitive to telepathic messages from other devils and obey their mental commands.

Combat

Lemures surge toward anything they meet and try to claw it apart. Only a telepathic command from other devils or the complete destruction of the lemures can make them stop.

Mindless (Ex): Lemures are immune to all mind-influencing effects.

IMP

Imps are insidious devils often found serving lawful evil spellcasters as councilors and spies.

In their natural forms, imps look like tiny humanoids with leathery batwings, barbed tails, and sharp, twisted horns. Their skin is dark red, their horns and jagged teeth gleaming white. Imps stand 2 feet tall and weigh about 8 pounds.

Combat

Imps are craven, but not so timid as to pass up an opportunity for a surprise attack (their *invisibility* and *polymorph* abilities often create opportunities). In its natural form, an imp attacks with the wicked stinger on its tail. It quickly flies out of reach if a foe manages to strike back effectively.

Spell-Like Abilities: At will—*detect good*, *detect magic*, and *invisibility* (self only); 1/day—*suggestion*. These abilities are as the spells cast by a 6th-level sorcerer (save DC 10 + spell level).

Once per week an imp can use *commune* to ask six questions. The ability otherwise works as the spell cast by a 12th-level cleric.

Poison (Ex): Sting, Fortitude save (DC 13); initial damage 1d4 temporary Dexterity, secondary damage 2d4 temporary Dexterity.

Polymorph (Su): An imp can assume other forms at will as a standard action. This ability functions as *polymorph self* cast by a 12th-level sorcerer, except that an individual imp can assume only one or two forms no larger than Medium-size. Common forms include monstrous spider, raven, rat, and boar.

Regeneration (Ex): Imps take normal damage from acid, and from holy and blessed weapons (if silver or enchanted).

OSYLUTH

Osyluths often serve as Baator's police and informers, monitoring other devils' activities and reporting on their service.

An osyluth looks bony and wretched, almost a husk of a humanoid form, topped with a fearsome skull whose sickly, dried skin is stretched tight. It has a tail like a scorpion's and exudes a foul odor of decay. Osyluths stand about 9 feet tall.

Combat

Osyluths hate all other creatures and attack ruthlessly. They freely use *wall of ice* to keep the enemy divided.

Spell-Like Abilities: At will—*animate dead, charm person, dimensional anchor, doom, fly, invisibility* (self only), *major image, suggestion,* and *wall of ice.* These abilities are as the spells cast by a 7th-level sorcerer (save DC 12 + spell level).

An osyluth can also *teleport without error* (self plus 50 pounds of objects only) at will as the spell cast by a 12th-level sorcerer.

Fear Aura (Su): Osyluths can radiate a 5-foot-radius fear aura as a free action. Affected creatures must succeed at a Will save (DC 14) or be affected as though by a *fear* spell cast by a 7th-level sorcerer. A creature that successfully saves cannot be affected again by the same osyluth's aura for one day. Other baatezu are immune to the aura.

Poison (Ex): Sting, Fortitude save (DC 14); initial damage 1d6 temporary Strength, secondary damage 2d6 temporary Strength.

Summon Baatezu (Sp): Once per day an osyluth can attempt to summon 2d10 lemures with a 50% chance of success, or another osyluth with a 35% chance of success.

Know Alignment (Su): Osyluths always know the alignment of any creature they look upon.

KYTON

Many people mistakenly believe the chain-shrouded kytons to be undead, likening them to the traditional shackle-rattling spirit. In fact, they are devils resembling humans, wrapped in chains instead of clothing.

Kytons speak Infernal and Common.

Combat

A kyton attacks by flailing away with the spiked chains that serve as clothing, armor, and weapons. Kytons savor fear and terror so much that they may stalk victims for hours, building dread and panic prior to attacking.

Dancing Chains (Su): A kyton's most awesome attack is its ability to control all chains within 20 feet as a standard action, making them dance or move as it wishes. In addition, the

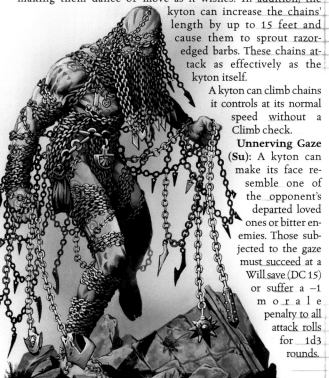

kyton can increase the chains' length by up to 15 feet and cause them to sprout razoredged barbs. These chains attack as effectively as the kyton itself.

A kyton can climb chains it controls at its normal speed without a Climb check.

Unnerving Gaze (Su): A kyton can make its face resemble one of the opponent's departed loved ones or bitter enemies. Those subjected to the gaze must succeed at a Will save (DC 15) or suffer a –1 morale penalty to all attack rolls for 1d3 rounds.

Regeneration (Ex): Kytons take normal damage from fire, acid, and blessed weapons.

A kyton that loses a piece of its body regrows it in 2d6×10 minutes. Holding the severed member against the stump enables it to reattach instantly.

Skills: Kytons receive a +8 racial bonus to Craft skills involving metalwork.

HELLCAT

These fierce devils, also called bezekiras, move about almost silently, constantly on the watch for some chance to do evil.

Hellcats measure some 7 feet long and have eyes that gleam with feral cunning and ravenous hunger. They are more than intelligent enough to set ambushes and otherwise outwit enemies.

Hellcats use a natural telepathy to communicate with one another and those they encounter.

Combat

A hellcat can hold its own in combat thanks to sharp claws and wicked fangs. It prefers to leap upon opponents, just as a lion does.

Pounce (Ex): If a hellcat leaps upon a foe during the first round of combat, it can make a full attack even if it has already taken a move action.

Improved Grab (Ex): To use this ability, the hellcat must hit with its bite attack. If it gets a hold, it can rake.

Rake (Ex): A hellcat can make two rake attacks (+12 melee) against a held creature with its hind legs for 1d4+3 damage each. If the hellcat pounces on an opponent, it can also rake.

Invisible in Light (Ex): A hellcat is invisible in any area lit well enough for a human to see. In a darkened area, it shows up as a faintly glowing outline visible up to 30 feet away (60 feet if the viewer has low-light vision). Magical *darkness* smothers the glow and conceals the outline.

Skills: Hellcats receive a +4 racial bonus to Listen and Move Silently checks.

BARBAZU

Barbazu serve as elite shock troops, spearheading attacks by masses of lemures. Every barbazu carries a saw-toothed glaive.

A barbazu is a foul, humanoid creature about 6 feet tall, with a long tail, clawed hands and feet, pointed ears, and a snaky, disgusting beard. Its skin is moist, though scaly like a reptile's.

Combat

Barbazu are aggressive and love to fight. They use *produce flame* to attack opponents they cannot otherwise reach, but they prefer melee. Their *fear* touch scatters groups that put up an effective defense.

Spell-Like Abilities: At will—*animate dead, charm person, command, desecrate, magic weapon, major image, produce flame,* and *suggestion.* Barbazu also can induce *fear* by touch as the spell, except it affects only the creature touched. These abilities are as cast by an 8th-level sorcerer (save DC 10 + spell level).

A barbazu can *teleport without error* (self plus 50 pounds of objects only) at will as the spell cast by a 12th-level sorcerer.

Wound (Su): A hit from a barbazu's glaive causes a bleeding wound. The injured creature loses 2 additional hit points each round until the wound is bound (a DC 10 Heal check) or the creature dies. This is an ability of the barbazu, not of the weapon.

Beard (Ex): If a barbazu hits a single opponent with both claw attacks, it automatically hits with its beard. The affected creature must succeed at a Fortitude save (DC 14) or be infected with a vile disease called devil chills (incubation period 1d4 days, damage 1d4 points of temporary Strength). Damage is dealt each day until the afflicted creature succeeds at three consecutive Fortitude saves, the disease is cured magically, or the creature dies (see Disease, page 74 in the *DUNGEON MASTER'S Guide*).

Battle Frenzy (Ex): A barbazu can work itself into a battle frenzy similar to the barbarian's rage ability (+4 Strength, +4 Constitution, +2 morale bonus to Will saves, –2 AC penalty), for a +2 morale bonus to attacks and damage and 12 extra hit points. The frenzy lasts 6 rounds, and the barbazu suffers no ill effects afterward.

Summon Baatezu (Sp): Once per day a barbazu can attempt to summon 2d10 lemures with a 50% chance of success, or another barbazu with a 35% chance of success.

ERINYES

Like their demonic counterparts, the succubi, erinyes seek to tempt mortals into depravity.

Unlike other devils, erinyes appear attractive to humans, resembling very comely women except for their huge, feathery wings and sinister eyes. They are about 6 feet tall.

Combat

Erinyes prefer to avoid combat when they can. If forced to fight, they use their charm person ability to turn foes against one another and entangle those they cannot charm.

Spell-Like Abilities: At will—*animate dead, charm monster, desecrate, invisibility* (self only), *magic circle against good* (self only), *major image, polymorph self, produce flame, see invisibility, suggestion,* and *unholy blight.* These abilities are as the spells cast by an 8th-level sorcerer (save DC 15 + spell level).

An erinyes also can *teleport without error* (self plus 50 pounds of objects only) at will as the spell cast by a 12th-level sorcerer.

Charm Person (Su): An erinyes can charm a humanoid creature with a look. This is not a gaze attack, and the target need not meet the erinyes's eye. The ability has a range of 60 feet; an affected opponent must succeed at a Will save (DC 18) or become utterly loyal to the erinyes. The victim will do anything to protect the erinyes, even if that means slaying his or her companions or facing certain death. The ability is otherwise similar to *charm person* cast by an 8th-level sorcerer.

Entangle (Ex): Each erinyes carries a stout rope some 50 feet long that entangles opponents of any size as an *animate rope* spell cast by a 16th-level sorcerer. The erinyes can hurl the rope 30 feet with no range penalty.

Summon Baatezu (Sp): Once per day an erinyes can attempt to summon 2d10 lemures with a 50% chance of success, or 1d4 barbazu with a 35% chance of success.

Tongues (Su): An erinyes has a permanent tongues ability as the spell cast by a 12th-level sorcerer. Erinyes usually use verbal communication when dealing with mortals and save telepathic communication for conversing with other fiends.

HAMATULA

Hamatulas are 7-foot-tall humanoids covered with sharp barbs, right down to the tips of their long, meaty tails. They serve as guardians and patrol troops.

A hamatula has unusually long, sharp claws on its hands. Its keen eyes shift and dart about, making it look perpetually nervous.

Combat

Hamatulas eagerly fight with their claws, trying to impale their opponents. They use *hold person* to immobilize those who avoid their hug attacks.

Spell-Like Abilities: At will—*animate dead, charm person, desecrate, doom, hold person, major image, produce flame, pyrotechnics,* and *suggestion;* 1/day—*order's wrath* or *unholy blight.* These abilities are as the spells cast by a 9th-level sorcerer (save DC 10 + spell level).

A hamatula can *teleport without error* (self plus 50 pounds of objects only) at will as the spell cast by a 12th-level sorcerer.

Fear (Su): A creature hit by a hamatula must succeed at a Will save (DC 14) or be affected as though by *fear* cast by a 9th-level sorcerer. Whether or not the save is successful, that creature cannot be affected again by that hamatula's fear ability for one day.

Improved Grab (Ex): To use this ability, the hamatula must hit with a claw attack. If it gets a hold, it can impale the opponent on its barbed body.

Impale (Ex): A hamatula deals 3d4+4 points of damage to a grabbed opponent with a successful grapple check.

Summon Baatezu (Sp): Once per day a hamatula can attempt to summon 2d10 lemures with a 50% chance of success, or another hamatula with a 35% chance of success.

CORNUGON

Cornugons serve as elite defense forces and are terrible to look upon—even for devils.

A cornugon is 9 feet tall, only vaguely humanoid, and covered with hideous scales. Its huge wings and snaking, prehensile tail add to its intimidating appearance.

Combat

Cornugons are bold fighters. They rarely retreat, even against overwhelming odds. They love to fight with their whips, usually singling out the most powerful foes to stun and eliminate quickly.

Spell-Like Abilities: At will—*animate dead, charm person, desecrate, detect good, detect magic, detect thoughts, dispel chaos, dispel good, magic circle against good, major image, produce flame, pyrotechnics, suggestion,* and *teleport without error* (self plus 50 pounds of objects only); 3/day—*fireball* and *lightning bolt;* 1/day—*wall of fire.* These abilities are as the spells cast by a 12th-level sorcerer (save DC 12 + spell level).

Fear Aura (Su): As a free action, a cornugon can create an aura of fear in a 5-foot radius. It is otherwise identical with *fear* cast by a 12th-level sorcerer (save DC 17). If the save is successful, that creature cannot be affected again by that cornugon's fear aura for one day. Other baatezu are immune to the aura.

Stun (Su): Whenever a cornugon hits with a whip attack, the opponent must succeed at a Fortitude save (DC 17) or be stunned for 1d4 rounds.

Wound (Su): A hit from a cornugon's tail attack causes a bleeding wound. The injured creature loses 2 additional hit points each round until the wound is bound (a DC 10 Heal check) or the creature dies.

Summon Baatezu (Sp): Once per day a cornugon can attempt to summon 2d10 lemures or 1d6 barbazu with a 50% chance of success, 1d6 hamatulas with a 35% chance of success, or another cornugon with a 20% chance of success.

Regeneration (Ex): Cornugons take normal damage from acid, and from holy and blessed weapons of at least +2 enchantment.

GELUGON

Gelugons serve almost exclusively as superelite guards and spies. They look like tall, alien insects.

A gelugon has clawed hands and feet, powerful mandibles, and a long, thick tail covered in razor-sharp spikes. Gelugons are about 12 feet tall.

Combat

Gelugons prefer to fight only when it serves their mission but never hesitate to attack when they deem it necessary.

Spell-Like Abilities: At will—*animate dead, charm monster, cone of cold, desecrate, detect good, detect magic, fly, magic circle against good, major image, polymorph self, suggestion, teleport without error* (self plus 50 pounds of objects only), *unholy aura,* and *wall of ice.* These abilities are as the spells cast by a 13th-level sorcerer (save DC 13 + spell level).

Fear Aura (Su): As a free action, a gelugon can create an aura of fear in a 10-foot radius. It is otherwise identical with *fear* cast by a 13th-level sorcerer (save DC 19). If the save is successful, that creature cannot be affected again by that gelugon's fear aura for one day. Other baatezu are immune to the aura.

Cold (Su): A hit from a gelugon's tail or spear attack induces numbing cold. The opponent must succeed at a Fortitude save (DC 21) or be affected as though by a *slow* spell for 1d6 rounds.

Summon Baatezu (Sp): Once per day a gelugon can attempt to summon 2d10 lemures or 1d6 barbazu with a 50% chance of success, 2d4 osyluths or 1d6 hamatulas with a 35% chance of success, or another gelugon with a 20% chance of success.

Regeneration (Ex): Gelugons take normal damage from holy and blessed weapons of at least +2 enchantment.

PIT FIEND

Pit fiends are the undisputed leaders of the baatezu. Terrible, winged humanoids some 12 feet tall, they often appear wreathed in flames.

A pit fiend has vast bat wings that it often wraps around itself like a grotesque cloak. Its large fangs drip with a vile green liquid, and its hulking body is covered in red scales.

Combat

Pit fiends are wily and resourceful fighters, using *improved invisibility* to gain the upper hand and biting at foes who seem able to see them. They don't hesitate to blanket an area with *fireballs* and frequently surround themselves with *walls of fire.*

Spell-Like Abilities: At will—*animate dead, blasphemy, charm person, create undead, desecrate, detect good, detect magic, dispel magic, fireball, hold person, improved invisibility, magic circle against good, major image, produce flame, polymorph self, pyrotechnics, suggestion, teleport without error* (self plus 50 pounds of objects only), *unholy aura, unhallow,* and *wall of fire;* 1/day—*meteor swarm* (any) and *symbol* (any). These abilities are as the spells cast by a 17th-level sorcerer (save DC 13 + spell level).

Once per year a pit fiend can use *wish* as the spell cast by a 20th-level sorcerer.

Fear Aura (Su): As a free action, a pit fiend can create an aura of fear in a 20-foot radius. It is otherwise identical with *fear* cast by a 15th-level sorcerer (save DC 19). If the save is successful, that creature cannot be affected again by that pit fiend's fear aura for one day. Other baatezu are immune to the aura.

Poison (Ex): Bite, Fortitude save (DC 21); initial damage 1d6 temporary Constitution, secondary damage death.

Disease (Su): Even if an affected creature saves against the poison, it must succeed at a Fortitude save (DC 14) or be infected with a vile disease called devil chills (incubation period 1d4 days, damage 1d4 points of temporary Strength). See Disease, page 74 in the DUNGEON MASTER's Guide.

Improved Grab (Ex): To use this ability, the pit fiend must hit a Medium-size or smaller opponent with its tail slap attack. If it gets a hold, it can constrict.

Constrict (Ex): A pit fiend deals 2d4+10 points of damage with a successful grapple check against Medium-size or smaller creatures.

Summon Baatezu (Sp): Twice per day a pit fiend can automatically summon two lemures, osyluths, or barbazu, or one erinyes, cornugon, or gelugon.

Regeneration (Ex): Pit fiends take normal damage from holy and blessed weapons of at least +3 enchantment.

DEVOURER

Illus. by C. Arellano

Large Undead
Hit Dice: 12d12 (78 hp)
Initiative: +4 (Improved Initiative)
Speed: 30 ft.
AC: 18 (–1 size, +9 natural)
Attacks: 2 claws +11 melee
Damage: Claw 1d6+5
Face/Reach: 5 ft. by 5 ft./10 ft.
Special Attacks: Energy drain, trap essence, spell-like abilities
Special Qualities: Undead, spell deflection, SR 21
Saves: Fort +4, Ref +4, Will +11
Abilities: Str 21, Dex 10, Con —, Int 16, Wis 16, Cha 17
Skills: Climb +10, Concentration +18, Jump +17, Listen +17, Move Silently +12, Spot +17
Feats: Alertness, Blind-Fight, Combat Casting, Expertise, Improved Initiative, Weapon Focus (claw)

Climate/Terrain: Any land and underground
Organization: Solitary
Challenge Rating: 11
Treasure: None
Alignment: Always neutral evil
Advancement: 13 HD (Large); 14–27 HD (Huge)

Devourers are massive creatures every bit as evil as they look. They lurk in the Ethereal and Astral Planes, stalking both natives and travelers with equal sadistic glee.

The devourer appears as a tall, skeletal figure with strands of mummified flesh hanging from its bones. Imprisoned within the creature's rib cage is a tiny figure, clearly in agony. This pitiful being is the trapped essence of a slain opponent, which is consumed like firewood to sustain the monster's unnatural life.

COMBAT

Even if it had no special abilities, the devourer would be a terrible opponent, for its bony claws can flay enemies alive.

Energy Drain (Su): Living creatures hit by a devourer's claw attack or *spectral hand* ability receive one negative level. The Fortitude save to remove the negative level has a DC of 19.

Trap Essence (Su): The devourer is named for its ability to consume an enemy's life essence. To do so, it must forgo its normal melee attacks and make a trap essence attack. This requires a normal attack roll to hit but deals no damage. The affected creature must succeed at a Fortitude save (DC 19) or die instantly.

The slain creature's essence is trapped within the devourer's ribs, and the diminutive figure takes on that victim's features. The trapped essence cannot be raised or resurrected, but a *limited wish*, *miracle*, or *wish* spell frees it, as does destroying the devourer. A devourer can hold only one essence at a time.

The trapped essence provides the devourer with enough power to use five spell-like abilities per HD or level of the trapped creature. As this energy is expended, the twisted soul fades away until it evaporates completely. The trapped essence receives one negative level for every five spell-like uses. When the number of negative levels equals the creature's total HD or level, the essence is destroyed. If an essence is freed, the restored creature must succeed at a Fortitude save (DC 17) for each negative level or lose that level permanently.

Spell-Like Abilities: At the start of any encounter, the trapped essence within a devourer is assumed to have 3d4+3 levels (enough fuel for 30 to 75 uses). Once per round, the devourer can use one of following as the spell cast by an 18th-level sorcerer (save DC 13 + spell level): *confusion, control undead, ghoul touch, lesser planar ally, ray of enfeeblement, spectral hand, suggestion,* and *true seeing*.

Undead: Immune to mind-influencing effects, poison, sleep, paralysis, stunning, and disease. Not subject to critical hits, subdual damage, ability damage, energy drain, or death from massive damage.

Spell Deflection (Su): The trapped essence provides a measure of magical protection. If any of the following spells are cast at the devourer and overcome its spell resistance, they affect the imprisoned essence instead: *banishment, chaos hammer, confusion, detect thoughts, dispel evil, dominate person, emotion, fear, geas/quest, holy word, hypnosis, imprisonment, magic jar, maze, suggestion, trap the soul,* or any form of charm or compulsion. In many cases, this effectively neutralizes the spell (charming a trapped essence, for example, is useless). Some of them (*banishment*, for example), might eliminate the trapped essence, robbing the devourer of its magical powers until it can consume another.

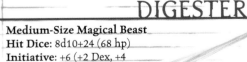

DIGESTER

Medium-Size Magical Beast
Hit Dice: 8d10+24 (68 hp)
Initiative: +6 (+2 Dex, +4 Improved Initiative)
Speed: 60 ft.

AC: 17 (+2 Dex, +5 natural)
Attacks: Rake +11 melee
Damage: Rake 1d8+4
Face/Reach: 5 ft. by 5 ft./5 ft.
Special Attack: Acid spray
Special Qualities: Scent, acid immunity
Saves: Fort +9, Ref +8, Will +3
Abilities: Str 17, Dex 15, Con 17, Int 2, Wis 12, Cha 10
Skills: Hide +11, Listen +6, Jump +7, Spot +6
Feats: Alertness, Improved Initiative

Climate/Terrain: Temperate and warm land and underground
Organization: Solitary or pack (3–6)
Challenge Rating: 6
Treasure: None
Alignment: Always neutral
Advancement: 9–12 HD (Medium-size); 13–24 HD (Large)

These swift predators spray an acid that can reduce a human to a pool of glop in seconds.

Digesters lurk almost anywhere there is prey to be found, from barren deserts to steaming jungles. A digester resembles a carnivorous dinosaur with powerful hind legs and a long tail. It has a narrow head with a sucking mouth and an orifice in its forehead that squirts acid.

A digester stands about 5 feet tall and is 8 feet long from snout to tail.

COMBAT

A digester is a hunting and eating machine. When it is not hungry (which is rarely), it lies low and avoids most other creatures. When hunting, it looks about for a likely target, then charges forth and delivers a gout of acid. If the initial attack is insufficient to kill the prey, the digester attacks with its hind feet until it can spray acid again.

Acid Spray (Ex): A digester can spray acid in a cone 20 feet long, dealing 4d8 points of damage to everything in the area. Once a digester uses this ability, it can't use it again until 1d4 rounds later. The creature can also produce a concentrated stream of acid that deals 8d8 points of damage to a single target within 5 feet. In either case, a successful Reflex save (DC 17) halves the damage.

Skills: The digester's coloration gives it a +4 racial bonus to Hide checks. It also has a +4 racial bonus to Jump checks.

	Deinonychus Large Beast	Elasmosaurus Huge Beast (Aquatic)	Megaraptor Huge Beast
Hit Dice:	4d10+12 (34 hp)	5d10+25 (52 hp)	8d10+32 (76 hp)
Initiative:	+2 (Dex)	+2 (Dex)	+2 (Dex)
Speed:	60 ft.	20 ft., swim 50 ft.	60 ft.
AC:	16 (−1 size, +2 Dex, +5 natural)	13 (−2 size, +2 Dex, +3 natural)	16 (−2 size, +2 Dex, +6 natural)
Attacks:	Rake +6 melee, 2 claws +1 melee, bite +1 melee	Bite +9 melee	Rake +9 melee, 2 claws +4 melee, bite +4 melee
Damage:	Rake 2d6+4, claw 1d3+2, bite 2d4+2	Bite 2d8+12	Rake 2d8+5, claw 1d4+2, bite 2d6+2
Face/Reach:	5 ft. by 5 ft./10 ft.	10 ft. by 20 ft./10 ft.	10 ft. by 10 ft./15 ft.
Special Qualities:	Scent	Scent	Scent
Saves:	Fort +7, Ref +6, Will +2	Fort +9, Ref +6, Will +2	Fort +10, Ref +8, Will +4
Abilities:	Str 19, Dex 15, Con 17, Int 2, Wis 12, Cha 10	Str 26, Dex 14, Con 20, Int 2, Wis 13, Cha 9	Str 21, Dex 15, Con 19, Int 2, Wis 15, Cha 10
Skills:	Hide +7, Jump +13, Listen +11, Spot +11, Wilderness Lore +9	Listen +2, Spot +5	Hide +5, Jump +14, Listen +12, Spot +12, Wilderness Lore +10
Climate/Terrain:	Warm forest, hill, plains, and marsh	Warm aquatic	Warm forest, hill, plains, and marsh
Organization:	Solitary, pair, or pack (3–6)	Solitary or pair	Solitary, pair, or pack (3–6)
Challenge Rating:	3	5	6
Treasure:	None	None	None
Alignment:	Always neutral	Always neutral	Always neutral
Advancement:	5–8 HD (Large)	6–15 HD (Huge)	9–16 HD (Huge); 17–24 HD (Gargantuan)

	Triceratops Huge Beast	Tyrannosaurus Huge Beast
Hit Dice:	16d10+112 (200 hp)	18d10+72 (171 hp)
Initiative:	−1 (Dex)	+1 (Dex)
Speed:	30 ft.	40 ft.
AC:	18 (−2 size, −1 Dex, +11 natural)	14 (−2 size, +1 Dex, +5 natural)
Attacks:	Gore +15 melee	Bite +20 melee
Damage:	Gore 2d8+7	Bite 5d8+13
Face/Reach:	10 ft. by 20 ft./10 ft.	10 ft. by 10 ft./15 ft.
Special Attacks:	Charge for double damage, trample	Improved grab, swallow whole
Special Qualities:	Scent	Scent
Saves:	Fort +17, Ref +9, Will +6	Fort +15, Ref +12, Will +8
Abilities:	Str 20, Dex 9, Con 25, Int 1, Wis 12, Cha 7	Str 28, Dex 12, Con 19, Int 2, Wis 15, Cha 10
Skills:	Listen +8, Spot +8	Listen +11, Spot +11
Climate/Terrain:	Warm forest, hill, and plains	Warm forest, hill, plains, and marsh
Organization:	Solitary, pair, or herd (5–8)	Solitary or pair
Challenge Rating:	7	8
Treasure:	None	None
Alignment:	Always neutral	Always neutral
Advancement:	17–32 HD (Gargantuan); 33–48 HD (Colossal)	19–36 HD (Gargantuan); 37–54 HD (Colossal)

Dinosaurs, or terrible lizards, are ancient beasts that may be related to dragons.

Among the traits that predatory dinosaurs share with many dragons are sharp teeth, savage dispositions, a well-developed sense of territory, and a ruthless capacity to hunt. The herbivorous dinosaurs usually are not aggressive unless wounded or defending their young, but may attack if startled or harassed.

Dinosaurs come in many sizes and shapes. Bigger species have drab colors, while smaller dinosaurs have a wide variety of more colorful markings. Most dinosaurs have a pebbly skin texture.

Dinosaurs most often live in rugged or isolated areas that humanoids seldom visit: remote mountain valleys, inaccessible plateaus, tropical islands, and deep fens.

COMBAT

Dinosaurs take full advantage of their size and speed. The swift carnivores stalk prey, staying hidden in cover until they can get into charge range and rush to the attack. The great herbivores frequently overrun and trample their opponents.

DEINONYCHUS

This fast carnivore is sometimes called a velociraptor, though that name properly belongs to a much smaller creature.

Despite being 12 feet long, this dinosaur is only about 6 feet tall. Its tail extends straight out behind itself, held aloft by an intricate structure of bony supports, thus allowing its weight to be carried entirely by the back legs. It weighs about 600 pounds.

A deinonychus has a brightly colored hide, making it look like a tropical bird. The dinosaur is bright green, orange, yellow, or red along its back and flanks, with a much lighter shade of the same color on its underside. The body has darker spots or stripes.

Combat

A deinonychus uses a terrible combination of speed, grasping forearms, large teeth, and hind legs with ripping talons. It hunts by running at prey, leaping, and raking with its rear talons as it claws and bites. The rakes count as one attack. A deinonychus often jumps on top of a larger creature and holds on with its front claws while continuing to rake with the rear talons.

The deinonychus has a relatively large brain for a dinosaur, and its pack hunts with cunning tactics. When charging, it uses only its rake attack, dealing 2d6+6 points of damage.

Skills: A deinonychus receives a +8 racial bonus to Hide, Jump, Listen, Spot, and Wilderness Lore checks.

ELASMOSAURUS

An elasmosaurus has a thick, ovoid body with fins instead of legs and a long, snaky tail and neck. Its neck makes up one-half its total length of 50 feet. An elasmosaurus weighs about 5,000 pounds. Observers who see only its head or tail might easily mistake it for a massive snake.

Combat

An elasmosaurus is aggressive and attacks anything it notices. The creature is strong, fast, and highly maneuverable, able to turn quickly and lunge at prey. When hunting, it travels with its head out of the water, snapping down quickly to seize prey.

MEGARAPTOR

This creature is simply a larger version of the deinonychus, with the same habits and abilities. When charging, a megaraptor uses only its rake attack, dealing 2d8+7 points of damage.

TRICERATOPS

This massive herbivore is fairly short-tempered and aggressive. It has a huge front plate of bone protecting its 6-foot-long head, from which project two great horns (each over 3 feet long), while a shorter horn juts from its nose. A triceratops has a body about 24 feet long and weighs about 20,000 pounds.

Combat

These creatures are likely to charge and skewer any creature of at least Large size that infringes on their territory. A triceratops uses its trample attack on smaller opponents.

Trample (Ex): A triceratops can trample Medium-size or smaller creatures for 2d12+5 points of damage. Opponents who do not make attacks of opportunity against the triceratops can attempt a Reflex save (DC 23) to halve the damage.

TYRANNOSAURUS

This ravenous creature is the most fearsome of all carnivorous dinosaurs.

Despite its huge size and 8-ton weight, a tyrannosaurus is a swift runner. Its huge head is nearly 6 feet long, and its teeth are from 3 to 6 inches in length. It is more than 50 feet long from nose to tail.

A tyrannosaurus eats almost anything it can sink its teeth into, and spends a great deal of its time scavenging for carrion and chasing smaller carnivores away from their kills.

Combat

A tyrannosaurus pursues and eats just about anything it sees. Its tactics are simple—charge in and bite.

Improved Grab (Ex): To use this ability, the tyrannosaurus must hit a Medium-size or smaller opponent with its bite attack. If it gets a hold, it can try to swallow the foe.

Swallow Whole (Ex): A tyrannosaurus can try to swallow a Medium-size or smaller opponent by making a successful grapple check. The swallowed creature takes 2d8+8 points of crushing damage per round plus 8 points of acid damage from the tyrannosaurus's gizzard. A swallowed creature can cut its way out by using claws or a Small or Tiny slashing weapon to deal 25 points of damage to the gizzard (AC 20). Once the creature exits, muscular action closes the hole; another swallowed opponent must again cut its own way out.

The tyrannosaurus's gizzard can hold two Medium-size, four Small, eight Tiny, sixteen Diminutive, or thirty-two Fine or smaller opponents.

DIRE ANIMALS

	Rat Small Animal	Weasel Medium-Size Animal	Badger Medium-Size Animal
Hit Dice:	1d8+1 (5 hp)	3d8 (13 hp)	3d8+12 (25 hp)
Initiative:	+3 (Dex)	+4 (Dex)	+3 (Dex)
Speed:	40 ft., climb 20 ft.	40 ft.	30 ft., burrow 10 ft.
AC:	15 (+1 size, +3 Dex, +1 natural)	16 (+4 Dex, +2 natural)	16 (+3 Dex, +3 natural)
Attacks:	Bite +4 melee	Bite +6 melee	2 claws +4 melee, bite −1 melee
Damage:	Bite 1d4	Bite 1d6+3	Claw 1d4+2, bite 1d6+1
Face/Reach:	5 ft. by 5 ft./5 ft.	5 ft. by 5 ft./5 ft.	5 ft. by 5 ft./5 ft.
Special Attacks:	Disease	Attach, blood drain	Rage

Special Qualities:	Scent	Scent	Scent
Saves:	Fort +3, Ref +5, Will +3	Fort +3, Ref +7, Will +4	Fort +7, Ref +6, Will +4
Abilities:	Str 10, Dex 17, Con 12, Int 1, Wis 12, Cha 4	Str 14, Dex 19, Con 10, Int 2, Wis 12, Cha 11	Str 14, Dex 17, Con 19, Int 2, Wis 12, Cha 10
Skills:	Climb +11, Hide +11, Move Silently +6	Hide +9, Move Silently +10, Spot +5	Listen +6, Spot +6
Feats:	Weapon Finesse (bite)	Weapon Finesse (bite)	—
Climate/Terrain:	Any land and underground	Temperate forest, hill, mountains, plains, and underground	Temperate forest, hill, plains, and underground
Organization:	Solitary or pack (11–20)	Solitary or pair	Solitary or cete (2–5)
Challenge Rating:	1/3	2	2
Treasure:	None	None	None
Alignment:	Always neutral	Always neutral	Always neutral
Advancement:	2–3 HD (Small); 4–6 HD (Medium-size)	4–6 HD (Large); 7–9 HD (Huge)	4–6 HD (Large); 7–9 HD (Huge)

	Bat Large Animal	**Ape** Large Animal	**Wolverine** Large Animal
Hit Dice:	4d8+12 (30 hp)	5d8+10 (32 hp)	5d8+20 (42 hp)
Initiative:	+6 (Dex)	+2 (Dex)	+3 (Dex)
Speed:	20 ft., fly 40 ft. (good)	30 ft., climb 15 ft.	30 ft., climb 10 ft.
AC:	20 (–1 size, +6 Dex, +5 natural)	15 (–1 size, +2 Dex, +4 natural)	16 (–1 size, +3 Dex, +4 natural)
Attacks:	Bite +5 melee	2 claws +8 melee, bite +3 melee	2 claws +8 melee, bite +3 melee
Damage:	Bite 1d8+4	Claw 1d6+6, bite 1d8+3	Claw 1d6+6, bite 1d8+3
Face/Reach:	10 ft. by 5 ft./5 ft.	5 ft. by 5 ft./10 ft.	5 ft. by 10 ft./5 ft.
Special Attacks:	—	Rend 2d6+12	Rage
Special Qualities:	Blindsight	Scent	Scent
Saves:	Fort +7, Ref +10, Will +6	Fort +6, Ref +6, Will +5	Fort +8, Ref +7, Will +5
Abilities:	Str 17, Dex 22, Con 17, Int 2, Wis 14, Cha 6	Str 22, Dex 15, Con 14, Int 2, Wis 12, Cha 7	Str 22, Dex 17, Con 19, Int 2, Wis 12, Cha 10
Skills:	Listen +11*, Move Silently +11, Spot +11*	Climb +14, Move Silently +9, Spot +9	Climb +14, Listen +9, Spot +8
Climate/Terrain:	Temperate and warm desert, forest, hill, plains, and underground	Warm forest, warm mountains, and underground	Temperate forest, hill, plains, and underground
Organization:	Solitary or colony (5–8)	Solitary or company (5–8)	Solitary or pair
Challenge Rating:	2	3	4
Treasure:	None	None	None
Alignment:	Always neutral	Always neutral	Always neutral
Advancement:	5–12 HD (Huge)	6–15 HD (Large)	6–15 HD (Large)

	Wolf Large Animal	**Boar** Large Animal	**Lion** Large Animal
Hit Dice:	6d8+18 (45 hp)	7d8+21 (52 hp)	8d8+24 (60 hp)
Initiative:	+2 (Dex)	+0	+2 (Dex)
Speed:	50 ft.	40 ft.	40 ft.
AC:	14 (–1 size, +2 Dex, +3 natural)	15 (–1 size, +6 natural)	15 (–1 size, +2 Dex, +4 natural)
Attacks:	Bite +10 melee	Bite +12 melee	2 claws +12 melee, bite +7 melee
Damage:	Bite 1d8+10	Bite 1d8+12	Claw 1d6+7, bite 1d8+3
Face/Reach:	5 ft. by 10 ft./5 ft.	5 ft. by 10 ft./5 ft.	5 ft. by 10 ft./5 ft.
Special Attacks:	Trip	Ferocity	Pounce, improved grab, rake 1d6+3
Special Qualities:	Scent	Scent	Scent
Saves:	Fort +8, Ref +7, Will +6	Fort +8, Ref +5, Will +6	Fort +9, Ref +8, Will +7
Abilities:	Str 25, Dex 15, Con 17, Int 2, Wis 12, Cha 10	Str 27, Dex 10, Con 17, Int 2, Wis 13, Cha 8	Str 25, Dex 15, Con 17, Int 2, Wis 12, Cha 10
Skills:	Hide +5, Listen +6, Move Silently +5, Spot +6, Wilderness Lore +1*	Listen +9, Spot +8	Hide +5*, Jump +10, Listen +4, Move Silently +9, Spot +4
Climate/Terrain:	Any forest, hill, mountains, plains, and underground	Temperate and warm forest	Any forest, hill, mountains, plains, and underground
Organization:	Solitary or pack (5–8)	Solitary or herd (5–8)	Solitary, pair, or pride (6–10)
Challenge Rating:	3	4	5
Treasure:	None	None	None
Alignment:	Always neutral	Always neutral	Always neutral
Advancement:	7–18 HD (Large)	8–16 HD (Large); 17–21 HD (Huge)	9–16 HD (Large); 17–24 HD (Huge)

	Bear	Tiger	Shark
	Large Animal	Huge Animal	Huge Animal (Aquatic)
Hit Dice:	12d8+48 (102 hp)	16d8+48 (120 hp)	18d8+54 (135 hp)
Initiative:	+1 (Dex)	+2 (Dex)	+2 (Dex)
Speed:	40 ft.	40 ft.	Swim 90 ft.
AC:	17 (−1 size, +1 Dex, +7 natural)	16 (−2 size, +2 Dex, +6 natural)	17 (−2 size, +2 Dex, +7 natural)
Attacks:	2 claws +18 melee, bite +13 melee	2 claws +18 melee, bite +13 melee	Bite +17 melee
Damage:	Claw 2d4+10, bite 2d8+5	Claw 2d4+8, bite 2d6+4	Bite 2d6+9
Face/Reach:	10 ft. by 20 ft./10 ft.	10 ft. by 30 ft./10 ft.	10 ft. by 50 ft./10 ft.
Special Attacks:	Improved grab	Pounce, improved grab, rake 2d4+4	Improved grab, swallow whole
Special Qualities:	Scent	Scent	Keen scent
Saves:	Fort +12, Ref +9, Will +9	Fort +13, Ref +12, Will +11	Fort +14, Ref +13, Will +12
Abilities:	Str 31, Dex 13, Con 19,	Str 27, Dex 15, Con 17,	Str 23, Dex 15, Con 17,
	Int 2, Wis 12, Cha 10	Int 2, Wis 12, Cha 10	Int 1, Wis 12, Cha 10
Skills:	Listen +7, Spot +7, Swim +13	Hide +0*, Jump +11, Listen +3, Move Silently +9, Spot +3, Swim +11	Listen +7, Spot +7

Climate/Terrain:	Any forest, hill, mountains, plains, and underground	Any forest, hill, mountains, plains, and underground	Any aquatic
Organization:	Solitary or pair	Solitary or pair	Solitary or school (2–5)
Challenge Rating:	7	8	9
Treasure:	None	None	None
Alignment:	Always neutral	Always neutral	Always neutral
Advancement:	13–16 HD (Large); 17–36 HD (Huge)	17–32 HD (Huge); 33–48 (Gargantuan)	19–32 (Huge); 33–54 (Gargantuan)

Dire animals are larger, tougher, meaner versions of normal animals. They tend to have a feral, prehistoric look.

DIRE RAT

A dire rat can grow up to 3 feet long and weigh over 60 pounds.

Combat

Dire rat packs attack fearlessly, biting and chewing with their sharp incisors.

Disease (Ex): Filth fever—bite, Fortitude save (DC 12), incubation period 1d3 days; damage 1d3 temporary Dexterity and 1d3 temporary Constitution (see Disease, page 74 in the DUNGEON MASTER's Guide).

DIRE WEASEL

These aggressive hunters grow up to 6 feet long and can reach a weight of 400 pounds.

Combat

Dire weasels stalk their prey in the dark and then leap on it, biting and clawing.

Attach (Ex): A dire weasel that hits with its bite attack latches onto the opponent's body with its powerful jaws. An attached dire weasel loses its Dex bonus to AC and thus has an AC of 12.

Blood Drain (Ex): A dire weasel drains blood for 2d4 points of temporary Constitution damage each round it remains attached.

DIRE BADGER

The vicious dire badger grows from 5 to 7 feet in length and can weigh up to 500 pounds.

Combat

Dire badgers attack with their sharp claws and teeth.

Rage (Ex): A dire badger that takes damage in combat flies into a berserk rage on its next turn, clawing and biting madly until either it or its opponent is dead. It gains +4 Strength, +4 Constitution, and −2 AC. The creature cannot end its rage voluntarily.

DIRE BAT

These nocturnal hunters have wingspans of 8 to 9 feet.

Combat

Dire bats swoop down upon unsuspecting prey from above.

Blindsight: Dire bats can "see" by emitting high-frequency sounds, inaudible to most other creatures, that allow them to locate objects and creatures within 120 feet. A *silence* spell negates this ability and forces the bat to rely on its weak vision, which has a maximum range of 10 feet.

Skills: Dire bats receive a +4 racial bonus to Spot and Listen checks. *These bonuses are lost if blindsight is negated.

DIRE APE

These apes resemble large gorillas with long, ivory claws and razor-sharp teeth. They stand about 8 feet tall and weigh from 600 to 1,000 pounds.

Combat

Dire apes attack anything that enters their territory, even other dire apes. If an opponent's armor foils a dire ape's attacks, the creature will attempt to grapple and pin, then claw the prone opponent.

Rend (Ex): A dire ape that hits with both claw attacks latches onto the opponent's body and tears the flesh. This automatically deals an additional 2d6+12 points of damage.

DIRE WOLVERINE

These foul-tempered creatures grow to about 18 feet in length and can weigh as much as 2,500 pounds.

Combat

Dire wolverines attack opponents wantonly, fearing no other creatures.

Rage (Ex): A dire wolverine that takes damage in combat flies into a berserk rage on its next turn, clawing and biting madly until either it or its opponent is dead. An enraged dire wolverine gains +4 Strength, +4 Constitution, and −2 AC. The creature cannot end its rage voluntarily.

DIRE WOLF

A dire wolf is an immense gray or black wolf, about 8 feet long and weighing some 700 pounds.

Combat

Dire wolves prefer to attack in packs, surrounding and flanking the foe when they can.

Trip (Ex): A dire wolf that hits with a bite attack can attempt to trip the opponent as a free action (see page 139 in the *Player's Handbook*) without making a touch attack or provoking an attack of opportunity. If the attempt fails, the opponent cannot react to trip the dire wolf.

Skills: A dire wolf receives a +1 racial bonus to Listen, Move Silently, and Spot checks and a +2 racial bonus to Hide checks. *It also receives a +4 racial bonus to Wilderness Lore checks when tracking by scent.

DIRE BOAR

Dire boars grow up to 16 feet long and weigh as much as 2,000 pounds.

Combat

A dire boar charges its opponents, trying to rip them open with its tusks.

Ferocity (Ex): A dire boar is such a tenacious combatant that it continues to fight without penalty even while disabled or dying (see page 129 in the *Player's Handbook*).

DIRE LION

Dire lions grow up to 20 feet long and weigh up to 3,500 pounds.

Combat

A dire lion attacks by running at prey, leaping, and clawing and biting as it rakes with its rear claws. It often jumps onto a creature larger than itself.

Pounce (Ex): If a dire lion leaps upon a foe during the first round of combat, it can make a full attack even if it has already taken a move action.

Improved Grab (Ex): To use this ability, the dire lion must hit with its bite attack. If it gets a hold, it can rake.

Rake (Ex): A dire lion can make two rake attacks (+12 melee) against a held creature with its hind legs for 1d6+3 damage each. If the dire lion pounces on an opponent, it can also rake.

Skills: Dire lions receive a +4 racial bonus to Hide and Move Silently checks. *In areas of tall grass or heavy undergrowth, the Hide bonus improves to +8.

DIRE BEAR

Dire bears can grow up to 20 feet long and weigh as much as 6,000 pounds.

Combat

A dire bear attacks by rending opponents with its claws.

Improved Grab (Ex): To use this ability, the dire bear must hit with a claw attack.

DIRE TIGER

Dire tigers grow up to 35 feet long and can weigh up to 6,000 pounds.

Combat

A dire tiger attacks by running at prey, leaping, and clawing and biting as it rakes with its rear claws.

Pounce (Ex): If a dire tiger leaps upon a foe during the first round of combat, it can make a full attack even if it has already taken a move action.

Improved Grab (Ex): To use this ability, the dire tiger must hit with its bite attack. If it gets a hold, it can rake.

Rake (Ex): A dire tiger can make two rake attacks (+18 melee) against a held creature with its hind legs for 2d4+4 damage each. If the dire tiger pounces on an opponent, it can also rake.

Skills: Dire tigers receive a +4 racial bonus to Hide and Move Silently checks. *In areas of tall grass or heavy undergrowth, the Hide bonus improves to +8.

DIRE SHARK

This monstrous fish can grow to a length of 50 feet and weigh more than 20,000 pounds.

Combat

Dire sharks attack anything they perceive to be edible, even larger creatures. They bite with their powerful jaws, swallowing smaller creatures in one gulp.

Improved Grab (Ex): To use this ability, the dire shark must hit with its bite attack. If it gets a hold, it can try to swallow the foe.

Swallow Whole (Ex): A dire shark can try to swallow a grabbed opponent of Large or smaller size by making a successful grapple check. Once inside, the opponent takes 2d6+6 points of crushing damage plus 1d8+4 points of acid damage per round from the shark's digestive juices. A swallowed creature can cut its way out using claws or a light slashing weapon by dealing 25 points of damage to the shark's digestive tract (AC 20). Once the creature exits, muscular action closes the hole; another swallowed opponent must cut its own way out.

The shark's gullet can hold two Large, four Small, eight Tiny, sixteen Diminutive, or thirty-two Fine or smaller opponents.

Keen Scent (Ex): A dire shark can notice creatures by scent in a 180-foot radius and detect blood in the water at ranges of up to a mile.

DISPLACER BEAST

Large Magical Beast
Hit Dice: 6d10+18 (51 hp)
Initiative: +2 (Dex)
Speed: 40 ft.
AC: 16 (–1 size, +2 Dex, +5 natural)
Attacks: 2 tentacles +9 melee, bite +4 melee
Damage: Tentacle 1d6+4, bite 1d8 +2
Face/Reach: 5 ft. by 10 ft./5 ft. (15 ft. with tentacles)
Special Qualities: Displacement, resistance to ranged attacks
Saves: Fort +8, Ref +7, Will +3
Abilities: Str 18, Dex 15, Con 16, Int 5, Wis 12, Cha 8
Skills: Hide +12, Listen +3, Move Silently +7, Spot +6
Feats: Alertness, Dodge

Climate/Terrain: Temperate forest, hill, or
  mountains and underground
Organization: Solitary, pair, or pride (6–10)
Challenge Rating: 4
Treasure: 1/10 coins; 50% goods; 50% items
Alignment: Usually lawful evil
Advancement: 7–9 HD (Large); 10–18 HD
  (Huge)

The displacer beast is a savage and stealthy
carnivore that resembles a puma with six legs,
glowing green eyes, and two muscular tentacles growing from its
shoulders.

A displacer beast has luxurious, blue-black fur and a long,
feline body and head. It is the size of a Bengal tiger, about 10
feet long and weighing about 500 pounds. The tentacles end
in pads equipped with horny ridges.

Displacer beasts favor small game but will eat
anything they can catch. They regard all other creatures as prey and tend to attack anything they meet.
They have a deep-seated hatred of blink dogs, and
the two attack each other ruthlessly when their
paths cross.

COMBAT

Displacer beasts rake opponents with their
tentacles and bite foes that get close.

Displacement (Su): A light-bending glamer continually surrounds a displacer beast, making it difficult to sur-
mise the creature's true location. Any melee or ranged
attack directed at it has a 50% miss chance unless the attacker can locate the beast by some means other than sight.
A *true seeing* effect allows the user to see the beast's position,
but *see invisibility* has no effect.

Resistance to Ranged Attacks (Su): A displacer
beast gains a +2 resistance bonus to saves against any
ranged spell or ranged magical attack that specifically
targets it (except for ranged touch attacks).

Skills: A displacer beast receives a +8 racial bonus
to Hide checks, thanks to its displacement power.

DOPPELGANGER

Medium-Size Shapechanger
Hit Dice: 4d8+4 (22 hp)
Initiative: +1 (Dex)
Speed: 30 ft.
AC: 15 (+1 Dex, +4 natural)
Attacks: 2 slams +4 melee
Damage: Slam 1d6+1
Face/Reach: 5 ft. by 5 ft./5 ft.
Special Attacks: Detect thoughts
Special Qualities: Alter self, immunities
Saves: Fort +5, Ref +5, Will +6
Abilities: Str 12, Dex 13, Con 12, Int 13, Wis 14,
  Cha 13
Skills: Bluff +12*, Disguise +12*, Listen +11, Sense
  Motive +6, Spot +8
Feats: Alertness, Dodge

Climate/Terrain: Any land and underground
Organization: Solitary, pair, or gang (3–6)
Challenge Rating: 3
Treasure: Double standard
Alignment: Usually neutral
Advancement: By character class

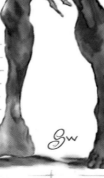

Doppelgangers are strange beings that are able to take on the
shapes of those they encounter.

Doppelgangers make excellent use of this natural mimicry to stage ambushes, bait traps, and infiltrate humanoid
society. Although not strictly evil, they are interested only
in themselves and regard all others as playthings to be
manipulated and deceived.

In its true form, a doppelganger has a more or less -
humanoid appearance. The flesh is pale and hairless,
feeling like oily buckskin. The large, bulging eyes are
white and lack a visible pupil. They are slender and
frail-looking, but doppelgangers are hardy things
with a natural agility not apparent from their gangly
limbs.

Because they can take the shape of any humanoid being between 4 and 8 feet tall, doppelgangers are natural spies and assassins. They can
sneak past sentries, slip into secured places, and
fool even lovers or close friends. They are cunning
and patient, willing to wait until an opportunity
presents itself instead of attacking rashly.

COMBAT

When in its natural form or in the guise of someone
unarmed, a doppelganger strikes with its powerful
fists. In the shape of a warrior or other armed person, it
attacks with whatever weapon is appropriate. In such
cases, it uses detect thoughts to employ the same tactics
and strategies as the person it is impersonating.

Detect Thoughts (Su): A doppelganger can continuously detect thoughts as the spell cast by an 18th-level
sorcerer (save DC 13). It can suppress or resume this ability as a free action.

Alter Self (Su): A doppelganger can assume the shape
of any Small or Medium-size humanoid. This works like
alter self as cast by an 18th-level sorcerer, but the doppelganger can remain in the chosen form indefinitely. It
can assume a new form or return to its own as a standard action.

Immunities (Ex): Doppelgangers are immune to sleep and charm effects.

Skills: A doppelganger receives a +4 racial bonus to Bluff and Disguise checks. *When using *alter self*, a doppelganger receives an additional +10 circumstance bonus to Disguise checks. If it can read an opponent's mind, it gets a further +4 circumstance bonus to Bluff and Disguise checks.

DRAGON

Dragons are winged, reptilelike creatures of ancient lineage. They are known and feared for their size, physical prowess, and magical abilities. The oldest dragons are among the most powerful creatures in the world.

Known varieties of dragons fall into two broad categories: chromatic and metallic. The chromatic dragons are black, blue, green, red, and white, all evil and extremely fierce. The metallic dragons are brass, bronze, copper, gold, and silver, who are good, usually noble, and highly respected by the wise.

All dragons gain more abilities and greater power as they age. They range in length from several feet upon hatching to more than 100 feet after attaining the status of great wyrm. The exact size varies according to age and variety.

DRAGON AGE CATEGORIES

	Category	Age (Years)
1	Wyrmling	0–5
2	Very young	6–15
3	Young	16–25
4	Juvenile	26–50
5	Young adult	51–100
6	Adult	101–200
7	Mature adult	201–400
8	Old	401–600
9	Very old	601–800
10	Ancient	801–1,000
11	Wyrm	1,001–1,200
12	Great wyrm	1,201+

Though they are fearsome predators, dragons scavenge when necessary and can eat almost anything if they are hungry enough. A dragon's metabolism operates like a highly efficient furnace and can metabolize even inorganic material. Some dragons have developed a taste for such fare.

Although goals and ideals vary among varieties, all dragons are covetous. They like to hoard wealth, collecting mounds of coins and gathering as many gems, jewels, and magic items as possible. Those with large hoards are loath to leave them for long, venturing out of their lairs only to patrol the immediate area or to get food. For dragons, there is never enough treasure: It's pleasing to look at, and they bask in its radiance. Dragons like to make beds of their hoards, shaping nooks and mounds to fit their bodies. By the time a dragon matures to the great wyrm stage, hundreds of gems and coins are embedded in its hide.

All dragons speak Draconic.

COMBAT

A dragon attacks with its powerful claws and bite, and can also use a breath weapon and special physical attacks, depending on its size. It prefers to fight on the wing, staying out of reach until it has worn down the enemy with ranged attacks. Older, more intelligent dragons are adept at sizing up the opposition and eliminating the most dangerous foes first (or avoiding them while picking off weaker enemies).

DRAGON FACE AND REACH

Size	Face	Reach
Tiny	2 1/2 ft. by 2 1/2 ft.	5 ft.*
Small	5 ft. by 5 ft.	5 ft.
Medium-size	5 ft. by 5 ft.	5 ft.
Large	5 ft. by 10 ft.	10 ft.*
Huge	10 ft. by 20 ft.	10 ft.
Gargantuan	20 ft. by 40 ft.	15 ft.
Colossal	40 ft. by 80 ft.	15 ft.

*Greater than normal reach for a creature of this size.

DRAGON ATTACKS

Size	1 Bite	2 Claws	2 Wings	1 Tail Slap	1 Crush	1 Tail Sweep
Tiny	1d4	1d3	—	—	—	—
Small	1d6	1d4	—	—	—	—
Medium-size	1d8	1d6	1d4	—	—	—
Large	2d6	1d8	1d6	1d8	—	—
Huge	2d8	2d6	1d8	2d6	2d8	—
Gargantuan	4d6	2d8	2d6	2d8	4d6	2d6
Colossal	4d8	4d6	2d8	4d6	4d8	2d8

Bite: Bite attacks deal the listed damage plus the dragon's Strength bonus. The dragon also can use its bite to snatch opponents (see the descriptions of feats below). Bite attacks use the full attack bonus.

Claw: Claw attacks deal the listed damage plus half the dragon's Strength bonus (round down). The dragon also can use its claws to snatch opponents (see the descriptions of feats below). Claw attacks are at –5 to the attack bonus.

Wing: The dragon can slam opponents with its wings, even when flying. Wing attacks deal the listed damage plus half the dragon's Strength bonus (round down) and are at –5 to the attack bonus.

Tail Slap: The dragon can slap one opponent each round with its tail. A tail slap deals the listed damage plus 1 1/2 times the dragon's Strength bonus (round down) and is at –5 to the attack bonus.

Crush: A flying or jumping dragon of at least Huge size can land on opponents as a standard action, using its whole body to crush them. Crush attacks are effective only against opponents three or more sizes smaller than the dragon (though it can attempt normal overrun or grapple attacks against larger opponents).

A crush attack affects as many creatures as can fit under the dragon's body (see Table 3: Dragon Face and Reach above). Creatures in the affected area must succeed at a Reflex save against a DC equal to that of the dragon's breath weapon or be pinned, automatically taking bludgeoning damage during the next round unless the dragon moves off them. If the dragon chooses to maintain the pin, treat it as a normal grapple attack. Pinned opponents take crush damage each round if they don't escape.

A crush attack deals the listed damage plus 1 1/2 times the dragon's Strength bonus (round down).

Tail Sweep: A dragon of at least Gargantuan size can sweep with its tail as a standard action. The sweep affects a half circle with a diameter of 30 feet, centered on the dragon's rear. A Colossal dragon's tail sweep has a 40-foot radius. Creatures within the swept area are affected if they are four or more sizes smaller than the dragon. The sweep automatically deals the listed damage plus 1 1/2 times the dragon's Strength bonus (round down). Affected creatures can attempt Reflex saves to take half damage, against a DC equal to that of the dragon's breath weapon.

Grappling: Dragons do not favor grapple attacks, though their crush attack and Snatch feat (see the descriptions of feats) use normal grapple rules.

If grappled by a creature the same size or larger, a dragon can return the attack with its bite and all four legs (the rear legs deal claw damage). If snatched or crushed by a larger dragon, a dragon can respond only with grapple attacks to try winning free, or with bite or breath weapon attacks. If grappled by a creature smaller than itself, the dragon can respond with any of its physical attacks other than a tail sweep.

The dragon can always use its breath weapon while grappling, as well as its spells and spell-like or supernatural abilities, provided it succeeds at Concentration checks.

Breath Weapon (Su): Using a breath weapon is a standard action. Once a dragon breathes, it can't breathe again until 1d4 rounds later. If the dragon has more than one type of breath weapon, it still can breathe only once every 1d4 rounds. A blast from a breath weapon always starts at the dragon's mouth and extends in a direction of the dragon's choice, with an area as noted below. If the breath weapon deals damage, creatures caught in the area can attempt Reflex saves to take half damage; the DC depends on the dragon's age and type, listed in the individual entry. Saves against nondamaging breath weapons use the same DC, but the types vary as noted in the variety descriptions.

Breath weapons come in two basic shapes, line and cone, whose areas vary with the dragon's size.

DRAGON BREATH WEAPONS

Dragon Size	Line* (Length)	Cone** (Length)
Tiny	30 ft.	15 ft.
Small	40 ft.	20 ft.
Medium-size	60 ft.	30 ft.
Large	80 ft.	40 ft.
Huge	100 ft.	50 ft.
Gargantuan	120 ft.	60 ft.
Colossal	140 ft.	70 ft.

*A line is always 5 feet high and 5 feet wide.
**A cone is as high and wide as its length.

Frightful Presence (Ex): A young adult or older dragon can unsettle foes with its mere presence. The ability takes effect automatically whenever the dragon attacks, charges, or flies overhead. Creatures within a radius of 30 feet × the dragon's age category are subject to the effect if they have fewer HD than the dragon.

A potentially affected creature that succeeds at a Will save (DC 10 + 1/2 dragon's HD + dragon's Charisma modifier) remains immune to that dragon's frightful presence for one day. On a failure, creatures with 4 or fewer HD become panicked for 4d6 rounds and those with 5 or more HD become shaken for 4d6 rounds. Dragons ignore the frightful presence of other dragons.

Spells: A dragon knows and casts arcane spells as a sorcerer of the level indicated in its variety description, gaining bonus spells for a high Charisma score. Some dragons can also cast spells from the cleric list or cleric domains as arcane spells.

Spell-Like Abilities: A dragon's spell-like abilities depend on its age and variety. It gains the abilities listed for its age category plus all previous ones, using its age category or its sorcerer caster level, whichever is higher, as the caster level. The save DC is 10 + dragon's Charisma modifier + spell level. All spell-like abilities are usable once per day unless otherwise specified.

Immunities (Ex): All dragons are immune to *sleep* and *paralysis* effects. Each variety of dragon is immune to one or two additional forms of attack no matter what its age, as listed in its description.

Spell Resistance (Ex): As dragons age, they become more resistant to spells and spell-like abilities, as listed in the variety descriptions.

Blindsight (Ex): A dragon can ascertain creatures by nonvisual means (mostly hearing and scent, but also by noticing vibration and other environmental clues) with a range of 30 feet × the dragon's age category.

Keen Senses (Ex): A dragon sees four times as well a human in low-light conditions and twice as well in normal light. It also has darkvision with a range of 100 feet × the dragon's age category.

Skills: All dragons start with 6 skill points per Hit Die, plus bonus points equal to Intelligence modifier × HD, and purchase the following skills at 1 rank per Hit Die: Listen, Spot, and Search. The remaining skill points are generally spent on Bluff, Concentration, Diplomacy, Escape Artist, Knowledge (any), and Scry at a cost of 1 skill point per rank. Dragons cannot purchase skills that are exclusive to a class.

Dragons that can cast spells have the Spellcraft skill for free at 1 rank per Hit Die, provided they have an Intelligence bonus of at least +1 (Intelligence score 12+).

Red, copper, gold, and silver dragons have the Jump skill for free at 1 rank per Hit Die.

Feats: All dragons have one feat, plus an additional feat per 4 HD. Dragons favor Alertness, Cleave (claw or tail slap attacks only), Improved Initiative, Power Attack, Sunder, Weapon Focus (claw or bite), and any metamagic feat that is available and useful to sorcerers. Dragons can also choose from the following feats:

Flyby Attack: See "Feats" in the Introduction.

Hover: When flying, a dragon can halt its forward motion and hover in place, fly straight down, or fly straight up regardless of its maneuverability.

While hovering, it can attack with its bite and all four feet (its hind feet deal claw damage) and can make tail slap attacks if normally allowed to do so. If it can make a tail sweep, it can do so while hovering but can make no other attacks. A hovering dragon cannot make wing attacks. It can use its breath weapon instead of making physical attacks.

If a dragon hovers close to the ground in an area with lots of loose debris, the draft from its wings creates a hemispherical cloud with a radius of 30 feet × the dragon's age category. The winds so generated can snuff torches, small campfires, exposed lanterns, and other small, open flames of nonmagical origin. The cloud obscures vision, and creatures caught within are blinded while inside and for 1 round after emerging. Those caught in the cloud must succeed at a Concentration check (DC 10 + 1/2 dragon's HD) to cast a spell.

Quicken Spell-Like Ability: The dragon can use one of its spell-like abilities each round as a free action.

Snatch: A dragon that hits with a claw or bite attack attempts to start a grapple as though it had the improved grab special attack. If the dragon gets a hold with a claw on a creature four or more sizes smaller, it squeezes each round for automatic claw damage. If it gets a hold with its bite on a creature three or more sizes smaller, it automatically deals bite damage each round, or if it does not move and takes no other action in combat, it deals double bite damage to the snatched creature. A snatched creature gets no saving throw against the dragon's breath weapon.

The dragon can drop a creature it has snatched as a free action or use a standard action to fling it aside. A flung creature travels 10 feet, and takes 1d6 points of damage, per age category of the dragon. If the dragon flings it while flying, the creature suffers this amount or falling damage, whichever is greater.

Wingover: A flying dragon can change direction quickly once each round. This feat allows it to turn up to 180 degrees regardless of its maneuverability, in addition to any other turns it is normally allowed. A dragon cannot gain altitude during the round it executes a wingover, but it can dive. For more information, see Tactical Aerial Movement, page 69 in the DUNGEON MASTER's *Guide*.

Dragon Overland Movement

Dragons are exceedingly strong flyers and can cover vast distances quickly.

DRAGON OVERLAND FLYING SPEEDS

Flight Speed	100 feet	150 feet	200 feet	250 feet
One Hour				
Normal	15 miles	20 miles	30 miles	40 miles
Hustle	24 miles	40 miles	60 miles	80 miles
One Day				
Normal	120 miles	160 miles	240 miles	320 miles

Dragons do not tire as quickly as other creatures when moving overland. If a dragon attempts a hustle or forced march (see page 143 in the *Player's Handbook*), check for subdual damage once every 2 hours instead of every hour.

DRAGON SOCIETY

Although all dragons are believed to have come from the same roots tens of thousands of years ago, the present varieties keep to themselves and cooperate only under extreme circumstances, such as a powerful mutual threat. Good dragons never work with evil dragons, however, though a few neutral specimens have been found with either. Gold dragons occasionally associate with silver dragons.

When evil dragons of different varieties encounter one another, they usually fight to protect their territories. Good dragons are more tolerant, though also very territorial, and usually try to work out differences in a peaceful manner.

Dragons follow a number of reproductive strategies to suit their needs and temperaments. These help assure the continuation of a dragon's bloodline, no matter what happens to the parent or the parent's lair. Young adults, particularly evil or less intelligent ones, tend to lay clutches of 1d4+1 eggs all around the countryside, leaving their offspring to fend for themselves. These hatch into clutches of dragons, usually juvenile or younger, which stick together until they can establish their own lairs.

Older and more intelligent dragons form families consisting of a mated pair and 1d4+1 young. Mated dragons are always adults or mature adults; offspring found with their parents are wyrmlings (01–10 on d%), very young (11–30), young (31–50), juvenile (51–90), or young adult (91–100). Shortly after a dragon reaches the young adult (or rarely, juvenile) stage, it leaves its parents to establish a lair of its own.

A pair of mated dragons beyond the mature adult stage usually splits up, independence and the lust for treasure driving them apart. Older females continue to mate and lay eggs, but only one parent stays in the lair to raise young. Often an older female lays many clutches of eggs, keeping one to tend herself and one for her mate, and leaving the rest untended. Sometimes a female dragon places an egg or wyrmling with nondraconic foster parents.

DRAGONHIDE

Armorsmiths can work with dragonhides to produce masterwork armor or shields for the normal cost (see Special and Superior Items, page 113 in the *Player's Handbook*).

One dragon produces enough hide for a single suit of masterwork hide armor for a creature up to one size smaller than the dragon. By selecting only choice scales and bits of hide, an armorsmith can produce one suit of masterwork banded mail for a creature up to two sizes smaller, one suit of masterwork half-plate for a creature three sizes smaller, or one masterwork breastplate or suit of full plate for a creature four sizes smaller. In each case, there is enough hide to produce a small or large masterwork shield in addition to the armor, provided that the dragon is of at least Large size.

CHROMATIC DRAGONS

Chromatic dragons form the evil branch of dragonkind. They are aggressive, greedy, vain, and nasty.

Black Dragon

Dragon (Water)

Climate/Terrain: Any marsh and underground

Organization: Wyrmling, very young, young, juvenile, and young adult: solitary or clutch (2–5); adult, mature adult, old, very old, ancient, wyrm, or great wyrm: solitary, pair, or family (1–2 and 2–5 offspring)

Challenge Ratings: Wyrmling 2; very young 3; young 4; juvenile 6; young adult 8; adult 10; mature adult 13; old 15; very old 17; ancient 18; wyrm 19; great wyrm 21

Treasure: Double standard

Alignment: Always chaotic evil

Advancement: Wyrmling 5–6 HD (Small); very young 8–9 HD (Medium-size); young 11–12 HD (Medium-size); juvenile 14–15 HD (Large); young adult 17–18 HD (Large); adult 20–21 HD (Huge); mature adult 23–24 HD (Huge); old 26–27 HD (Huge); very old 29–30 HD (Huge); ancient 32–33 HD (Gargantuan); wyrm 35–36 HD (Gargantuan); great wyrm 38+ HD (Gargantuan)

Black dragons are evil-tempered, cunning, and malevolent, characteristics that are reflected in their crafty, sinister faces. They are sometimes known as "skull dragons" because of their deep-socketed eyes and distinctive nasal opening.

Adding to the skeletal impression is the gradual deterioration of the hide around the horn base and cheekbones. This increases with age and does not harm the dragon. On hatching, a black dragon's scales are thin, small, and glossy. As the dragon ages, they become larger, thicker, and duller, helping it camouflage itself in swamps and marshes.

Black dragons lair in large, damp caves and multichambered subterranean caverns. They smell of rotting vegetation and foul

BLACK DRAGONS BY AGE

Age	Size	Hit Dice (hp)	AC	Attack Bonus	Fort Save	Ref Save	Will Save	Breath Weapon (DC)	Fear DC	SR
Wyrmling	T	4d12+4 (30)	15 (+2 size, +3 natural)	+6	+5	+4	+4	2d4 (13)	—	—
Very young	S	7d12+7 (52)	17 (+1 size, +6 natural)	+9	+6	+5	+5	4d4 (14)	—	—
Young	M	10d12+20 (85)	19 (+9 natural)	+12	+9	+7	+7	6d4 (17)	—	—
Juvenile	M	13d12+26 (110)	22 (+12 natural)	+16	+10	+8	+8	8d4 (18)	—	—
Young adult	L	16d12+48 (152)	24 (−1 size, +15 natural)	+19	+13	+10	+11	10d4 (22)	19	17
Adult	L	19d12+76 (199)	27 (−1 size, +18 natural)	+24	+15	+11	+12	12d4 (23)	20	18
Mature adult	H	22d12+110 (253)	29 (−2 size, +21 natural)	+28	+18	+13	+15	14d4 (26)	23	21
Old	H	25d12+125 (287)	32 (−2 size, +24 natural)	+32	+19	+14	+16	16d4 (27)	24	22
Very old	H	28d12+168 (350)	35 (−2 size, +27 natural)	+36	+22	+16	+19	18d4 (30)	27	23
Ancient	H	31d12+186 (387)	38 (−2 size, +30 natural)	+40	+23	+17	+20	20d4 (31)	28	25
Wyrm	G	34d12+238 (459)	39 (−4 size, +33 natural)	+42	+26	+19	+23	22d4 (34)	31	26
Great wyrm	G	37d12+296 (536)	42 (−4 size, +36 natural)	+46	+28	+20	+25	24d4 (36)	33	28

BLACK DRAGON ABILITIES BY AGE

Age	Speed	Str	Dex	Con	Int	Wis	Cha	Special Abilities	Caster Level
Wyrmling	60 ft., fly 100 ft. (average), swim 60 ft.	11	10	13	8	11	8	Acid immunity, water breathing	—
Very young	60 ft., fly 100 ft. (average), swim 60 ft.	13	10	13	8	11	8		—
Young	60 ft., fly 150 ft. (poor), swim 60 ft.	15	10	15	10	11	10		—
Juvenile	60 ft., fly 150 ft. (poor), swim 60 ft.	17	10	15	10	11	10	Darkness	—
Young adult	60 ft., fly 150 ft. (poor), swim 60 ft.	19	10	17	12	13	12	Damage reduction 5/+1	1st
Adult	60 ft., fly 150 ft. (poor), swim 60 ft.	23	10	19	12	13	12	Corrupt water	3rd
Mature adult	60 ft., fly 150 ft. (poor), swim 60 ft.	27	10	21	14	15	14	Damage reduction 10/+1	5th
Old	60 ft., fly 150 ft. (poor), swim 60 ft.	29	10	21	14	15	14	Plant growth	7th
Very old	60 ft., fly 150 ft. (poor), swim 60 ft.	31	10	23	16	17	16	Damage reduction 15/+2	9th
Ancient	60 ft., fly 150 ft. (poor), swim 60 ft.	33	10	23	16	17	16	Insect plague	11th
Wyrm	60 ft., fly 200 ft. (clumsy), swim 60 ft.	35	10	25	18	19	18	Damage reduction 20/+3	13th
Great wyrm	60 ft., fly 200 ft. (clumsy), swim 60 ft.	37	10	27	20	21	20	Charm reptiles	15th

water, with an acidic undertone. Older dragons hide the entrance to their lairs using *plant growth*. Black dragons dine primarily on fish, mollusks, and other aquatic creatures. They also hunt for red meat but like to "pickle" it by letting it lie in ponds within the lair for days before eating it.

Black dragons are especially fond of coins. Older dragons sometimes capture and question humanoids about stockpiles of gold, silver, and platinum coins before killing them.

Combat

Black dragons prefer to ambush their targets, using their surroundings as cover. When fighting in heavily forested swamps and marshes, they try to stay in the water or on the ground; trees and leafy canopies limit their aerial maneuverability. When outmatched, a black dragon attempts to fly out of sight, so as not to leave tracks, and hide in a deep pond or bog.

Breath Weapon (Su): A black dragon has one type of breath weapon, a line of acid.

Water Breathing (Ex): The dragon can breathe underwater indefinitely and can freely use its breath weapon, spells, and other abilities while submerged.

Corrupt Water (Sp): Once per day the dragon can stagnate 10 cubic feet of water, making it become still, foul, and unable to support animal life. The ability spoils liquids containing water. Magic items (such as potions) and items in a creature's possession must succeed at a Will save (DC equal to that of the dragon's frightful presence) or become fouled.

Charm Reptiles (Sp): The dragon can use this ability three times per day. It operates as a *mass charm* spell that works only on reptilian animals. The dragon can communicate with any charmed reptiles as though casting a *speak with animals* spell.

Other Spell-Like Abilities: 3/day—*darkness* (radius 10 feet per age category) and *insect plague*; 1/day—*plant growth*.

Illus. by T. Lockwood

DRAGON

Blue Dragon

Dragon (Earth)
Climate/Terrain: Temperate and warm desert and underground
Organization: Wyrmling, very young, young, juvenile, and young adult: solitary or clutch (2–5); adult, mature adult, old, very old, ancient, wyrm, or great wyrm: solitary, pair, or family (1–2 and 2–5 offspring)
Challenge Ratings: Wyrmling 2; very young 3; young 5; juvenile 7; young adult 10; adult 13; mature adult 15; old 17; very old 18; ancient 20; wyrm 22; great wyrm 24
Treasure: Double standard
Alignment: Always lawful evil
Advancement: Wyrmling 7–8 HD (Small); very young 10–11 HD (Medium-size); young 13–14 HD (Medium-size); juvenile 16–17 HD (Large); young adult 19–20 HD (Large); adult 22–23 HD (Huge); mature adult 25–26 HD (Huge); old 28–29 HD (Huge); very old 31–32 HD (Huge); ancient 34–35 HD (Gargantuan); wyrm 37–38 HD (Gargantuan); great wyrm 40+ HD (Gargantuan)

Blue dragons are vain and territorial. They are one of the dragon varieties best adapted to digging into sand.

A blue dragon is distinguished by dramatic frilled ears and a single, massive horn on its snout. Its scales vary in color from an iridescent azure to a deep indigo, polished to a glossy finish by blowing desert sands. The size of its scales increases little as the dragon ages, although they do become thicker and harder. Their hides tend to hum and crackle faintly with built-up static electricity. These effects intensify when the dragon is angry or about to attack, giving off an odor of ozone and sand.

Their vibrant color makes blue dragons easy to spot in barren desert surroundings. However, they often burrow into the sand so only part of their heads are exposed. Blue dragons love to soar in the hot desert air, usually flying in the daytime when temperatures are highest. Some nearly match the color of the desert sky and use this coloration to their advantage.

Blue dragons lair in vast underground caverns, where they also store their treasure. Although they collect anything that looks valuable,

Illus. by T. Lockwood

BLUE DRAGONS BY AGE

Age	Size	Hit Dice (hp)	AC	Attack Bonus	Fort Save	Ref Save	Will Save	Breath Weapon (DC)	Fear DC	SR
Wyrmling	S	6d12+6 (45)	16 (+1 size, +5 natural)	+8	+6	+5	+5	2d8 (14)	—	—
Very young	M	9d12+18 (76)	18 (+8 natural)	+11	+8	+6	+6	4d8 (16)	—	—
Young	M	12d12+24 (102)	21 (+11 natural)	+15	+10	+8	+9	6d8 (18)	—	—
Juvenile	L	15d12+45 (142)	23 (–1 size, +14 natural)	+18	+12	+9	+11	8d8 (20)	—	—
Young adult	L	18d12+72 (189)	26 (–1 size, +17 natural)	+23	+15	+11	+13	10d8 (23)	21	19
Adult	H	21d12+105 (241)	28 (–2 size, +20 natural)	+27	+17	+12	+15	12d8 (25)	23	21
Mature adult	H	24d12+120 (276)	31 (–2 size, +23 natural)	+31	+19	+14	+17	14d8 (27)	25	22
Old	H	27d12+162 (337)	34 (–2 size, +26 natural)	+35	+21	+15	+19	16d8 (29)	27	24
Very old	H	30d12+180 (375)	37 (–2 size, +29 natural)	+39	+23	+17	+21	18d8 (31)	29	25
Ancient	G	33d12+231 (445)	38 (–4 size, +32 natural)	+41	+25	+18	+23	20d8 (33)	31	27
Wyrm	G	36d12+288 (522)	41 (–4 size, +35 natural)	+45	+28	+20	+25	22d8 (36)	33	29
Great wyrm	G	39d12+312 (565)	44 (–4 size, +38 natural)	+49	+29	+21	+27	24d8 (37)	35	31

BLUE DRAGON ABILITIES BY AGE

Age	Speed	Str	Dex	Con	Int	Wis	Cha	Special Abilities	Caster Level*
Wyrmling	40 ft., fly 100 ft. (average), burrow 20 ft.	13	10	13	10	11	10	Electricity immunity, create/destroy water	—
Very young	40 ft., fly 150 ft. (poor), burrow 20 ft.	15	10	15	10	11	10		—
Young	40 ft., fly 150 ft. (poor), burrow 20 ft.	17	10	15	12	13	12		—
Juvenile	40 ft., fly 150 ft. (poor), burrow 20 ft.	19	10	17	14	15	14	Sound imitation	1st
Young adult	40 ft., fly 150 ft. (poor), burrow 20 ft.	23	10	19	14	15	14	Damage reduction 5/+1	3rd
Adult	40 ft., fly 150 ft. (poor), burrow 20 ft.	27	10	21	16	17	16	Ventriloquism	5th
Mature adult	40 ft., fly 150 ft. (poor), burrow 20 ft.	29	10	21	16	17	16	Damage reduction 10/+1	7th
Old	40 ft., fly 150 ft. (poor), burrow 20 ft.	31	10	23	18	19	18	Hallucinatory terrain	9th
Very old	40 ft., fly 150 ft. (poor), burrow 20 ft.	33	10	23	18	19	18	Damage reduction 15/+2	11th
Ancient	40 ft., fly 200 ft. (clumsy), burrow 20 ft.	35	10	25	20	21	20	Veil	13th
Wyrm	40 ft., fly 200 ft. (clumsy), burrow 20 ft.	37	10	27	20	21	20	Damage reduction 20/+3	15th
Great wyrm	40 ft., fly 200 ft. (clumsy), burrow 20 ft.	39	10	27	22	23	22	Mirage arcana	17th

*Can also cast cleric spells and those from the Air, Evil, and Law domains as arcane spells.

they are most fond of gems—especially sapphires. They are sometimes are forced to eat snakes, lizards, and desert plants to sate their great hunger but especially prefer herd animals such as camels. When they get the chance, they gorge themselves on these creatures, which they cook with their lightning breath.

Combat

Typically, blue dragons attack from above or burrow beneath the sands until opponents come within 100 feet. Older dragons use their special abilities, such as *hallucinatory terrain*, in concert with these tactics to mask the land and improve their chances to surprise the target. Blue dragons run from a fight only if they are severely damaged, since they view retreat as cowardly.

Breath Weapon (Su): A blue dragon has one type of breath weapon, a line of lightning.

Create/Destroy Water (Sp): The dragon can use this ability three times per day. It works like the *create water* spell, except that the dragon can decide to destroy water instead of creating it, which automatically spoils unattended liquids containing water. Magic items (such as potions) and items in a creature's possession must succeed at a Will save (DC equal to that of the dragon's frightful presence) or be ruined.

Sound Imitation (Ex): The dragon can mimic any voice or sound it has heard, anytime it likes. Listeners must succeed at a Will save (DC equal to that of the dragon's frightful presence) to detect the ruse.

Other Spell-Like Abilities: 3/day—*ventriloquism*; 1/day—*hallucinatory terrain*, *veil*, and *mirage arcana*.

Green Dragon

Dragon (Air)
Climate/Terrain: Temperate and warm forest and underground
Organization: Wyrmling, very young, young, juvenile, and young adult: solitary or clutch (2–5); adult, mature adult, old, very old, ancient, wyrm, or great wyrm: solitary, pair, or family (1–2 and 2–5 offspring)
Challenge Ratings: Wyrmling 2; very young 3; young 4; juvenile 7; young adult 10; adult 12;

mature adult 15; old 17; very old 18; ancient 20; wyrm 21; great wyrm 23
Treasure: Double standard
Alignment: Always lawful evil
Advancement: Wyrmling 6–7 HD (Small); very young 9–10 HD (Medium-size); young 12–13 HD (Medium-size); juvenile 15–16 HD (Large); young adult 18–19 HD (Large); adult 21–22 HD (Huge); mature adult 24–25 HD (Huge); old 27–28 HD (Huge); very old 30–31 HD (Huge); ancient 33–34 HD (Gargantuan); wyrm 36–37 HD (Gargantuan); great wyrm 39+ HD (Gargantuan)

Green dragons are belligerent and tend to attack without provocation. Their fierce, toothy jaws and arrogant crests warn other creatures of their aggressive nature.

A wyrmling green dragon's scales are thin, very small, and a deep shade of green that appears nearly black. As the dragon ages, the scales grow larger and lighter, turning shades of forest, emerald, and olive green, which helps it blend in with its wooded surroundings. Clusters of hornlets at the brows and chin enhance the fearsome appearance.

Green dragons make their lairs in forests; the older the forest and bigger the trees, the better. They prefer caves in cliffs or hillsides and can be detected by the stinging odor of chlorine. Although they have been known to eat practically anything, including shrubs and small trees when they are hungry enough, green dragons especially prize elves and sprites.

Combat

Green dragons initiate fights with little or no provocation, picking on creatures of any size. If the target is intriguing or seems formidable, the dragon stalks the creature to determine the best time to strike and the most appropriate tactics to use. If the target appears weak, the dragon makes its presence known quickly—it enjoys evoking terror. Sometimes the dragon elects to control a humanoid creature through

GREEN DRAGONS BY AGE

Age	Size	Hit Dice (hp)	AC	Attack Bonus	Fort Save	Ref Save	Will Save	Breath Weapon (DC)	Fear DC	SR
Wyrmling	S	5d12+5 (37)	15 (+1 size, +4 natural)	+7	+5	+4	+4	2d6 (13)	—	—
Very young	M	8d12+16 (68)	17 (+7 natural)	+10	+8	+6	+6	4d6 (16)	—	—
Young	M	11d12+22 (93)	20 (+10 natural)	+14	+9	+7	+8	6d6 (17)	—	—
Juvenile	L	14d12+42 (133)	22 (–1 size, +13 natural)	+17	+12	+9	+11	8d6 (20)	—	—
Young adult	L	17d12+68 (178)	25 (–1 size, +16 natural)	+22	+14	+10	+12	10d6 (22)	20	19
Adult	H	20d12+100 (230)	27 (–2 size, +19 natural)	+26	+17	+12	+15	12d6 (25)	23	21
Mature adult	H	23d12+115 (264)	30 (–2 size, +22 natural)	+30	+18	+13	+16	14d6 (26)	24	22
Old	H	26d12+156 (325)	33 (–2 size, +25 natural)	+34	+21	+15	+19	16d6 (29)	27	24
Very old	H	29d12+174 (362)	36 (–2 size, +28 natural)	+38	+22	+16	+20	18d6 (30)	28	25
Ancient	G	32d12+224 (432)	37 (–4 size, +31 natural)	+40	+25	+18	+23	20d6 (33)	31	27
Wyrm	G	35d12+280 (507)	40 (–4 size, +34 natural)	+44	+27	+19	+24	22d6 (35)	32	28
Great wyrm	G	38d12+304 (551)	43 (–4 size, +37 natural)	+48	+29	+21	+27	24d6 (37)	35	30

Green Dragon Abilities by Age

Age	Speed	Str	Dex	Con	Int	Wis	Cha	Special Abilities	Caster Level
Wyrmling	40 ft., fly 100 ft. (average), swim 40 ft.	13	10	13	10	11	10	Acid immunity, water breathing	—
Very young	40 ft., fly 150 ft. (poor), swim 40 ft.	15	10	15	10	11	10		—
Young	40 ft., fly 150 ft. (poor), swim 40 ft.	17	10	15	12	13	12		—
Juvenile	40 ft., fly 150 ft. (poor), swim 40 ft.	19	10	17	14	15	14		1st
Young adult	40 ft., fly 150 ft. (poor), swim 40 ft.	23	10	19	14	15	14	Damage reduction 5/+1	3rd
Adult	40 ft., fly 150 ft. (poor), swim 40 ft.	27	10	21	16	17	16	Suggestion	5th
Mature adult	40 ft., fly 150 ft. (poor), swim 40 ft.	29	10	21	16	17	16	Damage reduction 10/+1	7th
Old	40 ft., fly 150 ft. (poor), swim 40 ft.	31	10	23	18	19	18	Plant growth	9th
Very old	40 ft., fly 150 ft. (poor), swim 40 ft.	33	10	23	18	19	18	Damage reduction 15/+2	11th
Ancient	40 ft., fly 200 ft. (clumsy), swim 40 ft.	35	10	25	20	21	20	Dominate person	13th
Wyrm	40 ft., fly 200 ft. (clumsy), swim 40 ft.	37	10	27	20	21	20	Damage reduction 20/+2	15th
Great wyrm	40 ft., fly 200 ft. (clumsy), swim 40 ft.	39	10	27	22	23	22	Command plants	17th

intimidation and *suggestion*. Green dragons especially like to question adventurers to learn more about their society and abilities, what is going on in the countryside, and if there is treasure nearby.

Breath Weapon (Su): A green dragon has one type of breath weapon, a cone of corrosive (acid) gas.

Water Breathing (Ex): The dragon can breathe underwater indefinitely and can freely use its breath weapon, spells, and other abilities while submerged.

Spell-Like Abilities: 3/day—*suggestion* and *dominate person*; 1/day—*plant growth* and *command plants*.

Red Dragon

Dragon (Fire)

Climate/Terrain: Temperate and warm hill, mountains, and underground

Organization: Wyrmling, very young, young, juvenile, and young adult: solitary or clutch (2–5); adult, mature adult, old, very old, ancient, wyrm, or great wyrm: solitary, pair, or family (1–2 and 2–5 offspring)

Challenge Ratings: Wyrmling 3; very young 4; young 6; juvenile 9; young adult 12; adult 14; mature adult 17; old 19; very old 20; ancient 22; wyrm 23; great wyrm 25

Treasure: Double standard

Alignment: Always chaotic evil

Advancement: Wyrmling 8–9 HD (Medium-size); very young 11–12 HD (Large); young 14–15 HD (Large); juvenile 17–18 HD (Large); young adult 20–21 HD (Huge); adult 23–24 HD (Huge); mature adult 26–27 HD (Huge); old 29–30 HD (Gargantuan); very old 32–33 HD (Gargantuan); ancient 35–36 HD (Gargantuan); wyrm 38–39 HD (Gargantuan); great wyrm 41+ HD (Colossal)

Red dragons are the most covetous of all dragons, forever seeking to increase their treasure hoards. They are exceptionally vain, which is reflected in their proud bearing and disdainful expression.

The small scales of wyrmlings are a bright glossy scarlet, making them easily spotted by predators and hunters, so they stay underground and do not venture outside until they are more able to take care of themselves. Toward the end of their young stage the scales turn a deeper red, and the glossy texture is replaced by a smooth, dull finish. As the dragon grows older, the scales become large, thick, and strong as metal. The neck frill and wings are an ash blue or purple-gray toward the edges, becoming darker with age. The pupils of a red dragon fade as it ages; the oldest red dragons have eyes that resemble molten lava orbs.

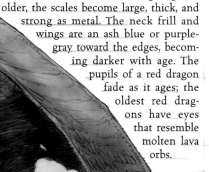

Illus. by T. Lockwood

RED DRAGONS BY AGE

Age	Size	Hit Dice (hp)	AC	Attack Bonus	Fort Save	Ref Save	Will Save	Breath Weapon (DC)	Fear DC	SR
Wyrmling	M	7d12+14 (59)	16 (+6 natural)	+10	+7	+5	+5	2d10 (15)	—	—
Very young	L	10d12+30 (95)	18 (–1 size, +9 natural)	+14	+10	+7	+8	4d10 (18)	—	—
Young	L	13d12+39 (123)	21 (–1 size, +12 natural)	+19	+11	+8	+9	6d10 (19)	—	—
Juvenile	L	16d12+64 (168)	24 (–1 size, +15 natural)	+24	+14	+10	+12	8d10 (22)	—	—
Young adult	H	19d12+95 (218)	26 (–2 size, +18 natural)	+27	+16	+11	+13	10d10 (24)	21	19
Adult	H	22d12+110 (253)	29 (–2 size, +21 natural)	+31	+18	+13	+17	12d10 (25)	24	21
Mature adult	H	25d12+150 (312)	32 (–2 size, +24 natural)	+34	+20	+14	+18	14d10 (28)	26	23
Old	G	28d12+196 (378)	33 (–4 size, +27 natural)	+36	+23	+16	+21	16d10 (30)	29	24
Very old	G	31d12+248 (449)	36 (–4 size, +30 natural)	+40	+25	+17	+23	18d10 (33)	31	26
Ancient	G	34d12+306 (527)	39 (–4 size, +33 natural)	+44	+28	+19	+26	20d10 (35)	34	28
Wyrm	G	37d12+370 (610)	42 (–4 size, +36 natural)	+48	+30	+20	+27	22d10 (38)	35	30
Great wyrm	C	40d12+400 (660)	41 (–8 size, +39 natural)	+49	+32	+22	+30	24d10 (40)	38	32

RED DRAGON ABILITIES BY AGE

Age	Speed	Str	Dex	Con	Int	Wis	Cha	Special Abilities	Caster Level
Wyrmling	40 ft., fly 150 ft. (poor)	17	10	15	10	11	10	Fire subtype	—
Very young	40 ft., fly 150 ft. (poor)	21	10	17	12	13	12		—
Young	40 ft., fly 150 ft. (poor)	25	10	17	12	13	12		1st
Juvenile	40 ft., fly 150 ft. (poor)	29	10	19	14	15	14	Locate object	3rd
Young adult	40 ft., fly 150 ft. (poor)	31	10	21	14	15	14	Damage reduction 5/+1	5th
Adult	40 ft., fly 150 ft. (poor)	33	10	21	16	19	16		7th
Mature adult	40 ft., fly 150 ft. (poor)	33	10	23	18	19	18	Damage reduction 10/+1	9th
Old	40 ft., fly 200 ft. (clumsy)	35	10	25	20	21	20	Suggestion	11th
Very old	40 ft., fly 200 ft. (clumsy)	37	10	27	22	23	22	Damage reduction 15/+2	13th
Ancient	40 ft., fly 200 ft. (clumsy)	39	10	29	24	25	24	Find the path	15th
Wyrm	40 ft., fly 200 ft. (clumsy)	41	10	31	24	25	24	Damage reduction 20/+3	17th
Great wyrm	40 ft., fly 200 ft. (clumsy)	45	10	31	26	27	26	Discern location	19th

*Can also cast cleric spells and those from the Chaos, Evil, and Fire domains as arcane spells.

Red dragons lair in large caves that extend deep into the earth, which shimmer with the heat of their bodies and are marked by a sulfurous, smoky odor. However, they always have a high perch nearby from which to haughtily survey their territory, which they consider to be everything in sight. This high perch sometimes intrudes upon the territory of a silver dragon, and for this reason red dragons and silver dragons are often enemies.

Red dragons are meat-eaters by preference, and their favorite food is a human or elven youth. Sometimes they charm villagers into regularly sacrificing maidens to them.

Combat

Because red dragons are so confident, they seldom pause to appraise an adversary. On spotting a target they make a snap decision whether to attack, using one of many strategies worked out ahead of time. A red dragon lands to attack small, weak creatures with its claws and bites rather than obliterating them with its breath weapon, so as not to destroy any treasure they might be carrying.

Breath Weapon (Su): A red dragon has one type of breath weapon, a cone of fire.

Fire Subtype (Ex): Fire immunity, double damage from cold except on a successful save.

Locate Object **(Sp):** The dragon can use this ability as the spell of the same name, once per day per age category.

Other Spell-Like Abilities: 3/day—*suggestion*; 1/day—*eyebite* and *discern location*.

Skills: Red dragons have the Jump skill for free at 1 rank per Hit Die.

White Dragon

Dragon (Cold)

Climate/Terrain: Any cold land and underground

Organization: Wyrmling, very young, young, juvenile, and young adult: solitary or clutch (2–5); adult, mature adult, old,

very old, ancient, wyrm, or great wyrm: solitary, pair, or family (1–2 and 2–5 offspring)

Challenge Ratings: Wyrmling 1; very young 2; young 3; juvenile 5; young adult 7; adult 9; mature adult 11; old 14; very old 16; ancient 17; wyrm 18; great wyrm 20

Treasure: Double standard

Alignment: Always chaotic evil

Advancement: Wyrmling 4–5 HD (Tiny); very young 7–8 HD (Small); young 10–11 HD (Medium-size); juvenile 13–14 HD (Medium-size); young adult 16–17 HD (Large); adult 19–20 HD (Large); mature adult 22–23 HD (Huge); old 25–26 HD (Huge); very old 28–29 HD (Huge); ancient 31–32 HD (Huge); wyrm 34–35 HD (Gargantuan); great wyrm 37+ HD (Gargantuan)

Among the smallest and least intelligent of dragonkind, most white dragons are simply animalistic predators. Their faces express single-minded ferocity rather than the shrewdness of their more powerful kin.

The scales of a wyrmling white dragon glisten like mirrors. As the dragon ages, the sheen disappears, and by very old age, scales of pale blue and light gray are mixed in with the white. A white dragon is distinguished by a beaked, crested head and is accompanied by a crisp, faintly chemical odor.

White dragons' lairs are usually icy caves and deep subterranean chambers that open away from the warming rays of the sun. They store all of their treasure within the lair, preferably in caverns coated in ice, which reflect the gems. White dragons are especially fond of diamonds.

Although white dragons, as all others, are able to eat nearly anything, they are very particular and will consume only food that has been frozen. Usually a dragon devours a creature killed by its breath weapon while the carcass is still stiff and frigid. It buries other kills in snowbanks until they are suitably frozen.

White dragons' natural enemies are frost giants, who kill the dragons for food and armor and capture them to use as guards.

Combat

White dragons prefer sudden assaults, swooping down from aloft or bursting from beneath water, snow, or ice. They loose their breath weapon, then try to knock out a single opponent with a follow-up attack.

Breath Weapon (Su): A white dragon has one type of breath weapon, a cone of cold.

Cold Subtype (Ex): Cold immunity, double damage from fire except on a successful save.

Icewalking (Ex): This ability works like the *spider climb* spell, but the surfaces the dragon climbs must be icy. It is always in effect.

Freezing Fog **(Sp):** The dragon can use this ability three times per day. It is similar to a *solid fog* spell but also causes a rime of slippery ice to form on any surface the fog touches, creating the effect of a *grease* spell. The dragon is immune to the *grease* effect because of its ice-walking ability.

Other Spell-Like Abilities: 3/day—*gust of wind, fog cloud, wall of ice*; 1/day—*control weather.*

WHITE DRAGONS BY AGE

Age	Size	Hit Dice (hp)	AC	Attack Bonus	Fort Save	Ref Save	Will Save	Breath Weapon (DC)	Fear DC	SR
Wyrmling	T	3d12+3 (22)	14 (+2 size, +2 natural)	+5	+4	+3	+3	1d6 (12)	—	—
Very young	S	6d12+6 (45)	16 (+1 size, +5 natural)	+8	+6	+5	+5	2d6 (14)	—	—
Young	M	9d12+18 (76)	18 (+8 natural)	+11	+8	+6	+6	3d6 (16)	—	—
Juvenile	M	12d12+24 (102)	21 (+11 natural)	+15	+10	+8	+8	4d6 (18)	—	—
Young adult	L	15d12+45 (142)	23 (−1 size, +14 natural)	+18	+12	+9	+9	5d6 (20)	16	16
Adult	L	18d12+72 (189)	26 (−1 size, +17 natural)	+23	+15	+11	+11	6d6 (23)	19	18
Mature adult	H	21d12+105 (241)	28 (−2 size, +20 natural)	+27	+17	+12	+13	7d6 (25)	21	20
Old	H	24d12+120 (276)	31 (−2 size, +23 natural)	+31	+19	+14	+15	8d6 (27)	23	21
Very old	H	27d12+162 (337)	34 (−2 size, +26 natural)	+35	+21	+15	+17	9d6 (29)	25	23
Ancient	H	30d12+180 (375)	37 (−2 size, +29 natural)	+39	+23	+17	+19	10d6 (31)	27	24
Wyrm	G	33d12+231 (445)	38 (−4 size, +32 natural)	+41	+25	+18	+20	11d6 (33)	29	25
Great wyrm	G	36d12+288 (522)	41 (−4 size, +35 natural)	+45	+28	+20	+24	12d6 (36)	32	27

WHITE DRAGON ABILITIES BY AGE

Age	Speed	Str	Dex	Con	Int	Wis	Cha	Special Abilities	Caster Level
Wyrmling	60 ft., fly 150 ft. (average), swim 60 ft., burrow 30 ft.	11	10	13	6	11	6	Cold subtype, icewalking	—
Very young	60 ft., fly 150 ft. (average), swim 60 ft., burrow 30 ft.	13	10	13	6	11	6		—
Young	60 ft., fly 200 ft. (poor), swim 60 ft., burrow 30 ft.	15	10	15	6	11	6		
Juvenile	60 ft., fly 200 ft. (poor), swim 60 ft., burrow 30 ft.	17	10	15	8	11	8	Fog cloud	—
Young adult	60 ft., fly 200 ft. (poor), swim 60 ft., burrow 30 ft.	19	10	17	8	11	8	Damage reduction 5/+1	—
Adult	60 ft., fly 200 ft. (poor), swim 60 ft., burrow 30 ft.	23	10	19	10	11	10	Gust of wind	1st
Mature adult	60 ft., fly 200 ft. (poor), swim 60 ft., burrow 30 ft.	27	10	21	12	13	12	Damage reduction 10/+1	3rd
Old	60 ft., fly 200 ft. (poor), swim 60 ft., burrow 30 ft.	29	10	21	12	13	12	Freezing fog	5th
Very old	60 ft., fly 200 ft. (poor), swim 60 ft., burrow 30 ft.	31	10	23	14	15	14	Damage reduction 15/+2	7th
Ancient	60 ft., fly 200 ft. (poor), swim 60 ft., burrow 30 ft.	33	10	23	14	15	14	Wall of ice	9th
Wyrm	60 ft., fly 250 ft. (clumsy), swim 60 ft., burrow 30 ft.	35	10	25	14	15	16	Damage reduction 20/+3	11th
Great wyrm	60 ft., fly 250 ft. (clumsy), swim 60 ft., burrow 30 ft.	37	10	27	18	19	18	Control weather	13th

METALLIC DRAGONS

Metallic dragons make up the good branch of dragonkind but are every bit as aggressive as their evil cousins when threatened or challenged. They also tend to be covetous and proud.

Brass Dragon

Dragon (Fire)
Climate/Terrain: Temperate and warm desert, plains, and underground
Organization: Wyrmling, very young, young, juvenile, and young adult: solitary or clutch (2–5); adult, mature adult, old, very old, ancient, wyrm, or great wyrm: solitary, pair, or family (1–2 and 2–5 offspring)
Challenge Ratings: Wyrmling 2; very young 3; young 5; juvenile 7; young adult 9; adult 11; mature adult 14; old 16; very old 18; ancient 19; wyrm 20; great wyrm 22
Treasure: Double standard
Alignment: Always chaotic good
Advancement: Wyrmling 5–6 HD (Tiny); very young 8–9 HD (Small); young 11–12 HD (Medium-size); juvenile 14–15 HD (Medium-size); young adult 17–18 HD (Large); adult 20–21 HD (Large); mature adult 23–24 HD (Huge); old 26–27 HD (Huge); very old 29–30 HD (Huge); ancient 32–33 HD (Huge); wyrm 35–36 HD (Gargantuan); great wyrm 38+ HD (Gargantuan)

Illus. by T. Lockwood

Brass dragons are talkative and have supple, expressive lips. They may have useful information, but usually share it only after long rambling and hinting for a gift.

At birth, a brass dragon's scales are a dull, mottled brown. As the dragon gets older, the scales become more brassy until they reach a warm, burnished appearance. Their grand head-plates are

BRASS DRAGONS BY AGE

Age	Size	Hit Dice (hp)	AC	Attack Bonus	Fort Save	Ref Save	Will Save	Breath Weapon (DC)	Fear DC	SR
Wyrmling	T	4d12+4 (30)	15 (+2 size, +3 natural)	+6	+5	+4	+4	1d6 (13)	—	—
Very young	S	7d12+7 (52)	17 (+1 size, +6 natural)	+9	+6	+5	+5	2d6 (14)	—	—
Young	M	10d12+20 (85)	19 (+9 natural)	+12	+9	+7	+8	3d6 (17)	—	—
Juvenile	M	13d12+26 (110)	22 (+12 natural)	+16	+10	+8	+9	4d6 (18)	—	—
Young adult	L	16d12+48 (152)	24 (−1 size, +15 natural)	+19	+13	+10	+12	5d6 (21)	20	18
Adult	L	19d12+76 (199)	27 (−1 size, +18 natural)	+24	+15	+11	+13	6d6 (23)	21	20
Mature adult	H	22d12+110 (253)	29 (−2 size, +21 natural)	+28	+18	+13	+16	7d6 (26)	24	22
Old	H	25d12+125 (287)	32 (−2 size, +24 natural)	+32	+19	+14	+17	8d6 (27)	25	24
Very old	H	28d12+168 (350)	35 (−2 size, +27 natural)	+36	+22	+16	+20	9d6 (30)	28	25
Ancient	H	31d12+186 (387)	38 (−2 size, +30 natural)	+40	+23	+17	+21	10d6 (31)	29	27
Wyrm	G	34d12+238 (459)	39 (−4 size, +33 natural)	+42	+26	+19	+24	11d6 (34)	32	28
Great wyrm	G	37d12+296 (536)	42 (−4 size, +36 natural)	+46	+28	+20	+25	12d6 (36)	33	30

BRASS DRAGON ABILITIES BY AGE

Age	Speed	Str	Dex	Con	Int	Wis	Cha	Special Abilities	Caster Level*
Wyrmling	60 ft., fly 150 ft. (average), burrow 30 ft.	11	10	13	10	11	10	Fire subtype, speak with animals	—
Very young	60 ft., fly 150 ft. (average), burrow 30 ft.	13	10	13	10	11	10		—
Young	60 ft., fly 200 ft. (poor), burrow 30 ft.	15	10	15	12	13	12		1st
Juvenile	60 ft., fly 200 ft. (poor), burrow 30 ft.	17	10	15	12	13	12	Endure elements	3rd
Young adult	60 ft., fly 200 ft. (poor), burrow 30 ft.	19	10	17	14	15	14	Damage reduction 5/+1	5th
Adult	60 ft., fly 200 ft. (poor), burrow 30 ft.	23	10	19	14	15	14	Suggestion	7th
Mature adult	60 ft., fly 200 ft. (poor), burrow 30 ft.	27	10	21	16	17	16	Damage reduction 10/+1	9th
Old	60 ft., fly 200 ft. (poor), burrow 30 ft.	29	10	21	16	17	16	Control winds	11th
Very old	60 ft., fly 200 ft. (poor), burrow 30 ft.	31	10	23	18	19	18	Damage reduction 15/+2	13th
Ancient	60 ft., fly 200 ft. (poor), burrow 30 ft.	33	10	23	18	19	18	Control weather	15th
Wyrm	60 ft., fly 250 ft. (clumsy), burrow 30 ft.	35	10	25	20	21	20	Damage reduction 20/+3	17th
Great wyrm	60 ft., fly 250 ft. (clumsy), burrow 30 ft.	37	10	27	20	21	20	Summon djinni	19th

*Can also cast cleric spells and those from the Chaos and Knowledge domains as arcane spells.

smooth and metallic, and they sport bladed chin horns that grow sharper with age. Wings and frills are mottled green toward the edges, darkening with age. As the dragon grows older, its pupils fade until the eyes resemble molten metal orbs.

Brass dragons love intense, dry heat and spend most of their time basking in the desert sun. They are accompanied by a tangy metallic or sandy odor. They lair in high caves, preferably facing east to enjoy the morning warmth, and their territories always contain several spots where they can sunbathe and trap unwary travelers in conversation.

Brass dragons can and will eat almost anything if the need arises but normally consume very little. They are able to get nourishment from the morning dew, a rare commodity in their habitat, and have been seen carefully lifting it off plants with their long tongues.

Because they share the same habitat, blue dragons are brass dragons' worst enemies. The larger blues have the advantage in one-on-one confrontations, so brass dragons usually try to evade them until they can rally their neighbors for a mass attack.

Combat

Brass dragons would rather talk than fight. If an intelligent creature tries to leave without engaging in conversation, the dragon might force compliance in a fit of pique, using *suggestion* or a dose of *sleep* gas. A creature put to sleep may wake to find itself pinned or buried to the neck in the sand until the dragon's thirst for small talk is slaked. When faced with real danger, younger brass dragons fly out of sight, then hide by burrowing into the sand. Older dragons spurn this ploy but prefer to have the advantage in combat.

Breath Weapon (Su): A brass dragon has two types of breath weapon, a line of fire or a cone of *sleep*. Creatures within the cone must succeed at a Will save or fall asleep, regardless of HD, for 1d6 rounds plus 1 round per age category of the dragon.

Fire Subtype (Ex): Fire immunity, double damage from cold except on a successful save.

Spell-Like Abilities: At will—*speak with animals*; 3/day—*endure elements* (radius 10 ft. × dragon's age category); 1/day—*suggestion*, *control winds*, and *control weather*.

Summon Djinni (Sp): This ability works like a *summon monster* spell, except that it summons one djinni.

Bronze Dragon

Dragon (Water)
Climate/Terrain: Temperate and warm aquatic and underground
Organization: Wyrmling, very young, young, juvenile, and young adult: solitary or clutch (2–5); adult, mature adult, old, very old, ancient, wyrm, or great wyrm: solitary, pair, or family (1–2 and 2–5 offspring)
Challenge Ratings: Wyrmling 2; very young 4; young 6; juvenile 8; young adult 11; adult 14; mature adult 16; old 18; very old 19; ancient 21; wyrm 22; great wyrm 24
Treasure: Double standard
Alignment: Always lawful good
Advancement: Wyrmling 7–8 HD (Small); very young 10–11 HD (Medium-size); young 13–14 HD (Medium-size); juvenile 16–17 HD (Large); young adult 19–20 HD (Large); adult 22–23 HD (Huge); mature adult 25–26 HD (Huge); old 28–29 HD (Huge); very old 31–32 HD (Huge); ancient 34–35 HD (Gargantuan); wyrm 37–38 HD (Gargantuan); great wyrm 40+ HD (Gargantuan)

Bronze dragons are inquisitive and enjoy polymorphing into small, friendly animals to observe adventurers. They are fascinated by warfare, eagerly joining an army for a just cause—and good pay.

A bronze wyrmling's scales are yellow tinged with green, showing only a hint of bronze. As the dragon approaches adulthood, its color deepens slowly to a darker,

Illus. by T. Lockwood

BRONZE DRAGONS BY AGE

Age	Size	Hit Dice (hp)	AC	Attack Bonus	Fort Save	Ref Save	Will Save	Breath Weapon (DC)	Fear DC	SR
Wyrmling	S	6d12+6 (45)	16 (+1 size, +5 natural)	+8	+6	+5	+7	2d6 (14)	—	—
Very young	M	9d12+18 (76)	18 (+8 natural)	+11	+8	+6	+8	4d6 (16)	—	—
Young	M	12d12+24 (102)	21 (+11 natural)	+15	+10	+8	+11	6d6 (18)	—	—
Juvenile	L	15d12+45 (142)	23 (−1 size, +14 natural)	+18	+12	+9	+13	8d6 (20)	—	—
Young adult	L	18d12+72 (189)	26 (−1 size, +17 natural)	+23	+15	+11	+15	10d6 (23)	23	20
Adult	H	21d12+105 (241)	28 (−2 size, +20 natural)	+27	+17	+12	+17	12d6 (25)	25	22
Mature adult	H	24d12+120 (276)	31 (−2 size, +23 natural)	+31	+19	+14	+19	14d6 (27)	27	23
Old	H	27d12+162 (337)	34 (−2 size, +26 natural)	+35	+21	+15	+21	16d6 (29)	29	25
Very old	H	30d12+180 (375)	37 (−2 size, +29 natural)	+39	+23	+17	+23	18d6 (31)	31	26
Ancient	G	33d12+231 (445)	38 (−4 size, +32 natural)	+41	+25	+18	+25	20d6 (33)	33	28
Wyrm	G	36d12+288 (522)	41 (−4 size, +35 natural)	+45	+28	+20	+28	22d6 (36)	36	29
Great wyrm	G	39d12+312 (565)	44 (−4 size, +38 natural)	+49	+29	+21	+29	24d6 (37)	37	31

BRONZE DRAGON ABILITIES BY AGE

Age	Speed	Str	Dex	Con	Int	Wis	Cha	Special Abilities	Caster Level
Wyrmling	40 ft., fly 100 ft. (average), swim 60 ft.	13	10	13	14	15	14	Electricity immunity, water breathing, speak with animals	—
Very young	40 ft., fly 150 ft. (poor), swim 60 ft.	15	10	15	14	15	14		—
Young	40 ft., fly 150 ft. (poor), swim 60 ft.	17	10	15	16	17	16	Polymorph self	1st
Juvenile	40 ft., fly 150 ft. (poor), swim 60 ft.	19	10	17	18	19	18		3rd
Young adult	40 ft., fly 150 ft. (poor), swim 60 ft.	23	10	19	18	19	18	Damage reduction 5/+1	5th
Adult	40 ft., fly 150 ft. (poor), swim 60 ft.	27	10	21	20	21	20	Create food and water, fog cloud	7th
Mature adult	40 ft., fly 150 ft. (poor), swim 60 ft.	29	10	21	20	21	20	Damage reduction 10/+1	9th
Old	40 ft., fly 150 ft. (poor), swim 60 ft.	31	10	23	22	23	22	Detect thoughts	11th
Very old	40 ft., fly 150 ft. (poor), swim 60 ft.	33	10	23	22	23	22	Damage reduction 15/+2	13th
Ancient	40 ft., fly 200 ft. (clumsy), swim 60 ft.	35	10	25	24	25	24	Control water	15th
Wyrm	40 ft., fly 200 ft. (clumsy), swim 60 ft.	37	10	27	26	27	26	Damage reduction 20/+3	17th
Great wyrm	40 ft., fly 200 ft. (clumsy), swim 60 ft.	39	10	27	26	27	26	Control weather	19th

*Can also cast cleric spells and those from the Animal, Law, and Water domains as arcane spells.

rich bronze tone. Very old dragons develop a blue-black tint to the edges of their scales. Powerful swimmers, they have webbed feet and smooth, flat scales. Its pupils fade as a dragon ages, until in the oldest the eyes resemble glowing green orbs.

Bronze dragons like to be near deep fresh water or salt water. They often visit the depths to cool off or hunt for pearls and sunken treasure. They prefer caves that are accessible only from the water, but their lairs are always dry—they do not lay eggs, sleep, or store treasure underwater. A smell of sea spray lingers about them. Bronze dragons eat aquatic plants and some varieties of seafood. They especially prize shark meat. They also dine on an occasional pearl.

Combat

Bronze dragons dislike killing animals and would rather bribe them (perhaps with food) or force them away magically. They use *detect thoughts* to learn intelligent creatures' intentions. When attacking they blind their opponents with *fog cloud* and then charge, or if flying, snatch them up. Against seafaring opponents they conjure up a storm or use their tails to smash the vessels' hulls. If a dragon is inclined to be lenient, ships might be merely becalmed, fogbound, or broken-masted.

Breath Weapon (Su): Bronze dragons have two types of breath weapon, a line of lightning or a cone of *repulsion* gas. Creatures within the cone must succeed at a Will save or be compelled to do nothing but move away from the dragon for 1d6 rounds plus 1 round per age category of the dragon. This is a mind-influencing compulsion enchantment.

Water Breathing (Ex): A bronze dragon can breathe underwater indefinitely and can freely use its breath weapon, spells, and other abilities while submerged.

Spell-Like Abilities: At will—*speak with animals;* 3/day—*create food and water, polymorph self, fog cloud, detect thoughts, control water;* 1/day—*control weather.* A bronze dragon's *polymorph self* ability works just like the spell, except that each use allows only one change, which lasts until the dragon assumes another form or reverts to its own (which does not count as a use of this ability).

Copper Dragon

Dragon (Earth)

Climate/Terrain: Temperate and warm desert, hill, mountains, and underground

Organization: Wyrmling, very young, young, juvenile, and young adult: solitary or clutch (2–5); adult, mature adult, old, very old, ancient, wyrm, or great wyrm: solitary, pair, or family (1–2 and 2–5 offspring)

Challenge Ratings: Wyrmling 2; very young 4; young 6; juvenile 8; young adult 10; adult 13; mature adult 15; old 18; very old 19; ancient 21; wyrm 22; great wyrm 24

Treasure: Double standard

Alignment: Always chaotic good

Advancement: Wyrmling 6–7 HD (Tiny); very young 9–10 HD (Small); young 12–13 HD (Medium-size); juvenile 15–16 HD (Medium-size); young adult 18–19 HD (Large); adult 21–22 HD (Large); mature adult 24–25 HD (Huge); old 27–28 HD (Huge); very old 30–31 HD (Huge); ancient 33–34 HD (Huge); wyrm 36–37 HD (Gargantuan); great wyrm 39+ HD (Gargantuan)

Copper dragons are incorrigible pranksters, joke tellers, and riddlers. Most are good-natured but also have a covetous, miserly streak. They are powerful jumpers and climbers, with massive thighs and shoulders.

At birth, a copper dragon's scales have a ruddy brown color with a metallic tint. As the dragon gets older, the scales become finer and more coppery, assuming a soft, warm gloss by the young adult stage. Very old dragons' scales pick up a green tint. A copper dragon's pupils fade with age, and the eyes of great wyrms resemble glowing turquoise orbs.

Copper dragons like dry, rocky uplands and mountains. They lair in narrow caves and often conceal the entrances using *move earth* and *stone shape.* Within the lair, they construct twisting mazes with open tops that allow the dragon to fly or jump over intruders.

Copper dragons are determined hunters, considering good sport at least as important as the food. They are known to eat almost anything, including metal ores. However, they prize monstrous scorpions and other large poisonous creatures (they say the venom sharpens their wit). The dragon's digestive system can

COPPER DRAGONS BY AGE

Age	Size	Hit Dice (hp)	AC	Attack Bonus	Fort Save	Ref Save	Will Save	Breath Weapon (DC)	Fear DC	SR
Wyrmling	T	5d12+5 (37)	16 (+2 size, +4 natural)	+7	+5	+4	+5	2d4 (13)	—	—
Very young	S	8d12+8 (60)	18 (+1 size, +7 natural)	+10	+7	+6	+7	4d4 (15)	—	—
Young	M	11d12+22 (93)	20 (+10 natural)	+13	+9	+7	+9	6d4 (17)	—	—
Juvenile	M	14d12+28 (119)	23 (+13 natural)	+17	+11	+9	+11	8d4 (19)	—	—
Young adult	L	17d12+51 (161)	25 (−1 size, +16 natural)	+20	+13	+10	+13	10d4 (21)	21	19
Adult	L	20d12+80 (210)	28 (−1 size, +19 natural)	+25	+16	+12	+15	12d4 (24)	23	21
Mature adult	H	23d12+115 (264)	30 (−2 size, +22 natural)	+29	+18	+13	+17	14d4 (27)	25	23
Old	H	26d12+130 (299)	33 (−2 size, +25 natural)	+33	+20	+15	+19	16d4 (28)	27	25
Very old	H	29d12+174 (362)	36 (−2 size, +28 natural)	+37	+22	+16	+21	18d4 (30)	29	26
Ancient	H	32d12+192 (400)	39 (−2 size, +31 natural)	+41	+24	+18	+23	20d4 (32)	31	28
Wyrm	G	35d12+245 (472)	40 (−4 size, +34 natural)	+43	+26	+19	+25	22d4 (34)	33	29
Great wyrm	G	38d12+304 (551)	43 (−4 size, +37 natural)	+47	+29	+21	+27	24d4 (37)	35	31

COPPER DRAGON ABILITIES BY AGE

Age	Speed	Str	Dex	Con	Int	Wis	Cha	Special Abilities	Caster Level
Wyrmling	40 ft., fly 100 ft. (average)	11	10	13	12	13	12	Acid immunity, spider climb	—
Very young	40 ft., fly 100 ft. (average)	13	10	13	12	13	12		—
Young	40 ft., fly 150 ft. (poor)	15	10	15	14	15	14		1st
Juvenile	40 ft., fly 150 ft. (poor)	17	10	15	14	15	14		3rd
Young adult	40 ft., fly 150 ft. (poor)	19	10	17	16	17	16	Damage reduction 5/+1	5th
Adult	40 ft., fly 150 ft. (poor)	23	10	19	16	17	16	Stone shape	7th
Mature adult	40 ft., fly 150 ft. (poor)	27	10	21	18	19	18	Damage reduction 10/+1	9th
Old	40 ft., fly 150 ft. (poor)	29	10	21	18	19	18	Transmute rock to mud/mud to rock	11th
Very old	40 ft., fly 150 ft. (poor)	31	10	23	20	21	20	Damage reduction 15/+2	13th
Ancient	40 ft., fly 150 ft. (poor)	33	10	23	20	21	20	Wall of stone	15th
Wyrm	40 ft., fly 200 ft. (clumsy)	35	10	25	22	23	22	Damage reduction 20/+3	17th
Great wyrm	40 ft., fly 200 ft. (clumsy)	37	10	27	22	23	22	Move earth	19th

*Can also cast cleric spells and those from the Chaos, Earth, and Trickery domains as arcane spells.

handle the venom safely, although injected venoms affect them normally.

Because copper dragons often inhabit hills in sight of red dragons' lairs, conflicts between the two varieties are inevitable. The smaller coppers usually run for cover until they can even the odds.

Combat

Copper dragons appreciate wit and don't usually harm creatures who can relate a joke, humorous story, or riddle they have not heard before. They quickly get annoyed with anyone who doesn't laugh at their jokes or accept their tricks with good humor. They like to taunt and annoy opponents into giving up or acting foolishly.

An angry copper dragon prefers to mire foes using *transmute rock to mud*. The dragon pushes trapped opponents into the mud or snatches and carries them aloft. A copper dragon tries to draw airborne enemies into narrow, stony gorges where it can use its *spider climb* ability and maneuver them into colliding with the walls.

Breath Weapon (Su): A copper dragon has two types of breath weapon, a line of acid or a cone of *slow* gas. Creatures within the cone must succeed at a Fortitude save or be slowed for 1d6 rounds plus 1 round per age category of the dragon.

Spider Climb (Ex): The dragon can climb on stone surfaces as though using the *spider climb* spell.

Spell-Like Abilities: 2/day—*stone shape*; 1/day—*transmute rock to mud* or *mud to rock*, *wall of stone*, and *move earth*.

Skills: Copper dragons have the Jump skill for free at 1 rank per Hit Die.

Illus. by T. Lockwood

Gold Dragon

Dragon (Fire)
Climate/Terrain: Any land and underground
Organization: Wyrmling, very young, young, juvenile, and young adult: solitary or clutch (2–5); adult, mature adult, old, very old, ancient, wyrm, or great wyrm: solitary, pair, or family (1–2 and 2–5 offspring)
Challenge Ratings: Wyrmling 4; very young 6; young 8; juvenile 10; young adult 13; adult 15; mature adult 18; old 20; very old 21; ancient 23; wyrm 24; great wyrm 26
Treasure: Double standard
Alignment: Always lawful good
Advancement: Wyrmling 9–10 HD (Medium-size); very young 12–13 HD (Large); young 15–16 HD (Large); juvenile 18–19 HD (Large); young adult 21–22 HD (Huge); adult 24–25 HD (Huge); mature adult 27–28 HD (Huge); old 30–31 HD (Gargantuan); very old 33–34 HD (Gargantuan); ancient 36–37 HD (Gargantuan); wyrm 39–40 HD (Colossal); great wyrm 42+ HD (Colossal)

Gold dragons are graceful, sinuous, and wise. They hate injustice and foul play, often embarking on self-appointed quests to promote good. A gold dragon usually assumes human or animal guise.

On hatching, a gold dragon's scales are dark yellow with golden metallic flecks. The flecks get larger as the dragon matures until, at the adult stage, the scales grow completely golden. Gold dragons' faces are bewhiskered and sagacious; as they age their pupils fade until the eyes resemble pools of molten gold. They smell of saffron and incense.

Gold dragons can live anywhere. Their lairs are secluded and always made of stone, whether caves or castles. These usually have loyal guards: animals appropriate to the terrain, storm giants, or good cloud giants. Giants usually form a mutual defensive agreement with a dragon.

Gold dragons usually sustain themselves on pearls or small gems. Such gifts are well received, as long as they are not bribes.

Combat

Gold dragons usually parley before fighting. When conversing with intelligent creatures they use *discern lies* and *detect gems* to gain the upper hand. In combat, they employ *bless* and their luck bonus; older dragons use their luck bonus at the start of each day. They make heavy use of spells in combat. Among their favorites are *cloudkill*, *delayed blast fireball*, *fire shield*, *globe of invulnerability*, *maze*, *slow*, and *stinking cloud*.

Breath Weapon (Su): A gold dragon has two forms of breath weapon, a cone of fire or a cone of weakening gas. Creatures within the latter must succeed at a Fortitude save or take 1 point of temporary Strength damage per age category of the dragon.

Fire Subtype (Ex): Fire immunity, double damage from cold except on a successful save.

Water Breathing (Ex): The dragon can breathe underwater indefinitely and can freely use its breath weapon, spells, and other abilities while submerged (the cone of fire becomes a cone of superheated steam underwater).

Luck Bonus (Sp): Once per day the dragon can touch one gem, usually embedded in the dragon's hide, and enchant it to bring good luck. As long as the dragon carries the gem, it and every good creature in a 10-foot radius per age category of the dragon receives a +1 luck bonus to all saving throws and similar dice rolls, as for a *stone of good luck* (see the item description on page 227 in the DUNGEON MASTER's Guide). If the dragon gives a gem to another creature, only that bearer gets the bonus. The enchantment lasts 1d3 hours plus 3 hours per age category of the dragon but ends if the gem is destroyed.

Detect Gems (Sp): The dragon can use this ability three times per day. This is a divination effect similar to a *detect magic* spell, except that it finds only gems. The dragon can scan a 60-degree arc each

GOLD DRAGONS BY AGE

Age	Size	Hit Dice (hp)	AC	Attack Bonus	Fort Save	Ref Save	Will Save	Breath Weapon (DC)	Fear DC	SR
Wyrmling	M	8d12+16 (68)	17 (+7 natural)	+11	+8	+6	+8	2d10 (16)	—	—
Very young	L	11d12+33 (104)	19 (–1 size, +10 natural)	+15	+10	+7	+10	4d10 (18)	—	—
Young	L	14d12+42 (133)	22 (–1 size, +13 natural)	+20	+12	+9	+12	6d10 (20)	—	—
Juvenile	L	17d12+68 (178)	25 (–1 size, +16 natural)	+25	+14	+10	+14	8d10 (22)	—	—
Young adult	H	20d12+100 (230)	27 (–2 size, +19 natural)	+28	+17	+12	+16	10d10 (25)	24	21
Adult	H	23d12+115 (264)	30 (–2 size, +22 natural	+32	+18	+13	+18	12d10 (26)	26	23
Mature adult	H	26d12+156 (325)	33 (–2 size, +25 natural)	+36	+21	+15	+20	14d10 (29)	28	25
Old	G	29d12+203 (391)	34 (–4 size, +28 natural)	+39	+23	+16	+23	16d10 (31)	31	27
Very old	G	32d12+256 (464)	37 (–4 size, +31 natural)	+43	+26	+18	+26	18d10 (34)	34	28
Ancient	G	35d12+315 (542)	40 (–4 size, +34 natural)	+47	+28	+19	+28	20d10 (36)	36	30
Wyrm	C	38d12+380 (627)	39 (–8 size, +37 natural)	+47	+31	+21	+31	22d10 (39)	39	31
Great wyrm	C	41d12+451 (717)	42 (–8 size, +40 natural)	+51	+33	+22	+33	24d10 (41)	41	33

GOLD DRAGON ABILITIES BY AGE

Age	Speed	Str	Dex	Con	Int	Wis	Cha	Special Abilities	Caster Level*
Wyrmling	60 ft., fly 200 ft. (poor), swim 60 ft.	17	10	15	14	15	14	Fire subtype, water breathing, polymorph self	—
Very young	60 ft., fly 200 ft. (poor), swim 60 ft.	21	10	17	16	17	16		—
Young	60 ft., fly 200 ft. (poor), swim 60 ft.	25	10	17	16	17	16		1st
Juvenile	60 ft., fly 200 ft. (poor), swim 60 ft.	29	10	19	18	19	18	Bless	3rd
Young adult	60 ft., fly 200 ft. (poor), swim 60 ft.	31	10	21	18	19	18	Damage reduction 5/+1	5th
Adult	60 ft., fly 200 ft. (poor), swim 60 ft.	33	10	21	20	21	20	Luck bonus	7th
Mature adult	60 ft., fly 200 ft. (poor), swim 60 ft.	35	10	23	20	21	20	Damage reduction 10/+1	9th
Old	60 ft., fly 250 ft. (clumsy), swim 60 ft.	39	10	25	24	25	24	Geas/quest, detect gems	11th
Very old	60 ft., fly 250 ft. (clumsy), swim 60 ft.	41	10	27	26	27	26	Damage reduction 15/+2	13th
Ancient	60 ft., fly 250 ft. (clumsy), swim 60 ft.	43	10	29	28	29	28	Sunburst	15th
Wyrm	60 ft., fly 250 ft. (clumsy), swim 60 ft.	45	10	31	30	31	30	Damage reduction 20/+3	17th
Great wyrm	60 ft., fly 250 ft. (clumsy), swim 60 ft.	47	10	33	32	33	32	Foresight	19th

*Can also cast cleric spells and those from the Law, Luck, and Good domains as arcane spells.

round: By concentrating for 1 round it knows if there are any gems within the arc; 2 rounds of concentration reveal the exact number of gems; and 3 rounds reveal their exact location, type, and value.

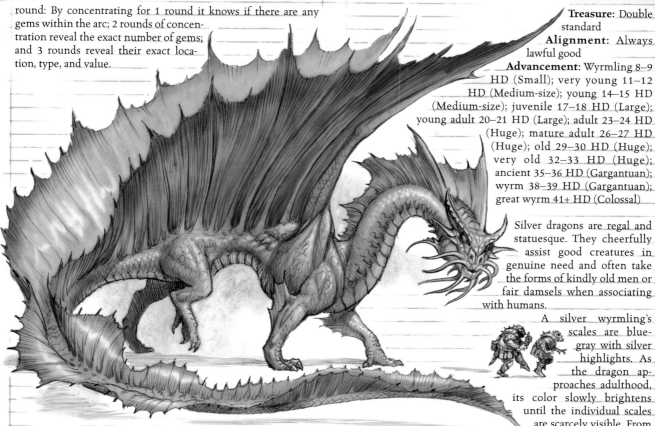

Treasure: Double standard

Alignment: Always lawful good

Advancement: Wyrmling 8–9 HD (Small); very young 11–12 HD (Medium-size); young 14–15 HD (Medium-size); juvenile 17–18 HD (Large); young adult 20–21 HD (Large); adult 23–24 HD (Huge); mature adult 26–27 HD (Huge); old 29–30 HD (Huge); very old 32–33 HD (Huge); ancient 35–36 HD (Gargantuan); wyrm 38–39 HD (Gargantuan); great wyrm 41+ HD (Colossal)

Silver dragons are regal and statuesque. They cheerfully assist good creatures in genuine need and often take the forms of kindly old men or fair damsels when associating with humans.

A silver wyrmling's scales are blue-gray with silver highlights. As the dragon approaches adulthood, its color slowly brightens until the individual scales are scarcely visible. From a distance, these dragons look as if they have been sculpted from pure metal. They are sometimes known as "shield dragons" because of the silvery plates on their heads. As a silver dragon grows older, its pupils fade until in the oldest the eyes resemble orbs of mercury.

Silver dragons prefer aerial lairs on secluded mountain peaks or amid the clouds themselves. A faint smell of rain always accompanies them. Even in clouds, though, the lair always has an enchanted area with a solid floor for laying eggs and storing treasure.

Silver dragons seem to prefer human form to their own, and they often have mortal companions, even forming deep friendships. Inevitably, however, a dragon resumes its true form and departs for a time. Silver dragons have a taste for human food and can live on such fare indefinitely.

Because they lair in similar territories, silver and red dragons often come into conflict. Duels between the two varieties are furious and deadly, but silver dragons generally get the upper hand by working together against their foes, often with human allies.

Other Spell-Like Abilities: 3/day—*polymorph self* and *bless*; 1/day—*geas/quest*, *sunburst*, and *foresight*. A gold dragon's *polymorph self* works just like the spell, except that each use allows only one change, which lasts until the dragon assumes another form or reverts to its own (which does not count as a use of this ability).

Skills: Gold dragons have the Jump skill for free at 1 rank per Hit Die.

Silver Dragon

Dragon (Air)

Climate/Terrain: Temperate and warm mountains and underground

Organization: Wyrmling, very young, young, juvenile, and young adult: solitary or clutch (2–5); adult, mature adult, old, very old, ancient, wyrm, or great wyrm: solitary, pair, or family (1–2 and 2–5 offspring)

Challenge Ratings: Wyrmling 3; very young 4; young 6; juvenile 9; young adult 12; adult 14; mature adult 17; old 19; very old 20; ancient 22; wyrm 23; great wyrm 25

Illus. by T. Lockwood

SILVER DRAGONS BY AGE

Age	Size	Hit Dice (hp)	AC	Attack Bonus	Fort Save	Ref Save	Will Save	Breath Weapon (DC)	Fear DC	SR
Wyrmling	S	7d12+7 (52)	17 (+1 size, +6 natural)	+9	+6	+5	+7	2d8 (14)	—	—
Very young	M	10d12+20 (85)	19 (+9 natural)	+12	+9	+7	+9	4d8 (17)	—	—
Young	M	13d12+26 (110)	22 (+12 natural)	+16	+10	+8	+11	6d8 (18)	—	—
Juvenile	L	16d12+48 (152)	24 (−1 size, +15 natural)	+19	+13	+10	+14	8d8 (21)	—	—
Young adult	L	19d12+76 (199)	27 (−1 size, +18 natural)	+24	+15	+11	+15	10d8 (23)	23	20
Adult	H	22d12+110 (253)	29 (−2 size, +21 natural)	+28	+18	+13	+18	12d8 (26)	26	22
Mature adult	H	25d12+125 (287)	32 (−2 size, +24 natural)	+32	+19	+14	+19	14d8 (27)	27	24
Old	H	28d12+168 (350)	35 (−2 size, +27 natural)	+36	+22	+16	+22	16d8 (30)	30	26
Very old	H	31d12+186 (387)	38 (−2 size, +30 natural)	+40	+23	+17	+24	18d8 (31)	32	27
Ancient	G	34d12+238 (459)	39 (−4 size, +33 natural)	+42	+26	+19	+27	20d8 (34)	35	29
Wyrm	G	37d12+333 (573)	42 (−4 size, +36 natural)	+47	+29	+20	+29	22d8 (36)	37	30
Great wyrm	C	40d12+400 (660)	41 (−8 size, +39 natural)	+48	+32	+22	+32	24d8 (39)	40	32

SILVER DRAGON ABILITIES BY AGE

Age	Speed	Str	Dex	Con	Int	Wis	Cha	Special Abilities	Caster Level
Wyrmling	40 ft., fly 100 ft. (average)	13	10	13	14	15	14	Cold and acid immunity, cloudwalking, polymorph self	—
Very young	40 ft., fly 150 ft. (poor)	15	10	15	14	15	14		—
Young	40 ft., fly 150 ft. (poor)	17	10	15	16	17	16		1st
Juvenile	40 ft., fly 150 ft. (poor)	19	10	17	18	19	18	Feather fall	3rd
Young adult	40 ft., fly 150 ft. (poor)	23	10	19	18	19	18	Damage reduction 5/+1	5th
Adult	40 ft., fly 150 ft. (poor)	27	10	21	20	21	20	Fog cloud	7th
Mature adult	40 ft., fly 150 ft. (poor)	29	10	21	20	21	20	Damage reduction 10/+1	9th
Old	40 ft., fly 150 ft. (poor)	31	10	23	22	23	22	Control winds	11th
Very old	40 ft., fly 150 ft. (poor)	33	10	23	24	25	24	Damage reduction 15/+2	13th
Ancient	40 ft., fly 200 ft. (clumsy)	35	10	25	26	27	26	Control weather	15th
Wyrm	40 ft., fly 200 ft. (clumsy)	39	10	29	28	29	28	Damage reduction 20/+3	17th
Great wyrm	40 ft., fly 200 ft. (clumsy)	43	10	31	30	31	30	Reverse gravity	19th

*Can also cast cleric spells and those from the Air, Good, Law, and Sun domains as arcane spells.

Combat

Silver dragons are not violent and avoid combat except when faced with highly evil or aggressive foes. If necessary, they use *fog cloud* or *control weather* to blind or confuse opponents before attacking. When angry, they use *reverse gravity* to fling enemies helplessly into the air, where they can be snatched. Against flying opponents, a silver dragon hides in clouds (creating some with *control weather* on clear days), then jumps to the attack when it has the advantage.

Breath Weapon (Su): A silver dragon has two types of breath weapon, a cone of cold or a cone of paralyzing gas. Creatures within the latter must succeed at a Fortitude save or be paralyzed for 1d6 rounds plus 1 round per age category of the dragon.

Cloudwalking (Su): The dragon can tread on clouds or fog as though on solid ground. The ability functions continuously but can be negated or resumed at will.

Spell-Like Abilities: 3/day—*polymorph self, fog cloud, control winds*; 2/day—*feather fall*; 1/day—*control weather* and *reverse gravity*. A silver dragon's *polymorph self* works just like the spell, except that each use allows only one change, which lasts until the dragon assumes another form or reverts to its own (which does not count as a use of this ability).

Skills: Silver dragons have the Jump skill for free at 1 rank per Hit Die.

DRAGON TURTLE

Huge Dragon (Aquatic)
Hit Dice: 12d12+60 (138 hp)
Initiative: +0
Speed: 20 ft., swim 30 ft.
AC: 20 (–2 size, +12 natural)
Attacks: Bite +18 melee, 2 claws +13 melee
Damage: Bite 4d6+8, claw 2d8+4
Face/Reach: 30 ft. by 40 ft./10 ft.
Special Attacks: Breath weapon, snatch, capsize
Special Qualities: Scent, fire immunity
Saves: Fort +13, Ref +8, Will +9
Abilities: Str 27, Dex 10, Con 21, Int 12, Wis 13, Cha 12*
Skills: Hide +7*, Intimidate +16, Intuit Direction +10, Listen +18, Search +16, Spot +18
Feats: Alertness, Blind-Fight, Cleave, Power Attack

Climate/Terrain: Temperate aquatic
Organization: Solitary
Challenge Rating: 9
Treasure: Triple standard
Alignment: Usually neutral
Advancement: 13–24 HD (Huge); 25–36 HD (Gargantuan)

Dragon turtles are one of the most beautiful, awesome, and feared creatures of the water. Deadly jaws, steaming breath, and a penchant for capsizing ships make them dreaded by mariners.

A surfacing dragon turtle is sometimes mistaken for the reflection of the sun or moon on the water. Its rough, deep green shell is much the same color as the deep water the monster favors, and the silver highlights that line the shell resemble light dancing on open water. The turtle's legs, tail, and head are a lighter green,

Illus. by T. Lockwood

flecked with golden highlights. The head is crested by golden spines with dark green webbing connecting them. An dragon adult turtle can measure over 40 feet from snout to tail, with a shell up to 30 feet in diameter, and can weigh 32,000 pounds.

Dragon turtles speak Aquan, Draconic, and Common.

COMBAT

Dragon turtles are fierce fighters and generally attack any creature that threatens their territory or looks like a potential meal.

Breath Weapon (Su): Cloud of superheated steam 20 feet high, 25 feet wide, and 50 feet long, every 1d4 rounds; damage 20d6, Reflex half DC 21; effective both on the surface and underwater.

Snatch (Ex): A dragon turtle that hits with a bite attack attempts to start a grapple as a free action without provoking an attack of opportunity. If it gets a hold on a creature three or more sizes smaller, it seizes the creature with its mouth and automatically deals bite damage each round. If it does not move and takes no other action in combat, it deals double bite damage to the snatched creature. A snatched creature gets no saving throw against the dragon turtle's breath weapon.

The dragon turtle can drop a creature it has snatched as a free action or use a standard action to fling it aside. A flung creature travels 60 feet and takes 6d6 points of damage.

Capsize (Ex): A submerged dragon turtle that surfaces under a boat or ship less than 20 feet long capsizes the vessel 95% of the time. It has a 50% chance to capsize a vessel from 20 to 60 feet long and a 20% chance to capsize one over 60 feet long.

Skills: *Dragon turtles receive a +8 racial bonus to Hide checks when submerged.

DRAGONNE

Large Magical Beast
Hit Dice: 9d10+27 (76 hp)
Initiative: +6 (+2 Dex, +4 Improved Initiative)
Speed: 40 ft., fly 30 ft. (poor)
AC: 18 (−1 size, +2 Dex, +7 natural)
Attacks: Bite +12 melee, 2 claws +7 melee
Damage: Bite 2d6+4, claw 2d4+2
Face/Reach: 5 ft. by 10 ft./5 ft.
Special Attacks: Roar
Special Qualities: Scent
Saves: Fort +9, Ref +8, Will +4
Abilities: Str 19, Dex 15, Con 17, Int 6, Wis 12, Cha 12
Skills: Listen +12, Spot +13
Feats: Blind-Fight, Improved Initiative

Climate/Terrain: Temperate and warm desert, hill, and underground
Organization: Solitary, pair, or pride (5–10)
Challenge Rating: 7
Treasure: Double standard
Alignment: Usually neutral
Advancement: 10–12 HD (Large); 13–27 HD (Huge)

Possessing some of the most dangerous qualities of a lion and a brass dragon, the dragonne is a vicious and deadly hunter.

From a distance, a dragonne looks much like a giant lion, with the notable exception of a pair of small, brass-colored wings that sprout from its shoulders. On closer inspection, other differences become apparent, too. It is covered with thick, brass-colored scales, much like a brass dragon, and its mane is much thicker and coarser than a lion's. The beast also possesses huge claws and fangs, and large eyes, usually the color of its scales. A dragonne is about 12 feet long and weighs about 700 pounds.

Dragonnes are not necessarily aggressive toward strangers. Their reputation as mindless devourers of helpless travelers is more the product of ignorance than well-researched fact. A dragonne almost always attacks a creature that invades its lair or threatens its territory, so adventurers who stumble across its cave or settlers in the area are often subject to fierce and immediate retaliation. Those not threatening the dragonne's lair or simply passing through its territory are usually left alone.

Dragonnes prefer herd animals such as goats for food, especially since they don't fight back as fiercely as humanoids. They attack humanoids only if no other game is available.

Dragonnes speak Draconic.

COMBAT

A dragonne's wings are useful only for short flights, carrying the creature for 10 to 30 minutes at a time. Nevertheless, it uses its wings effectively in battle. If opponents attempt to charge or encircle it, the dragonne simply takes to the air and finds a more defensible position. Dragonnes prefer not to fight in the air, since they are very slow and maneuver poorly compared to most other flying creatures.

Roar (Su): A dragonne can loose a terrifying roar every 1d4 rounds. All creatures (except dragonnes) within 120 feet must succeed at a Will save (DC 15) or be weakened with fear, losing half their current Strength scores for 2d6 rounds. Those within 30 feet become deafened for 2d6 rounds. Creatures with 8 or fewer HD get no saving throw, but others can negate the effect with a successful Fortitude save (DC 15). Deafened creatures cannot be affected again by the dragonne's roar.

Skills: Dragonnes receive a +2 racial bonus to Listen and Spot checks.

DRIDER

Illus. by C. Arellano

Large Aberration
Hit Dice: 6d8+18 (45 hp)
Initiative: +2 (Dex)
Speed: 30 ft., climb 15 ft.
AC: 17 (–1 size, +2 Dex, +6 natural)
Attacks: 2 short swords +3 melee, bite +0 melee; or shortbow +5 ranged
Damage: Short sword 1d6+2, short sword 1d6+1, bite 1d4+1; shortbow 1d6
Face/Reach: 10 ft. by 10 ft./5 ft.
Special Attacks: Spells, spell-like abilities, poison
Special Qualities: SR 14
Saves: Fort +5, Ref +4, Will +8
Abilities: Str 15, Dex 15, Con 16, Int 15, Wis 16, Cha 16
Skills: Climb +14, Concentration +10, Hide +8, Listen +9, Move Silently +7, Spellcraft +10, Spot +9
Feats: Ambidexterity, Combat Casting, Two-Weapon Fighting

Climate/Terrain: Underground
Organization: Solitary, pair, or troupe (1–2 plus 7–12 Medium-size monstrous spiders)
Challenge Rating: 7
Treasure: Double standard
Alignment: Always chaotic evil
Advancement: By character class

Driders are bloodthirsty creatures that lurk in the depths of the earth, seeking warm-blooded prey of any kind.

These strange beings have the head and torso of a drow and the legs and lower body of a giant spider. Driders are created by the drow's dark goddess, Lolth. When a dark elf of above-average ability reaches 6th level, the goddess may put him or her through a special test. Failures become driders.

Because they have failed their goddess's test, driders are outcasts from their own communities. Drow and driders hate one another passionately.

Driders speak Drow, Common, and Undercommon.

COMBAT

Driders seldom pass up an opportunity to attack other creatures, especially from ambush. They usually begin with a spell assault and often levitate out of the enemy's reach.

Spells: Driders may be 6th-level clerics, wizards, or sorcerers. Drider clerics can choose from the following domains: Chaos, Destruction, Evil, and Trickery.

Spell-Like Abilities: 1/day—*dancing lights, darkness, detect chaos, detect evil, detect good, detect law, detect magic, faerie fire,* and *levitate.* These abilities are as the spells cast by a 6th-level sorcerer (save DC 13 + spell level).

Once per day a drider cleric can additionally use *clairaudience/ clairvoyance, discern lies, dispel magic,* and *suggestion* as a 6th-level caster.

Poison (Ex): Bite, Fortitude save (DC 16), initial and secondary damage 1d6 temporary Strength.

Skills: A drider receives a +4 racial bonus to Hide and Move Silently checks.

DRYAD

Medium-Size Fey
Hit Dice: 2d6 (7 hp)
Initiative: +6 (+2 Dex, +4 Improved Initiative)
Speed: 30 ft.
AC: 12 (+2 Dex)
Attacks: Dagger +1 melee
Damage: Dagger 1d4
Face/Reach: 5 ft. by 5 ft./5 ft.
Special Attacks: Spell-like abilities
Special Qualities: Symbiosis
Saves: Fort +0, Ref +5, Will +5
Abilities: Str 10, Dex 15, Con 11, Int 14, Wis 15, Cha 18
Skills: Animal Empathy +9, Craft (any one) or Knowledge (any one) +6, Escape Artist +7, Hide +7, Listen +9, Move Silently +7, Sense Motive +7, Spot +9, Wilderness Lore +7
Feats: Alertness, Dodge, Improved Initiative

Climate/Terrain: Temperate and warm forest
Organization: Solitary or grove (4–7)
Challenge Rating: 1
Treasure: Standard
Alignment: Always chaotic good
Advancement: 3–4 HD (Medium-size)

Dryads are exquisitely beautiful tree sprites found deep in secluded woodlands. They sometimes aid adventurers and can prove a source of useful information.

These creatures remain something of a mystery even to other woodland beings. Tales tell of dryads who took a fancy to handsome elf or human men, charmed them, and held them captive. But since dryads rarely associate with any outside their own kind, these stories may be purely anecdotal.

A dryad's delicate features are much like an elf maiden's, with eyes always a striking color such as amber, violet, or emerald green. Complexion and hair color change with the seasons. During the spring and summer, the skin of a dryad is lightly tanned and the hair is green as oak leaves. In the fall, the hair turns golden or red, and the skin darkens to match. Finally, in the winter, both are white.

Although they are generally solitary, up to seven dryads have been encountered in one place on rare occasions.

Dryads speak Common, Elven, and Sylvan.

COMBAT

Shy, intelligent, and non-violent, dryads are as elusive as they are alluring—they shun combat and are rarely seen unless they wish to be. If threatened, a dryad uses *charm person*, attempting to gain control of the attacker(s) who could help the most against the rest. Any attack on her tree, however, will provoke the dryad into a frenzied defense.

Spell-Like Abilities: Dryads can communicate with plants at will (as *speak with plants*). They can also, at will, step inside any tree and use *dimension door* as cast by a 7th-level sorcerer to reach their own oak tree. A dryad can use *charm person* three times per day, as cast by a 4th-level sorcerer; targets must succeed at a Will save (DC 15) or be charmed for 4 hours.

Symbiosis (Su): Each dryad is mystically bound to a single, enormous oak tree and must never stray more than 300 yards from it. Any who do become ill and die within 4d6 hours. A dryad's oak does not radiate magic.

Medium-Size Humanoid (Dwarf)
Hit Dice: 1d8+1 (5 hp)
Initiative: +0
Speed: 15 ft. (scale mail); base 20 ft.
AC: 16 (+4 scale mail, +2 large shield)
Attacks: Dwarven waraxe +1 melee; or shortbow+1 ranged
Damage: Dwarven waraxe 1d10; shortbow 1d6
Face/Reach: 5 ft. by 5 ft./5 ft.
Special Attacks: Dwarven traits
Special Qualities: Dwarven traits
Saves: Fort +3, Ref +0, Will +0
Abilities: Str 11, Dex 10, Con 13, Int 10, Wis 10, Cha 8
Skills: Appraise +2, Craft (metalworking) +2, Listen +2, Spot +2
Feats: Exotic Weapon Proficiency (dwarven waraxe)

Climate/Terrain: Any hill, mountains, and underground
 Deep, derro, duergar—Any underground
 Mountain—Any mountains and underground
Organization: Team (2–4), squad (11–20 plus 2 3rd-level sergeants and 1 leader of 3rd–6th level), or clan (30–100 plus 30% noncombatants plus 1 3rd-level sergeant per 10 adults, 5 5th-level lieutenants, and 3 7th-level captains)
Challenge Rating: 1/2 (hill, deep, mountain) or 1 (derro, duergar)
Treasure: Standard coins; double goods; standard items
Alignment: Usually lawful good
 Deep—Usually lawful neutral or neutral
 Derro—Usually chaotic evil
 Duergar—Usually lawful evil
 Mountain— Usually lawful good
Advancement: By character class

Dwarves are noble warriors who excel at metalcraft, stoneworking, and war. They tend to be serious, determined, and very honorable.

Averaging 4 feet tall and weighing as much as an adult human, a dwarf is stocky and muscular. The skin of a dwarf is light brown or deeply tanned, cheeks ruddy, eyes bright. The long hair is usually black, gray, or brown; males have long, carefully groomed beards and mustaches. Dwarves' clothing favors earth tones and tends to be simple and functional. They prefer to spend their time making masterpieces of stone, steel, and precious metals. They create durable weapons, craft beautiful jewelry, and cut superior gems. However, they consider it bad taste to flaunt wealth, so few wear jewelry other than one simple piece.

Dwarves speak Dwarven and Undercommon. Most who travel outside dwarven lands (as traders, mercenaries, or adventurers) know the Common tongue, while warriors in the dwarven cities usually learn Goblin to better interrogate and spy on those evil denizens of the deep caves.

Most dwarves encountered outside their home are warriors; the information in the statistics block is for one of 1st level (see page 39 in the DUNGEON MASTER's Guide for more about the warrior class).

COMBAT

Dwarves are experts in combat, effectively using their environment and executing well-planned group attacks. They rarely use magic in fights, since they have few wizards or sorcerers (but dwarven clerics throw themselves into battle as heartily as their fellow warriors). If they have time to prepare, they may build deadfalls or other traps involving stone. In addition to the dwarven waraxe and thrown hammer, dwarves also use warhammers, picks, shortbows, heavy crossbows, and maces.

Dwarven Traits (Ex): Dwarves benefit from a number of racial traits.

- +1 racial bonus to attack rolls against orcs and goblinoids, through special combat training.
- +2 racial bonus to Will saves against spells and spell-like abilities.
- +2 racial bonus to Fortitude saves against all poisons.
- +4 dodge bonus against giants, through special defensive training.
- Darkvision up to 60 feet.
- Stonecunning: Dwarves receive a +2 racial bonus to checks to notice unusual stonework. Something that isn't stone but is disguised as stone also counts as unusual stonework. A dwarf who merely comes within 10 feet of unusual stonework can make a check as though actively searching and can use the Search skill to find stonework traps as a rogue can. A dwarf can also intuit depth, sensing the approximate distance underground as naturally as a human can sense which way is up.

  Skills: Dwarves receive a +2 racial bonus to Appraise checks and Craft or Profession checks that are related to stone or metal.

DWARF SOCIETY

Dwarves prefer living in underground cities that they build around mines (although some live on surface outposts). Carved into solid stone, these cities take centuries to complete but remain for ages. Dwarf society is organized into clans, with distinct family lines within each. A clan is led by a hereditary ruler, usually a king or queen and direct descendant of the clan's founder. Dwarves are strongly loyal to their family, clan, monarch, and people as a whole; in conflicts with other races, even objective dwarves tend to side with their kinfolk. These ties have helped the dwarves survive generations of warfare against the evil creatures that live under the earth.

A dwarven city has noncombatant members (usually the young, elderly, and a few adults) equal to 30% of the fighting population; dwarven females are as numerous as males and are accepted in any part of dwarf society, including warriors.

Dwarven clans usually focus on one or two types of craft, such as blacksmithing, making weapons or armor, creating jewelry, engineering, or stonework. To avoid becoming overspecialized, dwarves apprentice some of their young ones to other clans; this practice also helps foster unity. Since dwarves live a long time, these apprenticeships can last many years, even well into adulthood.

The chief dwarf deity is Moradin, the god who created their race and the patron of smiths and other skilled craftworkers.

SUBRACES

The information above is for hill dwarves, the most common variety. There are four other major dwarven subraces, which differ from hill dwarves as follows.

Deep Dwarves

These dwarves live far underground and tend to be more standoffish with nondwarves. They are the same height as other dwarves, but leaner. Their skin sometimes has a reddish tinge, and their large eyes lack the brightness of their kindred, being a washed-out blue. Their hair ranges from bright red to straw blond. They have little contact with surface dwellers, relying on hill or mountain dwarves to trade goods for them. They speak Dwarven and Goblin, and occasionally Draconic or Undercommon.

The typical ability scores for a deep dwarf are Str 11, Dex 10, Con 13, Int 10, Wis 10, Cha 6.

Deep Dwarf Traits (Ex): These are in addition to the basic dwarf traits, except where noted here.
- Racial bonus to Will saves against spells and spell-like abilities increases to +3.
- Racial bonus to Fortitude saves against all poisons increases to +3.
- Darkvision up to 90 feet.
- *Light Sensitivity (Ex)*: Deep dwarves suffer a –1 circumstance penalty to attack rolls in bright sunlight or within the radius of a *daylight* spell.

Derro

Derro are degenerate and evil human–dwarf crossbreeds who live in the Underdark. Incredibly cruel, they enjoy taking slaves and torturing surface dwellers (especially humans) to death. Their skin is white with bluish undertones, their hair is pale yellow, their staring eyes white with no irises or pupils. They have humanlike body hair, and males have mustaches but no beards. Their clothes are woven from animal fur, and their armor is leather studded with copper and brass.

Derro are encountered only in squads or platoons, carrying daggers, spiked bucklers, and repeating light crossbows that fire poisoned bolts. This poison is either greenblood oil (see Poison, page 79 in the *DUNGEON MASTER's Guide*) or a substance that causes initial and secondary damage of 2d6 points of temporary Strength (Fortitude negates DC 14).

Most derro revere Diirinka, a chaotic deity of magic and cruelty. Derro have very few clerics, but those who follow this path can choose two of the following domains: Chaos, Destruction, Evil, and Trickery.

The derro's leaders are spellcasters called savants, whom derro follow fanatically. Derro savants are at least 5th-level sorcerers; they have one to three Knowledge skills (usually arcana and other esoteric fields) and are able to use any magic item or weapon. (Most of a savant's treasure is magic items.) A savant is accompanied by two lower-level students, each of which has one minor magic item. Savants use their spells to confuse and frustrate rather than kill, preferring to make slaves of defeated foes.

The typical ability scores for derro are Str 9, Dex 14, Con 13, Int 10, Wis 10, Cha 6.

Derro Traits (Ex): These are in addition to the basic dwarf traits, except where noted here.
- Spell resistance 18.
- Darkvision up to 30 feet.
- *Sunlight Vulnerability (Ex)*: Derro take 1 point of temporary Constitution damage for every hour they are exposed to sunlight, dying when their Constitution reaches 0. Lost Constitution points are recovered at the rate of 1 per day out of the sun.
- Blind-Fight feat.

Duergar

Sometimes called gray dwarves, these evil beings live in the Underdark. They are emaciated and nasty-looking, with gray hair and skin. Most duergar are bald (even the females), and they dress in drab clothing that is designed to blend into stone. In their lairs they may wear jewelry, but it is always kept dull. They war with other dwarves, even allying with other Underdark dwellers from time to time.

The duergar revere the deity Laduguer, a joyless god who demands constant toil.

A duergar's typical ability scores are Str 11, Dex 10, Con 13, Int 10, Wis 10, Cha 6.

Duergar Traits (Ex): These are in addition to the basic dwarf traits, except where noted here.

- +4 racial bonus to Move Silently checks.
- Immune to paralysis, phantasms, and magical or alchemical poisons (but not normal poisons).
- *Spell-Like Abilities:* 1/day—*enlarge* and *invisibility* as a wizard twice the duergar's level (minimum 3rd level); these affect only the duergar and whatever it carries.
- Darkvision up to 120 feet.
- *Light Sensitivity* (Ex): Duergar suffer a –2 circumstance penalty to attack rolls, saves, and checks in bright sunlight or within the radius of a *daylight* spell.
- Listen +1, Spot +1.
- Alertness feat.

Mountain Dwarves

Mountain dwarves live deeper under the mountains than hill dwarves but generally not as far beneath as deep dwarves. They average about 4 1/2 feet tall and have lighter skin and hair than hill dwarves. They claim they were the first dwarven race and that all other dwarves are descended from them, an attitude that contributes to their isolationism.

DWARF CHARACTERS

A dwarf's favored class is fighter. Most dwarf leaders are fighters or fighter/clerics.

ELEMENTAL

	Air Elemental, Small Small Elemental (Air)	Air Elemental, Medium Medium-Size Elemental (Air)	Air Elemental, Large Large Elemental (Air)
Hit Dice:	2d8 (9 hp)	4d8+8 (26 hp)	8d8+24 (60 hp)
Initiative:	+7 (+3 Dex, +4 Improved Initiative)	+9 (+5 Dex, +4 Improved Initiative)	+11 (+7 Dex, +4 Improved Initiative)
Speed:	Fly 100 ft. (perfect)	Fly 100 ft. (perfect)	Fly 100 ft. (perfect)
AC:	17 (+1 size, +3 Dex, +3 natural)	18 (+5 Dex, +3 natural)	20 (–1 size, +7 Dex, +4 natural)
Attacks:	Slam +5 melee	Slam +8 melee	Slam +12/+7 melee
Damage:	Slam 1d4	Slam 1d6+1	Slam 2d6+3
Face/Reach:	5 ft. by 5 ft./5 ft.	5 ft. by 5 ft./5 ft.	5 ft. by 5 ft./10 ft.
Special Attacks:	Air mastery, whirlwind	Air mastery, whirlwind	Air mastery, whirlwind
Special Qualities:	Elemental	Elemental	Elemental, damage reduction 10/+1
Saves:	Fort +0, Ref +6, Will +0	Fort +3, Ref +9, Will +1	Fort +5, Ref +13, Will +2
Abilities:	Str 10, Dex 17, Con 10, Int 4, Wis 11, Cha 11	Str 12, Dex 21, Con 14, Int 4, Wis 11, Cha 11	Str 14, Dex 25, Con 16, Int 6, Wis 11, Cha 11
Skills:	Listen +5, Spot +5	Listen +7, Spot +7	Listen +11, Spot +11
Feats:	Flyby Attack, Improved Initiative, Weapon Finesse (slam)	Flyby Attack, Improved Initiative, Weapon Finesse (slam)	Dodge, Flyby Attack, Improved Initiative, Weapon Finesse (slam)

	Air Elemental, Huge Huge Elemental (Air)	Air Elemental, Greater Huge Elemental (Air)	Air Elemental, Elder Huge Elemental (Air)
Hit Dice:	16d8+64 (136)	21d8+84 (178 hp)	24d8+96 (204 hp)
Initiative:	+13 (+9 Dex, +4 Improved Initiative)	+14 (+10 Dex, +4 Improved Initiative)	+15 (+11 Dex, +4 Improved Initiative)
Speed:	Fly 100 ft. (perfect)	Fly 100 ft. (perfect)	Fly 100 ft. (perfect)
AC:	21 (–2 size, +9 Dex, +4 natural)	26 (–2 size, +10 Dex, +8 natural)	27 (–2 size, +11 Dex, +8 natural)
Attacks:	Slam +19/+14/+9 melee	Slam +23/+18/+13 melee	Slam +27/+22/+17/+12 melee
Damage:	Slam 2d8+6	Slam 2d8+7	Slam 2d8+9
Face/Reach:	10 ft. by 5 ft./15 ft.	10 ft. by 5 ft./15 ft.	10 ft. by 5 ft./15 ft.
Special Attacks:	Air mastery, whirlwind	Air mastery, whirlwind	Air mastery, whirlwind
Special Qualities:	Elemental, damage reduction 10/+2	Elemental, damage reduction 10/+2	Elemental, damage reduction 15/+3
Saves:	Fort +9, Ref +19, Will +5	Fort +11, Ref +22, Will +7	Fort +12, Ref +25, Will +8
Abilities:	Str 18, Dex 29, Con 18, Int 6, Wis 11, Cha 11	Str 20, Dex 31, Con 18, Int 6, Wis 11, Cha 11	Str 22, Dex 33, Con 18, Int 6, Wis 11, Cha 11
Skills:	Listen +18, Spot +18	Listen +23, Spot +23	Listen +26, Spot +26
Feats:	Dodge, Flyby Attack, Improved Initiative, Weapon Finesse (slam)	Dodge, Flyby Attack, Improved Initiative, Mobility, Weapon Finesse (slam)	Dodge, Flyby Attack, Improved Initiative, Mobility, Weapon Finesse (slam)

Elementals are incarnations of the elements that compose existence. They are as wild and dangerous as the forces that birthed them.

COMBAT

Elementals have varied combat abilities and tactics, but all have the same elemental qualities.

Elemental: Immune to poison, sleep, paralysis, and stunning. Not subject to critical hits.

AIR ELEMENTAL

Air elementals are among the swiftest and most agile creatures in existence. They seldom leave their home plane except when summoned elsewhere by a spell.

An air elemental appears as an amorphous, shifting cloud. Darker bits of swirling vapor give the appearance of two eyes and a mouth.

Air elementals speak Auran, though they rarely choose to do so. Their voices sound like the high-pitched screech of a tornado or the low moan of a midnight storm.

Combat

Their rapid speed makes air elementals useful on vast battlefields or in extended aerial combat.

Air Mastery (Ex): Airborne creatures suffer a –1 penalty to attack and damage rolls against an air elemental.

Whirlwind (Su): The elemental can transform itself into a whirlwind once every 10 minutes and remain in that form for up to 1 round for every 2 HD it has. In this form, the elemental can move through the air or along a surface at its fly speed.

The whirlwind is 5 feet wide at the base, up to 30 feet wide at the top, and up to 50 feet tall, depending on the elemental's size. The elemental controls the exact height, but it must be at least 10 feet.

Creatures one or more sizes smaller than the elemental might take damage when caught in the whirlwind (see the following table for details) and may be lifted into the air. An affected creature must succeed at a Reflex save when it comes into contact with the whirlwind or take the listed damage. It must also succeed at a second Reflex save or be picked up bodily and held suspended in the powerful winds, automatically taking the listed damage each round. A creature that can fly is allowed a Reflex save each round to escape the whirlwind. The creature still takes damage but can leave if the save is successful. The DC for saves against the whirlwind's effects varies with the elemental's size.

The elemental can eject any carried creatures whenever it wishes, depositing them wherever the whirlwind happens to be. A summoned elemental always ejects trapped creatures before returning to its home plane.

If the whirlwind's base touches the ground, it creates a swirling cloud of debris. This cloud is centered on the elemental and has a diameter equal to half the whirlwind's height. The cloud obscures all vision, including darkvision, beyond 5 feet. Creatures 5 feet away have one-half concealment, while those farther away have total concealment (see Concealment, page 133 in the *Player's Handbook*). Those caught in the cloud must succeed at a Concentration check to cast a spell (DC equal to the Reflex save DC).

AIR ELEMENTAL SIZES

Elemental	Height	Weight	Save DC	Whirlwind Damage	Height
Small	4 ft.	1 lb.	11	1d4	10–20 ft.
Medium	8 ft.	2 lb.	13	1d6	10–30 ft.
Large	16 ft.	4 lb.	16	2d6	10–40 ft.
Huge	32 ft.	8 lb.	22	2d8	10–50 ft.
Greater	36 ft.	10 lb.	25	2d8	10–60 ft.
Elder	40 ft.	12 lb.	27	2d8	10–60 ft.

EARTH ELEMENTAL

Earth elementals are immensely strong and tough: The larger ones can pound almost anything into rubble. They seldom leave their home plane except when summoned elsewhere by a spell.

An earth elemental looks like a very large, stony humanoid. When summoned to the Material Plane, it is made of whatever types of dirt, stones, precious metals, and gems it was conjured from. The elemental always has a cold, expressionless face with a mouthlike opening, and two eyes that sparkle like multifaceted gems.

Earth elementals speak Terran but rarely choose to do so. Their voices sound like an echo in a deep tunnel, the rumbling of an earthquake, or the grinding of stone on stone.

	Earth Elemental, Small Small Elemental (Earth)	Earth Elemental, Medium Medium-Size Elemental (Earth)	Earth Elemental, Large Large Elemental (Earth)
Hit Dice:	2d8+2 (11 hp)	4d8+12 (30 hp)	8d8+32 (68 hp)
Initiative:	–1 (Dex)	–1 (Dex)	–1 (Dex)
Speed:	20 ft.	20 ft.	20 ft.
AC:	17 (+1 size, –1 Dex, +7 natural)	18 (–1 Dex, +9 natural)	18 (–1 size, –1 Dex, +10 natural)
Attacks:	Slam +5 melee	Slam +8 melee	Slam +12/+7 melee
Damage:	Slam 1d6+4	Slam 1d8+7	Slam 2d8+10
Face/Reach:	5 ft. by 5 ft./5 ft.	5 ft. by 5 ft./5 ft.	5 ft. by 5 ft./10 ft.
Special Attacks:	Earth mastery, push	Earth mastery, push	Earth mastery, push
Special Qualities:	Elemental	Elemental	Elemental, damage reduction 10/+1
Saves:	Fort +4, Ref –1, Will +0	Fort +7, Ref +0, Will +1	Fort +10, Ref +1, Will +2
Abilities:	Str 17, Dex 8, Con 13, Int 4, Wis 11, Cha 11	Str 21, Dex 8, Con 17, Int 4, Wis 11, Cha 11	Str 25, Dex 8, Con 19, Int 6, Wis 11, Cha 11
Skills:	Listen +5, Spot +5	Listen +7, Spot +7	Listen +11, Spot +11
Feats:	Power Attack	Power Attack	Cleave, Power Attack

	Earth Elemental, Huge Huge Elemental (Earth)	Earth Elemental, Greater Huge Elemental (Earth)	Earth Elemental, Elder Huge Elemental (Earth)
Hit Dice:	16d8+80 (152 hp)	21d8+105 (199 hp)	24d8+120 (228 hp)
Initiative:	–1 (Dex)	–1 (Dex)	–1 (Dex)
Speed:	20 ft.	20 ft.	20 ft.
AC:	18 (–2 size, –1 Dex, +11 natural)	20 (–2 size, –1 Dex, +13 natural)	22 (–2 size, –1 Dex, +15 natural)
Attacks:	Slam +19/+14/+9 melee	Slam +23/+18/+13 melee	Slam +27/+22/+17/+12 melee
Damage:	Slam 2d10+13	Slam 2d10+15	Slam 2d10+16
Face/Reach:	10 ft. by 5 ft./15 ft.	10 ft. by 5 ft./15 ft.	10 ft. by 5 ft./15 ft.
Special Attacks:	Earth mastery, push	Earth mastery, push	Earth mastery, push
Special Qualities:	Elemental, damage reduction 10/+2	Elemental, damage reduction 10/+2	Elemental, damage reduction 15/+3
Saves:	Fort +15, Ref +4, Will +5	Fort +17, Ref +6, Will +7	Fort +19, Ref +7, Will +8
Abilities:	Str 29, Dex 8, Con 21, Int 6, Wis 11, Cha 11	Str 31, Dex 8, Con 21, Int 6, Wis 11, Cha 11	Str 33, Dex 8, Con 21, Int 6, Wis 11, Cha 11
Skills:	Listen +18, Spot +18	Listen +23, Spot +23	Listen +26, Spot +26
Feats:	Cleave, Great Cleave, Power Attack, Sunder	Cleave, Great Cleave, Improved Critical (slam), Power Attack, Sunder	Cleave, Great Cleave, Improved Critical (slam), Power Attack, Sunder

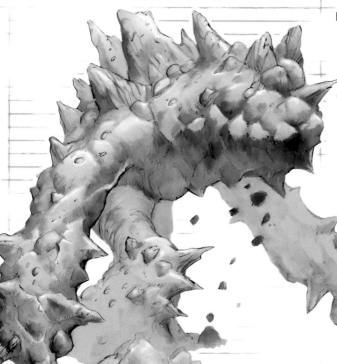

EARTH ELEMENTAL SIZES

Elemental	Height	Weight	Elemental	Height	Weight
Small	4 ft.	80 lb.	Huge	32 ft.	48,000 lb.
Medium	8 ft.	750 lb.	Greater	36 ft.	54,000 lb.
Large	16 ft.	6,000 lb.	Elder	40 ft.	60,000 lb.

Combat

Though an earth elemental moves slowly, it is a relentless opponent. It can travel though solid ground or stone as easily as humans walk on the earth's surface. It cannot swim, however, and must either walk around a body of water or go through the ground under it. An earth elemental can move along the bottom of a body of water but prefers not to.

Earth Mastery (Ex): An earth elemental gains a +1 attack and damage bonus if both it and its foe touch the ground. If an opponent is airborne or waterborne, the elemental suffers a –4 penalty to attack and damage. (These modifiers are not included in the statistics block.)

Push (Ex): An earth elemental can start a bull rush maneuver without provoking an attack of opportunity. The combat modifiers given in Earth Mastery, above, also apply to the elemental's opposed Strength checks.

FIRE ELEMENTAL

Fire elementals are fast and agile. The merest touch from their fiery bodies is sufficient to set many materials aflame.

A fire elemental looks like a tall sheet of flame with an armlike appendage on each side. These "arms" seem to flicker back into the

	Fire Elemental, Small Small Elemental (Fire)	Fire Elemental, Medium Medium-Size Elemental (Fire)	Fire Elemental, Large Large Elemental (Fire)
Hit Dice:	2d8 (9 hp)	4d8+8 (26 hp)	8d8+24 (60 hp)
Initiative:	+5 (+1 Dex, +4 Improved Initiative)	+7 (+3 Dex, +4 Improved Initiative)	+9 (+5 Dex, +4 Improved Initiative)
Speed:	50 ft.	50 ft.	50 ft.
AC:	15 (+1 size, +1 Dex, +3 natural)	16 (+0 size, +3 Dex, +3 natural)	18 (–1 size, +5 Dex, +4 natural)
Attacks:	Slam +3 melee	Slam +6 melee	Slam +10/+5 melee
Damage:	Slam 1d4 and 1d4 fire	Slam 1d6+1 and 1d6 fire	Slam 2d6+3 and 2d6 fire
Face/Reach:	5 ft. by 5 ft./5 ft.	5 ft. by 5 ft./5 ft.	5 ft. by 5 ft./10 ft.
Special Attacks:	Burn	Burn	Burn
Special Qualities:	Elemental, fire subtype	Elemental, fire subtype	Elemental, damage reduction 10/+1, fire subtype
Saves:	Fort +0, Ref +4, Will +0	Fort +3, Ref +7, Will +1	Fort +5, Ref +11, Will +2
Abilities:	Str 10, Dex 13, Con 10, Int 4, Wis 11, Cha 11	Str 12, Dex 17, Con 14, Int 4, Wis 11, Cha 11	Str 14, Dex 21, Con 16, Int 6, Wis 11, Cha 11
Skills:	Listen +5, Spot +5	Listen +7, Spot +7	Listen +11, Spot +11
Feats:	Improved Initiative, Weapon Finesse (slam)	Improved Initiative, Weapon Finesse (slam)	Dodge, Improved Initiative, Weapon Finesse (slam)

	Fire Elemental, Huge Huge Elemental (Fire)	Fire Elemental, Greater Huge Elemental (Fire)	Fire Elemental, Elder Huge Elemental (Fire)
Hit Dice:	16d8+64 (136 hp)	21d8+84 (178 hp)	24d8+96 (204 hp)
Initiative:	+11 (+7 Dex, +4 Improved Initiative)	+12 (+8 Dex, +4 Improved Initiative)	+13 (+9 Dex, +4 Improved Initiative)
Speed:	50 ft.	50 ft.	50 ft.
AC:	19 (–2 size, +7 Dex, +4 natural)	24 (–2 size, +8 Dex, +8 natural)	25 (–2 size, +9 Dex, +8 natural)
Attacks:	Slam +17/+12/+7 melee	Slam +21/+16/+11 melee	Slam +25/+20/+15/+10 melee
Damage:	Slam 2d8+6 and 2d8 fire	Slam 2d8+7 and 2d8 fire	Slam 2d8+9 and 2d8 fire
Face/Reach:	10 ft. by 5 ft./15 ft.	10 ft. by 5 ft./15 ft.	10 ft. by 5 ft./15 ft.
Special Attacks:	Burn	Burn	Burn
Special Qualities:	Elemental, damage reduction 10/+2, fire subtype	Elemental, damage reduction 10/+2, fire subtype	Elemental, damage reduction 15/+3, fire subtype
Saves:	Fort +9, Ref +17, Will +5	Fort +11, Ref +20, Will +7	Fort +12, Ref +23, Will +8
Abilities:	Str 18, Dex 25, Con 18, Int 6, Wis 11, Cha 11	Str 20, Dex 27, Con 18, Int 6, Wis 11, Cha 11	Str 22, Dex 29, Con 18, Int 6, Wis 11, Cha 11
Skills:	Listen +18, Spot +18	Listen +23, Spot +23	Listen +26, Spot +26
Feats:	Dodge, Improved Initiative, Mobility, Weapon Finesse (slam)	Dodge, Improved Initiative, Mobility, Spring Attack, Weapon Finesse (slam)	Dodge, Improved Initiative, Mobility, Spring Attack, Weapon Finesse (slam)

creature's flaming body, only to spring out again seconds later. The only facial features of a fire elemental are two large glowing patches of brilliant blue flame, which seem to function as eyes.

A fire elemental cannot enter water or any other nonflammable liquid. A body of water is an impassible barrier unless the fire elemental can step or jump over it.

Fire elementals speak Ignan, though they rarely choose to do so. When one does, its voice sounds like the crackle and hiss of a great fire.

Fire Elemental Sizes

Elemental	Height	Weight	Burn Save DC
Small	4 ft.	1 lb.	11
Medium	8 ft.	2 lb.	14
Large	16 ft.	4 lb.	17
Huge	32 ft.	8 lb.	22
Greater	36 ft.	10 lb.	24
Elder	40 ft.	12 lb.	26

Combat

A fire elemental is a fierce opponent that attacks its enemies directly and savagely. It takes joy in burning the creatures and objects of the Material Plane to ashes.

Burn (Ex): Those hit by a fire elemental's slam attack must succeed at a Reflex save or catch fire. The flame burns for 1d4 rounds (see Catching on Fire, page 86 in the Dungeon Master's Guide). The save DC varies with the elemental's size. A burning creature can take a move-equivalent action to put out the flame.

Creatures hitting a fire elemental with natural weapons or unarmed attacks take fire damage as though hit by the elemental's attack, and also catch fire unless they succeed at a Reflex save.

Fire Subtype (Ex): Fire immunity, double damage from cold except on a successful save.

WATER ELEMENTAL

A water elemental can be as ferocious and powerful as a stormy sea.

It looks like a high, crested wave with smaller waves for arms. Two orbs of deep green peer out of the front of the wave, serving as eyes. A water elemental can't venture more than 180 feet from the body of water from which it was conjured.

Water elementals speak Aquan but rarely choose to do so. When one does, its voice sounds like the crashing of waves on rocky shores or the howls of an ocean gale.

	Water Elemental, Small Small Elemental (Water)	Water Elemental, Medium Medium-Size Elemental (Water)	Water Elemental, Large Large Elemental (Water)
Hit Dice:	2d8+2 (11 hp)	4d8+12 (30 hp)	8d8+32 (68 hp)
Initiative:	+0	+1 (Dex)	+2 (Dex)
Speed:	20 ft., swim 90 ft.	20 ft., swim 90 ft.	20 ft., swim 90 ft.
AC:	17 (+1 size, +0 Dex, +6 natural)	19 (+1 Dex, +8 natural)	20 (−1 size, +2 Dex, +9 natural)
Attacks:	Slam +4 melee	Slam +6 melee	Slam +10/+5 melee
Damage:	Slam 1d6+3	Slam 1d8+4	Slam 2d8+7
Face/Reach:	5 ft. by 5 ft./5 ft.	5 ft. by 5 ft./5 ft.	5 ft. by 5 ft./10 ft.
Special Attacks:	Water mastery, drench, vortex	Water mastery, drench, vortex	Water mastery, drench, vortex
Special Qualities:	Elemental	Elemental	Elemental, damage reduction 10/+1
Saves:	Fort +4, Ref +0, Will +0	Fort +7, Ref +2, Will +1	Fort +10, Ref +4, Will +2
Abilities:	Str 14, Dex 10, Con 13, Int 4, Wis 11, Cha 11	Str 16, Dex 12, Con 17, Int 4, Wis 11, Cha 11	Str 20, Dex 14, Con 19, Int 6, Wis 11, Cha 11
Skills:	Listen +5, Spot +5	Listen +7, Spot +7	Listen +11, Spot +11
Feats:	Power Attack	Power Attack	Cleave, Power Attack

	Water Elemental, Huge Huge Elemental (Water)	Water Elemental, Greater Huge Elemental (Water)	Water Elemental, Elder Huge Elemental (Water)
Hit Dice:	16d8+80 (152 hp)	21d8+105 (199 hp)	24d8+120 (228 hp)
Initiative:	+4 (Dex)	+5 (Dex)	+6 (Dex)
Speed:	20 ft., swim 90 ft.	20 ft., swim 90 ft.	20 ft., swim 90 ft.
AC:	21 (−2 size, +4 Dex, +9 natural)	22 (−2 size, +5 Dex, +9 natural)	23 (−2 size, +6 Dex, +9 natural)
Attacks:	Slam +17/+12/+7 melee	Slam +21/+16/+11 melee	Slam +25/+20/+15/+10 melee
Damage:	Slam 2d10+10	Slam 2d10+12	Slam 2d10+13
Face/Reach:	10 ft. by 5 ft./15 ft.	10 ft. by 5 ft./15 ft.	10 ft. by 5 ft./15 ft.
Special Attacks:	Water mastery, drench, vortex	Water mastery, drench, vortex	Water mastery, drench, vortex
Special Qualities:	Elemental, damage reduction 10/+2, fire immunity	Elemental, damage reduction 10/+2, fire immunity	Elemental, damage reduction 15/+3, fire immunity
Saves:	Fort +15, Ref +9, Will +5	Fort +17, Ref +12, Will +7	Fort +19, Ref +14, Will +8
Abilities:	Str 24, Dex 18, Con 21, Int 6, Wis 11, Cha 11	Str 26, Dex 20, Con 21, Int 6, Wis 11, Cha 11	Str 28, Dex 22, Con 21, Int 6, Wis 11, Cha 11
Skills:	Listen +18, Spot +18	Listen +23, Spot +23	Listen +26, Spot +26
Feats:	Cleave, Great Cleave, Power Attack, Sunder	Cleave, Great Cleave, Improved Critical (slam), Power Attack, Sunder	Cleave, Great Cleave, Improved Critical (slam), Power Attack, Sunder

Climate/Terrain: Any land and underground
Organization: Solitary
Challenge Rating: Small 1; medium 3; large 5; huge 7; greater 9; elder 11
Treasure: None
Alignment: Usually neutral
Advancement: Small 3 HD (Small); medium 5–7 HD (Medium-size); large 9–15 HD (Large); huge 17–20 HD (Huge); greater 22–23 HD (Huge); elder 25+ HD (Huge)

Combat

A water elemental prefers to fight in a large body of water where it can disappear beneath the waves and suddenly swell up behind its opponents.

Water Mastery (Ex): A water elemental gains a +1 attack and damage bonus if both it and its opponent touch water. If the opponent or elemental is landbound, the elemental suffers a –4 penalty to attack and damage. (These modifiers are not included in the statistics block.)

A water elemental can be a serious threat to a ship that crosses its path. The elemental can easily overturn small craft (5 feet of length per Hit Die of the elemental) and stop larger vessels (10 feet long per HD). Even large ships (20 feet long per HD) can be slowed to half speed.

Drench (Ex): The elemental's touch puts out torches, campfires, exposed lanterns, and other open flames of nonmagical origin if these are of Large size or smaller. The creature can dispel magical fire it touches as *dispel magic* cast by a sorcerer whose level equals the elemental's HD total.

Vortex (Su): The elemental can transform itself into a whirlpool once every 10 minutes, provided it is underwater, and remain in that form for up to 1 round for every 2 HD it has. In vortex form, the elemental can move through the water or along the bottom at its swim speed.

The vortex is 5 feet wide at the base, up to 30 feet wide at the top, and 10 feet or more tall, depending on the elemental's size. The elemental controls the exact height, but it must be at least 10 feet.

Creatures one or more sizes smaller than the elemental might take damage when caught in the vortex (see the table below for details) and may be swept up by it. An affected creature must succeed at a Reflex save when it comes into contact with the vortex or take the listed damage. It must also succeed at a second Reflex save or be picked up bodily and held suspended in the powerful currents, automatically taking damage each round. A creature that can swim is allowed a Reflex save each round to escape the vortex. The creature still takes damage, but can leave if the save is successful. The DC for saves against the vortex's effects varies with the elemental's size.

The elemental can eject any carried creatures whenever it wishes, depositing them wherever the vortex happens to be. A summoned elemental always ejects trapped creatures before returning to its home plane.

If the vortex's base touches the bottom, it creates a swirling cloud of debris. This cloud is centered on the elemental and has a diameter equal to half the vortex's height. The cloud obscures all vision, including darkvision, beyond 5 feet. Creatures 5 feet away have one-half concealment, while those farther away have total concealment (see Concealment, page 133 in the *Player's Handbook*). Those caught in the cloud must succeed at a Concentration check to cast a spell (DC equal to the Reflex save DC).

WATER ELEMENTAL SIZES

| | | | | | Vortex | |
Elemental	Height	Weight	Save DC	Damage	Height
Small	4 ft.	34 lb.	13	1d4	10–20 ft.
Medium	8 ft.	280 lb.	15	1d6	10–30 ft.
Large	16 ft.	2,250 lb.	19	2d6	10–40 ft.
Huge	32 ft.	18,000 lb.	25	2d8	10–50 ft.
Greater	36 ft.	21,000 lb.	26	2d8	10–60 ft.
Elder	40 ft.	24,000 lb.	29	2d8	10–60 ft.

Medium-Size Humanoid (Elf)
Hit Dice: 1d8–1 (3 hp)
Initiative: +1 (Dex)
Speed: 30 ft.
AC: 15 (+1 Dex, +3 studded leather, +1 small shield)
Attacks: Longsword +1 melee; or longbow +2 ranged
Damage: Longsword 1d8; or longbow 1d8
Face/Reach: 5 ft. by 5 ft./5 ft.
Special Qualities: Elven traits
Saves: Fort +1, Ref +1, Will +0
Abilities: Str 10, Dex 13, Con 8, Int 11, Wis 11, Cha 11
Skills: Hide +1, Listen +3, Search +3, Spot +2
Feats: Weapon Focus (longbow)

Climate/Terrain: Temperate forest
    Half-elf—Any land
    Aquatic—Temperate aquatic
    Drow—Any underground
    Gray—Temperate forest and mountains
    Wild—Temperate and warm forest
    Wood—Temperate forest
Organization: Company (2–4), squad (11–20 plus 2 3rd-level sergeants and 1 leader of 3rd–6th level), or band (30–100 plus 20% noncombatants plus 1 3rd-level sergeant per 10 adults, 5 5th-level lieutenants, and 3 7th-level captains)
Challenge Rating: 1/2 or 1 (drow)
Treasure: Standard
Alignment: Usually chaotic good
    Drow—Usually neutral evil
    Wood—Usually neutral
Advancement: By character class

Elves are aloof guardians of the forests, studying magic and swordplay for the duration of their long lives.

Elves are attractive humanlike beings that average 5 feet tall and typically weigh just over 100 pounds. They tend to be pale-skinned and dark-haired, with deep green eyes, and do not grow facial hair. They live on fruits, grains, and occasional hunting. Elves prefer colorful clothes, usually with a green-and-gray cloak that blends well with the colors of the forest. They like beautiful things, from elegant jewelry to attractive flowers to decorated clothing and tools.

Elves speak Elven, and most also know Common and Sylvan. Like dwarves, elves are craftmasters, although they work in wood and metal rather than metal and stone. Elven items are prized by other races, and many elven communities have become prosperous by trading crafted goods with other peoples in and out of the forests.

Most elves encountered outside their homes are warriors; the information in the statistics block is for one of 1st level (see page 39 in the DUNGEON MASTER'S *Guide* for more about the warrior class).

COMBAT

Elves are cautious warriors and take time to analyze their opponents and the location of the fight if at all possible, maximizing their advantage by using ambushes, snipers, and camouflage. They prefer to fire from cover and retreat before they are found, repeating this maneuver until all of their enemies are dead. They prefer longbows, shortbows, rapiers, and longswords. In melee, elves are graceful and deadly, using complex maneuvers that are beautiful to observe. Their wizards often use *sleep* spells during combat because these won't affect other elves.

Elven Traits (Ex): Elves benefit from a number of racial traits.

- Proficient with longsword, rapier, longbow, composite longbow, shortbow, and composite shortbow, regardless of character class.
- Immunity to magic *sleep* spells and effects.
- +2 racial bonus to Will saves against enchantment spells or effects.
- Low-Light Vision: Elves can see twice as far as a human in starlight, moonlight, torchlight, etc.
- +2 racial bonus to Search, Spot, and Listen checks. An elf who merely passes within 5 feet of a secret or concealed door is entitled to a Search check as though actively looking for it.

ELF SOCIETY

Elves believe that independence and freedom for the individual are more important than the rigid structures of civilization, so they tend to live and travel in small bands. These bands accept the loose authority of a noble, who in turn owes allegiance to an elven monarch (who rules his or her own band directly).

Elves live in harmony with nature, building temporary camps that blend into the trees—or are in the branches of the trees, away from prying eyes. They frequently have animal guardians or giant eagles watching their homes. An elven settlement contains noncombatants (mostly children) equal to 20% of the fighting population. Elf society is very egalitarian, and males or females may be found in almost any role.

Their long life span gives elves a patient perspective and allows them to take pleasure in the enduring beauty of the natural world. They don't see the point in short-term gains and instead learn things that will provide joy for years to come, such as stories, music, art, and dance. Treasures such as elven music and crafts disguise the fact that elves are dedicated warriors determined to check the spread of evil in the forests.

Elves eat little, and although they are omnivorous, they eat more plants than meat. This is partly because of their affinity with nature (they believe a harvested plant causes less disruption to nature than a slain animal) and partly because their fondness for roving requires food that is preserved more easily.

The chief elf deity is Corellon Larethian, who is the creator and protector of the race.

SUBRACES

The above information describes the high elf, the most common variety. There are five other major subraces of elf, in addition to half-elves, who share enough elven characteristics to be included here.

Half-Elves

Half-elves are not truly an elven subrace, but they are often mistaken for elves. They may be outcasts from their parents' societies or welcomed into the elven or human community, depending on the attitudes the two groups have for each other. Half-elves usually inherit a good blend of their parents' physical characteristics, so a half-aquatic elf has greenish skin, a half-drow has dusky skin and light hair, and so on. A half-elf can choose any class as his or her favored class.

Half-Elven Traits (Ex): These are in addition to the basic elf traits, except where noted here.
- Racial bonus to Search, Spot, and Listen checks decreases to +1. Half-elves cannot notice secret doors just by being near them.

Aquatic Elves

Also called sea elves, these are water-breathing cousins to land-dwelling elves. They cavort amid the waves and the ocean depths with allies such as dolphins and whales. Their skin is usually greenish silver, with hair that ranges from emerald green to deep blue; their fingers and toes are partially webbed. They fight underwater with tridents, spears, and nets.

The typical ability scores for an aquatic elf are Str 10, Dex 13, Con 10, Int 9, Wis 11, Cha 11. An aquatic elf's favored class is fighter.

Many aquatic elves revere Deep Sashelas, an undersea god of knowledge and beauty.

Aquatic Elf Traits (Ex): These are in addition to the basic elf traits, except where noted here.
- Swim 40 feet.
- Gills: Aquatic elves can survive out of the water for 1 hour per point of Constitution (after that, refer to the suffocation rules on page 88 in the *Dungeon Master's Guide*).
- Low-Light Vision: Aquatic elves can see four times as far as a human in starlight, moonlight, torchlight, and similar conditions of low illumination.

Drow

Also known as dark elves, drow are a depraved and evil subterranean offshoot. They have jet-black skin and pale hair, with white being common. They tend to be smaller and thinner than other sorts of elves, and their eyes are usually a vivid red. Their society is matriarchal and rigidly controlled by the priesthood.

The drow's patron deity is the spider goddess Lolth. Female drow favor the cleric class rather than wizard and have access to two of the following domains: Chaos, Destruction, Evil, and Trickery.

Typical ability scores for males are Str 10, Dex 13, Con 8, Int 13, Wis 11, Cha 9. Typical scores for females are Str 10, Dex 13, Con 8, Int 13, Wis 11, Cha 13. Drow usually coat their arrows with a potent venom.

Poisoned Arrows: Fortitude save (DC 17) or fall unconscious. After 1 minute, the subject must succeed at another Fortitude save (DC 17) or remain unconscious for 2d4 hours.

Drow Traits (Ex): These are in addition to the basic elf traits, except where noted here. Drow do not get the usual elven weapon proficiencies.
- Spell resistance 11 + class level.
- +2 racial bonus to Will saves against spells and spell-like abilities.
- Spell-Like Abilities: 1/day—*dancing lights*, *darkness*, and *faerie fire*. These abilities are as the spells cast by a sorcerer of the drow's character level.
- Darkvision up to 120 feet. This replaces elven low-light vision.
- *Light Blindness (Ex):* Abrupt exposure to bright light (such as sunlight or a *daylight* spell) blinds drow for 1 round. In addition, they suffer a −1 circumstance penalty to all attack rolls, saves, and checks while operating in bright light.

Gray Elves

These are the most noble and regal of all elves. Taller and grander in physical appearance than others, gray elves have a reputation of being aloof and arrogant (even by elven standards). They certainly are more reclusive than high elves, living in isolated mountain citadels and allowing entry only to a select few outsiders. They have either silver hair and amber eyes or pale golden hair and violet eyes. They prefer clothing of white, silver, yellow, or gold, with cloaks of deep blue or purple.

Their typical ability scores are Str 8, Dex 13, Con 8, Int 13, Wis 10, Cha 11.

Wild Elves

Wild elves, also known as grugach, are barbaric and tribal. Their skin tends to be dark brown, and their hair ranges from black to light brown, lightening to silvery white with age. They dress in simple clothing of animal skins and basic plant weaves. Though the others consider them savages, they contend that they are the true elves, for the rest have lost their primal elven essence in needing to build. Nomadic and rugged, wild elves favor the sorcerer class rather than wizard, although many are barbarians as well.

Their typical ability scores are Str 10, Dex 13, Con 10, Int 9, Wis 10, Cha 11.

Wood Elves

Also called sylvan elves, members of this subrace live deep in primordial forests. Their hair is yellow or coppery red, and they are more muscular than other elves. Their clothing is in dark shades of green and earth tones to better blend with their natural surroundings. Their homes are often guarded by giant owls or sometimes leopards or pumas (use leopard statistics). Wood elves favor the ranger class.

Their typical ability scores are Str 12, Dex 13, Con 8, Int 9, Wis 11, Cha 9.

ELF CHARACTERS

An elf's favored class is wizard. Elf leaders are usually wizards.

ETHEREAL FILCHER

Medium-Size Aberration
Hit Dice: 5d8 (22 hp)
Initiative: +8 (+4 Dex, +4 Improved Initiative)
Speed: 40 ft.
AC: 17 (+4 Dex, +3 natural)
Attacks: Bite +3 melee
Damage: Bite 1d4
Face/Reach: 5 ft. by 5 ft./5 ft.
Special Qualities: Ethereal jaunt, detect magic
Saves: Fort +1, Ref +5, Will +5
Abilities: Str 10, Dex 18, Con 11, Int 7, Wis 12, Cha 10
Skills: Listen +8, Pick Pocket +12, Spot +8
Feats: Improved Initiative

Climate/Terrain: Any land and underground
Organization: Solitary
Challenge Rating: 3
Treasure: No coins; standard goods; double items
Alignment: Usually neutral
Advancement: 6–7 HD (Medium-size); 8–15 HD (Large)

Ethereal filchers are bizarre-looking creatures with a penchant for snatching trinkets from passersby. Their ability to move quickly between the Ethereal and the Material Planes makes them spectacular pickpockets.

Ethereal filchers dwell on the Material Plane, where they stuff lairs with all manner of refuse. They prefer secluded, inaccessible spots, such as the bottoms of abandoned wells or mine shafts, alpine caves, or the basements of ruined buildings.

A filcher looks like a creature from a nightmare. It is 4 1/2 feet tall and has a baglike body, with a thick neck and a bulbous head. It has four long arms and a single leg that ends in a prehensile foot. It is pearly gray overall with metallic blue and turquoise markings. Ethereal filchers do not speak.

Illus. by B. Despain

COMBAT

An ethereal filcher lurks on the Ethereal Plane waiting for a likely mark. Upon locating one, it shifts to the Material Plane, attempting to catch its victim unawares. The creature attempts to snatch an item, then retreats quickly back to the Ethereal. It is not above delivering a bite to distract its target. Once it secures a trinket, it scurries back to its lair to admire its prize. When badly wounded, the filcher escapes rather than continue the fight.

Any number of simple ruses can blunt a filcher's attack. Quick-thinking individuals often can recover a stolen item simply by snatching it back before the filcher can escape. Others keep a few cheap baubles available for the local filcher to snatch. Filchers are known to have noses for magic, so items enchanted with *Nystul's magic aura* or *continual flame* spells often prove irresistible, especially if they also are gaudy. Fortunately, a filcher usually is satisfied with a single prize.

Ethereal Jaunt (Su): An ethereal filcher can shift from the Ethereal to the Material Plane as part of any move action, and shift back again as a free action. It can remain on the Ethereal Plane for 1 round before returning to the Material. The ability is otherwise identical with *ethereal jaunt* cast by a 15th-level sorcerer.

Detect Magic (Su): Ethereal filchers continuously *detect magic* as the spell cast by a 5th-level sorcerer. A filcher can suppress or restart the ability once per round as a free action.

ETHEREAL MARAUDER

Medium-Size Magical Beast
Hit Dice: 2d10 (11 hp)
Initiative: +5 (+1 Dex, +4 Improved Initiative)
Speed: 40 ft.
AC: 14 (+1 Dex, +3 natural)
Attacks: Bite +4
Damage: Bite 1d6+3
Face/Reach: 5 ft. by 5 ft./5 ft.
Special Qualities: Ethereal jaunt
Saves: Fort +3, Ref +4, Will +1
Abilities: Str 14, Dex 12, Con 11, Int 7, Wis 12, Cha 10
Skills: Listen +6, Move Silently +6, Spot +6
Feats: Improved Initiative

Climate/Terrain: Any land and underground
Organization: Solitary
Challenge Rating: 3
Treasure: None
Alignment: Always neutral
Advancement: 5–7 HD (Medium-size); 8–15 HD (Large)

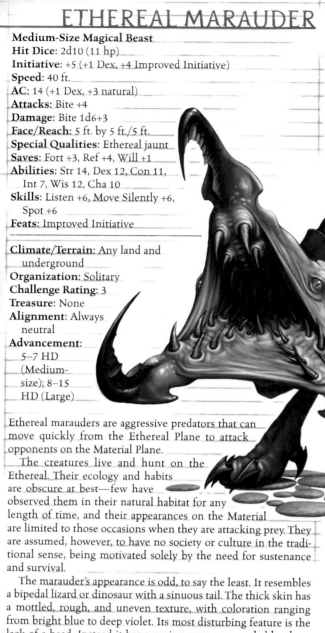

Ethereal marauders are aggressive predators that can move quickly from the Ethereal Plane to attack opponents on the Material Plane.

The creatures live and hunt on the Ethereal. Their ecology and habits are obscure at best—few have observed them in their natural habitat for any length of time, and their appearances on the Material are limited to those occasions when they are attacking prey. They are assumed, however, to have no society or culture in the traditional sense, being motivated solely by the need for sustenance and survival.

The marauder's appearance is odd, to say the least. It resembles a bipedal lizard or dinosaur with a sinuous tail. The thick skin has a mottled, rough, and uneven texture, with coloration ranging from bright blue to deep violet. Its most disturbing feature is the lack of a head. Instead it has a gaping maw surrounded by three powerful mandibles; gleaming, jet-black teeth line the inner mouth. Three small eyes ring the maw, interspersed with the mandibles.

Ethereal marauders speak no known languages. Survivors of their attacks on the Material Plane claim that they emit an eerie, high whine that varies in pitch depending on the creature's speed and health.

COMBAT

Once a marauder locates prey, it shifts to the Material Plane to attack, attempting to catch its victim flat-footed. The creature bites its victim, then retreats quickly back to the Ethereal Plane. When badly hurt or wounded, the marauder escapes to its home plane rather than continue the fight.

Ethereal Jaunt (Su): An ethereal marauder can shift from the Ethereal to the Material Plane as a free action, and shift back again as a move-equivalent action (or as part of a move-equivalent action). The ability is otherwise identical with *ethereal jaunt* cast by a 15th-level sorcerer.

ETTERCAP

Medium-Size Aberration
Hit Dice: 5d8+5 (27 hp)
Initiative: +3 (Dex)
Speed: 30 ft., climb 30 ft.
AC: 14 (+3 Dex, +1 natural)
Attacks: Bite +3 melee, 2 claws +1 melee
Damage: Bite 1d8 and poison, claws 1d3
Face/Reach: 5 ft. by 5 ft./5 ft.
Special Attacks: Web, poison
Special Qualities: Low-light vision
Saves: Fort +2, Ref +4, Will +6
Abilities: Str 10, Dex 17, Con 13, Int 6, Wis 15, Cha 8
Skills: Climb +8, Craft (any one) +2, Hide +3*, Listen +10, Spot +10*
Feats: Multiattack

Climate/Terrain: Temperate and warm forests
Organization: Solitary, pair, or troupe (1–2 plus 2–4 Medium-size monstrous spiders)
Challenge Rating: 4
Treasure: Standard
Alignment: Usually neutral evil
Advancement: 6–7 HD (Medium-size); 8–15 HD (Large)

Although not very intelligent, ettercaps are cunning predators. Like the monstrous spiders in whose company they are often found, they are skilled hunters and trappers.

An ettercap is a revolting creature resembling a cross between a gangly human and a bloated spider. It stands 6 feet tall, with long, slender arms and legs protruding from a rounded, fleshy body. A pair of bulbous black eyes in its arachnid face allows it to see very well in even the dimmest light.

Lurking in dark shadows, ettercaps are solitary creatures that exist only to eat and breed. They often make their homes near well-traveled paths or game trails, where food is plentiful. They savor the taste of still-living flesh, often consuming incapacitated prey before it dies.

Ettercaps are very fond of spiders and often keep them as others keep bees. From time to time, however, an ettercap has a number of monstrous spiders as pets, which are as loyal to it as a dog to a human master.

Ettercaps speak Common.

COMBAT

Ettercaps are not brave creatures, but their cunning traps often ensure that the enemy never draws a weapon. When an ettercap does engage its enemies, it attacks with its keen-edged claws and venomous bite.

Web (Ex): An ettercap can cast a web eight times per day. This is similar to an attack with a net but has a maximum range of 50 feet, with a range increment of 10 feet, and is effective against targets of up to Medium-size (see page 102 in the *Player's Handbook* for details on net attacks). The web anchors the target in place, allowing no movement.

An entangled creature can escape with a successful Escape Artist check (DC 20) or burst the web with a successful Strength check (DC 26). The web has 6 hit points and takes double damage from fire.

Ettercaps can also create sheets of sticky webbing from 5 to 60 feet square. They usually position these to snare flying creatures but can also try to trap prey on the ground. Approaching creatures must succeed at a Spot check (DC 20) to notice a web or stumble into it and become trapped as though by a successful web attack. Attempts to escape or burst the webbing receive a +5 bonus if the trapped creature has something to walk on or grab while pulling free. Each 5-foot-square section has 6 hit points and takes double damage from fire.

An ettercap can move across its own sheet web at its climb speed and can determine the exact location of any creature touching the web.

Poison (Ex): Bite, Fortitude save (DC 13); initial damage 1d6 temporary Dexterity, secondary damage 2d6 temporary Dexterity.

Skills: *Ettercaps in shadow receive a +4 racial bonus to Hide and Spot checks.

ETTIN

Large Giant
Hit Dice: 10d8+20 (65 hp)
Initiative: +3 (–1 Dex, +4 Improved Initiative)
Speed: 40 ft.
AC: 18 (–1 size, –1 Dex, +7 natural, +3 hide)
Attacks: 2 greatclubs +12/+7 melee; or 2 longspears +5/+0 ranged
Damage: Greatclub 1d10+6; longspear 1d8+6
Face/Reach: 5 ft. by 5 ft./10 ft.
Special Attacks: Superior two-weapon fighting
Special Qualities: Darkvision 90 ft.
Saves: Fort +9, Ref +2, Will +3
Abilities: Str 23, Dex 8, Con 15, Int 6, Wis 10, Cha 11
Skills: Listen +10, Search +0, Spot +10
Feats: Alertness, Improved Initiative, Power Attack

Climate/Terrain: Cold and temperate hill, mountains, and underground
Organization: Solitary, gang (2–4), troupe (1–2 plus 1–2 brown bears), band (3–5 plus 1–2 brown bears), or colony (3–5 plus 1–2 brown bears and 7–12 orcs or 9–16 goblins)
Challenge Rating: 5
Treasure: Standard

Alignment: Usually chaotic evil
Advancement: By character class

Ettins, or two-headed giants, are vicious and unpredictable hunters that stalk the night. Their two heads make them exceptionally sharp-eyed and alert. They are excellent guardians and scouts.

An ettin has orclike facial features and pink to brownish skin. It never bathes if it can help it, which usually leaves it so grimy and dirty its skin resembles thick, gray hide (ettins that don't smell bad are rare indeed). An ettin has long, stringy, unkempt hair and large, yellowing, often rotten teeth. Adult ettins are about 13 feet tall and weigh 5,200 pounds. They live about 75 years.

Ettins have no language of their own but speak a pidgin of Orc, Goblin, and Giant. Creatures that can speak any of these languages must succeed at an Intelligence check (DC 15) to communicate with an ettin. Check once for each bit of information: If the other creature speaks two of these languages, the DC is 10, and for someone who speaks all three, the DC is 5. Ettins talk among themselves without difficulty, despite their low Intelligence, and a lone ettin often whiles away the hours chatting with itself.

COMBAT

Though ettins aren't very intelligent, they are cunning fighters. They prefer to ambush their victims rather than charge into a straight fight, but once the battle has started, an ettin usually fights furiously until all enemies are dead.

Superior Two-Weapon Fighting (Ex): An ettin fights with a club or spear in each hand. Because each of its two heads controls an arm, the ettin does not suffer an attack or damage penalty for attacking with two weapons.

Skills: An ettin's two heads give it a +2 racial bonus to Listen, Spot, and Search checks.

ETTIN SOCIETY

Ettins like to establish their lairs in remote, rocky areas. They dwell in dark, underground caves that stink of decaying food and offal. They tolerate other creatures, such as orcs, if these can be useful in some way. Otherwise, ettins tend to be violently isolationist, crushing trespassers without question.

Ettins are generally solitary, and mated pairs stay together for only a few months after a child is born. Young ettins mature quickly. Within eight to ten months after birth, they are self-sufficient enough to go off on their own.

On rare occasions, a particularly strong ettin may gather a small group, or gang, of ettins. This gang stays together only as long as the leader is undefeated. Any major defeat shatters the leader's hold over the others, and they go their separate ways.

Ettins place little value on wealth but are canny enough to understand its value to others. They collect treasure only because it can buy them the services of goblins or orcs. These lesser creatures sometimes build traps around ettins' lairs, or help them fight off powerful opponents.

FORMIAN

	Worker Small Outsider (Lawful)	Warrior Medium-Size Outsider (Lawful)	Taskmaster Medium-Size Outsider (Lawful)
Hit Dice:	1d8+1 (5 hp)	4d8+8 (26 hp)	6d8+12 (39 hp)
Initiative:	+2 (Dex)	+3 (Dex)	+7 (+3 Dex, +4 Improved Initiative)
Speed:	40 ft.	40 ft.	40 ft.
AC:	17 (+1 size, +2 Dex, +4 natural)	18 (+3 Dex, +5 natural)	19 (+3 Dex, +6 natural)
Attacks:	Bite +3 melee	Sting +7 melee, 2 claws +5 melee, bite +5 melee	Sting +10 melee, 2 claws+5 melee
Damage:	Bite 1d4+1	Sting 2d4+3, claw 1d6+1, bite 1d4+1	Sting 2d4+4, claw 1d6+2
Face/Reach:	5 ft. by 5 ft./5 ft.	5 ft. by 5 ft./5 ft.	5 ft. by 5 ft./5 ft.
Special Attacks:	Hive mind	Hive mind, poison	Hive mind, poison, dominate person, dominated creature
Special Qualities:	Immunities, resistances, make whole, heal	Immunities, resistances, SR 18	Immunities, resistances, telepathy, SR 21
Saves:	Fort +3, Ref +4, Will +2	Fort +6, Ref +7, Will +5	Fort +7, Ref +8, Will +8
Abilities:	Str 13, Dex 14, Con 13, Int 6, Wis 10, Cha 9	Str 17, Dex 16, Con 14, Int 10, Wis 12, Cha 11	Str 18, Dex 16, Con 14, Int 14, Wis 16, Cha 19
Skills:	Craft (any one) +3, Climb +3	Climb +10, Hide +10, Listen +7, Move Silently +10, Spot +6	Climb +13, Hide +12, Listen +12, Move Silently +12, Search +8, Sense Motive +12, Spot +12
Feats:	Skill Focus (craft)	Dodge, Multiattack	Improved Initiative, Spell-Like Ability Focus (enchantment)
Climate/Terrain:	Any land and underground	Any land and underground	Any land and underground
Organization:	Team (2–4) or crew (7–18)	Solitary, team (2–4), or troop (6–11)	Solitary (1 plus 1 dominated creature) or conscription team (2–4 plus 1 dominated creature each)
Challenge Rating:	1/2	3	7
Treasure:	None	None	Standard
Alignment:	Always lawful neutral	Always lawful neutral	Always lawful neutral
Advancement:	2 HD (Medium-size)	5–8 HD (Medium-size); 9–12 HD (Large)	7–9 HD (Medium-size); 10–12 HD (Large)

	Myrmarch Large Outsider (Lawful)	Queen Large Outsider (Lawful)
Hit Dice:	12d8+48 (102 hp)	20d8+100 (190 hp)
Initiative:	+8 (+4 Dex, +4 Improved Initiative)	−5
Speed:	40 ft.	0 ft.
AC:	28 (−1 size, +4 Dex, +15 natural)	23 (−1 size, +14 natural)
Attacks:	Sting +15 melee, bite +13 melee; or javelin +15/+10 ranged	—
Damage:	Sting 2d4+4, bite 2d6+2; or javelin 1d6+4 and poison	—
Face/Reach:	5 ft. by 10 ft./5 ft.	5 ft. by 10 ft./5 ft.
Special Attacks:	Hive mind, poison, spell-like abilities	Hive mind, spells, spell-like abilities
Special Qualities:	Immunities, resistances, fast healing 2, SR 25	Immunities, resistances, fast healing 2, telepathy, SR 30
Saves:	Fort +12, Ref +12, Will +11	Fort +19, Ref —, Will +19
Abilities:	Str 19, Dex 18, Con 18, Int 16, Wis 16, Cha 17	Str —, Dex —, Con 20, Int 20, Wis 20, Cha 21
Skills:	Climb +18, Craft (any one) +9, Diplomacy +15, Hide +15, Knowledge (any one) +16, Listen +18, Move Silently +19, Search +17, Sense Motive +18, Spot +18	Appraise +22, Bluff +28, Concentration +22, Diplomacy +28, Knowledge (any three) +28, Listen +30, Scry +28, Sense Motive +28, Spellcraft +28, Spot +30
Feats:	Dodge, Improved Initiative, Mobility, Multiattack	Alertness, Great Fortitude, Iron Will, item creation feat (any one), Quicken Spell, Spell Focus (Enchantment)
Climate/Terrain:	Any land and underground	Any land and underground
Organization:	Solitary, team (2–4), or platoon (1 plus 7–18 workers and 6–11 warriors)	Solitary or hive (1 plus 100–400 workers, 11–40 warriors, 4–7 taskmasters with 1 dominated creature each, and 5–8 myrmarchs)
Challenge Rating:	10	18
Treasure:	Standard	Double standard
Alignment:	Always lawful neutral	Always lawful neutral
Advancement:	13–18 HD (Large); 19–24 HD (Huge)	21–30 HD (Huge); 31–40 HD (Gargantuan)

Formians hail from planes devoted to law. They seek to colonize all that they see and incorporate all living things into their hive as workers.

Expansionist in the extreme, their goal is to spread colonies until they have taken over everything and their order is unquestioned. To further this end, they attack all other creatures, usually to put them to work building and expanding cities. Formians maintain these "conscripted" workers as well as those mentally dominated by the power of their taskmasters.

A formian resembles a cross between an ant and a centaur. All formians are covered in a brownish-red carapace—their size and appearance varies by type.

COMBAT

Formians are generally aggressive, seeking to subdue all they encounter. If they perceive even the slightest threat to their hive-city or to their queen, they attack immediately and fight to the death. Any formian also attacks immediately if ordered to do so by a superior.

Hive Mind (Ex): All formians within 50 miles of their queen are in constant communication. If one is aware of a particular danger, they all are. If one in a group is not flat-footed, none of them are. No formian in a group is considered flanked unless all of them are.

Immunities (Ex): Formians have poison, petrification, and cold immunity.

Resistances (Ex): All formians have fire, electricity, and sonic resistance 20.

FORMIAN SOCIETY

Formians build fabulous hive-cities in which hundreds of the creatures dwell. They are born into their station, with no ability to progress. Workers obey orders given by warriors, myrmarchs, or the queen. Warriors carry out the will of their myrmarch commanders or the queen. Myrmarchs take orders only from the queen herself, although they have different ranks depending on services rendered. These are not positions of power but of prestige. The most prestigious of the myrmarchs guard the queen. Taskmasters are equal in rank to warriors but seldom interact with other formians.

WORKER

Workers are the lowest-ranking and most common formians. They exist only to serve, performing all the necessary, lowly tasks that the hive needs. While they cannot speak, they can convey simple concepts (such as danger) by body movements. Through the hive mind, however, they can communicate just fine—although their intelligence still limits the concepts that they can grasp.

Workers are about the size of dogs, with clumsy claws usable only for manual labor.

Combat

Formian workers fight only to defend the hive-cities, using their mandibled bite.

Make Whole (Sp): Three workers together can repair an object as though with *make whole* cast by a 7th-level cleric. This is a full-round action for all three workers.

Heal (Sp): Eight workers together can heal a creature's wounds as though with *cure serious wounds* cast by a 7th-level cleric. This is a full-round action for all eight workers.

WARRIOR

Warriors exist only to fight. Just slightly above the workers, warriors can communicate more efficiently through the hive mind, but only to communicate battle plans and make reports to their commanders. They cannot speak otherwise.

Warriors are the size of ponies, and their claws are designed specifically for combat.

Combat

Warriors are wicked combatants, using claws, bite, and a poisonous sting all at once. Through the hive mind, they attack with coordinated and extremely efficient tactics.

Poison (Ex): Sting, Fortitude save (DC 14); initial and secondary damage 1d6 temporary Strength.

TASKMASTER

Taskmasters resemble warriors with no mandibles—no apparent mouth at all, in fact. These formians communicate only telepathically and derive sustenance from the mental energies of those they dominate.

A taskmaster's duty is to gather and control nonformians for integration into the hive. Put simply, taskmasters enslave other creatures. They do not enjoy controlling others but believe it is the only efficient way to spread the hive to all places, a desirable end for all rational creatures. If a taskmaster can manage to "conscript" a laborer without using its dominate person ability, it will.

Those few souls who have escaped refer to formian hive-cities as "work pits." While the formians are not cruel, they are still emotionless—and pitiless.

Combat

Taskmasters rely on their dominated slaves to fight for them if at all possible. If necessary, though, they can defend themselves with vicious claws and a poison stinger.

Dominate Person (Su): Taskmasters can use dominate person on any creature as the spell cast by a 10th-level sorcerer (save DC 19), although the subject may be of any type and may be up to Large size. A single taskmaster can dominate up to four subjects at a time.

Dominated Creature (Ex): A taskmaster is never encountered alone: One dominated nonformian creature always accompanies it (choose or determine randomly any creature of CR 4).

Poison (Ex): Sting, Fortitude save (DC 15); initial and secondary damage 1d6 temporary Strength.

Telepathy (Su): Taskmasters can communicate telepathically with any intelligent creature within 100 feet.

MYRMARCH

Myrmarchs are the elite of formian society. Much more than those beneath them, these creatures are individuals, with goals, desires, and creative thought. Very rarely do these ever conflict with the wishes of the queen, though—most myrmarchs are still very loyal to her.

Myrmarchs are commanders in formian armies and leaders in formian communities. They are the hands of the queen, carrying out her direct orders and making sure everything goes as exactly as she desires. Myrmarchs also have a secondary role: stamping out chaos wherever and whenever they can. Those who foment disorder, and particularly creatures that revere or exemplify it (such as slaadi), are the hated foes of myrmarchs.

Myrmarchs are the size of horses and have claws capable of fine manipulation, like human hands. They wear bronze helms to signify their position (the more elaborate the helm, the more prestige).

Myrmarchs speak Formian and Common.

Combat

Myrmarchs' claws are like hands and thus serve no combat purpose. Myrmarchs occasionally employ javelins for ranged attacks, coated with poison from their own stingers.

They fight intelligently, aiding those under them (if any such are present) and commanding them through the hive mind. If chaotic creatures are present, however, a myrmarch is single-minded in its quest to destroy them.

Poison (Ex): Sting, Fortitude save (DC 20); initial and secondary damage 2d6 temporary Dexterity.

Spell-Like Abilities: At will—*charm monster, clairaudience/clairvoyance, detect chaos, detect thoughts, magic circle against chaos,* and *teleport without error;* 1/day—*dictum* and *order's wrath.* These abilities are as the spells cast by a 12th-level sorcerer (save DC 13 + spell level).

QUEEN

The queen sits at the center of the hive-city, her bloated form never moving from the royal chamber. She is served and guarded by twenty of the most loyal myrmarchs.

The queen is half again as big as a myrmarch, with atrophied legs—she cannot move. With her telepathic abilities, though, she can send instructions to and get reports from any formian within her range.

The queen speaks Formian and Common, although she can communicate with any creature telepathically.

Combat

The queen does not fight. She has no ability to move. If necessary, a team of workers and myrmarchs (or dominated slaves) haul her enormous bulk to where she needs to go. This is very rare, however, and most of the time the queen remains within her well-defended chambers.

Despite her utter lack of physical activity, the queen can cast spells and use spell-like abilities to great effect in her own defense as well as the defense of the hive-city.

Spells: The queen casts arcane spells as a 17th-level sorcerer.

Spell-Like Abilities: At will—*calm emotions, charm monster, clairaudience/clairvoyance, detect chaos, detect thoughts, dictum, divination, hold monster, magic circle against chaos, order's wrath, shield of law,* and *true seeing.* These abilities are as the spells cast by a 17th-level sorcerer (save DC 15 + spell level).

Telepathy (Su): The queen can communicate telepathically with any intelligent creature within fifty miles whose presence she is aware of.

FROST WORM

Huge Magical Beast (Cold)
Hit Dice: 14d10+70 (147 hp)
Initiative: +4 (Improved Initiative)
Speed: 30 ft., burrow 10 ft.
AC: 18 (−2 size, +10 natural)
Attacks: Bite +20 melee
Damage: Bite 2d6+12 and 1d8 cold
Face/Reach: 5 ft. by 40 ft./10 ft.
Special Attacks: Trill, cold, breath weapon
Special Qualities: Cold subtype, death throes
Saves: Fort +14, Ref +9, Will +6
Abilities: Str 26, Dex 10, Con 20, Int 3, Wis 11, Cha 5
Skills: Hide +3*, Listen +5, Spot +4
Feats: Alertness, Improved Initiative, Iron Will

Climate/Terrain: Any cold land
Organization: Solitary
Challenge Rating: 12
Treasure: None
Alignment: Usually neutral
Advancement: 15–21 HD (Huge); 22–42 HD (Gargantuan)

Terror of the frozen lands, the frost worm is a long, blue-white creature with huge mandibles and a strange nodule from which it makes a trilling sound.

The frost worm spends most of its life burrowing through the ice, snow, and even the frozen earth. It surfaces only to attack its prey. Frost worms eat yaks, polar bears, walruses, seals, moose, and mammoths.

Sages cannot agree whether this horrible monster is related to the purple worm or to the remorhaz. Perhaps the answer is neither. It is true that frost worms hate remorhazes and attack them on sight in a colossal battle that might very well lay waste to a large area. Remorhazes are frequently the victors in such battles.

Frost worms lay eggs that to the untrained observer appear to be simply oval-shaped ice formations. Hatchling frost worms must immediately fend for themselves, growing to maturity in three to five years. Tribesfolk of the cold wastes can sometimes train young frost worms to help protect the community and even to be ridden using magic, cold-resistant saddles.

COMBAT

Frost worms lurk under the snow, waiting for prey to come near. They begin their attack with trilling and then attack helpless prey with their bite.

Trill (Su): The frost worm can emit a noise that forces its prey to stand motionless. This sonic, mind affecting compulsion affects all creatures other than frost worms within a 100-foot spread. Creatures must succeed at a Will save (DC 17) or be stunned for as long as the worm trills, even if they are attacked. However, if attacked or violently shaken (a full-round action), a victim is allowed another saving throw. Once a creature has resisted or broken the effect, it cannot be affected again by that frost worm for one day. The effect's caster level is 14.

Cold (Ex): Frost worms' bodies generate intense cold, dealing 1d8 points of damage with their touch. Creatures attacking a frost worm unarmed or with natural weapons take cold damage each time their attacks hit.

Breath Weapon (Su): Cone of cold, 30 feet long, once per hour; damage 15d6, Reflex half DC 22. Opponents held motionless by the frost worm's trill get no saving throw.

Cold Subtype (Ex): Cold immunity; double damage from fire except on a successful save.

Death Throes (Ex): When killed, a frost worm turns to ice and shatters in an explosion that deals 12d6 points of cold damage and 8d6 points of piercing damage to everything within 100 feet (Reflex half DC 22).

Skills: *A frost worm, due to its coloration and its affinity for burying itself in the snow, receives a +10 racial bonus to Hide checks in its native environment.

FUNGUS

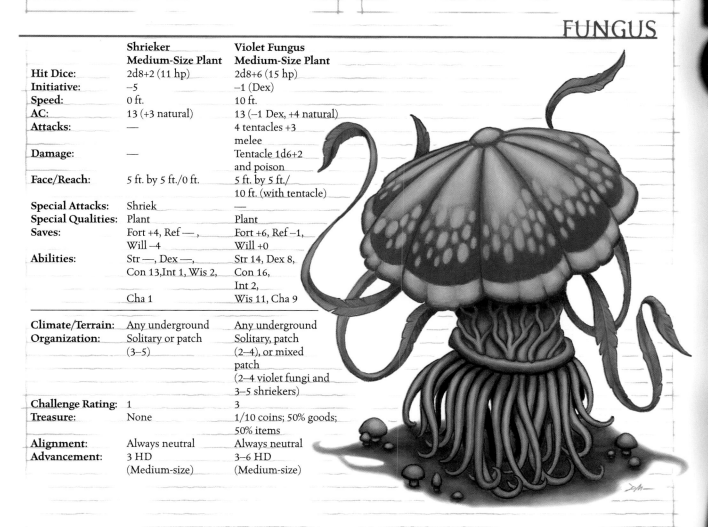

	Shrieker Medium-Size Plant	Violet Fungus Medium-Size Plant
Hit Dice:	2d8+2 (11 hp)	2d8+6 (15 hp)
Initiative:	−5	−1 (Dex)
Speed:	0 ft.	10 ft.
AC:	13 (+3 natural)	13 (−1 Dex, +4 natural)
Attacks:	—	4 tentacles +3 melee
Damage:	—	Tentacle 1d6+2 and poison
Face/Reach:	5 ft. by 5 ft./0 ft.	5 ft. by 5 ft./ 10 ft. (with tentacle)
Special Attacks:	Shriek	—
Special Qualities:	Plant	Plant
Saves:	Fort +4, Ref —, Will −4	Fort +6, Ref −1, Will +0
Abilities:	Str —, Dex —, Con 13, Int 1, Wis 2, Cha 1	Str 14, Dex 8, Con 16, Int 2, Wis 11, Cha 9
Climate/Terrain:	Any underground	Any underground
Organization:	Solitary or patch (3–5)	Solitary, patch (2–4), or mixed patch (2–4 violet fungi and 3–5 shriekers)
Challenge Rating:	1	3
Treasure:	None	1/10 coins; 50% goods; 50% items
Alignment:	Always neutral	Always neutral
Advancement:	3 HD (Medium-size)	3–6 HD (Medium-size)

Unlike normal fungi, which are harmless to other living creatures, these two specimens can be dangerous to unwary adventurers.

A fungus lacks chlorophyll, a true stem, roots, or leaves. Incapable of photosynthesis, it exists as a parasite, breaking down organic matter slowly. While both species occur individually, shriekers and violet fungi often coexist in the same environment.

COMBAT

Shriekers and violet fungi often work together to attract and kill prey. When the shriekers' hellish racket attracts a curious creature, the violet fungus tries to kill it. Both enjoy the fruits of a successful hunt.

Plant: Immune to mind-influencing effects, poison, sleep, paralysis, stunning, and polymorphing. Not subject to critical hits.

SHRIEKER

A shrieker is a stationary fungus that emits a loud noise to attract prey or when disturbed. Shriekers live in dark, underground places, often in the company of violet fungi, whose poison they are immune to. They resemble human-sized mushrooms of various shades of purple.

Combat

A shrieker has no means of attack. Instead, it lures prey to its vicinity by emitting a piercing loud noise (hence its name).

Shriek (Ex): Movement or a light source within 10 feet of a shrieker causes the fungus to emit a piercing sound that lasts for 1d3 rounds. The sound attracts nearby creatures that are disposed to investigate it. Some creatures that live near shriekers learn that the fungus's noise means there is food nearby.

VIOLET FUNGUS

Violet fungi resemble shriekers and are often found growing among them.

A violet fungus looks like a human-sized mushroom with four tendril-like tentacles and a mass of small, rootlike feelers at its base that allow slow movement. Its coloration ranges from purple overall to dull gray or violet covered with purple spots.

Combat

A violet fungus flails about with its tentacles at living creatures that come within its reach.

Poison (Ex): Tentacle, Fortitude save (DC 14); initial and secondary damage 1d4 temporary Strength and 1d4 temporary Constitution.

GARGOYLE

Medium-Size Magical Beast (Earth)
Hit Dice: 4d10+16 (38 hp)
Initiative: +2 (Dex)
Speed: 45 ft., fly 75 ft. (average)
AC: 16 (+2 Dex, +4 natural)
Attacks: 2 claws +6 melee, bite +4 melee, gore +4 melee
Damage: Claw 1d4, bite 1d6, gore 1d6
Face/Reach: 5 ft. by 5 ft./5 ft.
Special Qualities: Damage reduction 15/+1, freeze
Saves: Fort +8, Ref +6, Will +1
Abilities: Str 11, Dex 14, Con 18, Int 6, Wis 11, Cha 7
Skills: Hide +9*, Listen +4, Spot +4
Feats: Multiattack, Weapon Finesse (claw, bite, gore)

Climate/Terrain: Any land, aquatic, and underground
Organization: Solitary, pair, or wing (5–16)
Challenge Rating: 4
Treasure: Standard
Alignment: Always chaotic evil
Advancement: 5–6 HD (Medium-size); 7–12 HD (Large)

A gargoyle is a vicious flying predator that enjoys torturing creatures weaker than itself.

Gargoyles appear to be winged stone statues, for they can perch indefinitely without moving and use this disguise to surprise their foes. They require no food, water, or air but often eat their fallen foes out of fondness for inflicting pain. When not enjoying their favorite pastime, a gang of gargoyles can be found waiting silently for prey or bragging among themselves. Gargoyles speak Common and Terran.

A marine variety of gargoyle, the kapoacinth, uses its wings to swim at the listed fly speed.

COMBAT

Gargoyles either remain still, then suddenly attack, or dive onto their prey.

Freeze (Ex): A gargoyle can hold itself so still it appears to be a statue. An observer must succeed at a Spot check (DC 20) to notice the gargoyle is really alive.

Skills: *Gargoyles receive a +8 racial bonus to Hide checks when concealed against a background of worked stone.

GENIE

	Janni Medium-Size Outsider	Djinni Large Outsider (Air, Chaotic, Good)	Efreeti Large Outsider (Evil, Fire, Lawful)
Hit Dice:	6d8+6 (33 hp)	7d8+14 (45 hp)	10d8+20 (65 hp)
Initiative:	+6 (+2 Dex, +4 Improved Initiative)	+8 (+4 Dex, +4 Improved Initiative)	+7 (+3 Dex, +4 Improved Initiative)
Speed:	20 ft., fly 10 ft. (perfect) in chainmail; base 30 ft., fly 20 ft. (perfect)	20 ft., fly 60 ft. (perfect)	20 ft., fly 40 ft. (perfect)
AC:	18 (+2 Dex, +1 natural, +5 chainmail)	16 (−1 size, +4 Dex, +3 natural)	18 (−1 size, +3 Dex, +6 natural)
Attacks:	Scimitar +9/+4 melee; or longbow +8/+3 ranged	Slam +10/+5 melee	Slam +15/+10 melee
Damage:	Scimitar 1d8+4; or longbow 1d8	Slam 1d8+6	Slam 1d8+9 and 1d6 fire
Face/Reach:	5 ft. by 5 ft./5 ft.	5 ft. by 5 ft./10 ft.	5 ft. by 5 ft./10 ft.
Special Attacks:	Spell-like abilities	Spell-like abilities, air mastery, whirlwind	Spell-like abilities, heat

Special Qualities:	Plane shift, telepathy, fire resistance 30, elemental endurance	Plane shift, telepathy, acid immunity	Plane shift, telepathy
Saves:	Fort +6, Ref +7, Will +7	Fort +7, Ref +9, Will +7	Fort +9, Ref +10, Will +9
Abilities:	Str 16, Dex 15, Con 12, Int 14, Wis 15, Cha 13	Str 18, Dex 19, Con 14, Int 14, Wis 15, Cha 15	Str 23, Dex 17, Con 14, Int 12, Wis 15, Cha 15
Skills:	Appraise +8, Concentration +7, Craft (any two) +7, Escape Artist +6, Listen +8, Move Silently +6, Ride +6, Sense Motive +6, Spot +8	Appraise +9, Concentration +9, Craft (any one) +11, Escape Artist +11, Knowledge (any one) +9, Listen +9, Move Silently +9, Sense Motive +9, Spellcraft +9, Spot +9	Bluff +12, Concentration +16, Escape Artist +13, Intimidate +11, Listen +12, Move Silently +13, Sense Motive +11, Spellcraft +11, Spot +12
Feats:	Combat Reflexes, Dodge, Improved Initiative, Mobility	Combat Casting, Combat Reflexes, Dodge, Improved Initiative	Combat Casting, Combat Reflexes, Dodge, Improved Initiative
Climate/Terrain:	Any land	Any land	Any land
Organization:	Solitary, company (2–4), or band (6–15)	Solitary, company (2–4), or band (6–15)	Solitary, company (2–4), or band (6–15)
Challenge Rating:	4	5	8
Treasure:	Standard	Standard	Standard coins; double goods; standard items
Alignment:	Usually neutral	Always chaotic good	Always lawful evil
Advancement:	7–9 HD (Medium-size); 10–18 HD (Large)	8–10 HD (Large); 11–21 (Huge)	11–15 HD (Large); 16–30 HD (Huge)

Genies are humanlike beings who dwell on the elemental planes. They are famous for their strength, guile, and skill with illusion magic.

Genies sometimes use the Material Plane as a neutral ground for meeting (or fighting) others of their kind or collecting goods not readily available on their home planes.

COMBAT

Genies prefer to outmaneuver and outthink their foes. They are not too proud to flee if it means they'll live to fight another day. If trapped, they bargain, offering treasure or favors in return for their lives and freedom.

Plane Shift (Sp): A genie can enter any of the elemental planes, the Astral Plane, or the Material Plane. This ability transports the genie and up to six other creatures, provided they all link hands with the genie. It is otherwise similar to the spell of the same name.

Telepathy (Su): A genie can communicate telepathically with any creature within 100 feet that has a language.

JANNI

The jann (singular *janni*) are the weakest of the genies. Jann are formed out of all four elements and must therefore spend most of their time on the Material Plane. They favor forlorn deserts and hidden oases, where they have both privacy and safety.

Jann society is very open, treating males and females as equals. Each tribe is ruled by a sheik and one or two viziers. Exceptionally powerful sheiks are given the title of *amir*, and in times of need they gather and command large forces of jann (and sometimes allied humans).

Many jann bands are nomadic, traveling with herds of camels, goats, or sheep from oasis to oasis. These itinerant jann appear human in every respect and are often mistaken for them, unless they are attacked. The territory of a jann tribe can extend hundreds of miles in any direction.

Jann speak Common, plus Auran, Aquan, Ignan, or Terran, plus Celestial, Abyssal, or Infernal.

Combat

Jann are physically strong and courageous, and do not take kindly to insult or injury. If they meet a foe they cannot defeat in a stand-up fight, they use flight and *invisibility* to regroup and maneuver to a more advantageous position.

Spell-Like Abilities: 3/day—*invisibility*; 2/day—*enlarge* or *reduce* and *speak with animals*. These abilities are as the spells cast by a 12th-level sorcerer (save DC 11 + spell level). Once per day a janni can *create food and water* as a 7th-level priest and can use *ethereal jaunt* for 1 hour as the spell cast by a 12th-level priest.

Elemental Endurance (Ex): Jann can survive on the Elemental Planes of Air, Earth, Fire, or Water for up to 48 hours. Failure to return to the Material Plane after that time deals 1 point of damage per additional hour to a janni, until it dies or returns to the Material Plane.

DJINNI

The djinn (singular *djinni*) are genies from the Elemental Plane of Air. They live on floating islands of earth and rock, anywhere from 1,000 yards to several miles across, crammed with buildings, courtyards, gardens, fountains, and sculptures. Each island is ruled by a local sheik.

The structure of djinn society is based on rule by a caliph served by various nobles and officials (viziers, beys, amirs, sheiks, sharifs, and maliks). A caliph rules all djinn estates within two days' travel and is advised by six viziers who help maintain the balance of the landholds.

If a large force attacks a landhold, a messenger (usually the youngest djinni) is sent to the next landhold, which sends aid and dispatches two more messengers to warn the next landholds, thus alerting the entire nation.

A djinni is about 10 1/2 feet tall and weighs about 100 pounds. Djinn speak Auran, Celestial, Common, and Ignan.

Noble Djinn

Some djinn (1% of the total population) are "noble" and can grant three *wishes* to any being (nongenies only) who captures them. Noble djinn perform no other services and, upon granting the third *wish*, are free of their servitude. Noble djinn are as strong as efreet (see below), with 10 HD.

Combat

Djinn disdain physical combat, preferring to use their magical powers and aerial abilities against foes. A djinni overmatched in combat usually takes flight and becomes a whirlwind to harass those who follow.

Air Mastery (Ex): Airborne creatures suffer a –1 circumstance penalty to attack and damage rolls against a djinni.

Whirlwind (Su): The djinni can transform itself into a whirlwind once every 10 minutes and remain in that form for up to 7 rounds. In this form, it can move through the air or along a surface at its fly speed.

The whirlwind is 5 feet wide at the base, up to 30 feet wide at the top and up to 50 feet tall. The djinni controls the exact height, but it must be at least 10 feet.

Medium-size or smaller creatures might take damage when caught in the whirlwind and be lifted into the air. An affected creature must succeed at a Reflex save (DC 20) when it comes into contact with the whirlwind or take 3d6 points of damage. It must also succeed at a second Reflex save or be picked up bodily and held suspended in the powerful winds, automatically taking 1d8 points of damage each round. A creature that can fly is allowed a Reflex save (DC 20) each round to escape the whirlwind. The creature still takes damage but can leave if the save is successful.

The djinni can eject any carried creatures whenever it wishes, depositing them wherever the whirlwind happens to be.

If the whirlwind's base touches the ground, it creates a swirling cloud of debris. This cloud is centered on the djinni and has a diameter equal to half the whirlwind's height. The cloud obscures all vision, including darkvision, beyond 5 feet. Creatures 5 feet away have one-half concealment, while those farther away have total concealment (see Concealment, page 133 in the *Player's Handbook*). Those caught in the cloud must succeed at a Concentration check (DC 20) to cast a spell.

Spell-Like Abilities: 1/round—*invisibility* (self only); 1/day—*create food and water*, *create wine* (as *create water*, but wine instead), *major creation* (created vegetable matter is permanent), *persistent image*, and *wind walk*. These abilities are as the spells cast by a 20th-level sorcerer (save DC 12 + spell level). Once per day, a djinni can assume *gaseous form* (as the spell) for up to 1 hour.

EFREETI

The efreet (singular *efreeti*) are genies from the Elemental Plane of Fire. They are said to be made of basalt, bronze, and congealed flames. Efreet are infamous for their hatred of servitude, desire for revenge, cruel nature, and ability to beguile and mislead. Their primary home is the fabled City of Brass, but there are many efreet outposts throughout the Plane of Fire, military stations for watching or harassing others on the plane. They are enemies of the djinn and attack them whenever they meet.

The efreet are ruled by a grand sultan who makes his home in the City of Brass. He is advised by a variety of beys, amirs, and maliks concerning actions on the plane, and by six great pashas who deal with efreet business on the Material.

The City of Brass is a huge citadel that is home to the majority of efreet. It hovers in the hot regions of the plane and is bordered by seas and lakes of glowing magma. The city sits upon a hemisphere of glowing brass some forty miles across. From the upper towers rise the minarets of the great bastion of the sultan's palace, which is said to hold vast riches. The city's population far outnumbers any of the great cities of the Material Plane.

An efreeti stands about 12 feet tall and weighs about 2,000 pounds. Efreet speak Ignan, Common, Auran, and Infernal.

Combat

Efreet love to mislead, befuddle, and confuse their foes. They do so for enjoyment as well as a battle tactic.

Spell-Like Abilities: At will—*produce flame* and *pyrotechnics*; 1/day—grant up to three *wishes* (to nongenies only), *detect magic*, *enlarge*, *gaseous form*, *invisibility*, *permanent image*, *polymorph self*, and *wall of fire*. These abilities are as the spells cast by an 18th-level sorcerer (save DC 12 + spell level).

Heat (Ex): An efreeti's red-hot body deals 1d6 points of additional fire damage whenever it hits in melee, or when grappling, each round it maintains a hold.

Fire Subtype (Ex): Fire immunity, double damage from cold except on a successful save.

	Ghoul	Ghast
	Medium-Size Undead	**Medium-Size Undead**
Hit Dice:	2d12 (13 hp)	4d12 (26 hp)
Initiative:	+2 (Dex)	+2 (Dex)
Speed:	30 ft.	30 ft.
AC:	14 (+2 Dex, +2 natural)	16 (+2 Dex, +4 natural)
Attacks:	Bite +3 melee; 2 claws +0 melee	Bite +4 melee; 2 claws +1 melee
Damage:	Bite 1d6+1 and paralysis; claw 1d3 and paralysis	Bite 1d8+1 and paralysis; claw 1d4 and paralysis
Face/Reach:	5 ft. by 5 ft./5 ft.	5 ft. by 5 ft./5 ft.
Special Attacks:	Paralysis, create spawn	Stench, paralysis, create spawn
Special Qualities:	Undead, +2 turn resistance	Undead, +2 turn resistance
Saves:	Fort +0, Ref +2, Will +5	Fort +1, Ref +3, Will +6
Abilities:	Str 13, Dex 15, Con —, Int 13, Wis 14, Cha 16	Str 13, Dex 15, Con —, Int 13, Wis 14, Cha 16
Skills:	Climb +6, Escape Artist +7, Hide +7, Intuit Direction +3, Jump +6, Listen +7, Move Silently +7, Search +6, Spot +7	Climb +6, Escape Artist +8, Hide +8, Intuit Direction +3, Jump +6, Listen +8, Move Silently +7, Search +6, Spot +8
Feats:	Multiattack, Weapon Finesse (bite)	Multiattack, Weapon Finesse (bite)
Climate/Terrain:	Any land, aquatic, and underground	Any land and underground
Organization:	Solitary, gang (2–4), or pack (7–12)	Solitary, gang (2–4), or pack (2–4 plus 7–12 ghouls)
Challenge Rating:	1	3
Treasure:	None	Standard
Alignment:	Always chaotic evil	Always chaotic evil
Advancement:	3 HD (Medium-size)	5–6 HD (Medium-size)

Ghouls haunt graveyards, battlefields, and other places rich with the carrion they hunger for. These terrible creatures lurk wherever the stench of death hangs heavy, ready to devour the unwary.

Ghouls are said to be created on the death of a living man or woman who savored the taste of the flesh of people. This may or may not be true, but it does explain the disgusting behavior of these anthropophagous undead. Some believe that anyone of exceptional debauchery and wickedness runs the risk of becoming a ghoul.

That ghouls were once people is obvious to those with the courage to look upon them. Although they still appear more or less humanoid, their mottled, decaying flesh is drawn tight across clearly visible bones. The transformation from living beings into fell things of the night has warped their minds, making them cunning and feral. Their eyes burn like hot coals in their sunken sockets.

Ghouls speak the languages they spoke in life (usually Common).

COMBAT

Ghouls try to attack with surprise whenever possible. They strike from behind tombstones, leap from mausoleums, and burst from shallow graves.

Paralysis (Ex): Those hit by a ghoul's bite or claw attack must succeed at a Fortitude save (DC 14) or be paralyzed for 1d6+2 minutes. Elves are immune to this paralysis.

Create Spawn (Su): In most cases, ghouls devour those they kill. From time to time,

however, the bodies of their humanoid victims lie where they fell, to rise as ghouls themselves in 1d4 days. Casting *protection from evil* on a body before the end of that time averts the transformation. (The statistics above are for human ghouls and ghasts. Ghouls and ghasts may vary depending on their original race or kind.)

Undead: Immune to mind-influencing effects, poison, sleep, paralysis, stunning, and disease. Not subject to critical hits, subdual damage, ability damage, energy drain, or death from massive damage.

LACEDON

These aquatic cousins of the ghoul lurk near hidden reefs or other places where ships are likely to meet their end. They have a swim speed of 30 feet.

GHAST

Although these creatures look just like their lesser kin, they are far more deadly and cunning.

Combat

Stench (Ex): The stink of death and corruption surrounding these creatures is sickening. Those within 10 feet must succeed at a Fortitude save (DC 15) or be wracked with nausea, suffering a −2 circumstance penalty to all attacks, saves, and skill checks for 1d6+4 minutes.

Paralysis (Ex): Those hit by a ghast's bite or claw attack must succeed at a Fortitude save (DC 15) or be paralyzed for 1d6+4 minutes. Even elves are vulnerable to this paralysis.

Illus. by B. Snoddy

	Hill Giant Large Giant	Stone Giant Large Giant (Earth)	Frost Giant Large Giant (Cold)
Hit Dice:	12d8+48 (102 hp)	14d8+56 (119 hp)	14d8+70 (133 hp)
Initiative:	–1 (Dex)	+2 (Dex)	–1 (Dex)
Speed:	40 ft.	40 ft.	40 ft.
AC:	20 (–1 size, –1 Dex, +9 natural, +3 hide)	25 (–1 size, +2 Dex, +11 natural, +3 hide)	21 (–1 size, –1 Dex, +9 natural, +4 chain shirt)
Attacks:	Huge greatclub +16/+11 melee; or rock +8/+3 ranged	Huge greatclub +17/+12 melee; or rock +12/+7 ranged	Huge greataxe +18/+13 melee; or rock +9/+4 ranged
Damage:	Huge greatclub 2d6+10; or rock 2d6+7	Huge greatclub 2d6+12; or rock 2d8+8	Huge greataxe 2d8+13; or rock 2d6+9
Face/Reach:	5 ft. by 5 ft./10 ft.	5 ft. by 5 ft./10 ft.	5 ft. by 5 ft./10 ft.
Special Attacks:	Rock throwing	Rock throwing, and see text	Rock throwing
Special Qualities:	Rock catching	Rock catching	Rock catching, cold subtype
Saves:	Fort +12, Ref +3, Will +4	Fort +13, Ref +6, Will +4	Fort +14, Ref +3, Will +4
Abilities:	Str 25, Dex 8, Con 19, Int 6, Wis 10, Cha 17	Str 27, Dex 15, Con 19, Int 10, Wis 10, Cha 11	Str 29, Dex 9, Con 21, Int 10, Wis 10, Cha 11
Skills:	Climb +9, Jump +9, Spot +4	Climb +10, Hide +0*, Jump +10, Spot +3	Climb +13, Jump +13, Spot +6
Feats:	Cleave, Power Attack, Weapon Focus (greatclub)	Combat Reflexes, Point Blank Shot, Power Attack, Precise Shot	Cleave, Great Cleave, Power Attack, Sunder

Climate/Terrain:	Any hill, mountains, and underground	Any mountains	Any cold land and underground
Organization:	Solitary, gang (2–5), band (6–9 plus 35% noncombatants), hunting/raiding party (6–9 plus 2–4 dire wolves), or tribe (21–30 plus 35% noncombatants plus 12–30 dire wolves, 2–4 ogres, and 12–22 orcs)	Solitary, gang (2–5), band (6–9 plus 35% noncombatants), hunting/raiding/trading party (6–9 plus 1 elder), or tribe (21–30 plus 35% noncombatants plus 1–3 elders and 3–6 dire bears)	Solitary, gang (2–5), band (6–9 plus 35% noncombatants plus 1 adept or cleric of 1st or 2nd level), hunting/raiding party (6–9 plus 35% noncombatants plus 1 adept or sorcerer of 3rd–5th level plus 2–4 winter wolves and 2–3 ogres), or tribe (21–30 plus 1 adept, cleric, or sorcerer of 6th or 7th level plus 12–30 winter wolves, 12–22 ogres, and 1–2 young white dragons)
Challenge Rating:	7	8	9
Treasure:	Standard	Standard	Standard
Alignment:	Often chaotic evil	Usually neutral	Often chaotic evil
Advancement:	By character class	By character class	By character class

	Fire Giant Large Giant (Fire)	Cloud Giant Huge Giant (Air)	Storm Giant Huge Giant (Electricity)
Hit Dice:	15d8+75 (142 hp)	17d8+102 (178 hp)	19d8+114 (199 hp)
Initiative:	–1 (Dex)	+1 (Dex)	+2 (Dex)
Speed:	30 ft. (chainmail); base 40 ft.	50 ft.	40 ft., swim 30 ft. (breastplate); base 50 ft., swim 40 ft.
AC:	21 (–1 size, –1 Dex, +8 natural, +5 chainmail)	21 (–2 size, +1 Dex, +12 natural)	27 (–2 size, +2 Dex, +12 natural, +5 breastplate)
Attacks:	Huge greatsword +20/+15/+10 melee; or rock +10/+5/+0 ranged	Gargantuan morningstar +22/+17/+12 melee; or rock +12/+7/+2 ranged	Gargantuan greatsword +26/+21/+16 melee; or Gargantuan mighty composite longbow (+14) +14/+9/+4 ranged
Damage:	Huge greatsword 2d8+15; or rock 2d6+10 and 2d6 fire	Gargantuan morningstar 4d6+18; or rock 2d8+12	Gargantuan greatsword 4d6+21; or Gargantuan mighty composite longbow (+14) 2d8+14
Face/Reach:	5 ft. by 5 ft./10 ft.	10 ft. by 10 ft./15 ft.	10 ft. by 10 ft./15 ft.
Special Attacks:	Rock throwing	Rock throwing, spell-like abilities	Spell-like abilities
Special Qualities:	Rock catching, fire subtype	Rock catching, scent	Electricity immunity, rock catching, freedom of movement, water breathing
Saves:	Fort +14, Ref +4, Will +5	Fort +16, Ref +6, Will +6	Fort +17, Ref +8, Will +9
Abilities:	Str 31, Dex 9, Con 21, Int 10, Wis 10, Cha 11	Str 35, Dex 13, Con 23, Int 12, Wis 12, Cha 13	Str 39, Dex 14, Con 23, Int 16, Wis 16, Cha 15
Skills:	Climb +11, Jump +11, Spot +7	Climb +16, Jump +16, Listen +10, Spot +10	Climb +18, Concentration +12, Jump +12, Perform (chant, dance, drama, harp, recorder) +7, Spot +8
Feats:	Cleave, Great Cleave, Power Attack, Sunder	Alertness, Cleave, Great Cleave, Power Attack	Cleave, Combat Reflexes, Great Cleave, Power Attack, Sunder

Climate/Terrain:	Any land and underground	Temperate and warm mountains and aquatic	Temperate and warm mountains
Organization:	Solitary, gang (2–5), band (6–9 plus 35% noncombatants plus 1 adept or cleric of 1st or 2nd level), hunting/raiding party (6–9 plus 1 adept or sorcerer of 3rd–5th level plus 2–4 hell hounds and 2–3 trolls or ettins), or tribe (21–30 plus 1 adept, cleric, or sorcerer of 6th or 7th level plus 12–30 hell hounds, 12–22 trolls, 5–12 ettins, and 1–2 young red dragons)	Solitary, gang (2–4), family (2–4 plus 35% noncombatants plus 1 sorcerer or cleric of 4th–7th level plus 2–5 griffons or 2–8 dire lions), or band (6–9 plus 1 sorcerer or cleric of 4th–7th level plus 2–5 griffons or 2–8 dire lions)	Solitary or family (2–4 plus 35% noncombatants plus 1 sorcerer or cleric of 7th–10th level plus 1–2 rocs, 2–5 griffons, or 2–8 sea lions)
Challenge Rating:	10	11	13
Treasure:	Standard	Standard coins; double goods; standard items	Standard coins; double goods; standard items
Alignment:	Often lawful evil	Usually neutral good or neutral evil	Often chaotic good
Advancement:	By character class	By character class	By character class

Giants combine great size with even greater strength, giving them an unparalleled ability to wreak destruction upon anyone or anything unfortunate enough to get in their way.

Giants have a reputation for crudeness and stupidity that is not undeserved, especially among the evil varieties. Most rely on their legendary strength to solve problems: Any difficulty that won't succumb to brute force isn't worth worrying about. Giants usually subsist by hunting and raiding, taking what they like from creatures weaker than themselves.

All giants speak Giant. Those with Intelligence scores of at least 10 also speak Common.

COMBAT

Giants relish melee combat. They favor massive two-handed weapons and wield them with impressive skill. They possess enough cunning to soften up a foe with ranged attacks first, if they can. A giant's favorite ranged weapon is a big rock.

Rock Throwing (Ex): Adult giants are accomplished rock throwers and receive a +1 racial bonus to attack rolls when throwing rocks. A giant of at least Large size can hurl rocks weighing 40 to 50 pounds each (Small objects) up to 5 range increments. The size of the range increment varies with the giant's variety. A Huge giant can hurl rocks of 60 to 80 pounds (Medium-size objects).

Rock Catching (Ex): A giant of at least Large size can catch Small, Medium-size, or Large rocks (or projectiles of similar shape). Once per round, a giant that would normally be hit by a rock can make a Reflex save to catch it as a free action. The DC is 15 for a Small rock, 20 for a Medium-size one, and 25 for a Large one. (If the projectile has a magical bonus to attack, the DC increases by that amount.) The giant must be ready for and aware of the attack.

GIANT SOCIETY

Solitary giants are usually young adults striking out on their own. Gangs are usually made up of young adults who hunt or raid (or both) together. Giant bands are usually large or extended families. Sometimes a band contains unrelated young adults that the band has taken in as mates, servants, or guards.

Giant clans and tribes are similar to bands but have more members, plus contingents of guard animals and nongiant servants.

GIANTS' BAGS

Most giants carry big leather shoulder sacks to hold their personal possessions. It is a common myth that giant's bags are stuffed with gold (always at least 1,000 gp by some accounts). In truth, they usually hold a few battered and smelly personal items, a supply of throwing rocks, some less than fresh rations, and a few trinkets. However, giants sometimes carry magic treasures that are too small for them to use, and many adventurers find looting a giant's bag worthwhile. The table below shows typical mundane items; roll d% or choose from the list. The exact number of items varies according to the giant variety (see each entry).

MUNDANE GIANT'S BAG CONTENTS

d%	Item
01–02	Berries or fruit
03–08	Bowl and spoon
09–10	Candles (1d6)
11–14	Hand-held chopper
15–16	Sticks or charcoal (1d6) or quills and ink
17–18	Chunk of cheese
19–20	Chunk of wood, whittled or carved
21–23	Cup or tankard
24–27	Cloak
28–29	Comb or brush
30–31	Cooking pot
32–33	Container of grease or grease paint
34–35	Drinking horn
36–37	Bag of flour or meal (5 pounds)
38–39	Piece of fur or hide
40–41	Hairpins
42–47	Knife
48–53	Knucklebones or dice
54–57	Haunch of meat
58–59	Incense or dried animal dung
60–65	100 to 200 feet of strong rope
66–67	Bag of salt (1 pound)
68–73	Shoes, sandals, or boots
74–76	Sewing needle
77–81	String or thread
82–86	Beads, stones, teeth, or tusks
87–93	Tinderbox (flint, steel, and tinder)
94–96	Lump of wax
97–00	Whetstone

Parties include guard animals and giants from a nearby tribe, or from several bands, working together.

About a third of the giants in a band or tribe are children. Giant children can be formidable creatures in their own right. When a group of giants includes children, roll d% for each child to determine maturity: 01–25 = infant (no combat ability); 26–50 = juvenile (two sizes smaller than an adult, 8 fewer HD, Strength and Constitution scores –8, and 1 rank in each skill that an adult has); and 51–100 = adolescent (one size smaller than an adult, 4 fewer HD, Strength and Constitution scores –4, and 2, 3, or 4 ranks in each skill that an adult has). Giant children can throw rocks if they meet the minimum size requirement (see above). Except where noted here, giant children are identical with adults of their variety.

HILL GIANT

Hill giants are selfish, cunning brutes who survive through hunting and raiding.

Hill giants have an oddly simian appearance, with overlong arms, stooped shoulders, low foreheads, and thick, powerful limbs. Their skin color ranges from light tan to deep ruddy brown. Their hair is brown or black, with eyes the same color. Hill giants wear layers of crudely prepared hides with the fur left on. They seldom wash or repair their garments, preferring to simply add more hides as their old ones wear out.

Adults are about 10 1/2 feet tall and weigh about 1,100 pounds. Hill giants can live to be 200 years old.

A hill giant's bag usually contains 2d4 throwing rocks, 1d4+4 mundane items, and the giant's personal wealth. These possessions tend to be well worn, filthy, and stinky. The items are usually crude and often jury-rigged or salvaged from some similar item. Examples include a hand chopper made from a broken battleaxe head, a wooden bowl and spoon, or a drinking cup made from a big gourd or a skull.

Combat

Hill giants prefer to fight from high, rocky outcroppings where they can pelt opponents with rocks and boulders while limiting the risk to themselves. Their thrown rocks have a range increment of 120 feet.

Hill giants love to make overrun attacks against smaller creatures when they first join battle. Thereafter, they stand fast and swing away with their massive clubs.

Hill Giant Society

Although hill giants prefer temperate areas, they can be found in practically any climate where there is an abundance of hills and mountains. Individuals and bands tend to be aggressive and prefer taking what they want over trading. Tribes (and some bands) often trade with other giants or with groups of ogres or orcs to get foodstuffs, trinkets, and servants.

STONE GIANT

Stone giants have a largely undeserved reputation as rock-throwing hooligans. In fact, they tend to be somewhat shy around strangers.

Stone giants resemble lean, muscular humans. Their hard, hairless flesh is smooth and gray, making it easy for them to blend in with their mountainous surroundings. They have gaunt facial features and deep-sunken, black eyes that make them seem perpetually grim. Stone giants prefer thick leather garments, dyed shades of brown and gray to match the stone around them.

Adults are about 12 feet tall and weigh about 1,500 pounds. Stone giants can live to be 800 years old.

Stone giants tend to be shy around strangers, but are by no means timid. Many stone giants have an artistic streak. Some draw and paint scenes of their lives on the walls of their lairs and on tanned hide scrolls. Some are fond of music and play stone flutes and drums. Others make simple jewelry, fashioning painted stone beads into necklaces.

Most stone giants are playful, especially at night. They are fond of rock-throwing contests and other games that test their might. Groups of giants often gather to toss rocks at each other, the losing side being those who are hit more often. Travelers' reports of such contests have given stone giants their reputation for wildness.

A stone giant's bag usually contains 2d12 throwing rocks, 1d4+6 mundane items, and the giant's personal wealth. A stone giant's possessions are nether particularly clean nor particularly dirty, but most of them are made from stone.

Combat

Stone giants fight from a distance whenever possible, but if they can't avoid melee, they use gigantic clubs chiseled out of stone. They use both hands to hurl rocks, with a range increment of 180 feet. A stone giant gains a +4 racial bonus when attempting to catch a thrown rock.

A favorite tactic of stone giants is to stand nearly motionless, blending in with the background, then move forward to throw rocks and surprise their foes.

Skills: *A stone giant gains a +8 racial bonus to Hide checks in rocky terrain.

Stone Giant Elders

Some stone giants develop special abilities related to their environment. These giant elders have Charisma scores of at least 15 and spell-like abilities, which they use as 10th-level sorcerers. Once per day they can use *stone shape*, *stone tell*, and either *transmute rock to mud* or *transmute mud to rock*. One in ten elders is a sorcerer, usually of 3rd to 6th level.

Stone Giant Society

Stone giants prefer to dwell in deep caves high on rocky, storm-swept mountains. Usually, groups live fairly close together (no more than a day's travel apart) for a sense of community and protection. Most stone giant lairs have 2d4 neighboring lairs. Some older stone giants choose to live in solitude, meditating and creating artwork. Many of them become elders after several decades.

Most groups of stone giants subsist by hunting, gathering, and herding mountain animals such as sheep or goats. They trade with any other nearby communities, exchanging foodstuffs and stone goods for cloth, pottery, and manufactured items. Groups of evil giants often go raiding or extort tolls from mountain travelers.

FROST GIANT

Frost giants are justifiably feared as brutal and wantonly destructive raiders.

They look like beefy, muscular humans with snow-white or ivory skin. Their hair is light blue or dirty yellow, with matching eyes. They dress in skins and pelts, along with any jewelry they own. Frost giant warriors add chain shirts and metal helmets decorated with horns or feathers.

An adult male is about 15 feet tall and weighs about 2,800 pounds. Females are slightly shorter and lighter, but otherwise identical with males. Frost giants can live to be 250 years old.

A frost giant's bag usually contains 1d4+1 throwing rocks, 3d4 mundane items, and the giant's personal wealth. Everything in a frost giant's bag is old, worn, dirty, and smelly, making the identification of any valuable items difficult.

Combat

Frost giants usually start combat at a distance, throwing rocks until they run out of ammunition or the opponent closes, then wading in with their enormous battleaxes. Their thrown rocks have a range increment of 120 feet.

A favorite strategy is to lay an ambush by hiding buried in the snow at the top of an icy or snowy slope, where opponents will have difficulty reaching them.

Cold Subtype (Ex): Cold immunity; double damage from fire except on a successful save.

Frost Giant Society

Frost giants live in frigid, arctic lands of glaciers and heavy snowfall. They make their lairs in crude castles or frigid caverns. Tribal leaders call themselves "jarls." Frost giant groups depend on hunting and raiding, though they sometimes make trading and defensive alliances with neighboring giants.

Frost giants often take captives. For each ten adult giants in a band or clan, there is a 20% chance that the lair has 1d2 captives. These can be of any sort.

Frost Giant Characters

Many groups of frost giants include clerics with access to any two of the following domains: Chaos, Destruction, Evil, and War (most choose Destruction or War).

FIRE GIANT

Fire giants are brutal, ruthless, and militaristic. They are tall but squat, resembling huge dwarves.

They have coal-black skin, flaming red or bright orange hair, and prognathous jaws that reveal dirty ivory or yellow teeth. An adult male is 12 feet tall, has a chest that measures 9 feet around, and weighs about 7,000 pounds. Females are slightly shorter and lighter. Fire giants can live to be 350 years old.

Fire giants wear sturdy cloth or leather garments colored red, orange, yellow, or black. Warriors wear helmets and chainmail of blackened steel.

A typical fire giant's bag contains 1d4+1 throwing rocks, 3d4 mundane items, a tinderbox, and the giant's personal wealth. Everything a fire giant owns is battered, dirty, and often singed from great heat.

Combat

Fire giants' thrown rocks have a range increment of 120 feet. Fire giants heat their rocks in fires, geysers, or lava pools, so that they deal additional damage. They favor magic flaming swords in melee (when they can get them). They are also fond of grabbing smaller opponents and tossing them somewhere very hot.

Fire Subtype (Ex): Fire immunity, double damage from cold except on a successful save.

Fire Giant Society

Fire giants dwell only in hot places. They prefer volcanic regions or areas with hot springs. They live in well-organized military groups, occupying large castles or caverns. Tribal leaders call themselves "kings" and "queens." Fire giants usually engage in ongoing military campaigns to subjugate the areas around them and often receive tribute from creatures living nearby.

Fire giants often take captives. For each ten adult giants in a band or clan, there is a 30% chance that the lair has 1d2 captives. These can be of any sort.

Fire Giant Characters

Most groups of fire giants include clerics with access to any two of the following domains: Evil, Law, Trickery, and War (most choose Trickery or War).

CLOUD GIANT

Cloud giants consider themselves above all others, except storm giants, whom they regard as equals. They are creative, appreciate fine things, and are master strategists in battle.

Cloud giants have muscular humanoid builds and handsome, well-defined features. Cloud giants' skin ranges in color from milky white tinged with blue to light sky blue. Their hair is silvery white or brass, and their eyes are iridescent blue. Adult males are about 18 feet tall and weigh about 5,000 pounds. Females are slightly shorter and lighter. Cloud giants can live to be 400 years old.

Cloud giants dress in the finest clothing available and wear jewelry. To many, appearance indicates station: The better the clothes and the finer the jewelry, the more important the wearer. They also appreciate music, and most can play one or more instruments (the harp is a favorite).

Unlike most other giant varieties, cloud giants leave their treasure in their lairs. Their bags contain food, 1d4+1 throwing rocks, 3d4 mundane items, a modest amount of cash (no more than 10d10 coins), and a musical instrument. A cloud giant's possessions are usually well made and maintained.

Combat

Cloud giants fight in well-organized units, using carefully developed battle plans. They prefer to fight from a position above their opponents. A favorite tactic is to circle the enemy, barraging them with rocks while the giants with magical abilities assault them with spells. A cloud giant's thrown rocks have a range increment of 140 feet.

Spell-Like Abilities: Cloud giants who dwell on cloud islands (see below) can use the following as the spells cast by a 15th-level sorcerer: 3/day—*levitate* (self plus 2,000 pounds) and *obscuring mist*; 1/day—*fog cloud*.

Skills and Feats: Cloud giants have EHD as though they were large creatures.

Cloud Giant Society

The majority of cloud giants dwell on cloud-covered mountain peaks, making their lairs in crude castles. They live in small groups but know the location of 1d8 other groups and band together with some of these for celebrations, battles, or trade. About 10% of the population builds castles on enchanted cloud islands and tends to be isolated from other cloud giants.

Cloud islands are fantastic places with giant-sized gardens of fruit trees. According to legend, some giants mine their clouds for small chunks of the purest silver.

Good cloud giants trade with humanoid communities for food, wine, jewelry, and cloth. Some establish such good relations that they come to a community's aid if it is endangered. Evil cloud giants raid communities to get what they want.

Cloud Giant Characters

Some cloud giant groups include sorcerers or clerics. Good clerics have access to any two of the following domains: Good, Healing, Strength, and Sun. Evil clerics have access to any two of the following domains: Death, Evil, and Trickery.

STORM GIANT

Storm giants are gentle and reclusive. They are usually tolerant of others but can be very dangerous when angry.

Storm giants resemble well-formed humans of enormous proportions. They have pale, light green or (rarely) violet skin. Green-skinned storm giants have dark green hair and glittering emerald eyes. Violet-skinned storm giants have deep violet or blue-black hair with silvery gray or purple eyes. Adults are about 21 feet tall and weigh about 12,000 pounds. Storm giants can live to be 600 years old.

Storm giants' garb is usually a short, loose tunic belted at the waist, sandals or bare feet, and a headband. They wear a few pieces of simple but finely crafted jewelry, anklets (favored by barefoot giants), rings, or circlets being most common. They live quiet, reflective lives and spend their time musing about the world, composing and playing music, and tilling their land or gathering food.

Storm giants usually carry pouches attached to their belts instead of shoulder sacks. These hold a simple musical instrument (usually a pan pipe or harp) and 2d4 mundane items. Other than the jewelry they wear, they prefer to leave their wealth in their lairs. A storm giant's possessions are usually simple (if not downright primitive), but well crafted and maintained.

Combat

Storm giants use weapons and spell-like abilities instead of hurling rocks. Their outsize composite longbows have a range increment of 180 feet.

Illus. by T. Lockwood

Spell-Like Abilities: Once per day a storm giant can *call lightning* as a 15th-level druid and use *chain lighting* as a 15th-level sorcerer. Twice per day a storm giant can *control weather* as a 20th-level druid and *levitate* as a 20th-level sorcerer. Save DC is 12 + spell level.

Freedom of Movement (Su): Storm giants continuously have freedom of movement as the spell.

Water Breathing (Ex): Storm giants can breathe underwater indefinitely and can freely use their spell-like abilities while submerged.

Skills and Feats: Storm giants have EHD as though they were large creatures. Storm giants ignore all weight penalties for gear carried when swimming.

Storm Giant Society

Storm giants live in castles built on cloud islands (01–70 on d%), mountain peaks (71–90), or underwater (91–00). They live off the land in the immediate vicinity of their lairs. If the natural harvest is not enough to sustain them, they create and carefully till large gardens, fields, and vineyards. They do not keep animals for food, preferring to hunt. Land- and air-dwelling storm giants usually are on good terms with neighboring silver dragons and good cloud giants, and cooperate with them for mutual defense. Aquatic storm giants have similar relationships with merfolk and bronze dragons.

Storm Giant Characters

About 20% of adult storm giants are sorcerers or clerics. Storm giant clerics can choose two of the following domains: Chaos, Good, Protection, and War.

GIANT EAGLE

Large Magical Beast
Hit Dice: 4d10+4 (26 hp)
Initiative: +3 (Dex)
Speed: 10 ft., fly 80 ft. (average)
AC: 15 (−1 size, +3 Dex, +3 natural)
Attacks: 2 claws +7 melee, bite +2 melee
Damage: Claw 1d6+4, bite 1d8+2
Face/Reach: 5 ft. by 5 ft./5 ft.
Special Qualities: Evasion
Saves: Fort +5, Ref +7, Will +3
Abilities: Str 18, Dex 17, Con 12, Int 10, Wis 14, Cha 10
Skills: Knowledge (nature) +2, Listen +5, Sense Motive +8, Spot +11*, Wilderness Lore +8
Feats: Alertness

Climate/Terrain: Any forest, hill, mountains, and plains
Organization: Solitary or pair
Challenge Rating: 3
Treasure: None
Alignment: Usually neutral good
Advancement: 5–8 HD (Huge); 9–12 HD (Gargantuan)

Giant eagles are intelligent, keen-eyed birds of prey that sometimes associate with good creatures.

They attack creatures that appear threatening, especially those intent on raiding the eagles' nest for eggs or fledglings, which fetch a handsome price in many civilized areas. Young eagles can be trained and are prized as aerial mounts.

A typical giant eagle stands about 10 feet tall, has a wingspan of up to 20 feet, and resembles its smaller cousins in nearly every way except size.

Giant eagles speak Common and Auran.

COMBAT

A giant eagle typically attacks from a great height, diving earthward at tremendous speed. When it cannot dive, it uses its powerful talons and slashing beak to strike at its target's head and eyes.

A solitary giant eagle is typically hunting or patrolling in the vicinity of its nest and generally ignores creatures that do not appear threatening. A mated pair will attack in concert, making repeated diving attacks to drive away intruders, and will fight to the death to defend their nests or hatchlings.

Skills: *Giant eagles receive a +4 racial bonus to Spot checks during daylight hours.

TRAINING A GIANT EAGLE

Training a giant eagle as an aerial mount requires a successful Handle Animal check (DC 24 for a young creature, or DC 29 for an adult) and that the creature be willing.

Giant eagle eggs are worth 2,500 gp apiece on the open market, while chicks are worth 4,000 gp each. Professional trainers charge 1,000 gp to rear or train a giant eagle, and riding one requires an exotic saddle. A giant eagle can fight while carrying a rider, but the rider cannot also attack unless he or she succeeds at a Ride check (see Ride, page 72 in the *Player's Handbook*).

Carrying Capacity: A light load for a giant eagle is up to 300 pounds; a medium load, 301–600 pounds; and a heavy load, 601–900 pounds.

GIANT OWL

Large Magical Beast
Hit Dice: 4d10+4 (26 hp)
Initiative: +3 (Dex)
Speed: 10 ft., fly 70 ft. (average)
AC: 15 (–1 size, +3 Dex, +3 natural)
Attacks: 2 claws +7 melee, bite +2 melee
Damage: Claw 1d6+4, bite 1d8+2
Face/Reach: 5 ft. by 5 ft./5 ft.
Special Qualities: Superior low-light vision
Saves: Fort +5, Ref +7, Will +3
Abilities: Str 18, Dex 17, Con 12, Int 10, Wis 14, Cha 10
Skills: Knowledge (nature) +6, Listen +16, Move Silently +9*, Spot +10*
Feats: Alertness

Climate/Terrain: Any forest, hill, mountains and plains
Organization: Solitary, pair, or company (2–5)
Challenge Rating: 3
Treasure: None
Alignment: Usually neutral good
Advancement: 5–8 HD (Huge); 9–12 HD (Gargantuan)

Giant owls are nocturnal birds of prey, feared for their ability to hunt and attack in near silence. They are intelligent, and though naturally suspicious, sometimes associate with good creatures.

They attack creatures that appear threatening, especially those intent on raiding the owls' nest for eggs or fledglings, which fetch a handsome price in many civilized areas. Young owls can be trained and are prized as aerial mounts.

A typical giant owl stands about 9 feet tall, has a wingspan of up to 20 feet, and resembles its smaller cousins in nearly every way except size.

Giant owls speak Common and Sylvan.

COMBAT

A giant owl attacks by gliding silently just a few feet above its prey and plunging to strike when directly overhead.

A solitary giant owl is typically hunting or patrolling in the vicinity of its nest and generally ignores creatures that do not appear threatening. A mated pair of giant owls will attack in concert and fight to the death to defend their nest. Several giant owls sometimes operate as a company for some specific purpose, such as driving away a group of evil humanoids.

Superior Low-Light Vision (Ex): A giant owl can see five times as far as a human can in dim light.

Skills: Giant owls receive a +8 racial bonus to Listen checks. *They also receive a +4 racial bonus to Spot checks in dusk and darkness; when in flight, they gain a +8 bonus to Move Silently checks.

TRAINING A GIANT OWL

Training a giant owl as an aerial mount requires a successful Handle Animal check (DC 24 for a young creature, or DC 29 for an adult) and that the creature be willing.

Giant owl eggs are worth 2,500 gp apiece on the open market, while chicks are worth 4,000 gp each. Professional trainers charge 1,000 gp to rear or train a giant owl, and riding one requires an exotic saddle. A giant owl can fight while carrying a rider, but the rider cannot also attack unless he or she succeeds at a Ride check (see Ride, page 72 in the *Player's Handbook*).

Carrying Capacity: A light load for a giant owl is up to 300 pounds; a medium load, 301–600 pounds; and a heavy load, 601–900 pounds.

GIBBERING MOUTHER

Medium-Size Aberration
Hit Dice: 4d8+4 (22 hp)
Initiative: +1 (Dex)
Speed: 10 ft., swim 20 ft.
AC: 19 (+1 Dex, +8 natural)
Attacks: 6 bites +4 melee
Damage: Bite 1
Face/Reach: 5 ft. by 5 ft./5 ft.
Special Attacks: Gibbering, spittle, improved grab, blood drain, engulf, ground manipulation
Special Qualities: Amorphous
Saves: Fort +2, Ref +2, Will +5
Abilities: Str 10, Dex 13, Con 12, Int 4, Wis 13, Cha 13
Skills: Listen +8, Spot +12
Feats: Weapon Finesse (bite)

Climate/Terrain: Any land, aquatic, and underground
Organization: Solitary
Challenge Rating: 5
Treasure: None
Alignment: Usually neutral
Advancement: 5–12 HD (Large)

A gibbering mouther is a horrible creature seemingly drawn from a lunatic's nightmares. Although not evil, it thirsts after bodily fluids and seems to prefer the blood of intelligent creatures.

It is difficult to describe the mouther. While its body has the form and fluid motion of an amoeba, its surface has the color (but not the consistency) of human flesh. Countless eyes and toothy mouths constantly form and disappear all over the creature, often retreating into its body even as they become apparent. Sometimes their arrangement resembles a face, but just as often they have no relationship to one another.

Gibbering mouthers can speak Common, but seldom say anything other than gibbering.

COMBAT

Gibbering mouthers attack by shooting out strings of protoplasmic flesh, each ending in one or more eyes and a mouth that bites at the enemy. A mouther can send out a total of six such members in any round.

Gibbering (Su): As soon as a mouther spots something edible, it begins a constant gibbering as a free action. All creatures (other than mouthers) within a 60-foot spread must succeed at a Will save (DC 13) or be affected as though by a *confusion* spell for 1d2 rounds. This is a sonic, mind-affecting compulsion effect. Opponents who successfully save cannot be affected by the same gibbering mouther's gibbering for one day.

Spittle (Ex): At the start of every combat, and every 2 rounds thereafter, a gibbering mouther looses a stream of spittle. This ignites on contact with the air, creating a blinding flash of light. All sighted creatures within 60 feet must succeed at a Fortitude save (DC 13) or be blinded for 1d3 rounds.

Improved Grab (Ex): To use this ability, the gibbering mouther must hit with a bite attack.

Blood Drain (Ex): On a second successful grapple check after grabbing, that mouth attaches to the opponent. It automatically deals bite damage and drains blood, dealing 1 point of temporary Constitution damage each round. A mouth can be ripped off (dealing 1 point of damage) with a successful Strength check (DC 12) or severed by a normal attack that deals at least 2 points of damage (AC 18). A severed mouth continues to bite and drain blood for 1d4 rounds after such an attack.

A creature whose Constitution is reduced to 0 is killed and absorbed by the mouther, which gains 1 hit point and adds another mouth and pair of eyes to its body.

Engulf (Ex): A gibbering mouther can try to engulf a Medium-size or smaller opponent grabbed by three or more mouths. The opponent must succeed at a Reflex save (DC 14) or fall and be engulfed. On the next round, the mouther makes twelve bite attacks instead of six (each with a +4 attack bonus). An engulfed creature cannot attack the

mouther from within. The previously attached mouths are now free to attack others.

Ground Manipulation (Su): At will, as a standard action, a gibbering mouther can cause stone and earth within 5 feet of it to become a morass akin to quicksand. Softening earth, sand, or the like takes 1 round, while stone takes 2 rounds. Anyone other than the mouther in that area must take a move-equivalent action to avoid becoming mired (treat as being pinned).

Amorphous (Ex): A gibbering mouther is not subject to critical hits. It has no clear front or back, so it cannot be flanked.

Skills: Thanks to their multiple eyes, gibbering mouthers receive a +4 racial bonus to Spot checks.

GIRALLON

Large Beast
Hit Dice: 7d10+14 (52 hp)
Initiative: +3 (Dex)
Speed: 40 ft., climb 40 ft.
AC: 16 (–1 size, +3 Dex, +4 natural)
Attacks: 4 claws +12 melee, bite +7 melee
Damage: Claw 1d4+8, bite 1d8+4
Face/Reach: 5 ft. by 5 ft./10 ft.
Special Attacks: Rend 2d4+12
Special Qualities: Scent
Saves: Fort +7, Ref +8, Will +3
Abilities: Str 26, Dex 17, Con 14, Int 3, Wis 12, Cha 7
Skills: Climb +16, Move Silently +8, Spot +7

Climate/Terrain: Warm forest, mountains, and underground
Organization: Solitary or company (5–8)
Challenge Rating: 5
Treasure: None
Alignment: Always chaotic evil
Advancement: 8–10 HD (Large); 11–21 HD (Huge)

Girallons are savage cousins of the gorilla. They are aggressive, bloodthirsty, highly territorial, and incredibly strong.

These creatures look very much like albino gorillas at first glance, but even a casual observer will note their four arms. Adults of both sexes are about 8 feet tall, broad-chested, and covered in thick, pure white fur. When moving on the ground, they walk on their legs and lower arms. They have razor-sharp teeth and long, ripping claws.

COMBAT

Girallons attack anything that enters their territory, even others of their kind. Their senseless belligerence is the one characteristic that keeps their numbers in check. Still, the creatures show some cunning.

A solitary girallon usually conceals itself in the branches of a tree or under a pile of leaves and brush, with only its nose showing. When it spots or scents prey, it charges to the attack. The girallon picks up prey that is small enough to carry and withdraws, often vanishing into the trees before the victim's companions can do anything to retaliate. Against larger foes, the girallon seeks to tear a single opponent to bits as quickly as it can.

Rend (Ex): A girallon that hits with both claw attacks latches onto the opponent's body and tears the flesh. This attack automatically deals an additional 2d4+12 points of damage.

GNOLL

Medium-Size Humanoid (Gnoll)
Hit Dice: 2d8+2 (11 hp)
Initiative: +0
Speed: 20 ft. (scale mail), base 30 ft.
AC: 17 (+1 natural, +4 scale, +2 large shield)
Attacks: Battleaxe +3 melee; or shortbow +1 ranged
Damage: Battleaxe 1d8+2; or shortbow 1d6
Face/Reach: 5 ft. by 5 ft./5 ft.
Special Qualities: Darkvision 60 ft.
Saves: Fort +4, Ref +0, Will +0
Abilities: Str 15, Dex 10, Con 13, Int 8, Wis 11, Cha 8
Skills: Listen +3, Spot +3
Feats: Power Attack

Climate/Terrain: Temperate or warm land and underground
Organization: Solitary, pair, gang (2–5), band (10–100 plus 50% noncombatants plus 1 3rd-level sergeant per 20 adults and 1 leader of 4th–6th level), or tribe (20–200 plus 1 3rd-level ser-

geant per 20 adults, 1 or 2 lieutenants of 4th or 5th level, 1 leader of 6th–8th level, and 6–10 dire lions; underground lairs also have 1–3 trolls)
Challenge Rating: 1
Treasure: Standard
Alignment: Usually chaotic evil
Advancement: By character class

Gnolls are hyena-headed, evil humanoids that wander in loose tribes.

A gnoll stands 7 1/2 feet tall, with greenish-gray skin, a furry body, and a head like a hyena's, with a reddish gray to dirty yellow mane. It is a nocturnal carnivore, preferring intelligent creatures for food because they scream more. Gnolls tend to think with their stomachs, and any alliances they make (usually with bugbears, hobgoblins, ogres, orcs, or trolls) often fall apart when the gnolls get hungry. They dislike giants and most other humanoids, and they disdain manual labor. They do not like bright light, but it causes no harm to them.

COMBAT

Gnolls like to attack when they have the advantage of numbers, using horde tactics and their great strength to overwhelm and knock down their opponents. They show little discipline when fighting unless they have a strong leader, at which times they can maintain ranks and fight as a unit. While they do not usually prepare traps, they do use ambushes and try to attack from a flanking or rear position. Because of its armor and shield, a gnoll's Hide score is –6, which means gnolls always take special care to seek favorable conditions when laying ambushes (such as darkness, heavy cover, or some other form of concealment).

Girallon illus. by A. Waters

105

GNOLL SOCIETY

Gnolls are ruled by the strongest member of the group, who uses fear, intimidation, and strength to remain in power. If a chieftain is killed, the stronger members of the tribe fight to be the new chieftain; if these combats take too long or several combatants die, the tribe may break up into a number of packs that go their separate ways. Gnolls revere the phases of the moon, but most tribes have no true priests.

A band or tribe includes as many noncombatant young as there are adults. Gnoll lairs are fortified surface encampments or underground complexes. Gnolls take slaves, and any lair will have one slave for every ten adults, if not more. Slaves are usually humans, orcs, or hobgoblins and suffer a high attrition rate because of the gnolls' appetites.

Gnolls speak Gnoll and sometimes Goblin or Orc.

Their special patron is the demon lord Yeenoghu, who looks like a gaunt gnoll. Most gnolls serve and revere Yeenoghu rather than worshiping a deity.

GNOLL CHARACTERS

A gnoll's favored class is ranger; gnoll leaders are usually rangers. Gnoll clerics usually worship Erythnul, deity of slaughter.

GNOME

LOCKWOOD

Small Humanoid (Gnome)
Hit Dice: 1d8+1 (5 hp)
Initiative: +0
Speed: 20 ft.
AC: 16 (+1 size, +4 chain shirt, +1 small shield)
Attacks: Short sword +2 melee; or light crossbow +2 ranged
Damage: Short sword 1d6–1; or light crossbow 1d8
Face/Reach: 5 ft. by 5 ft./5 ft.
Special Attacks: Gnome traits, spells
Special Qualities: Gnome traits, speak with animals
Saves: Fort +3, Ref +0, Will +0
Abilities: Str 8, Dex 10, Con 12, Int 11, Wis 11, Cha 11
Skills: Listen +4, Spot +2
Feats: Weapon Focus (short sword)

Climate/Terrain: Any forest, hill, and underground
Organization: Company (2–4), squad (11–20 plus 1 leader of 3rd–6th level and 2 3rd-level lieutenants), or band (30–50 plus 1 3rd-level sergeant per 20 adults, 5 5th-level lieutenants, 3 7th-level captains, and 2–5 dire badgers)
Challenge Rating: 1/2 or 1 (svirfneblin)
Treasure: Standard
Alignment: Usually neutral good
Advancement: By character class

Gnomes are inveterate explorers, tricksters, and inventors. They have a knack for both illusion and alchemy.

Gnomes stand 3 to 3 1/2 feet tall and weigh 40 to 45 pounds. Their skin color ranges from dark tan to woody brown, their hair is fair, and their eyes can be any shade of blue. Gnome males prefer short, carefully trimmed beards. Gnomes generally wear leather or earth tones, though they decorate their clothes with intricate stitching or fine jewelry. Gnomes reach adulthood at about age 40, and they live about 350 years, though some can live almost 500 years.

Gnomes are inquisitive. They love to learn by personal experience. At times they're even reckless. Their curiosity makes them skilled engineers, as they are always trying new ways to build things. Sometimes a gnome pulls a prank just to see how the people involved will react.

Gnomes speak their own language, Gnome. Most gnomes who travel outside gnome lands (as traders, tinkers, or adventurers) know Common, while warriors in gnome settlements usually learn Goblin or Kobold.

Most gnomes encountered outside their home are warriors; the information in the statistics block is for one of 1st level. (See page 39 in the DUNGEON MASTER'S Guide for more about the warrior class.)

COMBAT

Gnomes prefer misdirection and deception over direct confrontation. They would rather befuddle or embarrass foes (other than goblinoids or kobolds) than kill them. Gnomes make heavy use of illusion magic and carefully prepared ambushes and traps whenever they can.

Spells: Gnomes with Intelligence scores of 10 or higher may cast *dancing lights*, *ghost sound*, and *prestidigitation*, each once per day as a 1st-level wizard (spell failure penalties for armor apply).

Speak with Animals (Sp): Once per day a gnome can use *speak with animals* as a 1st-level druid to communicate with a burrowing mammal (badger, fox, rabbit, etc.).

Gnome Traits (Ex): Gnomes benefit from a number of racial traits.

- *Small:* Gnomes gain a +1 size bonus to AC and attack rolls and a +4 size bonus to Hide checks, but they must use smaller weapons than humans use, and their lifting and carrying limits are three-quarters of those of Medium-size creatures.
- *Low-light Vision.* Gnomes can see twice as far as a human in starlight, moonlight, torchlight, and similar conditions of poor illumination.
- +2 racial bonus to saving throws against illusions.
- +1 racial bonus to attack rolls against kobolds and goblinoids.
- +4 dodge bonus against giants.

Skills: Gnomes receive a +2 racial bonus to Listen checks, for their keen hearing, and to Alchemy checks, because their sensitive noses allow them to monitor alchemical processes by smell.

GNOME SOCIETY

Gnomes get along well with dwarves, who share their love of precious things, their curiosity about mechanical devices, and their hatred of goblins and giants. They enjoy the company of halflings, especially those who are easygoing enough to put up with pranks and jests. Most gnomes are a little suspicious of the taller races—humans, elves, half-elves, and half-orcs—but they are rarely hostile or malicious.

Gnomes make their homes in hilly, wooded lands. They live underground but get more fresh air than dwarves, enjoying the natural, living world on the surface whenever they can. Their homes are well hidden, both by clever construction and illusions. Those who come to visit and are welcome are ushered into the bright, warm burrows. Those who are not welcome never find the burrows in the first place.

The chief gnome god is Garl Glittergold, the Watchful Protector. His clerics teach that gnomes are to cherish and support their communities. Pranks, for example, are seen as ways to lighten spirits and to keep gnomes humble, not ways for pranksters to triumph over those they trick.

SUBRACES

The information above is for rock gnomes, the most common variety. There are two other major gnome subraces, which differ from rock gnomes as follows.

Svirfneblin

Also called deep gnomes, svirfneblin are said to dwell in great cities deep underground. They keep the location of these cities secret to protect them from their deadly foes: drow, kuo-toa, and mind flayers.

Svirfneblin have wiry, gnarled physiques. Their skin is rock-colored, usually medium brown to brownish gray, and their eyes are gray. Males are bald; females have stringy gray hair. The average svirfneblin lifespan is 250 years. They speak Gnome, Common, Terran, and Undercommon. Most also speak the language of drow or kuo-toa.

The typical ability scores for a svirfneblin are Str 8, Dex 12, Con 10, Int 10, Wis 12, Cha 6.

Spell-Like Abilities: Svirfneblin have no special skill with or resistance to illusions, but they can use *blindness*, *blur*, and *change self* each once per day. These abilities are as the spells cast by a wizard of the svirfneblin's character level (save DC 10 + spell level).

Nondetection (Su): Svirfneblin have a continuous nondetection ability as the spell.

Svirfneblin Traits (Ex): These are in addition to the basic gnome traits, except where noted here.

- Stonecunning: Like dwarves, svirfneblin receive a +2 racial bonus to checks to notice unusual stonework. Something that isn't stone but that is disguised as stone also counts as unusual stonework. A deep gnome who merely comes within 10 feet of unusual stonework can make a check as though actively searching and can use the Search skill to find stonework traps as a rogue can. A svirfneblin can also intuit depth, sensing the approximate distance underground as naturally as a human can sense which way is up.
- Darkvision up to 120 feet.
- Spell resistance of 11 + character level.
- +2 racial bonus to all saving throws.
- +4 dodge bonus against all creatures (no special bonus against giants).

Skills: Svirfneblin receive a +2 racial bonus to Hide checks, which improves to +4 in darkened areas underground.

Forest Gnomes

Shy and elusive, forest gnomes shun contact with other races except when dire emergencies threaten their beloved forest homes. They are the smallest of all the gnomes, averaging 2 to 2 1/2 feet in height, with bark-colored, gray-green skin, dark hair, and blue, brown, or green eyes. A very long-lived people, they have an average life expectancy of 500 years.

In addition to Gnome, forest gnomes speak Elf, Sylvan, and a simple language that enables them to communicate on a very basic level with forest animals.

Forest Gnome Traits (Ex): These are in addition to the basic gnome traits, except where noted here.

- Forest gnomes have the innate ability to *pass without trace* (as the spell).
- +1 racial bonus to attack rolls against kobolds, goblinoids, orcs, and reptilian humanoids.

Skills: Forest gnomes receive a +4 racial bonus to Hide checks, which improves to +8 in a wooded area.

GNOME CHARACTERS

A gnome's favored class is illusionist. Most gnome leaders are illusionists or illusionist/rogues.

GOBLIN

Small Humanoid (Goblinoid)
Hit Dice: 1d8 (4 hp)
Initiative: +1 (Dex)
Speed: 30 ft.
AC: 15 (+1 size, +1 Dex, +3 studded leather)
Attacks: Morningstar +1 melee; or javelin +3 ranged
Damage: Morningstar 1d8–1; or javelin 1d6–1
Face/Reach: 5 ft. by 5 ft./5 ft.
Special Qualities: Darkvision 60 ft.
Saves: Fort +2, Ref +1, Will +0
Abilities: Str 8, Dex 13, Con 11, Int 10, Wis 11, Cha 8
Skills: Hide +6, Listen +3, Move Silently +4, Spot +3
Feats: Alertness

Climate/Terrain: Temperate and warm land and underground
Organization: Gang (4–9), band (10–100 plus 100% noncombatants plus 1 3rd-level sergeant per 20 adults and 1 leader of 4th–6th level), warband (10–24 with worg mounts), or tribe (40–400 plus 1 3rd-level sergeant per 20 adults, 1 or 2 lieutenants of 4th or 5th level, 1 leader of 6th–8th level, 10–24 worgs, and 2–4 dire wolves)
Challenge Rating: 1/4
Treasure: Standard
Alignment: Usually neutral evil
Advancement: By character class

Goblins are small humanoids that many consider little more than a nuisance. However, if they are unchecked, their great numbers, rapid reproduction, and evil dispositions enable them to overrun and despoil civilized areas.

Goblins have flat faces, broad noses, pointed ears, wide mouths, and small, sharp fangs. Their foreheads slope back, and their eyes are usually dull and glazed, varying in color from red to yellow. They walk upright, but their arms hang down almost to their knees. Goblins' skin color ranges from yellow through any shade of orange to a deep red; usually all members of a single tribe are about the same color. They wear clothing of dark leather, tending toward drab, soiled-looking colors.

Goblins speak Goblin; those with Intelligence scores of 12 or above also speak Common.

Most goblins encountered outside their homes are warriors; the information in the statistics block is for one of 1st level. (See page 39 in the *Dungeon Master's Guide* for more about the warrior class.)

COMBAT

Being bullied by bigger, stronger creatures has taught goblins to exploit what few advantages they have: sheer numbers and malicious ingenuity. The concept of a fair fight is meaningless in their society. They favor ambushes, overwhelming odds, dirty tricks, and any other edge they can devise.

Goblins have a poor grasp of strategy and are cowardly by nature, tending to flee the field if a battle turns against them. With proper supervision, though, they can implement reasonably complex plans, and in such circumstances their numbers can be a deadly advantage.

Skills: Goblins gain a +4 racial bonus to Move Silently checks. Goblin cavalry (mounted on worgs) gain a +6 bonus to Ride checks and the Mounted Combat feat (neither of these benefits is included in the statistics block).

GOBLIN SOCIETY

Goblins are tribal. Their leaders are generally the biggest, strongest, and sometimes even the smartest around. They have almost no concept of privacy, living and sleeping in large common areas; only the leaders live separately. Goblins survive by raiding and stealing (preferably from those who cannot defend themselves easily), sneaking into lairs, villages, and even towns by night to take what they can. They are not above waylaying travelers on the road or in forests and stripping them of all possessions, up to and including the clothes on their backs. Goblins sometimes capture slaves to perform hard labor in the tribe's lair or camp.

These creatures live wherever they can, from dank caves to dismal ruins, and their lairs are always smelly and filthy due to an utter lack of sanitation. Goblins often settle near civilized areas to raid for food, livestock, tools, weapons, and supplies. Once a tribe has despoiled a locale, it simply packs up and moves on to the next convenient area. Hobgoblins and bugbears are sometimes found in the company of goblin tribes, usually as bullying leaders. Some goblin tribes form alliances with worgs, which carry them into combat.

Goblin bands and tribes have noncombatant young equal in number to the adults.

The chief goblin deity is Maglubiyet, who urges his worshipers to expand their numbers and overwhelm their competitors.

GOBLIN CHARACTERS

A goblin's favored class is rogue; goblin leaders tend to be rogues or fighter/rogues. Goblin clerics worship Maglubiyet and can choose two of the following domains: Chaos, Evil, and Trickery. Most goblin spellcasters, however, are adepts (see page 37 in the DUNGEON MASTER'S GUIDE). Goblin adepts favor spells that fool or confuse enemies.

GOLEM

	Flesh	Clay	Stone
	Large Construct	Large Construct	Large Construct
Hit Dice:	9d10 (49 hp)	11d10 (60 hp)	14d10 (77 hp)
Initiative:	−1 (Dex)	−1 (Dex)	−1 (Dex)
Speed:	30 ft. (can't run)	20 ft. (can't run)	20 ft. (can't run)
AC:	18 (−1 size, −1 Dex, +10 natural)	22 (−1 size, −1 Dex, +14 natural)	26 (−1 size, −1 Dex, +18 natural)
Attacks:	2 slams +10 melee	2 slams +14 melee	2 slams +18 melee
Damage:	Slam 2d8+5	Slam 2d10+7	Slam 2d10+9
Face/Reach:	5 ft. by 5 ft./10 ft.	5 ft. by 5 ft./10 ft.	5 ft. by 5 ft./10 ft.
Special Attacks:	Berserk	Berserk, wound	Slow
Special Qualities:	Construct, magic immunity, damage reduction 15/+1	Construct, magic immunity, damage reduction 20/+1, immune to piercing and slashing, haste	Construct, magic immunity, damage reduction 30/+2
Saves:	Fort +3, Ref +2, Will +3	Fort +3, Ref +2, Will +3	Fort +4, Ref +3, Will +4
Abilities:	Str 21, Dex 9, Con —, Int —, Wis 11, Cha 1	Str 25, Dex 9, Con —, Int —, Wis 11, Cha 1	Str 29, Dex 9, Con —, Int —, Wis 11, Cha 1
Climate/Terrain:	Any land and underground	Any land and underground	Any land
Organization:	Solitary or gang (2–4)	Solitary or gang (2–4)	Solitary or gang (2–4)
Challenge Rating:	7	10	11
Treasure:	None	None	None
Alignment:	Always neutral	Always neutral	Always neutral
Advancement:	10–18 HD (Large); 19–27 HD (Huge)	12–18 HD (Large); 19–33 HD (Huge)	15–21 HD (Large); 22–42 (Huge)

	Iron
	Large Construct
Hit Dice:	18d10 (99 hp)
Initiative:	−1 (Dex)
Speed:	20 ft. (can't run)
AC:	30 (−1 size, −1 Dex, +22 natural)
Attacks:	2 slams +23 melee
Damage:	Slam 2d10+11
Face/Reach:	5 ft. by 5 ft./10 ft.
Special Attacks:	Breath weapon
Special Qualities:	Construct, magic immunity, damage reduction 50/+3, rust vulnerability
Saves:	Fort +6, Ref +5, Will +6
Abilities:	Str 33, Dex 9, Con —, Int —, Wis 11, Cha 1

Climate/Terrain:	Any land
Organization:	Solitary or gang (2–4)
Challenge Rating:	13
Treasure:	None
Alignment:	Always neutral
Advancement:	19–24 HD (Large); 25–54 HD (Huge)

Golems are magically created automatons of great power. Constructing one involves the employment of mighty magic and elemental forces.

The animating force for a golem is a spirit from the Elemental Plane of Earth. The process of creating the golem binds the unwilling spirit to the artificial body and subjects it to the will of the golem's creator.

COMBAT

Golems are tenacious in combat and prodigiously strong as well. Being mindless, they do nothing without orders from their creators. They follow instructions explicitly and are incapable of any strategy or tactics. They are emotionless in combat and cannot be easily provoked.

A golem's creator can command it if the golem is within 60 feet and can see and hear its creator. If uncommanded, the golem usually follows its last instruction to the best of its ability, though if attacked it returns the attack. The creator can give the golem a simple program to govern its actions in his or her absence, such as "Remain in an area and attack all creatures that enter" (or only a specific type of creature), "Ring a gong and attack," or the like.

Since golems do not need to breathe and are immune to most forms of energy, they can press an attack against an opponent almost anywhere, from the bottom of the sea to the frigid top of the tallest mountain.

Construct: Immune to mind-influencing effects, poison, disease, and similar effects. Not subject to critical hits, subdual damage, ability damage, energy drain, or death from massive damage.

Magic Immunity (Ex): Golems completely resist most magical and supernatural effects, except where otherwise noted below.

CONSTRUCTION

The cost listed for each golem includes that of the physical body and all the materials and spell components that are consumed or become a permanent part of it.

The first task is carving or assembling the golem's physical body. The golem's creator can assemble the body or hire someone else to do the job. The builder must have the appropriate skill, which varies with the golem.

The real work of creating a golem involves extended magical rituals that require two months to complete. Understanding the rituals requires a character of the required level with the Craft Magic Arms and Armor and Craft Wondrous Item feats. The creator must labor for at least 8 hours each day in a specially prepared laboratory or workroom. The chamber is similar to an alchemist's laboratory and costs 500 gp to establish.

When not working on the rituals, the creator must rest and can perform no other activities except eating, sleeping, or talking. If personally constructing the golem's body, the creator can perform the building and rituals together. If the creator misses a day of rituals, the process fails and must be started again. Money spent is lost, but XP spent are not. The golem's body can be reused, as can the laboratory.

Completing the ritual drains the appropriate XP from the creator and requires casting any spells on the final day. The creator must cast the spells personally, but they can come from outside sources, such as scrolls.

FLESH GOLEM

A flesh golem is a ghoulish collection of stolen human body parts, stitched together into a single composite form. It stands 8 feet tall and weighs almost 500 pounds.

Its skin is the sickly green or yellow of partially decayed flesh. A flesh golem smells faintly of freshly dug earth and dead flesh, and no natural animal willingly tracks one. The golem wears whatever clothing its creator desires, usually just a ragged pair of trousers. It has no possessions and no weapons. The golem cannot speak, although it can emit a hoarse roar of sorts. It walks and moves with a stiff-jointed gait, as if not in complete control of its body.

Combat

Flesh golems often fare poorly in combat thanks to their fairly low AC, though they can easily crush foes that lack magic weaponry. A flesh golem supported by an ally that can launch electrical attacks is fearsome indeed.

Berserk (Ex): When a flesh golem enters combat, there is a cumulative 1% chance each round that its elemental spirit breaks free and goes berserk. The uncontrolled golem goes on a rampage, attacking the nearest living creature or smashing some object smaller than itself if no creature is within reach, then moving on to spread more destruction. The golem's creator, if within 60 feet, can try to regain control by speaking firmly and persuasively to the golem, which requires a successful Charisma check (DC 19). It takes 1 minute of rest by the golem to reset the golem's berserk chance to 0%.

Magic Immunity (Ex): Flesh golems are immune to all spells, spell-like abilities, and supernatural effects, except as follows. Fire- and cold-based effects *slow* them (as the spell) for 2d6 rounds, with no saving throw. An electricity effect breaks any *slow* effect on the golem and cures 1 point of damage for each 3 points of damage it would otherwise deal. For example, a flesh golem hit by a *lightning bolt* cast by a 5th-level wizard gains back 6 hit points if the damage total is 18. The golem rolls no saving throw against electricity effects.

Construction

The pieces of a flesh golem must come from normal human corpses that have not decayed significantly. Assembly requires a minimum of six different bodies, one for each limb, the torso (with head), and the brain. In some cases, more bodies may be necessary.

The golem costs 50,000 gp to create, which includes 500 gp for the construction of the body. Assembling the body requires a successful Craft (leatherworking) or Heal check (DC 13).

The creator must be 14th level and able to cast arcane spells. Completing the ritual drains 1,000 XP from the creator and requires *bull's strength, geas/quest, limited wish, polymorph any object,* and *protection from arrows.*

CLAY GOLEM

This golem has a humanoid body made from clay and stands about 18 inches taller than a normal human. It weighs around 600 pounds.

The golem's features are grossly distorted from the human norm. Its chest is overly large, with arms attached by thick knots of muscle at the shoulder, hanging down to its knees, and ending in short, stubby fingers. It has no neck, and the large head has broad, flat features. Its legs are short and bowed, with wide, flat feet. A clay golem wears no clothing except for a metal or stiff leather garment around its hips. It smells faintly of clay. The golem cannot speak or make any vocal noise. It walks and moves with a slow, clumsy gait.

Combat

Clay golems are fairly effective combatants, thanks to their immunities and their haste ability.

Berserk (Ex): When a clay golem enters combat, there is a cumulative 1% chance each round that its elemental spirit breaks free and goes berserk. The uncontrolled golem goes on a rampage, attacking the nearest living creature or smashing some object smaller than itself if no creature is within reach, then moving on to spread more destruction. Once the golem goes berserk, no known method can reestablish control.

Wound (Ex): The damage a clay golem deals doesn't heal naturally. Only a *heal* spell or a Healing spell of 6th level or higher can heal it.

Immune to Slashing and Piercing (Ex): Slashing and piercing weapons, even enchanted ones, deal no damage to a clay golem.

Magic Immunity (Ex): Clay golems are immune to all spells, spell-like abilities, and supernatural effects, except as follows. A *move earth* spell drives the golem back 120 feet and deals 3d12 points of damage to it. A *disintegrate* spell slows the golem (as the *slow* spell) for 1d6 rounds and deals 1d12 points of damage. An *earthquake* cast directly at a clay golem stops it from moving that round and deals 5d10 points of damage. The golem gets no saving throw against any of these effects.

Haste (Su): After it has engaged in at least 1 round of combat, a clay golem can haste itself once per day as a free action. The effect lasts 3 rounds and is otherwise the same as the spell.

Construction

A clay golem's body must be sculpted from a single block of clay weighing at least 1,000 pounds.

The golem costs 60,000 gp to create, including 1,500 gp for the body and 30,000 gp for vestments, which can be reused. Creating the body requires a successful Craft (sculpting or masonry) check (DC 15).

The ritual requires a 16th-level creator who can cast divine spells. Completing the ritual drains 1,200 XP from the creator and requires *animate objects, bless, commune, prayer,* and *resurrection.*

STONE GOLEM

A stone golem is 9 feet tall and weighs around 2,000 pounds. Its body is of roughly chiseled stone, frequently stylized to suit its creator. For example, it might look like it is wearing armor, with a particular symbol carved on the breastplate, or have designs worked into the stone of its limbs.

Combat

Stone golems are formidable opponents, being physically powerful and difficult to harm.

Slow (Su): A stone golem can use slow as a free action once every 2 rounds. The effect has a range of 10 feet and a duration of 7 rounds, requiring a successful Will save (DC 13) to negate. The ability is otherwise the same as the spell.

Magic Immunity (Ex): A stone golem is immune to all spells, spell-like abilities, and supernatural effects, except as follows. A *transmute rock to mud* spell slows it (as the *slow* spell) for 2d6 rounds, with no saving throw, while *transmute mud to rock* heals all of its lost hit points. A *stone to flesh* spell does not actually change the golem's structure but makes it vulnerable to any normal attack for the following round (this does not include spells, except those that cause damage).

Construction

A stone golem's body is chiseled from a single block of hard stone, such as granite, weighing at least 3,000 pounds.

The golem costs 80,000 gp to create, which includes 1,000 gp for the body. Assembling the body requires a successful Craft (sculpting or masonry) check (DC 17).

The creator must be 16th level and able to cast arcane spells. Completing the ritual drains 1,600 XP from the creator and requires *geas/quest, limited wish, polymorph any object,* and *slow.*

IRON GOLEM

An iron golem is twice the height of a normal human and weighs around 5,000 pounds. It can be fashioned in any manner, just like a stone golem, although it almost always displays armor of some sort. Its features are much smoother than those of a stone golem. Iron golems sometimes have a short sword (relative to their size) in one hand.

The iron golem cannot speak or make any vocal noise, nor does it have any distinguishable odor. It moves with a ponderous but smooth gait at half the speed of a normal human. Each step causes the floor to tremble unless it is on a thick, solid foundation.

Combat

Iron golems are mighty combatants. They strike with deadly accuracy and incredible force. Their bodies are nearly invulnerable but can be reduced to piles of rubbish by rust monsters.

Breath Weapon (Su): First or second round of combat—cloud of poisonous gas, 10-foot cube directly in front of the golem lasting 1 round, free action every 1d4+1 rounds; Fortitude save (DC 17), initial damage 1d4 temporary Constitution, secondary damage death.

Magic Immunity (Ex): An iron golem is immune to all spells, spell-like abilities, and supernatural effects, except as follows. An electricity effect slows it (as the *slow* spell) for 3 rounds, with no saving throw. A fire effect breaks any slow effect on the golem and cures 1 point of damage for each 3 points of damage it would otherwise deal. For example, a flesh golem hit by a *fireball* cast by a 5th-level wizard gains back 6 hit points if the damage total is 18. The golem rolls no saving throw against fire effects.

Rust Vulnerability (Ex): An iron golem is affected normally by rust attacks, such as that of a rust monster or a *rusting grasp* spell.

Construction

An iron golem's body is sculpted from 5,000 pounds of pure iron.

The golem costs 100,000 gp to create, which includes 1,500 gp for the body. Assembling the body requires a successful Craft (armorsmithing or weaponsmithing) check (DC 20).

The creator must be 16th level and able to cast arcane spells. Completing the ritual drains 2,000 XP from the creator and requires *cloudkill*, *geas/quest*, *limited wish*, and *polymorph any object*.

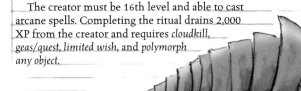

Large Magical Beast
Hit Dice: 8d10+24 (68 hp)
Initiative: +4 (Improved Initiative)
Speed: 30 ft.
AC: 18 (−1 size, +9 natural)
Attacks: Gore +12 melee
Damage: Gore 1d8+7
Face/Reach: 5 ft. by 10 ft./5 ft.
Special Attacks: Breath weapon, trample 1d8+7
Special Qualities: Scent
Saves: Fort +9, Ref +6, Will +3
Abilities: Str 21, Dex 10, Con 17, Int 2, Wis 12, Cha 9
Skills: Listen +8, Spot +8
Feats: Alertness, Improved Initiative

Climate/Terrain: Temperate and warm land and underground
Organization: Solitary, pair, pack (2–4), or herd (5–13)
Challenge Rating: 8
Treasure: None
Alignment: Always neutral
Advancement: 9–15 HD (Large); 16–24 HD (Huge)

Gorgons are bull-like creatures that guard their territory fiercely. They are fond of rocky areas, especially underground labyrinths.

A typical gorgon stands over 6 feet tall at the shoulder and measures 8 feet from snout to tail. Although built like a bull, the gorgon is covered with metallic black scales and has silver horns. Its eyes burn red, giving the impression of two hot coals set beneath its heavy brow.

Gorgons are nothing if not aggressive. They attack intruders on sight, attempting to trample, gore, or petrify them. There is no way to calm these furious beasts, and they are impossible to domesticate.

COMBAT

Whenever possible, a gorgon begins any encounter by charging at its opponents.

Breath Weapon (Su): Turn to stone permanently, cone, 60 feet, every 1d4 rounds (but no more than five times per day); Fortitude save (DC 17).

Trample (Ex): A gorgon can trample Small or smaller creatures for 1d8+7 points of damage. Opponents who do not make attacks of opportunity against the gorgon can attempt a Reflex save (DC 23) to halve the damage.

GRAY RENDER

Large Beast
Hit Dice: 10d10+70 (125 hp)
Initiative: +0
Speed: 30 ft.
AC: 19 (–1 size, +10 natural)
Attacks: Bite +12 melee, 2 claws +7 melee
Damage: Bite 2d6+6, claw 1d6+3
Face/Reach: 5 ft. by 5 ft./10 ft.
Special Attacks: Improved grab, rend 3d6+9
Special Qualities: Scent
Saves: Fort +14, Ref +7, Will +4
Abilities: Str 23, Dex 10, Con 24, Int 3, Wis 12, Cha 8
Skills: Hide +7, Spot +8

Climate/Terrain: Any land and underground
Organization: Solitary
Challenge Rating: 8
Treasure: None
Alignment: Usually neutral
Advancement: 11–15 HD (Large); 16–30 HD (Huge)

Bestial and savage, the gray render is a deadly predator found in remote wilderness areas.

These beasts are thought to be composed of dense muscle and bone, granting them the strength and stamina of a giant. Rangers have reported seeing renders uproot trees 3 feet in diameter with their jaws and tear them into splinters in just minutes.

A gray render stands 9 feet tall, despite its stooped frame, and 4 feet broad. Its hairless skin is a uniform dull gray, and its sloped forehead bears six small, yellowish eyes. The mouth is wide and powerful, filled with black teeth.

Gray renders are never found in groups. Each of these asexual creatures produces one offspring and carries it for a time in a pouch, but thereafter the young render must fend for itself.

A unique quality of the gray render is its tendency to bond with, protect, and provide for another creature (or group of creatures) native to its surroundings. This strange behavior seems contrary to its otherwise savage nature, yet gray renders have been found with wolves, lions, horses, displacer beasts, owlbears, unicorns, hippogriffs, and occasionally even humanoid groups. Whether accepted or not, the render always attempts to remain fairly close, watching over its adopted charge(s) and daily bringing an offering of meat. It never willingly harms adopted creatures and retreats if they attack it. Most creatures, however, quickly begin to appreciate having such a powerful ally and accept and even rely on the gray render.

COMBAT

A gray render attacks to kill, whether to bring down prey or to protect itself or those it has adopted. When hunting, it sometimes attempts to hide and wait for prey to wander close.

Improved Grab (Ex): To use this ability, the gray render must hit with its bite attack.

Rend (Ex): A gray render that gets a hold latches onto the opponent's body and tears the flesh. This attack automatically deals 3d6+9 points of damage.

Skills: Gray renders receive a +4 racial bonus to Spot checks due to their six keen eyes.

GRICK

Medium-Size Aberration
Hit Dice: 2d8 (9 hp)
Initiative: +2 (Dex)
Speed: 30 ft., climb 20 ft.
AC: 16 (+2 Dex, +4 natural)
Attacks: 4 tentacle rakes +3 melee, bite –2 melee
Damage: Tentacle rake 1d4+2, bite 1d3+1
Face/Reach: 5 ft. by 5 ft./5 ft.
Special Qualities: Scent, damage reduction 15/+1
Saves: Fort +0, Ref +2, Will +5
Abilities: Str 14, Dex 14, Con 11, Int 3, Wis 14, Cha 5
Skills: Climb +10, Hide +4*, Listen +7, Spot +7
Feats: Alertness

Climate/Terrain: Underground
Organization: Solitary or cluster (2–4)
Challenge Rating: 3
Treasure: 1/10 coins; 50% goods; 50% items
Alignment: Usually neutral
Advancement: 3–4 HD (Medium-size); 5–6 HD (Large)

Gricks are stealthy underground predators that infest dungeons, caves, and other shadowed places under the earth, waiting patiently for prey to come within reach.

Gricks lair in any sheltered space that can accommodate their bodies, including holes, burrows, ledges, and crevices. They do not collect treasure, but their lairs are likely to contain the uneaten possessions of their victims. When prey is scarce, gricks venture aboveground and hunt in the wilderness, using tactics similar to those they employ underground. These creatures are not comfortable under the open sky, however, and return to the subterranean world as quickly as possible.

A grick's body grows to a length of about 3 feet, and its tentacles add another 2 feet to its overall length. An adult creature weighs some 200 pounds. Its body coloration is uniformly dark, shading to dull gray on its underbelly. The monster's tentacles, located on its head just above its jaws, are segmented like the body of an earthworm and are the color of dark mud.

COMBAT

Gricks attack when hungry or threatened. They hunt by holing up near high-traffic areas, using their natural coloration to blend into convenient shadows. When prey (virtually anything that moves) ventures near, they lash out with their tentacles. A grick's rubbery body seems to shed blows of any kind. Its jaws are relatively small and weak compared to its body mass, so rather than consume its kill immediately, the grick normally drags its victim back to its lair to be eaten at its leisure.

Multiple gricks do not fight in concert: Each attacks the prey closest to it, and breaks off the fight as soon as it can drag dead or unconscious prey away.

Skills: *Their coloration affords gricks a +8 racial bonus to Hide checks when in natural rocky areas.

SARDINHA

Griffon illus. by A. Waters

GRIFFON

Climate/Terrain: Temperate and warm hill and mountains
Organization: Solitary, pair, or pride (6–10)
Challenge Rating: 4
Treasure: None
Alignment: Always neutral
Advancement: 8–10 HD (Large); 11–21 HD (Huge)

Large Beast
Hit Dice: 7d10+21 (59 hp)
Initiative: +2 (Dex)
Speed: 30 ft., fly 80 ft. (average)
AC: 17 (–1 size, +2 Dex, +6 natural)
Attacks: Bite +8 melee, 2 claws +3 melee
Damage: Bite 2d6+4, claw 1d4+2
Face/Reach: 5 ft. by 10 ft./5 ft.
Special Attacks: Pounce, rake 1d6+2
Special Qualities: Scent
Saves: Fort +8, Ref +7, Will +3
Abilities: Str 18, Dex 15, Con 16, Int 5, Wis 13, Cha 8
Skills: Jump +8, Listen +6, Spot +11*

Griffons are powerful, majestic creatures with the characteristics of both lions and eagles. They prey on all manner of beasts but favor the flesh of horses above all else. The body of a griffon resembles that of a muscular lion. Its head and front legs are those of an eagle.

From nose to tail, an adult griffon can measure as much as 8 feet. Neither males nor females are endowed with a mane. A pair of broad, golden wings emerge from the creature's back and span 25 feet or more.

113

Griffons make their homes in high places, swooping down with a shrill, eaglelike cry to attack their prey. Although both aggressive and territorial, they are also intelligent enough to avoid obviously powerful enemies. They almost always attack horses, however, and any who attempt to protect horses from a hungry griffon often end up on the menu themselves.

COMBAT

Griffons prefer to pounce on their prey, either diving to the attack or leaping from above.

Pounce (Ex): If a griffon dives or leaps upon a foe during the first round of combat, it can make a full attack even if it has already taken a move action.

Rake (Ex): A griffon that pounces on an opponent can make two rake attacks (+8 melee) with its hind legs for 1d6+2 slashing damage each.

Skills: Griffons receive a +4 racial bonus to Jump checks. *They also receive a +4 racial bonus to Spot checks in daylight.

TRAINING A GRIFFON

Training a griffon as an aerial mount requires a successful Handle Animal check (DC 21 for a young creature, or DC 28 for an adult) and that the creature be willing. Griffons mature in about two years. Trainers can reduce the DC by 5 and the rearing time by one-half by using a magic bridle enchanted for this purpose.

Griffon eggs are worth 3,500 gp apiece on the open market, while young are worth 7,000 gp each. Professional trainers charge 1,500 gp to rear or train a griffon. Riding a trained griffon requires an exotic saddle. A griffon can fight while carrying a rider, but the rider cannot also attack unless he or she succeeds at a Ride check (see Ride, page 72 in the *Player's Handbook*).

Carrying Capacity: A light load for a griffon is up to 300 pounds; a medium load, 301–600 pounds; and a heavy load, 601–900 pounds.

GRIMLOCK

Medium-Size Monstrous Humanoid
Hit Dice: 2d8+2 (11 hp)
Initiative: +1 (Dex)
Speed: 30 ft.
AC: 15 (+1 Dex, +4 natural)
Attacks: Battleaxe +4 melee
Damage: Battleaxe 1d8+3
Face/Reach: 5 ft. by 5 ft./5 ft.
Special Attacks: Blindsight
Special Qualities: Immunities, scent
Saves: Fort +1, Ref +4, Will +2
Abilities: Str 15, Dex 13, Con 13, Int 10, Wis 8, Cha 6
Skills: Climb +7, Hide +6*, Listen +6, Search +5, Spot +3
Feats: Alertness

Climate/Terrain: Any mountains and underground
Organization: Gang (2–4), pack (10–20), tribe (10–60 plus 1 leader of 3rd–5th level per 10 adults), or cult (10–80 plus 1 leader of 3rd–5th level per 10 adults and 1 mind flayer or medusa)
Challenge Rating: 1
Treasure: Standard coins; standard goods (gems only); standard items
Alignment: Always neutral evil
Advancement: By character class

Grimlocks are muscular humanoids with thick, gray, scaly skin and no visible eyes. Though blind, they have superior senses of smell and hearing to compensate.

Grimlocks are natives of the deep places beneath the earth but come to the surface to raid for slaves and pillage. While there, they lurk in mountainous terrain, which hides them well. They prefer raw, fresh meat—preferably human.

Extremely xenophobic, grimlocks are normally encountered in small patrols or packs on the surface. Underground, they may form larger communities that are led by powerful grimlocks or by a more intelligent creature, such as a medusa or mind flayer. Grimlocks are invulnerable to medusas' gaze attacks, while mind flayers consume only brains, leaving the flesh for their grimlock followers.

COMBAT

Grimlocks are blind, but their exceptional senses of smell and hearing allow them to locate foes nearby. As a result, they usually shun ranged weapons and rush to the attack, brandishing their stone battleaxes.

Blindsight (Ex): Grimlocks can ascertain all foes within 40 feet as a sighted creature would. Beyond that range, they treat all targets as totally concealed (see Concealment, page 133 in the *Player's Handbook*).

Grimlocks are susceptible to sound- and scent-based attacks, however, and are affected normally by loud noises and sonic spells (such as *ghost sound* or *silence*) and overpowering odors (such as *stinking cloud* or incense-heavy air). Negating a grimlock's sense of smell or hearing reduces this ability to normal Blind-Fight (as the feat). If both are negated, the grimlock is effectively blinded.

Immunities: Grimlocks are immune to gaze attacks, visual effects, illusions, and other attack forms that rely on sight.

Skills: *A grimlock's dull gray skin helps it hide in its native terrain, conferring a +10 racial bonus to Hide checks when in mountains or underground.

GRIMLOCK CHARACTERS

Grimlocks favor the barbarian class. Independent groups of grimlocks are usually led by barbarians, while those in the service of mind flayers are often rangers.

	Sea Hag	Annis	Green Hag
	Large Monstrous Humanoid (Aquatic)	Large Monstrous Humanoid	Medium-Size Monstrous Humanoid
Hit Dice:	3d8+3 (16 hp)	7d8+14 (45 hp)	9d8+9 (49 hp)
Initiative:	+1 (Dex)	+1 (Dex)	+1 (Dex)
Speed:	30 ft., swim 40 ft.	40 ft.	30 ft., swim 30 ft.
AC:	13 (−1 size, +1 Dex, +3 natural)	20 (−1 size, +1 Dex, +10 natural)	22 (+1 Dex, +11 natural)
Attacks:	2 claws +6 melee	2 claws +13 melee, bite +8 melee	2 claws +13 melee
Damage:	Claw 1d4+4	Claw 1d6+7, bite 1d6+3	Claw 1d4+4
Face/Reach:	5 ft. by 5 ft./10 ft.	5 ft. by 5 ft./10 ft.	5 ft. by 5 ft./5 ft.
Special Attacks:	Horrific appearance, evil eye	Improved grab, rend 2d6+14, spell-like abilities	Spell-like abilities, weakness, mimicry
Special Qualities:	SR 14, water breathing	SR 19, steely skin	SR 18, darkvision 90 ft.
Saves:	Fort +2, Ref +4, Will +4	Fort +4, Ref +6, Will +6	Fort +6, Ref +7, Will +7
Abilities:	Str 19, Dex 12, Con 12, Int 10, Wis 13, Cha 10	Str 25, Dex 12, Con 14, Int 13, Wis 13, Cha 10	Str 19, Dex 12, Con 12, Int 13, Wis 13, Cha 10
Skills:	Craft or Knowledge (any one) +4, Hide +3, Listen +9, Spot +9	Concentration +12, Hide +7, Listen +11, Spot +11	Concentration +13, Craft or Knowledge (any one) +5, Hide +11, Listen +11, Spot +11
Feats:	Alertness	Alertness, Blind-Fight, Combat Casting	Alertness, Blind-Fight, Combat Casting, Great Fortitude
Climate/Terrain:	Any aquatic	Any land and underground	Temperate and warm forest and marsh
Organization:	Solitary or covey (3 hags of any type plus 1–8 ogres and 1–4 evil giants)	Solitary or covey (3 hags of any type plus 1–8 ogres and 1–4 evil giants)	Solitary or covey (3 hags of any type plus 1–8 ogres and 1–4 evil giants)
Challenge Rating:	4 or 12 (covey)	6 or 12 (covey)	5 or 12 (covey)
Treasure:	Standard	Standard	Standard
Alignment:	Always chaotic evil	Always chaotic evil	Always chaotic evil
Advancement:	By character class	By character class	By character class

Hags are horrible creatures whose love of evil is equaled only by their ugliness.

Although they often plot and scheme for power or some malevolent end, hags also appear to do evil for its own sake. They may use their dark magic and knowledge of fell things to serve a more powerful evil being, but they are seldom faithful. They may turn on their master if they see a chance to seize power for themselves.

Although different hags are unique in appearance and mannerism, they have many things in common. All take the form of crones whose bent shapes belie their fierce power and swiftness. Despite faces cracked by wrinkles and heavy with cruelty, their eyes shine with villainy and cunning. Their long nails have the strength of steel and are as keen as any knife.

Hags speak Giant and Common.

COMBAT

Hags are tremendously strong. They are naturally resistant to spells and can cast magic of their own. Hags often gather to form coveys. A covey, usually containing one hag of each type, can use powers beyond those of the individual members.

SEA HAG

Perhaps the most wretched of hags, the sea hag is found in the water of seas or overgrown lakes. Its flesh is sickly and yellow, covered with warts and oozing sores. Its long, filthy hair resembles rotting seaweed.

Combat

Sea hags are not subtle and prefer a direct approach to combat. They usually remain in hiding until they can affect as many foes as possible with their horrific appearance.

Horrific Appearance (Su): The sight of a sea hag is so revolting that anyone who sets eyes upon one must succeed at a Fortitude save (DC 11) or instantly be weakened, taking 2d8 points of temporary Strength damage. This cannot reduce a victim to a negative Strength score, but anyone reduced to Strength 0 is helpless. Creatures who successfully save cannot be affected again by the same hag's horrific appearance for one day.

Evil Eye (Su): Three times per day a sea hag can cast its dire gaze upon any single creature within 30 feet. The target must succeed at a Fortitude save (DC 11). Creatures who fail have a 25% chance of dying instantly from fright; even if they survive, they fall into a whimpering catatonia for three days, although *remove curse* or *dispel evil* can restore sanity sooner.

Water Breathing (Ex): Sea hags can breathe underwater indefinitely and can freely use their abilities while submerged.

ANNIS

The dreaded annis may be the most horrible of hags. It has deep blue skin and filthy black hair, and stands some 8 feet tall. An annis commonly uses its *change self* ability to take the form of an exceptionally tall human, a fair giant, or an ogre.

Combat

Though physically powerful, these hags do not favor simple assaults but try to divide and confuse their foes before combat. They love to pose as commoners or gentlefolk to lull their victims into a sense of false security before they attack.

Improved Grab (Ex): To use this ability, the annis must hit a Large or smaller creature with a claw attack.

Rend (Ex): An annis that hits with both claw attacks latches onto the opponent's body and tears the flesh. This attack automatically deals an additional 2d6+14 points of damage.

Tear (Ex): An annis automatically hits a held opponent with all its melee attacks each round it maintains the hold.

Spell-Like Abilities: 3/day—*change self* and *fog cloud*. These abilities are as the spells cast by an 8th-level sorcerer.

Steely Skin (Ex): The steely skin of an annis reduces damage dealt by slashing and piercing weapons by 1 point of damage per hit. Conversely, their brittle bones increase damage dealt by bludgeoning weapons by 1 point per hit. (Treat combination weapons such as morningstars as bludgeoning weapons.)

GREEN HAG

Green hags are found in desolate swamps and dark forests. They have a sickly green complexion with dark, tangled hair that looks almost like a twisted vine.

Combat

Green hags prefer to attack from hiding, usually after distracting foes. They often use darkvision to their advantage by attacking during moonless nights.

Spell-Like Abilities: At will—*change self, dancing lights, ghost sound, invisibility, pass without trace, tongues,* and *water breathing.* These abilities are as the spells cast by an 8th-level sorcerer (save DC 10 + spell level).

Weakness (Su): The green hag can weaken a foe by making a special touch attack. The affected opponent must succeed at a Fortitude save (DC 13) or take 2d4 points of temporary Strength damage.

Mimicry (Ex): Green hags can imitate the sounds of almost any animal found near their lairs.

HAG COVEY

From time to time, a trio of hags gathers as a covey. Usually this foul triune includes one hag of each type, but this is not always the case.

Combat

Hags in a covey rely on deception and their boosted magical abilities in combat.

A covey of hags is 80% likely to be guarded by 1d8 ogres and 1d4 evil giants who do their bidding. These are often *polymorphed* into less hostile forms and sent forth as spies. Such minions often (60%) carry magic stones known as *hag eyes* (see below).

Spell-Like Abilities: 3/day—*animate dead, bestow curse, control weather, dream, forcecage, mind blank, mirage arcana, polymorph other, veil,* and *vision.* These abilities are as the spells cast by a 9th-level sorcerer (save DC 13 + spell level). To use one of these abilities, all three hags must be within 10 feet of one another. This is a full-round action.

Once per month, a covey that does not have a *hag eye* can create one from a gem worth at least 20 gp (see below).

Hag Eye

A *hag eye* is a magic gem created by a covey. It appears to be nothing more than a semiprecious stone, but a *gem of seeing* or other such effect reveals it as a disembodied eye. Often, a *hag eye* is worn as a ring, brooch, or other adornment. Any of the three hags who created the *hag eye* can see through it whenever they wish, so long as it is on the same plane as the hag. Destroying a *hag eye* deals 1d10 points of damage to each member of the covey and blinds the one who sustained the greatest damage for 24 hours.

HALFLING

Small Humanoid (Halfling)
Hit Dice: 1d8 (4 hp)
Initiative: +1 (Dex)
Speed: 20 ft.
AC: 15 (+1 size, +1 Dex, +3 studded leather)
Attacks: Longsword +2 melee; or heavy crossbow +3 ranged
Damage: Longsword 1d8–1; or heavy crossbow 1d10
Face/Reach: 5 ft. by 5 ft./5 ft.
Special Attacks: Halfling traits
Special Qualities: Halfling traits
Saves: Fort +3, Ref +2, Will +1
Abilities: Str 8, Dex 13, Con 10, Int 11, Wis 11, Cha 11
Skills: Climb +0, Hide +5, Jump +0, Listen +3, Move Silently +4
Feats: Weapon Focus (longsword)

Climate/Terrain: Any land and underground
Organization: Company (2–4), squad (11–20 plus 2 3rd-level sergeants and 1 leader of 3rd–6th level), or band (30–100 plus 100% noncombatants plus 1 3rd-level sergeant per 20 adults, 5 5th-level lieutenants, 3 7th-level captains, 6–10 dogs, and 2–5 riding dogs)
Challenge Rating: 1/2
Treasure: Standard
Alignment: Usually neutral
Advancement: By character class

Halflings are cunning, resourceful survivors and opportunists who find room for themselves wherever they can. They might be reliable, hard-working citizens or thieves just waiting for their big chance.

Halflings stand about 3 feet tall and usually weigh between 30 and 35 pounds. Their skin is ruddy, their hair black and straight. They have brown or black eyes. Halfling men often have long sideburns, but beards are rare among them and mustaches almost unseen. They prefer simple, comfortable, and practical clothes. Unlike members of most races, they prefer actual comfort to shows of wealth. Halflings reach adulthood in their early twenties and generally live into the middle of their second century.

Halflings speak Halfling and Common. Most halflings encountered outside their home are warriors; the information in the statistics block is for one of 1st level. (See page 39 in the DUNGEON MASTER's Guide for more about the warrior class.)

COMBAT

Halflings prefer to fight defensively, usually hiding and launching ranged attacks as the foe approaches. There tactics are very much like those of elves but place more emphasis on cover and concealment and less on mobility.

Halfling Traits (Ex): Halflings benefit from a number of racial traits.

- Small: Halflings gain a +1 size bonus to AC and attack rolls and a +4 size bonus to Hide checks, but they must use smaller weapons than humans use, and their lifting and carrying limits are three-quarters of those of Medium-size creatures.

- +1 racial bonus to all saving throws.
- +2 morale bonus to saving throws against fear. (This bonus stacks with the halfling's +1 bonus to saving throws in general.)
- +1 racial attack bonus with a thrown weapon.

Skills: Halflings are agile, surefooted, and athletic. They receive a +2 racial bonus to Climb, Jump, and Move Silently checks. Their keen hearing bestows a +2 racial bonus to Listen checks.

HALFLING SOCIETY

Halflings try to get along with everyone else. They are adept at fitting into communities of humans, dwarves, elves, or gnomes and making themselves valuable and welcome. Since human society changes faster than the society of the longer-lived races, it most frequently offers opportunities to exploit, and halflings are often found in or around human lands.

Halflings often form tight-knit communities in human or dwarven cities. While they work readily with others, they often make friends only among themselves. Halflings also settle into secluded places where they set up self-reliant villages. Halfling communities, however, are known to pick up and move en masse to some place that offers some new opportunity, such as where a new mine has opened up or to a land where a devastating war has made skilled workers hard to find. If these opportunities are temporary, the community may pick up and move again once the opportunity is gone, or once a better one presents itself. If the opportunity is lasting, they settle and form a new village. Some communities, on the other hand, take to traveling as a way of life, driving wagons or guiding boats from place to place, with no permanent home.

The chief halfling deity is Yondalla, the Blessed One, protector of the halflings. Yondalla promises blessings and protection to those who heed her guidance, defend their clans, and cherish their families.

SUBRACES

The information above is for the lightfoot, the most common halfling variety. There are two other major halfling subraces, which differ from lightfeet as follows.

Tallfellows

Taller (4 feet or more in height) and slimmer than their kin, with fair skin and hair, tallfellows are somewhat rare among halfling folk. They generally speak Elven in addition to the usual halfling languages, and they greatly enjoy the company of elves. Their typical ability scores are the same as those of the lightfoot.

Tallfellow Traits (Ex): These are in addition to the basic halfling traits, except where noted here.

- +2 racial bonus to Search, Spot, and Listen checks. Like an elf, a tallfellow who merely passes within 5 feet of a secret or concealed door is entitled to a Search check as though actively looking for it.

Skills: Tallfellows are less athletic than lightfeet and do not receive any bonus to Climb, Jump, and Move Silently checks.

Deep Halflings

These halflings are shorter and stockier than the more common lightfeet. Deep halflings take great pleasure in gems and fine masonry, often working as jewelers or stonecutters. They rarely mix with humans and elves but enjoy the company of dwarves and speak Dwarven fluently. Their typical ability scores are the same as lightfeet.

Deep Halfling Traits (Ex): These are in addition to the basic halfling traits, except where noted here.

- Darkvision up to 60 feet.
- Stonecunning: Like dwarves, deep halflings receive a +2 racial bonus to checks to notice unusual stonework. Something that isn't stone but that is disguised as stone also counts as unusual stonework. A deep halfling who merely comes within 10 feet of unusual stonework can make a check as though actively searching and can use the Search skill to find stonework traps as a rogue can. A deep halfling can also intuit depth, sensing the approximate distance underground as naturally as a human can sense which way is up.

Skills: Deep halflings receive a +2 racial bonus to Appraise checks and Craft checks that are related to stone or metal. They are less athletic than lightfeet and do not receive any bonus to Climb, Jump, and Move Silently checks.

HALFLING CHARACTERS

A halfling's favored class is rogue. Halfling leaders are usually multiclass rogues.

Illus. by D. Bader

HARPY

Medium-Size Monstrous Humanoid
Hit Dice: 7d8 (31 hp)
Initiative: +2 (Dex)
Speed: 20 ft., fly 80 ft. (average)
AC: 13 (+2 Dex, +1 natural)
Attacks: Club +7/+2 melee, or 2 claws +2 melee
Damage: Club 1d4, or claw 1d3
Face/Reach: 5 ft. by 5 ft./5 ft.
Special Attacks: Captivating song
Saves: Fort +2, Ref +7, Will +5
Abilities: Str 10, Dex 15, Con 10, Int 7, Wis 10, Cha 15
Skills: Bluff +8, Listen +7, Perform (buffoonery, chant, epic, limericks, melody, ode, storytelling) +9, Spot +6
Feats: Dodge, Flyby Attack

Climate/Terrain: Temperate and warm land and underground
Organization: Solitary, pair, or flight (7–12)
Challenge Rating: 4
Treasure: Standard
Alignment: Usually chaotic evil
Advancement: By character class

A more malignant and wretched creature than the harpy is difficult to imagine. Taking great glee in causing suffering and death, the sadistic harpy is always watching for new victims.

A harpy resembles an evil-faced old human with the lower body, legs, and wings of a birdlike dinosaur. Its hair is tangled and filthy, crusted with the blood of its victims. A harpy's coal-black eyes clearly reflect its evil soul, as do the wicked talons on its knotty fingers. These vile creatures wear no clothing and often wield large, heavy bones as though they were clubs.

Harpies like to entrance hapless travelers with their magical songs and lead them to unspeakable torments. Only when a harpy has finished playing with its new "toys" will it release them from suffering by killing and consuming them.

COMBAT

When a harpy engages in battle, it prefers to use Flyby Attack and strike with a melee weapon.

Captivating Song (Su): The most insidious ability of the harpy is its song. When a harpy sings, all creatures (other than harpies) within a 300-foot spread must succeed at a Will save (DC 15) or become utterly captivated. This is a sonic, mind-affecting charm. If the save is successful, that creature cannot be affected again by that harpy's song for one day.

A captivated victim walks toward the harpy, taking the most direct route available. If the path leads into a dangerous area (through flame, off a cliff, etc.), that creature gets a second saving throw. Captivated creatures can take no actions other than to defend themselves. (Thus, a fighter cannot run away or attack but suffers no defensive penalties.) A victim within 5 feet of the harpy stands there and offers no resistance to the monster's attacks. The effect continues for as long as the harpy sings. A bard's countersong ability allows the captivated creature to attempt a new Will save.

Hell hounds are aggressive, fire-breathing canines of extraplanar origin. Specimens are frequently brought to the Material to serve evil beings, and many have established indigenous breeding populations.

A hell hound resembles a large, powerfully built dog with short, rust-red or reddish-brown fur; its markings, teeth, and tongue are sooty black. It is easily distinguished from normal hounds by its red, glowing eyes. A typical hell hound stands 4 1/2 feet high at the shoulder and weighs 120 pounds.

Hell hounds do not speak but understand Infernal.

COMBAT

Hell hounds are efficient hunters. A favorite pack tactic is to surround prey quietly, then attack with one or two hounds, driving it with their fiery breath toward the rest. If the prey doesn't run, the pack closes in. Hell hounds track fleeing prey relentlessly.

Breath Weapon (Su): Cone of fire, 30 feet, every 2d4 rounds; damage 1d4+1, Reflex half DC 13. The fiery breath also ignites any flammable materials within the cone. Hell hounds can use their breath weapon while biting.

Fire Subtype (Ex): Fire immunity, double damage from cold except on a successful save.

Skills: Hell hounds receive a +5 racial bonus to Hide and Move Silently checks. *They also receive a +8 racial bonus to Spot checks and Wilderness Lore checks when tracking by scent, due to their keen sense of smell.

HELL HOUND

Medium-Size Outsider (Evil, Fire, Lawful)
Hit Dice: 4d8+4 (22 hp)
Initiative: +5 (+1 Dex, +4 Improved Initiative)
Speed: 40 ft.
AC: 16 (+1 Dex, +5 natural)
Attacks: Bite +5 melee
Damage: Bite 1d8+1
Face/Reach: 5 ft. by 5 ft./5 ft.
Special Attacks: Breath weapon
Special Qualities: Scent, fire subtype
Saves: Fort +5, Ref +5, Will +4
Abilities: Str 13, Dex 13, Con 13, Int 6, Wis 10, Cha 6
Skills: Hide +11, Listen +5, Move Silently +13, Spot +7*, Wilderness Lore +0*
Feats: Improved Initiative, Track

Climate/Terrain: Any land and underground
Organization: Solitary, pair, or pack (5–12)
Challenge Rating: 3
Treasure: None
Alignment: Always lawful evil
Advancement: 5–8 HD (Large)

HIPPOGRIFF

Large Beast
Hit Dice: 3d10+9 (25 hp)
Initiative: +2 (Dex)
Speed: 50 ft., fly 100 ft. (average)
AC: 15 (–1 size, +2 Dex, +4 natural)
Attacks: 2 claws +5 melee, bite +0 melee
Damage: Claw 1d4+4, bite 1d8+2
Face/Reach: 5 ft. by 10 ft./5 ft.
Saves: Fort +6, Ref +5, Will +2
Abilities: Str 18, Dex 15, Con 16, Int 4, Wis 13, Cha 8
Skills: Listen +4, Spot +7*

Climate/Terrain: Temperate and warm hill and plains
Organization: Solitary, pair, or flight (7–12)
Challenge Rating: 2
Treasure: None
Alignment: Always neutral
Advancement: 4–6 HD (Large); 7–9 HD (Huge)

Hippogriffs are aggressive flying creatures that combine features of horses and giant eagles. Voracious omnivores, hippogriffs will hunt humanoids as readily as any other meal.

These beasts are very territorial, defending their preferred hunting and grazing areas against intruders with unusual ferocity. Their range usually extends about 5d10 miles from their nest, in which the young remain while the adults hunt. Hippogriffs never leave their young undefended, however: Discovering a hippogriff nest always means encountering adult creatures.

A hippogriff has the torso and hindquarters of a horse and the forelegs, wings, and head of a giant eagle. A typical specimen grows to 9 feet long, has a wingspread of 20 feet, and weighs 1,000 pounds.

COMBAT

Hippogriffs dive at their prey and strike with their taloned forelegs. When they cannot dive, they slash with claws and beak.

Mated pairs and flights of these creatures attack in concert, diving repeatedly to drive away or kill intruders. Hippogriffs fight to the death to defend their nests and their hatchlings, which are prized as aerial mounts and fetch a handsome price in many civilized areas.

Skills: *Hippogriffs receive a +4 racial bonus to Spot checks during daylight hours.

TRAINING A HIPPOGRIFF

Training a hippogriff as an aerial mount requires a successful Handle Animal check (DC 21 for a young creature, or DC 28 for an adult) and that the creature be willing. Hippogriffs mature at the same rate as horses. Trainers can reduce the DC by 5 and the rearing time by one-half by using a magic bridle enchanted for this purpose.

Hippogriff eggs are worth 2,000 gp apiece on the open market, while young are worth 3,000 gp each. Professional trainers charge 1,000 gp to rear or train a hippogriff. Riding a trained hippogriff requires an exotic saddle. A hippogriff can fight while carrying a rider, but the rider cannot also attack unless he or she succeeds at a Ride check (see Ride, page 72 in the *Player's Handbook*).

Carrying Capacity: A light load for a hippogriff is up to 300 pounds; a medium load, 301–600 pounds; and a heavy load, 601–900 pounds.

HOBGOBLIN

Medium-Size Humanoid (Goblinoid)
Hit Dice: 1d8+1 (5 hp)
Initiative: +1 (Dex)
Speed: 30 ft.
AC: 15 (+1 Dex, +3 studded leather, +1 small shield)
Attacks: Longsword +1 melee; or javelin +2 ranged
Damage: Longsword 1d8; or javelin 1d6
Face/Reach: 5 ft. by 5 ft./5 ft.
Special Qualities: Darkvision 60 ft.
Saves: Fort +3, Ref +1, Will +0
Abilities: Str 11, Dex 13, Con 13, Int 10, Wis 10, Cha 10

Skills: Hide +1, Listen +3, Move Silently +3, Spot +3
Feats: Alertness

Climate/Terrain: Temperate and warm land and underground
Organization: Gang (4–9), band (10–100 plus 50% noncombatants plus 1 3rd-level sergeant per 20 adults and 1 leader of 4th–6th level), warband (10–24), or tribe (30–300 plus 1 3rd-level sergeant per 20 adults, 1 or 2 lieutenants of 4th or 5th level, 1 leader of 6th–8th level, 2–4 dire wolves, and 1–4 ogres or 1–2 trolls)
Challenge Rating: 1/2
Treasure: Standard
Alignment: Usually lawful evil
Advancement: By character class

Hobgoblins are larger cousins of goblins. They are far more aggressive and organized than their smaller relatives and wage a perpetual war with other humanoids, particularly elves.

Hobgoblins are burly humanoids standing 6 1/2 feet tall. Their hairy hides range in coloration from dark reddish-brown to dark gray, with dark or red-orange skin. Large males have blue or red noses. Hobgoblin eyes are yellowish or dark brown, while their teeth are yellow. Their garments tend to be brightly colored, often blood red with black-tinted leather. Hobgoblin weaponry is kept polished and in good repair.

Hobgoblins speak Goblin and Common.

Most hobgoblins encountered outside their homes are warriors; the information in the statistics block is for one of 1st level (see page 39 in the Dungeon Master's Guide for more about the warrior class).

COMBAT

These creatures have a strong grasp of strategy and tactics and are capable of carrying out sophisticated battle plans. Under the leadership of a skilled strategist or tactician, their discipline can prove a deciding factor. Hobgoblins hate elves and attack them first, in preference to other opponents.

Skills: Hobgoblins receive a +4 racial bonus to Move Silently checks.

HOBGOBLIN SOCIETY

Hobgoblins are a military breed: They live for war and believe strongly in strength and martial prowess as the most desirable qualities for individuals and leaders alike. A hobgoblin leader is likely to be the biggest and strongest in the group, maintaining authority by enforcing strict discipline. Hobgoblins are often leaders among tribes of goblins and orcs, whom they bully and treat as inferiors. Hobgoblin mercenaries sometimes enter the service of wealthy evil humanoids.

Hobgoblin society is organized into tribal bands, each intensely jealous of its reputation and status. Meetings between rival bands are likely to erupt in violence if the troops are not restrained. Only an exceptionally powerful leader can force them to cooperate for any length of time. Each band has a distinctive battle standard that it carries into combat to inspire, rally, and signal the troops. A hobgoblin gang or band contains twice as many children as adults. Children are noncombatants unless they or their lair is threatened directly.

These creatures usually lair in places that either boast natural defenses or can be fortified: Cavern complexes, dungeons, ruins, and forests are among their favorites. Typical lair defenses include ditches, fences, gates, guard towers, pit traps, and crude catapults or ballistas.

Most hobgoblins revere Maglubiyet, who is also the patron deity of goblins.

HOBGOBLIN CHARACTERS

A hobgoblin's favored class is fighter, and hobgoblin leaders tend to be fighters or fighter/rogues. Hobgoblin clerics worship Maglubiyet and can choose two of the following domains: Evil, Destruction, and Trickery. Most hobgoblin spellcasters, however, are adepts (see page 37 in the DUNGEON MASTER's GUIDE). Hobgoblin adepts favor spells that deal damage.

HOMUNCULUS

Tiny Construct
Hit Dice: 2d10 (11 hp)
Initiative: +2 (Dex)
Speed: 20 ft., fly 50 ft. (good)
AC: 14 (+2 Dex, +2 size)
Attacks: Bite +2 melee
Damage: Bite 1d4–1 and poison
Face/Reach: 2 1/2 ft. by 2 1/2 ft./0 ft.
Special Attacks: Poison
Special Qualities: Construct
Saves: Fort +0, Ref +2, Will +1
Abilities: Str 8, Dex 15, Con —, Int 10, Wis 12, Cha 7

Climate/Terrain: Any land and underground
Organization: Solitary
Challenge Rating: 1
Treasure: None
Alignment: Any (same as creator)
Advancement: 3–6 HD (Tiny)

A homunculus is a diminutive servant created by a wizard. These creatures are weak combatants but make effective spies, messengers, and scouts.

Homunculi are little more than tools designed to carry out assigned tasks. They are extensions of their creators, sharing the same alignment and basic nature. A homunculus cannot speak, but the process of creating one links it telepathically with its creator. It knows what its master knows and can convey to him or her everything it sees and hears, up to a range of 500 yards. A homunculus never travels beyond this range willingly, though it can be removed forcibly. If this occurs, the creature does everything in its power to regain contact with its master. An attack that destroys a homunculus deals its master 2d10 points of damage. If the creature's master is slain, the homunculus also dies, and its body swiftly melts away into a pool of ichor.

A homunculus has a vaguely humanoid form. The creator determines an individual's precise features, but in general one stands about 18 inches tall and has a wingspan of about 2 feet. A homunculus's skin is often rough and sometimes warty, varying in color depending on the materials used to create it. Its mouth is filled with sharp, needlelike teeth that deliver a weak venom.

COMBAT

Homunculi land on their victims and bite with their venomous fangs.

Poison (Ex): Bite, Fortitude save (DC 11); initial damage sleep for 1 minute, secondary damage sleep for another 5d6 minutes.

Construct: Immune to mind-influencing effects, poison, disease, and similar effects. Not subject to critical hits, subdual damage, ability damage, energy drain, or death from massive damage.

CONSTRUCTION

A homunculus costs 100 gp to create, including 20 gp for the body. This cost includes all the materials and spell components that are consumed by or become a permanent part of the creation.

The first task is shaping the creature from a mixture of clay, ashes, mandrake root, spring water, and one pint of the creator's own blood. The creature's master may assemble the body or hire someone else to do the job. Creating the body requires a Craft (sculpture or masonry) check (DC of 12).

After the body is sculpted, it is animated through an extended magical ritual that requires a 7th-level character with the Craft Wondrous Item feat. This ritual requires a week to complete: The creator must labor for at least 8 hours each day in a specially prepared laboratory or workroom, similar to an alchemist's laboratory and costing 500 gp to establish. If the creator is personally constructing the creature's body, the building and ritual can be performed together.

A character not actively working on the ritual must rest and can perform no other activities except eating, sleeping, or talking. If he or she misses a day, the process fails, and the ritual must be started anew; any gp spent on the failed ritual is lost (but not XP). The previously crafted body can be reused, as can the laboratory.

Completing the ritual requires casting *arcane eye*, *mirror image*, and *mending* on the final day of the ritual and drains 25 XP from the creator. He or she must cast the spells personally, but they can come from outside sources, such as scrolls.

HOWLER

Large Outsider (Chaotic, Evil)
Hit Dice: 6d8+12 (39 hp)
Initiative: +7 (+3 Dex, +4 Improved Initiative)
Speed: 60 ft.
AC: 17 (–1 size, +3 Dex, +5 natural)
Attacks: Bite +10 melee, 1d4 quills +5 melee
Damage: Bite 2d8+5, quill 1d4+2
Face/Reach: 5 ft. by 10 ft./5 ft.
Special Attacks: Quills, howl
Saves: Fort +7, Ref +8, Will +7
Abilities: Str 21, Dex 17, Con 15, Int 6, Wis 14, Cha 8
Skills: Climb +10, Hide +8, Listen +11, Move Silently +8, Search +1, Spot +11
Feats: Alertness, Improved Initiative

Climate/Terrain: Any land and underground
Organization: Solitary, gang (2–4), or pack (6–10)
Challenge Rating: 3
Treasure: None
Alignment: Always chaotic evil
Advancement: 7–9 HD (Large); 11–18 HD (Huge)

Howlers live in dark planes where chaos and evil hold sway. These beasts hunt in packs, racing through caverns to wear down their prey and rend it to bits.

Long-legged and spiky-haired, howlers are bestially humanoid in appearance. Although they are surprisingly intelligent, howlers do not speak—they only howl. If there is a language within the howls, as some have suggested, even spells cannot decipher it.

COMBAT

Howlers attack in groups, for they are cowardly and cruel. They prefer to charge into combat, race out, and then charge in again.

Quills (Ex): The howler's neck bristles with long quills. While biting, the creature thrashes about, striking with 1d4 of them. An opponent hit by the howler's quill attack must make a Reflex save (DC 16) or have the quill break off in his or her flesh. A lodged quill imposes a –1 circumstance penalty to attacks, saves, and checks. Removing the quill deals 1d6 additional points of damage.

Howl (Ex): All beings other than outsiders that hear the creature's howling for an hour or more are subject to its effect, though it does not help the howler in combat. Those within a 100-foot spread must succeed at a Will save (DC 12) or take 1 point of temporary Wisdom damage. The save must be repeated for each hour of exposure. This is a sonic, mind-affecting attack; deafened creatures are not subject to it.

TRAINING A HOWLER

Small and Medium-size infernal creatures such as quasits, abyssal orcs, or even succubi sometimes use howlers as mounts or pack animals—they are particularly useful underground. Larger and more powerful demons use them like hunting dogs.

Training a howler requires a successful Handle Animal check (DC 23 for a young creature, or DC 30 for an adult) and that the creature be willing. Trainers can reduce the DC by 5 and the rearing time by one-half by using a magic harness enchanted for the purpose. Riding a howler requires an exotic saddle. A howler can fight while carrying a rider, but the rider cannot also attack unless he or she succeeds at a Ride check (see Ride, page 72 in the *Player's Handbook*).

Carrying Capacity: A light load for a howler is up to 460 pounds; a medium load, 461–920 pounds; and a heavy load, 921–1,380 pounds. A howler can drag 6,900 pounds.

HYDRA

	Five-Headed Huge Beast	Six-Headed Huge Beast	Seven-Headed Huge Beast
Hit Dice:	5d10+25 (52 hp)	6d10+30 (63 hp)	7d10+35 (73 hp)
Initiative:	+1 (Dex)	+1 (Dex)	+1 (Dex)
Speed:	20 ft., swim 10 ft.	20 ft., swim 10 ft.	20 ft., swim 10 ft.
AC:	15 (–2 size, +1 Dex, +6 natural)	15 (–2 size, +1 Dex, +6 natural)	15 (–2 size, +1 Dex, +6 natural)
Attacks:	5 bites +4 melee	6 bites +5 melee	7 bites +7 melee
Damage:	Bite 1d10+3	Bite 1d10+3	Bite 1d10+4
Face/Reach:	20 ft. by 20 ft./10 ft.	20 ft. by 20 ft./10 ft.	20 ft. by 20 ft./10 ft.
Special Qualities:	Scent	Scent	Scent
Saves:	Fort +9, Ref +5, Will +1	Fort +10, Ref +6, Will +2	Fort +10, Ref +6, Will +2
Abilities:	Str 17, Dex 12, Con 20, Int 3, Wis 10, Cha 9	Str 17, Dex 12, Con 20, Int 3, Wis 10, Cha 9	Str 19, Dex 12, Con 20, Int 3, Wis 10, Cha 9
Skills:	Listen +5, Spot +6	Listen +6, Spot +6	Listen +6, Spot +7
Feats:	Combat Reflexes	Combat Reflexes	Combat Reflexes

	Eight-Headed	**Nine-Headed**	**Ten-Headed**
	Huge Beast	Huge Beast	Huge Beast
Hit Dice:	8d10+40 (84 hp)	9d10+45 (94 hp)	10d10+50 (105 hp)
Initiative:	+1 (Dex)	+1 (Dex)	+1 (Dex)
Speed:	20 ft., swim 20 ft.	20 ft., swim 20 ft.	20 ft., swim 20 ft.
AC:	15 (−2 size, +1 Dex, +6 natural)	15 (−2 size, +1 Dex, +6 natural)	15 (−2 size, +1 Dex, +6 natural)
Attacks:	8 bites +8 melee	9 bites +9 melee	10 bites +10 melee
Damage:	Bite 1d10+4	Bite 1d10+5	Bite 1d10+5
Face/Reach:	20 ft. by 20 ft./10 ft.	20 ft. by 20 ft./10 ft.	20 ft. by 20 ft./10 ft.
Special Qualities:	Scent	Scent	Scent
Saves:	Fort +11, Ref +7, Will +2	Fort +11, Ref +7, Will +3	Fort +12, Ref +8, Will +3
Abilities:	Str 19, Dex 12, Con 20, Int 3, Wis 10, Cha 9	Str 21, Dex 12, Con 20, Int 3, Wis 10, Cha 9	Str 21, Dex 12, Con 20, Int 3, Wis 10, Cha 9
Skills:	Listen +7, Spot +7	Listen +7, Spot +8	Listen +8, Spot +8
Feats:	Combat Reflexes	Combat Reflexes	Combat Reflexes

	Eleven-Headed	**Twelve-Headed**
	Huge Beast	Huge Beast
Hit Dice:	11d10+55 (115 hp)	12d10+60 (126 hp)
Initiative:	+1 (Dex)	+1 (Dex)
Speed:	20 ft., swim 20 ft.	20 ft., swim 20 ft.
AC:	15 (−2 size, +1 Dex, +6 natural)	15 (−2 size, +1 Dex, +6 natural)
Attacks:	11 bites +12 melee	12 bites +13 melee
Damage:	Bite 1d10+6	Bite 1d10+6
Face/Reach:	20 ft. by 20 ft./10 ft.	20 ft. by 20 ft./10 ft.
Special Qualities:	Scent	Scent
Saves:	Fort +12, Ref +8, Will +3	Fort +13, Ref +9, Will +4
Abilities:	Str 23, Dex 12, Con 20, Int 3, Wis 10, Cha 9	Str 23, Dex 12, Con 20, Int 3, Wis 10, Cha 9
Skills:	Listen +8, Spot +9	Listen +9, Spot +9
Feats:	Combat Reflexes	Combat Reflexes

Climate/Terrain: Any marsh and underground

Organization: Solitary

Challenge Rating: Five-headed 4 (normal); 6 (pyro- or cryo-); 7 (Lernaean); or 8 (Lernaean pyro- or cryo-)

Six-headed 5 (normal); 7 (pyro- or cryo-); 8 (Lernaean); or 9 (Lernaean pyro- or cryo-)

Seven-headed 6 (normal); 8 (pyro- or cryo-); 9 (Lernaean); or 10 (Lernaean pyro- or cryo-)

Eight-headed 7 (normal); 9 (pyro- or cryo-); 10 (Lernaean); or 11 (Lernaean pyro- or cryo-)

Nine-headed 8 (normal); 10 (pyro- or cryo-); 11 (Lernaean); or 12 (Lernaean pyro- or cryo-)

Ten-headed 9 (normal); 11 (pyro- or cryo-); 12 (Lernaean); or 13 (Lernaean pyro- or cryo-)

Eleven-headed 10 (normal); 12 (pyro- or cryo-); 13 (Lernaean); or 14 (Lernaean pyro- or cryo-)

Twelve-headed 11 (normal); 13 (pyro- or cryo-); 14 (Lernaean); or 15 (Lernaean pyro- or cryo-)

Treasure: 1/10 coins; 50% goods; 50% items

Alignment: Usually neutral

Advancement: —

Hydras are reptilelike monsters with multiple heads.

A hydra is gray-brown to dark brown, with a light yellow or tan underbelly. The eyes are amber and the teeth are yellow-white. It is about 20 feet long and weighs about 4,000 pounds. Hydras do not speak.

MAGICAL BEASTS

Three special kinds of hydras—the Lernaean hydra, the pyrohydra, and the cryohydra—are magical beasts rather than beasts. They have all the same characteristics and statistics blocks that ordinary hydras have, and in addition they possess special abilities that are described in the text on the following page.

LOCKWOOD

COMBAT

Hydras can attack with all their heads at no penalty, even if they move or charge during the round.

A hydra can be killed either by severing all its heads or by slaying its body. To sever a head, an opponent must hit the monster's neck with a slashing weapon and deal damage equal to the hydra's original hit point total, divided by its original number of heads, in one blow. (The player says where the attack is aimed just before making the attack roll.) For example, if a five-headed hydra has 52 hp, a single blow dealing 10 or more points of damage severs a head (52 ÷ 5 = 10.4, rounded down to 10). Any excess damage is lost. A severed head dies, and a natural reflex seals the neck shut to prevent further blood loss. The hydra can no longer attack with the severed head but suffers no other penalties. A severed head regrows in about a month.

Skills: Hydras receive a +2 racial bonus to Listen and Spot checks, thanks to their multiple heads.

Feats: A hydra's Combat Reflexes feat allows it to use all its heads for attacks of opportunity each round.

LERNAEAN HYDRA

These hydras have bodies that are immune to all attacks (but see below). The only way to slay a Lernaean hydra normally is to sever all its heads. However, each time a head is severed, two new heads spring from the stump in 1d4 rounds. A Lernaean hydra can never have more than twice its original number of heads at any one time, and any extra heads it gains beyond its original number wither and die within a day.

To prevent a severed head from growing back into two, at least 5 points of fire or acid damage must be dealt to the stump (AC 19) before the new heads appear.

Spells such as *disintegrate, finger of death,* and *slay living* kill a Lernaean hydra outright if they succeed. If the spell deals damage on a successful save, that damage is directed against one of the hydra's heads.

PYROHYDRA

These reddish hydras can breathe jets of fire 10 feet high, 10 feet wide, and 20 feet long. All heads breathe once every 1d4 rounds. Each jet deals 3d6 damage per head. A successful Reflex save halves the damage. The save DC is 10 + 1/2 hydra's original number of heads + the hydra's Constitution modifier.

Fire Subtype (Ex): Fire immunity; double damage from cold except on a successful save.

A pyrohydra may also be of the Lernaean form.

CRYOHYDRA

These purplish hydras can breathe jets of frost 10 feet high, 10 feet wide, and 20 feet long. All heads breathe once every 1d4 rounds. Each jet deals 3d6 damage per head. A successful Reflex save halves the damage. The save DC is 10 + 1/2 hydra's original number of heads + the hydra's Constitution modifier.

Cold Subtype (Ex): Cold immunity; double damage from fire except on a successful save.

A cryohydra may also be of the Lernaean form.

INVISIBLE STALKER

Large Elemental (Air)
Hit Dice: 8d8+16 (52 hp)
Initiative: +8 (+4 Dex, +4 Improved Initiative)
Speed: 30 ft., fly 30 ft. (perfect)
AC: 17 (–1 size, +4 Dex, +4 natural)
Attacks: Slam +10/+5
Damage: Slam 2d6+6
Face/Reach: 5 ft. by 5 ft./10 ft.
Special Qualities: Elemental, natural invisibility, improved tracking
Saves: Fort +4, Ref +10, Will +4
Abilities: Str 18, Dex 19, Con 14, Int 14, Wis 15, Cha 11

Skills: Listen +11, Move Silently +15, Search +11, Spot +13
Feats: Combat Reflexes, Improved Initiative, Weapon Focus (slam)

Climate/Terrain: Any land and underground
Organization: Solitary
Challenge Rating: 7
Treasure: None
Alignment: Usually neutral
Advancement: 9–12 HD (Large); 13–24 HD (Huge)

Invisible stalkers are creatures native to the Elemental Plane of Air. They sometimes serve wizards and sorcerers, who summon them to fulfill specific tasks.

A summoned stalker performs whatever task the summoner commands, even if the task sends it hundreds or thousands of miles away. The creature follows a command until the task is completed and obeys only the summoner. However, it resents prolonged missions or complex tasks and seeks to pervert its instructions accordingly.

Invisible stalkers have an amorphous form. A *see invisibility* spell shows only a dim outline of a cloud, while a *true seeing* spell reveals a roiling cloud of vapor.

These creatures speak only Auran but can understand Common.

COMBAT

An invisible stalker attacks by using the air itself as a weapon. It creates a sudden, intense vortex of wind that pounds a single target on the same plane as the creature.

Invisible stalkers can be killed only when on the Elemental Plane of Air. When performing tasks elsewhere, they automatically return to their home plane when they suffer sufficient damage to destroy them.

Elemental: Immune to poison, sleep, paralysis, and stunning. Not subject to critical hits.

Natural Invisibility (Su): This ability is constant, allowing the stalker to remain invisible even when attacking. This ability is inherent and not subject to the *invisibility purge* spell.

Improved Tracking (Ex): Invisible stalkers are consummate trackers and make Spot checks instead of the usual Wilderness Lore checks to trace a creature's passage.

KOBOLD

Small Humanoid (Reptilian)
Hit Dice: 1/2 d8 (2 hp)
Initiative: +1 (Dex)
Speed: 30 ft.
AC: 15 (+1 size, +1 Dex, +1 natural, +2 leather)
Attacks: Halfspear –1 melee; or light crossbow +2 ranged
Damage: Halfspear 1d6–2; or light crossbow 1d8
Face/Reach: 5 ft. by 5 ft./5 ft.
Special Qualities: Darkvision 60 ft., light sensitivity
Saves: Fort +0, Ref +1, Will +2
Abilities: Str 6, Dex 13, Con 11, Int 10, Wis 10, Cha 10
Skills: Craft (trapmaking) +2, Hide +8, Listen +2, Move Silently +4, Search +2, Spot +2
Feats: Alertness

Illus. by T. Lockwood

Climate/Terrain: Any forest and underground
Organization: Gang (4–9), band (10–100 plus 100% noncombatants plus 1 3rd-level sergeant per 20 adults and 1 leader of 4th–6th level), warband (10–24 plus 2–4 dire weasels), tribe (40–400 plus 1 3rd-level sergeant per 20 adults, 1 or 2 lieutenants of 4th or 5th level, 1 leader of 6th–8th level, and 5–8 dire weasels)
Challenge Rating: 1/6
Treasure: Standard
Alignment: Usually lawful evil
Advancement: By character class

Kobolds are short, reptilian human-oids with cowardly and sadistic tendencies.

A kobold's scaly skin ranges from dark rusty brown to a rusty black color. It has two small light-colored horns on its doglike head, glowing red eyes, and a non-prehensile tail like that of a rat. Kobolds wear ragged cloth-ing, favoring red and orange, and speak Draconic with voices that sound like yapping dogs. They eat plants or animals but are not averse to eating intelligent beings. They spend most of their time fortifying the land around their lairs with traps and warning devices (such as spiked pits, tripwires attached to crossbows, and other mechanical contraptions).

Kobolds hate almost every other sort of humanoid or fey, especially gnomes and sprites.

COMBAT

Kobolds like to attack with overwhelming odds (at least two to one) or trickery; should the odds fall below this threshold, they usually flee. However, they attack gnomes on sight if their numbers are equal.

They begin a fight by slinging bullets, closing only when they can see that their foes have been weakened. Whenever they can, kobolds set up ambushes near trapped areas. They aim to drive enemies into the traps, where other kobolds wait to pour flaming oil over them, shoot them, or drop poisonous vermin onto them.

Light Sensitivity (Ex): Kobolds suffer a –1 penalty to attack rolls in bright sunlight or within the radius of a *daylight* spell.

Skills: Kobolds receive a +2 racial bonus to Craft (trapmaking), Profession (mining), and Search checks.

KOBOLD SOCIETY

Kobolds live in dark places: underground locations and overgrown forests. They are good miners and often live in the mines they're developing. A kobold tribe comprises up to ten clans, which form war parties that patrol within a ten-mile radius from their lair, attacking any intelligent creatures that enter their territory. They usually kill prisoners for food but occasionally sell some of them as slaves. Their nasty habits and distrust of most other beings mean that they have many enemies.

A kobold lair has one noncombatant child and one egg per ten adults.

The patron deity of the kobolds is Kurtulmak, who despises all living creatures except kobolds.

KOBOLD CHARACTERS

A kobold's favored class is sorcerer; most kobold leaders are sor-cerers. Kobold clerics are fairly rare and usually found only with very large tribes; adepts are more common (see page 37 in the *Dungeon Master's Guide*). Kobold clerics worship Kurtulmak and can choose any two of the following domains: Evil, Law, Luck, and Trickery.

KRAKEN

Gargantuan Magical Beast (Aquatic)
Hit Dice: 20d10+180 (290 hp)
Initiative: +4 (Improved Initiative)
Speed: Swim 20 ft.
AC: 20 (–4 size, +14 natural)
Attacks: 2 tentacle rakes +28 melee, 6 arms +23 melee, bite +23 melee
Damage: Tentacle rake 2d8+12, arm 1d6+6, bite 4d6+6
Face/Reach: 20 ft. by 40 ft./10 ft. (100 ft. with tentacle)
Special Attacks: Improved grab, constrict 2d8+12 or 1d6+6
Special Qualities: Jet, ink cloud, spell-like abilities
Saves: Fort +21, Ref +12, Will +13
Abilities: Str 34, Dex 10, Con 29, Int 21, Wis 20, Cha 10
Skills: Concentration +19, Knowledge (geography) +10, Knowl-edge (nature) +10, Listen +15, Search +15, Spot +15
Feats: Alertness, Blind-Fight, Expertise, Improved Critical (tentacle), Improved Initiative, Improved Trip, Iron Will

SARDINHA

Climate/Terrain: Any aquatic
Organization: Solitary
Challenge Rating: 12
Treasure: Triple standard
Alignment: Always neutral evil
Advancement: 21–32 HD (Gargantuan); 33–60 HD (Colossal)

Aggressive, cruel, and highly intelligent, krakens rule entire undersea regions. Though these behemoths are rarely seen on the surface, stories tell of ships dragged under and islands scoured of life by these monsters.

Krakens make their lairs thousands of feet below the ocean surface. They frequently inhabit huge cavern complexes that include sections filled with breathable air, where they imprison and breed humanoid slaves to serve and feed them.

A kraken resembles an immense squid, but with only eight tentacles. Its body is approximately 90 feet long and protected by layers of thick muscle. Six of the beast's tentacles are shorter arms about 50 feet long; the remaining two are nearly 100 feet long and covered with cruel barbs. Its beaklike mouth is located where the tentacles meet the lower portion of its body.

Krakens speak Common and Aquan.

COMBAT

Krakens strike their opponents with their barbed tentacles, then grab and crush with their arms or drag victims into their huge jaws.

Improved Grab (Ex): To use this ability, the kraken must hit an opponent of up to Huge size with an arm or tentacle attack. If it gets a hold, it can constrict.

Constrict (Ex): A kraken deals automatic arm or tentacle damage with a successful grapple check against Huge or smaller creatures.

Jet (Ex): A kraken can jet backward once per round as a double move action, at a speed of 280 feet.

Ink Cloud (Ex): A kraken can emit a cloud of jet-black ink 80 feet high by 80 feet wide by 120 feet long once per minute as a free action. The cloud provides total concealment, which the kraken normally uses to escape a losing fight. Creatures within the cloud suffer the effects of total darkness.

Spell-Like Abilities: 1/day—*control weather, control winds, dominate animal,* and *resist elements.* These abilities are as the spells cast by a 9th-level druid (save DC 15 + spell level).

KRENSHAR

Medium-Size Magical Beast
Hit Dice: 2d10 (11 hp)
Initiative: +2 (Dex)
Speed: 40 ft.
AC: 15 (+2 Dex, +3 natural)
Attacks: Bite +2 melee, 2 claws +0 melee
Damage: Bite 1d6, claw 1d4
Face/Reach: 5 ft. by 5 ft./5 ft.
Special Attacks: Scare
Special Qualities: Scent
Saves: Fort +3, Ref +5, Will +1
Abilities: Str 11, Dex 14, Con 11,
  Int 6, Wis 12, Cha 13
Skills: Hide +4, Jump +4, Listen
  +4, Move Silently +6
Feats: Multiattack

Climate/Terrain: Temperate and warm forest and plains
Organization: Solitary, pair, or pride (6–10)
Challenge Rating: 1
Treasure: None
Alignment: Always neutral
Advancement: 3–4 HD (Medium-size); 5–8 HD (Large)

The krenshar is a strange, catlike carnivore with extremely flexible skin.

A typical individual measures 4 or 5 feet in length with a long, narrow head. Males and females hunt together in packs, preferring herd animals for food but attacking humanoids when game becomes scarce. Krenshars are very social among their own kind, and occasional attempts to domesticate cubs have produced fierce and loyal companions. They otherwise behave much like mundane great cats. A lair contains cubs numbering half the adult total.

COMBAT

Krenshars use solitary scouts to drive prey into the waiting clutches of the pack. The scout appears from hiding, uses its scare ability, then chases the fleeing target to join the attack.

Scare (Ex or Su): As a standard action, a krenshar can pull the skin back from its head, revealing the musculature and bony structures of its skull. This alone is usually sufficient to scare away foes (treat as a Bluff check with a +3 bonus).

Combining this scare ability with a loud screech produces an unsettling effect that works like *scare* cast by a 3rd-level sorcerer (save DC 12). If the save is successful, that opponent cannot be affected again by that krenshar's scare ability for one day. The shriek does not affect other krenshars.

KUO-TOA

Medium-Size Monstrous Humanoid (Aquatic)
Hit Dice: 2d8+2 (11 hp)
Initiative: +0
Speed: 20 ft., swim 50 ft.
AC: 18 (+6 natural, +2 large shield)
Attacks: Spear +3 melee, bite –2 melee; or spear +2 ranged
Damage: Spear 1d8+1, bite 1d4
Special Attacks: Lightning bolt, pincer staff
Special Qualities: Keen sight, slippery, adhesive, immunities,
  electricity resistance 30, light blindness, amphibious
Saves: Fort +3, Ref +3, Will +5
Abilities: Str 13, Dex 10, Con 13, Int 13, Wis 14, Cha 8
Skills: Escape Artist +18, Knowledge or Craft (any one) +6,
  Listen +9, Move Silently +3, Search +10, Spot +11
Feats: Alertness, Great Fortitude

Climate/Terrain: Any aquatic and underground
Organization: Patrol (2–4 plus 1 3rd-level whip), squad (6–11 plus 1 or 2 3rd-level whips, 1 or 2 4th-level monitors, and 1 8th-level fighter), band (20–50 plus 100% non-combatants plus 2 3rd-level whips, 2 8th-level fighters, and 1 10th-level fighter), or tribe (40–400 plus 1 3rd-level whip per 20 adults, 1 4th-level monitor, 4 8th-level fighters, 1 10th-level whip, and 2 10th-level fighters)

Challenge Rating: 2
Treasure: Standard
Alignment: Often neutral evil
Advancement: By character class

The kuo-toa are an ancient line of aquatic humanoids noted for their sinister nature and diabolical tendencies.

Although most people shun contact with these loathsome creatures, sometimes avoiding them is simply not possible. Kuo-toas know much about long-forgotten, ancient evils dwelling in the deepest parts of the ocean.

An average kuo-toa stands roughly 5 feet tall and has a more or less humanoid appearance. Its rounded body is covered with fine scales giving it the appearance of being pudgy or bloated. The arms and legs are slender, almost willowy, ending in broad hands and distended feet that look very much like flippers. The bullet-shaped heads are piscine, with bulging, silver-black eyes and wide mouths full of needle-sharp teeth. Although kuo-toas are generally a silver-gray color, their pigmentation changes with their mood. An angry kuo-toa is dark red, while a frightened one becomes pale gray or even white. The air around a kuo-toa carries the almost overwhelming odor of rotting fish.

Kuo-toas speak Kuo-Toan, Undercommon, and Aquan.

COMBAT

Kuo-toan tactics and weapons vary greatly depending upon the training and skills of the individual encountered. A group of kuo-toa warriors usually fight in formation, throwing their spears before closing to melee range.

Lightning Bolt (Su): Two or more kuo-toa clerics (known as "whips") operating together can generate a stroke of lightning every 1d4 rounds. The whips must join hands to launch the bolt but need merely remain within 30 feet of one another while it builds. The lightning bolt deals 1d6 points of damage per whip, but a successful Reflex save halves this amount (save DC 13 + number of whips).

Pincer Staff: Many kuo-toa fighters and all whips above 6th level carry this Large exotic weapon. A pincer staff deals 1d10 points of bludgeoning damage, threatens a critical hit on a 20, and deals double damage on a critical hit. It has a 10-foot reach and cannot be used against an adjacent opponent. A wielder that hits an opponent of at least Small but no larger than Large size attempts to start a grapple as a free action without provoking an attack of opportunity. If the wielder gets a hold, the staff grabs the opponent and deals 1d10 points of damage each round the hold is maintained.

Keen Sight (Ex): Kuo-toas have excellent vision thanks to their two independently focusing eyes. Their eyesight is so keen that they can spot a moving object or creature even if it is invisible, ethereal, or astral. Only by remaining perfectly still can such objects or creatures avoid their notice.

Slippery (Ex): All kuo-toas secrete an oily film that makes them difficult to grapple or snare. Webs, magic or otherwise, don't affect kuo-toas, and they usually can wriggle free from most other forms of confinement.

Adhesive (Ex): Kuo-toas use their own body oil and other materials to give their shields a finish almost like flypaper, holding fast any creatures or items touching them. Anyone who makes an *unsuccessful* melee attack against a kuo-toa must succeed at a Reflex save (DC 14), or the attacker's weapon sticks to the shield and is yanked out of the wielder's grip. Creatures using natural weapons are automatically grappled if they get stuck.

Immunities (Ex): Kuo-toas are immune to poison and paralysis. The various *hold* spells also have no effect on them, and their keen sight automatically detects figments for what they are.

Light Blindness (Ex): Abrupt exposure to bright light (such as sunlight or a *daylight* spell) blinds kuo-toas for 1 round. In addition, they suffer a –1 circumstance penalty to all attack rolls, saves, and checks while operating in bright light.

Amphibious (Ex): Although kuo-toas breathe by means of gills, they can survive indefinitely on land.

Skills: Kuo-toas receive a +15 racial bonus to Escape Artist checks and a +4 racial bonus to Spot and Search checks.

KUO-TOAN SOCIETY

Kuo-toas dwell in subterranean communities that are well supplied with pools for recreation and breeding. They spawn as fish do, raising their young in special pools until their amphibian qualities develop (about a year after hatching).

Thanks to the efforts of the whips, virtually all kuo-toas are devoted worshipers of the goddess Blibdoolpoolp, whom they refer to as the Sea Mother. Every kuo-toan community has at least one shrine to the Sea Mother. Larger communities with major temples serve as hubs for clusters of smaller settlements. These are also centers for intergroup trade and politics. Virtually all kuo-toan communities are open to drow and their servants, who provide useful goods and services, although the drow are both feared and hated by the kuo-toa. This enmity leads to many minor skirmishes and frequent kidnappings between the peoples.

KUO-TOAN CHARACTERS

A kuo-toa's favored class is rogue. Most kuo-toan leaders are cleric/rogues or clerics (whips). Whips worship Blibdoolpoolp and can choose any two of the following domains: Destruction, Evil, and Water. Kuo-toan monks, called monitors, also exist.

LAMIA

Medium-Size Magical Beast
Hit Dice: 9d10+9 (58 hp)
Initiative: +2 (Dex)
Speed: 60 ft.
AC: 17 (+2 Dex, +5 natural)
Attacks: Touch +9 melee; or dagger +11/+6 melee
Damage: Touch 1 permanent Wisdom drain; or dagger 1d4
Face/Reach: 5 ft. by 5 ft./5 ft.
Special Attacks: Spell-like abilities, Wisdom drain
Saves: Fort +7, Ref +8, Will +7
Abilities: Str 10, Dex 15, Con 12, Int 13, Wis 15, Cha 12
Skills: Bluff +13, Concentration +11, Hide +14
Feats: Dodge, Iron Will, Mobility, Weapon Finesse (dagger)

Climate/Terrain: Any desert, hill, and underground
Organization: Solitary, pair, or gang (2–4)
Challenge Rating: 6
Treasure: Standard
Alignment: Usually chaotic evil
Advancement: 10–13 HD (Large); 14–27 HD (Huge)

Lamias are evil and cruel creatures that take great pleasure in causing suffering and spreading evil. They particularly target those who serve the cause of good for horrible deaths.

Most lamias appear as a cross between a stunningly attractive human and a sleek lion. Less commonly, the human torso might be found atop the body of a deer or goat.

COMBAT

Though a lamia appears to have an array of powerful natural weapons, its legs and claws (or hooves) are not very strong. Lamias wield daggers in combat when not using their Wisdom drain.

Lamias make excellent use of their magical abilities when hunting. They set illusions to lure would-be heroes into perilous situations, then attack from behind.

Spell-Like Abilities: 1/day—*charm person, major image, mirror image,* and *suggestion.* These abilities are as the spells cast by a 9th-level sorcerer (save DC 11 + spell level).

Wisdom Drain (Su): By making a successful touch attack, a lamia permanently drains 1 point of Wisdom. Lamias try to use this power early in an encounter to make foes more susceptible to *charm person* and *suggestion.*

LAMMASU

Large Magical Beast
Hit Dice: 7d10+21 (59 hp)
Initiative: +0
Speed: 30 ft., fly 60 ft.
(average)
AC: 14 (–1 size, +5 natural)
Attacks: 2 claws +12
melee
Damage: Claw
1d6+6
Face/Reach: 5 ft.
by 10 ft./5 ft.
Special Attacks:
Spells, pounce,
rake 1d6+3
Special Qualities: Magic circle
against evil, spell-like abilities
Saves: Fort +8, Ref +7, Will +7
Abilities: Str 23, Dex 10, Con 17, Int 16,
Wis 17, Cha 14
Skills: Concentration +12, Knowledge
(arcana) +12, Listen +8
Sense Motive +12, Spot +8*
Feats: Blind-Fight, Combat Casting, Flyby Attack, Iron Will,
Lightning Reflexes

Climate/Terrain: Any warm land and underground
Organization: Solitary
Challenge Rating: 8
Treasure: Standard
Alignment: Always lawful good
Advancement: 8–10 HD (Large); 11–21 HD (Huge)

Lammasus are noble creatures that are concerned with the welfare and safety of all good beings.

These creatures dwell most often in old, abandoned temples and ruins located in remote areas, where they contemplate how best to combat the influence of evil in the world. Adventurers sometimes seek them out to gain the benefit of their wisdom and their knowledge of ancient mysteries. Lammasus receive good beings and creatures cordially and usually offer assistance if the visitor is directly combating evil. They tolerate neutral beings but watch them carefully. They do not tolerate the presence of evil beings, attacking them on sight.

A lammasu has the golden-brown body of a lion, the wings of a giant eagle, and the face of a human. It is about 10 feet long and weighs about 600 pounds. Lammasus' bearing and demeanor are both noble and stern, though they can be quite compassionate.

Lammasus speak Common, Draconic, and Celestial.

COMBAT

Lammasus attack with spells or their razor-sharp claws. They almost always enter combat if they observe a good being that is threatened by evil.

Spells: A lammasu casts spells as a 7th-level cleric, choosing from any two of the following domains: Good, Healing, Knowledge, and Law. Save DC is 13 + spell level.

Magic Circle against Evil (Su): A lammasu has a continuous magic circle against evil that affects a 20-foot radius. The aura can be dispelled, but the lammasu can create it again as a free action on its next turn.

Spell-Like Abilities: 2/day—*improved invisibility;* 1/day—*dimension door.* These abilities are as the spells cast by a 7th-level sorcerer.

Pounce (Ex): If a lammasu leaps upon a foe during the first round of combat, it can make a full attack even if it has already taken a move action.

Rake (Ex): A lammasu that pounces on a creature can make two rake attacks (+12 melee) with its hind legs for 1d6+3 slashing damage each.

Skills: *Lammasus gain a +2 racial bonus to Spot checks during daylight hours.

Lamia illus. by B. Despain

LILLEND

Large Outsider (Chaotic, Good)
Hit Dice: 7d8+14 (45 hp)
Initiative: +3 (Dex)
Speed: 20 ft., fly 70 ft. (average)
AC: 17 (–1 size, +3 Dex, +5 natural)
Attacks: Sword +11/+6 melee, tail slap +6 melee
Damage: Sword 1d8+5, tail slap 2d6+2
Face/Reach: 5 ft. by 5 ft./10 ft.
Special Attacks: Improved grab, constrict 2d6+5, spells, spell-like abilities
Special Qualities: Poison immunity, fire resistance 20
Saves: Fort +7, Ref +8, Will +8
Abilities: Str 20, Dex 17, Con 15, Int 14, Wis 16, Cha 18
Skills: Appraise +12, Concentration +12, Knowledge (arcana) +12, Listen +13, Perform (any ten) +14, Spellcraft +12, Wilderness Lore +17
Feats: Combat Casting, Extend Spell

Climate/Terrain: Any land and underground
Organization: Solitary or covey (2–4)
Challenge Rating: 7
Treasure: Standard
Alignment: Always chaotic good
Advancement: 8–10 HD (Large); 11–21 HD (Huge)

Lillends are mysterious visitors from another plane. Many are skilled in one or more forms of artistic expression.

A lillend looks like a human or elf female (rarely a male) with the lower torso of a multicolored serpent and huge, strikingly patterned wings like a bird's. The typical lillend's coils are 20 feet long.

Lillends are lovers of music and art. Gold, even food, means little to them, while a song, story, or piece of artwork holds great value. The destruction of art and ill treatment of artists enrages them. Their grudges are infamous, and they are often encountered seeking violent retribution against enemies of their favorite arts.

Lillends also have a great love of unspoiled wilderness. The wilds remind them of the natural beauty of their home plane, and they occasionally visit and enjoy similar regions. A lillend is as protective of its chosen wilderness as it is of the arts. These beings sometimes form temporary alliances with rangers, druids, and bards to defend their favorite retreats against the encroachment of civilization. Sometimes a covey of lillends adopts a tract of wilderness, using any means necessary to drive off despoilers.

Lillends speak Celestial, Infernal, Abyssal, and Common.

COMBAT

Lillends are generally peaceful unless they intend vengeance against someone they believe guilty of harming, or even threatening, a favored art form, artwork, or artist. Then they become implacable foes. They use their spells and spell-like abilities to confuse and weaken opponents before entering combat. A covey of lillends usually discusses strategy before a battle.

Spells: A lillend casts arcane spells as a 6th-level bard. Save DC is 14 + spell level.

Spell-Like Abilities: 3/day—*darkness, hallucinatory terrain, knock,* and *light;* 1/day—*charm person, speak with animals,* and *speak with plants.* These abilities are as the spells cast by a 10th-level bard (save DC 14 + spell level).

A lillend also has the bardic music ability as a 6th-level bard.

Improved Grab (Ex): To use this ability, the lillend must hit an opponent of up to Medium-size with its tail slap attack. If it gets a hold, it can constrict.

Constrict (Ex): A lillend deals 2d6+5 points of damage with a successful grapple check against opponents of up to Medium-size. This uses the entire lower portion of its body, so it cannot take any move actions when constricting, though it can still attack with its sword.

Fire Resistance (Ex): A lillend is immune to nonmagical fire and has magic fire resistance 20.

Skills: Lillends receive a +4 racial bonus to Wilderness Lore checks.

LIZARDFOLK

Medium-Size Humanoid (Aquatic, Reptilian)
Hit Dice: 2d8+2 (11 hp)
Initiative: +0
Speed: 30 ft.
AC: 15 (+5 natural) or 17 (+5 natural, +2 large shield)
Attacks: 2 claws +2 melee (or greatclub +2 melee), bite +0 melee; or javelin +1 ranged
Damage: Claw 1d4+1, greatclub 1d10+1, bite 1d4, or javelin 1d6+1
Face/Reach: 5 ft. by 5 ft./5 ft.
Saves: Fort +1, Ref +3, Will +0
Abilities: Str 13, Dex 10, Con 13, Int 9, Wis 10, Cha 10
Skills: Balance +4, Jump +7, Swim +9
Feats: Multiattack

Climate/Terrain: Temperate and warm marsh
Organization: Gang (2–3), band (6–10 plus 50% noncombatants plus 1 leader of 3rd–6th level), or tribe (30–60 plus 2 lieutenants of 3rd–6th level and 1 leader of 4th–10th level)
Challenge Rating: 1
Treasure: 50% coins; 50% goods; 50% items
Alignment: Usually neutral
Advancement: By character class

Lizardfolk are primitive reptilian humanoids that can be very dangerous if provoked.

Lizardfolk are usually 6 to 7 feet tall with green, gray, or brown scales. Their tails are used for balance and are 3 to 4 feet long. They can hold their breath for twice as long as a human. Although they are omnivores, they prefer meat, particularly human flesh. Some more advanced tribes build huts and use weapons and shields; leaders of these tribes may even have equipment stolen or traded from other intelligent creatures.

Lizardfolk speak Draconic.

COMBAT

Lizardfolk fight as unorganized individuals. They prefer frontal assaults and massed rushes, sometimes trying to force foes into the water, where the lizardfolk have an advantage. If outnumbered or if their territory is being invaded, they set snares, plan ambushes, and make raids to hinder enemy supplies. Advanced tribes use more sophisticated tactics and have better traps and ambushes.

Skills: Thanks to their tails, lizardfolk receive a +4 racial bonus to Jump, Swim, and Balance checks (the numbers in the statistics block do not reflect check penalties for large shields).

LIZARDFOLK SOCIETY

Lizardfolk have a patriarchal society in which the most powerful member rules the others. Shamans offer advice but rarely become leaders themselves. Survival is the utmost concern of lizardfolk, and a threatened or starving tribe will go to incredible lengths (even committing deeds considered abominable by other humanoids) to ensure its continued existence.

Most tribes live in swamps, but about a third of the population lives in underwater air-filled caves. Local tribes often unite against a greater threat (including hostile lizardfolk tribes) and occasionally make alliances with locathahs or serve more powerful creatures such as nagas or dragons. In isolated areas they survive by fishing, gathering, and scavenging, while those that live near other humanoids make raids for food, supplies, and slaves. A lizardfolk lair has half as many noncombatant hatchlings as adults, and one egg per ten adults.

The patron deity of lizardfolk is Semuanya, whose chief concern is their survival and propagation.

LIZARDFOLK CHARACTERS

A lizardfolk's favored class is druid; most lizardfolk leaders are druids. Lizardfolk clerics (shamans) worship Semuanya and can choose any two of the following domains: Animal, Plant, and Water.

LOCATHAH

Medium-Size Humanoid (Aquatic)
Hit Dice: 2d8 (9 hp)
Initiative: +1 (Dex)
Speed: 10 ft., swim 60 ft.
AC: 14 (+1 Dex, +3 natural)
Attacks: Longspear +1 melee; or light crossbow +2 ranged
Damage: Longspear 1d8; or light crossbow 1d8
Face/Reach: 5 ft. by 5 ft./5 ft.
Saves: Fort +3, Ref +1, Will +1
Abilities: Str 10, Dex 12, Con 10, Int 13, Wis 13, Cha 11
Skills: Craft (any one) +3, Listen +4, Spot +4
Feats: Blind-Fight

Climate/Terrain: Warm aquatic
Organization: Company (2–4), patrol (11–20 plus 2 3rd-level sergeants and 1 leader of 3rd–6th level), or tribe (30–100 plus 100% noncombatants plus 1 3rd-level sergeant per 10 adults, 5 5th-level lieutenants, and 3 7th-level captains)
Challenge Rating: 1/2
Treasure: Standard
Alignment: Usually neutral
Advancement: By character class

The nomadic locathahs dwell in warm coastal waters, hunting fish and gathering crustaceans for food. Although humanoid, they are clearly more fish than human.

The average locathah stands 5 feet tall and weighs 175 pounds. Locathahs are slender, with fine, yellow-green scales that shimmer in the sunlight. Females and males look very much alike, although the former can be recognized by the two ochre stripes marking their egg sacs.

Locathahs are not particularly aggressive but do not trust surface dwellers—far too many of their kind have been swept up in fishing nets.

COMBAT

Any battle with locathahs usually begins with the creatures loosing a volley of bolts from their crossbows. If they have managed to set up an ambush or other trap, they continue to employ these weapons for as long as possible. Otherwise, they close to bring their long, tridentlike spears into play. Although primarily used for fishing, these spears make formidable weapons.

Locathahs lack teeth, claws, and other natural weapons, so they are not especially dangerous if unarmed. A weaponless locathah will generally turn and flee.

LOCATHAH SOCIETY

Locathah clans usually move with each change of season, going where they can find food. They make their encampments in caves, rocky areas, or seaweed beds—locales that afford some concealment and protection. Patrols are usually hunting parties after small game, but they also keep a lookout for enemies trespassing in clan hunting areas. Larger groups are generally found tracking big animals or engaged in similar activities. Entire tribes come together to trade or hold council.

Locathahs revere the deity Eadro, who created both them and the merfolk.

LOCATHAH CHARACTERS

A locathah's favored class is barbarian, and most locathah leaders are barbarians. Most locathah spellcasters are adepts (see page 37 in the DUNGEON MASTER'S Guide). Locathah clerics worship Eadro and can choose two of the following domains: Animal, Protection, and Water.

MAGMIN

Small Elemental (Fire)
Hit Dice: 2d8 (9 hp)
Initiative: +1 (Dex)
Speed: 30 ft.
AC: 14 (+1 size, +1 Dex, +2 natural)
Attacks: Burning touch +1 melee
Damage: Burning touch 1d8 fire and combustion
Face/Reach: 5 ft. by 5 ft./5 ft.
Special Attacks: Combustion, fiery aura
Special Qualities: Elemental, fire subtype, melt weapons, damage reduction 15/+1
Saves: Fort +0, Ref +4, Will +0
Abilities: Str 9, Dex 13, Con 11, Int 8, Wis 10, Cha 10
Skills: Climb +4, Escape Artist +5, Jump +4, Spot +4

Climate/Terrain: Any land and underground
Organization: Solitary , gang (2–4), or squad (6–10)
Challenge Rating: 3
Treasure: Standard coins; standard goods (nonflammables only); standard items (nonflammables only)
Alignment: Always chaotic neutral
Advancement: 3–4 HD (Small); 5–6 HD (Medium-size)

Magmins are small, human-shaped beings that appear to have been sculpted from molten rock and flowing lava. They radiate intense heat and are wreathed in an aura of searing flames.

Although not truly evil, these fiery creatures are extremely mischievous. They like to watch things burn, perhaps lacking the ability to understand that flames are painful or even deadly to other creatures.

A typical magmin is 4 feet tall and weighs 1 pound. Magmins speak Ignan.

COMBAT

Although small, magmins are dangerous opponents. Their touch is effective against those who lack protection or immunity from heat and flames, but if faced with opponents who are immune to fire, magmins are reduced to unarmed attacks. In any case, magmins are not valiant fighters. They usually flee if injured, although often only far enough to set up a fiery ambush for their enemies.

Combustion (Ex): Anyone a magmin touches must succeed at a Reflex save (DC 11) or take an additional 1d8 points of fire damage as clothes ignite or armor becomes searing hot. The damage continues for another 1d4+2 rounds after the magmin's last successful attack. Magmins can also ignite flammable materials with a touch.

Fiery Aura (Ex): Anyone within 30 feet of a magmin must succeed at a Fortitude save (DC 11) or suffer 1d6 points of heat damage from the intense heat. Treat this effect as an emanation (see Aiming a Spell, page 148 in the Player's Handbook).

Elemental: Immune to poison, sleep, paralysis, and stunning. Not subject to critical hits.

Fire Subtype (Ex): Fire immunity, double damage from cold except on a successful save.

Melt Weapons (Ex): Any metal weapon that strikes a magmin must succeed at a Fortitude save (DC 11) or melt away into slag.

MANTICORE

Huge Magical Beast
Hit Dice: 6d10+24 (57 hp)
Initiative: +2 (Dex)
Speed: 30 ft., fly 50 ft. (clumsy)
AC: 16 (–2 size, +2 Dex, +6 natural)
Attacks: 2 claws +9 melee, bite +7 melee; or 6 spikes +6 ranged
Damage: Claw 2d4+5, bite 1d8+2; or spike 1d8+2
Face/Reach: 10 ft. by 20 ft./10 ft.
Special Attacks: Spikes
Special Qualities: Scent
Saves: Fort +9, Ref +7, Will +3
Abilities: Str 20, Dex 15, Con 19, Int 7, Wis 12, Cha 9
Skills: Listen +9, Spot +9*
Feat: Multiattack

Climate/Terrain: Warm and temperate land and underground
Organization: Solitary, pair, or pride (3–6)
Challenge Rating: 5
Treasure: Standard
Alignment: Usually lawful evil
Advancement: 7–16 HD (Huge); 17–18 HD (Gargantuan)

Manticores are fierce monsters that hunt widely for living flesh. They are cunning and evil, with keen, logical minds. A manticore can be a deadly enemy or a powerful ally.

A manticore is a monster in every sense of the word. It has the head of a vaguely humanoid beast, the body of a lion, and the wings of a dragon. The creature's back is set with curved barbs, and its long tail ends in a cluster of deadly spikes.

COMBAT

A manticore begins most attacks with a volley of spikes, then closes. In the outdoors, it often uses its powerful wings to stay aloft during battle.

The medusa is a hateful, repulsive creature that petrifies living beings with its gaze. It prizes art objects, fine jewelry, and wealth. Its activities often revolve around obtaining these items.

A medusa is indistinguishable from a normal human at distances greater than 30 feet (or closer, if its face is concealed). Once the creature is clearly visible, its true nature becomes apparent. Its hideous face is crowned with a mass of writhing, hissing snakes instead of hair, and its eyes glow a deep, feral red. In contrast, its body is perfectly proportioned and exceptionally attractive, although scaly and earthen-colored. The creature often wears garments that enhance its body while hiding its face behind a hood or veil. A typical medusa is 5 to 6 feet tall.

Medusas are found in nearly every climate. Some dwell in large cities, becoming active in the criminal underworld to gain their desires. A few medusas have formed robbery rings or organized smuggling cabals.

Spikes (Ex): With a snap of its tail, a manticore can loose a volley of six spikes as a standard action. This attack has a range of 180 feet with no range increment. A spike threatens a critical hit on a natural attack roll of 19 or 20. The creature can launch only twenty-four spikes in any one day.

Skills: *Manticores receive a +4 racial bonus to Spot checks in daylight.

MEDUSA

Medium-Size Monstrous Humanoid
Hit Dice: 6d8 +6 (33 hp)
Initiative: +2 (Dex)
Speed: 30 ft.
AC: 15 (+2 Dex, +3 natural)
Attacks: Shortbow +8/+3 ranged; or dagger +6/+1 melee, snakes +3 melee
Damage: Shortbow 1d6; or dagger 1d4, snakes 1d4 and poison
Face/Reach: 5 ft. by 5 ft./5 ft.
Special Attacks: Petrifying gaze, poison
Saves: Fort +3, Ref +7, Will +6
Abilities: Str 10, Dex 15, Con 12, Int 12, Wis 13, Cha 15
Skills: Bluff +11, Disguise +11, Move Silently +9, Spot +10
Feats: Point Blank Shot, Precise Shot, Weapon Finesse (snakes)

Climate/Terrain: Any land and underground
Organization: Solitary or covey (2–4)
Challenge Rating: 7
Treasure: Double standard
Alignment: Usually lawful evil
Advancement: By character class

COMBAT

A medusa tries to disguise its true nature until the intended victim is within range of its petrifying gaze, using subterfuge and bluffing games to convince the target that there is no danger. It uses normal weapons to attack those who avert their eyes or survive its gaze, while its poisonous snakes strike at adjacent opponents.

Petrifying Gaze (Su): Turn to stone permanently, 30 feet, Fortitude save (DC 15).

Poison (Ex): Snakes, Fortitude save (DC 14); initial damage 1d6 temporary Strength, secondary damage 2d6 temporary Strength.

Illus. by C. Arellano

	Air Mephit **Small Outsider (Air)**	**Dust Mephit** **Small Outsider (Air)**	**Earth Mephit** **Small Outsider (Earth)**
Hit Dice:	3d8 (13 hp)	3d8 (13 hp)	3d8+3 (16 hp)
Initiative:	+7 (+3 Dex, +4 Improved Initiative)	+7 (+3 Dex, +4 Improved Initiative)	−1 (Dex)
Speed:	30 ft., fly 60 ft. (perfect)	30 ft., fly 50 ft. (perfect)	30 ft., fly 40 ft. (average)
AC:	17 (+1 size, +3 Dex, +3 natural)	17 (+1 size, +3 Dex, +3 natural)	16 (+1 size, −1 Dex, +6 natural)
Attacks:	2 claws +4 melee	2 claws +4 melee	2 claws +7 melee
Damage:	Claw 1d3	Claw 1d3	Claw 1d3+3
Face/Reach:	5 ft. by 5 ft./5 ft.	5 ft. by 5 ft./5 ft.	5 ft. by 5 ft./5 ft.
Special Attacks:	Breath weapon, spell-like abilities, summon mephit	Breath weapon, spell-like abilities, summon mephit	Breath weapon, spell-like abilities, summon mephit
Special Qualities:	Fast healing 2, damage reduction 5/+1	Fast healing 2, damage reduction 5/+1	Fast healing 2, damage reduction 10/+1
Saves:	Fort +3, Ref +6, Will +3	Fort +3, Ref +6, Will +3	Fort +4, Ref +2, Will +3
Abilities:	Str 10, Dex 17, Con 10, Int 12, Wis 11, Cha 15	Str 10, Dex 17, Con 10, Int 12, Wis 11, Cha 15	Str 17, Dex 8, Con 13, Int 12, Wis 11, Cha 15
Skills:	Bluff +6, Hide +12, Listen +6, Move Silently +9, Spot +6	Bluff +6, Hide +12, Listen +6, Move Silently +9, Spot +6	Bluff +5, Hide +9, Listen +6, Move Silently +5, Spot +6
Feats:	Improved Initiative	Improved Initiative	Power Attack

	Fire Mephit **Small Outsider (Fire)**	**Ice Mephit** **Small Outsider (Air, Cold)**	**Magma Mephit** **Small Outsider (Fire)**
Hit Dice:	3d8 (13 hp)	3d8 (13 hp)	3d8 (13 hp)
Initiative:	+5 (+1 Dex, +4 Improved Initiative)	+7 (+3 Dex, +4 Improved Initiative)	+5 (+1 Dex, +4 Improved Initiative)
Speed:	30 ft., fly 50 ft. (average)	30 ft., fly 50 ft. (perfect)	30 ft., fly 50 ft. (average)
AC:	16 (+1 size, +1 Dex, +4 natural)	18 (+1 size, +3 Dex, +4 natural)	16 (+1 size, +1 Dex, +4 natural)
Attacks:	2 claws +4 melee	2 claws +4 melee	2 claws +4 melee
Damage:	Claw 1d3 and 2 fire	Claw 1d3 and 2 cold	Claw 1d3 and 2 fire
Face/Reach:	5 ft. by 5 ft./5 ft.	5 ft. by 5 ft./5 ft.	5 ft. by 5 ft./5 ft.
Special Attacks:	Breath weapon, spell-like abilities, summon mephit	Breath weapon, spell-like abilities, summon mephit	Breath weapon, spell-like abilities, summon mephit
Special Qualities:	Fire subtype, fast healing 2, damage reduction 5/+1	Cold subtype, fast healing 2, damage reduction 5/+1	Fire subtype, fast healing 2, damage reduction 5/+1
Saves:	Fort +3, Ref +4, Will +3	Fort +3, Ref +6, Will +3	Fort +3, Ref +4, Will +3
Abilities:	Str 10, Dex 13, Con 10, Int 12, Wis 11, Cha 15	Str 10, Dex 17, Con 10, Int 12, Wis 11, Cha 15	Str 10, Dex 13, Con 10, Int 12, Wis 11, Cha 15
Skills:	Bluff +5, Hide +11, Listen +6, Move Silently +7, Spot +6	Bluff +6, Hide +12, Listen +6, Move Silently +9, Spot +6	Bluff +5, Hide +11, Listen +6, Move Silently +7, Spot +6
Feats:	Improved Initiative	Improved Initiative	Improved Initiative

	Ooze Mephit **Small Outsider (Water)**	**Salt Mephit** **Small Outsider (Earth)**	**Steam Mephit** **Small Outsider (Fire)**
Hit Dice:	3d8+3 (16 hp)	3d8+3 (16 hp)	3d8 (13 hp)
Initiative:	+0	−1 (Dex)	+5 (+1 Dex, +4 Improved Initiative)
Speed:	30 ft., fly 40 ft. (average)	30 ft., fly 40 ft. (average)	30 ft., fly 50 ft. (average)
AC:	16 (+1 size, +5 natural)	16 (+1 size, −1 Dex, +6 natural)	16 (+1 size, +1 Dex, +4 natural)
Attacks:	2 claws +6 melee	2 claws +7 melee	2 claws +4 melee
Damage:	Claw 1d3+2	Claw 1d3+3	Claw 1d3 and 2 fire
Face/Reach:	5 ft. by 5 ft./5 ft.	5 ft. by 5 ft./5 ft.	5 ft. by 5 ft./5 ft.
Special Attacks:	Breath weapon, spell-like abilities, summon mephit	Breath weapon, spell-like abilities, summon mephit	Breath weapon, spell-like abilities, summon mephit
Special Qualities:	Fast healing 2, damage reduction 5/+1	Fast healing 2, damage reduction 10/+1	Fire subtype, fast healing 2, damage reduction 5/+1
Saves:	Fort +4, Ref +3, Will +3	Fort +4, Ref +2, Will +3	Fort +3, Ref +4, Will +3
Abilities:	Str 14, Dex 10, Con 13, Int 12, Wis 11, Cha 15	Str 17, Dex 8, Con 13, Int 12, Wis 11, Cha 15	Str 10, Dex 13, Con 10, Int 12, Wis 11, Cha 15
Skills:	Bluff +6, Hide +9, Listen +6, Move Silently +6, Spot +6	Bluff +6, Hide +8, Listen +6, Move Silently +5, Spot +6	Bluff +6, Hide +11, Listen +6, Move Silently +6, Spot +6
Feats:	Power Attack	Power Attack	Improved Initiative

Mephits are minor elemental creatures drawn from the basic components of creation. They are more curious than evil, although their natures vary with the essence of what birthed them.

All mephits appear as small, winged creatures with more or less humanoid features. While they are often described as impish, their elemental nature is apparent at first glance.

	Water Mephit
	Small Outsider (Water)
Hit Dice:	3d8+3 (16 hp)
Initiative:	+0
Speed:	30 ft., fly 40 ft. (average)
AC:	16 (+1 size, +5 natural)
Attacks:	2 claws +6 melee
Damage:	Claw 1d3+2
Face/Reach:	5 ft. by 5 ft./5 ft.
Special Attacks:	Breath weapon, spell-like abilities, summon mephit
Special Qualities:	Fast healing 2, damage reduction 5/+1
Saves:	Fort +4, Ref +3, Will +3
Abilities:	Str 14, Dex 10, Con 13, Int 12, Wis 11, Cha 15
Skills:	Bluff +6, Hide +9, Listen +6, Move Silently +6, Spot +6
Feats:	Power Attack
Climate/Terrain:	Any land and underground
Organization:	Solitary (1), gang (2–4 mephits of mixed types), or swarm (5–12 mephits of mixed types)
Challenge Rating:	3
Treasure:	Standard
Alignment:	Usually neutral
Advancement:	4–6 HD (Small); 7–9 HD (Medium-size)

COMBAT

All mephits fight by biting and clawing or by using a dangerous breath weapon, the nature and effects of which vary from creature to creature.

Breath Weapon: A mephit can use its breath weapon once every 1d4 rounds as a standard action. See the individual descriptions for details.

Spell-Like Abilities: All mephits have one or more spell-like abilities (save DC 12 + spell level). See the individual descriptions for details.

Summon Mephit (Sp): Once per day, all mephits can summon other mephits much as though casting a *summon monster* spell, but they have only a 25% chance of success to summon one mephit of the same type. Roll d%: On a failure, no creature answers the summons. A mephit that has just been summoned cannot use its own summon ability for 1 hour.

Fast Healing (Ex): Mephits heal 2 points of damage each round, provided they are still alive and certain other conditions are met. See the individual descriptions for details.

MEPHIT GANGS AND SWARMS

Groups of similar mephits (for example, water, ooze, and ice) sometimes congregate in any locale they all find comfortable.

AIR MEPHIT

Air mephits look like cloud-white humans with whirlwinds instead of legs. They are about 4 feet tall and weigh about 1 pound.

Combat

Breath Weapon (Su): Cone of dust and grit, 15 feet; damage 1d8, Reflex half DC 12.

Spell-Like Abilities: Once per hour an air mephit can surround itself with vapor, duplicating the effects of a *blur* spell as cast by a 3rd-level sorcerer. Once per day it can use *gust of wind* as the spell cast by a 6th-level sorcerer.

Fast Healing (Ex): An air mephit heals only if exposed to moving air, be it a breeze, a draft, a spell effect, or even the mephit fanning itself.

DUST MEPHIT

Dust mephits are gaunt, tragic-looking figures who dress only in black and have a morbid fascination with death and suffering. They are about 4 feet tall and weigh about 2 pounds.

Combat

Breath Weapon (Su): Cone of irritating particles, 10 feet; damage 1d4, Reflex half DC 12. Living creatures that fail their saves are tormented by itching skin and burning eyes. This imposes a –4 morale penalty to AC and a –2 morale penalty to attack rolls for 3 rounds.

Spell-Like Abilities: Once per hour a dust mephit can surround itself with a plume of dust, duplicating the effects of a *blur* spell cast by a 3rd-level sorcerer. Once per day it can create a mass of roiling dust that duplicates the effect of *wind wall* as cast by a 6th-level sorcerer.

Fast Healing (Ex): A dust mephit heals only if in an arid, dusty environment.

EARTH MEPHIT

These creatures are heavy, stocky things as stubborn as they are rugged. They are about 4 feet tall and weigh about 80 pounds.

Combat

Breath Weapon (Su): Cone of rock shards and pebbles, 15 feet; damage 1d8, Reflex half DC 12.

Spell-Like Abilities: 1/hour—*enlarge*; 1/day—*soften earth and stone*. These abilities are as the spells cast by a 6th-level sorcerer.

Fast Healing (Ex): An earth mephit heals only if it is underground or buried up to its waist in earth.

FIRE MEPHIT

These creatures look for all the world like miniature devils, wreathed in flame and cackling with mischief. They are about 4 feet tall and weigh about 1 pound.

Combat

Breath Weapon (Su): Cone of fire, 15 feet; damage 1d8, Reflex half DC 12.

Spell-Like Abilities: 1/hour—*magic missile* as the spell cast by a 3rd-level sorcerer; 1/day—*heat metal* as the spell cast by a 6th-level sorcerer.

Illus. by M. Mitchell

Fire Subtype (Ex): Fire immunity, double damage from cold except on a successful save.

Fast Healing (Ex): A fire mephit heals only if it is touching a flame at least as large as a torch.

ICE MEPHIT

Ice mephits are creatures of snow and ice with translucent skin and cold, aloof manners. They are about 4 feet tall and weigh about 30 pounds.

Combat

Breath Weapon (Su): Cone of ice shards, 10 feet; damage 1d4, Reflex half DC 12. Living creatures that fail their saves are tormented by frostbitten skin and frozen eyes unless they are immune to or protected from cold. This imposes a –4 morale penalty to AC and a –2 morale penalty to attack rolls for 3 rounds.

Spell-Like Abilities: 1/hour—*magic missile* as the spell cast by a 3rd-level sorcerer; 1/day—*chill metal* as the spell cast by a 6th-level sorcerer.

Cold Subtype (Ex): Cold immunity; double damage from fire except on a successful save.

Fast Healing (Ex): An ice mephit heals only if it is touching a piece of ice of at least Tiny size or if the ambient temperature is freezing or below.

MAGMA MEPHIT

Composed of molten stone and glowing lava, these creatures are slow-witted and brutish. They are about 4 feet tall and weigh about 60 pounds.

Combat

Breath Weapon (Su): Cone of magma, 10 feet; damage 1d4, Reflex half DC 12. Living creatures that fail their saves are tormented by burned skin and seared eyes unless they are immune to or protected from fire. This imposes a –4 morale penalty to AC and a –2 morale penalty to attack rolls for 3 rounds.

Spell-Like Abilities: Once per hour, a magma mephit can *shapechange* into a pool of lava 3 feet in diameter and 6 inches deep. The mephit's damage reduction improves to 20/+1. The mephit can't attack while in lava form but can use other spell-like abilities. It can move at a speed of 10 feet, but it can't "run." In this form the mephit can pass through small holes or narrow openings, even mere cracks. The pool's touch ignites flammable materials such as paper, straw, or dry wood.

Once per day a magma mephit can use *pyrotechnics* as the spell cast by a 6th-level sorcerer. It can use itself as the fire source without harm.

Fire Subtype (Ex): Fire immunity, double damage from cold except on a successful save.

Fast Healing (Ex): A magma mephit heals only if it is touching magma, lava, or a flame at least as large as a torch.

OOZE MEPHIT

These loathsome creatures are composed of muck and filth. Ooze mephits are green things of dribbling slime that give off a terribly offensive odor and seem constantly on the verge of liquefaction. They are about 4 feet tall and weigh about 30 pounds.

Combat

Breath Weapon (Su): Cone of caustic liquid, 10 feet; damage 1d4, Reflex half DC 12. Living creatures that fail their saves are tormented by itching skin and burning eyes. This imposes a –4 morale penalty to AC and a –2 morale penalty to attack rolls for 3 rounds.

Spell-Like Abilities: Once per hour an ooze mephit can hurl an acidic blob that functions like *Melf's acid arrow* cast by a 3rd-level sorcerer. Once per day it can create a mass of smelly fog that duplicates the effect of *stinking cloud* as cast by a 6th-level sorcerer.

Fast Healing (Ex): An ooze mephit heals only if in a wet or muddy environment.

SALT MEPHIT

Salt mephits are pale humanoids with bleary red eyes and crystalline flesh. They are sarcastic creatures who loathe water and moisture of any kind. Salt mephits are about 4 feet tall and weigh about 80 pounds.

Combat

Breath Weapon (Su): Cone of salt crystals, 10 feet; damage 1d4, Reflex half DC 12. Living creatures that fail their saves are tormented by itching skin and burning eyes. This imposes a –4 morale penalty to AC and a –2 morale penalty to attack rolls for 3 rounds.

Spell-Like Abilities: Once per hour a salt mephit can use *glitterdust* as the spell cast by a 3rd-level sorcerer. Once per day it can draw the moisture from an area in a 20-foot radius centered on itself. Living creatures within range take 2d8 points of damage (Fortitude half DC 15). This is especially devastating to aquatic creatures and plants, which receive a –2 racial penalty to their saving throws.

Fast Healing (Ex): A salt mephit heals only if in an arid environment.

STEAM MEPHIT

Steam mephits are bossy creatures who consider themselves the lords of all their kind. These hot-tempered creatures release a plume of steam when they breathe and trail scalding water when they walk. They are about 4 feet tall and weigh about 2 pounds.

Combat

Unlike the others, steam mephits rush into combat eagerly, driven by an oversized ego.

Breath Weapon (Su): Cone of steam, 10 feet; damage 1d4, Reflex half DC 12. Living creatures that fail their saves are tormented by burned skin and seared eyes unless they are immune to or protected from fire. This imposes a –4 morale penalty to AC and a –2 morale penalty to attack rolls for 3 rounds.

Spell-Like Abilities: Once per hour a steam mephit can surround itself with a plume of vapor, duplicating the effects of a *blur* spell cast by a 3rd-level sorcerer. Once per day it can create a rainstorm of boiling water that affects an area 20 feet square. Living creatures caught in the storm take 2d6 points of damage (Reflex half DC 15).

Fire Subtype (Ex): Fire immunity, double damage from cold except on a successful save.

Fast Healing (Ex): A steam mephit heals only if it is touching boiling water or is in a hot, humid area.

WATER MEPHIT

Water mephits are jaunty creatures with an unflagging sense of humor who quickly get on the nerves of everyone around them. They resemble miniature fish-people, covered with scales and viewing the world through black, bulbous eyes. They are about 4 feet tall and weigh about 30 pounds.

Combat

Breath Weapon (Su): Cone of caustic liquid, 15 feet; damage 1d8, Reflex half DC 12.

Spell-Like Abilities: Once per hour a water mephit can hurl an acidic blob that functions like *Melf's acid arrow* cast by a 3rd-level sorcerer. Once per day it can create a mass of smelly fog that duplicates the effect of *stinking cloud* as cast by a 6th-level sorcerer.

Fast Healing (Ex): A water mephit heals only if it is exposed to rain or submerged up to its waist in water.

MERFOLK

Medium-Size Humanoid (Aquatic)
Hit Dice: 1d8+1 (5 hp)
Initiative: +1 (Dex)
Speed: 5 ft., swim 50 ft.
AC: 13 (+1 Dex, +2 leather)
Attacks: Trident +1 melee; or heavy crossbow +2 ranged
Damage: Trident 1d8; or heavy crossbow 1d10
Face/Reach: 5 ft. by 5 ft./5 ft.
Special Qualities: Low-light vision
Saves: Fort +3, Ref +1, Will +0
Abilities: Str 10, Dex 12, Con 12, Int 11, Wis 11, Cha 13
Skills: Listen +4, Spot +4
Feats: Alertness

Climate/Terrain: Temperate aquatic
Organization: Company (2–4), patrol (11–20 plus 2 3rd-level lieutenants and 1 leader of 3rd–6th level), or band (30–60 plus 1 3rd-level sergeant per 20 adults, 5 5th-level lieutenants, 3 7th-level captains, and 10 porpoises)
Challenge Rating: 1/2
Treasure: Standard
Alignment: Usually neutral
Advancement: By character class

The merfolk are playful, marine-dwelling people. Although wary of surface dwellers, they are not usually hostile: They prefer sunning themselves on rocks to engaging in warfare.

Merfolk have the upper bodies, arms, and heads of fair-featured humans. Instead of legs, however, they have the scaled tails of great fish. Both males and females decorate themselves with shells, coral, and other underwater adornments.

Adventurers who encounter merfolk are often the victims of pranks and mischief. The sport of merfolk can be cruel, although they are not actually evil. Should surface dwellers do them harm, however, these creatures can be formidable enemies.

Merfolk speak Common and Aquan.

Most merfolk encountered outside their home are warriors; the information in the statistics block is for one of 1st level (see page 39 in the DUNGEON MASTER's *Guide* for more about the warrior class).

COMBAT

Merfolk favor heavy crossbows of shell and coral that fire bolts fashioned from blowfish spines, with an underwater range of 30 yards. Merfolk often barrage their enemies before closing, when they resort to tridents.

MERFOLK SOCIETY

Merfolk live in semipermanent communities located near choice fishing and hunting areas. They often keep company with porpoises. Surface dwellers who come face to face with merfolk commonly encounter a scouting or hunting party.

The merfolk revere the deity Eadro, who created both them and the locathahs.

MERFOLK CHARACTERS

A merfolk's favored class is bard; most merfolk leaders are bards. Merfolk spellcasters who are not bards are generally adepts (see page 37 in the DUNGEON MASTER's *Guide*). Merfolk clerics worship Eadro and can choose two of the following domains: Animal, Protection, and Water.

MIMIC

Large Aberration
Hit Dice: 7d8+21 (52 hp)
Initiative: +1 (Dex)
Speed: 10 ft.
AC: 13 (–1 size, +1 Dex, +3 natural)
Attacks: Slam +8 melee
Damage: Slam 1d8+6
Face/Reach: 5 ft. by 5 ft./10 ft.
Special Attacks: Adhesive
Special Qualities: Mimic shape, acid immunity
Saves: Fort +5, Ref +3, Will +6
Abilities: Str 19, Dex 12, Con 17, Int 10, Wis 13, Cha 10
Skills: Climb +9, Disguise +12, Listen +11, Spot +6
Feats: Skill Focus (Disguise)

Climate/Terrain: Any land and underground
Organization: Solitary
Challenge Rating: 4
Treasure: 1/10th coins; 50% goods; 50% items
Alignment: Usually neutral
Advancement: 8–10 HD (Large); 11–21 HD (Huge)

Mimics are strange and deadly creatures that can change their pigmentation and shape. They use this ability to lure hapless victims close enough to slay.

It is said that mimics are not natural creatures but were created long ago by a now-forgotten wizard. Ever since, these terrible things have served to guard treasures. Mimics speak Common.

COMBAT

A mimic often surprises the unsuspecting adventurer, lashing out with a heavy pseudopod. Mimics are smart enough to avoid fights to the death by extorting treasure or food from a party.

Adhesive (Ex): A mimic exudes a thick slime that acts as a powerful adhesive, holding fast any creatures or items touching it. An adhesive-covered mimic automatically grapples any creature it hits with its slam attack. Opponents so grappled cannot get free while the mimic is alive without removing the adhesive first. A mimic makes one automatic slam attack each round against any creature stuck to it.

Illus. by R. Guay

135

A weapon that strikes an adhesive-coated mimic is also stuck fast unless the wielder succeeds at a Reflex save (DC 16). A successful Strength check (DC 16) is needed to pry it off.

Strong alcohol dissolves the adhesive. A pint of wine or a similar liquid weakens it, but the mimic still has a +4 bonus to grapple checks. A mimic can dissolve its adhesive at will, and the substance breaks down 5 rounds after the creature dies.

Mimic Shape (Ex): A mimic can assume the general shape of any object that fills roughly 150 cubic feet (5 feet by 5 feet by 6 feet), such as a massive chest, a stout bed, or a wide door frame. The creature cannot substantially alter its size, though. A mimic's body is hard and has a rough texture, no matter what appearance it might present. Anyone who examines the mimic can detect the ruse with a successful Spot check opposed by the mimic's Disguise check. Of course, by this time it is generally far too late.

Illus. by T. Lockwood

MIND FLAYER

Medium-Size Aberration
Hit Dice: 8d8+8 (44 hp)
Initiative: +6 (+2 Dex, +4 Improved Initiative)
Speed: 30 ft.
AC: 15 (+2 Dex, +3 natural)
Attacks: 4 tentacles +8 melee
Damage: Tentacle 1d4+1
Face/Reach: 5 ft. by 5 ft./5 ft.
Special Attacks: Mind blast, psionics, improved grab, extract
Special Qualities: SR 25, telepathy
Saves: Fort +3, Ref +4, Will +9
Abilities: Str 12, Dex 14, Con 12, Int 19, Wis 17, Cha 17
Skills: Bluff +8, Concentration +12, Hide +8, Intimidate +10, Knowledge (any two) +9, Listen +10, Move Silently +7, Spot +10
Feats: Alertness, Combat Casting, Dodge, Improved Initiative, Weapon Finesse (tentacle)

Climate/Terrain: Any underground
Organization: Solitary, pair, inquisition (3–5), or cult (3–5 plus 6–10 grimlocks)
Challenge Rating: 8
Treasure: Double standard
Alignment: Usually lawful evil
Advancement: By character class

Mind flayers (also called illithids) are so insidious, diabolical, and powerful that all denizens of the dark fear them. They bend others to their will and shatter enemies' minds.

A mind flayer is a strange creature, standing some 6 feet tall, that is humanoid only in the most general terms. Its flesh is rubbery and mauve, glistening with chill slime. The creature's head looks rather like a four-tentacled octopus, made all the more horrible by a pair of bloated, white eyes. Its mouth, a revolting thing like a lamprey's maw, constantly drips an oily slime when it is not siphoning out the brains of living prey.

In addition to being highly intelligent, wholly evil, and terribly sadistic, mind flayers are utterly self-serving. If an encounter turns against the creature, it flees at once, caring nothing for the fate of its companions or servitors.

Mind flayers speak Undercommon but prefer to communicate telepathically.

COMBAT

Mind flayers like to fight from a distance, using their psionic abilities, particularly their *mind blast*. If pressed into melee combat, a mind flayer lashes its enemies with the tentacles ringing its mouth.

Mind Blast (Sp): This attack is a cone 60 feet long. Anyone caught in this cone must succeed at a Will save (DC 17) or be stunned for 3d4 rounds. Mind flayers often hunt using this power and then drag off one or two of their stunned victims to feed upon.

Psionics (Sp): At will—*astral projection, charm monster, detect thoughts, levitate, plane shift,* and *suggestion.* These abilities are as the spells cast by an 8th-level sorcerer (save DC 13 + spell level).

Improved Grab (Ex): To use this ability, the mind flayer must hit a Small to Large creature with its tentacle attack. If it gets a hold, it attaches the tentacle to the opponent's head. A mind flayer can grab a Huge or larger creature, but only if it can somehow reach the foe's head.

After a successful grab, the mind flayer can try to attach its remaining tentacles with a single grapple check. The opponent can escape with a single successful grapple check or Escape Artist check, but the mind flayer gets a +2 circumstance bonus for every tentacle that was attached at the beginning of the opponent's turn.

Extract (Ex): A mind flayer that begins its turn with all four tentacles attached and successfully maintains its hold automatically extracts the opponent's brain, instantly killing that creature.

Telepathy (Su): Mind flayers can communicate telepathically with any creature within 100 feet that has a language.

MIND FLAYER SOCIETY

Mind flayers congregate in underground cities of two hundred to two thousand inhabitants, plus at least two slaves apiece. Slaves obey their masters without question. The center of a community is its elder-brain, a pool of briny fluid that contains the brains of the city's dead mind flayers.

Although they constantly vie for power, mind flayers are quite willing to work together. A small group of these creatures, known as an inquisition, often forms to root out some dark and terrible secret. In many ways, a mind flayer inquisition is not unlike a party of adventurers, with each member contributing its own skills and knowledge to the group.

When a task is too great for an inquisition to handle, mind flayers generally form a cult. A pair of illithids commands the group, each struggling for supremacy. Exactly why no individual assumes leadership of a cult is unknown.

MINOTAUR

Large Monstrous Humanoid
Hit Dice: 6d8+12 (39 hp)
Initiative: +0
Speed: 30 ft.
AC: 14 (−1 size, +5 natural)
Attacks: Huge greataxe +9/+4 melee, gore +4 melee
Damage: Huge greataxe 2d8+4, gore 1d8+2
Face/Reach: 5 ft. by 5 ft./10 ft.
Special Attacks: Charge 4d6+6
Special Qualities: Scent, natural cunning
Saves: Fort +6, Ref +5, Will +5
Abilities: Str 19, Dex 10, Con 15, Int 7, Wis 10, Cha 8
Skills: Intimidate +5, Jump +8, Listen +8, Search +6, Spot +8
Feats: Great Fortitude, Power Attack

Climate/Terrain: Any underground
Organization: Solitary or gang (2–4)
Challenge Rating: 4
Treasure: Standard
Alignment: Usually chaotic evil
Advancement: By character class

Minotaurs are strong, fiercely territorial creatures often found in vast underground labyrinths.

A minotaur's natural cunning and feral instincts enable it to find its way easily through even the most confusing tunnel complexes—an ability it puts to great use in hunting, tormenting, and ultimately destroying intruders.

A minotaur looks very much like a powerfully muscled human with the head of a bull, standing well over 7 feet tall and covered in shaggy fur. The dark eyes of these beasts gleam with savage fury.

Minotaurs speak Giant.

COMBAT

Minotaurs prefer melee combat, where their great strength serves them well.

Charge (Ex): A minotaur typically begins a battle by charging at an opponent, lowering its head to bring its mighty horns into play. In addition to the normal benefits and hazards of a charge, this allows the beast to make a single gore attack that deals 4d6+6 points of damage.

Natural Cunning (Ex): Although minotaurs are not especially intelligent, they possess innate cunning and logical ability. This makes them immune to *maze* spells, prevents them from ever becoming lost, and enables them to track enemies. Further, they are never caught flat-footed.

Skills: Minotaurs receive a +4 racial bonus to Search, Spot, and Listen checks.

MOHRG

Medium-Size Undead
Hit Dice: 14d12 (91 hp)
Initiative: +5 (+1 Dex, +4 Improved Initiative)
Speed: 30 ft.
AC: 15 (+1 Dex, +4 natural)
Attacks: 2 slams +12 melee, tongue touch +7 melee
Damage: Slam 1d6+5, tongue paralysis
Face/Reach: 5 ft. by 5 ft./5 ft.
Special Attacks: Improved grab, paralyzing touch, create spawn
Special Qualities: Undead
Saves: Fort +4, Ref +5, Will +9
Abilities: Str 21, Dex 13, Con —, Int 11, Wis 10, Cha 10
Skills: Climb +11, Hide +15, Listen +12, Move Silently +15, Spot +12, Swim +10
Feats: Alertness, Dodge, Improved Initiative, Mobility

Climate/Terrain: Any land and underground
Organization: Solitary, gang (2–4), or mob (2–4 plus 5–10 zombies)
Challenge Rating: 8
Treasure: None
Alignment: Always chaotic evil
Advancement: 15–21 HD (Medium-size); 22–28 HD (Large)

Mohrgs are the animated corpses of mass murderers or similar villains who die without atoning for their crimes. Tortured by all-consuming hatred of living things, they long to live again.

A mohrg looks like a gaunt, nearly skeletal corpse and is easily mistaken for a zombie or ghoul. The creature's tongue is its most noteworthy feature—long, cartilaginous, and clawed.

COMBAT

Like zombies, mohrgs attack by slamming enemies with their powerful fists. They often catch opponents flat-footed, for they move much faster than zombies.

Improved Grab (Ex): To use this ability, the mohrg must hit with its slam attack.

Paralyzing Touch (Su): A mohrg lashes out with its tongue in combat. An opponent the tongue touches must succeed at a Fortitude save (DC 17) or become paralyzed for 1d4 minutes.

Create Spawn (Su): Creatures killed by a mohrg rise after 1d4 days as zombies under the mohrg's control. They do not possess any of the abilities they had in life.

MUMMY

Medium-Size Undead
Hit Dice: 6d12+3 (42 hp)
Initiative: −1 (Dex)
Speed: 20 ft.
AC: 17 (−1 Dex, +8 natural)
Attacks: Slam +6 melee
Damage: Slam 1d6+4 and mummy rot
Face/Reach: 5 ft. by 5 ft./5 ft.
Special Attacks: Despair, mummy rot
Special Qualities: Undead, resistant to blows, damage reduction 5/+1, fire vulnerability
Saves: Fort +2, Ref +1, Will +7
Abilities: Str 17, Dex 8, Con —, Int 6, Wis 14, Cha 15
Skills: Hide +8, Listen +9 Move Silently +8, Spot +9
Feats: Alertness, Toughness

Climate/Terrain: Any desert and underground
Organization: Solitary, wardens (2–4), or guardians (6–10)
Challenge Rating: 3
Treasure: Standard
Alignment: Always lawful evil
Advancement: 7–12 HD (Medium-size); 13–18 HD (Large)

Mummies are preserved corpses animated through the auspices of dark desert gods best forgotten. They usually inhabit great tombs or temple complexes, maintaining a timeless vigil and destroying would-be graverobbers.

Physically, mummies are withered and desiccated, with features hidden beneath centuries-old funereal wrappings. They move with a slow, shambling gait and groan with the weight of the ages. These horrid creatures are often marked with symbols of the dire gods they serve. While other undead often stink of carrion, the herbs and powders used to create a mummy give off a sharp, pungent odor like that of a spice cabinet.

Mummies attack intruders without pause or mercy. They never attempt to communicate with their enemies and never retreat. An encounter with a mummy can end only with the utter destruction of one side or the other.

COMBAT

In melee combat, a mummy delivers a powerful blow. Even if it had no other abilities, its great strength and grim determination would make it a formidable opponent.

Despair (Su): At the mere sight of a mummy, the viewer must succeed at a Will save (DC 15) or be paralyzed with fear for 1d4 rounds. Whether or not the save is successful, that creature cannot be affected again by that mummy's despair ability for one day.

Mummy Rot (Su): Supernatural disease—slam, Fortitude save (DC 20), incubation period 1 day; damage 1d6 temporary Constitution. Unlike normal diseases, mummy rot continues until the victim reaches Constitution 0 (and dies) or receives a *remove disease* spell or similar magic (see Disease, page 74 in the Dungeon Master's Guide).

An afflicted creature that dies shrivels away into sand and dust that blow away into nothing at the first wind unless both a *remove disease* and *raise dead* are cast on the remains within 6 rounds.

Undead: Immune to mind-influencing effects, poison, sleep, paralysis, stunning, and disease. Not subject to critical hits, subdual damage, ability damage, energy drain, or death from massive damage.

Resistant to Blows (Ex): Physical attacks deal only half damage to mummies. Apply this effect before damage reduction.

Fire Vulnerability (Ex): A mummy takes double damage from fire attacks unless a save is allowed for half damage. A successful save halves the damage and a failure doubles it.

NAGA

	Water Naga	Spirit Naga	Dark Naga
	Large Aberration (Aquatic)	Large Aberration	Large Aberration
Hit Dice:	7d8+28 (59 hp)	9d8+36 (76 hp)	9d8+18 (58 hp)
Initiative:	+1 (Dex)	+1 (Dex)	+2 (Dex)
Speed:	30 ft., swim 50 ft.	40 ft.	40 ft.
AC:	15 (−1 size, +1 Dex, +5 natural)	16 (−1 size, +1 Dex, +6 natural)	14 (−1 size, +2 Dex, +3 natural)
Attacks:	Bite +7 melee	Bite +9 melee	Sting +7 melee, bite +2 melee
Damage:	Bite 2d6+4 and poison	Bite 2d6+6 and poison	Sting 2d4+2 and poison, bite 1d4+1
Face/Reach:	5 ft. by 5 ft. (coiled)/10 ft.	5 ft. by 5 ft. (coiled)/10 ft.	5 ft. by 5 ft. (coiled)/10 ft.
Special Attacks:	Poison, spells	Poison, charming gaze, spells	Poison, detect thoughts, spells
Special Qualities:	—	—	Poison immunity, guarded thoughts, charm resistance
Saves:	Fort +6, Ref +5, Will +8	Fort +7, Ref +6, Will +9	Fort +5, Ref +7, Will +8
Abilities:	Str 16, Dex 13, Con 18, Int 10, Wis 17, Cha 15	Str 18, Dex 13, Con 18, Int 12, Wis 17, Cha 17	Str 14, Dex 15, Con 14, Int 16, Wis 15, Cha 17
Skills:	Concentration +12, Listen +10, Spellcraft +8, Spot +10	Concentration +13, Listen +15, Spellcraft +10, Spot +15	Bluff +9, Concentration +13, Listen +11, Sense Motive +8, Spellcraft +12, Spot +11
Feats:	Lightning Reflexes	Alertness, Lightning Reflexes	Alertness, Combat Casting, Dodge, Lightning Reflexes

Climate/Terrain:	Temperate and warm aquatic and underground	Temperate and warm land and underground	Temperate and warm land and underground
Organization:	Solitary or nest (2–4)	Solitary or nest (2–4)	Solitary or nest (2–4)
Challenge Rating:	7	9	8
Treasure:	Standard	Standard	Standard
Alignment:	Usually neutral	Usually chaotic evil	Usually lawful evil
Advancement:	8–10 HD (Large); 11–21 HD (Huge)	10–13 HD (Large); 14–27 HD (Huge)	10–13 HD (Large); 14–27 HD (Huge)

	Guardian Naga Large Aberration
Hit Dice:	11d8+44 (93 hp)
Initiative:	+2 (Dex)
Speed:	40 ft.
AC:	18 (–1 size, +2 Dex, +7 natural)
Attacks:	Bite +12 melee
Damage:	Bite 2d6+7 and poison
Face/Reach:	5 ft. by 5 ft. (coiled)/10 ft.
Special Attacks:	Poison, spit, spells
Saves:	Fort +7, Ref +7, Will +11
Abilities:	Str 21, Dex 14, Con 19, Int 16, Wis 19, Cha 18
Skills:	Bluff +12, Concentration +15, Listen +13, Sense Motive +13, Spellcraft +11, Spot +13
Feats:	Alertness, Combat Casting, Dodge, Lightning Reflexes, Spell Focus (any one school)

Climate/Terrain:	Temperate and warm land and underground
Organization:	Solitary or nest (2–4)
Challenge Rating:	10
Treasure:	Standard
Alignment:	Usually lawful good
Advancement:	12–16 HD (Large); 17–33 HD (Huge)

Nagas are highly intelligent creatures with a variety of magical powers. They are natural masters of those around them, using subtle wards and clever traps to keep intruders from disturbing their peace.

All nagas have long, snakelike bodies covered with glistening scales and more or less human faces. They range in length from 10 to 20 feet. The eyes of a naga are bright and intelligent, burning with an almost hypnotic inner light.

COMBAT

Nagas favor spells over other forms of combat. Because they are almost always found in the lairs they guard and know well, they can arrange most encounters to suit their wishes.

WATER NAGA

A water naga is a beautiful creature with reticulated emerald-green patterns running the length of its body. Fiery red and orange spines jut from its backbone, rising like hackles when the naga becomes angry.

Combat

Water nagas prefer to stay mostly concealed in a body of water while they launch a spell attack.

Poison (Ex): Bite, Fortitude save (DC 17); initial and secondary damage 1d8 temporary Constitution.

Spells: Water nagas cast spells as 7th-level sorcerers but never use fire spells.

SPIRIT NAGA

A spirit naga has a black body banded by swaths of bright crimson. The odor of the carrion it savors hangs heavy in the air about it.

Combat

Spirit nagas meet foes boldly so as to use their gaze attacks to best effect. They quickly slither forward to bite foes that avert their eyes.

Poison (Ex): Bite, Fortitude save (DC 18); initial and secondary damage 1d8 temporary Constitution.

Charming Gaze (Su): As charm person, 30 feet, Will save (DC 17).

Spells: Spirit nagas cast spells as 7th-level sorcerers, and can also cast cleric spells and spells from the domains of Chaos and Evil as arcane spells.

DARK NAGA

Dark nagas are a deep purple in color and have fine scales on a rubbery leather hide. They look more like giant eels than snakes.

A dark naga's tail ends in a barbed stinger that injects a narcotic venom.

Combat

Dark nagas prefer to fight from an elevated position where they get a good view of the battlefield while also staying out of reach.

Detect Thoughts (Su): A dark naga can continuously detect thoughts as the spell cast by a 9th-level sorcerer (DC 15). This ability is always active.

Poison (Ex): Sting, Fortitude save (DC 16) or lapse into a nightmare-haunted sleep for 2d4 minutes.

Guarded Thoughts (Ex): Dark nagas are immune to any form of mind reading.

Charm Resistance: Dark nagas receive a +2 racial bonus to saving throws against all charm effects (not included in the statistics block).

Spells: Dark nagas cast spells as 7th-level sorcerers.

GUARDIAN NAGA

A guardian naga is green-gold in color and gives off the sweet scent of flowers.

Combat

Guardian nagas usually warn off intruders before attacking. If the warning is ignored, they may begin a spell assault or spit poison.

Poison (Ex): Bite, Fortitude save (DC 19); initial and secondary damage 2d8 temporary Constitution.

Spit (Ex): A guardian naga can spit its venom up to 30 feet as a standard action. The attack ignores armor and has no range increment. Opponents hit by this attack must attempt saves against the naga's poison, as above.

Spells: Guardian nagas cast spells as 9th-level sorcerers, and can also cast cleric spells and spells from the Good and Law domains as arcane spells.

NIGHT HAG

Medium-Size Outsider (Evil)
Hit Dice: 8d8+8 (44 hp)
Initiative: +1 (Dex)
Speed: 20 ft.
AC: 20 (+1 Dex, +9 natural)
Attacks: Bite +12 melee
Damage: Bite 2d6+6 and disease
Face/Reach: 5 ft. by 5 ft./5 ft.
Special Attacks: Spell-like abilities, dream haunting
Special Qualities: Immunities, SR 25, damage reduction 20/+3
Saves: Fort +9, Ref +9, Will +10
Abilities: Str 19, Dex 12, Con 12, Int 15, Wis 15, Cha 12
Skills: Bluff +11, Concentration +12, Intimidate +11, Listen +14, Ride +11, Sense Motive +12, Spellcraft +13, Spot +14
Feats: Alertness, Combat Casting, Mounted Combat

Climate/Terrain: Any land and underground
Organization: Solitary, mounted (1, on nightmare), or covey (3, on nightmares)
Challenge Rating: 9
Treasure: Standard
Alignment: Always neutral evil
Advancement: 9–16 HD (Medium-size)

Merciless and utterly evil, night hags are creatures from the lower planes that constantly hunger for the flesh and souls of innocent men and women.

A night hag looks like a hideously ugly human woman. Its flesh is the blue-violet of a deep bruise and covered with warts, blisters, and open sores. It has straggly jet-black hair and jagged, yellow teeth as deadly as a lion's. The eyes burn like hot coals, throwing out a thick, red radiance that fairly speaks of the evil thoughts behind them.

Night hags speak Infernal, Abyssal, and Celestial.

COMBAT

Night hags attack good creatures on sight if the odds of success are favorable.

These creatures rip through armor and flesh with their deadly teeth. They love to use *sleep* and then strangle those who are overcome by it.

Disease (Ex): Demon fever—bite, Fortitude save (DC 18), incubation period 1 day; damage 1d6 temporary Constitution. Each day thereafter, on a failed save, the creature must immediately succeed at another Fortitude save or suffer 1 point of permanent Constitution drain (see Disease, page 74 in the DUNGEON MASTER'S *Guide*).

Spell-Like Abilities: At will—*detect chaos, detect evil, detect good, detect law, detect magic, magic missile, polymorph self, ray of enfeeblement,* and *sleep.* These abilities are as the spells cast by an 8th-level sorcerer (save DC 11 + spell level). A night hag can use *etherealness* at will as a 16th-level sorcerer so long as it possesses its *heartstone* (see below).

Dream Haunting (Su): Night hags can visit the dreams of chaotic or evil individuals by using a special periapt known as a *heartstone* to become ethereal, then hovering over the creature. Once the hag invades someone's dreams, it rides on the victim's back until dawn. The sleeper suffers from tormenting dreams and suffers 1 point of permanent Constitution drain upon awakening. A sleeper reduced to a Constitution score of 0 dies. Only another ethereal being can stop these nocturnal intrusions, by confronting and defeating the night hag.

Immunities (Ex): Night hags are immune to fire and cold, and to charm, sleep, and fear effects.

HEARTSTONE

All night hags carry this periapt, which instantly cures any disease contracted by the holder. In addition, a *heartstone* imparts a +2 resistance bonus to all saving throws. A night hag that loses this charm can no longer use *etherealness* until it can manufacture another (which takes one month). Good-aligned creatures can also benefit from the *heartstone*'s powers, but the periapt shatters after ten uses and does not bestow *etherealness*.

NIGHTMARE

Large Outsider (Evil)
Hit Dice: 6d8+18 (45 hp)
Initiative: +6 (+2 Dex, +4 Improved Initiative)
Speed: 40 ft., fly 90 ft. (good)
AC: 24 (–1 size, +2 Dex, +13 natural)
Attacks: 2 hooves +9 melee, bite +4 melee
Damage: Hoof 1d8+4 and 1d4 fire, bite 1d8+2
Face/Reach: 5 ft. by 10 ft./5 ft.
Special Attacks: Flaming hooves, smoke
Special Qualities: Astral projection, etherealness
Saves: Fort +8, Ref +7, Will +6
Abilities: Str 18, Dex 15, Con 16, Int 13, Wis 13, Cha 12
Skills: Intuit Direction +10, Listen +12, Move Silently +11, Search +10, Sense Motive +10, Spot +12
Feats: Alertness, Improved Initiative

Climate/Terrain: Any land and underground
Organization: Solitary
Challenge Rating: 5
Treasure: None
Alignment: Always neutral evil
Advancement: 7–10 HD (Large); 11–18 HD (Huge)

Nightmares are proud equine creatures with hearts as black and evil as the dark abysses from which they come.

At first glance, a nightmare looks like a large, powerful horse with a jet-black coat. A closer look, however, reveals its true nature. Flames wreathe its steely hooves, trail from its flared nostrils, and smolder in the depths of its dark eyes.

Nightmares are wild and restless creatures. They roam the world doing evil and haunting the dreams of all who dared cross them. Although they have no wings, they can fly with great speed. They seldom allow others to ride them, but particularly powerful and evil creatures have been known to make mounts of nightmares.

COMBAT

Nightmares do battle by biting with their viperish fangs and kicking with their powerful legs. A nightmare can fight while mounted, but the rider cannot also fight unless he or she succeeds at a Ride check (see Ride, page 72 in the *Player's Handbook*).

Flaming Hooves (Su): A blow from a nightmare's hooves sets combustible materials alight.

Smoke (Su): During the excitement of battle, a nightmare often snorts and neighs with rage. This fills a 15-foot cone with a hot, sulfurous smoke that chokes and blinds opponents. Anyone in the cone must succeed at a Fortitude save (DC 16) or suffer a –2 morale penalty to all attack and damage rolls until 1d6 minutes after they leave the cone. The nightmare gains one-half concealment against creatures 5 feet away and total concealment against creatures 10 feet away. The smoke does not obscure the nightmare's vision at all. The nightmare can suppress the smoke as a free action.

Astral Projection and Etherealness (Su): These function just like the spells of the same names as cast by a 20th-level sorcerer.

Carrying Capacity: A light load for a nightmare is up to 300 pounds; a medium load, 301–600 pounds; and a heavy load, 601–900 pounds.

NIGHTSHADE

Illus. by Todd Lockwood

	Nightwing Huge Undead	Nightwalker Huge Undead	Nightcrawler Gargantuan Undead
Hit Dice:	17d12 (110 hp)	21d12 (136 hp)	25d12 (162 hp)
Initiative:	+8 (+4 Dex, +4 Improved Initiative)	+6 (+2 Dex, +4 Improved Initiative)	+4 (Improved Initiative)
Speed:	20 ft., fly 60 ft. (good)	40 ft., fly 20 ft. (poor)	30 ft., burrow 60 ft.
AC:	28 (–2 size, +4 Dex, +16 natural)	26 (–2 size, +2 Dex, +16 natural)	28 (–4 size, +22 natural)
Attacks:	Bite +15 melee	2 slams +20 melee	Bite +25 melee, sting +20 melee
Damage:	Bite 2d6+13 and transformation	Slam 2d6+12	Bite 4d6+17, sting 2d8+8 and poison
Face/Reach:	20 ft. by 10 ft./10 ft.	10 ft. by 10 ft./15 ft.	30 ft. by 30 ft. (coiled)/10 ft.
Special Attacks:	Nightshade abilities, magic drain	Nightshade abilities, crush item, evil gaze	Nightshade abilities, improved grab, swallow whole, energy drain, poison
Special Qualities:	Undead, nightshade abilities	Undead, nightshade abilities	Undead, nightshade abilities, tremorsense
Saves:	Fort +5, Ref +9, Will +15	Fort +7, Ref +9, Will +17	Fort +8, Ref +8, Will +21
Abilities:	Str 29, Dex 18, Con —, Int 20, Wis 20, Cha 18	Str 35, Dex 14, Con —, Int 20, Wis 20, Cha 18	Str 45, Dex 10, Con —, Int 20, Wis 20, Cha 18
Skills:	Concentration +16, Intuit Direction +19, Listen +22, Move Silently +20, Spellcraft +19, Spot +22	Concentration +19, Hide +12*, Listen +22, Move Silently +19, Spellcraft +19, Spot +22	Concentration +18, Intuit Direction +7, Listen +22, Move Silently +20, Spellcraft +17, Spot +22
Feats:	Alertness, Blind-Fight, Combat Casting, Combat Reflexes, Dodge, Flyby Attack, Improved Critical (bite), Improved Initiative, Power Attack	Alertness, Blind-Fight, Cleave, Combat Casting, Combat Reflexes, Great Cleave, Improved Critical (slam), Improved Initiative, Power Attack, Sunder	Alertness, Blind-Fight, Combat Casting, Improved Critical (bite), Improved Critical (sting), Improved Initiative, Iron Will, Power Attack
Climate/Terrain:	Any land and underground	Any land and underground	Any land and underground
Organization:	Solitary, pair, or flock (3–6)	Solitary, pair, or gang (2–4)	Solitary or pair
Challenge Rating:	14	16	18
Treasure:	Standard	Standard	Standard
Alignment:	Always chaotic evil	Always chaotic evil	Always chaotic evil
Advancement:	18–25 HD (Huge); 26–51 HD (Gargantuan)	22–31 HD (Huge); 32–63 HD (Gargantuan)	26–75 HD (Colossal)

Nightshades are powerful undead composed of equal parts darkness and absolute evil. Their chilling malevolence hangs heavily about them, along with the smell of an open grave on a winter's morning.

Nightshades can read and understand all forms of communication; however, they communicate with others by telepathy.

COMBAT

Each of the three known varieties of night-shade is a terrible creature with unique powers and abilities. Their tactics vary according to their abilities, but they all make liberal use of *haste*.

Undead: Immune to mind-influencing effects, poison, sleep, paralysis, stunning, and disease. Not subject to critical hits, subdual damage, ability damage, energy drain, or death from massive damage.

Nightshade Abilities

All nightshades share the following special abilities.

Chill Aura (Su): All nightshades radiate a 60-foot-radius aura of utter cold. While this aura does not damage living things, it spoils any food and drink it touches. In addition, it ruins holy water and magic potions, oils, and ointments unless the items succeed at a Fortitude save (DC 22). Items that successfully save cannot be affected again by the same nightshade's aura for one day.

This bone-numbing cold is so distinctive that anyone exposed to it once instantly recognizes it in the future, so it is difficult for a nightshade to surprise someone who has previously encountered such a beast.

Spell-Like Abilities: At will—*cause disease, charm person, cloudkill, confusion, darkness, dispel magic, haste, hold person,* and *invisibility*; once per night—*finger of death*. These abilities are as the spells cast by a sorcerer whose level equals the nightshade's HD total (save DC 14 + spell level).

Summon Undead (Su): A nightshade can summon undead creatures once every 4 hours: 2–5 shadows, 1–2 wraiths, 1 spectre, or 1 ghost. The undead arrive in 1d10 rounds and serve for 1 hour or until released.

Aversion to Daylight (Ex): Nightshades are creatures of utter darkness. While they loathe all light, if exposed to natural daylight (not merely a *daylight* spell), they suffer a –4 morale penalty to all attack rolls.

Cold Immunity (Ex): Nightshades suffer no damage from cold.

Resistances (Ex): Nightshades have acid, fire, and electricity resistance 50.

Spell Immunity (Su): Nightshades ignore the effects of spells and spell-like abilities of 6th level or lower, just as if the spellcaster had failed to overcome spell resistance.

Detect Magic (Su): A nightshade can continuously detect magic as the spell cast by a 20th-level sorcerer. It can suppress or resume this ability as a free action.

See Invisibility (Su): A nightshade can continuously see invisibility as the spell cast by a 20th-level sorcerer. It can suppress or resume this ability as a free action.

Telepathy (Su): Nightshades can communicate telepathically with any creature within 100 feet that has a language.

Damage Reduction (Su): All nightshades have damage reduction 25/+3.

NIGHTWING

These horrible creatures appear as great bats composed of utter darkness.

Combat

Nightwings prowl the night sky and dive onto their victims. They are all but invisible, detectable only because of the stars they obscure in their passing.

Magic Drain (Su): A nightwing can weaken magic armor, weapons, and shields by making a successful touch attack. The target item must succeed at a Fortitude save (DC 20) or lose one "plus" (for example, a +2 *sword* becomes a +1 *sword*). An item that is completely drained becomes normal in all respects and loses any other powers (such as *flame tongue*) as well. Casting *dispel evil* upon the item reverses the effects of the magic drain, provided this occurs within a number of days after the attack equal to the caster's level.

NIGHTWALKER

A nightwalker is a 20-foot-tall humanoid giant composed of pure darkness.

Combat

Nightwalkers lurk in dark areas where they can almost always surprise the unwary or those who do not recognize the absolute cold radiating from the creatures.

Crush Item (Su): A nightwalker can destroy any weapon or item of Large size or smaller (even magic ones, but not artifacts) by picking it up and crushing it between its hands. This is a standard action. The nightshade must make a successful disarm attack to grab an item held by an opponent.

Evil Gaze (Su): Curse, 30 feet, Will save (DC 24). Cursed opponents suffer a –4 morale penalty to all attack rolls, checks, and saving throws. *Dispel evil* or *remove curse* eliminates the effect.

Skills: *When hiding in a dark area, a nightwalker receives a +8 racial bonus to Hide checks.

NIGHTCRAWLER

A nightcrawler is a massive behemoth similar to a purple worm, though utterly black in color. It measures about 7 feet in diameter and is 100 feet long from its toothy maw to the tip of its stinging tail.

Combat

A nightcrawler attacks by burrowing through the ground and emerging to strike. The ground blocks the creature's distinctive chill until it emerges to attack.

Improved Grab (Ex): To use this ability, the nightcrawler must hit with its bite attack. If it gets a hold, it automatically deals bite damage and can try to swallow the opponent.

Swallow Whole (Ex): A nightcrawler can try to swallow a grabbed opponent of Huge or smaller size by making a successful grapple check. Once inside, the opponent takes 2d8+12 points of crushing damage plus 1d8 points of acid damage per round from the nightcrawler's gizzard, and is subject to the creature's energy drain. A swallowed creature can climb out of the gizzard with a successful grapple check. This returns it to the nightcrawler's maw, where another successful grapple check is needed to get free. A swallowed creature can also cut its way out by using claws or a Small or Tiny slashing weapon to deal 35 points of damage to the gizzard (AC 24). Once the creature exits, muscular action closes the hole; another swallowed opponent must cut its own way out.

The nightcrawler's interior can hold two Huge, four Large, eight Medium-size, sixteen Small, or thirty-two Tiny or smaller opponents.

Energy Drain (Su): Living creatures inside a nightcrawler's gizzard receive one negative level each round. The Fortitude save to remove a negative level has a DC of 24.

Poison (Ex): Sting, Fortitude save (DC 22); initial and secondary damage 2d6 temporary Strength.

Tremorsense (Ex): A nightcrawler can automatically sense the location of anything within 60 feet that is in contact with the ground.

NYMPH

Medium-Size Fey
Hit Dice: 3d6 (10 hp)
Initiative: +1 (Dex)
Speed: 30 ft., swim 20 ft.
AC: 11 (+1 Dex)
Attacks: Dagger +1 melee
Damage: Dagger 1d4
Face/Reach: 5 ft. by 5 ft./5 ft.
Special Attacks: Blinding beauty, unearthly beauty
Special Qualities: Spell-like abilities
Saves: Fort +1, Ref +4, Will +8
Abilities: Str 10, Dex 13, Con 10, Int 16, Wis 17, Cha 19
Skills: Animal Empathy +10, Craft (any one) or Knowledge (any one) +7, Escape Artist +7, Heal +9, Hide +7, Listen +11, Move Silently +7, Sense Motive +9, Spot +11
Feats: Ability Focus (unearthly beauty), Alertness, Dodge, Iron Will

Climate/Terrain: Any land
Organization: Solitary
Challenge Rating: 6
Treasure: Standard
Alignment: Always chaotic good
Advancement: 4–9 HD (Medium-size)

Nymphs are nature's embodiment of physical beauty: They are so unbearably lovely that even a glimpse can blind or kill onlookers. Nymphs hate evil and ugliness.

These creatures inhabit only the most secluded and tranquil wilderness places and usually dwell near a body of pure, clear water—ocean grottoes, crystalline caverns, mountain streams, and the like. Nymphs believe in the sanctity of nature and try to keep their lairs safe and pure. Though normally solitary, they sometimes aid good beings in combating evil. Animals of all types flock to a nymph, ignoring their natural enemies; injured beasts know that a nymph will tend their wounds.

A nymph's beauty exceeds mere words. The appearance of individual nymphs varies, but all appear to be ever-young women of human size, with sleek figures, luxuriant hair, and perfect features. Their demeanor is charming and graceful, and their minds are quick and witty.

A nymph is likely to react favorably to very handsome humanoids, particularly elves, half-elves, and humans, and sometimes even rescues such beings if they appear to be in distress.

Nymphs speak Sylvan and Common.

COMBAT

Nymphs avoid combat whenever possible, fleeing when confronted by intruders or danger.

Blinding Beauty (Su): This ability operates continuously, affecting all humanoids within 60 feet of the nymph. Those who look directly at the nymph must succeed at a Fortitude save (DC 15) or be blinded permanently as though by the *blindness* spell. The nymph can suppress or resume this ability as a free action.

Unearthly Beauty (Su): The nymph can evoke this ability once every 10 minutes. Those within 30 feet of the nymph who look directly at it must succeed at a Will save (DC 17) or die.

Spell-Like Abilities: Nymphs can use *dimension door* once per day as cast by a 7th-level sorcerer. They can also replicate druid spells as 7th-level casters (save DC 13 + spell level).

	Ogre	Ogre Mage
	Large Giant	Large Giant
Hit Dice:	4d8+8 (26 hp)	5d8+15 (37 hp)
Initiative:	–1 (Dex)	+4 (Improved Initiative)
Speed:	30 ft.	30 ft., fly 40 ft. (good)
AC:	16 (–1 size, –1 Dex, +5 natural, +3 hide)	18 (–1 size, +5 natural, +4 chain shirt)
Attacks:	Huge greatclub +8 melee; or Huge longspear +1 ranged	Huge greatsword +7 melee; or Huge longbow +2 ranged
Damage:	Huge greatclub 2d6+7; or Huge longspear 2d6+5	Huge greatsword 2d8+7; or Huge longbow 2d6
Face/Reach:	5 ft. by 5 ft./10 ft. (15–20 ft. with longspear)	5 ft. by 5 ft./10 ft.
Special Attacks:	—	Spell-like abilities
Special Qualities:	—	Regeneration 2, SR 18
Saves:	Fort +6, Ref +0, Will +1	Fort +7, Ref +1, Will +3
Abilities:	Str 21, Dex 8, Con 15, Int 6, Wis 10, Cha 7	Str 21, Dex 10, Con 17, Int 14, Wis 14, Cha 17
Skills:	Climb +4, Listen +2, Spot +2	Concentration +6, Listen +5, Spellcraft +4, Spot +5
Feats:	Weapon Focus (greatclub)	Improved Initiative

Climate/Terrain:	Any land, aquatic, and underground	Any land and underground
Organization:	Solitary, pair, gang (2–4), or band (5–8)	Solitary, pair, or troupe (1–2 plus 2–4 ogres)
Challenge Rating:	2	8
Treasure:	Standard	Double standard
Alignment:	Usually chaotic evil	Usually lawful evil
Advancement:	By character class	By character class

Ogres are big, ugly, greedy creatures that live by raiding and scavenging. They join other monsters to prey on the weak and associate freely with ogre mages, giants, and trolls.

Lazy and bad-tempered, ogres solve problems by smashing them; what they can't smash, they either ignore or flee. Dwelling in small tribal groups, ogres occupy any convenient location and eat nearly anything they can catch, steal, or slay. Ogres sometimes accept mercenary service with other evil humanoids (including humans).

Adult ogres stand 9 to 10 feet tall and weigh 300 to 350 pounds. Their skin color ranges from dull yellow to dull brown. Their thick hides are often covered in dark, warty bumps, and their hair is long, unkempt, and greasy. Their clothing consists of poorly cured furs and hides, which add to their naturally repellent odor.

Ogres speak Giant, and those specimens who boast Intelligence scores of at least 10 also speak Common.

COMBAT

Ogres favor overwhelming odds, sneak attacks, and ambushes to a fair fight. They are intelligent enough to fire ranged weapons first to soften up their foes before closing, but ogre gangs and bands fight as unorganized individuals.

MERROW (AQUATIC OGRE)

The merrow are a variety of ogre that dwell in freshwater lakes and rivers. Apart from their habitat, speed (swim 40 ft.), and their penchant for longspears (attack +7 melee, damage 1d8+7), they are identical with their landbound cousins.

OGRE MAGE

The ogre mage is a more intelligent and dangerous variety of its mundane cousin. Rapacious and cruel by nature, ogre mages often lead organized raids for slaves, treasure, and food. These creatures dwell in fortified structures or underground lairs, usually living alone or with a small group of ogre followers. Status among ogre mages is measured by wealth. While they do not generally associate with their own kind, they often undertake raids and schemes in competition with one another to amass the most riches.

An ogre mage stands about 10 feet tall and weighs up to 600 pounds. Its skin varies in color from light green to light blue, and its hair is dark. A pair of short ivory horns protrude from its forehead. The eyes are dark with strikingly white pupils, and the teeth and claws are jet black. Ogre mages favor loose, comfortable clothing and lightweight armor.

Ogre mages speak Giant and Common.

Combat

Ogre mages rely on their spell-like abilities, resorting to physical combat only when necessary. When faced with obviously superior forces, they prefer to retreat in *gaseous form* rather than fight a losing battle. Ogre mages hold deep, abiding grudges, however, and the unwise person who crosses one would do well to keep looking over a shoulder.

Spell-Like Abilities: At will—*darkness* and *invisibility*; 1/day—*charm person, cone of cold, gaseous form, polymorph self,* and *sleep.* These abilities are as the spells cast by a 9th-level sorcerer (save DC 13 + spell level).

Flight (Su): An ogre mage can cease or resume flight as a free action. While in *gaseous form* it can fly at normal speed and has perfect maneuverability.

Regeneration (Ex): Ogre mages take normal damage from fire and acid.

An ogre mage that loses a limb or body part can reattach it by holding the severed member to the stump. Reattachment takes 1 minute. If the head or other vital organ is severed, it must be reattached within 10 minutes or the creature dies. Ogre mages cannot regrow lost body parts.

	Gray Ooze	Gelatinous Cube	Ochre Jelly
	Medium-Size Ooze	**Huge Ooze**	**Large Ooze**
Hit Dice:	3d10+10 (26 hp)	4d10+36 (58 hp)	6d10+27 (60 hp)
Initiative:	–5 (Dex)	–5 (Dex)	–5 (Dex)
Speed:	10 ft.	15 ft.	10 ft., climb 10 ft.
AC:	5 (–5 Dex)	3 (–2 size, –5 Dex)	4 (–1 size, –5 Dex)
Attacks:	Slam +3 melee	Slam +1 melee	Slam +5 melee
Damage:	Slam 1d6+1 and 1d6 acid	Slam 1d6+4 and 1d6 acid	Slam 2d4+3 and 1d4 acid
Face/Reach:	5 ft. by 5 ft./5 ft.	10 ft. by 10 ft./10 ft.	5 ft. by 10 ft./10 ft.
Special Attacks:	Improved grab, acid, corrosion, constrict 1d6+1 and 1d6 acid	Engulf, paralysis, acid	Improved grab, acid, constrict 2d4+3 and 1d4 acid
Special Qualities:	Blindsight, cold and fire immunity, ooze, camouflage	Blindsight, transparent, electricity immunity, ooze	Blindsight, split, ooze
Saves:	Fort +1, Ref –4, Will –4	Fort +5, Ref –4, Will –4	Fort +4, Ref –3, Will –3
Abilities:	Str 12, Dex 1, Con 11, Int —, Wis 1, Cha 1	Str 10, Dex 1, Con 19, Int —, Wis 1, Cha 1	Str 15, Dex 1, Con 15, Int —, Wis 1, Cha 1
Climate/Terrain:	Any marsh and underground	Any underground	Any marsh and underground
Organization:	Solitary	Solitary	Solitary
Challenge Rating:	4	3	5
Treasure:	None	1/10th coins, 50% goods (no nonmetal or nonstone), 50% items (no nonmetal or nonstone)	None
Alignment:	Always neutral	Always neutral	Always neutral
Advancement:	4–6 HD (Medium-size); 7–9 HD (Large)	5–12 HD (Huge); 13–24 HD (Gargantuan)	7–9 HD (Large); 10–18 HD (Huge)

	Black Pudding
	Huge Ooze
Hit Dice:	10d10+60 (115 hp)
Initiative:	–5 (Dex)
Speed:	20 ft., climb 20 ft.
AC:	3 (–2 size, –5 Dex)
Attacks:	Slam +8 melee
Damage:	Slam 2d6+4 and 2d6 acid
Face/Reach:	5 ft. by 20 ft./10 ft.
Special Attacks:	Improved grab, acid, constrict 2d6+4 and 2d6 acid
Special Qualities:	Blindsight, split, ooze
Saves:	Fort +7, Ref –2, Will –2
Abilities:	Str 17, Dex 1, Con 19, Int —, Wis 1, Cha 1
Climate/Terrain:	Any marsh and underground
Organization:	Solitary
Challenge Rating:	7
Treasure:	None
Alignment:	Always neutral
Advancement:	11–15 HD (Huge); 16–30 HD (Gargantuan)

Oozes are amorphous creatures that live only to eat. They inhabit underground areas throughout the world, scouring caverns, ruins, and dungeons in search of organic matter—living or dead.

COMBAT

Oozes attack any creatures they encounter. They lash out with pseudopods or simply engulf opponents with their bodies, which secrete acids that help them catch or digest their prey.

Blindsight (Ex): An ooze's entire body is a primitive sensory organ that can ascertain prey by scent and vibration within 60 feet.

Ooze: Immune to mind-influencing effects, poison, sleep, paralysis, stunning, and polymorphing. Not subject to critical hits.

GRAY OOZE

A gray ooze appears to be a harmless puddle of water, a patch of wet sand, or a section of damp stone—until it moves or strikes.

Gray oozes can grow to a length of up to 8 feet and a thickness of about 6 inches.

Combat

A gray ooze strikes like a snake, slamming opponents with its body.

Improved Grab (Ex): To use this ability, the gray ooze must hit with its slam attack. If it gets a hold, it can constrict.

Acid (Ex): A gray ooze secretes a digestive acid that quickly dissolves organic material and metal. Any melee hit deals acid damage.

Illus. by T. Lockwood

145

The ooze's acidic touch deals 40 points of damage per round to wood or metal objects. Armor or clothing dissolves and becomes useless immediately unless it succeeds at a Reflex save (DC 19). The acid cannot harm stone. A metal or wooden weapon that strikes a gray ooze also dissolves immediately unless it succeeds at a Reflex save (DC 19).

Constrict (Ex): A gray ooze deals automatic slam and acid damage with a successful grapple check. The opponent's clothing and armor suffer a –4 penalty to Reflex saves against the acid.

Camouflage (Ex): It takes a successful Spot check (DC 15) to recognize a motionless gray ooze for what it really is.

GELATINOUS CUBE

The nearly transparent gelatinous cube travels slowly along dungeon corridors and cave floors, absorbing carrion, creatures, and trash. Inorganic material remains trapped and visible inside the cube's body.

A typical gelatinous cube is 10 feet on a side and weighs 10,000 pounds, though much larger specimens are not unknown.

Combat

A gelatinous cube attacks by slamming its body into its prey. It is capable of lashing out with a pseudopod, but usually engulfs foes.

Engulf (Ex): Although it moves slowly, a gelatinous cube can simply mow down Large or smaller creatures as a standard action. It cannot make a slam attack during a round in which it engulfs. The gelatinous cube merely has to move over the opponents, affecting as many as it can cover. Opponents can make opportunity attacks against the cube, but if they do so they are not entitled to a saving throw. Those who do not attempt opportunity attacks must succeed at a Reflex save (DC 13) or be engulfed; on a success, they are pushed back or aside (opponent's choice) as the cube moves forward. Engulfed creatures are subject to the cube's paralysis and acid, and are considered to be grappled and trapped within its body.

Paralysis (Ex): Gelatinous cubes secrete an anesthetizing slime. A target hit by a cube's melee or engulf attack must succeed at a Fortitude save (DC 16) or be paralyzed for 3d6 rounds. The cube can automatically engulf a paralyzed opponent.

Acid (Ex): A gelatinous cube's acid does not harm metal or stone.

Transparent (Ex): Gelatinous cubes are hard to see, even under ideal conditions, and it takes a successful Spot check (DC 15) to notice one. Creatures who fail to notice a cube and walk into it are automatically engulfed.

OCHRE JELLY

An ochre jelly seeps along floors, walls, and ceilings with ease, squeezing its malleable body under doors and through cracks in search of meals.

This creature resembles a giant, dark yellow amoeba. It can grow to a length of about 12 feet and a thickness of about 6 inches, but can compress its body to fit into cracks as small as 1 inch wide.

Combat

Ochre jellies attempt to envelop and squeeze their prey.

Improved Grab (Ex): To use this ability, the ochre jelly must hit with its slam attack. If it gets a hold, it can constrict.

Acid (Ex): An ochre jelly secretes a digestive acid that dissolves only flesh. Any melee hit deals acid damage.

Constrict (Ex): An ochre jelly deals automatic slam and acid damage with a successful grapple check.

Split (Ex): Weapons and electricity attacks deal no damage to an ochre jelly. Instead the creature splits into two identical jellies, each with half the original's hit points (round down). A jelly with only 1 hit point cannot be further split.

BLACK PUDDING

Black puddings slither and undulate along underground terrain seeking sustenance. They resemble nothing so much as roundish blobs of inky black goo.

The average pudding measures 20 feet across and 2 feet thick.

Combat

Black puddings attack by grabbing and squeezing their prey.

Improved Grab (Ex): To use this ability, the black pudding must hit with its slam attack. If it gets a hold, it can constrict.

Acid (Ex): The pudding secretes a digestive acid that dissolves organic material and metal quickly. Any melee hit deals acid damage. The pudding's acidic touch deals 50 points of damage per round to wood or metal objects. The opponent's armor and clothing dissolve and become useless immediately unless they succeed at Reflex saves (DC 19). The acid can dissolve stone, dealing 20 points of damage per round of contact.

A metal or wooden weapon that strikes a black pudding also dissolves immediately unless it succeeds at a Reflex save (DC 19).

Constrict (Ex): A black pudding deals automatic slam and acid damage with a successful grapple check. The opponent's clothing and armor suffer a –4 penalty to Reflex saves against the acid.

Split (Ex): Weapons deal no damage to a black pudding. Instead the creature splits into two identical puddings, each with half the original's hit points (round down). A pudding with only 1 hit point cannot be further split.

ORC

Medium-Size Humanoid (Orc)
Hit Dice: 1d8 (4 hp)
Initiative: +0
Speed: 20 ft. (scale mail); base 30 ft.
AC: 14 (+4 scale mail)
Attacks: Greataxe +3 melee; or javelin +1 ranged
Damage: Greataxe 1d12+3; or javelin 1d6+2
Face/Reach: 5 ft. by 5 ft./5 ft.
Special Qualities: Darkvision 60 ft., light sensitivity
Saves: Fort +2, Ref +0, Will –1
Abilities: Str 15, Dex 10, Con 11, Int 9, Wis 8, Cha 8
Skills: Listen +2, Spot +2
Feats: Alertness

Climate/Terrain: Any land and underground
Organization: Gang (2–4), squad (11–20 plus 2 3rd-level sergeants and 1 leader of 3rd–6th level), or band (30–100 plus 150% noncombatants plus 1 3rd-level sergeant per 10 adults, 5 5th-level lieutenants, and 3 7th-level captains)
Challenge Rating: 1/2
Treasure: Standard
Alignment: Usually chaotic evil
Advancement: By character class

Orcs are aggressive humanoids that raid, pillage, and battle other creatures. They have a hatred of elves and dwarves that began generations ago, and often kill them on sight.

Orcs vary in appearance but in general look like primitive humans with gray skin, coarse hair, stooped postures, low foreheads, and porcine faces with prominent lower canines that resemble a boar's tusks. They have lupine ears, their eyes are reddish, and they wear vivid colors that most humans would consider unpleasant, such as blood red, mustard yellow, yellow-green, and deep purple. Their equipment is dirty and unkempt.

When not actually fighting other creatures, orcs are usually planning raids or practicing their fighting skills. Their language varies slightly from tribe to tribe but is understandable by anyone who speaks Orc. Some orcs know Goblin or Giant as well.

Most orcs encountered away from their homes are warriors; the information in the statistics block is for one of 1st level (see page 39 in the DUNGEON MASTER's Guide for more about the warrior class).

COMBAT

Orcs are familiar with the use of most weapons, preferring those that cause the most damage in the least time. They enjoy attacking from concealment and setting ambushes, and they obey the rules of war (such as honoring a truce) only as long as it is convenient for them.

Light Sensitivity (Ex): Orcs suffer a –1 penalty to attack rolls in bright sunlight or within the radius of a *daylight* spell.

ORC SOCIETY

Orcs believe that to survive, they must conquer as much territory as possible, which puts them at odds with all intelligent creatures that live near them. They are constantly warring with or preparing to war with humanoids, including other orc tribes. They can ally with other humanoids for a time but quickly rebel if not commanded by orcs. Their deities teach them that all other beings are inferior and that all worldly goods rightfully belong to the orcs, having been stolen by the others. Orc spellcasters are ambitious, and rivalries between them and warrior leaders sometimes tear a tribe apart.

Orc society is patriarchal: Females are prized possessions at best and chattel at worst. Male orcs pride themselves on the number of females they own and male children they sire, as well as their battle prowess, wealth, and amount of territory. They wear their battle scars proudly and ritually scar themselves to mark significant achievements and turning points in their lives.

An orc lair may be a cave, a series of wooden huts, a fort, or even a large city built above and below ground. A lair includes females (as many as there are males), young (half as many as there are females), and slaves (about one per 10 males).

The chief orc deity is Gruumsh, a one-eyed god who tolerates no sign of peaceability among his people.

HALF-ORCS

These orc-human crossbreeds can be found in either orc or human society (where their status varies according to local sentiments), or in communities of their own. Half-orcs usually inherit a good blend of the physical characteristics of their parents. They are as tall as humans and a little heavier, thanks to their muscle. They have greenish pigmentation, sloping foreheads, jutting jaws, prominent teeth, and coarse body hair. Half-orcs who have lived among or near orcs have scars, in keeping with orcish tradition.

The typical ability scores for a half-orc are Str 13, Dex 10, Con 11, Int 9, Wis 8, Cha 8. Half-orcs have 60-foot darkvision but are not sensitive to light.

ORC CHARACTERS

An orc's favored class is barbarian, and orc leaders tend to be barbarians. Orc clerics worship Gruumsh (favored weapon: any spear) and can choose two of the following domains: Chaos, Evil, Strength, and War. Most orc spellcasters, however, are adepts (see page 37 in the DUNGEON MASTER's Guide). Orc adepts favor spells that deal damage.

OTYUGH

Large Aberration
Hit Dice: 6d8+6 (33 hp)
Initiative: +0
Speed: 20 ft.
AC: 17 (–1 size, +8 natural)
Attacks: 2 tentacle rakes +3 melee, bite –2 melee
Damage: Tentacle rake 1d6, bite 1d4
Face/Reach: 5 ft. by 5 ft./10 ft. (15 ft. with tentacle)
Special Attacks: Improved grab, constrict 1d6, disease
Special Qualities: Scent
Saves: Fort +3, Ref +2, Will +6
Abilities: Str 11, Dex 10, Con 13, Int 5, Wis 12, Cha 6
Skills: Hide +5*, Listen +6, Spot +9
Feats: Alertness

Climate/Terrain: Any underground
Organization: Solitary, pair, or cluster (2–4)
Challenge Rating: 4
Treasure: Standard
Alignment: Always neutral
Advancement: 7–8 HD (Large); 9–15 HD (Huge)

Otyughs are grotesque subterranean monsters that lurk within heaps of refuse. Although primarily scavengers, they never object to a meal of fresh meat when the opportunity presents itself.

An otyugh is a bloated ovoid covered with a tough, rocklike skin, as well as dung, trash, and scraps of decaying organic matter from its lair. A vinelike stalk about 2 feet long rises from the top

Illus. by T. Lockwood

of the disgusting body and bears the creature's two eyes and olfactory organ. Its mouth—little more than a wide gash filled with razor-sharp teeth—is in the center of the mass. The creature shuffles about on three thick, sturdy legs and grasps objects with two long tentacles covered in rough, thorny protrusions. The tentacles end in leaflike appendages covered in more thorny growths. A typical otyugh's body is 6 feet in diameter and weighs 500 pounds.

Otyughs spend most of their time within their lairs with only their sensory stalks exposed, shoveling food into their mouths. Intelligent subterranean beings sometimes coexist with otyughs, which they regard as convenient garbage disposals: They dump their refuse in the lair of the otyugh, which generally refrains from attacking them.

Otyughs speak Common.

COMBAT

An otyugh attacks living creatures if it feels threatened or if it is hungry; otherwise it is content to remain hidden. Otyughs rake and squeeze opponents with their tentacles, which they also use to drag prey into their mouths.

Improved Grab (Ex): To use this ability, the otyugh must hit a Medium-size or smaller opponent with a tentacle attack. If it gets a hold, it can constrict.

Constrict (Ex): An otyugh deals automatic tentacle damage to a Medium-size or smaller opponent with a successful grapple check.

Disease (Ex): Filth fever—bite, Fortitude save (DC 12), incubation period 1d3 days; damage 1d3 temporary Dexterity and 1d3 temporary Constitution (see Disease, page 74 in the DUNGEON MASTER's GUIDE).

Skills: *An otyugh receives a +8 racial bonus to Hide checks when in its lair, due to its natural coloration.

Owlbears are extraordinarily vicious predators with a reputation for ferocity, aggression, and sheer ill temper. They tend to attack nearly anything that moves without provocation.

Scholars have long debated the exact origins of this creature. The most common theory is that a demented wizard created the first specimen by crossing a giant owl with a bear. An owlbear's coat is a thick mix of dark feathers and fur, ranging in color from brown-black to yellowish brown; its beak is a dull ivory color. A full-grown male can stand as high as 8 feet and weigh up to 1,500 pounds. Adventurers who have survived encounters with the creature often speak of the bestial madness they glimpsed in its red-rimmed eyes.

Owlbears inhabit wilderness areas, making their lairs within tangled forests or in shallow underground caverns. They can be active during the day or night, depending on the habits of the available prey. Adults live in mated pairs and hunt in packs, leaving their young in the lair. A lair usually has 1d6 young, fetching a price of 3,000 gp each in many civilized areas. While owlbears cannot be domesticated, they can still be placed in strategically important areas as free-roaming guardians. A professional trainer charges 2,000 gp to rear or train an owlbear (DC 23 for a young creature, DC 30 for an adult).

COMBAT

Owlbears attack prey—any creature bigger than a mouse—on sight, always fighting to the death. They slash with claws and beak, trying to grab their prey and rend it apart.

Improved Grab (Ex): To use this ability, the owlbear must hit with a claw attack.

OWLBEAR

Large Beast
Hit Dice: 5d10+20 (47 hp)
Initiative: +1 (Dex)
Speed: 30 ft.
AC: 15 (−1 size, +1 Dex, +5 natural)
Attacks: 2 claws +7 melee, bite +2 melee
Damage: Claw 1d6+5, bite 1d8+2
Face/Reach: 5 ft. by 10 ft./5 ft.
Special Attacks: Improved grab
Special Qualities: Scent
Saves: Fort +8, Ref +5, Will +2
Abilities: Str 21, Dex 12, Con 19, Int 5, Wis 12, Cha 10
Skills: Listen +8, Spot +7

Climate/Terrain: Temperate forest
Organization: Solitary, pair, or pack (5–8)
Challenge Rating: 4
Treasure: None
Alignment: Usually chaotic evil
Advancement: 6–8 HD (Large); 9–15 HD (Huge)

PEGASUS

Large Magical Beast
Hit Dice: 4d10+12 (34 hp)
Initiative: +2 (Dex)
Speed: 60 ft., fly 120 ft. (average)
AC: 14 (−1 size, +2 Dex, +3 natural)
Attacks: 2 hooves +7 melee, bite +2 melee
Damage: Hoof 1d6+4, bite 1d3+2
Face/Reach: 5 ft. by 10 ft./5 ft.
Special Qualities: Scent, spell-like abilities
Saves: Fort +7, Ref +6, Will +4
Abilities: Str 18, Dex 15, Con 16, Int 10, Wis 13, Cha 13
Skills: Listen +12, Sense Motive +7, Spot +12, Wilderness Lore +3
Feats: Iron Will

Climate/Terrain: Temperate and warm forest
Organization: Solitary, pair, or herd (6–10)
Challenge Rating: 3
Treasure: None
Alignment: Always chaotic good
Advancement: 5–8 HD (Large)

The pegasus is a magnificent winged horse that sometimes serves the cause of good. Though highly prized as aerial steeds, pegasi are wild and shy creatures not easily tamed.

Pegasi mate for life, building their nests in high, remote locations. A mated pair have either 1–2 eggs or 1–2 young in their nest.

A pegasus is larger than a normal horse and has two large, feathered wings. Its coat and wings are pure white, but rumors tell of brown and even black specimens. A typical pegasus stands 6 feet high at the shoulder, weighs 1,500 pounds, and has a wingspan of 20 feet.

COMBAT

Pegasi attack with their sharp hooves and powerful bite. Mated pairs and herds attack as a team, fighting to the death to defend their eggs and young, which fetch a handsome price in many civilized areas.

Spell-Like Abilities: Pegasi can *detect good* and *detect evil* at will within a 60-yard radius, as the spells cast by a 5th-level sorcerer.

Skills: Pegasi receive a +4 racial bonus to Listen and Spot checks.

TRAINING A PEGASUS

Pegasus eggs are worth 2,000 gp each on the open market, while young are worth 3,000 gp per head. Pegasi mature at the same rate as horses. Professional trainers charge 1,000 gp to rear or train a pegasus, which serves its master with absolute faithfulness for life.

Training a pegasus requires a successful Handle Animal check (DC 22 for a young creature, DC 29 for an adult) and that the creature be willing. Trainers can reduce the DC by 5 and the training time by half by using a magic bridle enchanted for the purpose. A pegasus can fight while carrying a rider, but the rider cannot also attack unless he or she succeeds at a Ride check (see Ride, page 72 in the *Player's Handbook*).

Carrying Capacity: A light load for a pegasus is up to 300 pounds; a medium load, 301–600 pounds; and a heavy load, 601–900 pounds.

PHANTOM FUNGUS

Medium-Size Plant
Hit Dice: 2d8+6 (15 hp)
Initiative: +0
Speed: 20 ft.
AC: 14 (+4 natural)
Attacks: Bite +3 melee
Damage: Bite 1d6+3
Special Qualities: Plant, Improved invisibility
Saves: Fort +6, Ref +0, Will +0
Abilities: Str 14, Dex 10, Con 16, Int 2, Wis 11, Cha 9
Skills: Move Silently +5

Climate/Terrain: Any underground
Organization: Solitary
Challenge Rating: 3
Treasure: None
Alignment: Always neutral
Advancement: 3–4 HD (Medium-size); 5–6 HD (Large)

This ambulatory fungus is naturally invisible, making it a feared predator among subterranean inhabitants.

A phantom fungus looks like a brown and greenish-brown mass, though it is visible only when dead. A cluster of nodules atop the main mass serve as sensory organs. The creature feeds and attacks with a gaping maw lined with rows of calcitic teeth. Four stumpy legs support the creature and allow it to move about.

COMBAT

Phantom fungi usually roam quietly, hunting for prey. They attack lone individuals almost anywhere, but when tackling groups they prefer open spaces where they are not readily evident.

Plant: Immune to mind-influencing effects, poison, sleep, paralysis, stunning, and polymorphing. Not subject to critical hits.

Improved Invisibility (Su): This ability is constant, allowing the phantom fungus to remain invisible even when attacking. This works just like *improved invisibility* cast by a 12th-level sorcerer, and lasts as long as the phantom fungus is alive. This ability is not subject to the *invisibility purge* spell. Once killed, a phantom fungus become visible after 1 minute.

Skills: Phantom fungus has a +5 racial bonus to Move Silently checks.

Illus. by C. Critchlow

PHASE SPIDER

Large Magical Beast
Hit Dice: 5d10+15 (42 hp)
Initiative: +7 (+3 Dex, +4 Improved Initiative)
Speed: 40 ft., climb 20 ft.
AC: 15 (–1 size, +3 Dex, +3 natural)
Attacks: Bite +7 melee
Damage: Bite 1d6+4 and poison
Face/Reach: 10 ft. by 10 ft./5 ft.
Special Attacks: Ethereal jaunt, poison
Saves: Fort +7, Ref +7, Will +2
Abilities: Str 17, Dex 17, Con 16, Int 7, Wis 13, Cha 10
Skills: Climb +12, Move Silently +11, Spot +9
Feats: Improved Initiative

Climate/Terrain: Any land and underground
Organization: Solitary or cluster (2–5)
Challenge Rating: 5
Treasure: None
Alignment: Always neutral
Advancement: 6–8 HD (Large); 9–15 HD (Huge)

Phase spiders are aggressive predators that can move quickly from the Ethereal Plane to attack opponents on the Material Plane.

These creatures resemble giant wolf spiders, except with larger heads and variegated markings in white, gray, and black over legs and backs. Their eight eyes are silver-white. A typical phase spider's body is 8 feet long.

Illus. by B. Despain

COMBAT

Phase spiders dwell and hunt on the Material Plane. Once a spider locates prey, however, it shifts to the Ethereal Plane to attack, attempting to catch its victim flat-footed. The spider shifts in, bites its victim, and retreats quickly back to the Ethereal Plane.

Ethereal Jaunt (Su): A phase spider can shift from the Ethereal to the Material Plane as a free action, and shift back again as a move-equivalent action (or during a move-equivalent action). The ability is otherwise identical with *ethereal jaunt* cast by a 15th-level sorcerer.

Poison (Ex): Bite, Fortitude save (DC 15); initial and secondary damage 2d6 temporary Constitution.

PHASM

Medium-Size Shapechanger
Hit Dice: 15d8+30 (97 hp)
Initiative: +6 (+2 Dex, +4 Improved Initiative)
Speed: 30 ft.
AC: 17 (+2 Dex, +5 natural)
Attacks: 2 slams +12 melee
Damage: Slam 1d3+1
Face/Reach: 5 ft. by 5 ft./5 ft.
Special Qualities: Amorphous, scent, alternate form, telepathy, tremorsense

Saves: Fort +11, Ref +11, Will +11
Abilities: Str 12, Dex 15, Con 15, Int 16, Wis 15, Cha 14
Skills: Bluff +15, Climb +7, Craft (any one) +7, Disguise +7*, Knowledge (any one) +7, Listen +10, Spot +10, Wilderness Lore +6
Feats: Alertness, Blind-Fight, Combat Reflexes, Dodge, Improved Initiative, Mobility, Skill Focus (Disguise)

Climate/Terrain: Any land and underground
Organization: Solitary
Challenge Rating: 7
Treasure: Standard
Alignment: Usually neutral
Advancement: 15–21 HD (Huge); 22–42 HD (Gargantuan)

Phasms are amorphous creatures that can assume the guise of almost any other creature or object.

Their shapeshifting ability frees phasms from most material needs, which usually leads them to lives of exploration, hedonism, or philosophical contemplation. There's no telling where a phasm will turn up, nor what it will do if discovered. They are natural spies but notoriously unreliable, since they feel no particular need to report what they learn. They have an affinity with doppelgangers and sometimes ally themselves with groups of them for security—or just for the fun of it.

A phasm in its natural form looks like a blob of multicolored goo about 5 feet across and 2 feet high at the center. Swirls of color indicate sensory organs. In this form, the phasm slithers about like an ooze and can attack with a pair of pseudopods.

Phasms can speak Common but prefer telepathic communication.

COMBAT

When faced with potential danger, a phasm is equally likely to retreat, parley, or attack, as its fancy strikes. Phasms value new experiences: fresh scents and tastes, obscure facts, gossip, odd bric-a-brac, and the like. Those who offer a phasm such things stand a good chance of avoiding a fight.

If pursued or harassed, a phasm transforms into the most fearsome creature it knows, such as an adult white dragon or a fire giant, and attacks. When seriously hurt, it changes to some fast or agile form and tries to escape.

Amorphous (Ex): A phasm in its natural form is immune to poison, sleep, paralysis, stun, and polymorph. It is not subject to critical hits and, having no clear front or back, cannot be flanked.

Alternate Form (Su): Phasms can assume the form of any corporeal creature or object from Diminutive to Large size as a standard action. This ability is otherwise similar to *shapechange* as cast by a 20th-level sorcerer.

Telepathy (Su): Phasms can communicate telepathically with any creature within 100 feet that has a language.

Tremorsense (Ex): A phasm can automatically sense the location of anything within 60 feet that is in contact with the ground, so long as it is touching the ground itself.

Skills: *When using alternate form, a phasm receives a +10 circumstance bonus to Disguise checks.

	Aasimar Medium-Size Outsider	Tiefling Medium-Size Outsider
Hit Dice:	1d8 (4 hp)	1d8 (4 hp)
Initiative:	+4 (Improved Initiative)	+1 (Dex)
Speed:	30 ft.	30 ft.
AC:	16 (+4 scale, +2 large shield)	15 (+1 Dex, +3 studded leather, +1 small shield)
Attacks:	Longsword +1 melee; or light crossbow +1 ranged	Rapier +2 melee; or light crossbow +2 ranged
Damage:	Longsword 1d8; or light crossbow 1d8	Rapier 1d6; or light crossbow 1d8
Face/Reach:	5 ft. by 5 ft./5 ft.	5 ft. by 5 ft./5 ft.
Special Attacks:	Light	Darkness
Special Qualities:	Acid, cold, and electricity resistance 5	Fire, cold, and electricity resistance 5
Saves:	Fort +2, Ref +2, Will +3	Fort +2, Ref +3, Will +2
Abilities:	Str 10, Dex 10, Con 10, Int 10, Wis 13, Cha 13	Str 10, Dex 13, Con 10, Int 13, Wis 11, Cha 8
Skills:	Heal +5, Knowledge (religion) +1, Listen +4, Ride +1, Spot +4	Bluff +1, Hide +3, Move Silently +2, Pick Pocket +3
Feats:	Improved Initiative	Weapon Finesse (rapier)
Climate/Terrain:	Any land and underground	Any land and underground
Organization:	Solitary or team (2–4)	Solitary or gang (2–4)
Challenge Rating:	1/2	1/2
Treasure:	Standard	Standard
Alignment:	Usually good (any)	Usually evil (any)
Advancement:	By character class	By character class

"Planetouched" is a general word to describe those who can trace their bloodline back to an outsider, usually a fiend or celestial.

The effects of having a supernatural being in one's heritage last many generations. Although not as dramatically altered as a half-celestial or a half-fiend, the planetouched still retain some special qualities.

The planetouched discussed here are the most common. Aasimars are humans with some trace of celestial blood in their veins, and tieflings have some fiendishness in their family tree.

There is no "typical" aasimar or tiefling. They do not have their own societies or cultures, instead blending into existing ones. Many have character classes.

AASIMAR

Graced with a touch of the holy, aasimars are usually tall, good-looking, and generally pleasant. Some have a minor physical trait suggesting their heritage, such as silver hair, golden eyes, or an unnaturally intense stare.

Most aasimars are decidedly good-aligned. They fight against evil causes and attempt to sway others to do the right thing. Occasionally they take on the vengeful, judgmental aspect of their celestial ancestor, but this is rare. They're rarely found in leadership positions and often live as loners due to their absolute dedication to goodness. Others are less fanatical and fit seamlessly into normal human society.

Combat

Aasimars usually like a fair, straightforward contest. Against a particularly evil foe, however, they fight with utter conviction and to the death.

Light (Sp): Aasimars can use *light* once per day as cast by a sorcerer of 1st level or their character level, whichever is higher.

Skills: Aasimars receive a +2 racial bonus to Spot and Listen checks.

Aasimar Characters

An aasimar's favored class is paladin.

Illus. by T. Diterlizzi

TIEFLING

Twisted, devious, and untrustworthy, tieflings more often than not follow their inherent traits and heed the call to evil. A few defy their nature, but still must fight against popular opinion (if their nature is known) or the feeling of otherworldly "wrongness" that seems to follow them wherever they go.

Beyond this aura that many find disturbing, many tieflings are indistinguishable from humans. Others have small horns, pointed teeth, red eyes, a whiff of brimstone about them, or even cloven feet. No two tieflings are the same.

In most human societies, tieflings maintain a low profile, operating as thieves, assassins, or spies. Occasionally they rise to a position of power, but when their nature is revealed they quickly become outcasts.

Combat

Tieflings are sneaky, subtle, and generally conniving. They prefer to strike from ambush and usually avoid a fair fight if they can.

Darkness (Sp): Tieflings can use *darkness* once per day as cast by a sorcerer of 1st level or their character level, whichever is higher.

Skills: Tieflings receive a +2 racial bonus to Bluff and Hide checks.

Tiefling Characters

A tiefling's favored class is rogue.

PSEUDODRAGON

Illus. by A. Waters

Tiny Dragon
Hit Dice: 2d12+2 (15 hp)
Initiative: +0
Speed: 15 ft., fly 60 ft. (good)
AC: 18 (+2 size, +6 natural)
Attacks: Sting +4 melee, bite –1 melee
Damage: Sting 1d3 and poison, bite 1
Face/Reach: 2 1/2 ft. by 2 1/2 ft./0 ft.
(5 ft. with tail)
Special Attacks: Poison
Special Qualities: See invisibility, telepathy, immunities, SR 19
Saves: Fort +4, Ref +3, Will +4
Abilities: Str 11, Dex 11, Con 13, Int 10, Wis 12, Cha 10
Skills: Hide +16*, Intuit Direction +3, Listen +5, Search +2, Spot +5
Feats: Alertness

Climate/Terrain: Temperate and warm forest
Organization: Solitary, pair, or clutch (3–5)
Challenge Rating: 1
Treasure: None
Alignment: Always neutral good
Advancement: 3–4 HD (Tiny)

Pseudodragons are tiny, playful members of the dragon family.

Pseudodragons resemble miniature red dragons, but are red-brown in color rather than deep red. They have fine scales and sharp horns and teeth. A pseudodragon's tail is about 2 feet long (twice as long as its body), barbed, and very flexible.

Pseudodragons can communicate telepathically and vocalize animal noises, such as a rasping purr (pleasure), a hiss (unpleasant surprise), a chirp (desire), or a growl (anger).

COMBAT

The pseudodragon can deliver a vicious bite, but its major weapon is its sting-equipped tail.

Poison (Ex): Sting, Fortitude save (DC 12); initial damage sleep for 1 minute, secondary damage sleep for 1d3 days.

See Invisibility (Ex): Pseudodragons continuously *see invisibility* as the spell, with a range of 60 feet.

Telepathy (Su): Pseudodragons can communicate telepathically with creatures that speak Common or Sylvan, provided they are within 60 feet.

Immunities (Ex): Pseudodragons are immune to sleep and paralysis effects.

Skills: Pseudodragons have a chameleonlike ability that grants them a +4 racial bonus to Hide checks. *In forests or overgrown areas, this bonus improves to +8.

PSEUDODRAGON COMPANIONS

A pseudodragon may very rarely seek humanoid companionship. It stalks a candidate silently for days, reading his or her thoughts and judging his or her deeds. If it finds the candidate promising, the pseudodragon presents itself as a potential companion and observes the other's reaction. If the candidate seems delighted and promises to take very good care of it, the pseudodragon accepts. Otherwise, it flies away.

A pseudodragon's personality has been described as catlike. At times it seems arrogant, demanding, and less than helpful. It is willing to serve—provided that it is well fed and groomed, and receives lots of attention. The companion must pamper it and make it feel like the most important thing in his or her life. If the pseudodragon is mistreated or insulted, it will leave—or worse, play pranks when least expected. Pseudodragons particularly dislike cruelty and will not serve cruel masters.

A pseudodragon egg can fetch a price of up to 10,000 gp, and a hatchling as much as 20,000 gp. Pseudodragons have a life span of 10 to 15 years. Like dragons, they are attracted to bright, shiny objects.

PURPLE WORM

Gargantuan Beast
Hit Dice: 16d10+112 (200 hp)
Initiative: –2 (Dex)
Speed: 20 ft., burrow 20 ft., swim 10 ft.
AC: 19 (–4 size, –2 Dex, +15 natural)
Attacks: Bite +20 melee, sting +15 melee
Damage: Bite 2d8+12, sting 2d6+6 and poison
Face/Reach: 30 ft. by 30 ft. (coiled)/15 ft.
Special Attacks: Improved grab, swallow whole, poison
Special Qualities: Tremorsense
Saves: Fort +17, Ref +8, Will +4
Abilities: Str 35, Dex 6, Con 25, Int 1, Wis 8, Cha 8
Skills: Climb +14

Climate/Terrain: Any aquatic and underground
Organization: Solitary
Challenge Rating: 12
Treasure: No coins, 50% goods (stone only), no items
Alignment: Always neutral
Advancement: 16–32 HD (Gargantuan); 33–45 HD (Colossal)

These massive scavengers attempt to consume any organic material they find. Purple worms are feared for swallowing their prey whole: Entire groups of adventurers have vanished down their gullets, one member after the other.

A mature purple worm is 5 feet in diameter and 80 feet long, weighing about 40,000 pounds. It has a toothy maw and a poisonous stinger in its tail. The worm's body is a dark purple.

A purple worm consumes great quantities of dirt and rock when tunneling. Its gizzard may hold gems and other acid-resistant items. In mineral-rich areas, purple worm castings might contain unrefined ores.

COMBAT

In battle, a purple worm forms into a coil 15 feet across, biting and stinging anything within reach.

Improved Grab (Ex): To use this ability, the purple worm must hit with its bite attack. If it gets a hold, it automatically deals bite damage and can attempt to swallow the foe.

Swallow Whole (Ex): A purple worm can try to swallow a grabbed opponent of Large or smaller size by making a successful grapple check. Once inside, the opponent takes 2d8+12 points of crushing damage plus 1d8 points of acid damage per round from the worm's gizzard. A swallowed creature can climb out of the gizzard with a successful grapple check. This returns it to the worm's maw, where another successful grapple check is needed to get free. A swallowed creature can also cut its way out by using claws or a Small or Tiny slashing weapon to deal 25 points of damage to the gizzard (AC 20). Once the creature exits, muscular action closes the hole; another swallowed opponent must cut its own way out.

The worm's interior can hold two Large, four Small, eight Tiny, sixteen Diminutive, or thirty-two Fine or smaller opponents.

Poison (Ex): Sting, Fortitude save (DC 24); initial damage 1d6 temporary Strength, secondary damage 2d6 temporary Strength.

Tremorsense (Ex): A purple worm can automatically sense the location of anything within 60 feet that is in contact with the ground.

RAKSHASA

Medium-Size Outsider (Evil, Lawful)
Hit Dice: 7d8+21 (52 hp)
Initiative: +2 (Dex)
Speed: 40 ft.
AC: 21 (+2 Dex, +9 natural)
Attacks: 2 claws +8 melee, bite +3 melee
Damage: Claw 1d4+1, bite 1d6
Face/Reach: 5 ft. by 5 ft./5 ft.
Special Attacks: Detect thoughts, spells
Special Qualities: Alternate form, spell immunity, vulnerable to blessed crossbow bolts, damage reduction 20/+3
Saves: Fort +8, Ref +7, Will +6
Abilities: Str 12, Dex 14, Con 16, Int 13, Wis 13, Cha 17
Skills: Bluff +16*, Disguise +17*, Listen +11, Move Silently +11, Perform (ballad, chant, drama, epic, plus any other five) +12, Sense Motive +10, Spot +12
Feats: Alertness, Dodge

Climate/Terrain: Warm forest and marsh
Organization: Solitary
Challenge Rating: 9
Treasure: Standard coins; double goods; standard items
Alignment: Always lawful evil
Advancement: 8–14 HD (Medium-size)

Some say rakshasas are the very embodiment of evil. Few beings are more malevolent.

Rakshasas look like humanoid tigers garbed in the clothes of nobility. They love rich living, gladly using their intelligence and power to maintain a decadent lifestyle at the expense of others. Although their bodies are like those of humans, except for the luxurious coat of tiger's fur, their hands are backward (with the palm where the back of the hand is on a human). While this doesn't detract from the creatures' manual dexterity, it makes them look very disturbing to those unfamiliar with them.

Rakshasas speak Common, Infernal, and Undercommon.

COMBAT

In close combat, which a rakshasa disdains as ignoble, it employs its sharp claws and powerful bite. Whenever possible, it uses its other abilities to make such encounters unnecessary.

Detect Thoughts (Su): A rakshasa can continuously detect thoughts as the spell cast by an 18th-level sorcerer (save DC 15). It can suppress or resume this ability as a free action.

Spells: A rakshasa casts spells as a 7th-level sorcerer, and can also cast 1st-level cleric spells as arcane spells.

Alternate Form (Su): A rakshasa can assume any humanoid form, or revert to its own form, as a standard action. This ability is similar to the *alter self* spell cast by an 18th-level sorcerer, but the rakshasa can remain in the new form indefinitely.

Spell Immunity (Su): Rakshasas ignore the effects of spells and spell-like abilities of 8th level or less, just as if the spellcaster had failed to overcome spell resistance.

Vulnerable to Blessed Crossbow Bolts (Ex): Any hit scored with a blessed crossbow bolt instantly slays a rakshasa.

Skills: A rakshasa receives a +4 racial bonus to Bluff and Disguise checks. *When using alternate form, it gains an additional +10 circumstance bonus to Disguise checks. If reading an opponent's mind, its circumstance bonus to Bluff and Disguise checks increases by a further +4.

RAST

Medium-Size Outsider (Fire)
Hit Dice: 4d8+4 (22 hp)
Initiative: +5 (+1 Dex, +4 Improved Initiative)
Speed: Fly 50 ft. (good)
AC: 15 (+1 Dex, +4 natural)
Attacks: 4 claws +6 melee; or bite +6 melee
Damage: Claw 1d4+2; or bite 1d8+3
Face/Reach: 5 ft. by 5 ft./5 ft.
Special Attacks: Paralyzing gaze, improved grab, blood drain
Special Qualities: Fire subtype, flight
Saves: Fort +5, Ref +5, Will +5
Abilities: Str 14, Dex 12, Con 13, Int 3, Wis 13, Cha 12
Skills: Hide +5, Listen +7, Move Silently +7
Feats: Dodge, Improved Initiative

Climate/Terrain: Any land and underground
Organization: Solitary, pair, or swarm (3–6)
Challenge Rating: 5
Treasure: None
Alignment: Usually neutral
Advancement: 5–6 HD (Medium-size); 7–12 HD (Large)

Rasts swarm in isolated pockets of distant planes, particularly the elemental planes. Floating, fleshy sacks of teeth and claws, these insatiable creatures eat almost continuously.

A rast has anywhere from ten to fifteen long, spindly claws that hang menacingly from its bulbous, floating body. Its round head is almost all mouth, and its mouth is almost all teeth.

At their heart, rasts are creatures of ash and cinder, but they feast on blood with a lust that would shame most normal beasts.

COMBAT

Rasts attack in swarms, with a frightening, brutal cunning. The creatures paralyze as many of their foes as possible, then attack any that are still moving. A rast can claw or bite, but cannot do both during the same round.

Paralyzing Gaze (Su): aralysis for 1d6 rounds, 30 feet, Fortitude save (DC 13).

Improved Grab (Ex): To use this ability, the rast must hit with its bite attack. If it gets a hold, it automatically deals bite damage.

Blood Drain (Ex): A rast drains blood from a grabbed opponent, dealing 1 point of temporary Constitution damage each round it maintains the hold.

Fire Subtype (Ex): Fire immunity, double damage from cold except on a successful save.

Flight (Su): A rast can fly as the spell cast by an 11th-level sorcerer, as a free action. A rast that loses this ability falls and can perform only partial actions.

RAVID

Medium-Size Outsider
Hit Dice: 3d8+3 (16 hp)
Initiative: +0
Speed: Fly 60 ft. (perfect)
AC: 25 (+15 natural)
Attacks: Tail slap +4 melee, claw +2 melee
Damage: Tail slap 1d6+1 and positive energy, claw 1d4 and positive energy
Face/Reach: 5 ft. by 5 ft./5 ft.
Special Attacks: Positive energy lash, animate objects
Special Qualities: Fire immunity, flight
Saves: Fort +4, Ref +3, Will +4
Abilities: Str 13, Dex 10, Con 13, Int 7, Wis 12, Cha 14
Skills: Listen +7, Move Silently +6, Spot +7
Feats: Multiattack*

Climate/Terrain: Any land and underground
Organization: Solitary (1 plus at least 1 animated object)
Challenge Rating: 5
Treasure: None
Alignment: Always neutral
Advancement: 4 HD (Medium-size); 5–9 HD (Large)

Ravids are extraplanar creatures embodying positive energy. These bizarre entities imbue creatures with energy by their touch and animate lifeless objects around them.

A ravid has a long, serpentine body that trails as it floats effortlessly through the air, and a single claw that juts forward near its head. Ravids that make their way to the Material Plane wander about aimlessly, followed by the objects to which they've given life.

COMBAT

Ravids fight only in self-defense. A ravid itself is not very powerful but is always accompanied by at least one animated object that defends it.

Positive Energy Lash (Su): A ravid can make a touch attack or hit with a claw or tail slap attack to infuse a target with positive energy. The energy produces an unpleasant tingle in living creatures, and against undead foes (even incorporeal ones) it deals 2d10 points of damage.

REMORHAZ

Huge Magical Beast
Hit Dice: 7d10+35 (73 hp)
Initiative: +1 (Dex)
Speed: 30 ft., burrow 20 ft.
AC: 20 (–2 size, +1 Dex, +11 natural)
Attacks: Bite +13 melee

Damage: Bite 2d8+12
Face/Reach: 10 ft. by 20 ft./10 ft.
Special Attacks: Improved grab, swallow whole
Special Qualities: Heat, tremorsense
Saves: Fort +10, Ref +6, Will +3
Abilities: Str 26, Dex 13, Con 21, Int 5, Wis 12, Cha 10
Skills: Listen +10, Spot +9
Feats: Power Attack

Climate/Terrain: Any cold land
Organization: Solitary
Challenge Rating: 7
Treasure: None
Alignment: Usually neutral
Advancement: 8–10 HD (Huge); 11–21 HD (Gargantuan)

Animate Objects (Su): Once per round, a random object within 20 feet of the ravid animates as though by the spell *animate objects* cast by a 20th-level cleric. These objects defend the ravid to the best of their ability, but the ravid isn't intelligent enough to give them specific commands.

Flight (Su): A ravid can fly as the spell cast by an 11th-level sorcerer, as a free action. A ravid that loses this ability falls and can perform only partial actions.

Feats: *Ravids have the Multiattack feat even through they do not have the requisite three natural weapons.

The remorhaz is an arctic monster, an aggressive predator that burrows through ice and earth.

A remorhaz looks like a huge worm with dozens of insectoid legs, faceted eyes, and a wide mouth brimming with jagged teeth. The back of the head bristles with a pair of winglike fins. Remorhazes are whitish-blue in color but pulse with a reddish glow from the heat their bodies produce.

Although wild remorhazes prey on frost giants (as well as polar bears, elk, and deer), the giants occasionally train or entice these beasts to guard their lairs.

COMBAT

Remorhazes hide under the snow and ice until they hear movement above them, then attack from below and surprise prey.

Improved Grab (Ex): To use this ability, the remorhaz must hit with its bite attack. If it gets a hold, it automatically deals bite damage and can attempt to swallow the opponent.

Swallow Whole (Ex): A remorhaz can try to swallow a grabbed opponent of Large or smaller size by making a successful grapple check. Once inside, the opponent takes 2d8+12 points of crushing damage plus 10d10 points of fire damage per round from the creature's blazing gut. A swallowed creature can cut its way out by using claws or a Small or Tiny slashing weapon to deal 25 points of damage to the remorhaz's gut (AC 20). Once the creature exits, muscular action closes the hole; another swallowed opponent must cut its own way out. The remorhaz's interior can hold two Large, four Small, eight Tiny, sixteen Diminutive, or thirty-two Fine or smaller opponents.

Heat (Ex): An enraged remorhaz generates heat so intense that anything touching its body takes 10d10 points of fire damage. This is usually enough to melt nonmagical weapons, but magic weapons get a Fortitude save (DC 18).

Tremorsense (Ex): A remorhaz can automatically sense the location of anything within 60 feet that is in contact with the ground.

Skills: Remorhazes receive a +4 racial bonus to Listen checks.

ROC

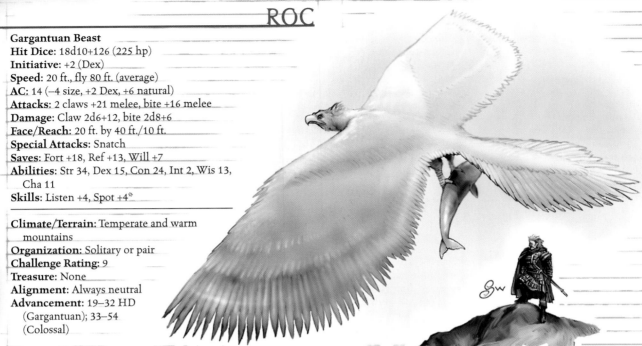

Gargantuan Beast
Hit Dice: 18d10+126 (225 hp)
Initiative: +2 (Dex)
Speed: 20 ft., fly 80 ft. (average)
AC: 14 (–4 size, +2 Dex, +6 natural)
Attacks: 2 claws +21 melee, bite +16 melee
Damage: Claw 2d6+12, bite 2d8+6
Face/Reach: 20 ft. by 40 ft./10 ft.
Special Attacks: Snatch
Saves: Fort +18, Ref +13, Will +7
Abilities: Str 34, Dex 15, Con 24, Int 2, Wis 13, Cha 11
Skills: Listen +4, Spot +4*

Climate/Terrain: Temperate and warm mountains
Organization: Solitary or pair
Challenge Rating: 9
Treasure: None
Alignment: Always neutral
Advancement: 19–32 HD (Gargantuan); 33–54 (Colossal)

Almost too big to be believed, rocs are huge birds of prey that dwell in warm mountainous regions and are known for carrying off large animals (cattle, horses, even elephants).

Rocs lair in vast nests made from trees, branches, lumber, and the like. They prefer to dwell high in the mountains, far from other rocs, to avoid straining their food supply; they hunt within a radius of about ten miles around their nests.

Rocs resemble large eagles, with plumage either dark brown or golden from head to tail. In a few rare instances, red, black, or white rocs are sighted, but they are often considered bad omens. These enormous creatures are 60 feet long from beak to tailfeathers, with wingspans as wide as 120 feet.

COMBAT

A roc attacks from the air, swooping earthward to snatch prey in its powerful talons and carry it off for itself and its young to devour. A solitary roc is typically hunting and will attack any Medium-size or larger creature that appears edible. A mated pair of rocs attack in concert, fighting to the death to defend their nests or hatchlings.

Snatch (Ex): A roc that hits a creature of at least Small size, but no larger than Huge, with a claw attack attempts to start a grapple as a free action without provoking an attack of opportunity. If the roc achieves a hold, it can fly off with its prey and automatically make a bite attack each round in lieu of a claw attack. It can drop a snatched creature as a free action or use a standard action to fling it aside.

A flung creature travels 90 feet and takes 9d6 points of damage. If the roc flings it while flying, the creature suffers this amount of damage or falling damage, whichever is greater.

Skills: *Rocs receive a +4 racial bonus to Spot checks during daylight hours.

ROPER

Large Magical Beast
Hit Dice: 10d10+30 (85 hp)
Initiative: +5 (+1 Dex, +4 Improved Initiative)
Speed: 10 ft.
AC: 24 (–1 size, +1 Dex, +14 natural)
Attacks: 6 strands +11 ranged, bite +8 melee
Damage: Strand (see text), bite 2d6+2
Face/Reach: 5 ft. by 5 ft./10 ft. (50 ft. with strand)
Special Attacks: Strands, attach, weakness
Special Qualities: Electricity immunity, cold resistance 30, fire vulnerability, SR 28
Saves: Fort +10, Ref +8, Will +8
Abilities: Str 19, Dex 13, Con 17, Int 12, Wis 16, Cha 12
Skills: Climb +7, Hide +10*, Listen +13, Spot +13
Feats: Alertness, Improved Initiative, Iron Will, Weapon Focus (strand)

Climate/Terrain: Any underground
Organization: Solitary, pair, or cluster (3–6)
Challenge Rating: 10
Treasure: No coins; 50% goods (stone only); no items
Alignment: Usually chaotic evil
Advancement: 11–15 HD (Large); 16–30 HD (Huge)

Ropers are hideous creatures that lurk in the deep caverns of the world. They are altogether evil and far more intelligent than most people would judge by their appearance.

A roper looks much like a naturally formed stalagmite. It stands some 9 feet tall and tapers from 3 or 4 feet in diameter at the base to 1 foot across at the top. The creature's great, gaping maw is lined with crystalline teeth capable of biting a Medium-size opponent in half. A roper's coloration and temperature change to match the surrounding cave.

COMBAT

A roper hunts by standing very still and imitating a bit of rock. This usually allows it to attack with surprise. When it notices prey, it lashes out with its strands and bites adjacent opponents with its powerful maw.

Strands (Ex): Most encounters with a roper begin when it fires its strong, sticky strands. The creature has six such members that can strike up to 50 feet away (no range increment).

Attach (Ex): If a roper hits with a strand attack, the strand latches onto the opponent's body. This deals no damage but draws the stuck opponent 10 feet closer each subsequent round (no attack of opportunity) unless that creature breaks free, which requires a successful Escape Artist check (DC 23) or Strength check (DC 19). The roper can draw in a creature within 10 feet of itself and bite with a +4 attack bonus, in that round.

A single attack with a slashing weapon that deals at least 10 points of damage severs a strand (AC 20).

Weakness (Ex): A roper's strands can sap an opponent's strength. Anyone caught by a strand must succeed at a Fortitude save (DC 18) or take 2d8 points of temporary Strength damage.

Fire Vulnerability (Ex): A roper takes double damage from fire attacks unless a save is allowed for half damage. A successful save halves the damage and a failure doubles it.

Skills: *Ropers receive a +8 racial bonus to Hide checks in stony or icy areas.

RUST MONSTER

Medium-Size Aberration
Hit Dice: 5d8+5 (27 hp)
Initiative: +3 (Dex)
Speed: 40 ft.
AC: 18 (+3 Dex, +5 natural)
Attacks: Antennae touch +3 melee, bite −2 melee
Damage: Antennae touch rust, bite 1d3
Face/Reach: 5 ft. by 5 ft./5 ft.
Special Attacks: Rust
Special Qualities: Scent
Saves: Fort +2, Ref +4, Will +5
Abilities: Str 10, Dex 17, Con 13, Int 2, Wis 13, Cha 8
Skills: Listen +9, Spot +9
Feats: Alertness

Climate/Terrain: Any underground
Organization: Solitary or pair
Challenge Rating: 3
Treasure: None
Alignment: Always neutral
Advancement: 6–8 HD (Medium-size); 9–15 HD (Large)

Most fighters would rather face an army of orcs than confront a rust monster. These creatures corrode and eat metal objects and have ruined the armor, shields, and weapons of countless adventurers.

The average rust monster measures 5 feet long and 3 feet high, weighing 200 pounds. Its squat body is protected by a thick, lumpy hide that varies in color from a yellowish tan underside to a rust-red upper back. Its tail is covered by armor plates and ends in a bony projection that looks like a double-ended paddle. The creature sports two prehensile antennae on its head, one beneath each eye, which rust metals on contact.

COMBAT

A rust monster can scent a metal object up to 90 feet away, dashing toward the source and attempting to strike it with its antennae. The creature is relentless, chasing adventurers over long distances if they still possess intact metal objects but usually ceasing its attacks to devour a freshly rusted meal. A clever (or desperate) adventurer can often distract a hungry rust monster by tossing it some metal objects, then fleeing while it consumes them.

The creature targets the largest metal object available, striking first at armor, then shields and smaller items. It prefers ferrous metals (steel or iron) over precious metals (such as gold or silver) but will devour the latter if given the opportunity.

Rust (Ex): A rust monster that makes a successful touch attack with its antennae causes the target metal to corrode, falling to pieces and becoming useless immediately. The size of the object is immaterial—a full suit of armor rusts away as quickly as a sword. Magic armor and weapons, and other enchanted items made of metal, must succeed at a Reflex save (DC 20) or be dissolved.

A metal weapon that deals damage to a rust monster also corrodes immediately. Wooden, stone, and other nonmetallic weapons are unaffected.

SAHUAGIN

Medium-Size Humanoid (Aquatic)
Hit Dice: 2d8+2 (11 hp)
Initiative: +1 (Dex)
Speed: 30 ft., swim 60 ft.
AC: 16 (+1 Dex, +5 natural)
Attacks: Trident +3 melee, 2 rakes +1 melee (or 2 rakes +3 melee, 2 claws +1 melee), bite +1 melee; or heavy crossbow +2 ranged
Damage: Trident 1d8+2, rake 1d4+2 (1d4+1 when a secondary attack), claw 1d2+1, bite 1d4+1; or heavy crossbow 1d10
Face/Reach: 5 ft. by 5 ft./5 ft.
Special Attacks: Blood frenzy
Special Qualities: Speak with sharks, underwater sense, light blindness, amphibious, freshwater sensitivity
Saves: Fort +4, Ref +1, Will +1
Abilities: Str 14, Dex 13, Con 12, Int 14, Wis 13, Cha 9
Skills: Animal Empathy +2, Hide +6*, Listen +7*, Profession (hunt) +2, Spot +7*, Wilderness Lore +1*
Feats: Multiattack

Climate/Terrain: Warm aquatic
Organization: Solitary, pair, team (5–8), patrol (11–20 plus 1 3rd-level lieutenant and 1–2 sharks), band (20–80 plus 100% noncombatants plus 1 3rd-level lieutenant and 1 4th-level chieftain per 20 adults plus 1–2 sharks), or tribe (70–160 plus 100% noncombatants plus 1 3rd-level lieutenant per 20 adults, 1 4th-level chieftain per 40 adults, 9 4th-level guards, 1–4 underpriestesses of 3rd–6th level, 1 7th-level priestess, and 1 baron of 6th–8th level plus 5–8 sharks)
Challenge Rating: 2
Treasure: Standard
Alignment: Always lawful evil
Advancement: By character class

Sahuagin are marine predators that are superbly adapted to undersea hunting. Also known as sea devils, these beings dwell in coastal waters, forming organized groups that raid shore communities.

Most sahuagin feature green coloration, darker along the back and lighter on the belly. Many have dark stripes, bands, or spots, but these tend to fade with age. Their great, staring eyes are deep black. They have scaly skin with webbed fingers and toes, and their mouths are filled with sharp fangs. An adult male sahuagin stands roughly 6 feet tall and weighs about 200 pounds.

Sahuagin are are the natural enemy of tritons. The two cannot coexist peacefully: Wars between them are prolonged, bloody affairs that sometimes interfere with shipping and maritime trade.

COMBAT

Sahuagin are savage fighters, asking for and giving no quarter. When swimming, a sahuagin rakes with its feet as it strikes with its claws or a weapon. About half of any group of sahuagin are also armed with nets.

When sahuagin raid surface dwellers' communities, they venture ashore on dark, moonless nights to slaughter the inhabitants and livestock for food. They attack ships by swarming up from all sides, leaving a portion of their forces in the water as reinforcements or to deal with opponents the raiders throw into the sea.

Blood Frenzy: Once per day a sahuagin that takes damage in combat can fly into a frenzy the following round, clawing and biting madly until either it or its opponent is dead. It gains +2 Constitution and +2 Strength, and suffers a –2 AC penalty. The sahuagin cannot end its frenzy voluntarily.

Speak with Sharks (Ex): Sahuagin can communicate telepathically with sharks up to 150 feet away. The communication is limited to fairly simple concepts such as "food," "danger," and "enemy." Sahuagin can use Animal Empathy to befriend and train sharks.

Underwater Sense (Ex): A sahuagin can locate creatures underwater within a 30-foot radius. This ability negates the effects of invisibility and poor visibility. It is less effective against creatures without central nervous systems, such as undead, oozes, and constructs; a sahuagin can locate such creatures only within a 15-foot radius. Sahuagin are not fooled by figments when underwater.

Light Blindness (Ex): Abrupt exposure to bright light (such as sunlight or a *daylight* spell) blinds sahuagin for 1 round. In addition to temporary blindness, they suffer a –1 morale penalty to all attack rolls, saves, and checks while operating in bright light.

Amphibious (Ex): Sahuagin can survive out of the water for 1 hour per 2 points of Constitution (after that, refer to the drowning rules on page 85 in the DUNGEON MASTER'S *Guide*).

Freshwater Sensitivity (Ex): A sahuagin fully immersed in freshwater must succeed at a Fortitude save (DC 15) or leave the water immediately. If the sahuagin fails and cannot escape, it suffers a –4 morale penalty to all attack rolls, saves, and checks. Even on a success, it must repeat the save attempt every 10 minutes it remains immersed.

Skills: Sahuagin receive a +4 racial bonus to Hide, Listen, and Spot checks. *Underwater, the bonus improves to +8. They receive a +8 bonus to Wilderness Lore and Profession (hunt) checks within fifty miles of their homes.

SAHUAGIN MUTANTS

About one in two hundred sahuagin has four arms. Such creatures can make four claw attacks or use extra weapons, in addition to the rake and bite attacks.

If a community of aquatic elves is located within a hundred miles of a sahuagin community, about one in one hundred sahuagin looks just like an aquatic elf. These creatures, called malenti, have a swim speed of 40 feet, can remain out of water for 1 hour per point of Constitution, and have freshwater and light

sensitivity (–1 to attack rolls). They are otherwise identical with sahuagin.

SAHUAGIN SOCIETY

The sea devils live by a code of ritualized behavior developed over millennia. Every member of a sahuagin community knows its place well—and remains there. The sahuagin pride themselves on self-sufficiency and strict adherence to their social code. Unfortunately for others, one of their core beliefs is that the survival of the sahuagin depends on ruthlessly eradicating anything that is not sahuagin.

Sahuagin dwell in communities of varying sizes, from villages to cities, built of stone and other natural materials deep beneath the ocean waves. The creatures employ a variety of defenses, both passive (such as seaweed camouflage) and active (such as traps and tame sharks), to protect their communities. Elite groups of senior males (especially the four-armed) rule each community: A baron governs a village, while a prince rules approximately twenty villages. Sahuagin kings rule much larger territories and dwell within cities having as many as six thousand inhabitants. A sahuagin kingdom generally covers an entire seacoast, with villages and towns at least 100 miles apart. Sahuagin clerics function as teachers and keepers of lore, controlling religious life in their communities. Despite the presence of these priestesses within their society, the superstitious sea devils distrust and fear magic.

The patron deity of sahuagin is Sekolah, a great devil shark

SAHUAGIN CHARACTERS

A male sahuagin's favored class is ranger, and most sahuagin leaders are rangers. Most sahuagin rangers choose humanoids (elves) as their favored enemy. Female sahuagin favor the cleric class. Sahuagin clerics worship Sekolah (favored weapon: trident) and can choose any two of the following domains: Evil, Law, Strength, and War.

Illus. by P. Jaquays

	Flamebrother	Average Salamander	Noble Salamander
	Small Outsider (Fire)	**Medium-Size Outsider (Fire)**	**Large Outsider (Fire)**
Hit Dice:	3d8+3 (16 hp)	7d8+7 (38 hp)	15d8+45 (112 hp)
Initiative:	+1 (Dex)	+1 (Dex)	+1 (Dex)
Speed:	20 ft.	20 ft.	20 ft.
AC:	19 (+1 size, +1 Dex, +7 natural)	18 (+1 Dex, +7 natural)	18 (−1 size, +1 Dex, +8 natural)
Attacks:	Halfspear +5 melee, tail slap +3 melee	Longspear +9/+4 melee, tail slap +7 melee	+3 *Huge longspear* +23/+18/+13 melee, tail slap +15 melee
Damage:	Halfspear 1d6+1 and 1d6 fire, tail slap 1d4 and 1d6 fire	Longspear 1d8+2 and 1d6 fire, tail slap 2d6+1 and 1d6 fire	+3 *Huge longspear* 2d8+9 and 1d8 fire, tail slap 2d8+3 and 1d8 fire
Face/Reach:	5 ft. by 5 ft./5 ft.	5 ft. by 5 ft./5 ft.	5 ft. by 5 ft./10 ft.
Special Attacks:	Heat, constrict 1d4 and 1d6 fire	Heat, constrict 2d6+1 and 1d6 fire	Heat, constrict 2d8+3 and 1d8 fire, spell-like abilities
Special Qualities:	Fire subtype	Fire subtype, damage reduction 10/+1	Fire subtype, damage reduction 20 /+2
Saves:	Fort +4, Ref +4, Will +5	Fort +6, Ref +6, Will +7	Fort +12, Ref +10, Will +11
Abilities:	Str 12, Dex 13, Con 12, Int 14, Wis 15, Cha 13	Str 14, Dex 13, Con 12, Int 14, Wis 15, Cha 13	Str 22, Dex 13, Con 16, Int 15, Wis 15, Cha 15
Skills:	Craft (metalworking) +11, Escape Artist +7, Hide +9, Listen +7, Search +7, Spot +7	Craft (metalworking) +16, Escape Artist +11, Hide +11, Listen +14, Move Silently +11, Search +12, Spot +14	Bluff +11, Craft (metalworking) +24, Diplomacy +13, Escape Artist +19, Hide +15, Listen +20, Move Silently +17, Search +20, Sense Motive +12, Spot +20
Feats:	Multiattack	Alertness, Multiattack	Cleave, Great Cleave, Multiattack, Power Attack
Climate/Terrain:	Any land and underground	Any land and underground	Any land and underground
Organization:	Solitary, pair, or cluster (3–5)	Solitary, pair, or cluster (3–5)	Solitary, pair, or noble party (9–14)
Challenge Rating:	2	5	9
Treasure:	Standard (nonflammables only)	Standard (nonflammables only)	Double standard (nonflammables only) and +3 *Huge longspear*
Alignment:	Usually evil (any)	Usually evil (any)	Usually evil (any)
Advancement:	4–6 HD (Small)	8–14 HD (Medium-size)	16–21 HD (Large); 22–45 HD (Huge)

The Elemental Plane of Fire is home to many strange creatures, including the fearsome legions of the salamanders. Serpentine beings, they dwell in metal cities glowing with supernatural heat.

Salamanders have muscular, red- and black-scaled arms and hawkish faces. They are selfish and cruel, and they enjoy tormenting others. They're rarely encountered without their heated metal spears, but sometimes wield other weapons.

When summoned to the Material Plane, salamanders often assist forge workers and smiths. Their ability to work metal while it's still in the fire makes them some of the best metalsmiths known anywhere.

Salamanders reproduce asexually, each producing a single larva every ten years and incubating the young in fire pits until they reach maturity. Flamebrothers and average salamanders are actually different species, while nobles rise from the ranks of the average.

Salamanders speak Ignan. Some average salamanders and all nobles also speak Common.

COMBAT

Salamanders use metal spears heated red-hot by their own furnacelike bodies. Bloodthirsty and sadistic, they are quick to attack. They prefer to take on those who appear strongest first, saving weaker enemies for slower, agonizing treatment later.

Heat (Ex): A salamander generates so much heat that its mere touch deals additional fire damage. Salamanders' metallic weapons also conduct this heat.

Constrict (Ex): A salamander deals automatic tail slap damage (including fire damage) with a successful grapple check against creatures up to one size larger than itself. A noble salamander can constrict multiple creatures simultaneously, provided they are all at least two sizes smaller than it.

Illus. by R. Sardinha

Spell-Like Abilities: (Noble salamanders only) 3/day—*burning hands, fireball, flaming sphere,* and *wall of fire;* 1/day—*dispel magic* and *summon monster VII* (huge fire elemental). These abilities are as the spells cast by a 15th-level sorcerer (save DC 12 + spell level).

Fire Subtype (Ex): Fire immunity, double damage from cold except on a successful save.

Skills: Salamanders receive a +4 racial bonus to Craft (metalworking) skill checks.

Feats: Salamanders have the Multiattack feat even without the requisite three natural weapons.

SALAMANDER SOCIETY

Flamebrothers, the smallest salamanders, are barbaric and tribal. Often more sophisticated salamanders force their civilization upon their smaller kin. Salamander nobility make a point of traveling through the planes, learning secrets to further their power. These experienced creatures eventually return to master their own kind and raise mighty kingdoms.

In a mixed society, status is determined by size and power—flamebrothers are the lowest class and the front ranks of salamander armies. Average salamanders are the middle class and the main fighting force, while noble salamanders are commanders.

Salamander nations do their best to resist the mighty elemental lords on their plane, and they disdain the azers, efreet, and other inhabitants. They often fail, though, and are enslaved by other fiery masters or conscripted into elemental armies.

SALAMANDER CHARACTERS

Flamebrothers have no favored class. They sometimes become adepts or warriors (see pages 37 and 39 in the DUNGEON MASTER'S *Guide* for more about these classes). Average or noble salamanders may be clerics, sorcerers, or fighters (their favored class).

SATYR

Medium-Size Fey
Hit Dice: 5d6+5 (22 hp)
Initiative: +1 (Dex)
Speed: 40 ft.
AC: 15 (+1 Dex, +4 natural)
Attacks: Gore +2 melee, dagger –3 melee; or shortbow +3 ranged
Damage: Gore 1d6, dagger 1d4; or shortbow 1d6
Face/Reach: 5 ft. by 5 ft./5 ft.
Special Attacks: Pipes
Saves: Fort +2, Ref +5, Will +5
Abilities: Str 10, Dex 13, Con 12, Int 12, Wis 13, Cha 13
Skills: Bluff +9, Hide +13, Listen +15, Move Silently +13, Perform (dance, pan pipes, plus any two others) +9, Spot +15
Feats: Alertness, Dodge, Mobility

Climate/Terrain: Temperate forest
Organization: Solitary, band (2–5), or troop (6–11)
Challenge Rating: 2 (without pipes) or 4 (with pipes)
Treasure: Standard
Alignment: Usually chaotic neutral
Advancement: 6–10 HD (Medium-size)

Satyrs, also known as fauns, are hedonistic creatures that frolic in the wild places of the world. They love fine food, strong drink, and passionate romance.

A satyr might best be described as a horned man with the legs of a goat. Its hair is red or chestnut brown, while its hooves and horns are jet black. Satyrs are far more likely to be found carrying musical instruments or bottles of wine than weapons.

For the most part, satyrs leave travelers alone. They are, however, more than a little mischievous and often seek fun at the expense of those who wander too near their woodland homes.

COMBAT

The keen senses of a satyr make it almost impossible to surprise one in the wild. Conversely, with their own natural grace and agility satyrs can sneak up on travelers who are not carefully watching the surrounding wilderness.

Once engaged in battle, an unarmed satyr attacks with a powerful head butt. A satyr expecting trouble is likely to be armed with a bow and a dagger and typically looses arrows from hiding, weakening an enemy before closing.

Pipes (Su): Satyrs can play a variety of magical tunes on their pan pipes. Usually, only one satyr in a group carries pipes. When it plays, all creatures within a 60-foot spread (except satyrs) must succeed at a Will save (DC 14) or be affected by *charm person, sleep,* or *fear,* as the spells cast by a 10th-level sorcerer (the satyr chooses the tune and its effect). In the hands of other beings, these pipes have no special powers. A creature that successfully saves against any of the pipe's effects cannot be affected by the same set of pipes again for one day.

A satyr often uses its pipes to charm and seduce especially comely women or to put a party of adventurers to sleep and then steal their valuables.

Skills: Satyrs receive a +4 racial bonus to Hide, Listen, Move Silently, Perform, and Spot checks.

SEA LION

Large Beast
Hit Dice: 6d10+18 (51 hp)
Initiative: +1 (Dex)
Speed: Swim 40 ft.
AC: 18 (–1 size, +1 Dex, +8 natural)
Attacks: 2 claws +7 melee, bite +2 melee
Damage: Claw 1d6+4, bite 1d8+2
Face/Reach: 5 ft. by 10 ft./5 ft.

Special Attacks: Rend 2d6+6
Special Qualities: Scent
Saves: Fort +8, Ref +6, Will +3
Abilities: Str 19, Dex 12, Con 17, Int 4, Wis 13, Cha 10
Skills: Listen +7, Spot +7

Climate/Terrain: Temperate and warm aquatic
Organization: Solitary, pair, or pride (5–12)
Challenge Rating: 4
Treasure: None
Alignment: Always neutral
Advancement: 7–9 HD (Large); 10–18 HD (Huge)

A sea lion is a fearsome aquatic creature with the head and fore-paws of a lion and the body and tail of a fish.

These predators inhabit shallow coastal waters, making their lairs in undersea caves or in the wreckage of ships. They hunt for fish, aquatic mammals, sea birds, and anything else they can catch and kill.

Sea lions are aggressively territorial, attacking any creature, regardless of size, that enters their domain. Their chief enemies and competitors are sharks, and sea lions go out of their way to attack them. Sometimes they form temporary prides to deal with particularly dangerous or resistant intruders. Their normal pride structure is much like that of terrestrial lions.

A typical sea lion is 12 feet long and weighs 800 pounds.

COMBAT

Sea lions attack on sight, either for food or to defend their territory, and use both claws and teeth to grab and rend their prey. They display tremendous courage, always fighting to the death, even against creatures many times their size. Pairs and prides of sea lions attack in concert, trying to wear the opponent down until one beast can dispatch it.

Rend (Ex): A sea lion that hits with both claw attacks latches onto the opponent's body and tears the flesh. This automatically deals an additional 2d6+6 points of damage.

SHADOW

Medium-Size Undead (Incorporeal)
Hit Dice: 3d12 (19 hp)
Initiative: +2 (Dex)
Speed: 30 ft., fly 40 ft. (good)
AC: 13 (+2 Dex, +1 deflection)
Attacks: Incorporeal touch +3 melee
Damage: Incorporeal touch 1d6 temporary Strength
Face/Reach: 5 ft. by 5 ft./5 ft.
Special Attacks: Strength damage, create spawn
Special Qualities: Undead, incorporeal, +2 turn resistance
Saves: Fort +1, Ref +3, Will +4
Abilities: Str —, Dex 14, Con —, Int 6, Wis 12, Cha 13
Skills: Hide +8, Intuit Direction +5, Listen +7, Spot +7
Feat: Dodge

Climate/Terrain: Any land and underground
Organization: Solitary, gang (2–5), or swarm (6–11)
Challenge Rating: 3
Treasure: None
Alignment: Always chaotic evil
Advancement: 4–9 HD (Medium-size)

Shadows are creatures of living darkness, hating life and light with equal fervor. Their touch bestows the painful chill of nonexistence, making them very dangerous opponents.

Shadows, as one might expect, look like shadows. They are more or less humanoid in shape, difficult to see in dark or gloomy areas but standing out starkly in brightly illuminated places.

Natural enemies of all that live, shadows are aggressive and predatory. They are quick to strike and make short work of those unprepared to deal with them.

COMBAT

Shadows lurk in dark places, waiting for living prey to happen by.

Strength Damage (Su): The touch of a shadow deals 1d6 points of temporary Strength damage to a living foe. A creature reduced to Strength 0 by a shadow dies.

Create Spawn (Su): Any humanoid reduced to Strength 0 by a shadow becomes a shadow under the control of its killer within 1d4 rounds.

Undead: Immune to mind-influencing effects, poison, sleep, paralysis, stunning, and disease. Not subject to critical hits, subdual damage, ability damage, energy drain, or death from massive damage.

Incorporeal: Can be harmed only by other incorporeal creatures, +1 or better magic weapons, or magic, with a 50% chance to ignore any damage from a corporeal source. Can pass through solid objects at will, and own attacks pass through armor. Always moves silently.

SHADOW MASTIFF

Medium-Size Outsider (Evil)
Hit Dice: 4d8+12 (30 hp)
Initiative: +5 (+1 Dex, +4 Improved Initiative)
Speed: 50 ft.
AC: 14 (+1 Dex, +3 natural)
Attacks: Bite +7 melee
Damage: Bite 1d6+4

Face/Reach: 5 ft. by 5 ft./5 ft.
Special Attacks: Bay, trip
Special Qualities: Shadow blend, scent
Saves: Fort +7, Ref +5, Will +5
Abilities: Str 17, Dex 13, Con 17, Int 4, Wis 12, Cha 13
Skills: Listen +8, Spot +8, Wilderness Lore +7*
Feats: Dodge, Improved Initiative

Climate/Terrain: Any land and underground
Organization: Solitary, pair, or pack (5–12)
Challenge Rating: 5
Treasure: None
Alignment: Always neutral evil
Advancement: 5–6 HD (Medium-size); 7–12 HD (Large)

Shadow mastiffs are great, black hounds that prowl the night, seeking any prey they can find. Their native plane is a place of shadow.

A shadow mastiff is as large as a St. Bernard, with a smooth coat and a sleek body.

COMBAT

Shadow mastiffs prefer fighting in shadows or dark conditions, which gives them a great advantage. A magical light source banishes the shadows they love, but shadow mastiffs are cunning enough to either move out of the light or back off and break up the opposition with their baying. They have been known to seize and carry off items enchanted with *daylight* spells.

Bay (Su): When a shadow mastiff howls or barks, all creatures except evil outsiders within a 300-foot spread must succeed at a Will save (DC 13) or become panicked for 2d4 rounds. This is a sonic, mind-affecting fear effect. Whether or not the save is successful, an affected creature is immune to that mastiff's bay for one day.

Trip (Ex): A shadow mastiff that hits with its bite attack can attempt to trip the opponent as a free action (see page 139 in the *Player's Handbook*) without making a touch attack or provoking an attack of opportunity. If the attempt fails, the opponent cannot react to trip the shadow mastiff.

Shadow Blend (Su): During any conditions other than full daylight, a shadow mastiff can disappear into the shadows, giving it nine-tenths concealment. Artificial illumination, even a *light* or *continual flame* spell, does not negate this ability. A *daylight* spell, however, will.

Skills: A shadow mastiff receives a +4 racial bonus to Wilderness Lore checks when tracking by scent.

SHAMBLING MOUND

Large Plant
Hit Dice: 8d8+24 (60 hp)
Initiative: +0
Speed: 20 ft.
AC: 20 (−1 size, +11 natural)
Attacks: 2 slams +10 melee
Damage: Slam 2d6+5
Face/Reach: 5 ft by 5 ft./10 ft.
Special Attacks: Improved grab, constrict 2d6+7
Special Qualities: Plant, electricity immunity, fire resistance 30
Saves: Fort +9, Ref +2, Will +2
Abilities: Str 21, Dex 10, Con 17, Int 7, Wis 10, Cha 9
Skills: Hide +0*, Listen +4, Move Silently +4

Climate/Terrain: Temperate and warm forest, marsh, and underground
Organization: Solitary
Challenge Rating: 6
Treasure: 1/10th coins; 50% goods; 50% items
Alignment: Always neutral
Advancement: 9–12 HD (Large); 13–24 HD (Huge)

Shambling mounds, or shamblers, appear to be heaps of rotting vegetation. They are actually intelligent plants, with a roughly humanoid shape and a brainlike control center in the "chest."

The carnivorous shambler is almost totally silent and invisible in its natural surroundings, often catching opponents flat-footed. It may lie partially submerged in a shallow bog, waiting patiently for some creature to walk onto it. Shamblers move easily through water as well, and they have been known to sneak into the camps of unsuspecting travelers at night.

Adventurers tell stories of shamblers moving about during intense electrical storms without so much as flinching from direct lightning strikes.

A shambler's lower half has an 8-foot girth, tapering to about 2 feet at its "head."

Illus. by S. Wood

COMBAT

A shambling mound batters or constricts its opponents with two huge, armlike appendages.

Improved Grab (Ex): To use this ability, the shambler must hit an opponent of up to Large size with both arm attacks. If it gets a hold, it can constrict.

Constrict (Ex): A shambler deals 2d6+7 points of damage with a successful grapple check against Large or smaller creatures. The shambler can still move but cannot take any attack actions when constricting.

Plant: Immune to mind-influencing effects, poison, sleep, paralysis, stunning, and polymorphing. Not subject to critical hits.

Electricity Immunity (Ex): Shamblers take no damage from electricity. Instead, any electrical attack (such as *shocking grasp* or *lightning bolt*) used against a shambler grants it 1d4 points of temporary Constitution. The shambler loses these points at the rate of 1 per hour.

Skills: Shamblers receive a +4 racial bonus to Hide, Listen, and Move Silently checks. *They receive a +12 bonus to Hide checks when in a swampy or forested area.

SHIELD GUARDIAN

Large Construct
Hit Dice: 15d10 (82 hp)
Initiative: +0
Speed: 30 ft.
AC: 24 (–1 size, +15 natural)
Attacks: Slam +16/+11/+6 melee
Damage: Slam 1d8+9
Face/Reach: 5 ft. by 5 ft./10 ft.
Special Attacks: Spell storing
Special Qualities: Construct, fast healing 5, shield other, guard, find master
Saves: Fort +5, Ref +5, Will +5
Abilities: Str 22, Dex 10, Con —, Int —, Wis 10, Cha 1

Climate/Terrain: Any land and underground
Organization: Solitary
Challenge Rating: 8
Treasure: None
Alignment: Always neutral
Advancement: 16–24 HD (Large); 25–45 HD (Huge)

Created by spellcasters to be bodyguards, shield guardians are constructs that protect their masters with spells and stamina.

A shield guardian is an imposing humanoid figure of metal, wood, and stone that, when fashioned, is keyed to a particular amulet. Henceforth, it regards the wearer of that amulet to be its master, protecting and following that person everywhere (unless specifically commanded not to do so).

A shield guardian obeys its master's verbal commands to the best of its ability, although it is not good for much beyond combat and possibly simple manual labor. It can also be keyed to perform specific tasks at specific times or when certain conditions are met. The wearer of the amulet can call the shield guardian from any distance, and it will come as long as it is on the same plane.

COMBAT

Shield guardians are straightforward in battle, bashing with their heavy stone fists. They are made for defense and are not particularly impressive on offense.

Spell Storing (Sp): The shield guardian can store one spell of 4th level or lower that is cast into it by another creature. It "casts" this spell when commanded or when a predetermined situation arises. Once this is used, it can store another spell (or the same spell).

Construct: Immune to mind-influencing effects, poison, disease, and similar effects. Not subject to critical hits, subdual damage, ability damage, energy drain, or death from massive damage.

Shield Other (Sp): The wearer of the keyed amulet can activate this defensive ability if within 100 feet of the shield guardian. Just as the spell of the same name, this transfers to the guardian half the damage that would be dealt to the amulet wearer (this ability does not provide the spell's AC or save bonuses, but see below).

Guard (Ex): The shield guardian moves swiftly to defend the amulet wearer by its side, blocking blows and disrupting foes. All attacks against the amulet wearer suffer a –2 deflection penalty.

Find Master (Su): No matter the distance, as long as they are on the same plane, the shield guardian can find the amulet wearer (or just the amulet, if it is removed after the guardian is called).

CONSTRUCTION

A shield guardian costs 100,000 gp to create. This cost includes the construct's physical body, the keyed amulet, and all the materials and spell components that are consumed or become a permanent part of them. This cost includes 1,000 gp for the body and 500 gp for the amulet.

The first task is creating the body, a humanoid figure of wood, bronze, stone, and steel. The construct's master can assemble the body or can hire someone else to do the job. Creating the body requires a successful Profession (engineering) or Craft (sculpture) check (DC 16).

The second requirement is creating the keyed amulet from bronze, which requires a successful Craft (metalworking) check (DC 12).

After the body and amulet are fashioned, the creature must be animated through an extended magical ritual that requires a week to complete. Understanding the ritual requires a 12th-level character with the Craft Wondrous Item feat. The creator must labor for at least 8 hours each day in a specially prepared laboratory or workroom. The chamber is similar to both an alchemist's laboratory and a smithy and costs 1,000 gp to establish.

When not working on the ritual, the character must rest and can perform no other activities except eating, sleeping, or talking. If personally constructing the creature's body, the creator can perform the building and ritual together. If the creator misses a day of the ritual, the process fails and must be started again. Money spent is lost, but XP spent are not. The shield guardian's body can be reused, as can the chamber.

Completing the ritual drains 2,000 XP from the creator and requires *limited wish*, *locate object*, *make whole*, *shield*, and *shield other*, which must be cast on the final day of the ritual. The creator must cast the spells personally, but they can come from outside sources, such as scrolls.

AMULET

If the keyed amulet is destroyed, the guardian ceases to function until a new one is created. If the wearer dies but the amulet is intact, the shield guardian carries out the last command given.

SHOCKER LIZARD

Small Magical Beast
Hit Dice: 2d10+2 (13 hp)
Initiative: +2 (Dex)
Speed: 40 ft., climb 20 ft., swim 20 ft.
AC: 16 (+1 size, +2 Dex, +3 natural)
Attacks: Bite +3 melee
Damage: Bite 1d4
Face/Reach: 5 ft. by 5 ft./5 ft.
Special Attacks: Stunning shock, lethal shock
Special Qualities: Electricity sense, electricity immunity
Saves: Fort +3, Ref +5, Will +1
Abilities: Str 10, Dex 15, Con 13, Int 5, Wis 12, Cha 6
Skills: Climb +12, Hide +11, Jump +4, Listen +4, Spot +4
Feats: Alertness

Climate/Terrain: Warm aquatic, marsh, and underground
Organization: Solitary, pair, clutch (3–5), or colony (6–11)
Challenge Rating: 2
Treasure: 1/10 coins; 50% goods; 50% items
Alignment: Usually neutral
Advancement: 3–4 HD (Medium-size); 5–6 HD (Large)

The shocker lizard is a sleek reptile whose body can generate intense electrical shocks.

A shocker lizard has a bullet-shaped head sporting a large pair of horns that sweep back from the sides like spiky ears. A similar structure appears on the tip of the tail. The creature has a pale gray or blue underside, shading to a darker hue on its back. It has blue-black markings along its back and tail.

Shocker lizards prefer warm and damp conditions, and often lurk in swamps, shaded riverbanks, and water-filled caves. They hunt fish, reptiles, and small animals, but also scavenge or take larger prey from time to time. They spend most of their time hiding and waiting for prey to happen by.

COMBAT

Unless it is very hungry, a shocker lizard dislikes fighting creatures larger than itself and usually tries to warn off intruders by emitting a series of rapid clicks. The sound is actually a low-power electrical discharge, and living creatures within 10 feet can feel the current tickling their skins and scalps. If the warning fails, the lizard raises its horns and tail to administer stunning shocks.

A shocker lizard relies on its electrical abilities in combat. A lizard tends to bite only after its shock has rendered an opponent unconscious or when the shock seems to have no effect at all. Lone lizards flee once they deliver their shocks, but if others are nearby, they all home in on their comrade's discharges and administer deadly shocks to the foe.

Stunning Shock (Su): Once per round, a shocker lizard can deliver an electrical shock to a single opponent within 5 feet. This attack deals 2d8 points of subdual damage to living opponents (Reflex half DC 12).

Lethal Shock (Su): Whenever two or more shocker lizards are within 25 feet of each other, they can work together to create a lethal shock. This effect has a radius of 25 feet, centered on any one contributing lizard. The shock deals 2d8 points of damage for each lizard contributing to it (Reflex half DC 10 + number of lizards contributing).

Electricity Sense (Ex): Shocker lizards automatically detect any electrical discharges within 100 feet.

Skills: Shocker lizards receive a +4 racial bonus to Hide checks due to their coloration.

	Tiny Skeleton **Tiny Undead**	**Small Skeleton** **Small Undead**	**Medium-Size Skeleton** **Medium-Size Undead**
Hit Dice:	1/4 d12 (1 hp)	1/2 d12 (3 hp)	1d12 (6 hp)
Initiative:	+5 (+1 Dex, +4 Improved Initiative)	+5 (+1 Dex, +4 Improved Initiative)	+5 (+1 Dex, +4 Improved Initiative)
Speed:	30 ft.	30 ft.	30 ft.
AC:	13 (+2 size, +1 Dex)	13 (+1 size, +1 Dex, +1 natural)	13 (+ 1 Dex, +2 natural)
Attacks:	2 claws +0 melee	2 claws +0 melee	2 claws +0 melee
Damage:	Claw 1d2–2	Claw 1d3–1	Claw 1d4
Face/Reach:	2 1/2 ft. by 2 1/2 ft./0 ft.	5 ft. by 5 ft./5 ft.	5 ft. by 5 ft./5 ft.
Special Qualities:	Undead, immunities	Undead, immunities	Undead, immunities
Saves:	Fort +0, Ref +1, Will +2	Fort +0, Ref +1, Will +2	Fort +0, Ref +1, Will +2
Abilities:	Str 6, Dex 12, Con —, Int —, Wis 10, Cha 11	Str 8, Dex 12, Con —, Int —, Wis 10, Cha 11	Str 10, Dex 12, Con —, Int —, Wis 10, Cha 11
Feats:	Improved Initiative	Improved Initiative	Improved Initiative

	Large Skeleton **Large Undead**	**Huge Skeleton** **Huge Undead**
Hit Dice:	2d12 (13 hp)	4d12 (26 hp)
Initiative:	+5 (+1 Dex, +4 Improved Initiative)	+5 (+1 Dex, +4 Improved Initiative)
Speed:	40 ft.	40 ft.
AC:	13 (–1 size, +1 Dex, +3 natural)	13 (–2 size, +1 Dex, +4 natural)
Attacks:	2 claws +2 melee	2 claws +4 melee
Damage:	Claw 1d6+2	Claw 1d8+4
Face/Reach:	5 ft. by 5 ft./10 ft.	10 ft. by 10 ft./15 ft.
Special Qualities:	Undead, immunities	Undead, immunities
Saves:	Fort +0, Ref +1, Will +3	Fort +1, Ref +2, Will +4
Abilities:	Str 14, Dex 12, Con —, Int —, Wis 10, Cha 11	Str 18, Dex 12, Con —, Int —, Wis 10, Cha 11
Feats:	Improved Initiative	Improved Initiative

	Gargantuan Skeleton **Gargantuan Undead**	**Colossal Skeleton** **Colossal Undead**
Hit Dice:	16d12 (104 hp)	32d12 (208 hp)
Initiative:	+5 (+1 Dex, +4 Improved Initiative)	+5 (+1 Dex, +4 Improved Initiative)
Speed:	40 ft.	40 ft.
AC:	13 (–4 size, +1 Dex, +6 natural)	13 (–8 size, +1 Dex, +10 natural)
Attacks:	2 claws +10 melee	2 claws +16 melee
Damage:	Claw 2d6+6	Claw 2d8+8
Face/Reach:	20 ft. by 20 ft./20 ft.	40 ft. by 40 ft./25 ft.
Special Qualities:	Undead, immunities	Undead, immunities
Saves:	Fort +5, Ref +6, Will +10	Fort +10, Ref +11, Will +18
Abilities:	Str 22, Dex 12, Con —, Int —, Wis 10, Cha 11	Str 26, Dex 12, Con —, Int —, Wis 10, Cha 11
Feats:	Improved Initiative	Improved Initiative

Climate/Terrain:	Any land and underground
Organization:	Any
Challenge Rating:	Tiny 1/6; Small 1/4; Medium-size 1/3; Large 1; Huge 2; Gargantuan 7; Colossal 9
Treasure:	None
Alignment:	Always neutral
Advancement:	Tiny, Small, and Medium-size —; Large 3 HD (Large); Huge 5–15 HD (Huge); Gargantuan 17–31 HD (Gargantuan); Colossal 33–64 HD (Colossal)

Illus. by B. Snoddy

Skeletons are the animated bones of the dead, mindless automatons that obey the orders of their evil masters.

These undead creatures are seldom garbed with anything more than the rotting remnants of any armor they were wearing when slain. Pinpoints of red light smolder in their empty eye sockets.

Skeletons do only what they are ordered to do. They can draw no conclusions of their own and take no initiative. Because of this limitation, their instructions must always be simple, such as "Kill anyone who enters this chamber."

The statistics block describes skeletons with humanlike forms. Skeletons with different forms may have different statistics.

COMBAT

Skeletons attack until destroyed, for that is what they were created to do. The threat posed by a group of skeletons depends primarily on its size.

Undead: Immune to mind-influencing effects, poison, sleep, paralysis, stunning, and disease. Not subject to critical hits, subdual damage, ability damage, energy drain, or death from massive damage.

Immunities (Ex): Skeletons have cold immunity. Because they lack flesh or internal organs, they take only half damage from piercing or slashing weapons.

SKUM

Medium-Size Aberration (Aquatic)

Hit Dice: 2d8+2 (11 hp)
Initiative: +1 (Dex)
Speed: 20 ft., swim 40 ft.
AC: 13 (+1 Dex, +2 natural)
Attacks: Bite +5 melee, 2 claws +0 melee, 2 rakes +0 melee
Damage: Bite 2d6+4, claw 1d4+2, rake 1d6+2
Face/Reach: 5 ft. by 5 ft./5 ft.
Special Qualities: Low-light vision
Saves: Fort +1, Ref +1, Will +3
Abilities: Str 19, Dex 13, Con 13, Int 10, Wis 10, Cha 6
Skills: Climb +9, Hide +6*, Listen +7*, Move Silently +3, Spot +7*
Feats: Alertness

Climate/Terrain: Temperate and warm aquatic and underground
Organization: Brood (2–5) or pack (6–15)
Challenge Rating: 2
Treasure: None
Alignment: Always lawful evil
Advancement: 3–4 HD (Medium-size); 5–6 HD (Large)

Skum are misbegotten creatures created by aboleths to serve as beasts of burden and slaves. They are derived from human stock, making them even more loathsome.

Skum look exactly like what they are: an abominable cross-breed of human and fish. Their fins have grown into twisted arms and legs; their bent backs are crowned with a long, spiny frill. A slender, muscular tail makes them powerful swimmers, while bulbous eyes give them good vision both in and out of the water.

Skum can breathe both air and water. They speak Aquan.

COMBAT

In the water, skum are dangerous enemies who attack by biting, clawing, and raking with their rear legs. On land they are less dangerous, for they cannot rake and suffer a –2 circumstance penalty to all attack rolls. Skum serving an aboleth are sometimes trained to fight with weapons, usually two-handed melee weapons with reach (such as longspears) and simple ranged weapons such as javelins, tridents, or slings.

Skills: *Skum receive a +4 racial bonus to Hide, Listen, and Spot checks underwater.

SLAAD

	Red Slaad	Blue Slaad	Green Slaad
	Large Outsider (Chaotic)	**Large Outsider (Chaotic)**	**Large Outsider (Chaotic)**
Hit Dice:	7d8+21 (52 hp)	8d8+24 (60 hp)	9d8+27 (67 hp)
Initiative:	+1 (Dex)	+2 (Dex)	+1 (Dex)
Speed:	30 ft.	30 ft.	30 ft.
AC:	16 (–1 size, +1 Dex, +6 natural)	18 (–1 size, +2 Dex, +7 natural)	20 (–1 size, +1 Dex, +10 natural)
Attacks:	Bite +10 melee, 2 claws +8 melee	4 rakes +11 melee, bite +9 melee	2 claws +12 melee, bite +10 melee
Damage:	Bite 2d8+4, claw 1d4+2 and implant	Rake 2d6+4, bite 2d8+2 and disease	Claw 1d6+4, bite 2d8+2
Face/Reach:	5 ft. by 5 ft./10 ft.	5 ft. by 5 ft./10 ft.	5 ft. by 5 ft./10 ft.
Special Attacks:	Pounce, implant, stunning croak, summon slaad	Spell-like abilities, disease, summon slaad	Spell-like abilities, summon slaad
Special Qualities:	Fast healing 5, resistances	Fast healing 5, resistances	Fast healing 5, resistances
Saves:	Fort +8, Ref +6, Will +3	Fort +9, Ref +8, Will +4	Fort +9, Ref +7, Will +6
Abilities:	Str 19, Dex 13, Con 17, Int 6, Wis 6, Cha 8	Str 19, Dex 15, Con 17, Int 6, Wis 6, Cha 10	Str 19, Dex 13, Con 17, Int 10, Wis 10, Cha 10
Skills:	Climb +14, Jump +14, Listen +6, Move Silently +5, Spot +8	Climb +14, Jump +15, Listen +8, Move Silently +9, Spot +8	Climb +16, Hide +9, Jump +16, Listen +12, Move Silently +13, Spot +12
Feats:	Dodge, Multiattack	Dodge, Mobility, Multiattack	Cleave, Multiattack, Power Attack
Climate/Terrain:	Any land and underground	Any land and underground	Any land and underground
Organization:	Solitary, gang (2–5), or pack (6–10)	Solitary, gang (2–5), or pack (6–10)	Solitary or gang (2–5)
Challenge Rating:	7	8	9
Treasure:	None	Standard	Standard
Alignment:	Always chaotic neutral	Always chaotic neutral	Always chaotic neutral
Advancement:	8–10 HD (Large); 11–21 HD (Huge)	9–12 HD (Large); 13–24 HD (Huge)	10–15 HD (Large); 16–27 HD (Huge)

	Gray Slaad	Death Slaad
	Medium-Size Outsider (Chaotic)	Medium-Size Outsider (Chaotic)
Hit Dice:	10d8+30 (75 hp)	15d8+45 (112 hp)
Initiative:	+1 (Dex)	+8 (+4 Dex, +4 Improved Initiative)
Speed:	30 ft.	30 ft.
AC:	22 (+1 Dex, +11 natural)	26 (+4 Dex, +12 natural)
Attacks:	2 claws +14 melee, bite +12 melee	2 claws +20 melee, bite +18 melee
Damage:	Claw 2d4+4, bite 2d8+2	Claw 3d6+5 and stun, bite 2d10+2
Face/Reach:	5 ft. by 5 ft./5 ft.	5 ft. by 5 ft./5 ft.
Special Attacks:	Spell-like abilities, summon slaad	Stun, spell-like abilities, summon slaad
Special Qualities:	Fast healing 5, damage reduction 10/+1, resistances, alternate form	Fast healing 5, damage reduction 20/+2, resistances, telepathy, alternate form
Saves:	Fort +10, Ref +8, Will +9	Fort +12, Ref +13, Will +13
Abilities:	Str 19, Dex 13, Con 17, Int 14, Wis 14, Cha 14	Str 20, Dex 18, Con 17, Int 18, Wis 18, Cha 18
Skills:	Climb +15, Hide +14, Jump +17, Knowledge (arcana) +13, Listen +15, Move Silently +14, Search +15, Spot +15	Climb +23, Escape Artist +22, Hide +22, Jump +23, Knowledge (any two) +22, Listen +22, Move Silently +22, Search +22, Spot +22
Feats:	Multiattack, item creation feats (any two)	Cleave, Improved Initiative, Multiattack, Power Attack

Climate/Terrain:	Any land and underground	Any land and underground
Organization:	Solitary or pair	Solitary or pair
Challenge Rating:	10	13
Treasure:	Double standard	Double standard
Alignment:	Always chaotic neutral	Usually chaotic neutral (sometimes chaotic evil)
Advancement:	11–15 HD (Medium-size); 16–30 HD (Large)	16–22 HD (Medium-size); 23–45 HD (Large)

The chaotic planes seethe and roil with random energy and bits of matter, and weaving their way amid the cacophony of light and sound are the slaadi.

Creatures of chaos, slaadi have been likened to humanoid toads, but that description belies their agility and fearsome fighting prowess.

All slaadi speak their own language, Slaad. Green, gray, and death slaadi also speak Common, and in addition death slaadi can communicate telepathically.

COMBAT

Slaadi generally attack with their claws and bite. They relish melee combat but are savvy enough to use their summoning and other spell-like abilities to good effect.

Resistances (Ex): All slaadi have acid, cold, electricity, fire, and sonic resistance 5.

Summon Slaad (Sp): Slaadi can summon other slaadi much as though casting a *summon monster* spell, but they have only a limited chance of success. Roll d%: On a failure, no slaadi answer the summons. Summoned creatures automatically return whence they came after 1 hour. A slaad that has just been summoned cannot use its own summon ability for 1 hour.

Most slaadi do not use this ability lightly, since they are generally distrustful and fearful of one another. In general, they use it only when necessary to save their own lives.

SLAADI CHARACTERS

Slaadi rarely have the focus to devote themselves to a character class. Grays sometimes become sorcerers, and the most powerful death slaadi take on evil aspects and train as rogues to take the assassin class (see page 29 in the DUNGEON MASTER's Guide).

RED SLAAD

Weakest of the slaadi, the reds wander about individually, often establishing secret lairs on other planes. Most seek to escape from the other more powerful and sometimes cruel slaadi.

Red slaadi are found in groups only when working for some greater power that somehow has mastered them. Even then, they don't coordinate actions well.

Combat

Red slaadi usually attack only when hungry or riled. Once aroused, however, a red slaad fights to the death.

Pounce (Ex): If a red slaad leaps upon a foe during the first round of combat, it can make a full attack even if it has already taken a move action.

Implant (Ex): A red slaad that hits with a claw attack can inject an egg pellet into the opponent's body. The affected creature must succeed at a Fortitude save (DC 17) to avoid implantation. Often the slaad implants an unconscious or otherwise helpless creature (which gets no saving throw). The egg gestates for one week before hatching into a blue slaad that eats its way out, killing the host. Twenty-four hours before the egg fully matures, the victim falls extremely ill (–10 to all ability scores). A *remove disease* spell rids a victim of the pellet, as does a successful Heal check (DC 20) by someone with that skill. If the check fails, the healer can try again, but each attempt (successful or not) deals 1d4 points of damage to the patient.

If the host is an arcane spellcaster, the egg pellet instead hatches into a green slaad.

Stunning Croak (Su): Once per day a red slaad can emit a loud croak. Every creature within 20 feet must succeed at a Fortitude save (DC 16) or be stunned for 1d3 rounds.

Summon Slaad (Sp): Once per day a red slaad can attempt to summon another red slaad with a 40% chance of success.

BLUE SLAAD

Blue slaadi gather to wage horrific battles against other societies and their own. They are bullies that value only strength and power.

These slaadi are most often found in groups and work well together—at least, better than red slaadi.

Combat

Blue slaadi are quick to anger and attack most other creatures on sight to prove their strength. In addition to its claws, a blue slaad has bone hooks on the back of its hands, giving it four rake attacks each round.

Spell-Like Abilities: At will—*hold person*, *passwall*, and *telekinesis*. These abilities are as the spells cast by a 10th-level sorcerer (save DC 10 + spell level).

Once per day three blue slaadi working together can produce *chaos hammer* (save DC 16) as the spell cast by a 15th-level sorcerer.

Disease (Ex): The bite of a blue slaad can cause a terrible transformation. Affected creatures must succeed at a Fortitude save (DC 17) or be infected with a disease that transforms the victim over the next week into a red slaad. The infected creature can attempt a new save each day to throw off the infection.

If the infected being is an arcane spellcaster, the disease instead produces a green slaad.

Summon Slaad (Sp): Once per day a blue slaad can attempt to summon another blue slaad with a 40% chance of success.

GREEN SLAAD

If a red slaad's egg pellet or a blue slaad's disease enters an arcane spellcaster, that host instead produces a green slaad.

Greens are self-centered, arrogant louts that think only of themselves. They lust after magical power, eventually transforming into grays (see below) if they find it.

Green slaadi work in groups if doing so suits their immediate needs.

Combat

Green slaadi prefer to use spell-like abilities over physical combat but aren't afraid to attack with tooth and claw if they must. They never fight to the death, though, if they can avoid it.

Spell-Like Abilities: At will—*chaos hammer, deeper darkness, detect magic, detect thoughts, dispel law, fear, protection from law, see invisibility,* and *shatter.* These abilities are as the spells cast by a 12th-level sorcerer (save DC 10 + spell level).

Alternate Form (Su): A green slaad can shift between its natural form and any humanoid form at will as a standard action. A green slaad whose personal treasure includes useful equipment or magic items will employ these when in humanoid form.

A green slaad remains in humanoid form indefinitely. The ability is otherwise similar to *polymorph self* cast by a 9th-level sorcerer.

Summon Slaad (Sp): Twice per day a green slaad can attempt to summon another green slaad with a 40% chance of success.

GRAY SLAAD

A green slaad that survives for more than a century retreats into isolation for at least a year. It returns as a smaller, leaner gray slaad and devotes most of its time and attention to magical study. Gray slaadi enjoy crafting magic items to further their own power.

Combat

Gray slaadi prefer to fight from a distance, using their spell-like abilities, although they don't shy away from melee.

Spell-Like Abilities: At will—*animate objects, chaos hammer, deeper darkness, detect magic, dispel law, fly, identify, invisibility, lightning bolt, magic circle against law, see invisibility, shatter,* and *power word blind.* These abilities are as the spells cast by a 15th-level sorcerer (save DC 12 + spell level).

Alternate Form (Su): A gray slaad can shift between its natural and any humanoid form at will as a standard action. A gray slaad whose personal treasure includes useful equipment or magic items will use these when in humanoid form.

A gray slaad remains in humanoid form indefinitely. The ability is otherwise similar to *polymorph self* cast by a 10th-level sorcerer.

Summon Slaad (Sp): Twice per day a gray slaad can attempt to summon 1–2 red slaadi or 1 blue slaad with a 40% chance of success, or 1 green slaad with a 20% chance of success.

DEATH SLAAD

Death slaadi are grays that undergo some mysterious ritual that transforms them into veritable killing machines. Although they have spell-like abilities like gray slaadi, death slaadi focus more on killing than on magical power.

All slaadi obey the command of a death slaad, out of fear more than anything else. Death slaadi represent a corruption of pure chaos by evil rather than true exemplars of it.

Combat

Although its prowess with its natural weapons is fearsome, a death slaad enjoys wielding a magic weapon if available (particularly if the slaad has a character class and has assumed a humanoid form).

Stun (Ex): A death slaad can use Stunning Fist as the feat, three times per day (see Stunning Fist, page 85 in the *Player's Handbook*). The save DC is 21.

Spell-Like Abilities: At will—*animate objects, circle of death, chaos hammer, cloak of chaos, deeper darkness, detect magic, dispel law, fear, finger of death, fireball, fly, identify, invisibility, magic circle against law, power word blind, see invisibility, shatter,* and *word of chaos;* 1/day—*implosion.* These abilities are as the spells cast by an 18th-level sorcerer (save DC 14 + spell level).

Alternate Form (Su): A death slaad can shift between its natural and any humanoid form at will as a standard action. A death slaad whose personal treasure includes magic weapons will use these when in humanoid form.

A death slaad remains in humanoid form indefinitely. The ability is otherwise similar to *polymorph self* cast by a 15th-level sorcerer.

Summon Slaad (Sp): Twice per day a death slaad can attempt to summon 1–2 red or blue slaadi with a 40% chance of success, or 1–2 green slaadi with a 20% chance of success.

Telepathy (Su): Death slaadi can communicate telepathically with any creature within 100 feet that has a language.

VARIANT SLAADI

Being creatures of chaos, no two slaadi look exactly alike. Aside from minor physical differences (height, build, eye position, etc.), many slaadi possess physical or magical traits that distinguish them significantly from their kin. Roll on the table below for every slaad encountered.

SLAADI CHAOTIC VARIATIONS

d%	Variation	Effect
01–40	No noticeable variation	—
41–42	Skin more yellow	—
43–44	Skin more blue	—
45–46	Skin white	—
47–48	Skin black	—
49–50	Blotches of different color	—
51–52	Tufts of long hair	—
53–54	Very narrow mouth	Bite damage –2
55–56	Vestigial wings	—
57–58	Extra arm	—
59–60	Tail	—
61–62	Thin	–2 Str, +2 Int
63–64	Very wide mouth	Bite damage +2
65–66	Wide eyes	Spot +1
67–68	Extra eye	Spot +2
69–70	Muscular legs	Speed 40 ft.
71–72	Large head (bigger brain)	Int +4
73–74	Bladelike claws	Claw damage +1d6
75–76	Extra arm	Extra claw attack
77–78	Snakelike hair	As medusa (see entry)
79–80	Horns	Gore 2d6 (use lowest attack bonus)
81–82	Thick skin	Natural armor +2
83–84	Scales	Natural armor +3
85–86	Long legs	Dex +2
87–88	Muscular arms	Str +2
89–90	Stout	Con +2
91	Working wings	Fly 30 ft. (clumsy)
92	Narrow eyes	Gaze attack as medusa (see entry)
93	Oozing pustules	Poison touch, Fortitude save (DC 15). Initial 1 temporary Int, secondary 1d6 temporary Int
94	Steaming pustules	Stench, Fortitude save (DC 15) or –2 morale penalty to attacks, saves, and checks for 10 rounds
95	Narrow mouth	Breath weapon: 20-ft. cone of acid, cold, electricity, fire, or sound. Damage 1d6 per point of slaad's Con bonus (minimum 1d6); Reflex half DC 10 + 1/2 slaad's HD + Con bonus
96	Magical nature	Can use any one 1st-level spell at will (caster level = HD)
97	Enhanced magical nature	Can use any one 2nd- or 3rd-level spell at will (caster level = HD)
98–00	Roll twice	

Medium-Size Undead (Incorporeal)
Hit Dice: 7d12 (45 hp)
Initiative: +7 (+3 Dex, +4 Improved Initiative)
Speed: 40 ft., fly 80 ft. (good)
AC: 15 (+3 Dex, +2 deflection)
Attacks: Incorporeal touch +6 melee
Damage: Incorporeal touch 1d8 and energy drain
Face/Reach: 5 ft. by 5 ft./5 ft.
Special Attacks: Energy drain, create spawn
Special Qualities: Undead, incorporeal, +2 turn resistance, unnatural aura, sunlight powerlessness
Saves: Fort +2, Ref +5, Will +7
Abilities: Str —, Dex 16, Con —, Int 14, Wis 14, Cha 15
Skills: Hide +13, Intimidate +12, Intuit Direction +10, Listen +13, Search +10, Spot +13
Feats: Alertness, Blind-Fight, Combat Reflexes, Improved Initiative

Climate/Terrain: Any land and underground
Organization: Solitary, gang (2–4), or swarm (6–11)
Challenge Rating: 7
Treasure: None
Alignment: Always lawful evil
Advancement: 8–14 HD (Medium-size)

Spectres are incorporeal undead often mistaken for ghosts or other such horrors. They haunt the places where they died, retaining their sentience but now hating all living things.

A spectre looks so much as it did in life that it can be easily recognized by those who knew the individual or have seen the individual in paintings and such. In many cases, the evidence of a violent death is visible on its semitransparent, faintly luminous body. The chill of death hangs in the air around spectres and lingers in the places they haunt.

COMBAT

In close combat a spectre attacks with its numbing, life-draining touch. It makes full use of its incorporeal nature, moving through walls, ceilings, and floors as it attacks.

Energy Drain (Su): Living creatures hit by a spectre's incorporeal touch attack receive two negative levels. The Fortitude save to remove a negative level has a DC of 15.

Create Spawn (Su): Any humanoid slain by a spectre becomes a spectre in 1d4 rounds. Spawn are under the command of the spectre that created them and remain enslaved until its death. They do not possess any of the abilities they had in life.

Undead: Immune to mind-influencing effects, poison, sleep, paralysis, stunning, and disease. Not subject to critical hits, subdual damage, ability damage, energy drain, or death from massive damage.

Incorporeal: Can be harmed only by other incorporeal creatures, +1 or better magic weapons, or magic, with a 50% chance to ignore any damage from a corporeal source. Can pass through solid objects at will, and own attacks pass through armor. Always moves silently.

Unnatural Aura (Su): Both wild and domesticated animals can sense the unnatural presence of a spectre at a distance of 30 feet. They do not willingly approach nearer than that and panic if forced to do so; they remain panicked as long as they are within that range.

Sunlight Powerlessness (Ex): Spectres are utterly powerless in natural sunlight (not merely a *daylight* spell) and flee from it. A spectre caught in sunlight cannot attack and can take only partial actions.

SPHINX

	Androsphinx	Criosphinx	Gynosphinx
	Large Magical Beast	Large Magical Beast	Large Magical Beast
Hit Dice:	12d10+48 (114 hp)	10d10+30 (85 hp)	8d10+8 (52 hp)
Initiative:	+0	+0	+5 (+1 Dex, +4 Improved Initiative)
Speed:	50 ft., fly 80 ft. (poor)	30 ft., fly 60 ft. (poor)	40 ft., fly 60 ft. (poor)
AC:	22 (−1 size, +13 natural)	20 (−1 size, +11 natural)	21 (−1 size, +1 Dex, +11 natural)
Attacks:	2 claws +18 melee	Butt +15 melee, 2 claws +10 melee	2 claws +11 melee
Damage:	Claw 2d4+7	Butt 2d6+6, claw 1d6+3	Claw 1d6+4
Face/Reach:	5 ft. by 10 ft./5 ft.	5 ft. by 10 ft./5 ft.	5 ft. by 10 ft./5 ft.
Special Attacks:	Pounce, rake 2d4+3, roar, spells	Pounce, rake 1d6+3	Pounce, rake 1d6+2, spell-like abilities
Saves:	Fort +12, Ref +8, Will +7	Fort +10, Ref +7, Will +3	Fort +7, Ref +7, Will +8
Abilities:	Str 25, Dex 10, Con 19, Int 16, Wis 17, Cha 17	Str 23, Dex 10, Con 17, Int 10, Wis 11, Cha 11	Str 19, Dex 12, Con 13, Int 18, Wis 19, Cha 19
Skills:	Intimidate +13, Knowledge (any one) +5, Listen +15, Spot +15, Wilderness Lore +13	Intimidate +8, Listen +10, Spot +10	Concentration +12, Intimidate +13, Listen +17, Spot +17
Feats:	Alertness, Cleave, Great Cleave, Flyby Attack, Power Attack, Track	Cleave, Flyby Attack, Power Attack	Alertness, Blind-Fight, Combat Casting, Flyby Attack, Improved Initiative, Iron Will
Climate/Terrain:	Any warm land	Warm forest	Any warm land
Organization:	Solitary	Solitary	Solitary or covey (2–4)
Challenge Rating:	9	7	8
Treasure:	Standard	Standard	Double standard
Alignment:	Always chaotic good	Always neutral	Always neutral
Advancement:	13–18 HD (Large); 19–36 HD (Huge)	11–15 HD (Large); 16–30 HD (Huge)	9–12 HD (Large); 13–24 HD (Huge)

	Hieracosphinx
	Large Magical Beast
Hit Dice:	9d10+18 (67 hp)
Initiative:	+2 (Dex)
Speed:	30 ft., fly 90 ft. (poor)
AC:	19 (−1 size, +2 Dex, +8 natural)
Attacks:	Bite +13 melee, 2 claws +8 melee
Damage:	Bite 1d10+5, claw 1d6+2
Face/Reach:	5 ft. by 10 ft./5 ft.
Special Attacks:	Pounce, rake 1d6+2
Saves:	Fort +8, Ref +8, Will +5
Abilities:	Str 21, Dex 14, Con 15, Int 6, Wis 15, Cha 10
Skills:	Listen +13, Spot +14*
Feats:	Alertness, Flyby Attack
Climate/Terrain:	Warm hill
Organization:	Solitary, pair, or flock (4–7)
Challenge Rating:	5
Treasure:	None
Alignment:	Always chaotic evil
Advancement:	10–14 HD (Large); 15–27 HD (Huge)

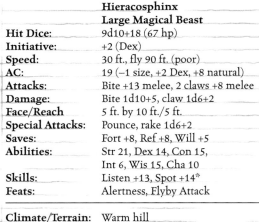

Sphinxes are enigmatic creatures with great, feathery wings and leonine bodies. All sphinxes are territorial, but the more intelligent ones can differentiate between deliberate intrusion and temporary or inadvertent trespass.

Sphinxes speak Sphinx, Common, and Draconic.

COMBAT

Most sphinxes fight on the ground, using their wings to help them leap much as lions do. If outnumbered by earthbound creatures, a sphinx takes wing and attacks on the fly.

Pounce (Ex): If a sphinx leaps upon a foe during the first round of combat, it can make a full attack even if it has already taken a move action.

Rake (Ex): A sphinx that pounces onto a creature can make two rake attacks with its hind legs. The individual description lists the attack bonus and damage.

ANDROSPHINX

These creatures resemble winged lions with humanoid facial features. They are always male. Androsphinxes are clever and generally good-natured, but they can be savage opponents.

Combat

In battle, an androsphinx rips apart enemies with its razor-sharp claws. It relies on its natural weaponry in a fight, employing its spells for defense or healing.

Rake (Ex): Attack bonus +18 melee, damage 2d4+3.

Roar (Su): Three times per day an androsphinx can loose a mighty roar. The first time it does this, all creatures within 500 feet must succeed at a Will save (DC 19) or be affected as though by a *fear* spell for 12 rounds.

If the sphinx roars a second time during the same encounter, all creatures within 250 feet must succeed at a Fortitude save (DC 19) or be paralyzed for 1d4 rounds, and all those within 90 feet are deafened for 2d6 rounds (no save).

If it roars a third time during the same encounter, all those within 250 feet must succeed at a Fortitude save (DC 19) or take 2d4 points of temporary Strength damage for 2d4 rounds. In addition, any Medium-size or smaller creature within 90 feet must succeed at a Fortitude save (DC 19) or be thrown to the ground and take 2d8 points of damage. The force of this roar is so great that it deals 50 points of damage to any stone or crystalline object within 90 feet. Magic items and held or carried items can avoid damage with a successful Reflex save (DC 19).

Other androsphinxes are immune to these effects.

Spells: An androsphinx casts divine spells as a 6th-level cleric from the cleric spell list and from the Good, Healing, and Protection domains.

CRIOSPHINX

These beasts have the bodies of winged lions and the heads of great rams. They are always male. Neither good nor evil, they lack the intelligence of the androsphinx. They constantly seek gynosphinxes, but if they cannot find one, they pursue wealth above all else. The best deal an adventurer can hope to strike with a criosphinx is safe passage in exchange for all of his or her treasure.

Combat

Criosphinxes attack with their claws and deadly bite, as do their kin, but they can also butt with their horns. They don't cast spells and employ only the most simple battle tactics.

Rake (Ex): Attack bonus +15 melee, damage 1d6+3.

GYNOSPHINX

These are the female counterparts of androsphinxes. They have the bodies of winged lions with female humanoid facial features. They gladly bargain for treasure or service but constantly seek out challenges for their staggering intellects. Riddles, puzzles, and other such things delight them to no end.

Combat

In close combat, gynosphinxes use their powerful claws to flay the flesh from their enemies. Despite their deadly nature, however, they prefer to avoid combat whenever possible.

Rake (Ex): Attack bonus +11 melee, damage 1d6+2.

Spell-Like Abilities: 3/day—*clairaudience/clairvoyance, detect magic, read magic,* and *see invisibility*; 1/day—*comprehend languages, locate object, dispel magic, remove curse,* and *legend lore.* These abilities are as the spells cast by a 14th-level sorcerer (save DC 14 + spell level).

Once per week a gynosphinx can create a *symbol of death, discord, insanity, pain, persuasion, sleep,* and *stunning* (one of each) as the spell cast by an 18th-level sorcerer (save DC 22).

HIERACOSPHINX

Of all the sphinxes, only these creatures are evil at heart. They are always male and have the body of a lion with the head of a great falcon or hawk. They spend much of their time searching for a gynosphinx but are generally just as happy to maul someone.

Combat

Hieracosphinxes can make short work of even the most dangerous opponents with their claws. They are not particularly intelligent, but are cunning enough to dive at their enemies from above with their limited flying ability.

Rake (Ex): Attack bonus +13 melee, damage 1d6+2.

Skills: *Hieracosphinxes gain a +4 racial bonus to Spot checks in daylight.

SPIDER EATER

Huge Magical Beast
Hit Dice: 4d10+20 (42 hp)
Initiative: +1 (Dex)
Speed: 30 ft., fly 60 ft. (good)
AC: 13 (–2 size, +1 Dex, +4 natural)
Attacks: Sting +7 melee, bite +2 melee
Damage: Sting 1d8+5 and poison, bite 1d8+2
Face/Reach: 10 ft. by 40 ft./ 10 ft.
Special Attack: Poison, implant
Special Qualities: Freedom of movement, scent
Saves: Fort +9, Ref +5, Will +2
Abilities: Str 21, Dex 13, Con 21, Int 2, Wis 12, Cha 10
Skills: Listen +7, Spot +7
Feats: Dodge

Climate/Terrain: Temperate and warm land and underground
Organization: Solitary
Challenge Rating: 5
Treasure: None
Alignment: Always neutral
Advancement: 5–12 HD (Huge)

These predators resemble great hornets and have temperaments to match. Nevertheless, they are valued as flying steeds. A company of bandits mounted on spider eaters is fearsome indeed.

Illus. by C. Critchlow

A spider eater resembles a giant, two-legged wasp with a pair of small forelimbs and huge bat wings. The creature gets its name from its ability to shrug off webs and its habit of laying eggs in the paralyzed bodies of enormous creatures, often arachnids.

COMBAT

A spider eater attacks with its venomous sting and powerful mandibles. Its usual tactic is to deliver a sting, then back off, hovering out of reach until the venom takes effect. Spider eaters do not like to give up their prey, and foes who harry them with spells or ranged attacks provoke a determined counterattack.

Poison (Ex): Bite, Fortitude save (DC 17); initial damage none, secondary damage paralysis for 1d8+5 weeks.

Implant (Ex): Female spider eaters lay their eggs inside paralyzed creatures of Huge or larger size. The young emerge about six weeks later, literally devouring the host from inside.

Freedom of Movement (Su): Spider eaters have freedom of movement as though from the spell cast by a 12th-level sorcerer. The effect can be dispelled, but the spider eater can create it again the next round as a free action. When the spider eater serves as a mount, this effect does not extend to its rider.

Skills: Spider eaters receive a +4 racial bonus to Listen and Spot checks.

TRAINING A SPIDER EATER

Training a spider eater as an aerial mount requires a successful Handle Animal check (DC 24 for a young creature, or DC 29 for an adult). A spider eater matures in six months.

Spider eater eggs are worth 2,000 gp apiece on the open market, while young are worth 3,000 gp each. Professional trainers charge 3,000 gp to rear or train a spider eater. Riding a trained spider eater requires an exotic saddle. A spider eater can fight while carrying a rider, but the rider cannot also attack unless he or she succeeds at a Ride check (see Ride, page 72 in the *Player's Handbook*).

Carrying Capacity: A light load for a spider eater is up to 612 pounds; a medium load, 613–1,224 pounds; and a heavy load, 1,225–1,840 pounds.

SPRITE

	Grig	Nixie	Pixie
	Tiny Fey	Small Fey	Small Fey
Hit Dice:	1/2 d6+1 (2 hp)	1d6 (3 hp)	1d6 (3 hp)
Initiative:	+4 (Dex)	+7 (+3 Dex, +4 Improved Initiative)	+4 (Dex)
Speed:	20 ft., fly 40 ft. (poor)	20 ft., swim 30 ft.	20 ft., fly 60 ft. (good)
AC:	18 (+2 size, +4 Dex, +2 natural)	14 (+1 size, +3 Dex)	16 (+1 size, +4 Dex, +1 natural)
Attacks:	Dagger +6 melee; or composite shortbow +6 ranged	Dagger +4 melee; or light crossbow +4 ranged	Dagger +5 melee; or composite shortbow +6 ranged
Damage:	Dagger 1d4–3; or composite shortbow 1d4	Dagger 1d4–2; or light crossbow 1d8	Dagger 1d4–2; or composite shortbow 1d6
Face/Reach:	2 1/2 ft. by 2 1/2 ft./0 ft.	5 ft. by 5 ft./5 ft.	5 ft. by 5 ft./5 ft.
Special Attacks:	Spell-like abilities, fiddle	Water breathing, charm person	Spell-like abilities, special arrows
Special Qualities:	SR 17	SR 16	SR 16, natural invisibility
Saves:	Fort +1, Ref +6, Will +3	Fort +0, Ref +5, Will +3	Fort +0, Ref +6, Will +4
Abilities:	Str 5, Dex 18, Con 13, Int 10, Wis 13, Cha 14	Str 7, Dex 16, Con 11, Int 12, Wis 13, Cha 18	Str 7, Dex 18, Con 11, Int 16, Wis 15, Cha 16
Skills:	Craft (any one) +4, Escape Artist +8, Hide +16, Jump +9, Listen +7, Move Silently +8*, Perform (dance, fiddle, melody, plus any other one) +6, Search +3, Spot +4	Animal Empathy +7, Bluff +8, Craft (any one) +5, Escape Artist +6, Handle Animal +8, Hide +10*, Listen +7, Perform (dance, melody, plus any other one) +7, Search +3, Sense Motive +5, Spot +7	Bluff +7, Concentration +4, Craft (any one) +7, Escape Artist +8, Heal +6, Hide +12, Listen +8, Move Silently +8, Ride +8, Search +9, Sense Motive +6, Spot +8
Feats:	Dodge, Weapon Finesse (dagger)	Dodge, Improved Initiative, Weapon Finesse (dagger)	Dodge, Point Blank Shot, Rapid Shot, Weapon Finesse (dagger), Weapon Focus (shortbow)
Climate/Terrain:	Temperate and warm forest	Temperate aquatic	Temperate forest
Organization:	Gang (2–4), band (6–11), or tribe (20–80)	Gang (2–4), band (6–11), or tribe (20–80)	Gang (2–4), band (6–11), or tribe (20–80)
Challenge Rating:	1	1	4
Treasure:	No coins; 50% goods; 50% items	No coins; 50% goods (metal or stone only); 50% items (no scrolls)	No coins; 50% goods; 50% items
Alignment:	Always neutral good	Always neutral	Always neutral good
Advancement:	1–3 HD (Tiny)	2–3 HD (Small)	2–3 HD (Small)

Sprites are reclusive fey. They go out of their way to fight evil and ugliness and to protect their homelands. Legend claims that sprites die only through injury or disease.

COMBAT

Sprites fight their opponents with spells and pint-sized weaponry. They prefer ambushes and other trickery to direct confrontation.

Skills: All sprites receive a +2 racial bonus to Search, Spot, and Listen checks.

GRIG

Grigs are mischievous and lighthearted. They have no fear of larger creatures and delight in playing tricks on them. Favorite pranks include stealing food, collapsing tents, and using *ventriloquism* to make objects talk.

A grig has a humanoid head, torso, and arms, with the wings, antennae, and legs of a cricket. Grigs can leap great distances. They have light blue skin, forest-green hair, and brown hairy legs, and usually wear tunics or brightly colored vests with buttons made from tiny gems. They stand a mere 1 1/2 feet tall.

Combat

Grigs are fierce by sprite standards, attacking opponents fearlessly with bow and dagger.

SPRITE

Spell-Like Abilities: 3/day—*change self, entangle, invisibility* (self only), *pyrotechnics,* and *ventriloquism.* These abilities are as the spells cast by a 9th-level sorcerer (save DC 12 + spell level).

Fiddle (Su): One grig in each band carries a tiny, grig-sized fiddle. When the fiddler plays, any non-sprite within 30 feet of the instrument must succeed at a Will save (DC 15) or be affected as though by *Otto's irresistible dance* as long as the playing continues.

Skills: Grigs receive a +8 racial bonus to Jump checks. *They also receive a +5 racial bonus to Move Silently checks in a forest setting.

NIXIE

Nixies are aquatic sprites who dwell in and protect pristine ponds and lakes. They are even more reclusive than most fey and tend to treat intruders with suspicion and hostility.

Nixies have webbed fingers and toes, pointed ears, and wide silver eyes. Most are slim and comely, with lightly scaled, pale green skin and dark green hair. Females often twine shells and pearl strings in their hair and dress in wraps woven from colorful seaweed. Males wear loincloths of the same materials. Nixies can breathe both water and air, and can travel on land, but they prefer not to leave their lakes. A nixie stands about 4 feet tall.

Combat

Nixies rely on their *charm person* ability to deter enemies, entering combat only to protect themselves and their territory.

Water Breathing (Sp): Once per day a nixie can use *water breathing* as the spell cast by a 6th-level sorcerer. (They usually bestow this effect on those they have charmed.)

Charm Person (Sp): A nixie can *charm person* three times per day as the spell cast by a 4th-level sorcerer. Those affected must succeed at a Will save (DC 15) or be charmed for 24 hours, performing heavy labor, guard duty, and other onerous tasks for the nixie community. Shortly before the effect wears off, the nixie escorts the charmed creature away and orders it to keep walking.

Skills: *Nixies receive a +5 racial bonus to Hide checks when in the water.

PIXIE

Pixies are merry pranksters who love to lead travelers astray. They can, however, be roused to surprising ire when dealing with evil creatures.

These sprites love to trick misers out of their wealth. They do not covet treasure themselves but use it to taunt and frustrate greedy folk. If a victim of pixie pranks exhibits no greed or demonstrates a good sense of humor, the tricksters may allow the individual to choose a reward from their hoard.

When visible, pixies resemble small elves, but with longer ears and gossamer wings. They wear bright clothing, often including a cap and shoes with curled and pointed toes. Pixies stand about 2 1/2 feet tall.

Combat

The normally carefree pixies ferociously attack evil creatures and unwanted intruders. They take full advantage of their invisibility and other abilities to harass and drive away opponents.

Natural Invisibility (Su): A pixie remains invisible even when it attacks. This ability is constant, but the pixie can suppress or resume it as a free action.

Spell-Like Abilities: 1/day—*confusion* (the pixie must touch the target), *dancing lights, detect chaos, detect good, detect evil, detect law, detect thoughts, dispel magic, entangle, permanent image* (visual and auditory elements only), and *polymorph self.* These abilities are as the spells cast by an 8th-level sorcerer (save DC 13 + spell level).

One pixie in ten can use *Otto's irresistible dance* once per day as cast by an 8th-level sorcerer.

Special Arrows (Ex): Pixies sometimes employ arrows that deal no damage but can erase memory or put a creature to sleep.

Memory Loss: An opponent struck by the arrow must succeed at a Fortitude save (DC 15) or lose all memory. The subject retains skills, languages, and class abilities but forgets everything else until he or she receives a *heal* spell or memory restoration with *limited wish, wish,* or *miracle.*

Sleep: Any opponent struck by the arrow, regardless of Hit Dice, must succeed at a Fortitude save (DC 15) or be affected as though by a *sleep* spell.

STIRGE

Tiny Beast
Hit Dice: 1d10 (5 hp)
Initiative: +4 (Dex)
Speed: 10 ft., fly 40 ft. (average)
AC: 16 (+2 size, +4 Dex)
Attacks: Touch +6
Damage: Touch 1d3–4
Face/Reach: 2 1/2 ft. by 2 1/2 ft./0 ft.
Special Attack: Attach, blood drain
Saves: Fort +2, Ref +6, Will +1
Abilities: Str 3, Dex 19, Con 10, Int 1, Wis 12, Cha 6
Skills: Hide +14
Feats: Weapon Finesse (touch)

Climate/Terrain: Temperate and warm forest and underground
Organization: Clutch (2–4), swarm (5–8), or flock (9–13)
Challenge Rating: 1/2
Treasure: None
Alignment: Always neutral
Advancement: —

Stirges are batlike creatures that feed on the blood of living beings. While just one poses little danger to most adventurers, multiple stirges can be a formidable threat.

A stirge resembles a cross between a bat and a giant mosquito. It has membranous bat wings, a short furry body, eight jointed legs that end in sharp pincers, and a needlelike proboscis. Coloration ranges from rust-red to reddish-brown, with a dirty yellow underside. The proboscis is pink at the tip, fading to gray at its base.

A stirge's body is about 1 foot long, with a wingspan of about 2 feet.

COMBAT

A stirge attacks by landing on a victim, finding a vulnerable spot, and plunging its proboscis into the flesh. This is a touch attack and can target only Small or larger creatures.

Attach (Ex): If a stirge hits with a touch attack, it uses its eight pincers to latch onto the opponent's body. An attached stirge has an AC of 12.

Blood Drain (Ex): A stirge drains blood, dealing 1d4 points of temporary Constitution damage each round it remains attached. Once it has drained 4 points of Constitution, it detaches and flies off to digest the meal.

TARRASQUE

Colossal Magical Beast
Hit Dice: 48d10+576 (840 hp)
Initiative: +7 (+3 Dex, +4 Improved Initiative)
Speed: 20 ft.
AC: 35 (−8 size, +3 Dex, +30 natural)
Attacks: Bite +57 melee, 2 horns +52 melee, 2 claws +52 melee, tail slap +52 melee
Damage: Bite 4d8+17, horn 1d10+8, claw 1d12+8, tail slap 3d8+8
Face/Reach: 40 ft. by 40 ft./25 ft.
Special Attacks: Frightful presence, rush, improved grab, swallow whole, augmented criticals
Special Qualities: Damage reduction 25/+5, carapace, immunities, regeneration 40, scent, SR 32
Saves: Fort +38, Ref +29, Will +20
Abilities: Str 45, Dex 16, Con 35, Int 3, Wis 14, Cha 14
Skills: Listen +21, Spot +21
Feats: Blind-Fight, Combat Reflexes, Dodge, Improved Initiative, Iron Will

Climate/Terrain: Any land
Organization: Solitary
Challenge Level: 20
Treasure: None
Alignment: Always neutral
Advancement: 49+ HD (Colossal)

The legendary tarrasque—fortunately, only one exists—is possibly the most dreaded monster of all (except for the largest dragons). None can predict where and when the creature will strike next.

The location of the tarrasque's lair is a mystery, and the beast remains dormant much of the time. Its torporous slumber usually lasts 6d4 months before it leaves its lair for a brief hunting foray lasting 1d3 days. Once every decade or so, the monster is particularly active, staying awake for 1d2 weeks. Thereafter, it slumbers for at least 4d6 years unless disturbed.

When active, the tarrasque is a perfect engine of destruction. It rampages across the land eating everything in its path, including plants, animals, humanoids, and even towns. Nothing is safe, and entire communities prefer to flee the ravening tarrasque rather than face its power.

Many legends surround the tarrasque's origins and purpose. Some hold it to be an abomination unleashed by ancient, forgotten gods to punish all of nature, while others tell of a conspiracy between evil wizards or merciless elemental powers. These tales are mere speculation, however, and the creature's true nature will probably remain a mystery. The tarrasque isn't in the habit of explaining itself, and it rarely leaves any living witnesses in its wake.

The tarrasque is a scaly biped 70 feet long and 50 feet tall, with two horns on its head, a lashing tail, and a reflective carapace. It weighs about 130 tons.

COMBAT

The tarrasque attacks with its claws, teeth, horns, and tail.

Frightful Presence (Su): The tarrasque can inspire terror by charging or attacking. Affected creatures must succeed at a Will save (DC 26) or become shaken, remaining shaken until they leave the area of effect.

Rush (Ex): Once per minute, the normally slow-moving tarrasque can move at a speed of 150 feet.

Improved Grab (Ex): To use this ability, the tarrasque must hit a Huge or smaller opponent with its bite attack. If it gets a hold, it can try to swallow the foe.

Swallow Whole (Ex): The tarrasque can try to swallow a grabbed opponent of Huge or smaller size by making a successful grapple check. Once inside, the opponent takes 2d8+8 points of crushing damage plus 2d8+6 points of acid damage per round from the tarrasque's digestive juices. A swallowed creature can cut its way out by dealing 50 points of damage to the tarrasque's digestive tract (AC 20). Once the creature exits, muscular action closes the hole; another swallowed opponent must cut its own way out.

The tarrasque's gullet can hold two Huge, four Large, eight Medium-size, or sixteen Small or smaller creatures.

Augmented Criticals (Ex): The tarrasque threatens a critical hit on a natural attack roll of 18–20, dealing triple damage on a successful critical hit.

Carapace (Ex): The tarrasque's armorlike carapace is exceptionally tough and highly reflective, deflecting all rays, lines, cones, and even *magic missile* spells. There is a 30% chance of reflecting any such effect back at the caster; otherwise, it is merely negated. Check for reflection before rolling to overcome the creature's spell resistance.

Illus. by C. Critchlow

Immunities (Ex): The tarrasque has fire, poison, and disease immunity.

Regeneration (Ex): No form of attack deals normal damage to the tarrasque. The tarrasque regenerates even if *disintegrated* or slain with death magic: These attack forms merely reduce it to –10 hit points. It is immune to effects that produce incurable or bleeding wounds, such as a *sword of wounding*, mummy rot, or a clay golem's wound ability. The tarrasque can be permanently slain only by reducing it to –30 hit points and using a *wish* or *miracle* spell to keep it dead.

If the tarrasque loses a limb or body part, the lost portion regrows in 1d6 minutes (the detached piece dies and decays normally). The creature can reattach the severed member instantly by holding it to the stump.

Skills: The tarrasque receives a +8 racial bonus to Listen and Spot checks.

TENDRICULOS

Huge Plant
Hit Dice: 9d8+54 (94 hp)
Initiative: –1 (Dex)
Speed: 20 ft.
AC: 16 (–2 size, –1 Dex, +9 natural)
Attacks: Bite +13 melee, 2 tendrils +8 melee
Damage: Bite 2d8+9, tendril 1d6+4
Face/Reach: 10 ft. by 40 ft./15 ft.
Special Attacks: Improved grab, swallow whole, paralysis
Special Qualities: Plant, regeneration 10
Saves: Fort +12, Ref +2, Will +2
Abilities: Str 28, Dex 9, Con 22, Int 3, Wis 8, Cha 3

Climate/Terrain: Temperate and warm forest, hill, and marsh
Organization: Solitary
Challenge Rating: 6
Treasure: 1/10th coins; 50% goods; 50% items
Alignment: Always neutral
Advancement: 10–16 HD (Huge); 17–27 HD (Gargantuan)

The tendriculos is a plant that may have been mutated by foul magic, or may have originated on another plane of existence—or possibly both of these theories are true.

Appearing most of the time as a massive mound of vegetation, the tendriculos can rear up to a height of 15 feet supported by limblike vines and branches. The mass has a huge mouthlike opening filled with "teeth" of sharp branches and long thorns.

The tendriculos is best known for its ability to grow and regrow its vegetable body extremely rapidly. Whole new leaves and vines appear in just a few minutes. The tendriculos accomplishes this by consuming vast quantities of meat.

Animals, beasts, and even other animate plants are unnerved by the presence of a tendriculos; they avoid it and any place it has been within the last 24 hours.

COMBAT

Prowling deep forests or waiting in vegetated areas (looking like nothing more than a small hillock), the tendriculos attacks savagely, showing no fear. It attempts to swallow as much flesh as it can, as quickly as it can.

Improved Grab (Ex): To use this ability, the tendriculos must hit with its bite attack. If it gets a hold, it automatically deals bite damage and can try to swallow the opponent.

A tendriculos that hits with a tendril attack grabs as above. If it gets a hold, it picks up the opponent and transfers it to the mouth as a partial action, automatically dealing bite damage as above.

Swallow Whole/Paralysis (Ex): A tendriculos can try to swallow a grabbed opponent of Large or smaller size by making a successful grapple check. Once inside the plant's mass, the opponent must succeed at a Fortitude save (DC 19) or be paralyzed for 3d6 rounds by the tendriculos's digestive juices, taking 2d6 points of acid damage per round. A new save is required each round inside the plant.

A swallowed creature that avoids paralysis can climb out of the mass with a successful grapple check. This returns it to the plant's maw, where another successful grapple check is needed to get free. A swallowed creature can also cut its way out by using claws or a Small or Tiny slashing weapon to deal 25 points of damage to the tendriculos's interior (AC 15). Once the creature exits, the plant's amazing regenerative capacity closes the hole; another swallowed opponent must again cut its own way out.

The tendriculos's interior can hold two Large, four Small, eight Tiny, sixteen Diminutive, or thirty-two Fine or smaller opponents.

Plant: Immune to mind-influencing effects, poison, sleep, paralysis, stunning, and polymorphing. Not subject to critical hits.

Regeneration (Ex): Bludgeoning weapons and acid deal normal damage to a tendriculos.

A tendriculos that loses part of its body mass can regrow it in 1d6 minutes. Holding the severed portion against the mass enables it to reattach instantly.

THOQQUA

Medium-Size Elemental (Earth, Fire)
Hit Dice: 3d8+3 (16 hp)
Initiative: +1 (Dex)
Speed: 30 ft., burrow 20 ft.
AC: 18 (+1 Dex, +7 natural)
Attacks: Slam +4 melee
Damage: Slam 1d6+3 and 2d6 fire
Face/Reach: 5 ft. by 5 ft./5 ft.
Special Attacks: Heat, burn
Special Qualities: Fire subtype, tremorsense
Saves: Fort +4, Ref +4, Will +2
Abilities: Str 15, Dex 13, Con 13, Int 6, Wis 12, Cha 10
Skills: Intuit Direction +4, Jump +6, Listen +6, Move Silently +5

Climate/Terrain: Any underground
Organization: Solitary or pair
Challenge Rating: 2
Treasure: None
Alignment: Usually neutral
Advancement: 4–9 HD (Large)

The thoqqua is a wormlike monster with a body hot enough to melt solid rock. It has a choleric mood and a foul temper.

A thoqqua's sinuous body is segmented like an earthworm's and glows with orange-white heat. The creature burrows through rock looking for minerals to eat.

A thoqqua is about 1 foot in diameter and 4 to 5 feet long.

COMBAT

When a thoqqua is disturbed, its first instinct is to attack. Its favored tactic is to spring directly at a foe, either by bursting out of the rock or by coiling up its body and launching itself like a spring. In either case, treat the maneuver as a charge.

Heat (Ex): Merely touching or being touched by a thoqqua automatically deals 2d6 fire damage.

Burn (Ex): When a thoqqua hits with its slam attack, the opponent must succeed at a Reflex save (DC 13) or catch fire. The flame burns for 1d4 rounds if not extinguished sooner. The burning creature can use a full-round action to put out the flame (see page 86 in the DUNGEON MASTER's Guide for more information on catching on fire).

Fire Subtype (Ex): Fire immunity, double damage from cold except on a successful save.

Tremorsense (Ex): Thoqquas can automatically sense the location of anything within 60 feet that is in contact with the ground.

TITAN

Huge Outsider (Chaotic, Good)
Hit Dice: 20d8+120 (210 hp)
Initiative: +1 (Dex)
Speed: 90 ft.
AC: 22 (–2 size, +1 Dex, +13 natural)
Attacks: Gargantuan warhammer +31/+26/+21/+16 melee; or Huge javelin +19/+14/+9/+4 ranged
Damage: Gargantuan warhammer 4d6+19; or Huge javelin 2d6+13
Face/Reach: 10 ft. by 10 ft./15 ft.
Special Attacks: Spell-like abilities, spells
Special Qualities: Damage reduction 15/+1, SR 25
Saves: Fort +18, Ref +13, Will +17
Abilities: Str 37, Dex 12, Con 23, Int 21, Wis 20, Cha 18
Skills: Bluff +27, Climb +21, Concentration +29, Craft (any one) +27, Jump +36, Knowledge (any one) +28, Knowledge (religion) +28, Listen +30, Perform (ballad, chant, dance, epic, harp, melody, ode, plus any other sixteen) +27, Sense Motive +28, Spot +30, Swim +36
Feats: Alertness, Blind-Fight, Cleave, Expertise, Great Cleave, Power Attack

Climate/Terrain: Any land and underground
Organization: Solitary or pair
Challenge Level: 21
Treasure: Triple standard
Alignment: Always chaotic good
Advancement: 21–30 HD (Huge); 31–60 HD (Gargantuan)

Titans are statuesque beings of heroic proportions. They have agile minds and powerful bodies.

A titan looks like a 25-foot-tall human of great physical strength and beauty. Titans favor loose, flowing clothing such as robes, togas, loincloths, and the like. They wear rare and valuable jewelry and generally make themselves seem beautiful and overpowering.

Titans are wild and chaotic, masters of their own fates. They are closer to the wellsprings of life than mere mortals and so revel in existence. They are prone to more pronounced emotions than humans and can experience deitylike fits of rage. They are, however, basically good and benevolent, so they tend not to take life even when angry.

Titans speak Common, Celestial, Draconic, Giant, and Sylvan.

COMBAT

Titans can wreak havoc with their massive warhammers, which are sometimes referred to as "mauls of the titans." In addition to their considerable battle prowess, titans possess great speed and considerable magical power. They enjoy combat and usually close first. If that proves ineffective, they swiftly back off and pelt the foe with spells and magical effects.

Spell-Like Abilities: At will—*alter self, bless, charm person or animal, commune with nature, cure light wounds, eyebite, fire storm, halt undead, hold monster, invisibility, levitate, light, magic circle against evil, mirror image, pass without trace, persistent image, produce flame, summon nature's ally II, remove curse, remove fear, shield, speak with plants, summon swarm,* and *whispering wind;* 2/day—*astral projection* and *ethereality.* These abilities are as the spells cast by a 20th-level sorcerer (save DC 14 + spell level). Once every other round, a titan can use *holy smite* as a 20th-level cleric.

Spells: A titan can use arcane spells as a 20th-level wizard or divine spells as a 20th-level cleric, from the cleric list and from the Chaos and Good domains.

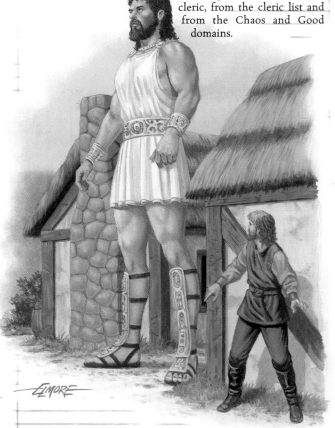

ELMORE

	Juvenile	Adult	Elder
	Small Outsider (Water)	**Medium-Size Outsider (Water)**	**Large Outsider (Water)**
Hit Dice:	3d8+6 (19 hp)	7d8+14 (45 hp)	15d8+60 (127 hp)
Initiative:	+1 (Dex)	+1 (Dex)	+1 (Dex)
Speed:	10 ft., swim 90 ft.	10 ft., swim 90 ft.	10 ft., swim 90 ft.
AC:	22 (+1 size, +1 Dex, +10 natural)	23 (+1 Dex, +12 natural)	24 (–1 size, +1 Dex, +14 natural)
Attacks:	Bite +6 melee, 2 claws +1 melee	Bite +10 melee, 2 claws +5 melee	Bite +20 melee, 2 claws +15 melee
Damage:	Bite 2d6+2, claw 1d4+1	Bite 2d8+3, claw 1d6+1	Bite 4d6+6, claw 1d8+3
Face/Reach:	5 ft. by 5 ft./5 ft.	5 ft. by 5 ft./5 ft.	10 ft. by 5 ft./5 ft.
Special Attack:	Improved grab, ink cloud	Improved grab, ink cloud	Improved grab, ink cloud
Special Qualities:	All-around vision, acid and cold immunity, fire and electricity resistance 20	All-around vision, acid and cold immunity, fire and electricity resistance 20	All-around vision, acid and cold immunity, fire and electricity resistance 20
Saves:	Fort +5, Ref +4, Will +4	Fort +7, Ref +6, Will +6	Fort +13, Ref +10, Will +10
Abilities:	Str 14, Dex 13, Con 15, Int 10, Wis 12, Cha 9	Str 16, Dex 13, Con 15, Int 10, Wis 12, Cha 9	Str 22, Dex 13, Con 19, Int 10, Wis 12, Cha 9
Skills:	Hide +11, Intuit Direction +7, Listen +7, Search +6, Spot +9	Escape Artist +11, Hide +11, Intimidate +5, Intuit Direction +11, Listen +11, Search +6, Spot +13	Escape Artist +19, Hide +15, Intimidate +17, Intuit Direction +19, Knowledge (Plane of Water) +13, Listen +19, Search +6, Spot +20
Feats:	Blind-Fight	Blind-Fight, Dodge	Blind-Fight, Cleave, Dodge, Power Attack
Climate/Terrain:	Any aquatic and underground	Any aquatic and underground	Any aquatic and underground
Organization:	Solitary or clutch (2–4)	Solitary or clutch (2–4)	Solitary or clutch (2–4)
Challenge Rating:	3	5	9
Treasure:	Standard	Standard	Standard
Alignment:	Always neutral	Always neutral	Always neutral
Advancement:	4–6 HD (Small)	8–14 HD (Medium-size)	16–24 HD (Large); 25–32 HD (Gargantuan)

Tojanidas are omnivores from the Elemental Plane of Water. Though they seem clumsy and innocuous at first glance, they are nimble swimmers and capable fighters.

A tojanida resembles a snapping turtle. It has a blue-green, spindle-shaped shell made up of hexagonal plates. Inside the shell is a fleshy body with seven stalks. Four of these stalks have paddles for locomotion, two are tipped with claws like a crab's, and one bears the creature's head. Each stalk is scaly and green, like a turtle. Eight vents in the shell, four at each end, allow the tojanida to thrust its stalks out in whatever configuration it finds convenient.

Juvenile tojanidas are one to twenty-five years old, with a shell about 3 feet long and weighing about 60 pounds. An adult is aged twenty-six to eighty years, with a shell about 6 feet long and weighing about 220 pounds. An elder is still hale and can reach 150 years of age. It has a shell about 9 feet long and weighs about 500 pounds.

Tojanidas speak Aquan and can be loquacious, but usually only on the subject of food.

COMBAT

Tojanidas are fairly even-tempered but can be ferocious if molested. They are very jealous of their food supplies and become testy if they suspect a newcomer is trying to beat them to a meal.

Improved Grab (Ex): To use this ability, the tojanida must hit with a bite or claw attack. If it gets a hold, it automatically deals that weapon's damage each round the hold is maintained. Underwater, a tojanida can tow a grabbed victim of its own size or smaller at top speed. A favorite tactic is to grab a single opponent, then withdraw, hauling the opponent away from its allies.

All-Around Vision (Ex): Tojanidas' multiple apertures allow them to look in any direction, bestowing a +4 racial bonus to Spot and Search checks. Opponents gain no flanking bonuses when attacking a tojanida.

Ink Cloud (Ex): A tojanida can emit a spherical cloud of jet-black ink with a radius of 30 feet once per minute as a free action. The effect is otherwise similar to *fog cloud* cast by an individual of a level equal to the tojanida's Hit Dice. Out of water, the ink emerges in a stream up to 30 feet long, which the tojanida can squirt into an opponent's eyes. The affected creature must succeed at a Reflex save or be blinded for 1 round. The save DC is 13 against a juvenile, 15 against an adult, and 19 against an elder.

TREANT

Huge Plant
Hit Dice: 7d8+35 (66 hp)
Initiative: –1 (Dex)
Speed: 30 ft.
AC: 20 (–2 size, –1 Dex, +13 natural)
Attacks: 2 slams +12 melee
Damage: Slam 2d6+9
Face/Reach: 10 ft. by 10 ft./15 ft.
Special Attacks: Animate trees, trample, double damage against objects
Special Qualities: Plant, fire vulnerability, half damage from piercing
Saves: Fort +10, Ref +1, Will +6
Abilities: Str 29, Dex 8, Con 21, Int 12, Wis 15, Cha 12
Skills: Hide –9*, Intimidate +8, Knowledge (any one) +8, Listen +9, Sense Motive +9, Spot +9, Wilderness Lore +9
Feats: Iron Will, Power Attack

Climate/Terrain: Any forest
Organization: Solitary or grove (4–7)
Challenge Rating: 8
Treasure: Standard
Alignment: Always neutral good
Advancement: 8–16 HD (Huge); 17–21 HD (Gargantuan)

Treants combine features of trees and humans. They are peaceful by nature but deadly when angered. They hate evil and the unrestrained use of fire, considering themselves guardians of the trees.

Treants are almost indistinguishable from trees. Their skin is thick and brown, with a barklike texture. Their arms are gnarled like branches, and their legs fit together when closed to look like the trunk of a tree. Above the eyes and along the head are dozens of smaller branches from which hang great leaves. In winter the leaves of a treant change color, but they rarely fall out.

Treants speak their own language, plus Common and Sylvan. Most also can manage a smattering of just about all other humanoid tongues—at least enough to say "Get out of my trees!"

COMBAT

Treants prefer to watch potential foes carefully before attacking. They often charge suddenly from cover to trample the despoilers of forests. If sorely pressed, they animate trees as reinforcements.

Animate Trees (Sp): A treant can animate trees within 180 feet at will, controlling up to two trees at a time. It takes a full round for a normal tree to uproot itself. Thereafter it moves at a speed of 10 and fights as a treant in all respects. Animated trees lose their ability to move if the treant who animated them is incapacitated or moves out of range. The ability is otherwise similar to *liveoak* as cast by a 12th-level druid.

Trample (Ex): A treant or animated tree can trample Medium-size or smaller creatures for 2d12+5 points of damage. Opponents who do not make attacks of opportunity against the treant or animated tree can attempt a Reflex save (DC 20) to halve the damage.

Double Damage against Objects (Ex): A treant or animated

tree that makes a full attack against an object or structure deals double damage.

Plant: Immune to mind-influencing effects, poison, sleep, paralysis, stunning, and polymorphing. Not subject to critical hits.

Fire Vulnerability (Ex): A treant or animated tree takes double damage from fire attacks unless the attack allows a save, in which case it takes double damage on a failure and no damage on a success.

Half Damage from Piercing (Ex): Piercing weapons deal only half damage to treants, with a minimum of 1 point of damage.

Skills: Treants receive skills as though they were fey*. They have a +16 racial bonus to Hide checks made in forested areas.

TRITON

Medium-Size Outsider (Water)
Hit Dice: 3d8+3 (16 hp)
Initiative: +0
Speed: Swim 40 ft.
AC: 16 (+6 natural)
Attacks: Trident +4 melee; or heavy crossbow +3 ranged
Damage: Trident 1d8+1; or heavy crossbow 1d10
Face/Reach: 5 ft. by 5 ft./5 ft.
Special Attacks: Spell-like abilities
Saves: Fort +4, Ref +3, Will +4
Abilities: Str 12, Dex 10, Con 12, Int 13, Wis 13, Cha 11
Skills: Craft (any one) +4, Hide +6, Listen +7, Ride +6, Spot +7
Feats: Mounted Combat

Climate/Terrain: Any aquatic
Organization: Company (2–5), squad (6–11), or band (20–80)
Challenge Rating: 4
Treasure: Standard
Alignment: Always neutral good
Advancement: 4–9 HD (Medium-size)

Tritons are rumored to be from the Elemental Plane of Water, on the Material Plane for some unknown purpose. They are sea dwellers, preferring warm waters but able to tolerate colder depths.

Tritons form communities, either in great undersea castles built of rock, coral, and other natural materials or in finely sculpted caverns. A hunter-gatherer people, tritons take from the sea's vast bounty only what they need to survive. They are naturally suspicious of surface dwellers and prefer not to deal with them if possible. However, tritons deal harshly with beings who intentionally invade their communities, capturing the intruders and setting them adrift without any possessions at least ten miles from any shoreline, left "to the mercy of the sea."

Tritons are the natural enemy of the cruel and evil sahuagin. The two cannot coexist peacefully: Wars between them are prolonged, bloody affairs that sometimes interfere with shipping and maritime trade.

A triton is roughly human-sized. Its lower half ends in two finned legs, while its torso, head, and arms are human. Tritons have silvery skin that fades into silver-blue scales on the lower half of their bodies. Their hair is deep blue or blue-green.

Tritons speak Common and Aquan.

COMBAT

The reclusive tritons prefer to avoid combat, but they fiercely defend their homes. They attack with either melee or ranged weapons as the circumstances warrant. When encountered outside their lair, they are 90% likely to be mounted on friendly sea creatures such as porpoises.

Spell-Like Abilities: A triton can use *summon nature's ally III* once per day as the spell cast by a 5th-level sorcerer, often choosing water elementals for their companions.

TROGLODYTE

Medium-Size Humanoid (Reptilian)
Hit Dice: 2d8+4 (13 hp)
Initiative: –1 (Dex)
Speed: 30 ft.
AC: 15 (–1 Dex, +6 natural)
Attacks: Longspear +1 melee (or 2 claws +1 melee), bite –1 melee; or javelin +1 ranged
Damage: Longspear 1d8, bite 1d4, claw 1d4; or javelin 1d6
Face/Reach: 5 ft. by 5 ft./5 ft. (10 ft. with longspear)
Special Attacks: Stench, darkvision 90 ft.
Saves: Fort +5, Ref –1, Will +0
Abilities: Str 10, Dex 9, Con 14, Int 8, Wis 10, Cha 10
Skills: Hide +6*, Listen +3
Feats: Multiattack, Weapon Focus (javelin)

Climate/Terrain: Any mountains and underground
Organization: Clutch (2–5), squad (6–11 plus 1–2 giant lizards), or band (20–80 plus 20% noncombatants plus 3–13 giant lizards)
Challenge Rating: 1
Treasure: 50% coins; 50% goods; 50% items
Alignment: Always chaotic evil
Advancement: By character class

Troglodytes are revolting lizard creatures as evil as the foulest of demons. They are very warlike and savor the taste of their enemies—especially humanoids.

Troglodytes (or trogs) look somewhat humanoid, standing about 5 feet tall and weighing about 150 pounds. They have spindly but muscular arms and walk erect on their squat legs, trailing a long, slender tail. Their heads are lizardlike and crowned with a frill that extends from the forehead to the base of the neck. Their eyes are black and beady and very sensitive to even the dimmest light.

Troglodytes are not especially intelligent, but their ferocity and natural cunning more than compensate for this deficiency. They often launch bloody raids against humanoid settlements or ambush caravans in warm climates. They guard their lairs aggressively, lashing out at anyone who comes too near.

Troglodytes speak Draconic.

COMBAT

Half of a group of troglodytes are armed only with claws and teeth; the rest carry one or two javelins and longspears. They normally conceal themselves, launch a volley of javelins, then close to attack. If the battle goes against them, they retreat and attempt to hide.

Stench (Ex): When a troglodyte is angry or frightened, it secretes an oily, musklike chemical that nearly every form of animal life finds offensive. All creatures (except troglodytes) within 30 feet of the trog must succeed at a Fortitude save (DC 13) or be overcome with nausea. This lasts for 10 rounds and deals 1d6 points of temporary Strength damage.

Skills: The skin of a troglodyte changes color somewhat, allowing it to blend in with surroundings like a chameleon and conferring a +4 racial bonus to Hide checks. *In rocky or subterranean settings, this bonus improves to +8.

TROGLODYTE SOCIETY

Troglodyte tribes are ruled by the largest and fiercest among them, with subchieftains who have distinguished themselves in battle. Trogs like to lair near humanoid settlements to prey on inhabitants and their livestock. They raid on moonless nights when their darkvision and camouflage are most effective.

Trogs prize steel above all else. Though individuals usually have no wealth, a lair may contain valuable items casually discarded, pushed into corners, or mixed in with refuse. The lair is usually a large cave with smaller caves for the hatchlings and eggs. A lair has hatchlings equal to one-fifth the number of adults and eggs equal to one-tenth.

The troglodytes revere Laogzed, a vile deity who resembles a cross between a toad and a lizard.

TROGLODYTE CHARACTERS

A troglodyte's favored class is cleric, and most troglodyte leaders are clerics. Troglodyte clerics worship Laogzed and can choose any two of the following domains: Chaos, Death, Destruction, and Evil.

TROLL

Large Giant
Hit Dice: 6d8+36 (63 hp)
Initiative: +2 (Dex)
Speed: 30 ft.
AC: 18 (−1 size, +2 Dex, +7 natural)
Attacks: 2 claws +9 melee, bite +4 melee
Damage: Claw 1d6+6, bite 1d6+3
Face/Reach: 5 ft. by 5 ft./10 ft.
Special Attacks: Rend 2d6+9
Special Qualities: Regeneration 5, scent, darkvision 90 ft.
Saves: Fort +11, Ref +4, Will +3
Abilities: Str 23, Dex 14, Con 23, Int 6, Wis 9, Cha 6
Skills: Listen +5, Spot +5
Feats: Alertness, Iron Will

Climate/Terrain: Any land, aquatic, and underground
Organization: Solitary or gang (2—4)
Challenge Rating: 5
Treasure: Standard
Alignment: Always chaotic evil
Advancement: By character class

Trolls are horrid carnivores found in all climes, from arctic wastelands to tropical jungles. Most creatures avoid these beasts, who know no fear and attack unceasingly when hungry.

Trolls have ravenous appetites, devouring everything from grubs to bears and humanoids. They often lair near settlements and hunt the inhabitants until they devour every last one.

A typical adult troll stands 9 feet tall and weighs 500 pounds. Its rubbery hide is moss green, mottled green and gray, or putrid gray. A writhing, hairlike mass grows out of the skull and is usually greenish black or iron gray. The arms and legs are long and ungainly. The legs end in great three-toed feet, the arms in wide, powerful hands with sharpened claws. Trolls can appear thin and frail but possess surprising strength. Females are larger and more powerful than their male counterparts.

Trolls walk upright but hunched forward with sagging shoulders. Their gait is uneven, and when they run, the arms dangle and drag along the ground.

For all this seeming awkwardness, trolls are very agile.

Trolls speak Giant.

COMBAT

Trolls have no fear of death: They launch themselves into combat without hesitation, flailing wildly at the closest opponent. Even when confronted with fire, they try to get around the flames and attack.

Rend (Ex): If a troll hits with both claw attacks, it latches onto the opponent's body and tears the flesh. This attack automatically deals an additional 2d6+9 points of damage.

Regeneration (Ex): Fire and acid deal normal damage to a troll.

If a troll loses a limb or body part, the lost portion regrows in 3d6 minutes. The creature can reattach the severed member instantly by holding it to the stump.

SCRAG

Scrags are a marine variety of troll that dwell in any body of water in any climate.

On land, scrags have a speed of 20 feet, and their swimming speed is 40 feet. They regenerate only if mostly immersed in water. Scrags are otherwise identical with their landbound cousins.

UMBER HULK

Large Aberration
Hit Dice: 8d8+32 (68 hp)
Initiative: +1 (Dex)
Speed: 20 ft., burrow 20 ft.
AC: 17 (−1 size, +1 Dex, +7 natural)
Attacks: 2 claws +11 melee, bite +9 melee
Damage: Claw 2d4+6, bite 2d8+3
Face/Reach: 5 ft. by 5 ft./10 ft.
Special Attacks: Confusing gaze
Special Qualities: Tremorsense
Saves: Fort +6, Ref +3, Will +6
Abilities: Str 23, Dex 13, Con 19, Int 9, Wis 11, Cha 13
Skills: Climb +17, Jump +14, Listen +11
Feats: Multiattack

Climate/Terrain: Any underground
Organization: Solitary or cluster (2—4)
Challenge Rating: 7
Treasure: Standard
Alignment: Always chaotic evil
Advancement: 9–12 HD (Large); 13–24 HD (Huge)

Umber hulks are massive creatures that dwell deep beneath the earth. Ripping through rock as though it were light underbrush, they rampage continuously—leaving a wake of destruction.

An umber hulk is powerfully built, looking something like a cross between a great ape and a beetle. The wedge-shaped creature stands roughly 8 feet tall and measures nearly 5 feet across, weighing about 800 pounds.

Armor plates cover virtually all of its chitinous body, whose scattered feelers resemble sparse hair. The low, rounded head is dominated by a massive pair of mandibles and rows of triangular teeth.

Umber hulks speak their own language.

COMBAT

An umber hulk can deliver blows powerful enough to crush almost any enemy. In addition, its mandibles are strong enough to bite through armor or exoskeletons with ease.

Despite its great bulk, the umber hulk is intelligent. When brute force won't overcome an enemy, it is more than capable of outthinking those who assume it to be a stupid beast. Umber hulks often use their tunneling ability to create deadfalls and pits for the unwary.

Confusing Gaze (Su): *Confusion* as cast by an 8th-level sorcerer, 30 feet, Will negates DC 15.

Tremorsense (Ex): Umber hulks can automatically sense the location of anything within 60 feet that is in contact with the ground.

UNICORN

Large Magical Beast
Hit Dice: 4d10+20 (42 hp)
Initiative: +3 (Dex)
Speed: 60 ft.
AC: 18 (–1 size, +3 Dex, +6 natural)
Attacks: Horn +11 melee, 2 hooves +3 melee
Damage: Horn 1d8+8, hoof 1d4+2
Face/Reach: 5 ft. by 10 ft./5 ft. (10 ft. with horn)
Special Qualities: Magic circle against evil, spell-like abilities, immunities
Saves: Fort +9, Ref +7, Will +6
Abilities: Str 20, Dex 17, Con 21, Int 10, Wis 21, Cha 24
Skills: Animal Empathy +11, Listen +11, Move Silently +9, Spot +11, Wilderness Lore +9*
Feats: Alertness

Climate/Terrain: Temperate forest
Organization: Solitary, pair, or grace (3–6)
Challenge Rating: 3
Treasure: None
Alignment: Always chaotic good
Advancement: 5–8 HD (Large)

These fierce, noble beasts shun contact with all but sylvan creatures (dryads, pixies, and the like), showing themselves only to defend their woodland homes.

Unicorns are powerful equines with gleaming white coats and deep sea-blue, violet, brown, or fiery gold eyes. Long, silky white hair hangs down from mane and forelock. Males sport a white beard, while females are slimmer. A single ivory-colored horn, 2 to 3 feet in length, grows from the center of the forehead. The hooves of a unicorn are cloven. A typical adult unicorn grows to 8 feet in length, stands 5 feet high at the shoulder, and weighs 1,200 pounds.

Unicorns mate for life, making their homes in open dells or glades in the forests they protect. Good and neutral travelers may pass freely through and even hunt for food in a unicorn's forest, but evil creatures do so at great risk. Likewise, a unicorn will attack any being it discovers killing for sport in its territory or damaging the forest maliciously.

Lone unicorns occasionally allow themselves to be tamed and ridden by good human or elven maidens of pure heart. Such a unicorn, if treated kindly, is the maiden's loyal steed and protector for life, even accompanying her beyond its forest.

A unicorn's horn is renowned for its healing properties. Evil and unscrupulous beings sometimes hunt a unicorn for its horn, which can fetch up to 2,000 gp, for use in various healing potions and devices. Most good creatures refuse to traffic in such things.

Unicorns speak Sylvan and Common.

COMBAT

Unicorns normally attack only when defending themselves or their forests. They either charge, impaling foes with their horns like lances (see Charge, page 124 in the *Player's Handbook*), or strike with their hooves. The horn is a +3 magic weapon, though its power fades if removed from the unicorn.

Magic Circle against Evil (Su): This ability continuously duplicates the effects of the spell. The unicorn cannot suppress this ability.

Spell-Like Abilities: Unicorns can *detect evil* at will as a free action. Once per day a unicorn can use *teleport without error* to move anywhere within its home. It cannot teleport beyond the forest boundaries nor back from outside.

A unicorn can use *cure light wounds* three times per day and *cure moderate wounds* once per day, as cast by a 5th-level druid, by touching a wounded creature with its horn. Once per day it can use *neutralize poison*, as cast by an 8th-level druid, with a touch of its horn.

Immunities (Ex): Unicorns are immune to all poisons and to charm and hold spells or abilities.

Skills: *Unicorns receive a +3 competence bonus to Wilderness Lore checks within the boundaries of their forest.

Illus. by T. Lockwood

VAMPIRE SPAWN

Medium-Size Undead
Hit Dice: 4d12 (26 hp)
Initiative: +6 (+2 Dex, +4 Improved Initiative)
Speed: 30 ft.
AC: 15 (+2 Dex, +3 natural)
Attacks: Slam +5 melee
Damage: Slam 1d6+4 and energy drain
Face/Reach: 5 ft. by 5 ft./5 ft.
Special Attacks: Charm, energy drain, blood drain
Special Qualities: Undead, +2 turn resistance, damage reduction 10/silver, cold and electricity resistance 10, gaseous form, spider climb, fast healing 2
Saves: Fort +1, Ref +5, Will +5
Abilities: Str 16, Dex 14, Con —, Int 13, Wis 13, Cha 14
Skills: Bluff +8, Climb +8, Craft (any one) or Profession (any one) +10, Hide +10, Jump +8, Listen +11, Move Silently +11, Search +8, Sense Motive +11, Spot +11
Feats: Alertness, Improved Initiative, Lightning Reflexes, Skill Focus (any Craft or Profession)

Climate/Terrain: Any land and underground
Organization: Solitary or pack (2–5)
Challenge Rating: 4
Treasure: Standard
Alignment: Always chaotic evil
Advancement: —

Vampire spawn are undead creatures that come into being when vampires slay mortals. Like their creators, spawn remain bound to their coffins and to the soil of their graves.

Vampire spawn appear just as they did in life, although their features are often hardened and feral, with a predatory look.

Vampire spawn speak Common.

COMBAT

Vampire spawn use their inhuman strength when engaging mortals, hammering their foes with powerful blows and dashing them against rocks or walls. They also use their gaseous form and flight abilities to strike where opponents are most vulnerable.

Charm (Su): This is similar to the vampire's domination ability (see the Vampire entry in Appendix 3: Templates), but the save DC is 14, and the effect is similar to *charm person* as cast by a 5th-level sorcerer. A charmed subject allows the vampire spawn to drain his or her blood (see below).

Energy Drain (Su): Living creatures hit by a vampire spawn's slam attack receive one negative level. The Fortitude save to remove the negative level has a DC of 14.

Blood Drain (Ex): A vampire spawn can suck blood from a living victim with its fangs by making a successful grapple check. If it pins the foe, it drains blood, inflicting 1d4 points of permanent Constitution drain each round.

Undead: Immune to mind-influencing effects, poison, sleep, paralysis, stunning, and disease. Not subject to critical hits, subdual damage, ability damage, energy drain, or death from massive damage.

Gaseous Form (Su): As a standard action, a vampire spawn can assume gaseous form at will, as the spell cast by a 6th-level sorcerer, but it can remain gaseous indefinitely and has a fly speed of 20 feet with perfect maneuverability.

Spider Climb (Ex): A vampire spawn can climb sheer surfaces as though with a *spider climb* spell.

Fast Healing (Ex): A vampire spawn heals 2 points of damage each round so long as it has at least 1 hit point. If reduced to 0 hit points in combat, it automatically assumes gaseous form and attempts to escape. It must reach its coffin home within 2 hours or be utterly destroyed. Once at rest in its coffin, it regains 1 hit point after 1 hour, then resumes healing at the rate of 2 hit points per round.

Skills: Vampire spawn receive a +4 racial bonus to Bluff, Hide, Listen, Move Silently, Search, Sense Motive, and Spot checks.

REPELLING AND SLAYING VAMPIRE SPAWN

Vampire spawn are equally vulnerable to attacks that slay vampires. For details, see the Vampire entry in Appendix 3: Templates.

VARGOUILLE

Small Outsider (Evil)
Hit Dice: 1d8+1 (5 hp)
Initiative: +1 (Dex)
Speed: Fly 30 ft. (good)
AC: 12 (+1 size, +1 Dex)
Attacks: Bite +3 melee
Damage: Bite 1d4 and poison
Face/Reach: 5 ft. by 5 ft./5 ft.
Special Attacks: Shriek, poison, kiss
Saves: Fort +3, Ref +3, Will +3
Abilities: Str 10, Dex 13, Con 12, Int 5, Wis 12, Cha 8
Skills: Listen +4, Spot +3
Feats: Weapon Finesse (bite)

Climate/Terrain: Any land and underground
Organization: Cluster (2–5) or swarm (6–11)
Challenge Rating: 2
Treasure: None
Alignment: Always neutral evil
Advancement: 2–3 HD (Small)

These revolting creatures come into the world from the deepest pits of the infernal planes. They haunt graveyards, ruins, and other places of death and decay.

A vargouille looks like a hideous, distorted human head suspended from leathery wings. In place of hair, it is crowned with writhing tendrils, and its eyes burn with a menacing green flame.

COMBAT

Vargouilles attack by biting with their jagged teeth. Their special attacks make them even more dangerous.

Shriek (Su): Instead of biting, a vargouille can open its distended mouth and let out a terrible shriek. Those within 60 feet (except other vargouilles) who both hear the shriek and can

Illus. by C. Arellano

clearly see the creature must succeed at a Fortitude save (DC 12) or be paralyzed with fear until the monster attacks them, goes out of range, or leaves their sight. A paralyzed creature is susceptible to the vargouille's kiss. If the save is successful, that opponent cannot be affected again by that vargouille's shriek for one day.

Poison (Ex): Bite, Fortitude save (DC 12) or be unable to heal the bite damage naturally or magically. A *neutralize poison* or *heal* spell removes the effect, while *delay poison* allows magical healing.

Kiss (Su): A vargouille can kiss a paralyzed target with a successful melee touch attack, beginning a terrible transformation. The affected opponent must succeed at a Fortitude save (DC 19) or begin to transform, losing all his or her hair 1d6 hours later. After another 1d6 hours, the ears grow into leathery wings, tentacles sprout on the chin and scalp, and the teeth become long, pointed fangs. During the next 1d6 hours, the victim suffers 1d6 points of permanent Intelligence and Charisma drain. The transformation is complete 1d6 hours later, when the head breaks free of the body (which promptly dies) and becomes a vargouille. This transformation is interrupted by sunlight, and even a *daylight* spell can delay death, but to reverse the transformation requires *remove disease*.

WIGHT

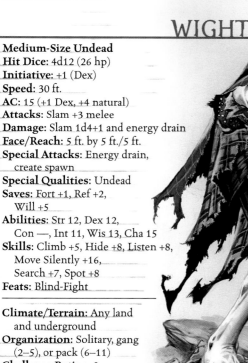

Medium-Size Undead
Hit Dice: 4d12 (26 hp)
Initiative: +1 (Dex)
Speed: 30 ft.
AC: 15 (+1 Dex, +4 natural)
Attacks: Slam +3 melee
Damage: Slam 1d4+1 and energy drain
Face/Reach: 5 ft. by 5 ft./5 ft.
Special Attacks: Energy drain, create spawn
Special Qualities: Undead
Saves: Fort +1, Ref +2, Will +5
Abilities: Str 12, Dex 12, Con —, Int 11, Wis 13, Cha 15
Skills: Climb +5, Hide +8, Listen +8, Move Silently +16, Search +7, Spot +8
Feats: Blind-Fight

Climate/Terrain: Any land and underground
Organization: Solitary, gang (2–5), or pack (6–11)
Challenge Rating: 3
Treasure: None
Alignment: Always lawful evil
Advancement: 5–8 HD (Medium-size)

In ages past, the term "wight" meant simply "man." As the years went by, however, the word came to be associated with these dark undead.

A wight's appearance is a weird and twisted reflection of the form it had in life. Wild, frantic eyes burn with malevolence. The leathery, desiccated flesh is drawn tight across its bones, and the teeth have grown into sharp, jagged needles.

Wights lurk in barrow-mounds, catacombs, and other places thick with the aura of death, where they nurture their hatred. They seek to destroy all life, filling graveyards with their victims and populating the world with their horrid progeny.

COMBAT

Wights attack by hammering with their fists.

Energy Drain (Su): Living creatures hit by a wight's slam attack receive one negative level. The Fortitude save to remove the negative level has a DC of 14.

Create Spawn (Su): Any humanoid slain by a wight becomes a wight in 1d4 rounds. Spawn are under the command of the wight that created them and remain enslaved until its death. They do not possess any of the abilities they had in life.

Undead: Immune to mind-influencing effects, poison, sleep, paralysis, stunning, and disease. Not subject to critical hits, subdual damage, ability damage, energy drain, or death from massive damage.

Skills: Wights receive a +8 racial bonus to Move Silently checks.

WILL-O'-WISP

Small Aberration (Air)
Hit Dice: 9d8 (40 hp)
Initiative: +13 (+9 Dex, +4 Improved Initiative)
Speed: Fly 50 ft. (perfect)
AC: 29 (+1 size, +9 Dex, +9 deflection)
Attacks: Shock +16 melee
Damage: Shock 2d8
Face/Reach: 5 ft. by 5 ft./5 ft.
Special Qualities: Spell immunity, natural invisibility
Saves: Fort +3, Ref +12, Will +9
Abilities: Str —, Dex 29, Con 10, Int 15, Wis 16, Cha 12
Skills: Bluff +11, Listen +17, Search +14, Spot +17
Feats: Alertness, Blind-Fight, Dodge, Improved Initiative

Climate/Terrain: Any swamp
Organization: Solitary or string (2–4)
Challenge Rating: 6
Treasure: 1/10 coins; 50% goods; 50% items
Alignment: Always chaotic evil
Advancement: 10–18 HD (Small)

Will-o'-wisps are evil creatures that feed on the powerful emotions associated with panic, horror, and death. They delight in luring travelers into deadly peril, then absorbing the resulting emanations.

Unless frightened, a will-o'-wisp appears as a faintly glowing sphere of yellow, white, green, or blue light. The creatures are easily mistaken for lanterns, especially in the foggy marshes and swamps where they reside.

A will-o'-wisp is a globe of semisolid vapor about 1 foot across and weighing about 3 pounds, and its glowing body sheds as much light as a torch. It has no vocal apparatus but can vibrate to create a ghostly voice. Will-o'-wisps speak Common and Auran, plus two bonus languages.

COMBAT

Will-o'-wisps usually avoid combat. They prefer to confuse and bewilder adventurers, luring them into morasses or other hazardous places. When they are forced to fight, they loose small electrical shocks, which act as normal melee attacks.

Spell Immunity (Ex): The only spells that can affect will-o'-wisps are *magic circle against chaos, magic circle against evil, magic missile, maze, protection from chaos,* and *protection from evil.*

Natural Invisibility (Ex): A startled or frightened will-o'-wisp can extinguish its glow, effectively becoming invisible as the spell.

WINTER WOLF

Large Magical Beast (Cold)
Hit Dice: 6d10+18 (51 hp)
Initiative: +5 (+1 Dex, +4 Improved Initiative)
Speed: 50 ft.
AC: 15 (−1 size, +1 Dex, +5 natural)
Attacks: Bite +9 melee
Damage: Bite 1d8+6
Face/Reach: 5 ft. by 10 ft./5 ft.
Special Attacks: Breath weapon, trip
Special Qualities: Scent, cold subtype
Saves: Fort +8, Ref +6, Will +3
Abilities: Str 18, Dex 13, Con 16, Int 9, Wis 13, Cha 10
Skills: Hide +6*, Listen +9, Move Silently +7, Spot +9, Wilderness Lore +1*
Feats: Alertness, Improved Initiative

Climate/Terrain: Any cold land and underground
Organization: Solitary, pair, or pack (2–5)
Challenge Rating: 5
Treasure: 1/10 coins; 50% goods; 50% items
Alignment: Always neutral evil
Advancement: 7–9 HD (Large); 10–18 HD (Huge)

Dangerous predators of the tundra and other chill regions, winter wolves pursue prey relentlessly. They rarely give up the chase until they bring down their quarry.

Winter wolves are more intelligent than their smaller cousins and sometimes associate with other evil creatures of their cold homelands, such as frost giants, whom they serve as scouts, hunters, and trackers.

The creature resembles a huge, white wolf with icy blue eyes. It grows about 8 feet long and stands about 4 1/2 feet at the shoulder.

Winter wolves can speak Giant and Common.

COMBAT

Winter wolves typically hunt in packs. Their size, cunning, and formidable breath weapon allow them to hunt and kill creatures much larger than themselves. A pack usually circles an opponent, each wolf attacking in turn to exhaust it. If they're in a hurry, white wolves try to pin their foes.

Breath Weapon (Su): Cone of cold, 15 ft., every 1d4 rounds; damage 4d6, Reflex half DC 16. Winter wolves can use their breath weapon while biting.

Trip (Ex): A winter wolf that hits with a bite attack can attempt to trip the opponent as a free action (see page 139 in the *Player's Handbook*) without making a touch attack or provoking an attack of opportunity. If the attempt fails, the opponent cannot react to trip the winter wolf.

Cold Subtype: Cold immunity; double damage from fire except on a successful save.

Skills: Winter wolves receive a +1 racial bonus to Listen, Move Silently, and Spot checks, and a +2 racial bonus to Hide checks. *Their natural coloration grants winter wolves a +7 racial bonus to Hide checks in areas of snow and ice. A winter wolf has a +4 racial bonus to Wilderness Lore checks when tracking by scent.

WORG

Medium-Size Magical Beast
Hit Dice: 4d10+8 (30 hp)
Initiative: +2 (Dex)
Speed: 50 ft.
AC: 14 (+2 Dex, +2 natural)
Attacks: Bite +7 melee
Damage: Bite 1d6+4
Face/Reach: 5 ft. by 5 ft./5 ft.
Special Attacks: Trip
Special Qualities: Scent
Saves: Fort +6, Ref +6, Will +3
Abilities: Str 17, Dex 15, Con 15, Int 6, Wis 14, Cha 10
Skills: Hide +7, Listen +9, Move Silently +7, Spot +9, Wilderness Lore +2*
Feats: Alertness

Climate/Terrain: Any forest, hill, plains, and mountains
Organization: Solitary, pair, or pack (6–11)
Challenge Rating: 2
Treasure: 1/10 coins; 50% goods; 50% items
Alignment: Always neutral evil
Advancement: 5–6 HD (Medium-size); 7–12 HD (Large)

Worgs are dire wolf off-shoots that have attained some intelligence and an evil disposition. They sometimes associate with other evil beings, particularly goblins, whom they serve as mounts and guardians.

Worgs typically live and hunt in packs. Their favored prey is large herbivores. Although they typically stalk and kill young, sick, or weak animals, they don't hesitate to hunt humanoids, particularly when game is scarce. Worgs may stalk humanoid prey for hours or even days before attacking, and choose the most advantageous terrain and time of day to do so (during the predawn hours, for example).

A worg looks like a black or gray wolf, with a malevolent intelligence in its face and eyes. The typical specimen grows to 5 feet long and stands 3 feet tall at the shoulder.

More intelligent than their smaller cousins, worgs speak their own language. Some can also speak Common and Goblin.

COMBAT

Mated pairs work together to bring down large game, while lone worgs usually chase down creatures smaller than themselves. Both often use hit-and-run tactics to exhaust their quarry. A pack usually circles a larger opponent: Each wolf attacks in turn, biting and retreating, until the creature is exhausted, at which point the pack moves in for the kill. If they get impatient or heavily outnumber the opponent, worgs attempt to pin it.

Trip (Ex): A worg that hits with a bite attack can attempt to trip the opponent as a free action (see page 139 in the *Player's Handbook*) without making a touch attack or provoking an attack of opportunity. If the attempt fails, the opponent cannot react to trip the worg.

Skills: A worg receives a +1 racial bonus to Listen, Move Silently, and Spot checks, and a +2 racial bonus to Hide checks. A worg has a +4 racial bonus to Wilderness Lore checks when tracking by scent.

WRAITH

Medium-Size Undead (Incorporeal)
Hit Dice: 5d12 (32 hp)
Initiative: +7 (+3 Dex, +4 Improved Initiative)
Speed: 30 ft., fly 60 ft. (good)
AC: 15 (+3 Dex, +2 deflection)
Attacks: Incorporeal touch +5 melee
Damage: Incorporeal touch 1d4 and 1d6 permanent Constitution drain
Face/Reach: 5 ft. by 5 ft./5 ft.
Special Attacks: Constitution drain, create spawn
Special Qualities: Undead, incorporeal, +2 turn resistance, unnatural aura, daylight powerlessness

Saves: Fort +1, Ref +4, Will +6
Abilities: Str —, Dex 16, Con —, Int 14, Wis 14, Cha 15
Skills: Hide +11, Intimidate +10, Intuit Direction +6, Listen +12, Search +10, Sense Motive +8, Spot +12
Feats: Alertness, Blind-Fight, Combat Reflexes, Improved Initiative

Climate/Terrain: Any land and underground
Organization: Solitary, gang (2–5), or pack (6–11)
Challenge Rating: 5
Treasure: None
Alignment: Always lawful evil
Advancement: 6–10 HD (Medium-size)

Wraiths are incorporeal creatures born of evil and darkness. They despise all living things, as well as the light that nurtures them.

Although composed of darkness, wraiths are more or less humanoid in shape. They are utterly featureless except for the glowing red pinpoints of their eyes. In some cases, the grim silhouette of a wraith might appear armored or outfitted with weapons. This does not affect the creature's AC or combat abilities but only reflects the shape it had in life.

COMBAT

Close combat with a wraith is dangerous, thanks to its deadly touch.

Constitution Drain (Su): Living creatures hit by a wraith's incorporeal touch attack must succeed at a Fortitude save (DC 14) or suffer 1d6 points of permanent Constitution drain.

Create Spawn (Su): Any humanoid slain by a wraith becomes a wight in 1d4 rounds. Spawn are under the command of the wraith that created them and remain enslaved until its death. They do not possess any of the abilities they had in life.

Unnatural Aura (Su): Both wild and domesticated animals can sense the unnatural presence of a wraith at a distance of 30 feet. They will not willingly approach nearer than that and panic if forced to do so; they remain panicked as long as they are within that range.

Undead: Immune to mind-influencing effects, poison, sleep, paralysis, stunning, and disease. Not subject to critical hits, subdual damage, ability damage, energy drain, or death from massive damage.

Incorporeal: Can be harmed only by other incorporeal creatures, +1 or better magic weapons, or magic, with a 50% chance to ignore any damage from a corporeal source. Can pass through solid objects at will, and own attacks pass through armor. Always moves silently.

Daylight Powerlessness (Ex): Wraiths are utterly powerless in natural sunlight (not merely a *daylight* spell) and flee from it.

WYVERN

Huge Dragon
Hit Dice: 7d12+14 (59 hp)
Initiative: +1 (Dex)
Speed: 20 ft., fly 60 ft. (poor)
AC: 17 (–2 size, +1 Dex, +8 natural)
Attacks: Sting +9 melee, bite +4 melee, 2 wings +4 melee; or 2 claws +9 melee
Damage: Sting 1d6+4 and poison, bite 2d8+2, wing 1d8+2; or claw 1d6+4
Face/Reach: 10 ft. by 20 ft./10 ft.
Special Attacks: Poison, improved grab, snatch
Special Qualities: Scent
Saves: Fort +7, Ref +6, Will +6
Abilities: Str 19, Dex 12, Con 15, Int 6, Wis 12, Cha 9
Skills: Listen +13, Move Silently +9, Spot +13*
Feats: Alertness, Flyby Attack

Climate/Terrain: Temperate and warm forest, hill, and mountains
Organization: Solitary, pair, or flight (3–6)
Challenge Rating: 6
Treasure: Standard
Alignment: Usually neutral
Advancement: 8–10 HD (Huge); 11–21 HD (Gargantuan)

A distant cousin to the dragon, the wyvern is a huge flying lizard with a poisonous stinger in its tail.

The 30-foot-long, dark brown to gray body of the wyvern is half tail, tipped with a thick knot of cartilage from which a stinger protrudes much like that of a scorpion. Its leathery bat wings measure over 50 feet from tip to tip. The huge jaws are filled with long, sharp teeth, and the eyes are red or orange. Unlike a dragon, it has only hind legs, which it uses as a hunting bird would. A wyvern does not have a strong odor, although its lair might smell of a recent kill. These beasts can make two sounds: a loud hiss and a deep-throated growl much like that of a bull alligator.

Some wyverns speak Draconic, but most are too stupid to understand any language.

COMBAT

Wyverns are rather stupid but always aggressive: They attack nearly anything that isn't obviously more powerful than themselves. A wyvern dives from the air, snatching the opponent with its claws and stinging it to death.

A wyvern can slash with its claws only when making a flyby attack, and it cannot make bite, sting, or wing attacks.

Poison (Ex): Sting, Fortitude save (DC 17); initial and secondary damage 2d6 temporary Constitution.

Improved Grab (Ex): To use this ability, the wyvern must hit with both claw attacks. If it gets a hold, it hangs on and stings.

Snatch: If a wyvern gets a hold on a creature four or more sizes smaller, it automatically deals damage with both claws and its sting attacks each round the hold is maintained.

The wyvern can drop a creature it has snatched as a free action or use a standard action to fling it aside. A flung creature travels 30 feet and takes 3d6 points of damage. If the wyvern flings it while flying, the creature suffers this amount or falling damage, whichever is greater.

Skills: *Wyverns receive a +3 racial bonus to Spot checks when flying during daylight hours.

XILL

Medium-Size Outsider (Evil, Lawful)
Hit Dice: 5d8+10 (32 hp)
Initiative: +7 (+3 Dex, +4 Improved Initiative)
Speed: 40 ft.
AC: 20 (+3 Dex, +7 natural)
Attacks: 2 short swords +7 melee, 2 claws +2 melee (or 4 claws +7 melee); or 1 or 2 longbows +8 ranged
Damage: Short sword 1d6+2, short sword 1d6+1, claw 1d4+1; claw 1d4+2, or longbow 1d8
Face/Reach: 5 ft. by 5 ft./5 ft.
Special Attacks: Improved grab, paralysis, implant
Special Qualities: SR 21, planewalk
Saves: Fort +6, Ref +7, Will +5
Abilities: Str 15, Dex 16, Con 15, Int 12, Wis 12, Cha 11
Skills: Escape Artist +11, Intuit Direction +6, Listen +9, Move Silently +11, Spot +9, Tumble +11
Feats: Improved Initiative, Multidexterity, Multiweapon Fighting

Climate/Terrain: Any land and underground
Organization: Solitary or gang (2–5)
Challenge Rating: 6
Treasure: Standard
Alignment: Always lawful evil
Advancement: 6–8 HD (Medium-size); 9–15 HD (Large)

Malevolent and extreme, xills are known for brutality and totalitarianism. They combine a healthy dose of evil with a keen love of cruelty.

A xill is quasireptilian, with four arms, bright red scales, and dark, penetrating eyes. It stands 4 to 5 feet tall and weighs about 100 pounds. Some xills are barbaric and fierce; others are more civilized creatures who rely on brutal order.

COMBAT

Xills are dangerous opponents, attacking with all four limbs at no penalty. More civilized ones use weapons, usually fighting with two at a time so as to leave two claws free for grab attacks.

Xills typically lie in wait on the Ethereal Plane for suitable prey to happen by, then ambush it using their planewalk ability. They make full use of their Tumble skill in combat: Usually, one or two distract physically powerful enemies by attacking, then assuming a defensive stance while their fellows maneuver to advantage.

Xills seldom destroy enemies in combat but take prisoners whenever they can, dragging them back to the Ethereal Plane and implanting them with eggs.

Improved Grab (Ex): To use this ability, the xill must hit with one or more claw attacks. The grapple check has a +2 bonus for each claw that hits. If it gets a hold and maintains it the next round, it automatically bites the foe at that time. The bite deals no damage but injects a paralyzing venom.

Paralysis (Ex): Those bitten by a xill must succeed at a Fortitude save (DC 14) or be paralyzed for 1d4 hours. Barbaric xills secrete enough venom to bite two opponents every 6 hours, while their civilized cousins can bite only once per day.

Planewalk (Su): These planar travelers like to slip between the folds of space to attack enemies as though from thin air. They can cross from the Ethereal Plane with a move action but take 2 rounds to cross back, during which time they are immobile. As a xill fades away, it becomes harder to hit: Opponents suffer a 20% miss chance on the first round and a 50% miss chance on the second.

Implant (Ex): Xills lay their eggs inside paralyzed creatures. The young emerge about 90 days later, literally devouring the host from inside. A *remove disease* spell rids a victim of the egg, as does a successful Heal check (DC 20) by someone with that skill. If the check fails, the healer can try again, but each attempt (successful or not) deals 1d4 points of damage to the patient.

Feats: A xill receives the Multiweapon Fighting feat as a bonus feat. With its Multidexterity and Multiweapon Fighting feats, it can attack with all its arms at no penalty as a racial ability.

XILL CHARACTERS

A gang of civilized xills is invariably led by a cleric. Xill clerics can choose any two of the following domains: Evil, Law, Strength, and Travel.

XORN

	Minor Xorn	Average Xorn	Elder Xorn
	Small Outsider (Earth)	**Medium-Size Outsider (Earth)**	**Large Outsider (Earth)**
Hit Dice:	3d8+6 (19 hp)	7d8+14 (45 hp)	15d8+60 (127 hp)
Initiative:	+0	+0	+0
Speed:	20 ft., burrow 20 ft.	20 ft., burrow 20 ft.	20 ft., burrow 20 ft.
AC:	23 (+1 size, +12 natural)	22 (+12 natural)	22 (–1 size, +13 natural)
Attacks:	Bite +6 melee, 3 claws +4 melee	Bite +10 melee, 3 claws +8 melee	Bite +21 melee, 3 claws +19 melee
Damage:	Bite 2d8+2, claw 1d3+1	Bite 4d6+3, claw 1d4+1	Bite 4d8+7, claw 1d6+3
Face/Reach:	5 ft. by 5 ft./5 ft.	5 ft. by 5 ft./5 ft.	10 ft. by 10 ft./10 ft.
Special Attacks:	Burrow	Burrow	Burrow
Special Qualities:	Xorn qualities	Xorn qualities	Xorn qualities
Saves:	Fort +5, Ref +3, Will +3	Fort +7, Ref +5, Will +5	Fort +13, Ref +9, Will +9
Abilities:	Str 15, Dex 10, Con 15, Int 10, Wis 11, Cha 10	Str 17, Dex 10, Con 15, Int 10, Wis 11, Cha 10	Str 25, Dex 10, Con 19, Int 10, Wis 11, Cha 10
Skills:	Hide +10, Intuit Direction +3, Listen +6, Move Silently +3, Search 6, Spot +8	Hide +10, Intuit Direction +10, Listen +10, Move Silently +10, Search +10, Spot +14	Hide +14, Intuit Direction +18, Knowledge (minerals) +12, Listen +18, Move Silently +18, Search +22, Spot +22
Feats:	Multiattack	Multiattack, Power Attack	Cleave, Great Cleave, Multiattack, Power Attack

Climate/Terrain:	Any land and underground	Any land and underground	Any land and underground
Organization:	Solitary, pair, or cluster (3–5)	Solitary, pair, or cluster (3–5)	Solitary, pair, or party (6–11)
Challenge Rating:	3	6	8
Treasure:	None	None	None
Alignment:	Usually neutral	Usually neutral	Usually neutral
Advancement:	4–6 HD (Small)	8–14 HD (Medium-size)	16–21 HD (Large); 22–45 HD (Huge)

Xorns are scavengers from the Elemental Plane of Earth.

The wide body of a xorn is made of a pebbly, stonelike material. It has a large, powerful mouth on top of its head, surrounded by three long arms, tipped with sharp talons, symmetrically positioned around it. Between the arms are large, stone-lidded eyes that see in all directions. At its base are three thick, short legs, each directly beneath an eye. The whole body is designed for burrowing, mouth first.

Minor xorns are about 3 feet tall and wide and weigh about 120 pounds. Average xorns are about 5 feet tall and wide, weighing about 1,100 pounds. Elder xorns are about 8 feet tall and wide and weigh about 9,000 pounds.

Xorns speak Terran and Common.

COMBAT

Xorns do not attack fleshly beings except to defend themselves or their property, since they cannot digest meat. Xorns are indifferent to creatures of the Material Plane—with the sole exception of anyone carrying a significant amount of precious metals or minerals, which xorns can smell up to 20 feet away. A xorn can be quite aggressive when seeking food, especially on the Material Plane, where such sustenance is harder to find than it is on its native plane.

A xorn's favorite mode of attack is to wait just beneath a stone surface until a foe comes within reach, then emerge suddenly. Groups of xorns often send one of their number to the surface to negotiate for food while the remainder position themselves for a surprise attack.

Burrow (Ex): A xorn can glide through stone, dirt, or almost any other sort of earth except metal as easily as a fish swims through water. Its burrowing leaves behind no tunnel or hole, nor does it create any ripple or other signs of its presence. A *move earth* spell cast on an area containing a burrowing xorn flings the xorn back 30 feet, stunning the creature for 1 round unless it succeeds at a Fortitude save.

Xorn Qualities

Immunities (Ex): Xorns are immune to fire and cold.

Resistances (Ex): Xorns have electricity resistance 10.

Half Damage from Slashing (Ex): Slashing weapons deal only half damage to xorns, with a minimum of 1 point of damage.

All-Around Vision (Ex): Xorns' symmetrically placed eyes allow them to look in any direction, bestowing a +4 racial bonus to Spot and Search checks. Xorns can't be flanked.

Tremorsense (Ex): Xorns can automatically sense the location of anything within 60 feet that is in contact with the ground.

YETH HOUND

Medium-Size Outsider (Evil)
Hit Dice: 3d8+6 (19 hp)
Initiative: +6 (+2 Dex, +4 Improved Initiative)
Speed: 40 ft., fly 70 ft. (good)
AC: 20 (+2 Dex, +8 natural)
Attacks: Bite +6 melee
Damage: Bite 1d8+4
Face/Reach: 5 ft. by 5 ft./5 ft.
Special Attacks: Bay, trip
Special Qualities: Scent, flight, damage reduction 10/silver
Saves: Fort +5, Ref +5, Will +5
Abilities: Str 17, Dex 15, Con 15, Int 6, Wis 14, Cha 10
Skills: Listen +8, Spot +8, Wilderness Lore +8*
Feats: Improved Initiative

Climate/Terrain: Any land and underground
Organization: Solitary, pair, or pack (6–11)
Challenge Rating: 3
Treasure: None
Alignment: Always neutral evil
Advancement: 4–6 HD (Medium-size); 7–9 HD (Large)

These fearsome flying hounds glide low over the countryside at night, seeking likely prey.

A yeth hound looks something like an oversized greyhound with dull black fur. It stands 5 feet tall at the shoulder and weighs about 400 pounds. Its eyes glow cherry red.

COMBAT

Yeth hounds hunt only at night. They fear the sun and never venture out in daylight, even if their lives depend on it.

Bay (Su): When a yeth hound howls or barks, all creatures except other evil outsiders within a 300-foot spread must succeed at a Will save (DC 12) or become panicked for 2d4 rounds. This is a sonic, mind-affecting fear effect. Whether or not the save is successful, an affected creature is immune to that hound's bay for one day.

Trip (Ex): A yeth hound that hits with its bite attack can attempt to trip the opponent as a free action (see page 139 in the *Player's Handbook*) without making a touch attack or provoking an attack of opportunity. If the attempt fails, the opponent cannot react to trip the yeth hound.

Flight (Su): A yeth hound can fly as the spell cast by an 11th-level sorcerer, as a free action. A yeth hound that loses this ability falls and can perform only partial actions.

Skills: *A yeth hound receives a +4 racial bonus to Wilderness Lore checks when tracking by scent.

YRTHAK

Huge Magical Beast
Hit Dice: 12d10+36 (102 hp)
Initiative: +6 (+2 Dex, +4 Improved Initiative)
Speed: 20 ft., fly 60 ft. (average)
AC: 18 (−2 size, +2 Dex, +8 natural)
Attacks: Bite +15 melee, 2 claws +13 melee
Damage: Bite 2d8+5, claw 1d6+2
Face/Reach: 10 ft. by 20 ft./10 ft.
Special Attacks: Sonic lance +12 ranged touch, explosion, snatch
Special Qualities: Blindsight, sonic vulnerability
Saves: Fort +11, Ref +10, Will +5
Abilities: Str 20, Dex 14, Con 17, Int 7, Wis 13, Cha 11
Skills: Listen +19, Move Silently +10
Feats: Flyby Attack, Improved Initiative, Multiattack

Climate/Terrain: Any hill and mountains
Organization: Solitary or clutch (2–4)
Challenge Rating: 9
Treasure: None
Alignment: Often neutral
Advancement: 13–16 HD (Huge); 17–36 HD (Gargantuan)

A strange predator from desolate wastelands, the yrthak terrorizes the area it inhabits as an always hungry dragon might.

Reptilian with fleshy wings, a long tail, and a large fin on its back, an yrthak is blind. It senses sound and movement with a special organ on its long tongue. A single hornlike protrusion on its crocodilian head emits powerfully focused beams of sound. The entire creature is a yellowish green color, with the wings and fin being more yellow and the head and body more green. The teeth are yellow.

Yrthaks are crafty and devious. They are omnivorous but prefer meat. An yrthak keeps a nest high in its isolated mountain lair and may travel for days in search of food, returning only infrequently. Yrthaks are sometimes seen swooping a hundred feet over the ground, attempting to sense prey.

Despite their intelligence, yrthaks do not speak.

COMBAT

An yrthak prefers to attack from the air, strafing the ground with sonic attacks or snatching up and dropping prey (eventually landing to devour the flattened mess).

Sonic Lance (Su): Every 2 rounds, an yrthak can focus sonic energy in a ray up to 60 feet long. This is a ranged touch attack that deals 6d6 points of damage to a single target.

Explosion (Su): The yrthak can fire its sonic lance at the ground, a large rock, a stone wall, or the like to create an explosion of shattered stone. This attack deals 2d6 points of piercing damage to all within 10 feet of the effect's center.

This counts as a use of the sonic lance and thus is usable only once every 2 rounds, and never on a round following a sonic lance attack.

Snatch (Ex): An yrthak that hits a Medium-size or smaller creature with a claw attack attempts to start a grapple as a free action without provoking an attack of opportunity. If it gets a hold, it can fly off with its prey and deal automatic claw damage, though it prefers to drop victims from a height. It can drop a snatched creature as a free action, which deals normal falling damage if the yrthak is flying.

Blindsight (Ex): An yrthak can ascertain all foes within 120 feet. Beyond that range it is considered blinded. Yrthaks are invulnerable to gaze attacks, visual effects of spells such as illusions, and other attack forms that rely on sight.

An yrthak whose sense of hearing is impaired is effectively blind, treating all targets as totally concealed (see Concealment, page 133 in the *Player's Handbook*).

Sonic Vulnerability (Ex): Yrthaks are affected by loud noises and sonic spells (such as *ghost sound* or *silence*) and are more susceptible to sound-based attacks, suffering a −2 racial penalty to all saves.

Skills: Yrthaks receive a +4 racial bonus to Listen checks.

YUAN-TI

	Pureblood Medium-Size Monstrous Humanoid	Halfblood Medium-Size Monstrous Humanoid	Abomination Large Monstrous Humanoid
Hit Dice:	6d8 (27 hp)	7d8+7 (38 hp)	9d8+27 (67 hp)
Initiative:	+5 (+1 Dex, +4 Improved Initiative)	+5 (+1 Dex, +4 Improved Initiative)	+5 (+1 Dex, +4 Improved Initiative)
Speed:	30 ft.	30 ft.	30 ft., climb 20 ft., swim 20 ft.
AC:	16 (+1 Dex, +1 natural, +2 leather, +2 masterwork large shield)	16 (+1 Dex, +1 natural, +2 leather, +2 masterwork large shield)	20 (−1 size, +1 Dex, +10 natural); or 21 (−1 size, +1 Dex, +10 natural, +1 masterwork small shield) with human arms
Attacks:	Masterwork scimitar +7/+2 melee; or masterwork longbow with masterwork arrows +9/+4 ranged	Masterwork scimitar +10/+5 melee (and bite if snake-headed +4 melee); or masterwork mighty composite longbow (+2) with masterwork arrows +10/+5 ranged	Masterwork falchion +13/+8 melee (human arms) (or bite +12 melee if snake-headed); or masterwork mighty composite longbow (+2) with masterwork arrows +11/+6 ranged (human arms)
Damage:	Masterwork scimitar 1d6; or masterwork longbow 1d8	Masterwork scimitar 1d6+2, bite 1d6+1 and poison; or masterwork mighty composite longbow (+2) 1d8+2	Masterwork falchion 2d4+6, bite 2d6+6 and poison; or masterwork mighty composite longbow (+2) 1d8+2
Face/Reach:	5 ft. by 5 ft./5 ft.	5 ft. by 5 ft./5 ft.	5 ft. by 5 ft./10 ft.
Special Attacks:	Spell-like abilities, psionics	Spell-like abilities, psionics	Spell-like abilities, psionics, improved grab (if snake-headed), constrict 1d6+6
Special Qualities:	SR 16	SR 16	SR 16
Saves:	Fort +2, Ref +6, Will +9	Fort +3, Ref +6, Will +9	Fort +6, Ref +7, Will +10
Abilities:	Str 11, Dex 13, Con 11, Int 18, Wis 18, Cha 16	Str 15, Dex 13, Con 13, Int 18, Wis 18, Cha 16	Str 19, Dex 13, Con 17, Int 18, Wis 18, Cha 16
Skills:	Concentration +9, Craft (any two) or Knowledge (any two) +9, Disguise +3*, Hide +7*, Listen +15, Spot +15	Concentration +11, Craft (any two) or Knowledge (any two) +9, Hide +8*, Listen +15, Spot +15	Concentration +11, 2 Craft (any two) or Knowledge (any two) +9, Hide +9*, Listen +15, Spot +15
Feats:	Alertness, Blind-Fight, Dodge, Expertise, Improved Initiative	Alertness, Blind-Fight, Dodge, Expertise, Improved Initiative	Alertness, Blind-Fight, Dodge, Expertise, Improved Initiative
Climate/Terrain:	Warm forest and underground	Warm forest and underground	Warm forest and underground
Organization:	Solitary, pair, gang (2–4), troupe (2–13 purebloods, 2–5 halfbloods, and 2–4 abominations), or tribe (20–160 purebloods, 10–80 halfbloods, and 10–40 abominations)		
Challenge Rating:	5	5	7
Treasure:	Double standard	Double standard	Double standard
Alignment:	Usually chaotic evil	Usually chaotic evil	Usually chaotic evil
Advancement:	By character class	By character class	By character class

The yuan-ti are descended from humans whose bloodlines have been mingled with those of snakes. Their evilness, cunning, and ruthlessness are legendary.

Yuan-ti constantly scheme to advance their own dark agendas. They are calculating and suave enough to form alliances with other evil creatures when necessary, but they always put their own interests first.

All yuan-ti possess some snakelike features, and many have snake body parts. Yuan-ti speak their own language, plus Common, Draconic, and Abyssal.

COMBAT

Yuan-ti are geniuses and fight as such. They plan elaborate traps and utilize their surroundings superbly in combat, preferring ambushes to direct confrontation. They also prefer ranged attacks and spells to melee, and they liberally use *cause fear* and aversion to keep foes at a distance.

In a mixed group, the least valuable and powerful attack first. This means that the purebloods go before the halfbloods, which go before the abominations. The group leader may order particular members forward before others if that makes for better strategy.

Spell-Like Abilities: (Human-headed) 1/day—*animal trance, cause fear, deeper darkness, entangle, neutralize poison, suggestion,* and *polymorph other.* These abilities are as the spells cast by an 8th-level sorcerer (save DC 13 + spell level).

Psionics (Sp): All yuan-ti can produce the following effects at will.

Detect Poison: As the spell cast by a 6th-level sorcerer.

Alternate Form: The yuan-ti can assume the form of a Tiny to Large viper (see the Snake entry in Appendix 1: Animals). This ability is similar to a *shapchange* spell cast by a 19th-level sorcerer but allows only viper forms. If the yuan-ti has a poisonous bite of its own, it uses its own or the viper's poison, whichever is more potent.

Chameleon Power: The yuan-ti can change the coloration of itself and its equipment to match its surroundings.

Produce Acid: The yuan-ti can exude acid from its body, dealing 1d6 points of damage to anything it touches. The acid becomes inert when it leaves the yuan-ti's body.

Aversion: The yuan-ti creates a compulsion effect targeting one creature within 30 feet. The subject must succeed at a Will save (DC 17) or gain an aversion to snakes for 10 minutes. Affected subjects must stay at least 20 feet from any snake or yuan-ti, alive or dead; if already within 20 feet, they move away. A subject can overcome the compulsion by succeeding at another DC 17 Will save, but still suffers deep anxiety. This causes a −4 reduction to Dexterity until the effect wears off or the subject is no longer within 20 feet of a snake or yuan-ti. This ability is otherwise similar to *antipathy* as cast by a 16th-level sorcerer.

Poison (Ex): Halfbloods and abominations with snake heads only—bite, Fortitude save (DC 17); initial and secondary damage 1d6 temporary Constitution.

Skills: *Yuan-ti using *chameleon power* receive a +8 circumstance bonus to Hide checks.

YUAN-TI HALFBLOOD FEATURES

1d6 Roll*	Feature	Effect
1	Snake head	Bite damage 1d6 and poison (save DC 14; initial and secondary damage 1d6 temporary Constitution)
2	Flexible torso	+1 racial bonus to Reflex saves
3	No legs, snake tail	Speed 20 ft., climb 15 ft., swim 15 ft; can constrict Medium-size or smaller creatures for 1d6+3 damage (see Abomination, below)
4	Snakes instead of arms	Gains 2 bite attacks (1d4 damage and poison as above)
5	Scales instead of skin	+4 natural armor
6	Legs and snake tail	Speed 30 ft., swim 15 ft.; can constrict Small or smaller creatures for 1d4+3 damage (see Abomination, below)

*Roll twice, ignoring duplicate or contradictory results.

YUAN-TI SOCIETY

The yuan-ti are devout worshipers of evil. They also hold all reptiles in high esteem. The center of yuan-ti life is the temple, and their rituals often involve bloody sacrifices. They tend toward isolated, old ruins but have been known to build even underneath human cities. Yuan-ti are always secretive about the location of a city or temple. Their architecture favors circles, with ramps and poles replacing stairs.

The abominations rule over the yuan-ti and are the temple leaders, with the high priest (always human-headed) above all. Purebloods take care of all outside negotiations, always pretending to be human.

The chief deity of the yuan-ti is Merrshaulk, who prompted and directed the formation of the line.

PUREBLOOD

Yuan-ti purebloods appear human at first glance. Their snakelike features tend to be subtle: reptilian eyes, forked tongues, pointed teeth, scaly patches on the neck or limbs, and the like. Thus, a pureblood gains a +5 racial bonus to Disguise checks when impersonating a human.

HALFBLOOD

Yuan-ti halfbloods always have obvious snake features. The most common of these are set out in the table above.

ABOMINATION

Yuan-ti abominations are all snake (01–50 on d%) or have a single human feature, either a head (51–75) or arms (76–00).

Improved Grab (Ex): To use this ability, a snake-headed abomination must hit with its bite attack. If it gets a hold, it can constrict.

Constrict (Ex): An abomination deals 1d6+6 points of damage with a successful grapple check (using the bite attack bonus if snake-headed) against Large or smaller creatures.

YUAN-TI CHARACTERS

The favored class for yuan-ti purebloods and halfbloods is ranger. Yuan-ti abominations favor the cleric class. Yuan-ti clerics worship Merrshaulk and can choose any two of the following domains: Chaos, Evil, Destruction, and Plant.

ZOMBIE

	Tiny Zombie Tiny Undead	Small Zombie Small Undead	Medium Zombie Medium-Size Undead
Hit Dice:	1/2 d12+3 (6 hp)	1d12+3 (9 hp)	2d12+3 (16 hp)
Initiative:	–1 (Dex)	–1 (Dex)	–1 (Dex)
Speed:	20 ft.	30 ft.	30 ft.
AC:	11 (+2 size, –1 Dex)	11 (+1 size, –1 Dex, +1 natural)	11 (–1 Dex, +2 natural)
Attacks:	Slam +2 melee	Slam +1 melee	Slam +2 melee
Damage:	Slam 1d3	Slam 1d4	Slam 1d6+1
Face/Reach:	2 1/2 ft. by 2 1/2 ft./0 ft.	5 ft. by 5 ft./5 ft.	5 ft. by 5 ft./5 ft.
Special Qualities:	Undead, partial actions only	Undead, partial actions only	Undead, partial actions only
Saves:	Fort +0, Ref –1, Will +2	Fort +0, Ref –1, Will +2	Fort +0, Ref –1, Will +3
Abilities:	Str 9, Dex 8, Con —, Int —, Wis 10, Cha 1	Str 11, Dex 8, Con —, Int —, Wis 10, Cha 1	Str 13, Dex 8, Con —, Int —, Wis 10, Cha 1
Feats:	Toughness	Toughness	Toughness

	Large Zombie		Huge Zombie		Gargantuan Zombie
	Large Undead		**Huge Undead**		**Gargantuan Undead**
Hit Dice:	4d12+3 (29 hp)		8d12+3 (55 hp)		24d12+3 (159 hp)
Initiative:	–1 (Dex)		–1 (Dex)		–1 (Dex)
Speed:	40 ft.		40 ft.		40 ft.
AC:	11 (–1 size, –1 Dex, +3 natural)		11 (–2 size, –1 Dex, +4 natural)		11 (–4 size, –1 Dex, +6 natural)
Attacks:	Slam +4 melee		Slam +7 melee		Slam +15 melee
Damage:	Slam 1d8+4		Slam 2d6+7		Slam 2d8+10
Face/Reach:	5 ft. by 5 ft./10 ft.		10 ft. by 10 ft./15 ft.		20 ft. by 20 ft./20 ft.
Special Qualities:	Undead, partial actions only		Undead, partial actions only		Undead, partial actions only
Saves:	Fort +1, Ref +0, Will +4		Fort +2, Ref +1, Will +6		Fort +8, Ref +7, Will +14
Abilities:	Str 17, Dex 8, Con —,		Str 21, Dex 8, Con —,		Str 25, Dex 8, Con —,
	Int —, Wis 10, Cha 1		Int —, Wis 10, Cha 1		Int —, Wis 10, Cha 1
Feats:	Toughness		Toughness		Toughness, Improved Critical (slam)

	Colossal Zombie
	Colossal Undead
Hit Dice:	48d12+3 (315 hp)
Initiative:	–2 (Dex)
Speed:	40 ft.
AC:	11 (–8 size, –2 Dex, +11 natural)
Attacks:	Slam +25 melee
Damage:	Slam 4d6+13
Face/Reach:	40 ft. by 40 ft./25 ft.
Special Qualities:	Undead, partial actions only
Saves:	Fort +16, Ref +14, Will +26
Abilities:	Str 29, Dex 6, Con —,
	Int —, Wis 10, Cha 3
Feats:	Toughness, Improved Critical (slam)

Climate/Terrain:	Any land and underground
Organization:	Tiny and Small: Squad (6–10) or mob (11–20); Medium-size: Gang (2–5), squad (6–10), or mob (11–20); Large and larger: Solitary, gang (2–5), squad, (6–10) or mob (11–20)
Challenge Rating:	Tiny 1/6; Small 1/4; Medium-size 1/2; Large 1; Huge 3; Gargantuan 6; Colossal 12
Treasure:	None
Alignment:	Always neutral
Advancement:	Tiny and Small —; Medium-size 3 HD (Medium-size); Large 5–7 HD (Large); Huge 9–23 HD (Huge); Gargantuan 25–47 HD (Gargantuan); Colossal 49–96 HD (Colossal)

Zombies are corpses reanimated through dark and sinister magic. These mindless automatons shamble about, doing their creator's bidding without fear or hesitation.

Zombies are not pleasant to look upon. Drawn from their graves, half decayed and partially consumed by worms, they wear the tattered remains of their burial clothes. A rank odor of death hangs heavy in the air around them.

Because of their utter lack of intelligence, the instructions given to a newly created zombie must be very simple, such as "Kill anyone who enters this room."

The statistics block describes zombies with humanlike forms. Zombies with different forms may have different statistics.

COMBAT

Zombies hammer enemies with their unnaturally strong fists. Because zombies move so slowly, however, experienced adventurers have little trouble dealing with them.

Undead: Immune to mind-influencing effects, poison, sleep, paralysis, stunning, and disease. Not subject to critical hits, subdual damage, ability damage, energy drain, or death from massive damage.

Partial Actions Only (Ex): Zombies have poor reflexes and can perform only partial actions. Thus they can move or attack, but can only do both if they charge (a partial charge).

	Ape	Baboon	Badger
	Large Animal	**Medium-Size Animal**	**Tiny Animal**
Hit Dice:	4d8+8 (26 hp)	1d8+1 (5 hp)	1d8+2 (6 hp)
Initiative:	+2 (Dex)	+2 (Dex)	+3 (Dex)
Speed:	30 ft., climb 30 ft.	40 ft., climb 30 ft.	30 ft., burrow 10 ft.
AC:	14 (−1 size, +2 Dex, +3 natural)	13 (+2 Dex, +1 natural)	15 (+2 size, +3 Dex)
Attacks:	2 claws +7 melee, bite +2 melee	Bite +2 melee	2 claws +5 melee, bite +0 melee
Damage:	Claw 1d6+5, bite 1d6+2	Bite 1d6+3	Claw 1d2−1, bite 1d3−1
Face/Reach:	5 ft. by 5 ft./5 ft.	5 ft. by 5 ft./5 ft.	2 1/2 ft. by 2 1/2 ft./0 ft.
Special Attacks:	—	—	Rage
Special Qualities:	Scent	Scent	Scent
Saves:	Fort +6, Ref +6, Will +2	Fort +3, Ref +4, Will +1	Fort +4, Ref +5, Will +1
Abilities:	Str 21, Dex 15, Con 14,	Str 15, Dex 14, Con 12,	Str 8, Dex 17, Con 15,
	Int 2, Wis 12, Cha 7	Int 2, Wis 12, Cha 4	Int 2, Wis 12, Cha 6
Skills:	Climb +18, Listen +6, Spot +6	Climb +13, Listen +5, Spot +5	Escape Artist +7, Listen +4, Spot +4
Feats:	—	—	Weapon Finesse (bite, claw)
Climate/Terrain:	Warm forest and mountains	Warm desert and plains	Temperate forest, hill, plains, and underground
Organization:	Solitary or company (2–5)	Solitary or troop (10–40)	Solitary or cete (2–5)
Challenge Rating:	2	1/2	1/2
Treasure:	None	None	None
Alignment:	Always neutral	Always neutral	Always neutral
Advancement:	5–8 HD (Large)	2–3 HD (Medium-size)	2 HD (Tiny)

APE

These powerful omnivores resemble gorillas but are far more aggressive; they kill and eat anything they can catch.

BABOON

Baboons are powerful and aggressive monkeys adapted to life on the ground. They prefer open spaces but climb trees to find safe places to rest overnight.

A typical baboon is the size of a big dog. Males can weigh as much as 90 pounds.

BADGER

The badger is a furry animal with a squat, powerful body. Its strong forelimbs are armed with long claws for digging.

Combat

Badgers attack with their sharp claws and teeth.

Rage (Ex): A badger that takes damage in combat flies into a berserk rage the following round, clawing and biting madly until either it or its opponent is dead. It gains +4 Strength, +4 Constitution, and −2 AC. The creature cannot end its rage voluntarily.

BAT

Bats are nocturnal flying mammals. The statistics presented here describe small, insectivorous bats.

Combat

Blindsight (Ex): Bats can "see" by emitting high-frequency sounds, inaudible to most other creatures, that allow them to locate objects and creatures within 120 feet. A *silence* spell negates

	Bat	Bear, Black	Bear, Brown
	Diminutive Animal	**Medium-Size Animal**	**Large Animal**
Hit Dice:	1/4 d8 (1 hp)	3d8+6 (19 hp)	6d8+24 (51 hp)
Initiative:	+2 (Dex)	+1 (Dex)	+1 (Dex)
Speed:	5 ft., fly 40 ft. (good)	40 ft.	40 ft.
AC:	16 (+4 size, +2 Dex)	13 (+1 Dex, +2 natural)	15 (−1 size, +1 Dex, +5 natural)
Attacks:	—	2 claws +6 melee, bite +1 melee	2 claws +11 melee, bite +6 melee
Damage:	—	Claw 1d4+4, bite 1d6+2	Claw 1d8+8, bite 2d8+4
Face/Reach:	1 ft. by 1 ft./0 ft.	5 ft. by 5 ft./5 ft.	5 ft. by 10 ft./5 ft.
Special Attacks:	—	—	Improved grab
Special Qualities:	Blindsight	Scent	Scent
Saves:	Fort +2, Ref +4, Will +2	Fort +5, Ref +4, Will +2	Fort +9, Ref +6, Will +3
Abilities:	Str 1, Dex 15, Con 10,	Str 19, Dex 13, Con 15,	Str 27, Dex 13, Con 19,
	Int 2, Wis 14, Cha 4	Int 2, Wis 12, Cha 6	Int 2, Wis 12, Cha 6
Skills:	Listen +9, Move Silently +6, Spot +9*	Climb +6, Listen +4, Spot +7, Swim +8	Listen +4, Spot +7, Swim +14
Climate/Terrain:	Temperate and warm desert, forest, hill, plains, and underground	Temperate and warm forest, hill, and mountains	Any forest, hill, mountains, and underground
Organization:	Colony (10–40) or swarm (10–50)	Solitary or pair	Solitary or pair
Challenge Rating:	1/10	2	4
Treasure:	None	None	None
Alignment:	Always neutral	Always neutral	Always neutral
Advancement:	—	4–5 HD (Medium-size)	7–10 HD (Large)

this and forces the bat to rely on its weak vision, which has a maximum range of 10 feet.

Skills: *Bats receive a +4 racial bonus to Spot and Listen checks. These bonuses are lost if Blindsight is negated.

BLACK BEAR

The black bear is a forest-dwelling omnivore that usually is not dangerous unless an interloper threatens its cubs or food supply.

Black bears can be pure black, blond, or cinnamon in color and are rarely more than 5 feet long.

BROWN BEAR

These massive carnivores weigh more than 1,800 pounds and stand nearly 12 feet tall when they rear up on their hind legs. They are bad-tempered and territorial. Brown bear statistics can be used for almost any big bear, including the North American grizzly.

POLAR BEAR

These long, lean carnivores are slightly taller than brown bears.

Combat

Polar bears fight just as brown bears do.

Skills: *A polar bear's white coat bestows a +12 racial bonus to Hide checks in snowy areas.

BISON

These herd animals can be very aggressive when protecting young and during the mating season, but they generally prefer flight to fighting.

Bison stand more than 6 feet tall at the shoulder and are 9 to 12 feet long. They weigh 1,800 to 2,400 pounds. Bison statistics can be used for almost any large herd animal.

Combat

Stampede (Ex): A frightened herd of bison flees as a group in a random direction (but always away from the perceived source of danger). They literally run over anything of size Large or smaller that gets in their way, dealing 1d12 points of damage for each five bison in the herd. A successful Reflex save (DC 16) halves the damage.

FAMILIARS

Some animals can become the familiar of a wizard or sorcerer character (see page 51 in the *Player's Handbook* for details). The animals and the special abilities they possess or impart to their master are as follows:

Familiar	Special
Bat	—
Cat	Master gains a +2 bonus to Move Silently checks
Hawk	—
Owl	Has low-light vision; master gains a +2 bonus to Move Silently checks
Rat	Master gains a +2 bonus to Fortitude saves
Raven	Speaks one language
Snake (Tiny)	Poisonous bite
Toad	Master gains +2 to Constitution score
Weasel	Master gains a +2 bonus to Reflex saves

BOAR

Though not carnivores, these wild swine are very bad-tempered and usually charge anyone who disturbs them.

A boar is covered in coarse, grayish-black fur. Adult males are about 4 feet long and 3 feet high at the shoulder.

Combat

Ferocity (Ex): A boar is such a tenacious combatant that it continues to fight without penalty even while disabled or dying (see page 129 in the *Player's Handbook*).

CAMEL

Camels are known for their ability to travel long distances without food or water.

The numbers presented here are for the dromedary, or one-humped camel, which thrives in warm deserts. Dromedaries stand about 7 feet tall at the shoulder, with a hump rising a foot higher.

The two-humped, or Bactrian, camel is suited to cooler, rocky areas. It is stockier, slower (speed 40), and has a better Constitution score (16).

	Bear, Polar	Bison	Boar
	Large Animal	**Large Animal**	**Medium-Size Animal**
Hit Dice:	8d8+32 (68 hp)	5d8+15 (37 hp)	3d8+9 (22 hp)
Initiative:	+1 (Dex)	+0	+0
Speed:	40 ft., swim 30 ft.	40 ft.	40 ft.
AC:	15 (−1 size, +1 Dex, +5 natural)	13 (−1 size, +4 natural)	16 (+6 natural)
Attacks:	2 claws +13 melee, bite +8 melee	Butt +6 melee	Gore +4 melee
Damage:	Claw 1d8+8, bite 2d8+4	Butt 1d8+6	Gore 1d8+3
Face/Reach:	5 ft. by 10 ft./5 ft.	5 ft. by 10 ft./5 ft.	5 ft. by 5 ft./5 ft.
Special Attacks:	Improved grab	Stampede	Ferocity
Special Qualities:	Scent	Scent	Scent
Saves:	Fort +10, Ref +7, Will +3	Fort +7, Ref +4, Will +1	Fort +6, Ref +3, Will +2
Abilities:	Str 27, Dex 13, Con 19, Int 2, Wis 12, Cha 6	Str 18, Dex 10, Con 16, Int 2, Wis 11, Cha 4	Str 15, Dex 10, Con 17, Int 2, Wis 13, Cha 4
Skills:	Hide −2*, Listen +4, Spot +7	Listen +8, Spot +5	Listen +7, Spot +5
Climate/Terrain:	Any cold land	Temperate plains	Temperate and warm forest
Organization:	Solitary or pair	Solitary or herd (6–30)	Solitary
Challenge Rating:	4	2	2
Treasure:	None	None	None
Alignment:	Always neutral	Always neutral	Always neutral
Advancement:	9–12 HD (Large)	6–7 HD (Large)	4–5 HD (Medium-size)

	Camel	Cat	Cheetah
	Large Animal	Tiny Animal	Medium-Size Animal
Hit Dice:	3d8+6 (19 hp)	1/2 d8 (2 hp)	3d8+6 (19 hp)
Initiative:	+3 (Dex)	+2 (Dex)	+4 (Dex)
Speed:	50 ft.	30 ft.	50 ft.
AC:	13 (−1 size, +3 Dex, +1 natural)	14 (+2 size, +2 Dex)	15 (+4 Dex, +1 natural)
Attacks:	Bite +5 melee	2 claws +4 melee, bite −1 melee	Bite +6 melee, 2 claws +1 melee
Damage:	Bite 1d4+6	Claw 1d2−4, bite 1d3−4	Bite 1d6+3, claw 1d2+1
Face/Reach:	5 ft. by 10 ft./5 ft.	2 1/2 ft. by 2 1/2 ft./0 ft.	5 ft. by 5 ft./5 ft.
Special Attacks:	—	—	Trip
Special Qualities:	Scent	—	Sprint
Saves:	Fort +5, Ref +6, Will +1	Fort +2, Ref +4, Will +1	Fort +5, Ref +7, Will +2
Abilities:	Str 18, Dex 16, Con 14,	Str 3, Dex 15, Con 10,	Str 16, Dex 19, Con 15,
	Int 1, Wis 11, Cha 4	Int 2, Wis 12, Cha 7	Int 2, Wis 12, Cha 6
Skills:	Listen +5, Spot +5	Balance +10, Climb +5, Hide +17*,	Hide +7, Listen +5,
		Listen +4, Move Silently +9, Spot +4	Move Silently +8, Spot +5
Feats:	—	Weapon Finesse (claw, bite)	Weapon Finesse (bite, claw)

	Camel	Cat	Cheetah
Climate/Terrain:	Any desert, hill, and mountains	Any land	Warm plains
Organization:	Solitary	Solitary	Solitary, pair, or family (3–5)
Challenge Rating:	1	1/4	2
Treasure:	None	None	None
Alignment:	Always neutral	Always neutral	Always neutral
Advancement:	—	—	4–5 HD (Medium-size)

	Crocodile	Crocodile, Giant	Dog
	Medium-Size Animal (Aquatic)	Huge Animal (Aquatic)	Small Animal
Hit Dice:	3d8+9 (22 hp)	7d8+28 (59 hp)	1d8+2 (6 hp)
Initiative:	+1 (Dex)	+1 (Dex)	+3 (Dex)
Speed:	20 ft., swim 30 ft.	20 ft., swim 30 ft.	40 ft.
AC:	15 (+1 Dex, +4 natural)	16 (−2 size, +1 Dex, +7 natural)	15 (+1 size, +3 Dex, +1 natural)
Attacks:	Bite +6 melee; or tail slap +6 melee	Bite +11 melee; or tail slap +11 melee	Bite +2 melee
Damage:	Bite 1d8+6; tail slap 1d12+6	Bite 2d8+12; tail slap 1d12+12	Bite 1d4+1
Face/Reach:	5 ft. by 5 ft./5 ft.	10 ft. by 20 ft./10 ft.	5 ft. by 5 ft./5 ft.
Special Attacks:	Improved grab	Improved grab	—
Special Qualities:	—	—	Scent
Saves:	Fort +6, Ref +4, Will +2	Fort +9, Ref +6, Will +3	Fort +4, Ref +5, Will +1
Abilities:	Str 19, Dex 12, Con 17,	Str 27, Dex 12, Con 19,	Str 13, Dex 17, Con 15,
	Int 2, Wis 12, Cha 2	Int 1, Wis 12, Cha 2	Int 2, Wis 12, Cha 6
Skills:	Hide +7*, Listen +5, Spot +5	Hide +0*, Listen +5, Spot +5	Listen +5, Spot +5, Swim +5,
			Wilderness Lore +1*

	Crocodile	Crocodile, Giant	Dog
Climate/Terrain:	Warm marsh and aquatic	Warm marsh and aquatic	Any land
Organization:	Solitary or colony (6–11)	Solitary or colony (6–11)	Solitary
Challenge Rating:	2	4	1/3
Treasure:	None	None	None
Alignment:	Always neutral	Always neutral	Always neutral
Advancement:	4–5 HD (Medium-size)	8–14 HD (Huge)	—

Carrying Capacity: A light load for a camel is up to 300 pounds; a medium load, 301–600 pounds; a heavy load, 601–900 pounds. A camel can drag 4,500 pounds.

CAT

The statistics presented here describe a common housecat.

Skills: Cats receive a +4 racial bonus to Hide and Move Silently checks and a +8 racial bonus to Balance checks. They use their Dexterity modifier for Climb checks. *In areas of tall grass or heavy undergrowth, the Hide bonus rises to +8.

CHEETAH

Cheetahs are swift feline predators of the plains. A cheetah is 3 to 5 feet long and weighs 110 to 130 pounds.

Combat

Cheetahs make sudden sprints to bring down prey.

Trip (Ex): A cheetah that hits with a claw or bite attack can attempt to trip the opponent as a free action (see page 139 in the *Player's Handbook*) without making a touch attack or provoking an attack of opportunity. If the attempt fails, the opponent cannot react to trip the cheetah.

Sprint (Ex): Once an hour, a cheetah can take a charge action to move ten times its normal speed (500 feet).

CROCODILE

These aggressive aquatic predators are 11 to 12 feet long. They lie mostly submerged in rivers or marshes, with only their eyes and nostrils showing, waiting for prey to come within reach.

Combat

Improved Grab (Ex): To use this ability, the crocodile must hit a Medium-size or smaller opponent with its bite attack. If it gets a hold, the crocodile grabs the opponent with its mouth and drags it into deep water, attempting to pin it to the bottom. The crocodile automatically deals bite damage each round it maintains the pin.

Skills: *A crocodile gains a +12 racial bonus to Hide checks when submerged.

Giant Crocodile

These huge creatures usually live in salt water and can be more than 20 feet long.

Giant crocodiles can grab and hold creatures of Large or smaller size but otherwise fight and behave like their smaller cousins.

DOG

The statistics presented here describe fairly small dogs such as terriers. They also can be used for small wild canines such as coyotes, jackals, and African wild dogs.

Skills: *Dogs receive a +8 racial bonus to Wilderness Lore checks when tracking by scent.

RIDING DOG

This category includes working breeds such as collies, huskies, and St. Bernards.

Combat

If trained for war, these animals can make trip attacks just as wolves do (see the Wolf entry). A riding dog can fight while carrying a rider, but the rider cannot also attack unless he or she succeeds at a Ride check (see Ride, page 72 in the *Player's Handbook*).

Carrying Capacity: A light load for a riding dog is up to 100 pounds; a medium load, 101–200 pounds; a heavy load, 201–300 pounds. A riding dog can drag 1,500 pounds.

Skills: *Riding dogs receive a +4 racial bonus to Wilderness Lore checks when tracking by scent.

DONKEY

These long-eared, horselike creatures are surefooted and sturdy. The statistics presented here could also describe burros.

Carrying Capacity: A light load for a donkey is up to 50 pounds; a medium load, 51–100 pounds; a heavy load, 101–150 pounds. A donkey can drag 750 pounds.

Skills: Donkeys receive a +2 racial bonus to Balance.

EAGLE

These birds of prey inhabit nearly every terrain and climate, though they all prefer high, secluded nesting spots.

A typical eagle is about 3 feet long and has a wingspan of about 7 feet. The statistics presented here can describe any similar-sized, diurnal bird of prey.

Skills: *Eagles receive a +8 racial bonus to Spot checks during daylight.

ELEPHANT

Massive herbivores of tropical lands, elephants are unpredictable but sometimes used as mounts or beasts of burden.

This entry describes an African elephant. Indian elephants are slightly smaller and weaker (Strength 28), but more readily trained (Wisdom 15). These statistics can also represent prehistoric creatures such as mammoths and mastodons.

Combat

Trample (Ex): An elephant can trample Medium-size or smaller creatures for automatic gore damage. Opponents who do not make attacks of opportunity against the elephant can attempt a Reflex save (DC 20) to halve the damage.

HAWK

These creatures are similar to eagles but slightly smaller: 1 to 2 feet long, with wingspans of 6 feet or less.

Combat

Hawks combine both claws into a single attack.

Skills: *Hawks gain a +8 racial bonus to Spot checks in daylight.

HEAVY HORSE

The statistics presented here describe large breeds of working horses such as Clydesdales. These animals are usually ready for heavy work by age three. A heavy horse cannot fight while carrying a rider.

Carrying Capacity: A light load for a heavy horse is up to 200 pounds; a medium load, 201–400 pounds; a heavy load, 401–600 pounds. A heavy horse can drag 3,000 pounds.

HEAVY WARHORSE

These animals are similar to heavy horses but are trained and bred for strength and aggression. A heavy warhorse can fight while carrying a rider, but the rider cannot also attack unless he or she succeeds at a Ride check (DC 10).

	Dog, Riding Medium-Size Animal	Donkey Medium-Size Animal	Eagle Small Animal
Hit Dice:	2d8+4 (13 hp)	2d8+2 (11 hp)	1d8+1 (5 hp)
Initiative:	+2 (Dex)	+1 (Dex)	+2 (Dex)
Speed:	40 ft.	30 ft.	10 ft., fly 80 ft. (average)
AC:	16 (+2 Dex, +4 natural)	13 (+1 Dex, +2 natural)	14 (+1 size, +2 Dex, +1 natural)
Attacks:	Bite +3 melee	Bite +1 melee	2 claws +3 melee, bite −2 melee
Damage:	Bite 1d6+3	Bite 1d2	Claw 1d3, bite 1d4
Face/Reach:	5 ft. by 5 ft./5 ft.	5 ft. by 5 ft./5 ft.	5 ft. by 5 ft./5 ft.
Special Qualities:	Scent	Scent	—
Saves:	Fort +5, Ref +5, Will +1	Fort +4, Ref +4, Will +0	Fort +3, Ref +4, Will +2
Abilities:	Str 15, Dex 15, Con 15, Int 2, Wis 12, Cha 6	Str 10, Dex 13, Con 12, Int 1, Wis 11, Cha 4	Str 10, Dex 15, Con 12, Int 2, Wis 14, Cha 6
Skills:	Listen +5, Spot +5, Swim +5 Wilderness Lore +1*	Balance +3, Listen +5, Spot +5	Listen +6, Spot +6*
Feats:	—	—	Weapon Finesse (claw, bite)
Climate/Terrain:	Any land	Temperate and warm desert, hill, plains, and mountains	Any forest, hill, plains, and mountains
Organization:	Solitary	Solitary	Solitary or pair
Challenge Rating:	1	1/6	1/2
Treasure:	None	None	None
Alignment:	Always neutral	Always neutral	Always neutral
Advancement:	—	—	2–3 HD (Medium-size)

	Elephant Huge Animal	Hawk Tiny Animal	Horse, Heavy Large Animal
Hit Dice:	11d8+55 (104 hp)	1d8 (4 hp)	3d8+6 (19 hp)
Initiative:	+0 (Dex)	+3 (Dex)	+1 (Dex)
Speed:	40 ft.	10 ft., fly 60 ft. (average)	50 ft.
AC:	15 (−2 size, +7 natural)	17 (+2 size, +3 Dex, +2 natural)	13 (−1 size, +1 Dex, +3 natural)
Attacks:	Slam +16 melee, 2 stamps +11 melee; or gore +16 melee	Claws +5 melee	2 hooves +3 melee
Damage:	Slam 2d6+10, stamp 2d6+5; gore 2d8+15	Claws 1d4−2	Hoof 1d6+2
Face/Reach:	10 ft. by 20 ft./10 ft.	2 1/2 ft. by 2 1/2 ft./0 ft.	5 ft. by 10 ft./5 ft.
Special Attacks:	Trample 2d8+15	—	
Special Qualities:	Scent		Scent
Saves:	Fort +12, Ref +7, Will +4	Fort +2, Ref +5, Will +2	Fort +5, Ref +4, Will +2
Abilities:	Str 30, Dex 10, Con 21, Int 2, Wis 13, Cha 7	Str 6, Dex 17, Con 10, Int 2, Wis 14, Cha 6	Str 15, Dex 13, Con 15, Int 2, Wis 12, Cha 6
Skills:	Listen +6, Spot +6	Listen +6, Spot +6*	Listen +6, Spot +6
Feats:	—	Weapon Finesse (claws)	
Climate/Terrain:	Warm forest and plains	Any forest, hill, plains, and mountains	Any land
Organization:	Solitary or herd (6–30)	Solitary or pair	Solitary
Challenge Rating:	8	1/3	1
Treasure:	None	None	None
Alignment:	Always neutral	Always neutral	Always neutral
Advancement:	12–22 HD (Huge)	—	—

	Horse, Heavy War Large Animal	Horse, Light Large Animal	Horse, Light War Large Animal
Hit Dice:	4d8+12 (30 hp)	3d8+6 (19 hp)	3d8+9 (22 hp)
Initiative:	+1 (Dex)	+1 (Dex)	+1 (Dex)
Speed:	50 ft.	60 ft.	60 ft.
AC:	14 (−1 size, +1 Dex, +4 natural)	13 (−1 size, +1 Dex, +3 natural)	14 (−1 size, +1 Dex, +4 natural)
Attacks:	2 hooves +6 melee; bite +1 melee	2 hooves +2 melee	2 hooves +4 melee; bite −1 melee
Damage:	Hoof 1d6+4; bite 1d4+2	Hoof 1d4+1	Hoof 1d4+3; bite 1d3+1
Face/Reach:	5 ft. by 10 ft./5 ft.	5 ft. by 10 ft./5 ft.	5 ft. by 10 ft./5 ft.
Special Qualities:	Scent	Scent	Scent
Saves:	Fort +7, Ref +5, Will +2	Fort +5, Ref +4, Will +2	Fort +6, Ref +4, Will +2
Abilities:	Str 18, Dex 13, Con 17, Int 2, Wis 13, Cha 6	Str 13, Dex 13, Con 15, Int 2, Wis 12, Cha 6	Str 16, Dex 13, Con 17, Int 2, Wis 13, Cha 6
Skills:	Listen +7, Spot +7	Listen +6, Spot +6	Listen +7, Spot +7
Climate/Terrain:	Any land	Any land	Any land
Organization:	Domesticated	Solitary	Solitary
Challenge Rating:	2	1	1
Treasure:	None	None	None
Alignment:	Always neutral	Always neutral	Always neutral
Advancement:	—	—	—

Carrying Capacity: A light load for a heavy warhorse is up to 300 pounds; a medium load, 301–600 pounds; a heavy load, 601–900 pounds. A heavy warhorse can drag 4,500 pounds.

LIGHT HORSE

The statistics presented here describe smaller breeds of working horses such as quarter horses and Arabians. These animals are usually ready for useful work by age two. A light horse cannot fight while carrying a rider.

Carrying Capacity: A light load for a light horse is up to 150 pounds; a medium load, 151–300 pounds; a heavy load, 301–450 pounds. A light horse can drag 2,250 pounds.

LIGHT WARHORSE

These animals or similar to light horses but are trained and bred for strength and aggression. They usually are not ready for warfare before age three. A light warhorse can fight while carrying a rider, but the rider cannot also attack unless he or she succeeds at a Ride check (DC 10).

Carrying Capacity: A light load for a light warhorse is up to 230 pounds; a medium load, 231–460 pounds; a heavy load, 461–690 pounds. A light warhorse can drag 3,450 pounds.

LEOPARD

These jungle cats are about 4 feet long and weigh about 120 pounds; they usually hunt at night.

The statistics presented here can describe any feline of similar size, such as jaguars, panthers, and mountain lions.

Combat

Pounce (Ex): If a leopard leaps upon a foe during the first round of combat, it can make a full attack even if it has already taken a move action.

Improved Grab (Ex): To use this ability, the leopard must hit with its bite attack. If it gets a hold, it can rake.

Rake (Ex): A leopard that gets a hold can make two rake attacks (+6 melee) with its hind legs for 1d3+1 damage each. If the leopard pounces on an opponent, it can also rake.

Skills: Leopards receive a +4 racial bonus to Hide and Move Silently checks and a +8 racial bonus to Balance checks. *In areas of tall grass or heavy undergrowth, the Hide bonus improves to +8.

LION

The statistics presented here describe a male African lion, which is 5 to 8 feet long and weighs 330 to 550 pounds. Females are slightly smaller, but use the same statistics.

Combat

Pounce (Ex): If a lion leaps upon a foe during the first round of combat, it can make a full attack even if it has already taken a move action.

Improved Grab (Ex): To use this ability, the lion must hit with its bite attack. If it gets a hold, it can rake.

Rake (Ex): A lion that gets a hold can make two rake attacks (+7 melee) with its hind legs for 1d4+2 damage each. If the lion pounces on an opponent, it can also rake.

Skills: Lions receive a +4 racial bonus to Balance, Hide, and Move Silently checks. *In areas of tall grass or heavy undergrowth, the Hide bonus improves to +12.

LIZARD

The statistics presented here describe small, nonvenomous lizards of perhaps a foot or two in length, such as an iguana.

Skills: Lizards use their Dexterity modifier for Climb checks and receive a +8 bonus to Balance checks.

GIANT LIZARD

This category includes fairly large, carnivorous creatures from 3 to 5 feet long, such as monitor lizards.

Skills: Giant lizards receive a +4 racial bonus to Hide and Move Silently checks. *In forested or overgrown areas, the Hide bonus improves to +8.

	Leopard Medium-Size Animal	Lion Large Animal	Lizard Tiny Animal
Hit Dice:	3d8+6 (19 hp)	5d8+10 (32 hp)	1/2 d8 (2 hp)
Initiative:	+4 (Dex)	+3 (Dex)	+2 (Dex)
Speed:	40 ft., climb 20 ft.	40 ft.	20 ft., climb 20 ft.
AC:	15 (+4 Dex, +1 natural)	15 (−1 size, +3 Dex, +3 natural)	14 (+2 size, +2 Dex)
Attacks:	Bite +6 melee; 2 claws +1 melee	2 claws +7 melee, bite +2 melee	Bite +4 melee
Damage:	Bite 1d6+3; claw 1d3+1	Claw 1d4+5, bite 1d8+2	Bite 1d4
Face/Reach:	5 ft. by 5 ft./5 ft.	5 ft. by 10 ft./5 ft.	2 1/2 ft. by 2 1/2 ft./0 ft.
Special Attacks:	Pounce, improved grab, rake 1d3+1	Pounce, improved grab, rake 1d4+2	—
Special Qualities:	Scent	Scent	—
Saves:	Fort +5, Ref +7, Will +2	Fort +6, Ref +7, Will +2	Fort +2, Ref +4, Will +1
Abilities:	Str 16, Dex 19, Con 15, Int 2, Wis 12, Cha 6	Str 21, Dex 17, Con 15, Int 2, Wis 12, Cha 6	Str 3, Dex 15, Con 10, Int 2, Wis 12, Cha 2
Skills:	Balance +12, Climb +11, Hide +9*, Listen +6, Move Silently +9, Spot +6	Balance +7, Hide +4*, Jump +5, Listen +5, Move Silently +11, Spot +5	Balance +10, Climb +12, Hide +13, Listen +4, Spot +4
Feats:	Weapon Finesse (bite, claw)	—	Weapon Finesse (bite)
Climate/Terrain:	Warm forest and plains	Warm plains	Any warm land
Organization:	Solitary or pair	Solitary, pair, or pride (6–10)	Solitary
Challenge Rating:	2	3	1/6
Treasure:	None	None	None
Alignment:	Always neutral	Always neutral	Always neutral
Advancement:	4–5 HD (Medium-size)	6–8 HD (Large)	—

	Lizard, Giant Medium-Size Animal	Monkey Tiny Animal	Mule Large Animal
Hit Dice:	3d8+9 (22 hp)	1d8 (4 hp)	3d8+9 (22 hp)
Initiative:	+2 (Dex)	+2 (Dex)	+1 (Dex)
Speed:	30 ft., swim 30 ft.	30 ft., climb 30 ft.	30 ft.
AC:	15 (+2 Dex, +3 natural)	14 (+2 size, +2 Dex)	13 (−1 size, +1 Dex, +3 natural)
Attacks:	Bite +5 melee	Bite +4 melee	2 hooves +4 melee
Damage:	Bite 1d8+4	Bite 1d3−4	Hoof 1d4+3
Face/Reach:	5 ft. by 5 ft./5 ft.	2 1/2 ft. by 2 1/2 ft./0 ft.	5 ft. by 10 ft./5 ft.
Special Attacks:	—	—	—
Special Qualities:	—	—	—
Saves:	Fort +6, Ref +5, Will +2	Fort +2, Ref +4, Will +1	Fort +6, Ref +4, Will +1
Abilities:	Str 17, Dex 15, Con 17, Int 2, Wis 12, Cha 2	Str 3, Dex 15, Con 10, Int 2, Wis 12, Cha 5	Str 16, Dex 13, Con 17, Int 2, Wis 11, Cha 6
Skills:	Climb +9, Hide +7*, Listen +4, Move Silently +6, Spot +4	Balance +10, Climb +13, Hide +13, Listen +4, Spot +4	Listen +6, Spot +6
Feats:	—	Weapon Finesse (bite)	—
Climate/Terrain:	Any warm land	Warm forest	Warm plains
Organization:	Solitary	Troop (10–40)	Solitary
Challenge Rating:	2	1/6	1
Treasure:	None	None	None
Alignment:	Always neutral	Always neutral	Always neutral
Advancement:	4–5 HD (Medium-size)	2–3 HD (Medium-size)	—

MONKEY

The statistics presented here can describe any arboreal monkey that is no bigger than a housecat, such as a colobus or capuchin.

Skills: Monkeys use their Dexterity modifier for Climb checks and receive a +8 racial bonus to Balance checks.

MULE

Mules are sterile crossbreeds of donkeys and horses. A mule is similar to a light horse, but slightly stronger and more surefooted.

Carrying Capacity: A light load for a mule is up to 230 pounds; a medium load, 231–460 pounds; a heavy load, 461–690 pounds. A mule can drag 3,450 pounds.

Skills: Mules receive a +2 racial bonus to Dexterity checks to avoid slipping or falling.

OCTOPUS

These bottom-dwelling sea creatures are dangerous only to their prey. If disturbed, they usually try to escape.

Combat

Improved Grab (Ex): To use this ability, the octopus must hit with its arms attack. If it gets a hold, it automatically deals bite damage each round the hold is maintained.

Ink Cloud (Ex): An octopus can emit a cloud of jet-black ink 10 feet high by 10 feet wide by 10 feet long once a minute as a free action. The cloud provides total concealment, which the octopus normally uses to escape a losing fight. Creatures within the cloud suffer the effects of total darkness.

Jet (Ex): An octopus can jet backward once a round as a double move action, at a speed of 200 feet.

Skills: An octopus can change colors, giving it a +4 racial bonus to Hide checks.

GIANT OCTOPUS

These creatures are aggressive and territorial hunters, with arms reaching 10 feet or more in length. Their tentacles are studded with barbs and sharp-edged suckers.

Combat

Improved Grab (Ex): To use this ability, the giant octopus must hit a Medium-size or smaller opponent with a tentacle rake attack. If it gets a hold, it can constrict.

Constrict (Ex): A giant octopus deals 2d8+6 points of damage with a successful grapple check against Medium-size or smaller creatures.

Ink Cloud (Ex): A giant octopus can emit a cloud of jet-black ink 20 feet high by 20 feet wide by 20 feet long once a minute as a free action. The cloud provides total concealment, which the octopus normally uses to escape a losing fight. Creatures within the cloud suffer the effects of total darkness.

Jet (Ex): A giant octopus can jet backward once a round as a double move action, at a speed of 200 feet.

Skills: A giant octopus can change colors, giving it a +4 racial bonus to Hide checks.

OWL

The statistics presented here describe nocturnal birds of prey from 1 to 2 feet long, with wingspans up to 6 feet. They combine both claws into a single attack.

Skills: Owls receive a +8 racial bonus to Listen checks, and a +14 to Move Silently checks. *They receive a +8 racial bonus to Spot checks in dusk and darkness.

PONY

The statistics presented here describe a small horse, under 5 feet tall at the shoulder. Ponies are otherwise similar to light horses and cannot fight while carrying a rider.

Carrying Capacity: A light load for a pony is up to 75 pounds; a medium load, 76–150 pounds; and a heavy load, 151–225 pounds. A pony can drag 1,125 pounds.

WARPONY

Warponies are bred for strength and aggression, and are similar to light warhorses. A warpony can fight while carrying a rider, but the rider cannot also attack unless he or she succeeds at a Ride check (see Ride, page 72 in the *Player's Handbook*).

Carrying Capacity: A light load for a warpony is up to 100 pounds; a medium load, 101–200 pounds; and a heavy load, 201–300 pounds. A warpony can drag 1,500 pounds.

	Octopus Small Animal (Aquatic)	Octopus, Giant Large Animal (Aquatic)	Owl Tiny Animal
Hit Dice:	2d8 (9 hp)	8d8+8 (44 hp)	1d8 (4 hp)
Initiative:	+3 (Dex)	+2 (Dex)	+3 (Dex)
Speed:	20 ft., swim 30 ft.	20 ft., swim 30 ft.	10 ft., fly 40 ft. (average)
AC:	16 (+1 size, +3 Dex, +2 natural)	18 (–1 size, +2 Dex, +7 natural)	17 (+2 size, +3 Dex, +2 natural)
Attacks:	8 arms +5 melee, bite +0 melee	8 tentacle rakes +10 melee, bite +5 melee	Claws +5 melee
Damage:	Arms 0, bite 1d3	Tentacle rake 1d4+5, bite 1d8+2	Claws 1d2–2
Face/Reach:	5 ft. by 5 ft./5 ft.	5 ft. by 5 ft./10 ft.	2 1/2 ft. by 2 1/2 ft./0 ft.
Special Attacks:	Improved grab	Improved grab, constrict	—
Special Qualities:	Ink cloud, jet	Ink cloud, jet	—
Saves:	Fort +3, Ref +6, Will +1	Fort +7, Ref +8, Will +3	Fort +2, Ref +5, Will +2
Abilities:	Str 12, Dex 17, Con 11, Int 2, Wis 12, Cha 3	Str 20, Dex 15, Con 13, Int 2, Wis 12, Cha 3	Str 6, Dex 17, Con 10, Int 2, Wis 14, Cha 4
Skills:	Hide +15, Listen +5, Spot +5	Hide +11, Listen +4, Spot +4	Listen +14, Move Silently +20, Spot +6*
Feats:	Weapon Finesse (arms, bite)	—	Weapon Finesse (claws)
Climate/Terrain:	Temperate and warm aquatic	Temperate and warm aquatic	Any forest, hill, plains, and mountains
Organization:	Solitary	Solitary	Solitary
Challenge Rating:	1	8	1/4
Treasure:	None	None	None
Alignment:	Always neutral	Always neutral	Always neutral
Advancement:	3–6 HD (Medium-size); 7 HD (Large)	9–12 HD (Large); 13–24 HD (Huge)	1 HD (Medium-size); 2 HD (Large)

PORPOISE

Porpoises are aquatic mammals that tend to be playful, friendly, and helpful.

A typical porpoise is 4 to 6 feet long and weighs 110 to 160 pounds. The statistics presented here can describe any small whale of similar size.

Combat

Blindsight (Ex): Porpoises can "see" by emitting high-frequency sounds, inaudible to most other creatures, that allow them to locate objects and creatures within 120 feet. A *silence* spell negates this and forces the porpoise to rely on its vision, which is approximately as good as a human's.

Skills: Porpoises gain a +4 racial bonus to Spot and Listen checks. *These bonuses are lost if blindsight is negated.

RAT

These omnivorous rodents thrive almost anywhere.

Skills: Rats receive a +4 racial bonus to Hide and Move Silently checks and a +8 racial bonus to Balance checks. They use their Dexterity modifier for Climb checks.

RAVEN

These glossy black birds are about 2 feet long and have wingspans of about 4 feet. They combine both claws into a single attack.

The statistics presented here can describe most nonpredatory birds of similar size.

RHINOCEROS

The rhinoceros is infamous for its bad temper and willingness to charge intruders.

The statistics presented here are based on the African black rhino, which is 6 to 14 feet long, 3 to 6 feet high at the shoulder, and weighs up to 6,000 pounds. These can describe any herbivore of similar size.

SHARK

These carnivorous fish are aggressive and liable to make unprovoked attacks against anything that approaches them.

Smaller sharks are from 5 to 8 feet long and not usually dangerous to creatures other than their prey. Large sharks can reach around 15 feet in length and are a serious threat. Huge sharks are true monsters, like great whites, that can exceed 20 feet in length.

Combat

Sharks circle and observe potential prey, then dart in and bite with their powerful jaws.

Keen Scent (Ex): A shark can notice creatures by scent in a 180-foot radius and detect blood in the water at ranges of up to a mile.

SNAKE

Snakes usually are not aggressive and flee when confronted. Venomous snakes, however, often bite before retreating.

Skills: Snakes receive a +4 racial bonus to Hide, Listen, and Spot checks and a +8 racial bonus to Balance checks. They can use either their Strength or Dexterity modifier for Climb checks, whichever is better.

CONSTRICTOR

Constrictor snakes hunt by grabbing prey with their mouths and then squeezing it with their powerful bodies.

Combat

Improved Grab (Ex): To use this ability, the constrictor snake must hit with its bite attack. If it gets a hold, it can constrict.

Constrict (Ex): A constrictor snake deals 1d3+4 points of damage with a successful grapple check against Medium-size or smaller creatures.

GIANT CONSTRICTOR

These creatures are more aggressive than their smaller cousins. They can constrict opponents of up to Large size, dealing 1d8+10 points of damage per round.

VIPER

These creatures rely on their venomous bites to kill prey and defend themselves.

Combat

Poison (Ex): Bite, Fortitude save (DC 11 for all sizes Large and smaller, DC 13 for a Huge viper); initial and secondary damage 1d6 temporary Constitution.

SQUID

These free-swimming mollusks are fairly aggressive. They are more feared than sharks in some locales.

	Pony	Pony, War	Porpoise
	Medium-Size Animal	Medium-Size Animal	Medium-Size Animal (Aquatic)
Hit Dice:	2d8+2 (11 hp)	2d8+4 (13 hp)	2d8+2 (11 hp)
Initiative:	+1 (Dex)	+1 (Dex)	+3 (Dex)
Speed:	40 ft.	40 ft.	Swim 80 ft.
AC:	13 (+1 Dex, +2 natural)	13 (+1 Dex, +2 natural)	15 (+3 Dex, +2 natural)
Attacks:	2 hooves +2 melee	2 hooves +3 melee	Butt +4 melee
Damage:	Hoof 1d3+1	Hoof 1d3+2	Butt 2d4
Face/Reach:	5 ft. by 5 ft./5 ft.	5 ft. by 5 ft./5 ft.	5 ft. by 5 ft./5 ft.
Special Qualities:	Scent	Scent	Blindsight
Saves:	Fort +4, Ref +4, Will +0	Fort +5, Ref +4, Will +0	Fort +4, Ref +6, Will +1
Abilities:	Str 13, Dex 13, Con 12, Int 2, Wis 11, Cha 4	Str 15, Dex 13, Con 14, Int 2, Wis 11, Cha 4	Str 11, Dex 17, Con 13, Int 2, Wis 12, Cha 6
Skills:	Listen +5, Spot +5	Listen +5, Spot +5	Listen +10*, Spot +10*
Feats:	—	—	Weapon Finesse (butt)
Climate/Terrain:	Any land	Any land	Any aquatic
Organization:	Solitary	Solitary	Solitary or school (2–20)
Challenge Rating:	1/4	1/4	1/2
Treasure:	None	None	None
Alignment:	Always neutral	Always neutral	Always neutral
Advancement:	—	—	3–4 HD (Medium-size); 5–6 HD (Large)

	Rat Tiny Animal	Raven Tiny Animal	Rhinoceros Large Animal
Hit Dice:	1/4 d8 (1 hp)	1/4 d8 (1 hp)	8d8+40 (76 hp)
Initiative:	+2 (Dex)	+2 (Dex)	+0 (Dex)
Speed:	15 ft., climb 15 ft.	10 ft., fly 40 ft. (average)	30 ft.
AC:	14 (+2 size, +2 Dex)	14 (+2 size, +2 Dex)	16 (−1 size, +7 natural)
Attacks:	Bite +4 melee	Claws +4 melee	Gore +13 melee
Damage:	Bite 1d3−4	Claws 1d2−5	Gore 2d6+12
Face/Reach:	2 1/2 ft. by 2 1/2 ft./0 ft.	2 1/2 ft. by 2 1/2 ft./0 ft.	5 ft. by 10 ft./5 ft.
Special Qualities:	Scent		
Saves:	Fort +2, Ref +4, Will +1	Fort +2, Ref +4, Will +2	Fort +11, Ref +6, Will +3
Abilities:	Str 2, Dex 15, Con 10, Int 2, Wis 12, Cha 2	Str 1, Dex 15, Con 10, Int 2, Wis 14, Cha 6	Str 26, Dex 10, Con 21, Int 2, Wis 13, Cha 2
Skills:	Balance +10, Climb +12, Hide +18, Move Silently +10	Listen +6, Spot +6	Listen +11
Feats:	Weapon Finesse (bite)	Weapon Finesse (claws)	—
Climate/Terrain:	Any land and underground	Any forest, hill, plains, and mountains	Warm plains
Organization:	Swarm (10–100)	Solitary	Solitary or herd (2–12)
Challenge Rating:	1/8	1/6	4
Treasure:	None	None	None
Alignment:	Always neutral	Always neutral	Always neutral
Advancement:	—	—	9–12 HD (Large); 13–24 HD (Huge)

	Shark, Medium-Size Medium-Size (Aquatic)	Shark, Large Large Animal (Aquatic)	Shark, Huge Huge Animal (Aquatic)
Hit Dice:	3d8+3 (16 hp)	7d8+7 (38 hp)	10d8+20 (65 hp)
Initiative:	+2 (Dex)	+2 (Dex)	+2 (Dex)
Speed:	Swim 60 ft.	Swim 60 ft.	Swim 60 ft.
AC:	15 (+2 Dex, +3 natural)	15 (−1 size, +2 Dex, +4 natural)	15 (−2 size, +2 Dex, +5 natural)
Attacks:	Bite +4 melee	Bite +7 melee	Bite +10 melee
Damage:	Bite 1d6+1	Bite 1d8+4	Bite 2d6+7
Face/Reach:	5 ft. by 5 ft./5 ft.	5 ft. by 10 ft./5 ft.	10 ft. by 20 ft./10 ft.
Special Qualities:	Keen scent	Keen scent	Keen scent
Saves:	Fort +4, Ref +5, Will +2	Fort +6, Ref +7, Will +3	Fort +9, Ref +9, Will +4
Abilities:	Str 13, Dex 15, Con 13, Int 1, Wis 12, Cha 2	Str 17, Dex 15, Con 13, Int 1, Wis 12, Cha 2	Str 21, Dex 15, Con 15, Int 1, Wis 12, Cha 2
Skills:	Listen +7, Spot +7	Listen +7, Spot +7	Listen +7, Spot +7
Feats:	Weapon Finesse (bite)	—	—
Climate/Terrain:	Any aquatic	Any aquatic	Any aquatic
Organization:	Solitary, school (2–5), or pack (6–11)	Solitary, school (2–5), or pack (6–11)	Solitary, school (2–5), or pack (6–11)
Challenge Rating:	1	2	4
Treasure:	None	None	None
Alignment:	Always neutral	Always neutral	Always neutral
Advancement:	4–6 HD (Medium-size)	8–10 HD (Large)	11–17 HD (Huge)

	Snake, Constrictor Medium-Size Animal	Snake, Giant Constrictor Huge Animal	Snake, Tiny Viper Tiny Animal
Hit Dice:	3d8+3 (16 hp)	11d8+11 (60 hp)	1/4 d8 (1 hp)
Initiative:	+3 (Dex)	+3 (Dex)	+3 (Dex)
Speed:	20 ft., climb 20 ft., swim 20 ft.	20 ft., climb 20 ft.	15 ft., climb 15 ft., swim 15 ft.
AC:	15 (+3 Dex, +2 natural)	15 (−2 size, +3 Dex, +4 natural)	17 (+2 size, +3 Dex, +2 natural)
Attacks:	Bite +5 melee	Bite +13 melee	Bite +5 melee
Damage:	Bite 1d3+4	Bite 1d8+10	Bite poison
Face/Reach:	5 ft. by 5 ft. (coiled)/5 ft.	15 ft. by 15 ft. (coiled)/10 ft.	2 1/2 ft. by 2 1/2 ft. (coiled)/0 ft.
Special Attacks:	Improved grab, constrict 1d3+4	Improved grab, constrict 1d8+10	Poison
Special Qualities:	Scent	Scent	Scent
Saves:	Fort +4, Ref +6, Will +2	Fort +8, Ref +10, Will +4	Fort +2, Ref +5, Will +1
Abilities:	Str 17, Dex 17, Con 13, Int 1, Wis 12, Cha 2	Str 25, Dex 17, Con 13, Int 1, Wis 12, Cha 2	Str 6, Dex 17, Con 11, Int 1, Wis 12, Cha 2
Skills:	Balance +11, Climb +14, Hide +11, Listen +9, Spot +9	Balance +11, Climb +18, Hide +3, Listen +9, Spot +9	Balance +11, Climb +12, Hide +18 Listen +8, Spot +8
Feats:	—	—	Weapon Finesse (bite)

Combat

Improved Grab (Ex): To use this ability, the squid must hit with its arms attack. If it gets a hold, it automatically deals bite damage each round the hold is maintained.

Ink Cloud (Ex): A squid can emit a cloud of jet-black ink 10 feet high by 10 feet wide by 10 feet long once a minute as a free action. The cloud provides total concealment, which the squid normally uses to escape a losing fight. Creatures within the cloud suffer the effects of total darkness.

Jet (Ex): A squid can jet backward once a round as a double move action, at a speed of 240 feet.

GIANT SQUID

These voracious creatures can have bodies more than 20 feet long and attack almost anything they meet.

	Snake, Constrictor	Snake, Giant Constrictor	Snake, Tiny Viper
Climate/Terrain:	Warm forest and aquatic	Warm forest and aquatic	Temperate and warm land, aquatic, and underground
Organization:	Solitary	Solitary	Solitary
Challenge Rating:	2	5	1/3
Treasure:	None	None	None
Alignment:	Always neutral	Always neutral	Always neutral
Advancement:	4–5 HD (Medium-size); 6–10 HD (Large)	12–16 HD (Huge); 17–33 HD (Gargantuan)	—

	Snake, Small Viper / Small Animal	Snake, Medium-Size Viper / Medium-Size Animal	Snake, Large Viper / Large Animal
Hit Dice:	1d8 (4 hp)	2d8 (9 hp)	3d8 (13 hp)
Initiative:	+3 (Dex)	+3 (Dex)	+3 (Dex)
Speed:	20 ft., climb 20 ft., swim 20 ft.	20 ft., climb 20 ft., swim 20 ft.	20 ft., climb 20 ft., swim 20 ft.
AC:	17 (+1 size, +3 Dex, +3 natural)	16 (+3 Dex, +3 natural)	15 (−1 size, +3 Dex, +3 natural)
Attacks:	Bite +4 melee	Bite +4 melee	Bite +4 melee
Damage:	Bite 1d2−2 and poison	Bite 1d4−1 and poison	Bite 1d4 and poison
Face/Reach:	5 ft. by 5 ft. (coiled)/5 ft.	5 ft. by 5 ft. (coiled)/5 ft.	5 ft. by 5 ft. (coiled)/10 ft.
Special Attacks:	Poison	Poison	Poison
Special Qualities:	Scent	Scent	Scent
Saves:	Fort +2, Ref +5, Will +1	Fort +3, Ref +6, Will +1	Fort +3, Ref +6, Will +2
Abilities:	Str 6, Dex 17, Con 11, Int 1, Wis 12, Cha 2	Str 8, Dex 17, Con 11, Int 1, Wis 12, Cha 2	Str 10, Dex 17, Con 11, Int 1, Wis 12, Cha 2
Skills:	Balance +11, Climb +12, Hide +15, Listen +9, Spot +9	Balance +11, Climb +11, Hide +12, Listen +9, Spot +9	Balance +11, Climb +11, Hide +8, Listen +9, Spot +9
Feats:	Weapon Finesse (bite)	Weapon Finesse (bite)	Weapon Finesse (bite)

Climate/Terrain:	Temperate and warm land, aquatic, and underground	Temperate and warm land, aquatic, and underground	Temperate and warm land, aquatic, and underground
Organization:	Solitary	Solitary	Solitary
Challenge Rating:	1/2	1	2
Treasure:	None	None	None
Alignment:	Always neutral	Always neutral	Always neutral
Advancement:	—	—	—

	Snake, Huge Viper / Huge Animal	Squid / Medium-Size Animal (Aquatic)	Squid, Giant / Huge Animal (Aquatic)
Hit Dice:	4d8+4 (22 hp)	3d8 (13 hp)	12d8+12 (66 hp)
Initiative:	+4 (Dex)	+3 (Dex)	+3 (Dex)
Speed:	20 ft., climb 20 ft., swim 20 ft.	Swim 60 ft.	Swim 80 ft.
AC:	15 (−2 size, +4 Dex, +3 natural)	16 (+3 Dex, +3 natural)	17 (−2 size, +3 Dex, +6 natural)
Attacks:	Bite +5 melee	10 arms +4 melee, bite −1 melee	10 tentacle rakes +15 melee, bite +10 melee
Damage:	Bite 1d4 and poison	Arms 0, bite 1d6+1	Tentacle 1d6+8, bite 2d8+4
Face/Reach:	15 ft. by 15 ft. (coiled)/10 ft.	5 ft. by 5 ft./5 ft.	10 ft. by 20 ft./10 ft. (40 ft. with tentacle)
Special Attacks:	Poison	Improved grab	Improved grab, constrict 1d6+8
Special Qualities:	Scent	Ink cloud, jet	Ink cloud, jet
Saves:	Fort +5, Ref +8, Will +2	Fort +3, Ref +6, Will +2	Fort +9, Ref +11, Will +5
Abilities:	Str 10, Dex 19, Con 13, Int 1, Wis 12, Cha 2	Str 14, Dex 17, Con 11, Int 1, Wis 12, Cha 2	Str 26, Dex 17, Con 13, Int 1, Wis 12, Cha 2
Skills:	Balance, +12, Climb +12, Hide +3, Listen +9, Spot +9	Listen +7, Spot +7	Listen +8, Spot +8
Feats:	Weapon Finesse (bite)	—	—

Climate/Terrain:	Temperate and warm land, aquatic, and underground	Any aquatic	Any aquatic
Organization:	Solitary	Solitary or school (6–11)	Solitary

Combat

Improved Grab (Ex): To use this ability, the giant squid must hit a Medium-size or smaller opponent with a tentacle rake attack. If it gets a hold, it can constrict.

Constrict (Ex): A giant squid deals automatic tentacle rake damage with a successful grapple check against Medium-size or smaller creatures.

Ink Cloud (Ex): A giant squid can emit a cloud of jet-black ink 20 feet high by 20 feet wide by 40 feet long once a minute as a free action. The cloud provides total concealment, which the squid normally uses to escape a losing fight. Creatures within the cloud suffer the effects of total darkness.

Jet (Ex): A giant squid can jet backward once a round as a double move action, at a speed of 320 feet.

TIGER

These great cats stand more than 3 feet tall at the shoulder and are about 9 feet long. They weigh from 400 to 600 pounds.

Combat

Pounce (Ex): If a tiger leaps upon a foe during the first round of combat, it can make a full attack even if it has already taken a move action.

Improved Grab (Ex): To use this ability, the tiger must hit with a claw or bite attack. If it gets a hold, it can rake.

Rake (Ex): A tiger that gets a hold can make two rake attacks (+9 melee) with its hind legs for 1d8+3 damage each. If the tiger pounces on an opponent, it can also rake.

Skills: Tigers receive a +4 racial bonus to Balance, Hide, and Move Silently checks. *In areas of tall grass or heavy undergrowth, the Hide bonus improves to +8.

TOAD

These diminutive amphibians are innocuous and beneficial, since they eat insects.

Skills: A toad's coloration gives it a +4 racial bonus to Hide checks.

WEASEL

The little mammals are aggressive predators but usually confine themselves to smaller prey. The statistics presented here can also apply to ferrets.

Combat

Attach (Ex): If a weasel hits with a bite attack, it uses its powerful jaws to latch onto the opponent's body and automatically deals bite damage each round it remains attached. An attached weasel has an AC of 12.

Skills: Weasels receive a +4 racial bonus to Move Silently checks and a +8 racial bonus to Balance checks. They use their Dexterity modifier for Climb checks.

WHALE

Blindsight (Ex): Whales can "see" by emitting high-frequency sounds, inaudible to most other creatures, that allow them to locate objects and creatures within 120 feet. A *silence* spell negates this and forces the whale to rely on its vision, which is approximately as good as a human's.

Skills: Whales gain a +4 racial bonus to Spot and Listen checks. *These bonuses are lost if Blindsight is negated.

BALEEN WHALE

The statistics presented here describe a plankton-feeding whale between 30 and 60 feet long, such as gray, humpback, and right whales.

These massive creatures are surprisingly gentle. If harassed or provoked, they are as likely to flee as they are to retaliate.

	Snake, Huge Viper	Squid	Squid, Giant
Challenge Rating:	3	1	9
Treasure:	None	None	None
Alignment:	Always neutral	Always neutral	Always neutral
Advancement:	5–6 HD (Huge);	4–6 HD (Medium-size);	13–18 HD (Huge);
	7–12 HD (Gargantuan)	7–11 HD (Large)	19–36 HD (Gargantuan)

	Tiger	Toad	Weasel
	Large Animal	Diminutive Animal	Tiny Animal
Hit Dice:	6d8+18 (45 hp)	1/4 d8 (1 hp)	1/2 d8 (2 hp)
Initiative:	+2 (Dex)	+1 (Dex)	+2 (Dex)
Speed:	40 ft.	5 ft.	20 ft., climb 20 ft.
AC:	14 (–1 size, +2 Dex, +3 natural)	15 (+4 size, +1 Dex)	14 (+2 size, +2 Dex)
Attacks:	2 claws +9 melee, bite +4 melee	—	Bite +4 melee
Damage:	Claw 1d8+6, bite 2d6+3	—	Bite 1d3–4
Face/Reach:	5 ft. by 10 ft./5 ft.	1 ft. by 1 ft./0 ft.	2 1/2 ft. by 2 1/2 ft./0 ft.
Special Attacks:	Pounce, improved grab, rake 1d8+3	—	Attach
Special Qualities:	—	—	Scent
Saves:	Fort +8, Ref +7, Will +3	Fort +2, Ref +3, Will +2	Fort +2, Ref +4, Will +1
Abilities:	Str 23, Dex 15, Con 17,	Str 1, Dex 12, Con 11,	Str 3, Dex 15, Con 10,
	Int 2, Wis 12, Cha 6	Int 1, Wis 14, Cha 4	Int 2, Wis 12, Cha 5
Skills:	Balance +6, Hide +5*, Listen +3, Move Silently +9, Spot +3, Swim +11	Hide +21, Listen +5, Spot +5	Balance +10, Climb +11, Hide +13, Move Silently +9, Spot +4
Feats:	—	—	Weapon Finesse (bite)
Climate/Terrain:	Any forest, hill, mountains, and plains	Temperate and warm land and aquatic	Temperate forest, hill, mountains, and plains
Organization:	Solitary	Swarm (10–100)	Solitary
Challenge Rating:	4	1/10	1/4
Treasure:	None	None	None
Alignment:	Always neutral	Always neutral	Always neutral
Advancement:	7–12 HD (Large); 13–18 HD (Huge)	—	—

	Whale, Baleen Gargantuan Animal (Aquatic)	Whale, Cachalot Gargantuan Animal (Aquatic)	Whale, Orca Huge Animal (Aquatic)
Hit Dice:	12d8+72 (126 hp)	12d8+84 (138 hp)	9d8+45 (85 hp)
Initiative:	+1 (Dex)	+1 (Dex)	+2 (Dex)
Speed:	Swim 40 ft.	Swim 40 ft.	Swim 50 ft.
AC:	16 (−4 size, +1 Dex, +9 natural)	16 (−4 size, +1 Dex, +9 natural)	16 (−2 size, +2 Dex, +6 natural)
Attacks:	Tail slap +17 melee	Bite +17 melee, tail slap +12 melee	Bite +12 melee
Damage:	Tail slap 1d8+18	Bite 4d6+12, tail slap 1d8+6	Bite 2d6+12
Face/Reach:	20 ft. by 40 ft./10 ft.	20 ft. by 40 ft./10 ft.	10 ft. by 20 ft./10 ft.
Special Qualities:	Blindsight	Blindsight	Blindsight
Saves:	Fort +14, Ref +9, Will +5	Fort +15, Ref +9, Will +6	Fort +11, Ref +8, Will +5
Abilities:	Str 35, Dex 13, Con 22, Int 2, Wis 12, Cha 6	Str 35, Dex 13, Con 24, Int 2, Wis 14, Cha 6	Str 27, Dex 15, Con 21, Int 2, Wis 14, Cha 6
Skills:	Listen +10*, Spot +11*	Listen +11*, Spot +12*	Listen +12*, Spot +12*
Climate/Terrain:	Any aquatic	Any aquatic	Any aquatic
Organization:	Solitary	Solitary or pod (6–11)	Solitary or pod (6–11)
Challenge Rating:	5	6	5
Treasure:	None	None	None
Alignment:	Always neutral	Always neutral	Always neutral
Advancement:	13–18 HD (Gargantuan); 19–36 HD (Colossal)	13–18 HD (Gargantuan); 19–36 HD (Colossal)	10–13 HD (Huge); 14–27 HD (Gargantuan)

	Wolf Medium-Size Animal	Wolverine Medium-Size Animal
Hit Dice:	2d8+4 (13 hp)	3d8+12 (25 hp)
Initiative:	+2 (Dex)	+2 (Dex)
Speed:	50 ft.	30 ft., burrow 10 ft., climb 10 ft.
AC:	14 (+2 Dex, +2 natural)	14 (+2 Dex, +2 natural)
Attacks:	Bite +3 melee	2 claws +4 melee; bite −1 melee
Damage:	Bite 1d6+1	Claw 1d4+2; bite 1d6+1
Face/Reach:	5 ft. by 5 ft./5 ft.	5 ft. by 5 ft./5 ft.
Special Attacks:	Trip	Rage
Special Qualities:	Scent	Scent
Saves:	Fort +5, Ref +5, Will +1	Fort +7, Ref +5, Will +2
Abilities:	Str 13, Dex 15, Con 15, Int 2, Wis 12, Cha 6	Str 14, Dex 15, Con 19, Int 1, Wis 12, Cha 10
Skills:	Hide +3, Listen +6, Move Silently +4, Spot +4, Wilderness Lore +1*	Climb +15, Listen +6, Spot +6
Feats:	Weapon Finesse (bite)	—
Climate/Terrain:	Any forest, hill, plains, and mountains	Cold and temperate forest and hill
Organization:	Solitary, pair, or pack (7–16)	Solitary
Challenge Rating:	1	2
Treasure:	None	None
Alignment:	Always neutral	Always neutral
Advancement:	3 HD (Medium-size); 4–5 HD (Large)	4–5 HD (Large)

CACHALOT WHALE

Also known as sperm whales, these creatures can be up to 60 feet long. They prey on giant squid.

ORCA

These ferocious creatures are about 30 feet long; they eat fish, squid, seals, and other whales.

WOLF

Wolves are pack hunters infamous for their persistence and cunning.

Combat

A favorite tactic is to send a few individuals against the foe's front while the rest of the pack circles and attacks from the flanks or rear.

Trip (Ex): A wolf that hits with a bite attack can attempt to trip the opponent as a free action (see page 139 in the *Player's Handbook*) without making a touch attack or provoking an attack of opportunity. If the attempt fails, the opponent cannot react to trip the wolf.

Skills: *Wolves receive a +4 racial bonus to Wilderness Lore checks when tracking by scent.

WOLVERINE

These creatures are similar to badgers but are bigger, stronger, and even more ferocious.

Combat

Rage (Ex): A wolverine that takes damage in combat flies into a berserk rage the following round, clawing and biting madly until either it or its opponent is dead. An enraged wolverine gains +4 Strength, +4 Constitution, and −2 AC. The creature cannot end its rage voluntarily.

	Giant Ant, Worker Medium-Size Vermin	Giant Ant, Soldier Medium-Size Vermin	Giant Ant, Queen Large Vermin
HD:	2d8 (9 hp)	2d8+2 (11 hp)	4d8+4 (22 hp)
Initiative:	+0	+0	−1 (Dex)
Speed:	50 ft., climb 20 ft.	50 ft., climb 20 ft.	40 ft.
AC:	17 (+7 natural)	17 (+7 natural)	17 (−1 size, −1 Dex, +9 natural)
Attacks:	Bite +1 melee	Bite +3 melee	Bite +5 melee
Damage:	Bite 1d6	Bite 2d4+3	Bite 2d6+4
Face/Reach:	5 ft. by 5 ft./5 ft.	5 ft. by 5 ft./5 ft.	5 ft. by 10 ft./5 ft.
Special Attacks:	Improved grab	Improved grab, acid sting	Improved grab
Special Qualities:	Vermin	Vermin	Vermin
Saves:	Fort +3, Ref +0, Will +0	Fort +4, Ref +0, Will +1	Fort +5, Ref +0, Will +2
Abilities:	Str 10, Dex 10, Con 10,	Str 14, Dex 10, Con 13,	Str 16, Dex 9, Con 13,
	Int —, Wis 11, Cha 9	Int —, Wis 13, Cha 11	Int —, Wis 13, Cha 11
Skills:	Climb +8, Listen +5, Spot +5	Climb +10, Listen +6, Spot +6	Listen +7, Spot +7
Climate/Terrain:	Temperate and warm desert, forest, hill, plains, and underground	Temperate and warm desert, forest, hill, plains, and underground	Temperate and warm desert, forest, hill, plains, and underground
Organization:	Gang (2–6) or crew (6–11 plus 1 giant ant soldier)	Solitary or gang (2–4)	Hive (1 plus 10–100 workers and 5–20 soldiers)
Challenge Rating:	1	2	2
Treasure:	None	None	1/10 coins; 50% goods; 50% items
Alignment:	Always neutral	Always neutral	Always neutral
Advancement:	3–4 HD (Medium-size); 5–6 HD (Large)	3–4 HD (Medium-size); 5–6 HD (Large)	5–6 HD (Large); 7–8 HD (Huge)

Vermin come in a variety of sizes and types that range from the merely annoying to the very deadly.

COMBAT

Except where noted, vermin attack whenever hungry or threatened.

Vermin: Immune to mind-influencing effects.

Poison (Ex): Many vermin have poisonous bites or stings. They are all injury type poisons. The Fortitude save DCs and damage are set out in the Vermin Poison table.

GIANT ANT

Giant ants are among the hardiest and most adaptable vermin. Soldiers and workers are about 6 feet long, while queens can grow to a length of 9 feet.

Combat

Giant ants fight with their powerful mandibles.

Improved Grab (Ex): To use this ability, the giant ant must hit with its bite attack. A giant ant soldier that gets a hold can sting.

Acid Sting (Ex): The giant ant soldier has a stinger and an acid-producing gland and in its abdomen. If it successfully grabs an opponent, it can attempt to sting each round using its full attack bonus. A hit with the sting attack deals 1d4+1 points of piercing damage and 1d4 points of acid damage.

GIANT BEE

Although they are many times larger, growing to a length of about 5 feet, giant bees behave generally the same as their smaller cousins.

Combat

Giant bees are usually not aggressive except when defending themselves or their hive.

Poison (Ex): See the Vermin Poison table, above. A bee that successfully stings another creature pulls away, leaving its stinger in the creature. The bee then dies.

VERMIN POISON

Poison	DC	Initial and Secondary Damage
Giant bee	13	1d6 Con
Giant wasp	18	1d6 Dex
Monstrous centipede		
Tiny	11	1 Dex
Small	11	1d2 Dex
Medium-size	13	1d3 Dex
Large	16	1d4 Dex
Huge	18	1d6 Dex
Gargantuan	26	1d8 Dex
Colossal	36	2d6 Dex
Monstrous scorpion		
Tiny	11	1d2 Str
Small	11	1d3 Str
Medium-size	15	1d4 Str
Large	18	1d6 Str
Huge	26	1d8 Str
Gargantuan	36	2d6 Str
Colossal	54	2d8 Str
Monstrous spider		
Tiny	11	1d2 Str
Small	11	1d3 Str
Medium-size	14	1d4 Str
Large	16	1d6 Str
Huge	22	1d8 Str
Gargantuan	31	2d6 Str
Colossal	35	2d8 Str

GIANT BOMBARDIER BEETLE

These creatures feed primarily on carrion and offal, gathering heaps of the stuff in which to build nests and lay eggs. A giant bombardier beetle is about 6 feet long.

Giant bombardier beetles have no interest in other creatures. They normally attack only to defend themselves, their nests, or their eggs.

Combat

Giant bombardier beetles bite with their mandibles and spray acid.

Acid Spray (Ex): When attacked or disturbed, a giant bombardier beetle can release a 10-foot cone of acidic vapor once per round. Those within the cone must succeed at a Fortitude save (DC 13) or take 1d4+2 points of damage.

GIANT FIRE BEETLE

These luminous nocturnal insects are prized by miners and adventurers. They have two glands, one above each eye, that produce a red glow. The glands' luminosity persists for 1d6 days after removal from the beetle, illuminating a roughly circular area with a 10-foot radius. Giant fire beetles are about 2 feet long.

Combat

When disturbed, giant fire beetles bite with their mandibles.

GIANT STAG BEETLE

These creatures are serious pests that greedily devour cultivated crops: A single beetle can strip an entire farm in short order. An adult giant stag beetle is about 10 feet long.

Combat

Giant stag beetles charge opponents, biting with their huge, horn-like mandibles.

Trample (Ex): A giant stag beetle can trample Medium-size or smaller creatures for 2d8+3 points of damage. Opponents who do not make attacks of opportunity against the giant stag beetle can attempt a Reflex save (DC 19) to halve the damage.

GIANT PRAYING MANTIS

This patient carnivore remains completely still as it waits for prey to come near.

Combat

A giant praying mantis uses both spiny claws as a single attack. It grabs smaller prey in its claws while it bites.

Improved Grab (Ex): To use this ability, the giant praying mantis must hit an opponent of Medium-size or smaller with its claws attack. If it gets a hold, it squeezes.

Squeeze (Ex): A giant praying mantis that gets a hold on a Medium-size or smaller opponent automatically deals 1d8+4 points of claw damage and bites at its full attack value of +6 each round the hold is maintained.

Skills: *Because of its camouflage, a mantis surrounded by foliage receives an additional +8 racial bonus to Hide checks.

GIANT WASP

Giant wasps are every bit as aggressive and territorial as their smaller cousins.

Combat

These creatures attack when hungry or threatened, stinging their prey to death. They take dead or incapacitated opponents back to their lairs as food for their unhatched young.

Poison (Ex): See the Vermin Poison table, page 205.

MONSTROUS CENTIPEDE

These creatures travel wherever hunger leads them. They prefer

	Giant Bee Medium-Size Vermin	Giant Beetle, Bombardier Medium-Size Vermin	Giant Beetle, Fire Small Vermin
HD:	3d8 (13 hp)	2d8+4 (13 hp)	1d8 (4 hp)
Initiative:	+2 (Dex)	+0	+0
Speed:	20 ft., fly 80 ft. (good)	30 ft.	30 ft.
AC:	14 (+2 Dex, +2 natural)	16 (+6 natural)	16 (+1 size, +5 natural)
Attacks:	Sting +2 melee	Bite +2 melee	Bite +1 melee
Damage:	Sting 1d4 and poison	Bite 1d4+1	Bite 2d4
Face/Reach:	5 ft. by 5 ft./5 ft.	5 ft. by 5 ft./5 ft.	5 ft. by 5 ft./5 ft.
Special Attacks:	Poison	Acid spray	—
Special Qualities:	Vermin	Vermin	Vermin
Saves:	Fort +3, Ref +3, Will +2	Fort +5, Ref +0, Will +0	Fort +2, Ref +0, Will +0
Abilities:	Str 11, Dex 14, Con 11, Int —, Wis 12, Cha 9	Str 13, Dex 10, Con 14, Int —, Wis 10, Cha 9	Str 10, Dex 11, Con 11, Int —, Wis 10, Cha 7
Skills:	Intuit Direction +6, Spot +6	Listen +5, Spot +5	Climb +4, Listen +3, Spot +3
Climate/Terrain:	Temperate and warm land and underground	Temperate and warm land and underground	Temperate and warm land and underground
Organization:	Solitary, swarm (2–5), or hive (11–20)	Cluster (2–5) or swarm (6–11)	Cluster (2–5) or swarm (6–11)
Challenge Rating:	1/2	2	1/3
Treasure:	No coins; 1/4 goods (honey only); no items	None	None
Alignment:	Always neutral	Always neutral	Always neutral
Advancement:	4–6 HD (Medium-size); 7–9 HD (Large)	3–4 HD (Medium-size); 5–6 HD (Large)	2–3 HD (Small)

	Giant Beetle, Stag Large Vermin	Giant Praying Mantis Large Vermin	Giant Wasp Large Vermin
HD:	7d8+21 (52 hp)	4d8+8 (26 hp)	5d8+10 (32 hp)
Initiative:	+0	−1 (Dex)	+1 (Dex)
Speed:	20 ft.	20 ft., fly 40 ft. (poor)	20 ft., fly 60 ft. (good)
AC:	19 (−1 size, +10 natural)	14 (−1 size, −1 Dex, +6 natural)	14 (−1 size, +1 Dex, +4 natural)
Attacks:	Bite +10 melee	Claws +6 melee, bite +1 melee	Sting +6 melee
Damage:	Bite 4d6+9	Claws 1d8+4, bite 1d6+2	Sting 1d3+6 and poison
Face/Reach:	5 ft. by 10 ft./5 ft.	5 ft. by 10 ft./5 ft.	5 ft. by 10 ft./5 ft.
Special Attacks:	Trample 2d8+3	Improved grab, squeeze	Poison

to feed on small animals but do not hesitate to attack humanoids or other larger prey. Monstrous centipedes are long and low:

MONSTROUS CENTIPEDE SIZES

Size	Body Length	Body Width*	Height
Tiny	2 feet	3 inches	1 1/2 inches
Small	4 feet	6 inches	3 inches
Medium-size	8 feet	1 foot	6 inches
Large	15 feet	2 feet	1 foot
Huge	30 feet	4 feet	2 feet
Gargantuan	60 feet	8 feet	4 feet
Colossal	120 feet	16 feet	8 feet

*The number includes the centipede's body and its legs; the actual body width is about a third of the total.

Combat

Monstrous centipedes tend to attack anything that resembles food, biting with their jaws and injecting their poison.

Poison (Ex): See the Vermin Poison table, page 205.

Skills: Monstrous centipedes receive a +4 racial bonus to Climb, Hide, and Spot checks.

MONSTROUS SCORPION

Monstrous scorpions are vicious predators that make unnerving scuttling noises as they speed across dungeon floors. A monstrous scorpion has a low, flat body:

MONSTROUS SCORPION SIZES

Size	Body Length	Body Width*	Height
Tiny	2 feet	1 foot	1 1/2 inches
Small	4 feet	2 feet	3 inches
Medium-size	6 feet	3 feet	6 inches
Large	10 feet	5 feet	1 1/2 feet
Huge	20 feet	10 feet	2 1/2 feet
Gargantuan	40 feet	20 feet	5 feet
Colossal	80 feet	40 feet	10 feet

*The number includes the scorpion's body and its legs; the actual body width is about a third of the total.

**The number indicates the height of the creature's body; the creature's stinger usually is held about as high off the ground as the creature is wide.

Combat

Monstrous scorpions are likely to attack any creature that approaches, and they usually charge prey.

Improved Grab (Ex): To use this ability, the monstrous scorpion must hit with its claw attack. If it gets a hold, it hangs on and stings.

Squeeze (Ex): A monstrous scorpion that gets a hold on an opponent of its size or smaller automatically deals damage with both claws, biting and stinging at its full attack value.

Poison (Ex): See the Vermin Poison table, page 205.

Skills: A monstrous scorpion receives a +4 racial bonus to Climb, Hide, and Spot checks.

	Giant Beetle, Stag	Giant Praying Mantis	Giant Wasp
Special Qualities:	Vermin	Vermin	Vermin
Saves:	Fort +8, Ref +2, Will +2	Fort +6, Ref +0, Will +3	Fort +6, Ref +2, Will +2
Abilities:	Str 23, Dex 17, Con 17,	Str 19, Dex 8, Con 15,	Str 18, Dex 12, Con 14,
	Int —, Wis 10, Cha 9	Int —, Wis 14, Cha 11	Int —, Wis 13, Cha 11
Skills:	Listen +8, Spot +7	Hide +1*, Listen +5, Spot +8	Intuit Direction +7, Spot +9
Climate/Terrain:	Temperate and warm forest and underground	Any land and underground	Temperate and warm land and underground
Organization:	Cluster (2–5) or swarm (6–11)	Solitary	Solitary, swarm (2–5), or nest (11–20)
Challenge Rating:	4	2	3
Treasure:	None	None	None
Alignment:	Always neutral	Always neutral	Always neutral
Advancement:	8–10 HD (Large); 11–21 HD (Huge)	5–8 HD (Large); 9–12 HD (Huge)	6–8 HD (Large); 9–15 HD (Huge)

	Monstrous Centipede, Tiny Tiny Vermin	Monstrous Centipede, Small Small Vermin	Monstrous Centipede, Medium-Size Medium-Size Vermin
Hit Dice:	1/4 d8 (1 hp)	1/2 d8 (2 hp)	1d8 (4 hp)
Initiative:	+2 (Dex)	+2 (Dex)	+2 (Dex)
Speed:	20 ft.	30 ft.	40 ft.
AC:	14 (+2 size, +2 Dex)	14 (+1 size, +2 Dex, +1 natural)	14 (+2 Dex, +2 natural)
Attacks:	Bite +4 melee	Bite +3 melee	Bite +2 melee
Damage:	Bite 1d3–5 and poison	Bite 1d4–3 and poison	Bite 1d6–1 and poison
Face/Reach:	2 1/2 ft. by 2 1/2 ft./0 ft.	5 ft. by 5 ft./5 ft.	5 ft. by 5 ft./5 ft.
Special Attacks:	Poison	Poison	Poison
Special Qualities:	Vermin	Vermin	Vermin
Saves:	Fort +2, Ref +2, Will +0	Fort +2, Ref +2, Will +0	Fort +2, Ref +2, Will +0
Abilities:	Str 1, Dex 15, Con 10,	Str 5, Dex 15, Con 10,	Str 9, Dex 15, Con 10,
	Int —, Wis 10, Cha 2	Int —, Wis 10, Cha 2	Int —, Wis 10, Cha 2
Skills:	Climb +3, Hide +17, Spot +7	Climb +5, Hide +13, Spot +7	Climb +8, Hide +8, Spot +8
Feats:	Weapon Finesse (bite)	Weapon Finesse (bite)	Weapon Finesse (bite)
Climate/Terrain:	Temperate and warm land and underground	Temperate and warm land and underground	Temperate and warm land and underground
Organization:	Colony (8–16)	Colony (2–5) or swarm (6–11)	Solitary or colony (2–5)
Challenge Rating:	1/8	1/4	1/2
Treasure:	None	None	None
Alignment:	Always neutral	Always neutral	Always neutral
Advancement:	—	—	—

MONSTROUS SPIDER

All monstrous spiders are aggressive predators.

Monstrous spiders come in two general types: hunters and web spinners. Hunters rove about, while web spinners usually attempt to trap prey. Hunting spiders are speedier than their web-spinning counterparts and use higher speed numbers shown in parentheses.

Monstrous spiders of both types have roughly circular bodies surrounded by outspread legs:

Combat

Monstrous spiders use their poisonous bite to subdue or kill prey.

Poison (Ex): See the Vermin Poison table, page 205.

Web (Ex): Both types of monstrous spiders often wait in their webs or in trees, then lower themselves silently on silk strands and leap onto prey passing beneath. A single strand is strong enough to support the spider and one creature of the same size.

Skills: *Monstrous spiders gain a +8 competence bonus to

Monstrous Spider Sizes

Size	Diameter*	Height
Tiny	2 feet	2 inches
Small	3 feet	3 inches
Medium-size	5 feet	6 inches
Large	10 feet	1 1/2 feet
Huge	15 feet	2 1/2 feet
Gargantuan	20 feet	5 feet
Colossal	40 feet	10 feet

*The number includes the spider's body and its legs; the actual body diameter is about a third of the total.

Hide and Move Silently checks when using their webs.

Web-spinning spiders can cast a web eight times per day. This is similar to an attack with a net but has a maximum range of 50 feet, with a range increment of 10 feet, and is effective against targets up to one size smaller that the spider (see page 102 in the

	Monstrous Centipede, Large Large Vermin	Monstrous Centipede, Huge Huge Vermin	Monstrous Centipede, Gargantuan Gargantuan Vermin
Hit Dice:	2d8 (9 hp)	4d8 (18 hp)	16d8 (72 hp)
Initiative:	+2 (Dex)	+2 (Dex)	+2 (Dex)
Speed:	40 ft.	40 ft.	40 ft.
AC:	14 (−1 size, +2 Dex, +3 natural)	16 (−2 size, +2 Dex, +6 natural)	18 (−4 size, +2 Dex, +10 natural)
Attacks:	Bite +2 melee	Bite +4 melee	Bite +13 melee
Damage:	Bite 1d8+1 and poison	Bite 2d6+4 and poison	Bite 2d8+7 and poison
Face/Reach:	5 ft. by 15 ft./5 ft.	10 ft. by 30 ft./10 ft.	15 ft. by 60 ft./10 ft.
Special Attacks:	Poison	Poison	Poison
Special Qualities:	Vermin	Vermin	Vermin
Saves:	Fort +3, Ref +2, Will +0	Fort +4, Ref +3, Will +1	Fort +10, Ref +7, Will +5
Abilities:	Str 13, Dex 15, Con 10, Int —, Wis 10, Cha 2	Str 17, Dex 15, Con 10, Int —, Wis 10, Cha 2	Str 21, Dex 15, Con 10, Int —, Wis 10, Cha 2
Skills:	Climb +10, Hide +3, Spot +8	Climb +11, Hide +1, Spot +7	Climb +13, Hide −3, Spot +7
Feats:	Weapon Finesse (bite)	—	—
Climate/Terrain:	Temperate and warm land and underground	Temperate and warm land and underground	Temperate and warm land and underground
Organization:	Solitary or colony (2–5)	Solitary or colony (2–5)	Solitary
Challenge Rating:	1	2	6
Treasure:	None	None	None
Alignment:	Always neutral	Always neutral	Always neutral
Advancement:	3 HD (Large)	5–15 HD (Huge)	17–31 HD (Gargantuan)

	Monstrous Centipede, Colossal Colossal Vermin	Monstrous Scorpion, Tiny Tiny Vermin	Monstrous Scorpion, Small Small Vermin
Hit Dice:	32d8 (144 hp)	1/2 d8+2 (4 hp)	1d8+2 (6 hp)
Initiative:	+2 (Dex)	+0	+0
Speed:	40 ft.	20 ft.	30 ft.
AC:	20 (−8 size, +2 Dex, +16 natural)	14 (+2 size, +2 natural)	14 (+1 size, +3 natural)
Attacks:	Bite +23 melee	2 claws +2 melee, sting −3 melee	2 claws +1 melee, sting −4 melee
Damage:	Bite 4d6+10 and poison	Claw 1d2−4, sting 1d2−4 and poison	Claw 1d3−1, sting 1d3−1 and poison
Face/Reach:	30 ft. by 120 ft./15 ft.	2 1/2 ft. by 2 1/2 ft./0 ft.	5 ft. by 5 ft./5 ft.
Special Attacks:	Poison	Improved grab, poison	Improved grab, squeeze, poison
Special Qualities:	Vermin	Vermin	Vermin
Saves:	Fort +18, Ref +12, Will +10	Fort +4, Ref +0, Will +0	Fort +4, Ref +0, Will +0
Abilities:	Str 25, Dex 15, Con 10, Int —, Wis 10, Cha 2	Str 3, Dex 10, Con 14, Int —, Wis 10, Cha 2	Str 9, Dex 10, Con 14, Int —, Wis 10, Cha 2
Skills:	Climb +15, Hide −7, Spot +7	Climb +4, Hide +15, Spot +7	Climb +6, Hide +12, Spot +7
Feats:	—	Weapon Finesse (claw, sting)	Weapon Finesse (claw, sting)
Climate/Terrain:	Temperate and warm land and underground	Temperate and warm land and underground	Temperate and warm land and underground
Organization:	Solitary	Colony (8–16)	Colony (2–5) or swarm (6–11)
Challenge Rating:	8	1/4	1/2
Treasure:	None	None	None
Alignment:	Always neutral	Always neutral	Always neutral
Advancement:	33–64 HD (Colossal)	—	—

	Monstrous Scorpion, Medium-Size Medium-Size Vermin	Monstrous Scorpion, Large Large Vermin	Monstrous Scorpion, Huge Huge Vermin
Hit Dice:	2d8+4 (13 hp)	4d8+8 (26 hp)	16d8+32 (104 hp)
Initiative:	+0	+0	+0
Speed:	40 ft.	50 ft.	50 ft.
AC:	14 (+4 natural)	14 (−1 size, +5 natural)	16 (−2 size, +8 natural)
Attacks:	2 claws +2 melee, sting −3 melee	2 claws +5 melee, sting +0 melee	2 claws +15 melee, sting +10 melee
Damage:	Claw 1d4+1, sting 1d4 and poison	Claw 1d6+3, sting 1d6+1 and poison	Claw 1d8+5, sting 2d4+2 and poison
Face/Reach:	5 ft. by 5 ft./5 ft.	5 ft. by 10 ft./5 ft.	10 ft. by 20 ft./10 ft.
Special Attacks:	Improved grab, squeeze, poison	Improved grab, squeeze, poison	Improved grab, squeeze, poison
Special Qualities:	Vermin	Vermin	Vermin
Saves:	Fort +5, Ref +0, Will +0	Fort +6, Ref +1, Will +1	Fort +12, Ref +5, Will +5
Abilities:	Str 13, Dex 10, Con 14, Int —, Wis 10, Cha 2	Str 17, Dex 10, Con 14, Int —, Wis 10, Cha 2	Str 21, Dex 10, Con 14, Int —, Wis 10, Cha 2
Skills:	Climb +8, Hide +8, Spot +7	Climb +11, Hide +3, Spot +7	Climb +12, Hide +0, Spot +7
Climate/Terrain:	Temperate and warm land and underground	Temperate and warm land and underground	Temperate and warm land and underground
Organization:	Solitary or colony (2–5)	Solitary or colony (2–5)	Solitary or colony (2–5)
Challenge Rating:	1	2	6
Treasure:	1/10 coins; 50% goods; 50% items	1/10 coins; 50% goods; 50% items	1/10 coins; 50% goods; 50% items
Alignment:	Always neutral	Always neutral	Always neutral
Advancement:	—	5–15 HD (Large)	17–31 HD (Huge)

	Monstrous Scorpion, Gargantuan Gargantuan Vermin	Monstrous Scorpion, Colossal Colossal Vermin	Monstrous Spider, Tiny Tiny Vermin
Hit Dice:	32d8+64 (208 hp)	64d8+128 (416 hp)	1/2 d8 (2 hp)
Initiative:	+0	+0	+3 (Dex)
Speed:	50 ft.	50 ft.	20 ft., climb 10 ft.
AC:	18 (−4 size, +12 natural)	20 (−8 size, +18 natural)	15 (+2 size, +3 Dex)
Attacks:	2 claws +27 melee, sting +22 melee	2 claws +49 melee, sting +44 melee	Bite +5 melee
Damage:	Claw 2d6+7, sting 2d6+3 and poison	Claw 2d8+9, sting 2d8+4 and poison	Bite 1d3−4 and poison
Face/Reach:	20 ft. by 40 ft./10 ft.	40 ft. by 80 ft./15 ft.	2 1/2 ft. by 2 1/2 ft./0 ft.
Special Attacks:	Improved grab, squeeze, poison	Improved grab, squeeze, poison	Poison, web
Special Qualities:	Vermin	Vermin	Vermin
Saves:	Fort +20, Ref +10, Will +10	Fort +36, Ref +21, Will +21	Fort +2, Ref +3, Will +0
Abilities:	Str 25, Dex 10, Con 14, Int —, Wis 10, Cha 2	Str 29, Dex 10, Con 14, Int —, Wis 10, Cha 2	Str 3, Dex 17, Con 10, Int —, Wis 10, Cha 2
Skills:	Climb +14, Hide −4, Spot +7	Climb +16, Hide −8, Spot +7	Climb +8, Hide +18, Jump −4*, Spot +7*
Feats:	—	—	Weapon Finesse (bite)
Climate/Terrain:	Temperate and warm land and underground	Temperate and warm land and underground	Temperate and warm land and underground
Organization:	Solitary	Solitary	Colony (8–16)
Challenge Rating:	9	11	1/4
Treasure:	1/10 coins; 50% goods; 50% items	1/10 coins; 50% goods; 50% items	None
Alignment:	Always neutral	Always neutral	Always neutral
Advancement:	33–63 HD (Gargantuan)	—	—

Player's Handbook for details on net attacks). The web anchors the target in place, allowing no movement.

An entangled creature can escape with a successful Escape Artist check or burst it with a Strength check. Both are standard actions whose DCs are listed in the accompanying table.

Web-spinning spiders often create sheets of sticky webbing from 5 to 60 feet square, depending on the size of the spider. They usually position these sheets to snare flying creatures but can also try to trap prey on the ground. Approaching creatures must succeed at a Spot check (DC 20) to notice a web; otherwise they stumble into it and become trapped as though by a successful web attack. Attempts to escape or burst the webbing gain a +5 bonus if the trapped creature has something to walk on or grab while pulling free. Each 5-foot section has the hit points listed on the table, and sheet webs have damage reduction 5/fire.

A monstrous spider can move across its own sheet web at its

MONSTROUS SPIDER WEBS

Spider Size	Escape DC	Break DC	Hit Points
Tiny	16	22	2
Small	18	24	4
Medium-size	20	26	6
Large	26	32	12
Huge	28	34	14
Gargantuan	30	36	16
Colossal	32	38	18

climb speed and can determine the exact location of any creature touching the web.

Skills: Monstrous spiders receive a +4 racial bonus to Hide and Spot checks.

*Hunting spiders receive a +6 racial bonus to Jump checks and a +8 racial bonus to Spot checks.

	Monstrous Spider, Small Small Vermin	Monstrous Spider, Medium-Size Medium-Size Vermin	Monstrous Spider, Large Large Vermin
Hit Dice:	1d8 (4 hp)	2d8+2 (11 hp)	4d8+4 (22 hp)
Initiative:	+3 (Dex)	+3 (Dex)	+3 (Dex)
Speed:	30 ft., climb 20 ft. (40 ft., climb 20 ft.)	30 ft., climb 20 ft. (40 ft., climb 20 ft.)	30 ft., climb 20 ft. (40 ft., climb 20 ft.)
AC:	14 (+1 size, +3 Dex)	14 (+3 Dex, +1 natural)	14 (−1 size, +3 Dex, +2 natural)
Attacks:	Bite +4 melee	Bite +4 melee	Bite +4 melee
Damage:	Bite 1d4−2 and poison	Bite 1d6 and poison	Bite 1d8+3 and poison
Face/Reach:	5 ft. by 5 ft./5 ft.	5 ft. by 5 ft./5 ft.	10 ft. by 10 ft./5 ft.
Special Attacks:	Poison, web	Poison, web	Poison, web
Special Qualities:	Vermin	Vermin	Vermin
Saves:	Fort +2, Ref +3, Will +0	Fort +4, Ref +3, Will +0	Fort +5, Ref +4, Will +1
Abilities:	Str 7, Dex 17, Con 10, Int —, Wis 10, Cha 2	Str 11, Dex 17, Con 12, Int —, Wis 10, Cha 2	Str 15, Dex 17, Con 12, Int —, Wis 10, Cha 2
Skills:	Climb +10, Hide +14, Jump −2*, Spot +7*	Climb +12, Hide +10, Jump +0*, Spot +7*	Climb +14, Hide +6, Jump +2*, Spot +7*
Feats:	Weapon Finesse (bite)	Weapon Finesse (bite)	—
Climate/Terrain:	Temperate and warm land and underground	Temperate and warm land and underground	Temperate and warm land and underground
Organization:	Colony (2–5) or swarm (6–11)	Solitary or colony (2–5)	Solitary or colony (2–5)
Challenge Rating:	1/2	1	2
Treasure:	None	1/10 coins; 50% goods; 50% items	1/10 coins; 50% goods; 50% items
Alignment:	Always neutral	Always neutral	Always neutral
Advancement:	—	3 HD (Medium-size)	6–9 HD (Large)

	Monstrous Spider, Huge Huge Vermin	Monstrous Spider, Gargantuan Gargantuan Vermin	Monstrous Spider, Colossal Colossal Vermin
Hit Dice:	10d8+10 (55 hp)	24d8+24 (132 hp)	48d8+48 (264 hp)
Initiative:	+3 (Dex)	+3 (Dex)	+3 (Dex)
Speed:	30 ft., climb 20 ft. (40 ft., climb 20 ft.)	30 ft., climb 20 ft. (40 ft., climb 20 ft.)	30 ft., climb 20 ft. (40 ft., climb 20 ft.)
AC:	16 (−2 size, +3 Dex, +5 natural)	18 (−4 size, +3 Dex, +9 natural)	20 (−8 size, +3 Dex, +15 natural)
Attacks:	Bite +9 melee	Bite +20 melee	Bite +36 melee
Damage:	Bite 2d6+6 and poison	Bite 2d8+9 and poison	Bite 4d6+12 and poison
Face/Reach:	15 ft. by 15 ft./10 ft.	20 ft. by 20 ft./10 ft.	40 ft. by 40 ft./15 ft.
Special Attacks:	Poison, web	Poison, web	Poison, web
Special Qualities:	Vermin	Vermin	Vermin
Saves:	Fort +8, Ref +6, Will +3	Fort +15, Ref +11, Will +8	Fort +27, Ref +19, Will +16
Abilities:	Str 19, Dex 17, Con 12, Int —, Wis 10, Cha 2	Str 23, Dex 17, Con 12, Int —, Wis 10, Cha 2	Str 27, Dex 17, Con 12, Int —, Wis 10, Cha 2
Skills:	Climb +16, Hide +2, Jump +4*, Spot +7*	Climb +18, Hide −2, Jump +6*, Spot +7*	Climb +20, Hide −6, Jump +8*, Spot +7*
Climate/Terrain:	Temperate and warm land and underground	Temperate and warm land and underground	Temperate and warm land and underground
Organization:	Solitary or colony (2–5)	Solitary	Solitary
Challenge Rating:	4	7	10
Treasure:	1/10 coins; 50% goods; 50% items	1/10 coins; 50% goods; 50% items	1/10 coins; 50% goods; 50% items
Alignment:	Always neutral	Always neutral	Always neutral
Advancement:	11–23 HD (Huge)	25–47 HD (Gargantuan)	49–64 HD (Colossal)

Appendix 3: Templates

Certain creatures have no type but are instead created by adding a "template" to an existing creature. The following rules set out the rules for building a templated creature, such as a vampire.

CELESTIAL CREATURES

Celestial creatures dwell in the upper planes, realms of good, although they resemble beings found on the Material Plane. They are more regal and more beautiful than their earthly counterparts.

Celestial creatures often come in metallic colors (usually silver, gold, or platinum). They can be mistaken for half-celestials, more powerful creatures that are created when a celestial mates with a noncelestial creature.

CREATING A CELESTIAL CREATURE

"Celestial" is a template that can be added to any corporeal creature of nonevil alignment (referred to hereafter as the "base creature"). Beasts or animals with this template become magical beasts, but otherwise the creature type is unchanged.

A celestial creature uses all the base creature's statistics and special abilities except as noted here.

Special Attacks: A celestial creature retains all the special attacks of the base creature and also gains the following.

Smite Evil (Su): Once per day the creature can make a normal attack to deal additional damage equal to its HD total (maximum of +20) against an evil foe.

Special Qualities: A celestial creature retains all the special qualities of the base creature and also gains the following ones:

- Darkvision with a range of 60 feet.
- Acid, cold, and electricity resistance (see the table below).
- Damage reduction (see the table below).
- SR equal to double the creature's HD (maximum 25).

	Acid, Cold, Electricity	
Hit Dice	Resistance	Damage Reduction
1–3	5	—
4–7	10	5/+1
8–11	15	5/+2
12+	20	10/+3

If the base creature already has one or more of these special qualities, use the better value.

Saves: Same as the base creature
Abilities: Same as the base creature, but Intelligence is at least 3.
Skills: Same as the base creature
Feats: Same as the base creature

Climate/Terrain: Any land and underground
Organization: Same as the base creature
Challenge Rating: Up to 3 HD, as base creature
4 HD to 7 HD, as base creature +1
8+ HD, as base creature +2
Treasure: Same as the base creature
Alignment: Always good (any)
Advancement: Same as the base creature

SAMPLE CELESTIAL CREATURE

Celestial Lion
Large Magical Beast
Hit Dice: 5d8+10 (32 hp)
Initiative: +3 (Dex)
Speed: 40 ft.
AC: 15 (–1 size, +3 Dex, +3 natural)
Attacks: 2 claws +7 melee; bite +2 melee
Damage: Claw 1d4+5; bite 1d8+2
Face/Reach: 5 ft. by 5 ft./5 ft.
Special Attacks: Pounce, improved grab, rake 1d4+2, smite evil
Special Qualities: Scent, darkvision 60 ft., damage reduction 5/+1, SR 10; acid, cold, and electricity resistance 10
Saves: Fort +6, Ref +7, Will +2
Abilities: Str 21, Dex 17, Con 15, Int 3, Wis 12, Cha 6
Skills: Balance +7, Hide +4*, Jump +5, Listen +5, Move Silently +11, Spot +5

Climate/Terrain: Any land and underground
Organization: Solitary, pair, or pride (6–10)
Challenge Rating: 3
Treasure: None
Alignment: Always good (any)
Advancement: 6–8 HD (Large)

Combat

Pounce (Ex): If a celestial lion leaps upon a foe during the first round of combat, it can make a full attack even if it has already taken a move action.

Improved Grab (Ex): To use this ability, the celestial lion must hit with its bite attack. If it gets a hold, it can rake.

Rake (Ex): A celestial lion that gets a hold can make two rake attacks (+7 melee) with its hind legs for 1d4+2 damage each. If the celestial lion pounces on an opponent, it can also rake.

Skills: Celestial lions receive a +4 racial bonus to Balance, Hide, and Move Silently checks. *In areas of tall grass or heavy undergrowth, the Hide bonus improves to +8.

FIENDISH CREATURES

Fiendish creatures dwell in the infernal planes, realms of evil, although they resemble beings found on the Material Plane. They are more fearsome in appearance than their earthly counterparts.

Fiendish creatures are often mistaken for half-fiends, more powerful creatures that are created when a fiend mates with a noncelestial creature, or though some foul infernal breeding project.

CREATING A FIENDISH CREATURE

"Fiendish" is a template that can be added to any corporeal creature of nongood alignment (referred to hereafter as the "base creature"). Beasts or animals with this template become magical beasts, but otherwise the creature type is unchanged. A fiendish creature uses all the base creature's statistics and special abilities except as noted here.

Special Attacks: A fiendish creature retains all the special attacks of the base creature and also gains the following.

Smite Good (Su): Once per day the creature can make a normal attack to deal additional damage equal to its HD total (maximum of +20) against a good foe.

Special Qualities: A fiendish creature retains all the special qualities of the base creature and also gains the following.

- Darkvision with a range of 60 feet.
- Cold and fire resistance (see the table below).
- Damage reduction (see the table below).
- SR equal to double the creature's HD (maximum 25).

	Cold, Fire	
Hit Dice	Resistance	Damage Reduction
1–3	5	—
4–7	10	5/+1
8–11	15	5/+2
12+	20	10/+3

If the base creature already has one or more of these special qualities, use the better value.

Saves: Same as the base creature

Abilities: Same as the base creature, but Intelligence is at least 3.

Skills: Same as the base creature

Feats: Same as the base creature

Climate/Terrain: Any land and underground

Organization: Same as the base creature

Challenge Rating: Up to 3 HD, as base creature

4 HD to 7 HD, as base creature +1

8+ HD, as base creature +2

Treasure: Same as the base creature

Alignment: Always evil (any)

Advancement: Same as the base creature

SAMPLE FIENDISH CREATURE

Abyssal Dire Rat

Small Magical Beast

Hit Dice: 1d8+1 (5 hp)

Initiative: +3 (Dex)

Speed: 40 ft., climb 20 ft.

AC: 15 (+1 size, +3 Dex, +1 natural)

Attacks: Bite +4 melee

Damage: Bite 1d4

Face/Reach: 5 ft. by 5 ft./5 ft.

Special Attacks: Disease, smite good

Special Qualities: Scent, darkvision 60 ft., cold and fire resistance 5, SR 2

Saves: Fort +3, Ref +5, Will +3

Abilities: Str 10, Dex 17, Con 12, Int 3, Wis 12, Cha 4

Skills: Climb +11, Hide +11, Move Silently +6

Feats: Weapon Finesse (bite)

Climate/Terrain: Any land and underground

Organization: Solitary or pack (11–20)

Challenge Rating: 1/2

Treasure: None

Alignment: Always evil (any)

Advancement: 2–3 HD (Small); 4–6 HD (Medium-size)

Combat

Disease (Ex): Filth fever—bite, Fortitude save (DC 12), incubation period 1d3 days; damage 1d3 temporary Dexterity and 1d3 temporary Constitution (see Disease, page 74 in the DUNGEON MASTER'S *Guide*).

GHOST

Ghosts are the spectral remnants of intelligent beings who, for one reason or another, cannot rest easily in their graves.

Some ghosts go about their business with little or no interest in the living. Others, however, are malevolent spirits who loathe all life and seek to destroy it whenever possible. Although ghosts can often be driven off or destroyed, they return again and again until they deal with the reason for their existence.

A ghost greatly resembles its corporeal shape in life, but in some cases, the spiritual form is somewhat altered. Some ghosts look angelic and sweet, while others are twisted and horrible things, showing clearly the agony of the undead. There is often—but not always—a correlation between a ghost's appearance and its alignment. Assumptions are dangerous.

A ghost's behavior usually matches its life. The spirit of a covetous person, for example, might continue to hoard wealth even though it has no use for such treasures. Similarly, a ghost is generally tied to the place where it died. If the aforementioned miser had died in a robbery, the ghost might remain in the counting house, tormenting the new owner and all who do business there. This is not a hard and fast rule, though: Many ghosts wander freely.

CREATING A GHOST

"Ghost" is a template that can be added to any aberration, animal, beast, dragon, giant, humanoid, magical beast, monstrous humanoid, or shapechanger. The creature (referred to hereafter as the "base creature") must have a Charisma score of at least 8. The creature's type changes to "undead." It otherwise uses all the base creature's statistics and special abilities except as noted here.

Hit Dice: Increase to d12.

Speed: Ghosts have a fly speed of 30 feet, unless the base creature has a higher fly speed, with perfect maneuverability.

AC: Natural armor is the same as the base creature but applies only to ethereal encounters. When the ghost manifests (see below) its natural armor value is +0, but it gains a deflection bonus equal to its Charisma modifier or +1, whichever is higher.

Attacks: The ghost retains all the attacks of the base creature, although those relying on physical contact do not affect nonethereal creatures.

Damage: Against ethereal creatures, a ghost uses the base creature's damage ratings. Against nonethereal creatures, the ghost usually cannot deal physical damage at all but can use its special attacks, if any, when it manifests (see below).

Special Attacks: The ghost retains all the special attacks of the base creature, although those relying on physical contact do not affect nonethereal creatures. The ghost also gains a manifestation ability plus 1d3 other special attacks described below. Saves have a DC of 10 + 1/2 ghost's HD + ghost's Charisma modifier unless noted otherwise.

Manifestation (Su): All ghosts have this ability. As ethereal creatures, they cannot affect or be affected by anything in the material world. When they manifest, ghosts become visible but remain incorporeal (see page 6). However, a manifested ghost can strike with its touch attack or a ghost touch weapon. A manifested ghost remains on the Ethereal Plane but can be attacked by opponents on both the Material and Ethereal planes. When a spellcasting ghost is on the Ethereal Plane, its spells cannot affect targets on the Material Plane, but they work normally against ethereal targets. When a spellcasting ghost manifests, its spells continue to affect ethereal targets and can affect targets on the Material Plane normally unless the spells rely on touch. A manifested ghost's touch spells don't work on material targets.

Corrupting Touch (Su): A ghost that hits a living target with its incorporeal attack deals 1d4 points of damage. Against ethereal opponents, it adds its Strength modifier to attack and damage rolls. Against material opponents, it adds its Dexterity modifier to attack rolls only.

Frightful Moan (Su): The ghost can moan as a standard action. All living creatures within a 30-foot spread must succeed at a Will save or become panicked for 2d4 rounds. This is a sonic, necromantic, mind-affecting fear effect. A creature that successfully saves against the moan cannot be affected by the same ghost's moan for one day.

Horrific Appearance (Su): Any living creature within 60 feet that views the ghost must succeed at a Fortitude save or immediately suffer 1d4 points of permanent Strength, 1d4 points of permanent Dexterity, and 1d4 points of permanent Constitution drain. A creature that successfully saves against this effect cannot be affected by the same ghost's horrific appearance for one day.

Corrupting Gaze (Su): The ghost can blast living beings with a glance, at a range of up to 30 feet. Creatures that meet the ghost's gaze must succeed at a Fortitude save or suffer 2d10 points of damage and 1d4 points of permanent Charisma drain.

Malevolence (Su): Once per round, an ethereal ghost can merge its body with a creature on the Material Plane. This ability is similar to *magic jar* as cast by a 10th-level sorcerer (or the ghost's character level, whichever is higher), except that it does not require a receptacle. If the attack succeeds, the ghost's body vanishes into the opponent's body. The target can resist the attack with a successful Will save (DC 15 + ghost's Charisma modifier). A creature that successfully saves is immune to that ghost's malevolence for one day.

Telekinesis (Su): The ghost can use *telekinesis* once per round as a free action, as cast by a sorcerer whose level equals the ghost's HD or 12, whichever is higher.

Special Qualities: A ghost has all the special qualities of the base creature and those listed below, and gains the undead type and incorporeal subtype (see page 6).

Rejuvenation (Su): In most cases, it's difficult to destroy a ghost through simple combat: The "destroyed" spirit will often restore itself in 2d4 days. Even the most powerful spells are often only temporary solutions. A ghost that would otherwise be destroyed returns to its old haunts with a successful level check (1d20 + ghost's level or HD) against DC 16. As a rule, the only way to get rid of a ghost for sure is to determine the reason for its existence and set right whatever prevents it from resting in peace. The exact means varies with each spirit and may require a good deal of research.

Turn Resistance (Ex): A ghost has +4 turn resistance (see page 10).

Saves: Same as the base creature

Abilities: Same as the base creature, except that the ghost has no Constitution score, and its Charisma score increases by +4.

Skills: Ghosts receive a +8 racial bonus to Hide, Listen, Search, and Spot checks. Otherwise same as the base creature.

Feats: Same as the base creature

Climate/Terrain: Any land and underground
Organization: Solitary, gang (2–4), or mob (7–12)
Challenge Rating: Same as the base creature +2
Treasure: None
Alignment: Any
Advancement: Same as the base creature

Ghostly Equipment

When a ghost forms, all its equipment and carried items usually become ethereal along with it. In addition, the ghost retains 2d4 items that it particularly valued in life (provided they are not in another creature's possession). The equipment works normally on the Ethereal Plane but passes harmlessly through material objects or creatures. A weapon of +1 or better enchantment, however, can harm material creatures when the ghost manifests, and enchanted weapons can harm the ghost.

The original material items remain behind, just as the ghost's physical remains do. If another creature seizes the original, the ethereal copy fades away. This invariably angers the ghost, who stops at nothing to return the item to its original resting place.

SAMPLE GHOST

This example uses a 5th-level human fighter as the base creature.

Ghost
Medium-Size Undead (Incorporeal)
Hit Dice: 5d12 (32 hp)
Initiative: +5 (+1 Dex, +4 Improved Initiative)
Speed: Fly 30 ft. (perfect)
AC: 12 (+1 Dex, +1 deflection); or 21 (+1 Dex, +8 full plate, +2 large shield)
Attacks: Incorporeal touch +6 melee (or masterwork bastard sword +10 melee); or masterwork shortbow +7 ranged
Damage: Incorporeal touch corruption 1d4 (1d4+3 vs. ethereal); masterwork bastard sword 1d10+4; masterwork shortbow 1d6
Face/Reach: 5 ft. by 5 ft./5 ft.
Special Attacks: Manifestation, corrupting touch, malevolence

Special Qualities: Undead, incorporeal, +4 turn resistance, rejuvenation
Saves: Fort +4, Ref +2, Will +2
Abilities: Str 16, Dex 13, Con —, Int 10, Wis 12, Cha 12
Skills: Climb +11, Hide +9, Listen +11, Ride +9, Search +8, Spot +11
Feats: Blind-Fight, Cleave, Exotic Weapon Proficiency (bastard sword), Improved Initiative, Power Attack, Weapon Focus (bastard sword)

The Will save against this ghost's malevolence has a DC of 16.

Undead: Immune to mind-influencing effects, poison, sleep, paralysis, stunning, and disease. Not subject to critical hits, subdual damage, ability damage, energy drain, or death from massive damage.

Incorporeal: Can be harmed only by other incorporeal creatures, +1 or better magic weapons, or magic, with a 50% chance to ignore any damage from a corporeal source. Can pass through solid objects at will, and own attacks pass through armor. Always moves silently.

Challenge Rating: 7

HALF-CELESTIAL

Celestials' magical nature allows them to crossbreed with virtually any creature. The offspring of the resulting unions, half-celestials, are glorious and wonderful beings.

To carry out their responsibilities, celestials sometimes spend great amounts of time in mortal realms. Being devoted and kind, they occasionally fall in love with mortals: humans, elves, unicorns, and similar creatures. The objects of celestial affection are never evil and are always intelligent. They always return the love of their immortal paramour and willingly conceive the child, usually caring for it since the celestial has other duties.

No matter the form, half-celestials are always comely and delightful to the senses, having golden skin, sparkling eyes, angelic wings, or some other sign of their higher nature.

Though noble and compassionate, half-celestials are often dismayed at the evil among their kin and take a stern, sometimes harsh, view of base instincts or malevolent actions. Never truly fitting into any mortal society, half-celestials are usually loners and wanderers attempting to right wrongs wherever they can.

CREATING A HALF-CELESTIAL

"Half-celestial" is a template that can be added to any corporeal creature with an Intelligence score of 4 or more and nonevil alignment (referred to hereafter as the "base creature"). The creature's type changes to "outsider." It uses all the base creature's statistics and special abilities except as noted here.

Speed: There is a 75% chance that a half-celestial has feathered wings. The creature can fly at twice the base creature's normal speed (good maneuverability).

AC: Natural armor improves by +1.

Special Attacks: A half-celestial retains all the special attacks of the base creature and also gains the supernatural ability to use *light* at will as the spell. Half-celestials with an Intelligence or Wisdom score of 8 or higher possess the following spell-like abilities, using their level as the caster level, as specified in the table below. Unless otherwise indicated, the ability is usable once per day.

Level	Abilities	Level	Abilities
1–2	*Protection from evil* 3/day, *bless*	9–10	*Dispel evil*
3–4	*Aid, detect evil*	11–12	*Holy word*
		13–14	*Holy aura* 3/day, *hallow*
5–6	*Cure serious wounds, neutralize poison*	15–16	*Symbol*
		17–18	*Summon monster IX* (celestials only)
7–8	*Holy smite, remove disease*	19+	*Resurrection*

Special Qualities: A half-celestial has all the special qualities of the base creature, plus low-light vision. Half-celestials are immune to acid, cold, disease, and electricity, and gain a +4 racial bonus to Fortitude saves against poison.

Saves: Same as the base creature

Abilities: Increase from the base creature as follows: Str +4, Dex +2, Con +4, Int +2, Wis +4, Cha +4.

Skills: A half-celestial has 8 skill points, plus its Intelligence modifier, per Hit Die. Treat skills from the base creature's list as class skills and other skills as cross-class. If the creature has a class, it gains skills for class levels normally.

Feats: Half-celestials have one feat for every four levels or the base creature's total of feats, whichever is greater.

Climate/Terrain: Same as either the base creature or the celestial
Organization: Same as the base creature
Challenge Rating: Same as the base creature +1
Alignment: Always good (any)
Treasure: Same as the base creature
Advancement: Same as the base creature

HALF-CELESTIAL CHARACTERS

Half-celestial humanoids often have a character class, favoring bards, clerics, fighters, and paladins. Nonhumanoids are also sometimes clerics or paladins. Half-celestial clerics serve good deities such as Ehlonna, Heironeous, Kord, or Pelor.

SAMPLE HALF-CELESTIAL

This example uses a unicorn as the base creature.

Half-Celestial/Half-Unicorn
Large Outsider (Chaotic, Good)
Hit Dice: 4d10+28 (50 hp)
Initiative: +4 (Dex)
Speed: 60 ft., fly 120 ft. (good)
AC: 20 (–1 size, +4 Dex, +7 natural)
Attacks: Horn +13 melee, 2 hooves +5 melee
Damage: Horn 1d8+10, hoof 1d4+3
Face/Reach: 5 ft. by 10 ft./5 ft. (10 ft. with horn)
Special Qualities: Magic circle against evil, light, spell-like abilities, immunities
Saves: Fort +11, Ref +8, Will +8
Abilities: Str 24, Dex 19, Con 25, Int 12, Wis 25, Cha 28
Skills: Animal Empathy +16, Diplomacy +10, Listen +16, Move Silently +11, Spot +15, Wilderness Lore +14*
Feats: Alertness

Climate/Terrain: Temperate forest
Organization: Solitary, pair, or grace (3–6)
Challenge Rating: 4
Treasure: None
Alignment: Always chaotic good
Advancement: 4–8 HD (Large)

Three out of four half-celestial/half-unicorns have elegant feathered wings on their backs. They often lead groups of other unicorns or act as their champions or defenders.

Combat

Half-celestial/half-unicorns normally attack only when defending themselves or their forests. They either charge, impaling foes with their horns like lances, or strike with their hooves. The horn is a +3 magic weapon, though its power fades if removed from the creature.

Magic Circle against Evil (Su): This ability continuously duplicates the effects of the *magic circle against evil* spell; the half-celestial/half-unicorn cannot suppress this power.

Light (Su): Half-celestial/half-unicorns can use *light* at will as a free action.

Spell-Like Abilities: Half-celestial/half-unicorns can *detect evil* at will as a free action. Once per day a half-celestial/half-unicorn can use *teleport without error* to move anywhere within its home. It cannot teleport beyond the forest boundaries nor back from outside.

A half-celestial/half-unicorn can use *cure light wounds* three times per day and *cure moderate wounds* once per day, as cast by a 5th-level druid, by touching a wounded creature with its horn. Once per day it can use *neutralize poison*, as cast by an 8th-level druid, with a touch of its horn. Further, it can use the following as a 4th-level cleric: 3/day—*protection from evil* (cast on others); 1/day—*bless* and *aid*.

Immunities: Half-celestial/half-unicorns are immune to acid, cold, disease, electricity, poison, and *charm* and *hold* spells or abilities.

Skills: *Half-celestial/half-unicorns receive a +3 racial bonus to Wilderness Lore checks within the boundaries of their forest.

HALF-DRAGON

Dragons' magical nature allows them to crossbreed with virtually any creature. This usually occurs while the dragon has changed its shape; it then abandons the crossbreed young.

Half-dragon creatures are always more formidable than their fellows, and their appearance betrays their nature—scales, elongated features, reptilian eyes, and exaggerated teeth and claws. Sometimes they have wings.

CREATING A HALF-DRAGON

"Half-dragon" is a template that can be added to any corporeal creature (referred to hereafter as the "base creature"). The creature's type becomes "dragon." It uses all the base creature's statistics and special abilities except as noted here.

Hit Dice: Increase by one die type, to a maximum of d12.

Speed: Half-dragons of Large or larger size have wings and can fly at their normal speed (average maneuverability). Smaller specimens have wings only if the base creature does.

AC: Natural armor improves by +4.

Damage: Half-dragons have bite and claw attacks. If the base creature does not have these attack forms, use the damage values in the table below. Otherwise, use the values below or the base creature's damage, whichever is greater.

Size	Bite Damage	Claw Damage
Fine	1	—
Diminutive	1d2	1
Tiny	1d3	1d2
Small	1d4	1d3
Medium-size	1d6	1d4
Large	1d8	1d6
Huge	2d6	2d8
Gargantuan	2d8	2d6
Colossal	4d6	2d8

Special Attacks: A half-dragon retains all the special attacks of the base creature and also gains a breath weapon based on the dragon variety, usable only once per day. Use all rules for dragon breath (see the Dragon entry) except as specified in the table below.

Dragon Variety	Breath Weapon	Damage (DC)
Black	Line* of acid	6d4 (17)
Blue	Line of lightning	6d8 (18)
Green	Cone** of gas	6d6 (17)
Red	Cone of fire	6d10 (19)
White	Cone of cold	3d6 (16)

Brass	Line of fire	3d6 (17)
Bronze	Line of lightning	6d6 (18)
Copper	Line of acid	6d4 (17)
Gold	Cone of fire	6d10 (20)
Silver	Cone of cold	6d8 (18)

*A line is always 5 ft. high, 5 ft. wide, and 60 ft. long.
**A cone is always 30 ft. long.

Special Qualities: A half-dragon has all the special qualities of the base creature, plus low-light vision and darkvision with a range of 60 feet. Half-dragons are immune to sleep and paralysis effects, and have additional immunities based on their dragon variety.

Dragon Variety	Immunity	Dragon Variety	Immunity
Black	Acid	Brass	Fire
Blue	Electricity	Bronze	Electricity
Green	Acid	Copper	Acid
Red	Fire	Gold	Fire
White	Cold	Silver	Cold

Saves: Same as the base creature
Abilities: Increase from the base creature as follows: Str +8, Dex +0, Con +2, Int +2, Wis +0, Cha +2.
Skills: A half-dragon has 6 skill points, plus its Intelligence modifier, per Hit Die. Treat skills from the base creature's list as class skills and other skills as cross-class. If the creature has a class, it gains skills for class levels normally.
Feats: Half-dragons have one feat for every four levels or the base creature's total of feats, whichever is greater. Half-dragons have access to, and usually favor, the dragon feats.

Climate/Terrain: Same as either the base creature or the dragon variety
Organization: Same as the base creature
Challenge Rating: Same as the base creature + 2
Treasure: Same as the base creature
Alignment: Same as the dragon variety
Advancement: Same as the base creature

HALF-DRAGON CHARACTERS
Half-dragons with a Charisma of 12 or higher are often sorcerers.

SAMPLE HALF-DRAGON
Here is an example of a red half-dragon using an ogre as the base creature.

Half-Dragon (Red)/Half-Ogre
Large Dragon
Hit Dice: 4d10+12 (34 hp)
Initiative: –1 (Dex)
Speed: 30 ft., fly 30 ft. (average)
AC: 20 (–1 size, –1 Dex, +9 natural, +3 hide)
Attacks: Huge greatclub +12 melee (or bite +11 melee, 2 claws +6 melee); or Huge longspear +1 ranged
Damage: Huge greatclub 2d6+13; Huge longspear 2d6+9; bite 1d8+9, claw 1d6+4
Face/Reach: 5 ft. by 5 ft./10 ft.
Special Attacks: Breath weapon
Special Qualities: Immunities, darkvision 60 ft., low-light vision
Saves: Fort +7, Ref +0, Will +1
Abilities: Str 29, Dex 8, Con 17, Int 8, Wis 10, Cha 9
Skills: Climb +12, Listen +7, Spot +7
Feats: Weapon Focus (greatclub)

Climate/Terrain: Any land, aquatic, and underground
Organization: Solitary, pair, gang (2–4), or band (5–8)

Challenge Rating: 4
Treasure: Standard
Alignment: Always chaotic evil
Advancement: By character class

Half-dragon/half-ogres speak Giant, Dragon, and Common.

Combat
Half-dragon/half-ogres use Huge two-handed (often exotic) weapons. Aggressive and temperamental, they're usually itching for a battle. They often lead other ogres but fight as individuals.
Breath Weapon (Su): Cone of fire, 30 feet, once per day; damage 6d10, Reflex half DC 19.
Immunities: Red half-dragons are immune to fire, *sleep*, and paralysis effects.

HALF-FIEND
Fiends' magical nature allows them to crossbreed with virtually any creature. Spawned deep in the dark, nether planes, these fiendish offspring are abominations that plague mortal creatures.

Demons and devils bring their progeny along to the Material Plane and loose them upon the world. Sometimes, however, fiends force themselves on mortal creatures to create evil half-breeds. The more depraved creatures are sometimes even willing to participate. Although half-fiend offspring are usually destroyed at birth, some survive to become grotesque mockeries of their mortal parents. All too rarely, though, one learns from and takes on the characteristics of its nonfiendish parent, turning from its evil heritage.

No matter the form, half-fiends are always hideous to behold, having dark scales, horns, glowing red eyes, batwings, a fetid odor, or some other obvious sign that they are tainted with evil.

Never truly fitting into any mortal society, half-fiends are usually loners. In the infernal planes, they are mistreated and derided for their impure nature. Among nonfiends, they are outcasts, hated corruptions of the natural order. Humanoid half-fiends are sometimes called "cambions." They often serve more powerful fiends or lead evil creatures on the Material Plane.

CREATING A HALF-FIEND
"Half-fiend" is a template that can be added to any corporeal creature (referred to hereafter as the "base creature"). The creature's type changes to "outsider." It uses all the base creature's statistics and special abilities except as noted here.

Speed: There is a 50% chance that a half-fiend has bat wings. The creature can fly at the base creature's normal speed (average maneuverability).

AC: Natural armor improves by +1.

Attacks: A half-fiend gains bite and claw attacks in addition to the base creature's attacks, if it did not have them already.

Damage: If the base creature does not have bite and claw attacks, use the damage values in the table below. Otherwise, use the values below or the base creature's damage, whichever is greater.

Size	Bite Damage	Claw Damage
Fine	1	—
Diminutive	1d2	1
Tiny	1d3	1d2
Small	1d4	1d3
Medium-size	1d6	1d4
Large	1d8	1d6
Huge	2d6	2d8
Gargantuan	2d8	2d6
Colossal	4d6	2d8

Special Attacks: A half-fiend retains all the special attacks of the base creature. Half-fiends with an Intelligence or Wisdom score of 8 or higher possess the following spell-like abilities, using their level as the caster level, as specified in the table below. Unless otherwise indicated, the ability is usable once per day.

Level	Abilities	Level	Abilities
1–2	*Darkness* 3/day	13–14	*Unholy aura* 3/day,
3–4	*Desecrate*		*unhallow*
5–6	*Unholy blight*	15–16	*Horrid wilting*
7–8	*Poison* 3/day	17–18	*Summon monster*
9–10	*Contagion*		*IX* (fiends only)
11–12	*Blasphemy*	19+	*Destruction*

Special Qualities: A half-fiend has all the special qualities of the base creature, plus darkvision with a range of 60 feet. Half-fiends are immune to poison, and have acid, cold, electricity, and fire resistance 20.

Saves: Same as the base creature

Abilities: Increase from the base creature as follows: Str +4, Dex +4, Con +2, Int +4, Wis +0, Cha +2.

Skills: A half-fiend has 8 skill points, plus its Intelligence modifier, per Hit Die. Treat skills from the base creature's list as class skills and other skills as cross-class. If the creature has a class, it gains skills for class levels normally.

Feats: Half-fiends have one feat for every four levels or the base creature's total of feats, whichever is greater.

Climate/Terrain: Same as either the base creature or the fiend
Organization: Same as the base creature
Challenge Rating: Same as the base creature +2
Alignment: Always evil (any)
Treasure: Same as the base creature
Advancement: Same as the base creature

HALF-FIEND CHARACTERS

Half-fiend humanoids often have a character class, favoring clerics, fighters, rogues, and sorcerers. Rogues and fighters frequently take the prestige classes assassin or blackguard, respectively. Non-humanoids are also sometimes clerics or sorcerers. Half-fiend clerics serve evil deities such as Erythnul, Gruumsh, Hextor, Nerull, or Vecna.

SAMPLE HALF-FIEND

This example uses a medusa as the base creature.

Half-Fiend/Half-Medusa
Medium-Size Outsider (Evil, Lawful)
Hit Dice: 6d8+12 (39 hp)
Initiative: +4 (Dex)
Speed: 30 ft., fly 30 ft. (average)
AC: 18 (+4 Dex, +4 natural)
Attacks: 2 claws +10 melee (or dagger +8/+3 melee), bite +3 melee, snakes +5 melee; or shortbow +10/+5 ranged
Damage: Claw 1d4+2; dagger 1d4+2; bite 1d6+1; snakes 1d4+1 and poison; shortbow 1d6
Face/Reach: 5 ft. by 5 ft./5 ft.
Special Attacks: Petrifying gaze, poison, spell-like abilities
Special Qualities: Poison immunity; acid, cold, electricity, and fire resistance 20
Saves: Fort +4, Ref +9, Will +6
Abilities: Str 14, Dex 19, Con 14, Int 16, Wis 13, Cha 17
Skills: Bluff +12, Diplomacy +8, Disguise +12, Knowledge (any one) +7, Listen +6, Move Silently +13, Sense Motive +6, Spot +10
Feats: Point Blank Shot, Precise Shot, Weapon Finesse (snakes)

Climate/Terrain: Any land and underground
Organization: Solitary or covey (2–4)
Challenge Rating: 9
Treasure: Double standard
Alignment: Always lawful evil
Advancement: 7–12 HD (Medium-size)

Unlike medusas, half-fiend/half-medusas are never mistaken for humans at any distance (the large bat wings give them away). Other medusas do not automatically reject these crossbreeds—in fact, they usually accept them as rulers.

Combat

More than their nonfiend siblings, half-fiend/half-medusas attack with aggressiveness and battle lust. They enjoy torturing their enemies.

Spell-Like Abilities: 3/day—*darkness*; 1/day—*desecrate* and *unholy blight*. These abilities are as the spells cast by a 6th-level cleric.

Petrifying Gaze (Su): Turn to stone permanently, 30 feet, Fortitude save (DC 15).

Poison (Ex): Snakes, Fortitude save (DC 15); initial damage 1d6 temporary Strength, secondary damage 2d6 temporary Strength.

LICH

Liches are undead spellcasters, usually wizards or sorcerers but sometimes clerics, who have used their magical powers to unnaturally extend their lives.

As a rule, these creatures are scheming and, some say, insane. They hunger for ever greater power, long-forgotten knowledge, and the most terrible of arcane secrets. Because the shadow of death does not hang over them, they often conceive plans taking years, decades, or even centuries to see fruition.

A lich is a gaunt and skeletal humanoid with withered flesh stretched tight across horribly visible bones. Its eyes have long ago been lost to decay, but bright pinpoints of crimson light burn on in the empty sockets. Even the least of these creatures was a powerful person in life, so they often are draped in grand clothing. Multiclass fighters or clerics may still bear the armor of a warrior. Like its body, however, the garb of a lich shows all too well the weight of years. Decay and corruption are its constant companions.

Liches speak Common plus any other languages they knew in life.

CREATING A LICH

"Lich" is a template that can be added to any humanoid creature (referred to hereafter as the "character"), provided it can create the required phylactery (see The Lich's Phylactery, below). The creature's type changes to "undead." It uses all the character's statistics and special abilities except as noted here.

Hit Dice: Increase to d12

Speed: Same as the character

AC: The lich has +5 natural armor or the character's natural armor, whichever is better.

Damage: Creatures without natural weapons gain a touch attack that uses negative energy to deal 1d8+5 points of damage to living creatures; a Will save with a DC of 10 + 1/2 lich's HD + lich's Charisma modifier reduces the damage by half. Creatures with natural attacks can use their natural weaponry or use the touch attack, as they prefer.

Special Attacks: A lich retains all the character's special attacks and also gains those listed below. Saves have a DC of 10 + 1/2 lich's HD + lich's Charisma modifier unless noted otherwise.

Fear Aura (Su): Liches are shrouded in a dreadful aura of death and evil. Creatures of less than 5 HD in a 60-foot radius that look at the lich must succeed at a Will save or be affected as though by *fear* as cast by a sorcerer of the lich's level.

Paralyzing Touch (Su): Any living creature the lich touches must succeed at a Fortitude save or be permanently paralyzed. *Remove paralysis* or any spell that can remove a curse can free the victim (see the *bestow curse* spell). The effect cannot be dispelled. Anyone paralyzed by a lich seems dead, though a successful Spot check (DC 20) or Heal check (DC 15) reveals that the victim is still alive. This power works in conjunction with the lich's damaging touch (see above).

Spells: The lich can cast any spells it could cast while alive.

Special Qualities: A lich retains all the character's special qualities and those listed below, and also gains the undead type (see page 6).

Turn Resistance (Ex): A lich has +4 turn resistance (see page 10).

Damage Reduction (Su): A lich's undead body is tough, giving the creature damage reduction 15/+1.

Immunities (Ex): Liches are immune to cold, electricity, polymorph, and mind-affecting attacks.

Saves: Same as the character

Abilities: A lich gains +2 to Intelligence, Wisdom, and Charisma, but being undead, has no Constitution score.

Skills: Liches receive a +8 racial bonus to Hide, Listen, Move Silently, Search, Sense Motive, and Spot checks. Otherwise same as the character.

Feats: Same as the character

Climate/Terrain: Any land and underground
Organization: Solitary or troupe (1 lich, plus 2–4 vampires and 5–8 vampire spawn)
Challenge Rating: Same as the character + 2
Treasure: Standard coins; double goods; double items
Alignment: Any evil
Advancement: By character class

LICH CHARACTERS

The process of becoming a lich is unspeakably evil and can be undertaken only by a character's own free will. The lich retains all class abilities it had in life.

THE LICH'S PHYLACTERY

An integral part of becoming a lich is creating a magic phylactery in which to store its life force. Unless the phylactery is located and destroyed, the lich reappears 1d10 days after its apparent death.

Each lich must make its own phylactery, which requires the Craft Wondrous Item feat. The character must be a sorcerer, wizard, or cleric of at least 11th level. The phylactery costs 120,000 gp and 4,800 XP to create and has a caster level equal to that of its creator at the time of creation.

The most common form of phylactery is a sealed metal box containing strips of parchment on which magical phrases have been transcribed. This typically has a leather strap so that the owner can wear it on the forearm or head. The box is Tiny and has a hardness rating of 20, 40 hit points, and a break DC of 40. Other types of phylacteries can exist, such as rings, amulets, or similar items.

SAMPLE LICH

This example uses an 11th-level human wizard as the character.

Lich
Medium-Size Undead
Hit Dice: 11d12+3 (74 hp)
Initiative: +3 (Dex)
Speed: 30 ft.
AC: 21 (+3 Dex, +5 natural, +2 *bracers of armor*, +1 *ring of protection*)
Attacks: Touch +5 melee (or quarterstaff +5 melee, or dagger +5 melee); or masterwork light crossbow with masterwork bolts +10 ranged

Damage: Touch 1d8+5 and paralysis; quarterstaff 1d6; dagger 1d4; light crossbow 1d8
Face/Reach: 5 ft. by 5 ft./5 ft.
Special Attacks: Damaging touch, fear aura, paralyzing touch, spells
Special Qualities: Undead, +4 turn resistance, damage reduction 15/+1, immunities
Saves: Fort +4, Ref +7, Will +10 (*cloak of resistance +1*)
Abilities: Str 10, Dex 16, Con —, Int 19, Wis 14, Cha 13
Skills: Concentration +15, Hide +15, Knowledge (arcana) +18, Listen +15, Move Silently +16, Scry +14, Search +16, Sense Motive +10, Spellcraft +18, Spot +15
Feats: Combat Casting, Craft Wondrous Item, Quicken Spell, Scribe Scroll, Silent Spell, Spell Focus (Evocation), Still Spell, Toughness

Climate/Terrain: Any land and underground
Organization: Solitary
Challenge Rating: 13
Treasure: Standard coins; double goods; double items
Alignment: Neutral evil
Advancement: By character class

Combat

Undead: Immune to mind-influencing effects, poison, sleep, paralysis, stunning, and disease. Not subject to critical hits, subdual damage, ability damage, energy drain, or death from massive damage.

Immunities (Ex): Liches are immune to cold, electricity, polymorph, and mind-affecting attacks.

The Will save against this lich's fear aura and damaging touch, and the Fortitude save against its paralyzing touch, have a DC of 16. The save DC against its spells is 14 + spell level.

Magic Items Carried: +2 *bracers of armor*, +1 *cloak of resistance*, 1 *potion of gaseous form*, +1 *ring of protection*, *scroll of summon monster IV* (8th level), *wand of magic missile* (50 charges, 9th level).

LYCANTHROPE

Lycanthropes are humanoids who can transform themselves into animals or hybrid monsters.

Evil lycanthropes often hide among normal folk, emerging in animal form at night (especially under the full moon) to spread terror and bloodshed.

CREATING A LYCANTHROPE

"Lycanthrope" is a template that can be added to any humanoid creature (referred to hereafter as the "character"). The creature's type changes to "shapechanger." The lycanthrope takes on the characteristics of some type of carnivorous animal (referred to hereafter as the "animal"). This can be any predator between the size of a small dog and a large bear. The most common are listed in the table below. Some kinds of lycanthropes can also adopt a hybrid shape that combines features of the character and the animal.

A lycanthrope uses either the character's or the animal's statistics and special abilities in addition to those set out below.

Hit Dice: Same as the character or animal, whichever produces the higher hit point total. If the lycanthrope's number of Hit Dice is important, as with a *sleep* spell, use the character's or animal's number of Hit Dice, whichever is greater.

Speed: Same as the character or animal, depending on which form the lycanthrope is using.

AC: The character's or animal's natural armor increases by +2, depending on which form the lycanthrope is using. (A wererat in hybrid form is an exception; see the entry below.)

Attacks: Same as the character or animal, depending on which form the lycanthrope is using. (A were-rat in hybrid form is an exception; see the entry below.)

Damage: Same as the character or animal, depending on which form the lycanthrope is using.

Special Attacks: A lycanthrope retains all the special attacks of the character or animal, depending on which form it is using, and also gains those listed below.

Lycanthropic Empathy (Ex): Lycanthropes can communicate and empathize with normal or dire animals of their animal form. This gives them a +4 racial bonus to checks when influencing the animal's attitude and allows the communication of simple concepts and (if the animal is friendly) commands, such as "friend," "foe," "flee," and "attack."

Curse of Lycanthropy (Su): Any humanoid hit by a lycanthrope's bite attack in animal form must succeed at a Fortitude save (DC 15) or contract lycanthropy. A wererat can spread lycanthropy with its bite or by hitting with a piercing or slashing weapon. Bludgeoning or nonpenetrating attacks do not transmit the condition.

Special Qualities: A lycanthrope retains all the special qualities of the character or animal and also gains those listed below.

Alternate Form (Su): All lycanthropes can shift into animal form as though using the *polymorph self* spell (though their gear does not change). Wererats, weretigers, and werewolves also can assume a bipedal hybrid form with prehensile hands and animalistic features. Changing to or from animal or hybrid form is a standard action. Upon assuming either form, the lycanthrope regains hit points as if having rested for a day. A slain lycanthrope reverts to its humanoid form, although it remains dead. Separated body parts retains their animal form, however. This shapeshifting ability can be difficult to control (see Lycanthropy as an Affliction, below).

Damage Reduction (Ex): A lycanthrope in animal or hybrid form gains damage reduction 15/silver.

Saves: The base saves are as for the character or animal, whichever is better. In addition, lycanthropes receive a +2 racial bonus to Fortitude and Will saves.

Abilities: For a lycanthrope in humanoid form, ability scores

COMMON LYCANTHROPES

Name	Animal Form	Ability Score Adjustments	Feats
Werebear	Brown bear	Str +16, Dex +2, Con +8	Blind-Fight, Multiattack, Power Attack
Wereboar	Boar	Str +4, Con +6	Blind-Fight, Improved Initiative
Wererat	Dire rat	Dex +6, Con +2	Multiattack (despite only one natural weapon), Weapon Finesse (bite), Weapon Finesse (any)
Weretiger	Tiger	Str +12, Dex +4, Con +6	Blind-Fight, Multiattack, Power Attack
Werewolf	Wolf	Str +2, Dex +4, Con +4	Blind-Fight, Improved Initiative, Weapon Finesse (bite)

are unchanged. In animal or hybrid form, a lycanthrope's ability scores improve by type, as set out in the table below.

Skills: Lycanthropes receive a +4 racial bonus to Search, Spot, and Listen checks when in humanoid form. In animal or hybrid form, these bonuses increase to +8. A lycanthrope in hybrid or animal form gains the same skills as a normal animal of its form in addition to the character's skills. If a lycanthrope has a skill in both its humanoid and animal forms, use the better score. Afflicted lycanthropes also can learn the Control Shape skill (see the sidebar) as a class skill.

Feats: Same as the character. When in hybrid or animal form, the lycanthrope gains any feats a normal animal of its form has. Lycanthropes also have the Improved Control Shape feat (see the sidebar). Lycanthropes in hybrid or animal form have additional feats as set out in the accompanying table.

Climate/Terrain: Same as either the character or animal
Organization: Solitary or pair, sometimes family (2–4), pack (6–10), or troupe (family plus related animals)
Challenge Rating: Same as the animal +2
Treasure: Standard
Alignment: Any; see examples below
Advancement: By character class

LYCANTHROPE CHARACTERS

Since they live in the wilderness, most lycanthropes become barbarians or rangers. Wererats tend to become rogues. Becoming a

---

CONTROL SHAPE (WIS)

Any character who has contracted lycanthropy and is aware of his or her condition can learn Control Shape as a class skill. This determines whether the afflicted lycanthrope can voluntarily control his or her shape. Natural lycanthropes instead have the Improved Control Shape feat, which gives them full control over their shapeshifting abilities.

Check: The afflicted character must make a check at moonrise each night of the full moon to resist involuntarily assuming animal form. An injured character must also check for an involuntary change after accumulating enough damage to reduce his or her hit points by one-quarter and again after each additional one-quarter lost (save DC same as for full moon).

Task	DC
Resist involuntary change	25
Return to humanoid form (full moon*)	25
Return to humanoid form (not full moon)	20
Voluntary change (full moon)	10
Voluntary change (not full moon)	15

*For game purposes, the full moon lasts three days every month.

Retry: Check for an involuntary change once each time a triggering event occurs.

On a failed check to return to humanoid form (see below), the character must remain in animal or hybrid form until the next dawn, when he or she automatically returns to humanoid form.

Special: An involuntary change to animal or hybrid form ruins the character's armor and clothing if the new form is larger than the character's natural form. Characters can hastily doff clothing while changing, but not armor. Magic armor survives the change if it succeeds at a Fortitude save (DC 15).

When returning to normal form after an involuntary change, the character attempts a Wisdom check (DC 15) to realize what has happened. If the check succeeds, the character becomes aware of the affliction and can now voluntarily attempt to change to animal or hybrid form, using the appropriate DC. An attempt is a standard action and can be made each round. Any voluntary change to animal or hybrid form immediately and permanently changes the character's alignment to that of the appropriate lycanthrope.

An afflicted character who is aware of his or her condition can also try to return to humanoid from after assuming animal or hybrid form, using the appropriate DC. Only one attempt is allowed, however, as described above.

lycanthrope does not change a character's favored class but usually changes alignment (see below). This may cause characters of certain classes to lose their class abilities, as noted in Chapter 3: Classes in the *Player's Handbook*.

Lycanthropy as an Affliction

When a character contracts lycanthropy through a lycanthrope's attack (see above), no symptoms appear until the first night of the next full moon. On that night, the afflicted character involuntarily assumes animal form and becomes a ravening beast, forgetting his or her own identity. The character remains in animal form, assuming the appropriate alignment, until dawn and remembers nothing about the incident.

Thereafter, the character is subject to involuntary transformation under the full moon and whenever damaged in combat. He or she feels an overwhelming rage building up and must succeed at a Control Shape check to resist changing into animal form (see the sidebar).

Many lycanthropes are born, not made, and are sometimes called "natural lycanthropes" to distinguish them from those who have contracted lycanthropy ("afflicted lycanthropes").

Curing Lycanthropy

An afflicted character who eats a sprig of belladonna (also called wolfsbane) within an hour of a lycanthrope's attack can attempt a Fortitude save (DC 20) to shake off the affliction. If a healer administers the herb, use the character's save or the healer's Heal check, whichever is higher. The character gets only one chance, no matter how much belladonna is consumed. The belladonna must be reasonably fresh (picked within the last week).

However, fresh or not, belladonna is toxic. The character must succeed at a Fortitude save (DC 13) or take initial damage of 1d6 points of temporary Strength. One minute later, the character must succeed at a second save or take an additional 2d6 points of temporary Strength damage.

A *remove disease* or *heal* spell cast by a cleric of at least 12th level also cures the affliction, provided the character receives the spell within three days of the lycanthrope's attack.

The only other way to remove the affliction is to cast *remove curse* or *break enchantment* on the character during one of the three days of the full moon. After receiving the spell, the character must succeed at a Will save (DC 20) to break the curse (the caster knows if the spell works). Otherwise the process must be repeated. Characters undergoing this cure are often kept bound or confined in cages until the cure takes effect.

Only afflicted lycanthropes can be cured of lycanthropy.

SAMPLE LYCANTHROPES

Below and on the next page are examples of the most common lycanthropes, using 1st-level human commoners as the characters.

In their natural forms, lycanthropes look like any other members of their people, though natural and long-time afflicted lycanthropes tend to have or acquire features reminiscent of their animal forms. In animal form, a lycanthrope resembles a powerful version of the normal animal, but on close inspection, its eyes show a faint spark of unnatural intelligence and often glow red in the dark.

	Werebear Medium-Size/Large Shapechanger	Wereboar Medium-Size Shapechanger	Wererat Medium-Size/Small Shapechanger
Hit Dice:	6d8+24 (51 hp)	3d8+9 (22 hp)	1d8+1 (5 hp)
Initiative:	+0; +1 (Dex) as bear	+0; +4 (Improved Initiative) as boar	+0; +3 (Dex) as rat
Speed:	30 ft.; 30 ft. as bear	30 ft.; 40 ft. as boar	30 ft.; 40 ft., climb 20 ft. as rat
AC:	12 (+2 natural); 17 (–1 size, +1 Dex, +7 natural) as bear	12 (+2 natural); 18 (+8 natural) as boar	12 (+2 natural); 16 (+3 Dex, +3 natural) as hybrid; 17 (+1 size, +3 Dex, +3 natural) as rat
Attacks:	Unarmed strike +0 melee; 2 claws +11 melee, bite +9 melee as bear	Unarmed strike +0 melee; gore +4 melee as boar	Unarmed strike +0 melee; rapier +3 melee, bite +1 melee as hybrid; bite +4 melee as rat
Damage:	Unarmed strike 1d3 subdual; claw 1d8+8, bite 2d8+4	Unarmed strike 1d3 subdual; gore 1d8+3	Unarmed strike 1d3 subdual; rapier 1d6; bite 1d4
Face/Reach:	5 ft. by 5 ft./5 ft; 5 ft. by 5 ft./10 ft as bear	5 ft. by 5 ft./5 ft; 5 ft. by 5 ft./5 ft as boar	5 ft. by 5 ft./5 ft.; 5 ft. by 5 ft./5 ft. as rat or hybrid
Special Attacks:	Improved grab, curse of lycanthropy as bear	Ferocity, curse of lycanthropy as boar	Curse of lycanthropy as rat or hybrid
Special Qualities:	Bear empathy; plus scent, damage reduction 15/silver as bear	Boar empathy; plus scent, damage reduction 15/silver as boar	Rat empathy; plus scent, damage reduction 15/silver as rat or hybrid
Saves:	Fort +11, Ref +6, Will +4	Fort +8, Ref +3, Will +3	Fort +5, Ref +5, Will +4
Abilities:	Str 27, Dex 13, Con 19, Int 10, Wis 10, Cha 10 as bear[1]	Str 15, Dex 11, Con 17, Int 10, Wis 10, Cha 10 (as boar[1])	Str 10, Dex 17, Con 13, Int 10, Wis 10, Cha 10 as rat or hybrid[1]
Skills:	Listen +11, Search +8, Spot +14, Swim +14 as bear[2]	Listen +15, Search +8, Spot +12 as boar[2]	Climb +14, Hide +11 as rat or +7 as hybrid, Listen +8. Move Silently +6, Search +8, Spot +8 as rat or hybrid[2],
Feats:	Blind-Fight, Multiattack, Power Attack as bear[3]	Blind-Fight, Improved Initiative as boar[3]	Multiattack, Weapon Finesse (bite), Weapon Finesse (rapier) as hybrid[3]
Climate/Terrain:	Any forest, hill, mountains, and underground	Temperate and warm forest	Any land and underground
Organization:	Solitary, pair, family (2–4), or troupe (2–4 plus 1–4 brown bears)	Solitary, pair, brood (2–4), or troupe (2–4 plus 1–4 boars)	Solitary, pair, pack (6–10), or troupe (2–5 plus 5–8 dire rats)
Challenge Rating:	5	3	2
Treasure:	Standard	Standard	Standard
Alignment:	Always lawful good	Always neutral	Always lawful evil
Advancement:	By character class	By character class	By character class

	Weretiger Medium-Size/Large Shapechanger	Werewolf Medium-Size Shapechanger
Hit Dice:	6d8+18 (45 hp)	2d8+4 (13 hp)
Initiative:	+0; +2 (Dex) as tiger or hybrid	+0; +6 (+2 Dex, +4 Improved Initiative) as wolf or hybrid
Speed :	30 ft.; 40 ft. as tiger or hybrid	30 ft.; 50 ft. as wolf or hybrid
AC:	12 (+2 natural); 17 (+2 Dex, +5 natural) as hybrid; 16 (−1 size, +2 Dex, +5 natural) as tiger	12 (+2 natural); 16 (+2 Dex, +4 natural) as wolf or hybrid
Attacks:	Unarmed strike +0 melee; 2 claws +10 melee, bite +8 melee as hybrid; 2 claws +9 melee, bite +7 melee as tiger	Unarmed strike +0 melee; bite +3 melee as wolf or hybrid
Damage:	Unarmed strike 1d3 subdual; claw 1d8+6; bite 2d6+3	Unarmed strike 1d3 subdual; bite 1d6+1
Face/Reach:	5 ft. by 5 ft./5 ft; 5 ft. by 10 ft./5 ft. as tiger or hybrid	5 ft. by 5 ft./5 ft; 5 ft. by 5 ft./5 ft. as wolf or hybrid
Special Attacks:	Pounce, improved grab, rake 1d8+3, curse of lycanthropy as tiger or hybrid	Trip, curse of lycanthropy as wolf or hybrid
Special Qualities:	Tiger empathy; plus scent, damage reduction 15/silver as tiger or hybrid	Wolf empathy; plus scent, damage reduction 15/silver as wolf or hybrid
Saves:	Fort +10, Ref +7, Will +4	Fort +7, Ref +5, Will +2
Abilities:	Str 23, Dex 15, Con 17, Int 10, Wis 10, Cha 10 as tiger or hybrid[1]	Str 13, Dex 15, Con 15, Int 10, Wis 10, Cha 10 as wolf or hybrid[1]
Skills:	Balance +6, Hide +9 as hybrid or +5 as tiger, Listen +10, Move Silently +9, Search +8, Spot +10, Swim +11 as tiger or hybrid[2]	Hide +3, Listen +14, Move Silently +4, Search +8, Spot +14, Wilderness Lore +0 as wolf or hybrid[2]
Feats:	Blind-Fight, Multiattack, Power Attack as tiger or hybrid[3]	Blind-Fight, Improved Initiative, Weapon Finesse (bite) as wolf or hybrid[3]
Climate/Terrain:	Any forest, hill, mountains, and plains	Any forest, hill, mountains, and plains
Organization:	Solitary or pair	Solitary, pair, pack (6–10), or troupe (2–5 plus 5–8 wolves)
Challenge Rating:	5	3
Treasure:	Standard	Standard
Alignment:	Always neutral	Always chaotic evil
Advancement:	By character class	By character class

[1]In human form, these lycanthropes have the following ability scores: Str 11, Dex 11, Con 11, Int 10, Wis 10, Cha 10.
[2]In human form, these lycanthropes have the skill Craft or Profession (any one) +6, Knowledge (any one) +4.
[3]In human form, these lycanthropes have the feat Skill Focus (any Craft or Profession).

Combat

Lycanthropes in their natural forms use whatever tactics are favored by their people, though they tend to be slightly more aggressive. Lycanthropes in animal or hybrid form fight like the animal they resemble.

WEREBEAR

Werebears in humanoid form tend to be stout, well-muscled, and hairy. Their brown hair is thick, and males usually wear beards. They may have reddish, blond, ivory, or black hair, matching the color of the ursine form. They dress in simple cloth and leather garments that are easy to remove, repair, or replace.

In their animal form, werebears are moody and grumpy. They desire only their own company and seek out evil creatures to slay.

Combat

Werebears fight just as brown bears do.

Improved Grab (Ex): To use this ability, the werebear must hit with a claw attack.

WEREBOAR

Wereboars in humanoid form tend to be stocky, muscular people of average height. Their hair is short and stiff. They dress in simple garments that are easy to remove, repair, or replace.

Combat

Wereboars are as ferocious as normal boars.

Ferocity (Ex): A wereboar is such a tenacious combatant that it continues to fight without penalty even while disabled or dying (see page 129 in the *Player's Handbook*).

WERERAT

The wererat in humanoid form tends to be a thin, wiry individual of shorter than average height. The eyes constantly dart around, and the nose and mouth may twitch if he or she is excited. Males often have thin, ragged moustaches.

Combat

Wererats can assume a hybrid form as well as an animal form.

Alternate Form (Su): A wererat can assume a bipedal hybrid form or the form of a dire rat. The bipedal form is Medium-size with head, torso, and tail identical to those of a rat, although the limbs remain human. The rat form is 2 feet long from nose to rump and is preferred for travel and spying on potential victims.

Skills: A wererat in rat or hybrid form uses its Dexterity modifier for Climb checks.

WERETIGER

Weretigers in humanoid form tend to be sleekly muscular, taller than average, and very agile.

Combat

Weretigers can assume a hybrid form as well as an animal form. In hybrid or tiger form, they can pounce and grab just as normal tigers do.

Alternate Form (Su): A weretiger can assume a bipedal hybrid form or the form of a tiger. The bipedal form is about 7 feet tall, with a 3-foot tail, and covered by tiger-striped hide. The legs are more feline than human, and this form walks on its toes. The fingernails grow into claws. The head is a mixture of features: Ears, nose, muzzle, and teeth are tigerlike, but the eyes and overall shape are human. If the human form's hair is long, it is still present. The animal form is that of a fully grown tiger without any trace of human features.

Pounce (Ex): If a weretiger in hybrid or tiger form leaps upon a foe during the first round of combat, it can make a full attack even if it has already taken a move action.

Improved Grab (Ex): To use this ability, the weretiger in hybrid or tiger form must hit with a claw or bite attack. If it gets a hold, it can rake.

Rake (Ex): A weretiger in hybrid or tiger form that gets a hold can make two rake attacks (+9 melee) with its hind legs for 1d8+3 damage each. If the weretiger pounces on an opponent, it can also rake.

Skills: In hybrid or tiger form, weretigers receive a +4 bonus to Balance, Hide, and Move Silently checks. *In areas of tall grass or heavy undergrowth, the Hide bonus improves to +8.

WEREWOLF

Werewolves in humanoid form have no distinguishing traits.

Combat

Werewolves can assume a hybrid form as well as an animal form. In hybrid or wolf form, they can trip just as normal wolves do.

Alternate Form (Su): A werewolf can assume a bipedal hybrid form or the form of a wolf. The bipedal form is about 6 feet tall, with a short tail, and covered in fur. The legs are like those of a wolf, and the head combines humanoid and lupine features in degrees that vary from one werewolf to the next. The animal form is that of a fully grown wolf without any trace of human features.

Trip (Ex): A werewolf that hits with a bite attack can attempt to trip the opponent as a free action (see page 139 in the *Player's Handbook*) without making a touch attack or provoking an attack of opportunity. If the attempt fails, the opponent cannot react to trip the werewolf.

Skills: A werewolf in hybrid or wolf form gains a +4 racial bonus to Wilderness Lore checks when tracking by scent.

VAMPIRE

Forever anchored to their coffins and the unholy earth of their graves, these nocturnal predators scheme constantly to strengthen themselves and fill the world with their foul progeny.

Vampires appear just as they did in life, although their features are often hardened and feral, with the predatory look of wolves. Like liches, they often embrace finery and decadence and may assume the guise of nobility. Despite their human appearance, vampires can be easily recognized, for they cast no shadows and throw no reflections in mirrors.

Vampires speak any languages they knew in life.

CREATING A VAMPIRE

"Vampire" is a template that can be added to any humanoid or monstrous humanoid creature (referred to hereafter as the "base creature"). The creature's type changes to "undead." It uses all the base creature's statistics and special abilities except as noted here.

Hit Dice: Increase to d12.

Speed: Same as the base creature. If the base creature has a swim speed, the vampire retains the ability to swim and is not vulnerable to immersion in running water (see below).

AC: The base creature's natural armor improves by +6.

Attacks: A vampire retains all the attacks of the base creature and also gains a slam attack if it didn't already have one.

Damage: Vampires have slam attacks. If the base creature does not have this attack form, use the damage values in the table below. Creatures with natural attacks retain their old damage ratings or use the values below, whichever is better.

Size	Damage
Fine	1
Diminutive	1d2
Tiny	1d3
Small	1d4
Medium-size	1d6
Large	1d8
Huge	2d6
Gargantuan	2d8
Colossal	4d6

Special Attacks: A vampire retains all the special attacks of the base creature and also gains those listed below. Saves have a DC of 10 + 1/2 vampire's HD + vampire's Charisma modifier unless noted otherwise.

Domination (Su): A vampire can crush an opponent's will just by looking onto his or her eyes. This is similar to a gaze attack, except that the vampire must take a standard action, and those merely looking at it are not affected. Anyone the vampire targets must succeed at a Will save or fall instantly under the vampire's influence as though by a *dominate person* spell cast by a 12th-level sorcerer. The ability has a range of 30 feet.

Energy Drain (Su): Living creatures hit by a vampire's slam attack suffer 2 negative levels.

Blood Drain (Ex): A vampire can suck blood from a living victim with its fangs by making a successful grapple check. If it pins the foe, it drains blood, inflicting 1d4 points of permanent Constitution drain each round the pin is maintained.

Children of the Night (Su): Vampires command the lesser creatures of the world and once per day can call forth a pack of 4d8 dire rats, a swarm of 10d10 bats, or a pack of 3d6 wolves as a standard action. These creatures arrive in 2d6 rounds and serve the vampire for up to 1 hour.

Create Spawn (Su): A humanoid or monstrous humanoid slain by a vampire's energy drain attack rises as a vampire spawn (see the Vampire Spawn entry, page 182) 1d4 days after burial.

If the vampire instead drains the victim's Constitution to 0 or less, the victim returns as a spawn if it had 4 or fewer HD and as a vampire if it had 5 or more HD. In either case, the new vampire or spawn is under the command of the vampire that created it and remains enslaved until its master's death.

Special Qualities: A vampire retains all the special qualities of the base creature and those listed below, and also gains the undead type (see page 6).

Damage Reduction (Su): A vampire's undead body is tough, giving the creature damage reduction 15/+1.

Turn Resistance (Ex): A vampire has +4 turn resistance (see page 10).

Resistance (Ex): A vampire has cold and electricity resistance 20.

Gaseous Form (Su): As a standard action, a vampire can assume *gaseous form* at will, as the spell cast by a 5th-level sorcerer, but can remain gaseous indefinitely and has a fly speed of 20 feet with perfect maneuverability.

Spider Climb (Ex): A vampire can climb sheer surfaces as though with a *spider climb* spell.

Alternate Form (Su): A vampire can assume the shape of a bat, dire bat, wolf, or dire wolf as a standard action. This ability is similar to a *polymorph self* spell cast by a 12th-level sorcerer, except that the vampire can assume only one of the forms listed here. It can remain in that form until it assumes another or until the next sunrise.

Fast Healing (Ex): A vampire heals 5 points of damage each round so long as it has at least 1 hit point. If reduced to 0 hit points or lower, a vampire automatically assumes *gaseous form* and attempts to escape. It must reach its coffin home within 2 hours or be utterly destroyed. (It can travel up to nine miles in 2 hours.) Once at rest in its coffin, it rises to 1 hit point after 1 hour, then resumes healing at the rate of 5 hit points per round.

Saves: Same as the base creature

Abilities: Increase from the base creature as follows: Str +6, Dex +4, Int +2, Wis +2, Cha +4. As undead creatures, vampires have no Constitution score.

Skills: Vampires receive a +8 racial bonus to Bluff, Hide, Listen, Move Silently, Search, Sense Motive, and Spot checks. Otherwise same as the base creature.

Feats: Vampires gain Alertness, Combat Reflexes, Dodge, Improved Initiative, and Lightning Reflexes, assuming the base creature meets the prerequisites and doesn't already have these feats.

Climate/Terrain: Any land and underground
Organization: Solitary, pair, gang (2–5), or troop (1–2 plus 2–5 vampire spawn)
Challenge Rating: Same as the base creature +2
Treasure: Double standard
Alignment: Always chaotic evil
Advancement: By character class

VAMPIRE WEAKNESSES

For all their power, vampires have a number of weaknesses.

Repelling A Vampire

Vampires cannot tolerate the strong odor of garlic and will not enter an area laced with it. Similarly, they recoil from a mirror or a strongly presented, holy symbol. These things don't harm the vampire—they merely keep it at bay.

Vampires are also unable to cross running water, although they can be carried over it while resting in their coffins or aboard a ship. They are utterly unable to enter a home or other building unless invited in by someone with the authority to do so. They may freely enter public places, since these are by definition open to all.

Slaying a Vampire

Simply reducing a vampire's hit points to 0 or below incapacitates but doesn't destroy it. However, certain attacks can slay vampires.

Exposing any vampire to direct sunlight disorients it: It can take only partial actions and is destroyed utterly on the next round if it cannot escape. Similarly, immersing a vampire in running water robs it of one-third of its hit points each round until it is destroyed at the end of the third round.

Driving a wooden stake through a vampire's heart instantly slays the monster. However, it returns to life if the stake is removed, unless the body is destroyed. A popular tactic is to cut off the creature's head and fill its mouth with holy wafers (or their equivalent).

VAMPIRE CHARACTERS

Vampires are always chaotic evil, which causes characters of certain classes to lose their class abilities, as noted in Chapter 3: Classes in the *Player's Handbook*. In addition, certain classes suffer additional penalties.

Clerics: Clerics lose their ability to turn undead but gain the ability to rebuke undead. This ability does not affect the vampire's controller or any other vampires that master controls.

Vampire clerics have access to the Chaos, Destruction, Evil, and Trickery domains.

Sorcerers and Wizards: These characters retain their class abilities, but if a character has a familiar (other than a rat or bat), the link between them is broken, and the familiar shuns its former companion. The character can summon another familiar, but it must be a rat or bat.

SAMPLE VAMPIRE

This example uses a 5th-level human fighter as the base creature.

Vampire
Medium-Size Undead
Hit Dice: 5d12 (32 hp)
Initiative: +7 (+3 Dex, +4 Improved Initiative)
Speed: 30 ft.
AC: 25 (+3 Dex, +6 natural, +4 masterwork chain shirt, +2 large shield)
Attacks: Slam +11 melee (or masterwork bastard sword +13 melee); or masterwork shortbow +9 ranged
Damage: Slam 1d6+6 and energy drain; bastard sword 1d10+11; or shortbow 1d6
Face/Reach: 5 ft. by 5 ft./5 ft.
Special Attacks: Charm, energy drain, blood drain, children of the night, create spawn
Special Qualities: Undead, damage reduction 15/+1, cold and electricity resistance 20, gaseous form, spider climb, alternate form, fast healing 5, vampire weaknesses
Saves: Fort +4, Ref +6, Will +4
Abilities: Str 22, Dex 17, Con —, Int 12, Wis 16, Cha 12
Skills: Bluff +9, Climb +10, Hide +11, Listen +17, Move Silently +11, Ride +11, Search +9, Sense Motive +11, Spot +17
Feats: Alertness, Blind-Fight, Combat Reflexes, Dodge, Exotic Weapon Proficiency (bastard sword), Improved Initiative, Lightning Reflexes, Mobility, Weapon Focus (bastard sword), Weapon Specialization (bastard sword)

Combat

Undead: Immune to mind-influencing effects, poison, sleep, paralysis, stunning, and disease. Not subject to critical hits, subdual damage, ability damage, energy drain, or death from massive damage.

The Will save against this vampire's charm, and the Fortitude save to regain levels lost to its energy drain, have a DC of 13.

Magic Items Carried: *Potion of haste.*
Challenge Rating: 7

Monsters Ranked by Challenge Ratings

Bat 1/10
Toad 1/10

Monstrous centipede, Tiny . . 1/8
Rat 1/8

Lizard 1/6
Monkey 1/6
Raven 1/6
Donkey 1/6
Kobold 1/6
Skeleton, Tiny 1/6
Zombie, Tiny 1/6

Cat 1/4
Goblin 1/4
Monstrous centipede, Small . 1/4
Monstrous scorpion, Tiny . . . 1/4
Monstrous spider, Tiny 1/4
Owl 1/4
Pony 1/4
Pony, war 1/4
Skeleton, Small 1/4
Weasel 1/4
Zombie, Small 1/4

Dire rat 1/3
Dog 1/3
Giant fire beetle 1/3
Hawk 1/3
Skeleton, Medium-size 1/3
Snake, Tiny viper 1/3

Aasimar 1/2
Abyssal dire rat 1/2
Animated object, Tiny 1/2
Baboon 1/2
Badger 1/2
Dwarf, deep 1/2
Dwarf, hill 1/2
Dwarf, mountain 1/2
Eagle 1/2
Elf (any subrace but drow) . . . 1/2
Giant bee 1/2
Gnome (forest or rock) 1/2
Halfling (any subrace) 1/2
Hobgoblin 1/2
Locathah 1/2
Merfolk 1/2
Monstrous centipede,
    Medium-size 1/2
Monstrous scorpion, Small . . 1/2
Monstrous spider, Small 1/2
Orc 1/2
Porpoise 1/2
Snake, Small viper 1/2
Stirge 1/2
Tiefling 1/2
Worker (formian) 1/2
Zombie, Medium-size 1/2

Air elemental, Small 1
Animated object, Small 1
Camel 1

Darkmantle 1
Derro (dwarf) 1
Dog, riding 1
Drow (elf) 1
Dryad 1
Duergar (dwarf) 1
Earth elemental, Small 1
Fire elemental, Small 1
Ghoul 1
Giant ant worker 1
Gnoll 1
Grimlock 1
Heavy horse 1
Homunculus 1
Krenshar 1
Lemure 1
Light horse 1
Light warhorse 1
Lizardfolk 1
Monstrous centipede, Large . . 1
Monstrous scorpion,
    Medium-size 1
Monstrous spider,
    Medium-size 1
Mule 1
Octopus 1
Pseudodragon 1
Shark, Medium-size 1
Shrieker 1
Skeleton, Large 1
Snake, Medium-size viper . . . 1
Sprite, grig 1
Sprite, nixie 1
Squid 1
Svirfneblin (gnome) 1
Troglodyte 1
Water elemental, Small 1
Wolf 1
Zombie, Large 1

Animated object, Medium-size . 2
Ape 2
Azer 2
Bison 2
Black bear 2
Blink dog 2
Boar 2
Bugbear 2
Cheetah 2
Choker 2
Crocodile 2
Dire badger 2
Dire bat 2
Dire weasel 2
Dretch 2
Giant ant queen 2
Giant ant soldier 2
Giant bombardier beetle 2
Giant lizard 2
Giant praying mantis 2
Heavy warhorse 2
Hippogriff 2
Imp 2
Kuo-toa 2

Lantern archon 2
Leopard 2
Monstrous centipede, Huge . . 2
Monstrous scorpion, Large . . . 2
Monstrous spider, Large 2
Ogre 2
Sahuagin 2
Salamander, flamebrother 2
Satyr [no pipes] 2
Shark, Large 2
Shocker lizard 2
Skeleton, Huge 2
Skum 2
Snake, constrictor 2
Snake, Large viper 2
Thoqqua 2
Vargouille 2
Wererat 2
Wolverine 2
Worg 2

Air elemental, Medium 3
Air mephit 3
Allip 3
Animated object, Large 3
Ankheg 3
Arrowhawk, juvenile 3
Assassin vine 3
Celestial lion 3
Centaur 3
Cockatrice 3
Deinonychus 3
Dire ape 3
Dire wolf 3
Doppelganger 3
Dust mephit 3
Earth elemental, Medium 3
Earth mephit 3
Ethereal filcher 3
Ethereal marauder 3
Fire elemental, Medium 3
Fire mephit 3
Gelatinous cube 3
Ghast 3
Giant eagle 3
Giant owl 3
Giant wasp 3
Grick 3
Hell hound 3
Howler 3
Ice mephit 3
Lion 3
Magma mephit 3
Magmin 3
Mummy 3
Ooze mephit 3
Pegasus 3
Phantom fungus 3
Quasit 3
Rust monster 3
Salt mephit 3
Shadow 3
Snake, Huge viper 3
Steam mephit 3

Tojanida, juvenile 3
Unicorn 3
Violet fungus 3
Warrior (formian) 3
Water elemental, Medium . . . 3
Water mephit 3
Wereboar 3
Werewolf 3
Wight 3
Xorn, minor 3
Yeth hound 3
Zombie, Huge 3

Aranea 4
Barghest 4
Brown bear 4
Carrion crawler 4
Dire boar 4
Dire wolverine 4
Displacer beast 4
Ettercap 4
Gargoyle 4
Genie, janni 4
Giant crocodile 4
Giant stag beetle 4
Gray ooze 4
Griffon 4
Half-celestial/half-unicorn . . . 4
Half-dragon(red)/half-ogre . . . 4
Harpy 4
Hound archon 4
Hydra, 5 heads 4
Mimic 4
Minotaur 4
Monstrous spider, Huge 4
Otyugh 4
Owlbear 4
Polar bear 4
Rhinoceros 4
Satyr [pipes] 4
Sea lion 4
Sea hag 4
Shark, Huge 4
Sprite, pixie 4
Tiger 4
Triton 4
Vampire spawn 4

Achaierai 5
Air elemental, Large 5
Animated object, Huge 5
Arrowhawk, adult 5
Baleen whale 5
Barghest, greater 5
Basilisk 5
Cloaker 5
Dire lion 5
Earth elemental, Large 5
Elasmosaurus 5
Ettin 5
Fire elemental, Large 5
Genie, djinni 5
Gibbering mouther 5
Girallon 5

Green hag 5
Hieracosphinx 5
Hydra, 6 heads 5
Manticore 5
Nightmare 5
Ochre jelly 5
Orca 5
Phase spider 5
Rast 5
Ravid 5
Salamander, average 5
Shadow mastiff 5
Snake, giant constrictor 5
Spider eater 5
Tojanida, adult 5
Troll 5
Water elemental, Large 5
Werebear 5
Weretiger 5
Winter wolf 5
Wraith 5
Yuan-ti, halfblood 5
Yuan-ti, pureblood 5

Annis 6
Belker 6
Cachalot whale 6
Digester 6
Hydra, 7 heads 6
Hydra, pyro/cryo, 5 heads 6
Kyton 6
Lamia 6
Megaraptor 6
Monstrous centipede,
    Gargantuan 6
Monstrous scorpion, Huge 6
Nymph 6
Osyluth 6
Shambling mound 6
Tendriculos 6
Will-o'-wisp 6
Wyvern 6
Xill 6
Xorn, average 6
Zombie, Gargantuan 6

Aboleth 7
Air elemental, Huge 7
Animated object, Gargantuan . . 7
Athach 7
Barbazu 7
Black pudding 7

Bulette 7
Chaos beast 7
Chimera 7
Chuul 7
Criosphinx 7
Dire bear 7
Dragonne 7
Drider 7
Earth elemental, Huge 7
Erinyes 7
Fire elemental, Huge 7
Flesh golem 7
Ghost (5th level) . . . 7 (level + 2)
Hellcat 7
Hill giant 7
Hydra, 8 heads 7
Hydra, Lern., 5 heads 7
Hydra, pyro/cryo, 6 heads 7
Invisible stalker 7
Lillend 7
Medusa 7
Monstrous spider,
    Gargantuan 7
Phasm 7
Remorhaz 7
Skeleton, Gargantuan 7
Slaad, red 7
Spectre 7
Taskmaster (formian) 7
Triceratops 7
Umber hulk 7
Vampire (5th level) . . 7 (level + 2)
Water elemental, Huge 7
Water naga 7
Yuan-ti, abomination 7

Arrowhawk, elder 8
Behir 8
Bodak 8
Dark naga 8
Destrachan 8
Dire tiger 8
Elephant 8
Genie, efreeti 8
Giant octopus 8
Gorgon 8
Gray render 8
Gynosphinx 8
Hamatula 8
Hydra, 9 heads 8
Hydra, Lern. p/c, 5 heads 8
Hydra, Lern., 6 heads 8

Hydra, p/c, 7 heads 8
Lammasu 8
Mind flayer 8
Mohrg 8
Monstrous centipede,
    Colossal 8
Ogre mage 8
Shield guardian 8
Slaad, blue 8
Stone giant 8
Treant 8
Tyrannosaurus 8
Xorn, elder 8

Air elemental, greater 9
Androsphinx 9
Avoral (guardinal) 9
Bebilith 9
Delver 9
Dire shark 9
Dragon turtle 9
Earth elemental, greater 9
Fire elemental, greater 9
Frost giant 9
Giant squid 9
Half-fiend/half-medusa 9
Hydra, 10 heads 9
Hydra, Lern. p/c, 6 heads 9
Hydra, Lern., 7 heads 9
Hydra, p/c, 8 heads 9
Monstrous scorpion,
    Gargantuan 9
Night hag 9
Rakshasa 9
Roc 9
Salamander, noble 9
Skeleton, Colossal 9
Slaad, green 9
Spirit naga 9
Succubus 9
Tojanida, elder 9
Water elemental, greater 9
Yrthak 9

Animated object, Colossal 10
Clay golem 10
Cornugon 10
Couatl 10
Fire giant 10
Guardian naga 10
Hydra, 11 heads 10
Hydra, Lern. p/c, 7 heads . . . 10

Hydra, Lern., 8 heads 10
Hydra, p/c, 9 heads 10
Monstrous spider, Colossal . . . 10
Myrmarch (formian) 10
Retriever 10
Roper 10
Slaad, gray 10

Air elemental, elder 11
Cloud giant 11
Devourer 11
Earth elemental, elder 11
Fire elemental, elder 11
Hydra, 12 heads 11
Hydra, Lern. p/c, 8 heads 11
Hydra, Lern., 9 heads 11
Hydra, p/c, 10 heads 11
Monstrous scorpion, Colossal . . 11
Stone golem 11
Water elemental, elder 11

Frost worm 12
Hydra, Lern. p/c, 9 heads 12
Hydra, Lern., 10 heads 12
Hydra, p/c, 11 heads 12
Kraken 12
Purple worm 12
Zombie, Colossal 12

Beholder 13
Gelugon 13
Ghaele (eladrin) 13
Hydra, Lern. p/c, 10 heads . . . 13
Hydra, Lern., 11 heads 13
Hydra, p/c, 12 heads 13
Iron golem 13
Lich (11th level) . . . 13 (level + 2)
Slaad, death 13
Storm giant 13
Vrock 13

Astral deva 14
Hezrou 14
Hydra, Lern. p/c, 11 heads . . . 14
Hydra, Lern., 12 heads 14
Nightwing 14
Trumpet archon 14

Glabrezu 15
Hydra, Lern. p/c, 12 heads . . . 15

Nalfeshnee 16
Nightwalker 16
Pit fiend 16
Planetar 16

Marilith 17

Balor 18
Nightcrawler 18
Queen (formian) 18

Solar 19

Tarrasque 20

Titan 21

DRAGON CRs BY AGE AND COLOR

Age	White	Black	Brass	Green	Blue	Copper	Bronze	Red	Silver	Gold
Wyrmling	1	2	2	2	2	2	2	3	3	4
Very young	2	3	3	3	3	4	4	4	4	6
Young	3	4	5	4	5	6	6	6	6	8
Juvenile	5	6	7	7	7	8	8	9	9	10
Young adult	7	8	9	10	10	10	11	12	12	13
Adult	9	10	11	12	13	13	14	14	14	15
Mature adult	11	13	14	15	15	15	16	17	17	18
Old	14	15	16	17	17	18	18	19	19	20
Very old	16	17	18	18	18	19	19	20	20	21
Ancient	17	18	19	20	20	21	21	22	22	23
Wyrm	18	19	20	21	22	22	22	23	23	24
Great wyrm	20	21	22	23	24	24	24	25	25	26